Skills for Accounting and Auditing Research

FASB Codification *and* eIFRS

Shelby Collins
University at Buffalo

With Tax Research Chapter By
Martha L. Salzman
University at Buffalo

Cambridge
BUSINESS PUBLISHERS

Cambridge Business Publishers, LLC

ISBN: 978-1-61853-074-5

Printed in Canada.
10 9 8 7 6 5 4 3 2 1

Foreword

For the past 16 years, I have taught the graduate accounting policy and research class at the University of Georgia's J. M. Tull School of Accounting. This experience has taught me first-hand what a challenging, albeit rewarding, topic accounting research is for students. Prior to this position, my 26 years with Ernst & Young and 10 years as Chairman of the Financial Accounting Standards Board (FASB) have shown me that despite this challenge, research and communication skills are what set graduates apart in practice.

In my class, students must prepare reports on real-world case studies and are expected to participate actively in class discussions of research and current events. However, these research and communication skills do not always come naturally to students. I'll never forget the time when, after assigning students a case involving revenue recognition at CBS Sports, a student approached me and said that he could not find "NFL Football" anywhere in the accounting literature. I hinted to him that terms such as "revenue recognition" or "licensing fees" were more likely to result in relevant information for this particular case. Frequently, even identifying the right keywords to search can involve practice and finesse.

While the introduction of the FASB Codification in 2009 has done a lot to facilitate guidance searches, accounting research remains a daunting challenge for many students. In part that's simply because of the sheer volume of guidance included within U.S. GAAP, and in part it is because accounting policy issues often don't have black or white answers.

It's therefore imperative that students are well trained in the resources that can help them make informed judgments. These include not only the authoritative literature, but also guidance for similar issues that may be relevant "by analogy" and nonauthoritative sources, such as examples from practice and interpretive guidance.

Shelby Collins is one of my former students, and a standout whom I had the privilege of nominating for a position at the FASB. When she approached me about a year ago with the idea for this book, I was immediately supportive. After all, in my 16 years of teaching, I have never found a resource that met the challenge of teaching accounting students the skills necessary to perform great research.

This book does just that. Shelby and I have worked closely on the content of this book, from outline to final chapters, and I am pleased to say that she has created a useful, and necessary resource that will enhance the quality of accounting research education—for students, instructors, and professional users alike.

With the help of this book, we can make this challenging, yet important, skill more attainable for our students.

Dennis R. Beresford
Executive in Residence, University of Georgia
Former Chairman of the Financial Accounting Standards Board

About the Authors

Shelby Collins is an adjunct instructor at the University at Buffalo School of Management, where she has taught the Masters-level accounting and auditing research course since 2011. To date, Shelby's career has focused specifically on performing and communicating technical accounting research, in a diversity of settings. Immediately after receiving her Bachelors' and Masters' degrees in Accountancy from the University of Georgia, Shelby went on to serve as a postgraduate technical assistant at the Financial Accounting Standards Board (FASB). From there, Shelby went on to work in KPMG's Accounting Advisory Services group, then in the Accounting Policy and Research group at Exelon Corporation in Chicago. In these roles, Shelby focused on the application of technical accounting guidance to complex and judgmental transactions.

Shelby's interest in teaching began early on, and she sought out the opportunity to serve as lead instructor of an introductory accounting course while pursuing her Masters' degree at the University of Georgia. While at Exelon, Shelby frequently taught CPE-eligible courses on new accounting guidance. Now at the University at Buffalo since 2011, and finding no textbook on the market that offered a hands-on, active learning approach to accounting research, she chose to create her own course materials including handouts, lecture slides, and case studies. Many of these materials have been incorporated into this book and its supplements.

Few professionals have the opportunity to hit the ground running with a career in research; accountants often get their first shot at higher-level research projects after several years on the job. Shelby's career is unique in that she started researching before she even had the depth of knowledge afforded by several years of experience. She quickly achieved that depth of knowledge through her work as a researcher. She therefore understands how to convey complex accounting concepts alongside the basic skills necessary for success in research, in a language that beginning researchers can understand. Her enthusiasm for teaching will serve as an asset to students utilizing this book.

Martha L. Salzman authored the tax research chapter of this book. Martha is a full-time adjunct assistant professor at the University at Buffalo School of Management, where she teaches the Masters-level professional tax research course and business law courses. Martha is a graduate of the University of Rochester (B.A., Political Science) and the University of Pennsylvania Law School (J.D.), and is licensed to practice law in the State of New York. Martha spent 18 years at the law firm of Phillips Lytle LLP, where her practice focused primarily on taxation, including advising clients regarding tax planning, compliance, audits and disputes. Martha enjoys using her real-world tax experience to better prepare students for their futures as tax and accounting professionals.

Preface

Increasingly, accounting research and communication skills are being regarded as fundamental to success in our profession. Professionals who excel in these areas will likely experience a *distinct competitive advantage* relative to their peers. At the same time, in today's highly regulated business climate, the consequences of inadequately researching and documenting accounting judgments can be severe (e.g., PCAOB or SEC enforcement actions). Recognizing the importance of research skills, the AICPA has made research simulations a key component of the national CPA exam in recent years. What's been missing, until now, is a high-quality, hands-on textbook that can teach students these important skills.

In this book, students will learn to confidently address and communicate accounting research issues, from start to finish. Students will not only take away the ability to identify the accounting problem (the "researchable question"), but will gain experience locating and applying guidance within key research tools (including the FASB Codification and eIFRS), in a variety of accounting environments. In learning to use these research tools, students will have the opportunity to apply guidance to a variety of actual accounting topics. Recognizing that students cannot learn to research simply by reading about research, the textbook offers students numerous opportunities to actively apply chapter lessons, throughout each chapter. Students will come away from this book armed with the research and critical thinking skills necessary for success as accounting professionals.

TARGET AUDIENCE

This book is intended to serve as the primary teaching materials for graduate and undergraduate courses in accounting research. The book may also be used to supplement materials used in an intermediate or advanced accounting course, given the many opportunities provided within the text to apply Codification guidance to related accounting topics (including, for example, lease classification, investment accounting, revenue recognition, and fair value measurements). Practitioners and staff training programs can also benefit from the research and communication strategies covered in this book, while gaining exposure to actual excerpts and topics covered in the Codification and other research databases.

Colleges and universities are increasingly including accounting research as a curriculum requirement for undergraduate and/or graduate-level accounting students. Often, students reaching this stage of their accounting program will have just completed their first accounting internship. Interns, as with new staff accountants, will quickly discover that they are expected to learn on the job (accounting can be a sink-or-swim environment). These students will likely have had just enough exposure to the challenges of research that they will crave more formal instruction on this critical skill. This book will offer that to students, in a format that is understandable and engaging.

Prerequisites for Users of this Book

To get the most value from this textbook, students studying this material should have already taken introductory-level accounting courses and—to the extent that the chapters on tax and auditing research will be covered—introductory tax and introductory auditing courses.

Users of this book will need access to the FASB Codification research tool. The American Accounting Association (AAA) provides academic access to the FASB *Accounting Standards Codification* and the Governmental Accounting Standards Board's *GARS Online* database for a low annual fee of $250 per year, per institution.

Instructors may also choose to require students to obtain a $20 annual subscription to eIFRS through the IAAER; alternatively, students can register on www.ifrs.org to obtain free access to individual standards.

To complete the exercises and case studies within the tax chapter of this book, it is suggested that users have access to an online tax research service, such as RIA Checkpoint or CCH IntelliConnect. Access to these services is often available at reduced rates (or free-of-charge) for students enrolled in a tax or tax research course. Information on RIA Checkpoint is available at: https://ria.thomsonreuters.com/TaxResearch/. For information on CCH IntelliConnect, go to www.cchgroup.com, then "Select a Solution" > Accounting Firms – Tax, then click on IntelliConnect.

OUTSTANDING FEATURES OF THIS BOOK

This book unites research techniques with actual technical accounting issues. Students will move their understanding of accounting issues and research techniques forward along the knowledge continuum, from simply "understanding" to having the ability to "critically think" about and "apply" accounting issues. The practical examples and exercises in this book will challenge students to actively learn while they read.

Instructors will value that this book allows students to independently read and practice the baseline skills necessary to become accounting researchers, leaving instructors free to expand lectures into discussions of accounting judgments, student presentations, current events, and classroom discussions of (or hands-on group practice with) case studies. In short, instructors will be able to actively engage students in classroom debates and discussions, because they can spend less of their valuable classroom time lecturing on basic research and communication skills.

Overview of the Book

Chapter 1 of this book introduces accounting research and key standard setters, including discussion of who performs accounting research and in what circumstances. Chapter 2 provides an in-depth introduction to the FASB Codification, including techniques for efficiently navigating the Codification. Students will learn to identify search terms and will learn in what circumstances each search method (Browse, Search, etc.) is generally most efficient.

Chapter 3 introduces the research process and fundamentals of effective technical writing, including the format of an accounting issues memorandum, techniques for effective email communication of research, and appropriate style for technical accounting writing. Chapter 4 teaches students how to properly use "nonauthoritative" resources, an essential but often overlooked skill for professionals learning to perform research. These include, for example, the FASB Concepts Statements, pre-Codification standards, peer benchmarking, and accounting firm publications.

While Chapters 1–4 of the book provide base knowledge necessary for understanding the rest of the book, the remaining chapters are written independently of one other, allowing instructors to choose to utilize only those chapters that fit their individual course needs.

Chapters 5–8 give students the opportunity to apply guidance to accounting issues following the order of "sections" in the Codification: first, issues involving scope (Ch. 5), then accounting recognition and derecognition (Ch. 6), followed by accounting measurement (Chs. 7 and 8). Chapter 8 focuses specifically on fair value measurements in the Codification, introducing key principles and select guidance from Topic 820 (Fair Value Measurements) and offering students extensive opportunities to apply principles from the guidance. Without formal instruction, the learning curve for practitioners applying scope, recognition, and measurement guidance can at times be steep. This book aims to speed students' journeys along that learning curve.

Chapters 9–12 introduce skills specific to performing research in other environments, including auditing and professional services research (Ch. 9), governmental accounting and auditing research (Ch. 10), tax research (Ch. 11), and international accounting and auditing research (Ch. 12). For each of these areas, the chapter begins by describing the research environment, including who performs accounting research and why. Next, these chapters introduce relevant research tools and guidance, including AICPA and PCAOB guidance, GARS Online and the GASB website, FASAB and GAO guidance, RIA Checkpoint and the IRS website, and eIFRS. Each of these chapters stands on its own, so instructors can choose to use only the chapters relevant to their own courses.

Finally, short and sweet Chapter 13 emphasizes the need for professionals to *stay current* as accounting requirements change. The chapter describes standard setters' "due process" for issuing new guidance and highlights resources that students can use to stay current as professionals. This chapter is a must-read, hopefully inspiring students to pursue continuous learning.

Engaging Pedagogy

Research is a skill that you learn by doing; accordingly, the pedagogy in this book is designed to foster active learning.

Chapter Opening Vignettes, Learning Objectives, and "Organization of This Chapter" Diagrams

Each chapter opens with a brief vignette placing students in the shoes of a beginning researcher. This opening vignette is followed by a list of the learning objectives for the chapter, and then by a diagram illustrating the organization of content within the chapter. These chapter-opening elements are intended to generate reader enthusiasm for chapter content, as well as provide students with an overview of the information to come.

Example Chapter Opening Vignette (from Chapter 5, regarding scope issues)

Printout in hand, Julie taps on her boss's door. She is feeling pretty good; she just found a paragraph in the guidance that appears to speak directly to the tax accrual issue her boss asked her to research. As she shows him the guidance, he taps his pen thoughtfully on the desk.

"Are you sure this guidance applies to our type of transaction?" he asks.

He continues, "I think the guidance for franchise taxes (which are based on net worth) differs from guidance for taxes based on income. You've brought me guidance specific to income taxes."

Julie shakes her head; she realizes that she forgot to review the scope section of the guidance that she had printed. "Let me double check the scope section for this guidance," she says. "I'll stop by again later to let you know what I've found."

Confirming that a transaction is within the scope of a Codification topic may seem like an extra step, but much of the guidance within the Codification includes specific instructions for its use. Reviewing the scope section is a critical step to analyzing potentially relevant accounting guidance. Don't get caught like Julie, forgetting to do the appropriate diligence work on guidance that may otherwise appear to be on point.

Example Learning Objectives (from Chapter 2, regarding the FASB Codification)

After reading this chapter and performing the exercises herein, you will be able to

1. **Understand** the role of the Codification in researching accounting issues.

2. **Describe** the difference between authoritative and nonauthoritative guidance.

3. **Identify** standard setters who have contributed to the current body of authoritative guidance.

4. **Understand** the organization of guidance within the Codification.

5. **Search** the Codification, using basic Browse, keyword, and glossary searches, and using the Cross Reference feature.

6. **Know** which sections of the guidance are considered "required reading" in order for a search effort to be thorough.

Example "Organization of This Chapter" Diagram (from Chapter 3, regarding the research process and effective communication)

This chapter begins by discussing the objectives of performing accounting research. This discussion is followed by guidance on the accounting research process, followed by discussion of how to communicate results of accounting research. The section on communication encompasses (1) drafting effective emails, (2) preparing accounting research memoranda, and (3) utilizing appropriate guidance references and proper style in these communications.

Two of the major lessons in this chapter—learning the process of performing research and learning to communicate research—may seem iterative. However, it is important to first understand *how to research* an issue before we can discuss *how to communicate* the research, as shown in the illustration.

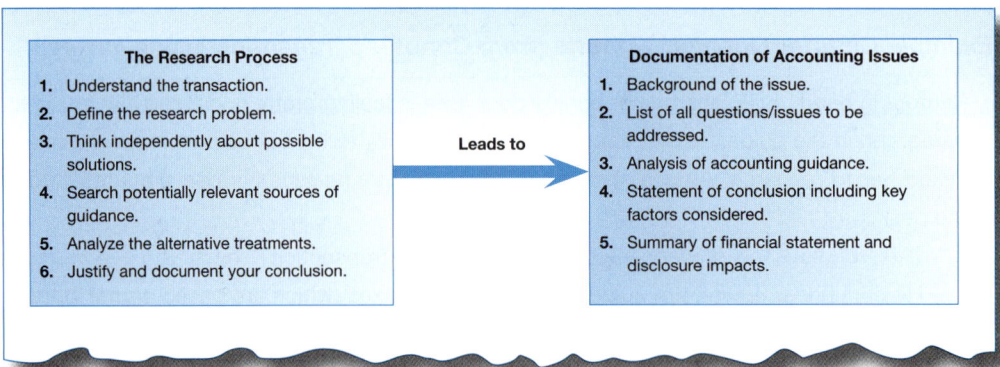

The Research Process
1. Understand the transaction.
2. Define the research problem.
3. Think independently about possible solutions.
4. Search potentially relevant sources of guidance.
5. Analyze the alternative treatments.
6. Justify and document your conclusion.

Leads to

Documentation of Accounting Issues
1. Background of the issue.
2. List of all questions/issues to be addressed.
3. Analysis of accounting guidance.
4. Statement of conclusion including key factors considered.
5. Summary of financial statement and disclosure impacts.

Chapter Features

Chapters are written in concise, easy to understand language, with boldfaced key terms to call students' attention to certain topics. In addition, chapters include extensive screenshots (from research tools, particularly the Codification) and diagrams illustrating key chapter concepts, intended to both engage students and improve their familiarity with research tools.

Chapters also include the following features, intended to engage students in active learning:

Now You Try

Throughout each chapter, following key content, students will be challenged to practice skills as they are taught (**Now YOU Try** questions). These exercises might involve, for example, a student being asked to "draw a picture" of a transaction, to "draft an email" describing an issue, to "show the search path you would use," or to "identify the journal entries" for a scenario, using guidance from the Codification as a guide for the appropriate accounting.

For example, following is a **Now YOU Try** from Chapter 3, on identifying the accounting problem (the "researchable question"), a key step in the accounting research process.

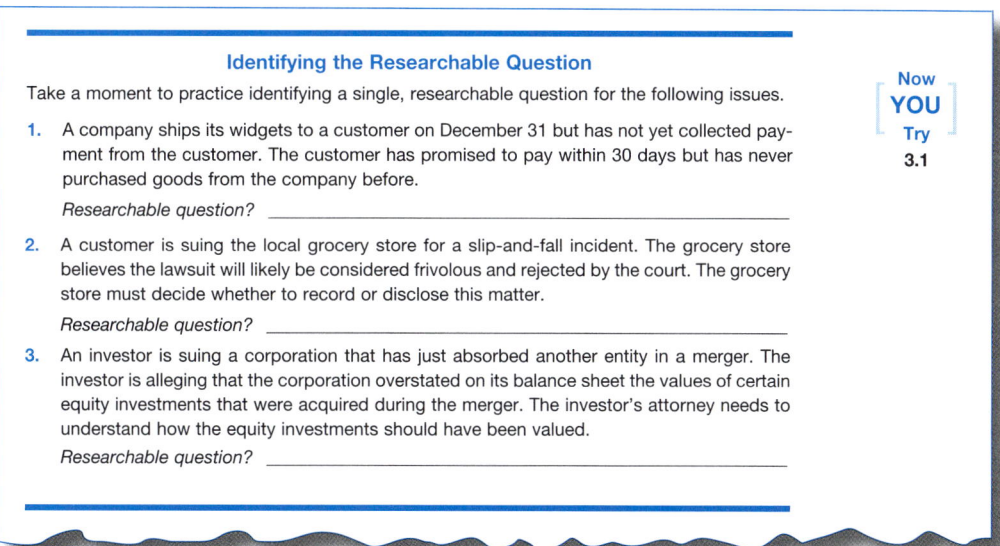

Identifying the Researchable Question

Take a moment to practice identifying a single, researchable question for the following issues.

Now YOU Try 3.1

1. A company ships its widgets to a customer on December 31 but has not yet collected payment from the customer. The customer has promised to pay within 30 days but has never purchased goods from the company before.

    Researchable question? _____

2. A customer is suing the local grocery store for a slip-and-fall incident. The grocery store believes the lawsuit will likely be considered frivolous and rejected by the court. The grocery store must decide whether to record or disclose this matter.

    Researchable question? _____

3. An investor is suing a corporation that has just absorbed another entity in a merger. The investor is alleging that the corporation overstated on its balance sheet the values of certain equity investments that were acquired during the merger. The investor's attorney needs to understand how the equity investments should have been valued.

    Researchable question? _____

Knowledge Checks

Knowledge Check questions are included within the body of each chapter, allowing students to check their understanding of chapter content before proceeding on to the next section of a chapter.

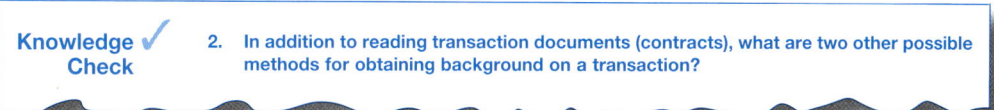

Knowledge Check ✓

2. In addition to reading transaction documents (contracts), what are two other possible methods for obtaining background on a transaction?

Tips from the Trenches

Periodically throughout the text, students will find **TIPS from the Trenches**, which offer additional insight on chapter content. These tips are designed to be like the insights you might hear an audit senior offer an audit staffer from across the table.

Your ultimate goal with the issues memo is to create a "one-stop shop" for knowledge about this transaction and its accounting. A reader, after picking up your memo, should not have to do additional digging to fully understand the background or the support for the accounting conclusion. After reading your memo, if a reader finds it necessary to get additional key facts from the contract, or to read additional guidance from the Codification, then you have failed to make your memo a one-stop shop.

TIP from the Trenches

End of Chapter Questions and Case Studies

At the conclusion of each chapter, review questions and exercises are provided, which instructors may choose to assign as homework.

- ■ The **review questions** encourage students to recall and apply key points from the reading.
- ■ The **exercises** provide students with an opportunity to practice their research skills using external resources, such as the FASB Codification, AICPA literature, eIFRS, or RIA Checkpoint.

In addition, **case study questions** are included at the end of each chapter, providing students with the opportunity to apply the research process to more involved accounting issues. Students are frequently asked to respond to these questions in the form of an email or by drafting an accounting issues memo. Cases of varying degrees of complexity are provided; accordingly, instructors may choose to assign case study questions as individual homework, or as group research assignments.

Example Case Study Question (from Chapter 3, regarding the research process and effective communication)

Inventory Valuation, Writing an Issues Memo You are in the controller's group of Charlie Corp. You have been asked to draft a (brief, 1 to 1.5 page) issues memorandum (a memo "to the files") documenting the accounting for the following issue.   3.3

> Charlie Corp has leased a mine, from which it recently extracted 100 kilograms of gypsum (a mineral that can be used to produce drywall). Charlie Corp plans to sell the gypsum to building materials manufacturers. Charlie Corp is analyzing whether its gypsum inventory can be carried at its selling price per **ASC 330-10-35-16(b)**. Assume that quoted market prices are generally available for gypsum, and that the market for gypsum is active.

Using the template for analyzing guidance with multiple conditions from Figure 3-5 of this chapter, analyze whether all necessary conditions are met for the accounting treatment proposed. If assumptions are needed to fully evaluate the guidance, identify those assumptions in your analysis. For this particular memo, you are not required to present alternative treatments; assume for this issue that you have solely been asked to document whether the conditions in **ASC 330-10-35-16(b)** are met. Present your response in the "standard memo format," including all required issues memo headings.

SUPPLEMENTS

All supplements for this book have been created by the book's authors.

Instructors Manual—Includes resources for instructors of this course, including sample course schedules and grading considerations, teaching tips for each chapter, a summary of chapter-end case studies, additional case studies, and links to external resources.

PowerPoint Slides—Available for each chapter, PowerPoint lecture slides reiterate and expand on key matter from each chapter. Lecture slides also highlight opportunities for class discussion of chapter concepts and offer additional in-class exercises, beyond those presented in the book, to engage students in active classroom learning.

Solutions Manual—Includes solutions to all end-of-chapter review questions, exercises, and case studies.

Now YOU Try and **Knowledge Check Responses**—Available to instructors, solutions to the **Now YOU Try** and **Knowledge Check** exercises may be shared with students as instructors deem appropriate. Alternatively, instructors may choose to keep these solutions to themselves, for reference in leading class discussions.

ACKNOWLEDGEMENTS

I would like to first thank Denny Beresford, for providing his support at every stage of this project, and whose ideas have helped to make this a great book. I am honored and grateful that he generously offered his time to support this project.

Martha and I would also like to thank our colleagues at SUNY-Buffalo for their comments on select chapters, and for their support of this project. In particular, thanks to Ron Huefner, Ann Cohen, Arlene Hibschweiler, and Susan Hamlen.

We were fortunate to receive review comments on this book from accounting research faculty from across the country, and we are sincerely grateful to these individuals for their time and important contributions to this book. These individuals are

Sheila Ammons, *Austin Community College*
Sumantra Chakravarty, *California State University*
Amanda Cromartie, *University of North Carolina at Greensboro*
Victoria Dickinson, *University of Mississippi*
Lynn Dikolli, *University of North Carolina at Chapel Hill*
Robert Elya, *Golden Gate University*
Patricia Fairfield, *Georgetown University*
Tim Firch, *California State University Stanislaus*
Carie Ford, *Baylor University*
Patricia Galletta, *College of Staten Island*
Hubert Glover, *Drexel University*
Rita Grant, *Grand Valley State University*
John Hassell, *Indiana University, IUPUI*
Leslie Hodder, *Indiana University*
Patrick Hopkins, *Indiana University*
Jeff Jones, *Auburn University*
Siyi Li, *University of Illinois at Chicago*
Elizabeth Oliver, *Washington and Lee University*
Terry Patton, *Midwestern State University*
Marlene Plumlee, *University of Utah*
Phil Rohrback, *University of Richmond*
Lee Schiffel, *Valparaiso University*
Changjiang Wang, *Florida International University*
Jeannie Welsh, *LaSalle University*
Jeff Wilks, *Brigham Young University,* and his students Jeff Bjorkman and Camila Antivilo

In particular, I would like to extend a heartfelt thanks to Sheila Ammons and Jeff Wilks, who have provided me with incredibly valuable feedback and counsel throughout the development of this book.

For their encouragement, I would like to thank my family, especially my husband Mathew.

A sincere thanks to the many institutions and corporations which permitted the use of their material in this book, especially the generosity of the Financial Accounting Foundation, PCAOB, and AICPA.

I would also like to thank George Werthman, Marnee Fieldman, Liz Haefele, and Jocelyn Mousel at Cambridge Business Publishers for their support, guidance, and dedication to this book. I never expected such a high level of support from my publishers, and I have been grateful for it every day.

Finally, a sincere thanks to the instructors, students, and firms using this book. I look forward to your comments and suggestions.

Shelby Collins

Brief Table of Contents

Contents

Chapter 1

Overview of Accounting Research

Each chapter in this book begins with an opening scenario, involving a beginning researcher who has been challenged to perform research. The opening scenario for this chapter is about *you*.

You are a senior or graduate-level accounting student, or you are an associate in an accounting firm. Your coursework and experiences to date have given you a strong accounting foundation; however, now you are being asked to perform accounting research. You are told that you'll need research skills for your upper-level coursework and for the CPA exam. Or, as a professional, your supervisor is already asking for your help researching client issues.

To perform this research, you will need the following skills:

- An understanding of which research tools apply in each research environment
- The ability to find relevant guidance within these tools
- The ability to understand the guidance you find
- The ability to effectively communicate your research results

You've come to the right place to obtain these skills. By actively participating in the lessons in this book, and by practicing your skills through research exercises and case studies, you can become an effective researcher. Get ready to roll up your sleeves—the ability to perform accounting research can pay dividends for your career, but mastering this skill requires practice.

After reading this chapter and performing the exercises herein, you will be able to

Learning Objectives

1. **Identify** parties who perform accounting research, and circumstances in which accounting research is required.

2. **Recognize** the different sources of guidance applicable to different research environments (e.g., financial, governmental, audit, tax, and international research).

3. **Identify** key standard setters involved in establishing U.S. accounting guidance.

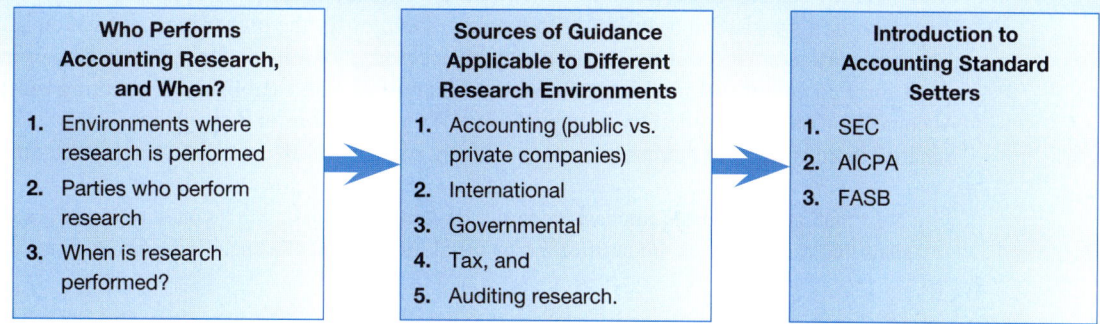

Who Performs Accounting Research, and When?	Sources of Guidance Applicable to Different Research Environments	Introduction to Accounting Standard Setters
1. Environments where research is performed 2. Parties who perform research 3. When is research performed?	1. Accounting (public vs. private companies) 2. International 3. Governmental 4. Tax, and 5. Auditing research.	1. SEC 2. AICPA 3. FASB

Organization of This Chapter

This chapter begins by identifying the circumstances in which accounting research is performed and the individuals responsible for performing this research. Next, the chapter summarizes which sources of guidance a researcher should consult in various research environments. Finally, the chapter introduces the key standard setters contributing to the existing body of financial accounting guidance.

The preceding graphic illustrates the organization of this chapter.

Following the introduction to accounting research presented in this chapter, Chapters 2-8 of this book focus on various aspects of financial accounting research, primarily related to U.S. public and nonpublic companies. Discussion of more specific areas of research, including guidance on governmental, international, tax, and auditing research, is provided in Chapters 9–12. Finally, Chapter 13 teaches readers the importance of staying current as our profession continually changes.

WHO PERFORMS ACCOUNTING RESEARCH, AND WHEN?

The term **accounting research** is used to describe two very different types of research:

- Research done in practice, by accountants and other interested parties, for example in conjunction with the preparation or review of financial statements or tax returns; and

- Academic research, primarily done by candidates pursuing—or academics who have obtained—a PhD in accounting.

This book focuses solely on the accounting research that is done in practice. Accountants often need to consult guidance requirements in order to determine the appropriate accounting treatment for a transaction or event, or to locate guidelines for the preparation of financial statements. In particular, accounting research may be necessary for transactions that are new or infrequent for a company, or for which a company does not have an established accounting practice. Accounting research is generally only performed for transactions and events that are considered material to an entity and that are therefore relevant to users of an entity's financial statements.

> "Information is **material** [emphasis added] if omitting it or misstating it could influence decisions that users make on the basis of the financial information of a specific reporting entity."[1]

Materiality can be evaluated based on the quantitative significance of an item or based on its qualitative significance. As a general rule of thumb, more resources are generally devoted to researching an entity's most material business issues, and less resources are generally devoted to less material issues.

[TIP] from the Trenches

Recognizing the importance of research skills, the uniform CPA exam tests candidates' research and other critical thinking skills through "task-based simulations" (or case studies). Task-based simulations have at times accounted for as much as 40–50% of candidates' exam scores on each of the regulation (REG), auditing (AUD), and financial accounting (FAR) sections of the exam.[2] Careful attention to the lessons in this book will help students develop the research skills necessary for success both professionally and on the CPA exam.

Environments in Which Accounting Research Is Performed

Accounting research is performed in a variety of environments, including in public and nonpublic companies (domestic and international), governments, and for purposes of researching tax requirements.

Public companies (e.g., companies that issue publicly traded debt or equity securities) are generally required to file financial statements with the SEC (Securities and Exchange Commission). By contrast, **nonpublic**, or **private**, **companies** are generally not required to file financial statements with the SEC; however, financial statements may be necessary to satisfy lenders, venture capitalists, or other stakeholders. In both cases, research is frequently necessary to ensure that the financial statements have been prepared in accordance with all applicable accounting standards.

Outside of the United States, accounting research is performed by public and nonpublic companies, as required by their national laws to issue financial statements. Many non-U.S. countries prepare their financial statements in accordance with IFRS (International Financial Reporting Standards); other countries continue to follow country-specific financial reporting guidance.

Governmental entities, including state, local, and federal governments and agencies, are frequently required to prepare financial statements to demonstrate how they have used the funds allocated to them. Accountants involved in the preparation of governmental financial statements must be able to research and understand requirements for their preparation.

---

[1] FASB Concepts Statement No. 8, *Conceptual Framework for Financial Reporting,* Chapter 1 (September 2010). Paragraph QC11.

[2] AICPA, *Content and Skill Specifications for the Uniform CPA Examination.* Approved by the Board of Examiners May 15, 2009 (Reference changes approved by the Board on January 19, 2011). Effective July 1, 2011. Page 35.

Tax research is performed by (and for) corporations and other entities that consider the tax consequences in planning transactions and that are required to report their activities to a government body (federal, state, and/or local). To understand tax reporting requirements, and to take advantage of all available tax incentive programs, researchers must become familiar with tax research sources ranging from the Internal Revenue Code to court decisions.

Parties Performing Accounting Research

Parties typically involved in performing accounting research (as illustrated in Figure 1-1) include

- *Corporate accountants*: Accountants working for a company may be involved in the preparation of the company's financial statements or tax returns, or may be involved in tax planning. These corporate accountants can also be referred to as "preparers" of financial statements or tax returns.

- *Auditors*: When audited financial statements are required, auditors must review whether a company's financial statements are presented fairly in conformity with GAAP (generally accepted accounting principles). This often involves researching whether a company's accounting positions are supportable based on requirements in the accounting guidance.

  In some cases (particularly for small companies), accounting firm personnel may be engaged to help companies prepare their accounting records and financial statements. This service may involve performing accounting research on behalf of a company.

- *Regulators*: Regulatory agencies (which can be either governmental or independent) are responsible for overseeing certain corporations and industries. Certain regulators, such as the SEC, routinely review the financial statements of companies they oversee. Regulators may need to perform research to understand positions taken in companies' financial statements.

- *Investors*: Professional investors often monitor accounting positions taken by companies and, in some cases, may raise concerns (or make adjustments to models they maintain) when a company's accounting positions are inconsistent with other companies in the same industry. Investors perform research as necessary to understand accounting guidance requirements, and alternative accounting methods. Investors may also be referred to as "users" of financial statements.

Parties Performing Accounting Research

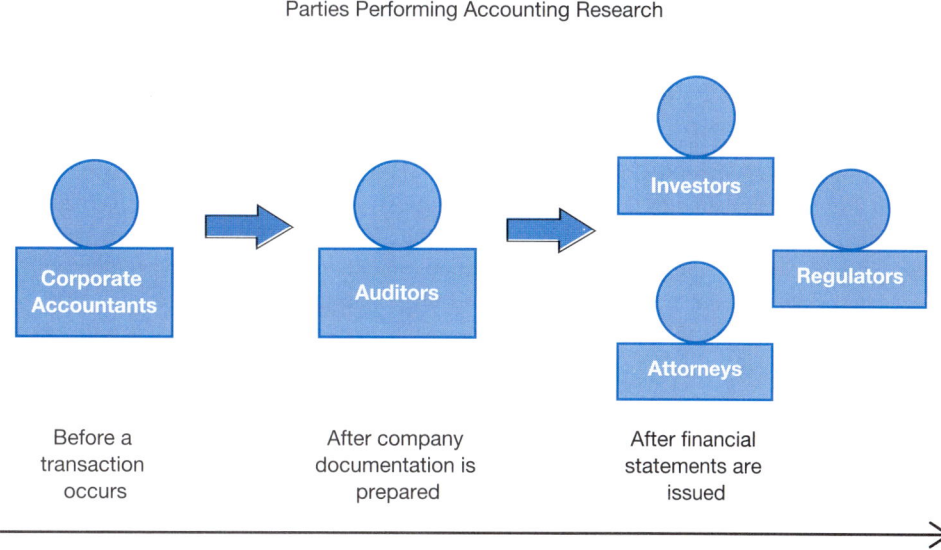

Figure 1-1

Parties performing accounting research

Will I Ever Perform Accounting Research?

Yes. No matter what accounting career path you pursue, you can expect to perform accounting research. In fact, you will likely be asked to research basic issues during your very first internship, or during your first year in the profession. At this early stage in your career, your research will generally be reviewed by a supervisor before it is relied on or shared with a client. That said, a well-documented, supportable, initial recommendation and research from you will open doors to higher-level projects.

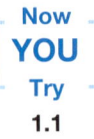

Now **YOU** Try **1.1**

Your Role as a Researcher

Based on the preceding descriptions of parties who perform accounting research, in what role(s) do you imagine that you might perform research?

_____

_____

When Is Research Performed?

Accounting research can occur at different stages in the financial reporting process, as described below. Ideally, as illustrated in Figure 1-1, companies with sufficient resources (often, public companies) will research the accounting for a transaction before the transaction takes place. However, the accounting research process may differ for small or nonpublic companies, which may be subject to more resource constraints and which generally have less user demand for financial statements. In these environments, research may only occur as financial statements are being prepared, or it may occur at the request of an auditor seeking further support for a company's accounting methods.

Regardless of the stage at which research is performed, you'll notice that documentation is one essential outcome of performing research. The importance of documentation is further discussed in Chapter 3 of this book.

Researching a Proposed Transaction

Performing accounting research before a transaction occurs is beneficial for a few reasons. This research allows

- Company management to evaluate whether the expected financial statement impacts of the transaction, as drafted, are acceptable.
- Management to adjust forecasted earnings to reflect the expected impacts of the transaction.
- The accounting team to prepare timely documentation of the expected accounting position.
- The audit team to review the proposed accounting treatment before the transaction is recorded.

Corporate management teams are frequently on the lookout for business opportunities that are profitable and aligned with their companies' strategic objectives. While management evaluates the merits of a potential transaction, the company's accounting team should be engaged concurrently to evaluate the accounting implications of the transaction. Management will take the expected financial statement impacts of the transaction into consideration when assessing whether the transaction is worth pursuing.

EXAMPLE

For example, assume that a company is closely monitoring its debt-to-equity ratio to remain compliant with its current debt covenants (promises to lenders). Said another way, assume the company has very little remaining "debt capacity" (ability to issue more debt under its current debt covenants).

If the company needs to raise additional capital, it would likely evaluate potential instruments to confirm that they would be accounted for as equity, not debt, before executing a final agreement with a bank. The company's accounting department would be responsible for researching the details of the capital issuance to determine whether the issuance would indeed be accounted for as equity instead of debt.

In addition to being responsible for reporting *past* transactions and events, corporate managers (particularly at public companies) are often held equally accountable for providing accurate short- and long-term earnings *forecasts*. Investors rely on corporate earnings forecasts in setting a reasonable share price for a company's stock. Accordingly, once management determines that a proposed transaction is worth pursuing, the company must adjust its future earnings expectations to reflect the anticipated financial statement impacts of the transaction. Figure 1-2 depicts an example in which management asks the accounting team to evaluate the financial statement impacts of a proposed transaction.

For their part, the accounting team must not only communicate the financial statement impacts of a transaction to management, but they must also document the research supporting their accounting conclusions. This documentation serves as support for the proposed accounting treatment shared with management and is the preliminary support for the accounting position to be reflected in the financial statements. This research should be saved in company files for future reference and updated with final contracts if the transaction is executed.

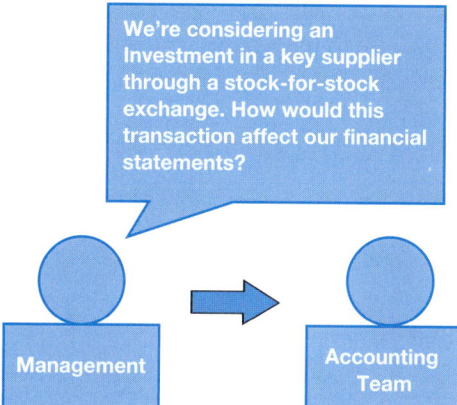

Figure 1-2

Reviewing the financial statement impacts of a proposed transaction

Certain accounting elections must be documented at the time a transaction is executed. For example, so-called contemporaneous, or concurrent, documentation requirements apply to entities electing hedge accounting for their derivative positions (this election reduces the income statement volatility resulting from changes in the fair value of derivative instruments).[3] In order to comply with this contemporaneous documentation requirement, companies should review draft transaction documents in advance of execution to evaluate whether the proposed instrument will meet all required criteria for hedge accounting.

Finally, researching and documenting the planned accounting for a transaction allows a company's auditors to offer their tentative concurrence with the proposed treatment before a transaction is recorded. While the accounting remains the responsibility of management (and auditors must take care to maintain their independence from management), it is often helpful for auditors to review draft agreements—as well as management's documentation of an accounting issue—in order to perform their own independent research and offer a preliminary view of management's position. Seeking this auditor "buy in" early in the process can minimize last-minute differences of opinion that could arise at quarter- or year-end, when financial statements are being finalized.

Researching a Past Transaction

When it is not possible to research a transaction before its execution, accounting research may be necessary at the time when, or after, a transaction occurs. The purpose of this research is simply to determine how to record the event in the financial statements, and to document this determination. Figure 1-3 illustrates a sample situation in which accountants must perform research related to a past transaction.

---

[3] FASB Accounting Standards Codification 815-20-25-3 (Derivatives and Hedging - Hedging).

Following are examples of circumstances in which research may be required at the time of, or after, a transaction is executed:

- The transaction was time-sensitive; therefore, there was not sufficient lead time to research its accounting treatment.

- The transaction was highly confidential; therefore, details of the transaction were only released to the accounting team after the transaction was executed.

- The transaction or event could not have been anticipated; for example, the company suffered from a building fire or natural disaster.

- Communication broke down between the dealmakers in the organization and the accounting team; consequently, the accounting team was only informed of the transaction after it was executed.

- The preparer has limited resources and therefore only performs research at the time financial statements are being prepared. For example, the company is a small or nonpublic company, and management is not required to prepare earnings forecasts.

- Finally, documentation (and—as necessary—research) prepared previously, for proposed transactions, should be updated to reflect final contract terms.

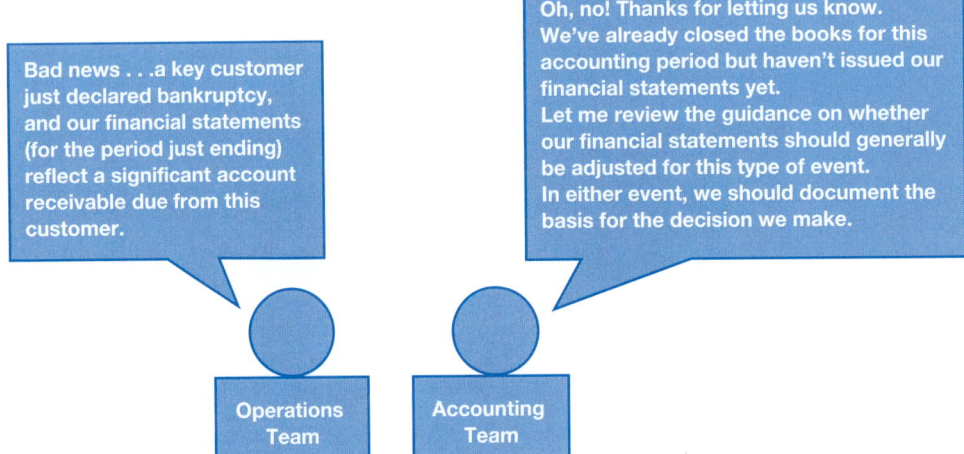

Figure 1-3

Researching a past transaction

Take particular note of the fourth bullet above; a communications failure between a company's operations teams and accounting team should be reviewed to determine what went wrong. To avoid a recurrence of the communications failure, a formal process in which material or unusual contracts are reviewed by the accounting team may need to be established.

As with the process for researching proposed transactions, accounting research performed for past transactions should be documented and shared with the company's audit team. This documentation and review process will support the accounting positions reflected in the financial statements.

Research Performed After Financial Statement Issuance

After financial statements have been issued, accounting research may be performed by various parties, as follows:

- Investors may research a company's choice of accounting methods and may seek to understand alternatives available in the literature. Using this information, investors may choose to adjust their internal models to improve consistency across companies they are evaluating.

- Regulators, such as the SEC, or industry-specific regulatory agencies like the Federal Railroad Administration, are frequently charged with the mission of protecting the public's interest by overseeing companies within their jurisdictions. To that end, certain regulators periodically review the amounts and disclosures presented in the financial statements of companies they oversee (see an example of an SEC review in Figure 1-4). To assess whether the companies' accounting judgments and disclosures are appropriate, certain regulators may perform research to familiarize themselves with accounting requirements.

■ Attorneys may perform accounting research as necessary to understand business issues related to accounting, including financial accounting, tax law, and securities law. Additionally, an attorney may perform accounting research in order to argue that a company's financial reporting has harmed an investor or other interested party; the attorney must support such arguments with citations from accounting guidance.

Questions from these parties may require corporate accountants to perform further research to explain or defend their accounting positions taken. Robust, timely documentation of accounting positions (before financial statement issuance) can assist corporate accountants in responding to such inquiries.

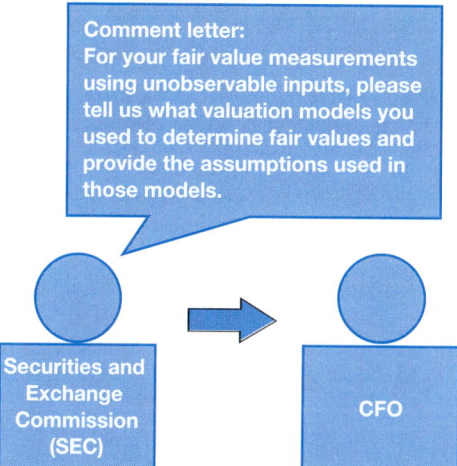

Figure 1-4

SEC inquiry regarding valuation disclosures presented in company financial statements

Research for the Purpose of Shaping Future Accounting Standards

Accounting standards are dynamic; that is, the current body of accounting guidance is continually being reviewed and is periodically revised. Many of the parties who perform accounting research (such as corporate accountants, investors, auditors, and regulators) also perform research for the purpose of shaping future accounting standards. This research could include, for example, reviewing existing guidance closely to provide the FASB (Financial Accounting Standards Board) with ideas for improvements to the guidance, or it could include reviewing existing guidance for areas of inconsistency.

The FASB's process for updating accounting guidance depends heavily on input from these "constituents" (a.k.a., interested parties). Chapter 13 introduces readers to the FASB's process for updating accounting guidance and describes steps that researchers can take to stay current.

1. Name one benefit of researching the accounting for a transaction *before* it occurs.
2. Name one circumstance in which it might not be possible to research the accounting for a transaction until *after* it has occurred.

 **Knowledge Check**

DIFFERENT GUIDANCE FOR EACH RESEARCH ENVIRONMENT

Each research environment (financial, governmental, tax, international, and audit) is subject to a different set of standards. Figure 1-5 identifies the rule makers (or "standard setters") for each research environment.

This book will introduce you to each of the preceding research environments and standard setters. In practice, you will likely specialize in only one or two of the boxes shown in Figure 1-5; for example, public company accountants and auditors will primarily perform research using FASB guidance (for accounting) and PCAOB (Public Company Accounting Oversight Board) guidance (for auditing).

Figure 1-5

Sources of accounting and auditing guidance

Preparer Type	Accounting Standard Setter	Audit Type	Auditing Standard Setter
Private companies	FASB*	Audits of private companies	AICPA
Public companies	FASB and SEC	Audits of public companies	PCAOB
Governmental entities—state and local	GASB (Governmental Accounting Standards Board)	Audits of state and local government entities	GAO (Government Accountability Office)
Governmental entities—federal	FASAB (Federal Accounting Standards Advisory Board)	Audits of federal government entities	GAO
International companies	IASB (International Accounting Standards Board), or other local standard-setter	Audits of international companies	IAASB (International Auditing and Assurance Standards Board), or other local standard setter

*The Private Company Council advisory body advises the FASB on standard-setting activities affecting private companies.

Tax research, by contrast, requires researchers to consult multiple sources including the Internal Revenue Code, tax regulations, IRS rulings and other guidance, and judicial rulings. Sources of tax research guidance are listed in Figure 1-6; note that this list is not all-inclusive. See Chapter 11 for a more complete discussion of tax sources.

Figure 1-6

Sources of tax research guidance

Sources for Tax Research	
Statutory Sources	• Internal Revenue Code • Other statutes with tax-related provisions (e.g., the Bankruptcy Code)
Administrative Sources	• Treasury regulations • IRS Revenue Rulings • Written administrative agency determinations
Judicial Sources	• U.S. Supreme Court • U.S. Court of Appeals • U.S. District Court • U.S. Court of Federal Claims • U.S. Tax Court

Following is an introduction to key U.S. accounting standard setters, which will set the stage for the accounting research topics discussed in Chapters 2–8. The standard setters responsible for creating auditing, tax, governmental, and international accounting guidance are introduced in Chapters 9–12.

ACCOUNTING STANDARD-SETTING BODIES

The next several chapters of this book (Chapters 2–8) provide in-depth coverage of the guidance and research process involved in performing U.S. accounting research. In preparation for these chapters, following is a brief history of—and introduction to—the standard-setting bodies primarily responsible for establishing U.S. accounting guidance. Having a basic familiarity with these standard setters provides context for understanding the accounting guidance applicable today.

This history follows a chronological order, beginning with the SEC—the first entity given formal authority to establish U.S. accounting standards. Figure 1-7 illustrates a timeline of key U.S. accounting standard setters.

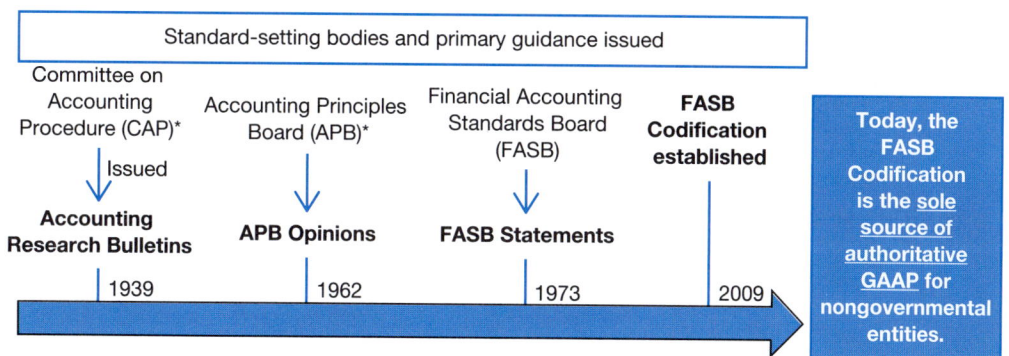

Figure 1-7

Brief timeline of key U.S. accounting standard setters

* A committee formed by the AICPA

The Securities and Exchange Commission

Following a crisis in investor confidence resulting from the Great Depression, the Securities Exchange Act of 1934 (the "1934 Act") created the SEC with the objective of providing investors with reliable financial information about public companies. First and foremost, the SEC's role is to act as a law enforcement agency, tasked with the authority to enforce securities laws in order to protect the investing public. The SEC describes the work of its Division of Enforcement, in part, as follows:

> *Each year the SEC brings hundreds of civil enforcement actions against individuals and companies for violation of the securities laws. Typical infractions include insider trading, accounting fraud, and providing false or misleading information about securities and the companies that issue them.*[4]

A second authority granted to the SEC in the 1934 Act was the authority to establish accounting standards. The SEC elected to delegate this responsibility—first to the AICPA (American Institute of Certified Public Accountants) and later to the FASB. (Notably, the Sarbanes-Oxley Act of 2002 established criteria—such as funding and independence requirements—related to the SEC's choice of standard-setter.) The FASB website describes its relationship to the SEC as follows:

> *The SEC has statutory authority to establish financial accounting and reporting standards for publicly held companies under the Securities Exchange Act of 1934. Throughout its history, however, the Commission's policy has been to rely on the private sector for this function to the extent that the private sector demonstrates ability to fulfill the responsibility in the public interest.*[5]

As noted, the SEC relies on the private sector to establish accounting guidance, on condition that the private sector demonstrates its "ability to fulfill" this responsibility. Accordingly,

---

[4] www.sec.gov, "About" - "What We Do." Accessed July 13, 2012

[5] www.fasb.org, "Facts about FASB." Accessed June 14, 2012.

SEC Chairman, Mary Jo White

Mary Jo White,
Chairman since 2013
(former prosecutor)

The SEC chairman is appointed by the
President, with the advice and consent of
the senate.

the SEC closely monitors the FASB's agenda and routinely provides input on tentative decisions reached by the FASB. The SEC also has the authority to decide whether the United States will adopt IFRS or, if not, what relationship should exist between U.S. GAAP and international accounting standards.

For its part, the SEC periodically issues accounting guidance applicable primarily to public companies. For example, the SEC establishes public company financial statement and disclosure requirements through its Regulations S-X and S-K. The SEC also periodically issues interpretive guidance on topics of key interest to the SEC, in the form of Staff Accounting Bulletins (SABs) and Financial Reporting Releases (FRRs).

Finally, it is worth noting that the SEC's Division of Corporation Finance reviews, at least every three years, the financial statements and disclosures of all companies with publicly traded securities.[6] These reviews can result in **comment letters** to corporations requesting additional explanation of a company's financial reporting. In some cases, unsatisfactory responses to comment letters, for material matters, can result in the SEC requesting that a company restate previously issued financial statements. Chapter 4, on nonauthoritative sources, describes how researchers can use the SEC website to search for company filings and SEC correspondence.

The SEC is headed by five commissioners, each appointed by the President of the United States, and each serving a five-year term. The President designates one of the commissioners to serve as Chairman of the SEC. Current SEC Chairman, Mary Jo White, is shown in Figure 1-8.

The American Institute of Certified Public Accountants

As noted, the SEC initially delegated its accounting standard-setting authority to the AICPA. Founded in 1887, the AICPA is the professional association for CPAs in the United States. In 1936, the AICPA formed the Committee on Accounting Procedure (CAP), and in 1959 replaced this committee with the Accounting Principles Board (APB). The membership of both entities consisted of volunteers who also maintained full-time positions with other employers. These early standard setters were criticized for their lack of independence, their slow response time to emerging issues, and for their failure to develop a conceptual framework to guide their decisions. The APB was dissolved in 1973 and was replaced by the FASB. Still today, a portion of the guidance issued by the CAP and the APB continues to be in effect within the FASB's *Accounting Standards Codification*.

Upon the dissolution of the APB, the AICPA formed an accounting standards committee to continue its participation in, and influence over, standard setting. In the years that followed, this committee issued guidance including AICPA Statements of Position (SOPs), industry-specific Audit and Accounting Guides (A&A Guides), and Practice Bulletins, some of which is still part of the body of GAAP today. In recent years, citing concerns about standards overload, the AICPA has limited its issuance of accounting guidance to industry-specific issues (through A&A Guides and related interpretive guidance), and—in 2013—introduced a "non-GAAP" financial reporting framework for small- and medium-sized private companies (see Chapter 4), while leaving broader accounting standard-setting responsibility to the FASB.

While its role in establishing GAAP has diminished over time, the AICPA remains a key authority in establishing standards for auditing and for accountants' professional conduct. This role is discussed further in Chapter 9.

---

[6] Sarbanes-Oxley Act of 2002, Sec. 408(c). Also known as Public Law 107-204. July 30, 2002.

The Financial Accounting Standards Board

The FASB was created in 1973, following the dissolution of the APB. The FASB is an independent organization focused on developing standards that result in decision-useful information for investors and other financial statement users. Both the SEC and the AICPA recognize the FASB as the entity with authority to set accounting standards for nongovernmental entities. To that end, the FASB developed and maintains the FASB *Accounting Standards Codification*, described in detail in the next chapter.

The FASB's seven full-time board members are required to represent a diversity of backgrounds. Specifically, board members must "collectively have knowledge and experience in investing, accounting, finance, business, accounting education, and research."[7] These board members are appointed by the FASB's parent organization, the Financial Accounting Foundation (FAF). The FAF oversees the operations of the FASB; its objective, in part, is to protect the independence and integrity of the standard-setting process.[8] Figure 1-9 depicts the current Chairman of the FASB, Russell G. Golden, who was appointed in 2013.

As required by the Sarbanes-Oxley Act, the FASB is primarily funded by **accounting support fees** assessed to public companies. Companies pay a share of this fee based on the size of their market capitalization (that is, the market value of a company's outstanding shares). This funding mechanism is designed to maintain the FASB's independence; that is, rather than rely on donations that could impair the Board's objectivity, public companies are required to participate in supporting the FASB's operations.

In response to criticism that compliance with GAAP is too burdensome for nonpublic companies, in 2012 the FAF created the **Private Company Council** (PCC). This Council has already begun to identify areas within existing GAAP that can be simplified for private companies and also plans to advise the FASB regarding private-company implications of its current projects. Chapter 13 provides further discussion of the FASB's "due process" for issuing new accounting guidance.

The standard setters responsible for establishing auditing, tax, international, and governmental accounting standards will be introduced in Chapters 9–12 of this book. For now, understanding the roles of these three U.S. accounting standard setters will provide the foundation for your next challenge: learning to perform *great* accounting research.

3. **Fill in the blanks: The SEC has _____ authority to establish accounting standards but has historically delegated this authority to the _____ sector.**
4. **What does the SEC view as its most important role?**
5. **What two committees did the AICPA form, which were at one point responsible for setting accounting standards?**
6. **What were some of the criticisms raised regarding these first two standard-setting bodies?**

✔ **Knowledge Check**

---

[7] FASB Rules of Procedure, amended and restated through January 1, 2012. Page 8.

[8] FASB Rules of Procedure, amended and restated through January 1, 2012. Page 6.

CHAPTER SUMMARY

Performing accounting research is integral to the work of many corporate accountants, auditors, investors, and regulators. Ideally, accounting research is performed before transactions take place; however, this is not always feasible given resource constraints. Sources of research vary based on the diverse research environments (accounting, governmental, audit, tax, and international); therefore, it is important for practitioners to understand which standard setter has authority before beginning research. Finally, it is important for beginning researchers to understand that no one organization is responsible for the vast population of accounting guidance available today—many organizations have been involved in creating and revising accounting guidance over time. Like the standard setters themselves, accounting guidance continually evolves in response to market and regulatory needs.

REVIEW QUESTIONS

1. Differentiate between the requirements for public (versus nonpublic) companies to prepare financial statements, and state why – in both cases – accounting research is frequently necessary.

2. Name two reasons for which accounting research should ideally be performed before a transaction is executed.

3. Identify four parties who typically perform accounting research and state why they perform research.

4. To what research environment do the following standards apply?
   a. Standards of the GASB
   b. Standards of the FASB
   c. Standards of the AICPA
   d. Standards of the IASB

5. List the organizations, in chronological order, that have historically been responsible for setting accounting standards.

6. Define "accounting support fees" and explain why these fees help the FASB maintain its independence.

EXERCISES

1. Perform an Internet search for the *Wall Street Journal*'s "Marketwatch" website. Enter the stock symbol "IBM" into the search bar on that site, and then click on the tab for "Analyst Estimates."
   a. What is the "mean" earnings per share estimate for this quarter? (Indicate what date your information is "as of"—i.e., the date on which you performed this search.)
   b. What is the mean EPS estimate for the next fiscal year? (Indicate what date your information is "as of.")
   c. Explain why performing accounting research before a transaction occurs might be important to IBM's management.

2. Go to www.wsj.com and type "Accounting Method" into the search bar. Summarize one of the headlines and issues discussed in the search results. Brainstorm (and explain) why readers of the *Wall Street Journal* might have an interest in this article.

3. Brainstorm an example of a financial accounting issue that would be researched before a transaction is finalized, an accounting issue that would be researched after a transaction has been executed, and an accounting issue that would be researched following financial statement issuance.

4. The chapter states that a communications failure between the company's accounting team and operations teams could result in company accountants evaluating the accounting for a transaction after it has occurred. Brainstorm a process that companies could put in place to encourage the timely communication of proposed transactions.

5. Go to www.fasb.org and locate (under "Latest News" on the bottom left side of the homepage) a recent news release. Describe the subject matter of the news release then identify *two parties* (such as parties depicted in Figure 1-1) who would be interested in this issue. Be as specific as possible, describing why the parties might be monitoring this issue.

6. The SEC has five divisions. Using www.sec.gov as a starting point, name these five divisions. Next, looking back at the chapter or using the SEC website, identify the division that the SEC believes is most important.

7. Using www.sec.gov, go to "Regulations" then "Staff Interpretations." Locate Staff Accounting Bulletin No. 99 ("SAB 99") and summarize the issue addressed by this guidance.

8. Using www.sec.gov, go to Divisions, then Division of Corporate Finance. Under Statutes, Rules, and Forms, go to Rules then to "Regulation S-K." Under Item 303 (Management's Discussion and Analysis) of Regulation S-K, list the five items (items 303(a)(1-5)) that must be included in a public company's MD&A disclosures. (*Hint:* The first item is "Liquidity.")

9. Go to www.sec.gov, then go to Division of Enforcement. Under Federal Court Actions, locate the June 29, 2012, enforcement action brought against Peter Madoff. Summarize the charges brought by the SEC against Mr. Madoff.

CASE STUDY QUESTIONS

Relationship Between the FASB and SEC The relationship between the FASB and the SEC has been dynamic over time. Given that the SEC is a government agency, and that it has delegated its standard-setting power to the FASB, the SEC has periodically been lobbied by both lawmakers and corporations who have disagreed with FASB decisions. Using an Internet search engine such as Google, locate one article involving both the FASB and SEC; the article does not have to be current. In approximately one page, double-spaced, summarize the issue raised in the article and the interplay you observe between these two organizations in the article. 1.1

Variation, Case 1-1(Alt.): See the instructions to Case 1-1 above; rather than documenting your observations about the interplay between these organizations, come to class prepared to describe your article and to discuss your observations to your fellow classmates. In this Case 1-1(Alt), you are *not* being asked to submit any documentation of your findings.

Researching Original FASB Standards Using the FASB website, locate the original ("pre-Codification" standard) FASB Statement No. 2, *Accounting for Research and Development Costs* (as amended). In approximately one paragraph, state how research and development costs "encompassed by this standard" should be accounted for, and cite the FASB standard and paragraph number that provides this guidance. State also which disclosures are required for entities engaging in research and development activities. Finally, summarize the background for this project; specifically, what was the Board's rationale (as described in Appendix A) for issuing guidance on research and development activities? 1.2

Parties Performing Accounting Research (FASB Comment Letters) In July 2010, the FASB solicited feedback on a proposed Accounting Standards Update related to loss contingency disclosures. The FASB issued this standard in response to financial statement users' concerns that existing loss contingency disclosures did not provide adequate, decision-useful information. The response from companies to this proposal was strong and swift. In this case study, you are asked to review a comment letter related to this proposal, then to respond to the questions below. Respond using complete sentences. 1.3

To begin, go to www.fasb.org then navigate to Projects, then Comment Letters. Click on the link next to Contingencies (Topic 450)–July 2010. Locate Comment Letter No. 70, from J.P. Morgan Chase. Read pages 1–3 of this comment letter, then respond to the following:

1. In the first paragraph, how does J.P. Morgan identify itself—as a "user" of financial statements, or as a preparer, or other? Explain.
2. What competing priorities does J.P. Morgan acknowledge that the Board must address in issuing this proposal?
3. What are some of the concerns that J.P. Morgan raises in its comments, related to the proposal?
4. Now read page five of the comment letter. What "user perspective" does J.P. Morgan share with the FASB on this page?

Chapter 2

The FASB Codification Research System

Jeremy is feeling anxious; he has been asked to research an issue related to his company's "volatility" assumption, one of the variables used to estimate the fair value of his company's outstanding stock compensation awards. Jeremy is a staff accountant, with only a limited understanding of stock compensation accounting.

He gets right to work. First, he asks his supervisor for more background on the issue then reviews a memo describing how the company has estimated this assumption in the past. Next, Jeremy logs into the FASB *Accounting Standards Codification* (the "Codification") and begins reading more about this assumption within the stock compensation topic. Before long, he has a basic understanding of the requirements for estimating volatility, and he is pleased to have learned something new in the process of researching this issue.

As you begin working with the Codification, your experience may be similar. You may be asked to research topics that you know very little about, and this may initially be uncomfortable; however, users of the Codification quickly learn that research is a skill you learn by doing.

After reading this chapter and performing the exercises herein, you will be able to

1. **Understand** the role of the Codification in researching accounting issues.
2. **Describe** the difference between authoritative and nonauthoritative guidance.
3. **Identify** standard setters who have contributed to the current body of authoritative guidance.
4. **Understand** the organization of guidance within the Codification.
5. **Search** the Codification, using basic Browse, keyword, and glossary searches, and using the Cross Reference feature.
6. **Know** which sections of the guidance are considered "required reading" in order for a search effort to be thorough.

Learning Objectives

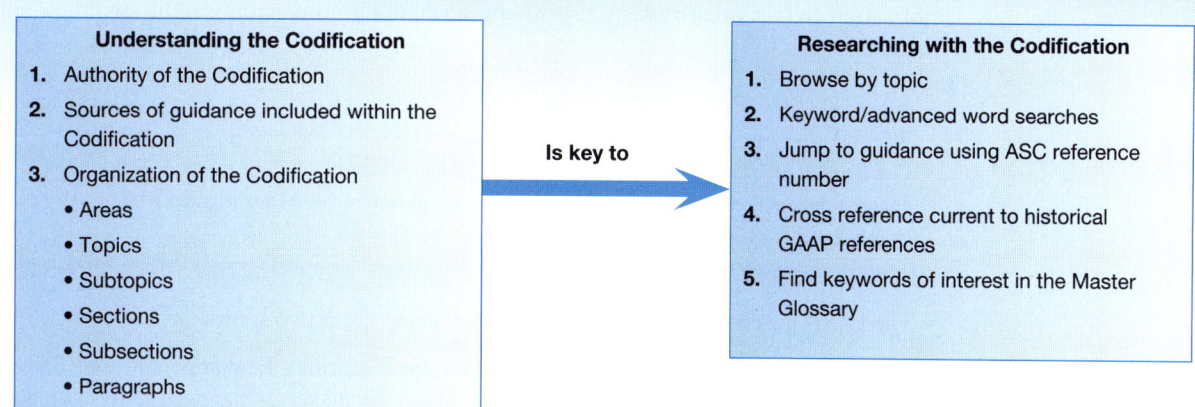

Understanding the Codification		Researching with the Codification
1. Authority of the Codification		1. Browse by topic
2. Sources of guidance included within the Codification	**Is key to**	2. Keyword/advanced word searches
3. Organization of the Codification		3. Jump to guidance using ASC reference number
• Areas		4. Cross reference current to historical GAAP references
• Topics		5. Find keywords of interest in the Master Glossary
• Subtopics		
• Sections		
• Subsections		
• Paragraphs		

Organization of This Chapter

This chapter begins by introducing readers to the FASB Codification, including (1) who created the Codification; (2) what its role is in accounting research; and (3) how guidance is organized within the Codification. Examples abound in this chapter, as it is critical for beginning researchers to develop a hands-on feel for how information is organized within this research tool.

Following the introduction to the Codification, the chapter describes several methods for performing searches of the Codification, including techniques for efficiently performing those searches. Readers will learn not only how to find information, but also what other steps must be performed to ensure that the research effort has been thorough. A checklist is provided to assist users with determining when a search effort is complete.

The two key themes in this chapter build upon one another. Properly understanding the Codification is key to efficiently performing research, as illustrated in the preceding diagram.

WHAT IS THE FASB CODIFICATION?

The FASB *Accounting Standards Codification* ("ASC" or the "Codification") is considered the sole source of **authoritative**, generally accepted accounting principles (GAAP) for non-governmental entities. The Codification became effective in 2009, and its primary objective is to simplify research. Prior to the issuance of the Codification, accounting guidance in the form of individual standards had piled up for nearly a century. Accounting practitioners often had to search several different standards to find guidance on a single topic. This created the risk that practitioners could miss important sources when searching for guidance. The Codification reduces that risk by organizing accounting guidance by topic, within a single research source.

> What does it mean for the Codification's guidance to be *authoritative*? It means that the Codification establishes GAAP. In order to receive an unqualified audit opinion, U.S. nongovernmental entities must prepare their financial statements in accordance with Codification guidance.

The FASB gets its authority to set GAAP primarily from two sources.

- First, the SEC, acting in its authority under the Securities Exchange Act and Sarbanes-Oxley, has identified the FASB as the designated private sector standard setter with authority to establish GAAP.[1]

- Second, in Rule 203-2 of its Code of Professional Conduct, the AICPA recognizes the FASB as the organization with the authority to establish GAAP for nongovernmental entities. An auditor may not issue an unqualified opinion for financial statements containing a material departure from GAAP.[2, 3]

Using this authority, the FASB has designated the Codification as the sole source of its authoritative guidance.

The term **nongovernmental entities** encompasses both public and nonpublic (private) entities, as well as not-for-profit entities. However, these entities are not always treated as equals within the Codification. That is, due to resource constraints and perceived lesser demand for nonpublic entity financial statements, nonpublic entities are exempt from some requirements (such as segment reporting requirements) and are frequently given longer transition periods for adopting new guidance. As noted in Chapter 1, the Private Company Council (PCC) was created in 2012 and has already begun to identify possible new exceptions and modifications within U.S. GAAP for nonpublic companies. Over the next few years, the work of the PCC is expected to increase the number of differences within U.S. GAAP between public and nonpublic entities.

---

[1] SEC Release No. 33-8221, *Policy Statement: Reaffirming the Status of the FASB as a Designated Private-Sector Standard Setter.* April 25, 2003.

[2] AICPA Code of Professional Conduct, Rule 203—*Accounting Principles*, par. 01: "A member shall not (1) express an opinion or state affirmatively that the financial statements or other financial data of any entity are presented in conformity with generally accepted accounting principles or (2) state that he or she is not aware of any material modifications that should be made to such statements or data in order for them to be in conformity with generally accepted accounting principles, if such statements or data contain any departure from an accounting principle promulgated by bodies designated by Council to establish such principles that has a material effect on the statements or data taken as a whole."

[3] AICPA Code of Professional Conduct, Rule 203-2—*Status of FASB, GASB and FASAB interpretations*, par. 03: "Council is authorized under Rule 203 [sec. 203 par. .01] to designate bodies to establish accounting principles. Council has designated the Financial Accounting Standards Board (FASB) as such a body and has resolved that FASB Accounting Standards Codification™ (ASC) constitutes accounting principles as contemplated in Rule 203 [sec. 203 par. .01]."

Accounting guidance for *industries*, including *not-for-profit entities*, also falls within the Codification's authority. However, as industries often have unique activities and transactions, industry-specific content must be followed *in addition to* the other general requirements of the Codification. That said, in limited cases, industry-specific content may indicate that it should be applied in lieu of a specified topic or paragraphs from the Codification's general requirements. Industries addressed in the Codification include airlines, financial services, not-for-profit entities, real estate, and software.

Students are often confused by the role of industry guidance in the Codification. Remember: Industry guidance in the Codification generally applies *in addition to* other general Codification content.

 TIP   from the Trenches

What Sources of Guidance Were Used to Populate the Codification?

The Codification is an aggregation of many, many accounting standards that have been issued over the course of the past century. These include, for example,[4]

- FASB Statements,
- FASB Interpretations,
- Emerging Issues Task Force (EITF) Abstracts, and
- AICPA Statements of Position.

Additionally, the Codification includes all still-effective guidance from the two standard-setting bodies that preceded the FASB, namely,

- The Committee on Accounting Procedure (CAP), which issued Accounting Research Bulletins (ARBs) between 1939 and 1962, and
- The Accounting Principles Board (APB), which issued APB Opinions between 1962 and 1973.

In 2009, when the guidance from these original standards was moved into the Codification, the original standards were superseded and became *nonauthoritative*. Today, these so-called "pre-Codification standards" still serve a limited role in research. This role is discussed further in Chapter 4, which describes the use of nonauthoritative guidance.

The Codification also includes certain content issued by the Securities and Exchange Commission (SEC), which is authoritative for public companies. This guidance is identified in the Codification with an "S" preceding the section reference number. However, not all SEC content has been incorporated within the Codification. Some SEC rules and requirements, such as management's discussion and analysis (MD&A) disclosure requirements, are also authoritative for public companies but are only available at www.sec.gov, and in related accounting research databases. Portions of the following SEC guidance have been included within the Codification:

- Regulation S-X (SX)
- Financial Reporting Releases (FRRs)/Accounting Series Releases (ASRs)
- Interpretive Releases (IRs)
- SEC Staff guidance in
  - Staff Accounting Bulletins (SABs)
  - EITF Topic D and SEC Staff Observer comments

---

[4] To view the complete list of guidance used to populate the Codification as of its adoption in 2009, consult the *Notice to Constituents* accessible from the home page of the Codification.

Figure 2-1 depicts the many sources of guidance used to populate the Codification.

Figure 2-1

Sources of guidance used to populate the Codification

Key standard setters and guidance issued

Committee on Accounting Procedure (1939–1962)
– Accounting Research Bulletins

Accounting Principles Board (1962–1973)
– APB Opinions, and related AICPA Accounting Interpretations (AIN)

Financial Accounting Standards Board (1973–present)
– FASB Statements, Interpretations, Technical Bulletins, Staff Positions, Staff Implementation Guides

Other standard-setting bodies and guidance issued

– **Emerging Issues Task Force:** EITF Abstracts, D-Topics

– **Derivatives Implementation Group:** "DIG" issues

– **AICPA:** Statements of Position, Practice Bulletins, plus certain content from Technical Inquiries and Audit & Accounting Guides

– **SEC:** Regulation S-X, Financial Reporting Releases, Accounting Series Releases, Interpretive Releases, Staff Accounting Bulletins, EITF D-Topics and SEC Staff Observer comments

These original standards were <u>superseded</u> when the Codification became effective. All guidance in the Codification has <u>equal authority</u>.

The FASB is responsible for maintaining the Codification. As the FASB issues new accounting standards (referred to as **Accounting Standards Updates**), the FASB amends or adds to the content in the Codification. Accounting Standards Updates are not authoritative in their own right; rather, they serve only to update or amend Codification content. The Codification includes links to proposed and final Accounting Standards Updates; these are also available on the FASB's website (www.fasb.org).

TIP from the Trenches

Students are often confused by the role of SEC guidance in the Codification. Here's what you need to know:

■ Guidance from the SEC *is authoritative for public companies*.

■ Portions—but not all—of the SEC's guidance have been included in the Codification. Companies can access the full population of SEC guidance at www.sec.gov.

■ Nonpublic companies may find it helpful, but are not required, to follow SEC guidance in the Codification.

Knowledge ✔ **Check**

1. What does it mean for the Codification's guidance to be considered "authoritative" for nongovernmental entities?
2. Name four standard-setting bodies whose guidance has been included within the Codification.
3. What type of entity must follow the guidance in the SEC sections of the Codification?

HOW IS INFORMATION ORGANIZED WITHIN THE CODIFICATION?

The Codification is organized into

■ Areas—nine broad categories from which to start your search, such as "Assets," "Liabilities," "Expenses," and "Presentation"

■ Topics—broadly describe the subject matter you are searching, such as "Leases"

- Subtopics—provide a more narrow definition of the subject matter, such as "Operating Leases"

- Sections—a standard set of section headers, such as Scope, Glossary, Initial Measurement, and Disclosure

- Subsections—headers within a topic that narrow a paragraph's applicability, such as "Lessees," or "Lessors"

- Paragraphs—where the guidance is found

The format for a Codification reference is as follows:

- Topic (**XXX**)-Subtopic (**YY**)-Section (**ZZ**)-Subsection (if applicable)-Paragraph (**PP**)

Here's an example of a Codification reference using this format:

> Leases (**Topic 840**)-Operating Leases (**Subtopic 20**)-Initial Measurement (**Section 30**)-Paragraph 1

In a memo, guidance on measuring a lessee's liability for residual value guarantees would be shown as **ASC 840-20-30-1** (Leases—Residual value guarantees). Figure 2-2 illustrates a browse search for this content.

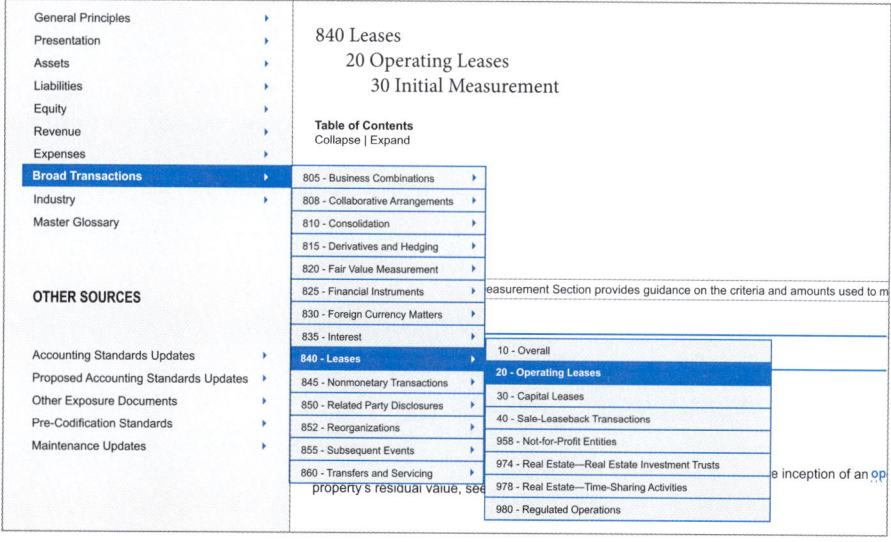

Figure 2-2

Illustration of Codification reference ASC 840-20-30-1

Reproduced with permission of the Financial Accounting Foundation.

Let's now take a closer look at each level of the Codification.

Areas and Topics

Guidance within the Codification is organized by **topic**. Topics are generally titled in a way that indicates the subject matter they cover. For example, if you have a question related to inventory valuation, begin by locating the topic "Inventory." Topics are organized into nine broad **areas**, all listed on the left-hand side of the Codification. For example, certain topics are organized by balance sheet category:

- The topic "Inventory" is available under the **Assets** area.
- For a search involving the topic "Debt," start by clicking on the **Liabilities** area.
- For a search involving the topic "Treasury Stock," start by clicking on the **Equity** area.

Straightforward, yes? However, where would you start a search for guidance on Leases? This topic is found under **Broad Transactions**. When you think about the different types of leases (e.g., capital, operating), you may notice that leases don't fit neatly into either area—Assets or Expenses—because they could be classified as either. Therefore, lease guidance is organized under a transaction-specific topic located in the Broad Transactions area of the Codification.

Where would you find guidance on employee pensions? This topic is found under **Expenses.** Costs related to paying employees are considered compensation expenses. Therefore, you would navigate to the Expenses area, then Compensation, to find the topic entitled "Compensation-Retirement Benefits." You'll find that locating the right starting point in the Codification requires a certain amount of trial and error. But after a fairly short period of experience, these starting points will become much more intuitive.

Here is a brief description of other Browse areas:

- The **General Principles** area includes information on broad conceptual matters.
  Example topic: Generally Accepted Accounting Principles

- The **Presentation** area includes topics related to how information is "presented" on the financial statements.
  Example topics: Balance Sheet, Income Statement, and Statement of Cash Flows

- The **Broad Transactions** area includes topics relating to specific transactions, or topics involving multiple financial statement accounts.
  Example topics: Business Combinations, Fair Value Measurement, and Derivatives

- The **Industry** area includes topics where the accounting is unique for an industry or type of activity.
  Example topics: Airlines, Software, and Real Estate

In particular, familiarize yourself with the list of topics located in the Broad Transactions area (see Figure 2-3). Topics listed under Broad Transactions are subject to specialized, transaction-specific guidance. It is inappropriate to apply general revenue recognition guidance, for example, to a transaction subject to transaction-specific accounting guidance.

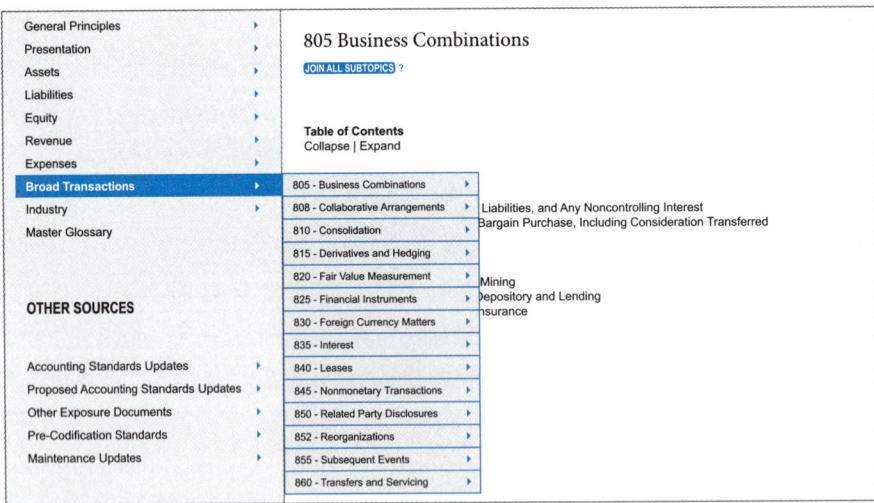

Figure 2-3

Topics available under the Broad Transactions area

Reproduced with permission of the Financial Accounting Foundation.

Finally, notice the link to access the "Master Glossary," shown on the left-hand side of Figure 2-3, immediately following the nine areas of the Codification. The Master Glossary is discussed later in this chapter.

Subtopics

Each topic is broken down into one or several **subtopics**. For example, the Leases topic (**ASC 840**) is broken down into subtopics including Overall ("**10**"), Operating Leases ("**20**"), Capital

Leases ("**30**"), Sale-Leaseback Transactions ("**40**"), and so on. It is important to understand how these subtopics interact.

Each topic contains an "Overall" subtopic ("**10**"), which often contains guidance that is pervasive to the topic. When researching accounting issues, take a moment to review guidance contained within the Overall subtopic. For example, even if you know with certainty that you are dealing with an operating lease (addressed in the "Operating Lease" subtopic), you're still responsible for complying with any guidance available under the Overall subtopic as well.

On the other hand, assume you are evaluating an arrangement and need to determine whether it qualifies for operating lease accounting. Since you have not yet determined which subtopic applies to your transaction (capital leases or operating leases), you would begin your search at "Overall." In this case, the Overall subtopic contains guidance for distinguishing between operating and capital leases.

In addition to transaction-specific subtopics, several industry-specific subtopics are available under Leases. Industry-specific content should be followed in addition to the other general content (unless stated otherwise). Assume that a not-for-profit entity is evaluating an operating lease. In this case, the researcher should check not only the "Not-For-Profit" subtopic, but also "Operating Leases" and, of course, "Overall" for guidance related to that transaction.

Identifying Subtopics to Review

Now **YOU** Try **2.1**

Assume that you are accounting for the sale of a product that has a right of return. You are trying to determine when it is appropriate to recognize revenue from the sale.

Following is an excerpt of subtopics available under the Revenue Recognition topic.

10 - Overall

15 - Products

20 - Services

25 - Multiple-Element Arrangements

28 - Milestone Method

30 - Rights to Use

Which two subtopics should you review in order to find potentially applicable guidance?

1. _____

2. _____

A final note: The subtopics listed under Revenue Recognition may describe accounting treatments that are unfamiliar to you (for example, "Rights to Use"). If a subtopic appears to be potentially relevant based on its title, read the Overview and Background of the subtopic to learn about common arrangements accounted for using this model.

Sections

Good news—guidance within the Codification is organized very logically, once you become familiar with the **sections**. Sections are used to organize guidance within each subtopic; each subtopic uses the same section titles, to the extent they apply.

Figure 2-4 illustrates a list of sections available under the subtopic Investments—Equity Method and Joint Ventures—Overall. Notice that each section includes a + sign, indicating that a user must click on the section title to be directed to content. Finally, notice that a user's search path is shown at the top of the screenshot. In this case, the search for the Investments topic began in the "Assets" area.

Home > Assets > 323 Investments—Equity Method and Joint Ventures > 10 Overall

323 Investments—Equity Method and Joint Ventures 10 Overall

To join all Sections within this Subtopic, click JOIN ALL SECTIONS.

JOIN ALL SECTIONS ?

Collapse I Expand

- 323 Investments—Equity Method and Joint Ventures
  - 10 Overall
    - 00 Status
    - 05 Overview and Background
    - 15 Scope and Scope Exceptions
    - 20 Glossary
    - 25 Recognition
    - 30 Initial Measurement
    - 35 Subsequent Measurement
    - 40 Derecognition
    - 45 Other Presentation Matters
    - 50 Disclosure
    - 55 Implementation Guidance and Illustrations
    - 60 Relationships
    - 65 Transition and Open Effective Date Information
    - 75 XBRL Elements
    - S00 Status
    - S45 Other Presentation Matters
    - S50 Disclosure
    - S55 Implementation Guidance and Illustrations
    - S99 SEC Materials

Reproduced with permission of the Financial Accounting Foundation.

So, how do you know which section is relevant to your search? Take a moment to understand what information is located within each section, as described below.

Section Number (xxx-yy-00)	Section Name	Description
00	Status	Provides references and links to Accounting Standards Updates that have changed the content of the subtopic.
05	Overview and Background	Provides general overview and background information for subtopics. Describes in general terms what transactions the subtopic is intended to address.
10	Objectives	States the high-level objectives of the subtopic.
15	Scope and Scope Exceptions	Answers the question: Does this guidance apply to my transaction? It is assumed that all transactions and entities are subject to guidance unless granted a scope exception.
20	Glossary	Defines all glossary terms used in a subtopic. The Codification also includes a Master Glossary, which includes all glossary terms used within the Codification.
25	Recognition	Describes *what* items can be recorded in the financial statements, *when* an item can be recorded, and *how* an item should be recorded.
30	Initial Measurement	Describes at what value (i.e., how much?) a financial statement item should be initially recognized. Also known as "day 1" measurement.
35	Subsequent Measurement	Provides guidance on how to change the value of an item after it is initially recorded. Also known as "day 2" measurement.

Continued

Section Number (xxx-yy-00)	Section Name	Description
40	Derecognition	Describes when and how a recorded item should be removed from the financial statements.
45	Other Presentation Matters	Provides additional guidance on how the transaction should be presented in the financial statements.
50	Disclosure	Provides disclosure requirements for a particular transaction or financial statement item.
55	Implementation Guidance and Illustrations	Includes (1) interpretive guidance describing how the guidance should be applied to specific scenarios and (2) illustrative examples.
60	Relationships	Provides references to other subtopics containing related guidance.
65	Transition and Open Effective Date Information	Provides transition guidance for content that has not yet become fully effective.
70	Grandfathered Guidance	Not generally relevant, but applies to practices that are no longer acceptable for new transactions but that some practitioners continue to apply to transactions that occurred prior to 2009 (when the Codification became effective).
75	XBRL Elements	Contains the XBRL-related elements for this subtopic. XBRL is a reporting format, for the benefit of financial statement users, in which companies "tag" certain financial statement data and information, allowing users to easily compile and compare information across companies.
S-00	"S" topics	Provides select SEC guidance, generally organized into sections similar to those described above. S-topics do not contain the full population of SEC guidance; limited guidance is provided for the convenience of Codification users.

Certain of these sections warrant additional discussion. Following is additional background and tips for reviewing these key sections.

Overview and Background (-05)

The **Overview and Background** section provides users with general knowledge about a Codification topic and highlights types of transactions covered by the guidance. Read this section to obtain a basic understanding of guidance that is new to you.

Try to avoid citing the Overview as a source. For example, this section may say: "This topic introduces the requirement that . . ." Beware: Quoting this sentence is not as impactful as quoting the requirement itself. You would be better off finding the actual requirement in the guidance, for example under a Recognition or Measurement section.

Objectives (-10)

The **Objectives** section answers the question: What were the standard setters hoping to achieve when they created these requirements? Like the Overview section, "Objectives" should not be read as actual requirements; rather, this section provides users with overarching principles to consider when applying guidance requirements.

Scope (-15)

The **Scope** section is one of the most critical sections of an accounting topic. It indicates which transactions or entities are subject to the guidance within the topic. However, beginning researchers often overlook this section, choosing instead to focus on the more "useful" guidance they expect to find under Recognition or Measurement. Pages and pages of professional literature have been devoted to analyzing nuances of the scope guidance contained within the Codification, as recognizing when you are within the scope of a standard is critical to properly applying the guidance.

For example, before you apply general multiple-element revenue accounting requirements, you must first review the list of multiple-element arrangements covered by other specific topics (**ASC 605-25-15**). Before you account for a 51% equity investment as a consolidated entity, you must first conclude that you are not within the scope of nontraditional, "variable-interest entity" consolidation guidance (**ASC 810-10-15**).

Scope guidance is commonly presented in one of two ways:

- The guidance may list transactions that are *not* within scope. For example, scope guidance in **ASC 350-10** (Intangibles—Goodwill and Other) states

> **15-3** The guidance in the Intangibles—Goodwill and Other Topic does not apply to the following transactions and activities: a. The accounting at acquisition for goodwill acquired in a business combination (for guidance see Subtopic **805-30**)...

- Alternatively, some scope guidance contains tests to determine what transactions should be included within the scope of the topic. For example, scope guidance in **ASC 840-10** (Leases) states

> **15-6** An arrangement [qualifies as a lease]...if any of the following conditions [are] met...

Therefore, before you even start the test to determine what type of lease you have (capital or operating), you should first ensure that you pass the test for the arrangement to fall within the scope of lease guidance.

See Chapter 5 of this book for additional discussion and illustrative examples of scope guidance in the Codification.

Recognition (-25)

Guidance in the **Recognition** section describes what, when, and how an item should be recorded in the financial statements. Following are examples of each issue:

- *What* should be recorded? Asset retirement obligation (ARO) guidance tells you that the obligation to pay money upon retirement of an asset must be recognized in the financial statements (**ASC 410-20-25**).
- *When* should items be recorded? Revenue recognition guidance tells you whether revenue can be recognized at the time of sale, for a product with a right of return attached (**ASC 605-15-25**).
- *How* should items be recorded? Derivatives guidance states that derivatives should be recognized as assets or liabilities in the balance sheet (**ASC 815-10-25**).

See Chapter 6 of this book for additional discussion and illustrative examples of recognition guidance in the Codification.

Initial Measurement (-30)

Guidance in the **Initial Measurement** section describes at what value (or for how much?) a financial statement item should be recognized. This value is also known as an item's "day 1" measurement.

For example, in general,

- Inventory is initially measured at cost (**ASC 330-10-30**).
- Guarantee liabilities are initially measured at fair value (**ASC 460-10-30**).
- Property, plant, and equipment is initially measured at historical cost, including interest (**ASC 360-10-30**).

Subsequent Measurement (-35)

Guidance in the **Subsequent Measurement** section describes how to change the value of an item after it is initially recorded. This value is also known as an item's "day 2" measurement.

For example, in general,

■ Inventory obsolescence would be considered in determining its "day 2" value (**ASC 330-10-35**).

■ Collectibility of an account receivable (for risk of uncollectible accounts) would be considered in determining its "day 2" value (**ASC 310-10-35**).

■ Depreciation of property, plant, and equipment is considered in determining its "day 2" value (**ASC 360-10-35**).

Chapters 7 and 8 of this book provide additional discussion and illustrative examples of measurement guidance in the Codification.

Other Presentation Matters (-45)

The **Other Presentation Matters** section provides additional guidance on how a transaction should be presented in the financial statements. This goes beyond the presentation guidance provided under the Recognition section.

For example,

■ Treasury Stock—Other Presentation Matters addresses where within the Equity section of the balance sheet to classify repurchased shares, when the repurchased shares may not be retired (**ASC 505-30-45**).

■ Earnings Per Share (EPS)—Other Presentation Matters states that entities with only common stock outstanding must present basic EPS for continuing operations and for net income on the face of the income statement (**ASC 260-10-45**).

Disclosure (-50)

The **Disclosure** section sets forth required and recommended disclosures for a particular transaction or financial statement item. This section provides disclosures related only to the specific subtopic being addressed; other general disclosure requirements are addressed in Topic **235**, (Notes to Financial Statements).

For example,

■ Inventory topic—This topic requires disclosure of "substantial and unusual losses" resulting from the application of the lower of cost or market rule (**ASC 330-10-50-2**).

■ Consolidation topic—This topic requires companies with consolidated financial statements to disclose the consolidation policy they are following (**ASC 810-10-50-1**).

Implementation Guidance and Illustrations (-55)

The **Implementation Guidance and Illustrations** section includes the following, as applicable to each topic:

■ Interpretive guidance describing how the guidance should be applied to specific scenarios.

■ Examples illustrating application of the guidance.

For example, according to the Recognition guidance in the topic "Loss Contingencies," an estimated loss from a loss contingency must be accrued if the loss is probable and reasonably estimable (**ASC 450-20-25-2**).

■ The Implementation Guidance section for loss contingencies identifies additional factors that should be considered in determining whether the "probable" threshold has been met (**ASC 450-20-55-12**).

■ Sample cases within the Implementation Guidance section illustrate appropriate accruals and disclosures for sample loss contingency cases.

Knowledge Check

4. Based on the preceding section descriptions, which section would you consult to determine whether lease guidance applies to natural resources, such as land with mineral deposits?
5. Which section might you read first if you are unfamiliar with a topic and need general information?
6. Which section might you consult if the requirements under the Recognition section seem vague, and you are looking for additional interpretive guidance?

Subsections and Paragraphs

Paragraphs are where the actual guidance is found within the Codification. Paragraphs are often organized into groups, called **subsections**. For example, within the Leases topic, under the Recognition section, you'll find a subsection containing guidance for Lessees, and a separate subsection containing guidance for Lessors. Whenever you find a paragraph with content that appears relevant to your search, be certain that you understand the context. That is, be sure you are reading guidance within a subsection that is relevant to your issue.

For example, assume you word search (ctrl + f) within the Leases topic for "contingent rent" and land in section "c" below.

Broad Transactions > Leases > Overall > Recognition

Lessees
a. Lessee application of lease classification criteria
b. Indemnifications
c. **Contingent rentals**
d. Lessee classification of a lease involving real estate

Lessors
a. Lessor application of lease classification criteria
b. Transfer-of-ownership criterion—lease involving integral equipment
c. . . .

Before you share this paragraph with your supervisor, wait! Consider the context. What if your company is actually the lessor in this arrangement? To avoid errors, be sure to scroll up and down on the page to understand all related section and subsection headers when you find guidance that appears to be on point.

In addition to understanding what subsection you are in within the guidance, you must also pay attention to paragraph groups, indicated by a header and >> notations. For example, paragraphs could be organized as follows:

Issue header
>Issue 1
>>Subissue A
>>Subissue B
>Issue 2

Assume that you encounter paragraphs organized in this fashion, and the guidance in Subissue B is relevant to your research. Since Subissues A and B are extensions of the guidance in Issue 1, it would not be appropriate to follow the guidance in Subissue B without also reading Issue 1. You would not be required to read Subissue A if it does not appear to be applicable.

Subsections and Paragraphs

Now
YOU
Try
2.2

Following is an example from **ASC 820** (Fair Value Measurement), showing the organization of paragraphs within the Subsequent Measurement section.

If you find guidance you are looking for under the header "Highest and Best Use for Nonfinancial Assets," what two other issues should you also read?

>Definition of Fair Value

>>The Asset or Liability
>>The Transaction
>>The Principal (or Most Advantageous) Market
>>Market Participants
>>The Price
>>Application to Nonfinancial Assets

>>>Highest and Best Use for Nonfinancial Assets
>>>Valuation Premise for Nonfinancial Assets

>>Application to Liabilities and Instruments Classified in a Reporting Entity's Shareholders' Equity

1. _____

2. _____

If you lose track of where you are in the Codification, you can hover your mouse over the paragraph number to be reminded of the subtopic and section number for your current location.

For example, by hovering your mouse over par. 15-6 (circled in the illustration), you'll see the "Currently Viewing" screen, which describes your location.

TIP from the Trenches

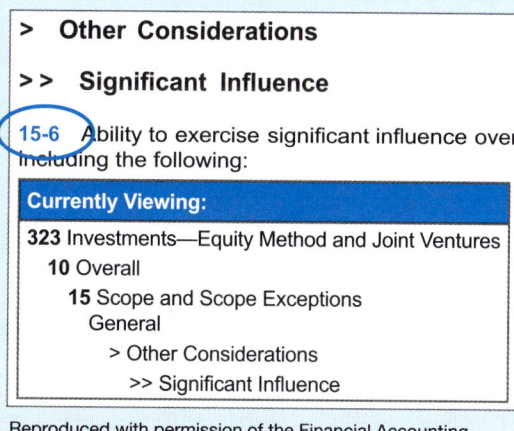

Reproduced with permission of the Financial Accounting Foundation (circle added).

Pending Content and Effective Dates

What is "Pending Content"?

When new guidance (that is, an "Accounting Standards Update") is issued by the FASB, it is added to the Codification as **pending content**.

Pending content shows up in a box, immediately following existing paragraphs in the Codification. Often, pending content has the same paragraph number as the content just above it, meaning that it will replace that guidance once it becomes fully effective. This process can take up to several years, given that companies can have different fiscal year-ends, and given that small or nonpublic entities are occasionally granted delayed effective dates. Once the pending content becomes fully effective, the previous (nonboxed) guidance will be removed from the Codification and the revised content will remain.[5]

If you see pending content directly under a paragraph that appears to be relevant to your research, click on the "Transition Guidance" link provided next to the pending content paragraph. Carefully read the transition guidance to determine whether the pending content will be effective for the transaction you are accounting for. If so, you should read the pending content in lieu of the identical paragraph number that precedes it. If pending content is in addition to existing content (for example, if there is existing content labeled par. 1-2, and pending content begins at par. 3), then consider whether this guidance should be followed in addition to existing content.

Understanding Effective Dates

As the FASB issues new guidance, it is common for that guidance to have a delay between its issuance date and its **effective date**. This gives companies time to review and implement the new guidance. Here are three examples of how effective dates are commonly worded:

a. For fiscal years ending after December 15, 20x1

b. For fiscal years beginning after December 15, 20x1

c. For fiscal quarters beginning after December 15, 20x1

Each implies quite a different time frame. For example, assume it is the year 20x1.

- A company with a calendar year-end would have to immediately apply any new guidance with the effective date described in (*a*) above (i.e., to its 12/31/20x1 financial statements).

- On the other hand, if new guidance was issued with the effective date described in (*b*), the company would first reflect the new guidance in its 12/31/20x2 financial statements.
  For an example of the effective date in (*c*) above, see the **Knowledge Check** that follows.

Knowledge Check

7. How can you determine whether pending content is relevant to your research question?

8. Assume it is the year 20x1, and your company has a calendar year-end. The FASB has just issued new guidance with the transition requirements described in (c) above. In what period's financial statements must this guidance first be applied?

Understanding Sections

Now YOU Try 2.3

Let's take a moment to practice your understanding of how guidance is organized within sections of the Codification. For this example, we'll use guidance from possibly one of the most daunting topics in the Codification—Derivatives (ASC 815).

As you'll notice in this example, the guidance within a topic becomes much more approachable once you understand how it is organized. In this example, your challenge is to match excerpts from the Derivatives topic to the section in which the excerpt is located.

That said, this example includes merely a sample of the extensive guidance included within Topic 815. For simplicity, many of the paragraphs included in this example have been excerpted.

---

[5] FASB *Notice to Constituents (v4.6) About the Codification.* January 9, 2012. Page 30.

Match the excerpt to the appropriate section (ASC 815)

1 An entity shall recognize all of its derivative instruments in its statement of financial position as either assets or liabilities depending on the rights or obligations under the contracts.

2 Definition of a derivative instrument
A derivative instrument is a financial instrument or other contract with all of the following characteristics. . . .

3 An entity with derivative instruments . . . shall disclose information to enable users of the financial statements to understand all of the following:
a. How and why an entity uses derivative instruments (or such nonderivative instruments)
b. How derivative instruments (or such nonderivative instruments) and related hedged items are accounted for under Topic 815 . . .

4 This section provides guidance on the following implementation matters:
a. Determining whether a contract is within the scope of this Subtopic
b. Unit of accounting—a transferrable option is considered freestanding, not embedded
c. Definition of derivative instrument
d. Instruments not within scope

5 All derivative instruments shall be measured initially at fair value.

6 1. All derivative instruments shall be measured subsequently at fair value.
2. . . . . Except as noted in the following paragraph, the gain or loss on a derivative instrument not designated as a hedging instrument shall be recognized currently in earnings.

7 Unless the conditions in paragraph 210-20-45-1 [Balance Sheet > Offsetting] are met, the fair value of derivative instruments in a loss position shall not be offset against the fair value of derivative instruments in a gain position.

A. Scope section
B. Recognition section
C. Initial measurement section
D. Subsequent measurement section
E. Other Presentation Matters section
F. Disclosure section
G. Implementation Guidance section

Sources: ASC 815-10, paragraphs 15-83, 25-1, 30-1, 35-1 and 35-2, 45-4, 50-1, 55-1.

Identify the section (A–G) corresponding to each numbered excerpt above.

1. _____ 2. _____ 3. _____ 4. _____ 5. _____ 6. _____ 7. _____

SEARCHING THE CODIFICATION

Please log into the Codification, and follow along while you read this section. Instructions for accessing the Codification are provided in the Preface to this book.

Several methods are available for searching the Codification:

1. **Browse** by topic, clicking through the left-hand menu hierarchy to reach the desired entry.
2. Search by **keyword**, using the Search/Advanced Search feature.

3. Jump directly to guidance using the FASB **ASC reference number** (e.g., type in **ASC 820-10-30-1** to jump directly to fair value measurement guidance).

4. **Cross-reference** by the "historical" GAAP designation (e.g., type in **FAS 157** to be directed to **ASC 820**).

5. Search using the **Master Glossary**, finding a keyword of interest and clicking on that word to be directed to the guidance.

Beginning researchers may have an initial tendency to search using the "Search" feature, as this feature has the same feel as a Google search. However, the FASB suggests that researchers use the "Browse" feature as a starting point when conducting research, when possible.[6] Indeed, experienced researchers will find that Browse searches are the most efficient search method, as the researcher can direct the search.

These five search methods are discussed further in the following section. Additionally, the following section addresses how to know when your search effort has been thorough. It is often not enough to navigate to guidance that appears to be on point, then to move on. We'll provide a checklist of sources that researchers should treat as "required reading."

Browse Feature

Now that you have a basic understanding of how the Codification is organized, you are capable of performing basic searches using the **Browse** feature.

The Browse feature is essentially a user-directed search. You, as the user, will click through a series of topics and subtopics that will, with a little experience, take you right to the appropriate guidance for a given transaction. As your understanding of the Codification increases, your efficiency in performing this search will improve.

The starting point in a Browse search is to locate the specific topic and subtopic that you are searching for. See Figure 2-5, illustrating a researcher browsing to the Loss Contingencies subtopic within the Codification. Once you reach the appropriate subtopic, you are ready to locate the appropriate sections and paragraphs that apply to your search.

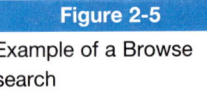
Figure 2-5

Example of a Browse search

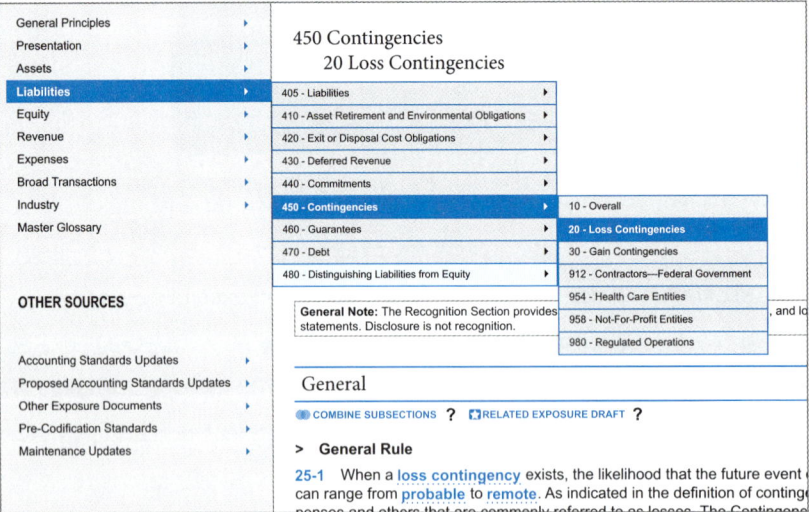

Reproduced with permission of the Financial Accounting Foundation.

As discussed earlier in this chapter, the first section you should read, if you are unfamiliar with a subtopic, is the Overview section (**05**). Next, consult the Scope section (**15**) to confirm that your specific transaction is within the scope of this guidance. Then, think about what question you are asking: Is it about Recognition? Initial Measurement?

---

[6] FASB *Notice to Constituents (v4.6) About the Codification.* January 9, 2012. Page 6.

Go to the appropriate section, and find guidance applicable to your search question. Let's assume that relevant guidance was available in par. 1 under Recognition. You've found your answer; you're done, right?

No. There are several important additional steps that you should "check off" before you can be confident that your research effort was thorough. In particular, treat any relevant Implementation Guidance and SEC content (particularly for public companies) as required reading. Often, the interpretive guidance located in these sections can confirm or change your view of how the guidance should be applied. While only public companies are *required* to follow SEC guidance, public and nonpublic companies alike can benefit from the SEC's interpretations of GAAP. Also, remember that these sections are equally as authoritative as other sections within the topic.

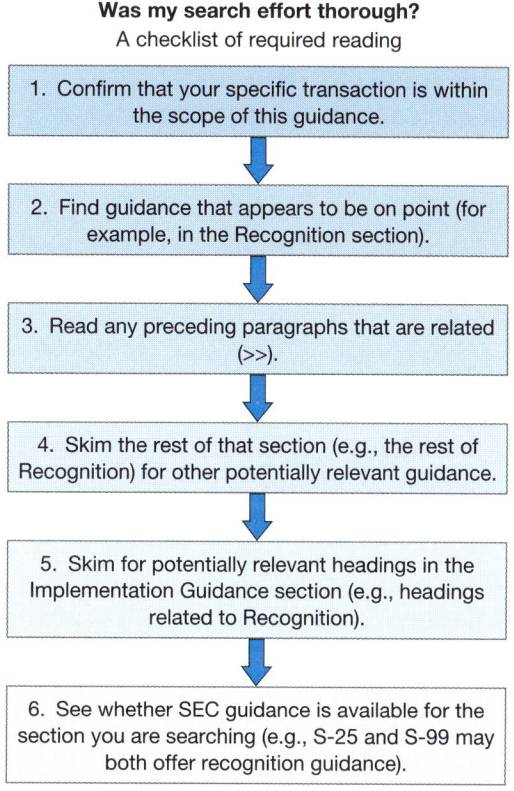

Was my search effort thorough?
A checklist of required reading

1. Confirm that your specific transaction is within the scope of this guidance.

2. Find guidance that appears to be on point (for example, in the Recognition section).

3. Read any preceding paragraphs that are related (>>).

4. Skim the rest of that section (e.g., the rest of Recognition) for other potentially relevant guidance.

5. Skim for potentially relevant headings in the Implementation Guidance section (e.g., headings related to Recognition).

6. See whether SEC guidance is available for the section you are searching (e.g., S-25 and S-99 may both offer recognition guidance).

Figure 2-6

A checklist of required reading

Figure 2-6 illustrates the following steps:

1. First, confirm that your transaction (or entity) is within the scope of the guidance you are searching.

2. Next, find guidance that appears to respond to your search question by navigating to the section that you anticipate is most relevant. For example, after confirming that your transaction is within the scope of a topic, head straight to "Recognition" for questions about recognizing an asset.

3. Ensure that you have read any preceding paragraphs that are related (for example, pay attention to the hierarchy of paragraphs, indicated by > >), as discussed earlier in this chapter.

4. Skim the rest of the section you are searching (for example, the Recognition section), to ensure that you have considered all relevant guidance. Subsequent paragraphs within that section may offer additional detail or situation-specific guidance that you should consider. Pay particular attention to boldfaced headings used to organize paragraphs, as they can assist you in quickly determining whether groups of paragraphs are potentially relevant.

5. Next, review the list of topics included within the Implementation Guidance section of the Codification (**55**). In some cases, the first paragraph of the Implementation Guidance section includes a list of the topics it addresses; in other cases, you may have to skim through the guidance, reviewing for potentially relevant headings. For example, look for headings related to recognition.

6. Finally, particularly for public companies, check whether relevant SEC guidance is available. For example, see whether a section numbered **S-25** (Recognition) is available for this topic. Beware: Creators of the Codification did not want to change content issued by the SEC; therefore, any content not fitting neatly within separate sections (e.g., **S-25** for recognition) is available under **S-99**. Researchers searching for recognition guidance should check both sections: **S-25** and **S-99**.

Be patient; it may initially be frustrating to use the Browse feature as your primary means for searching the Codification. However, it is essential that you learn how the guidance is organized. You will become more efficient with practice.

The following example illustrates how Implementation Guidance can assist in interpreting content within the Codification.

EXAMPLE

Understanding Why Implementation Guidance (Section 55) Is Integral to Your Browse Search

Assume that a customer slipped and fell in ABC Grocery, but the customer has not yet filed suit. Should ABC Grocery record a loss, due to the possibility that the customer will file a lawsuit? If the customer does file suit, the amount of loss is expected to be approximately $100,000.

ASC 450-20 (Loss Contingencies) states:

25-2 An estimated loss from a loss contingency shall be accrued by a charge to income if both of the following conditions are met:
   a. Information available before the financial statements are issued or are available to be issued . . . indicates that it is probable that an asset had been impaired or a liability had been incurred at the date of the financial statements . . .
   b. The amount of loss can be reasonably estimated.

The preceding guidance states that a loss should be recorded if it is probable that a liability has been incurred; this determination involves judgment. Experienced researchers know that additional guidance, when available, can assist in framing judgmental issues. After finding this guidance under Recognition, look for Recognition guidance in the Implementation Guidance section (**55**) of the Codification. There, you can find the following guidance even more specific to this issue:

Assessing Probability of the Incurrence of a Loss (**ASC 450-20**)
55-14 With respect to unasserted claims and assessments, an entity must determine the degree of probability that a suit may be filed or a claim or assessment may be asserted and the possibility of an unfavorable outcome. If an unfavorable outcome is probable and the amount of loss can be reasonably estimated, accrual of a loss is required by paragraph **450-20-25-2**.

Armed with this guidance, management should consider the probability that a suit will be filed, as well as the probability of an unfavorable outcome. Both guidance references (par. **25-2** and par. **55-14**) should be cited in a memo documenting the position taken. Note: Even if no accrual is made, it is a best practice to document the basis for such a judgment.

As noted, particularly for public companies, SEC content often can be equally as critical as FASB content.

EXAMPLE

Understanding Why SEC Content (Section "S") Can Be Integral to Your Browse Search

Consider the following requirements from the Codification regarding when revenue can be recognized.

ASC 605-10-25-1 (Recognition) requires that revenue, in order to be recognized, must be both realized or realizable and earned.

ASC 605-10-S99-1 (SEC guidance) states: "The staff [of the SEC] believes that revenue generally is realized or realizable and earned when all of the following criteria are met: . . ."

The SEC guidance goes on to list the following criteria for revenue recognition:

- Persuasive evidence of an arrangement exists.
- Delivery has occurred or services have been rendered.
- The seller's price to the buyer is fixed or determinable.
- Collectibility is reasonably assured.

If a public company is documenting its policy for recognizing revenue, the documentation would be lacking if it did not include consideration of both sources of literature just shown.

Notice how the preceding SEC guidance came from Section S-99? As noted under the research checklist in this chapter, SEC content not clearly fitting within a single section (such as S-25 for recognition) is available under S-99. A researcher in this case should check for SEC recognition guidance in both Sections: S-25 and S-99.

Finally, this section on Browse searching concludes with a **TIP from the Trenches**.

New researchers may find it helpful to take advantage of the "Join All Sections" button available for each subtopic. This button displays all subtopic content on one page. For example, assume you are looking for a term (e.g., "collectibility") that you know is somewhere within the revenue recognition overall subtopic. Select "join all sections" to put the full content of the subtopic on one page, then search the page for the term "collectibility" using "ctrl + F" (find).

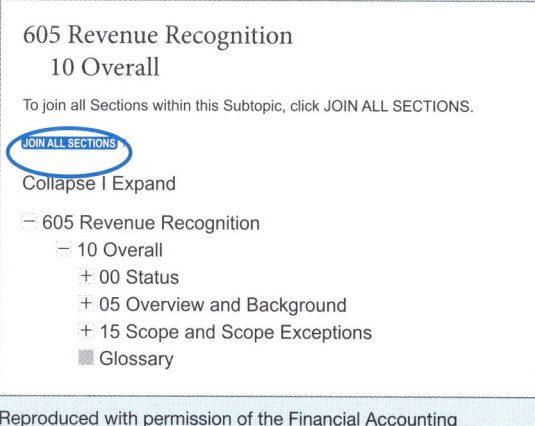

Reproduced with permission of the Financial Accounting Foundation.

9. Which Codification search method should you try to use most often (e.g., Browse, text search)?
10. Why is it critical to review Implementation Guidance (Section 55) and SEC content, if available?
11. Describe how, in the preceding contingent liability example, the Implementation Guidance (Section 55) goes beyond the Recognition guidance (Section 25).
12. What four conditions for revenue recognition are provided in the SEC content, but are not in the FASB content, as just listed?

Keyword Search (using the search bar, the advanced search tool, and identifying search terms)

A **keyword search** (i.e., a text search) is most useful when you are looking for a specific term in the guidance, or when you are uncertain where you would begin a browse search. For example, assume you want to find guidance on "involuntary conversions." Unless you have experience with this topic, you would likely not know that this term is addressed primarily in revenue recognition guidance. In this case, a keyword search would be appropriate.

When a researcher performs a keyword search, the results of the search are listed by topic and include an excerpt from the guidance containing the term. As this type of search allows researchers to see a term in multiple contexts, keyword searches can be a useful brainstorming tool. Researchers can choose to pursue one or several search results, or the results can be used to generate ideas for other search terms that might be effective.

Figure 2-7 illustrates a simple search for the term "involuntary conversion" (see search bar at top right). Notice that seven search results were found, in areas including Revenue Recognition, Liabilities, and Broad Transactions. Researchers seeking to narrow instances of this term to a single (or multiple) areas—or by related term—can use the "Narrow" option shown on the right-hand side of Figure 2-7.

Figure 2-7

Search results for the term "involuntary conversion"

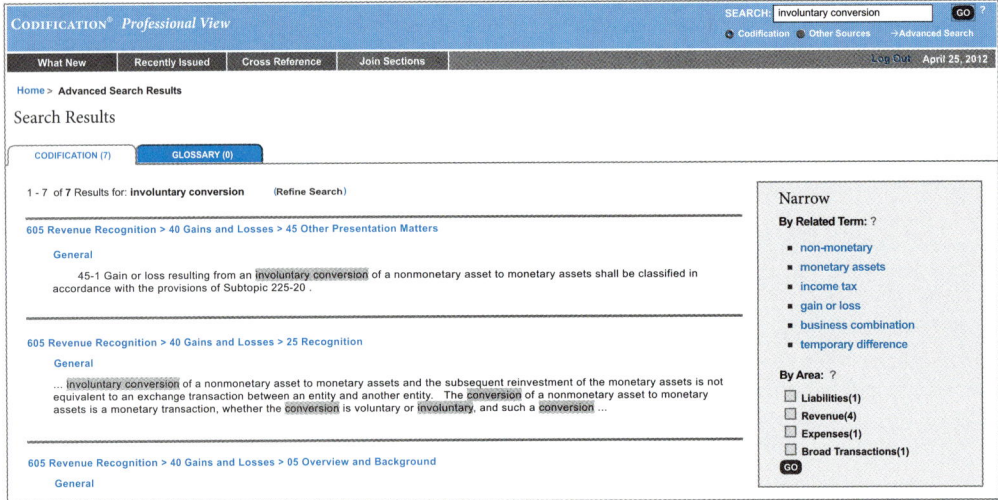

Reproduced with permission of the Financial Accounting Foundation.

Users can choose to conduct either simple or advanced searches. A simple search involves a simple empty search bar, similar to Google. This is the type of search illustrated in Figure 2-7. Note the following about the simple keyword search:[7]

- Multiple terms: Entering **troubled debt** is equivalent to searching for **troubled** and **debt**.
- Phrases: To search for an exact phrase, use quotes. For example, entering **"development stage"** returns results about **Development Stage Entities**.
- Singular/plural: A search for either **intangible** or **intangibles** will yield the same results.

An advanced search offers additional search options. For example, users can enter a phrase, such as **involuntary conversion** and can elect to search for

- "any" words (results will display any guidance containing the word **involuntary** OR **conversion**),
- "all" (results will display any guidance containing both **involuntary** AND **conversion**),

---

[7] Source: FASB Codification, Search Help. Accessed April 23, 2012.

- "exact phrase," or
- words that occur within "n" words of each other (for example, users can specify that **involuntary** and **conversion** must be within five words of each other).

The advanced search feature also allows users to choose a specific area to search; for example, a user could specify upfront that search results for **involuntary conversion** must be from the Revenue area. Figure 2-8 illustrates an advanced search for the exact phrase **involuntary conversion**, limited by area.

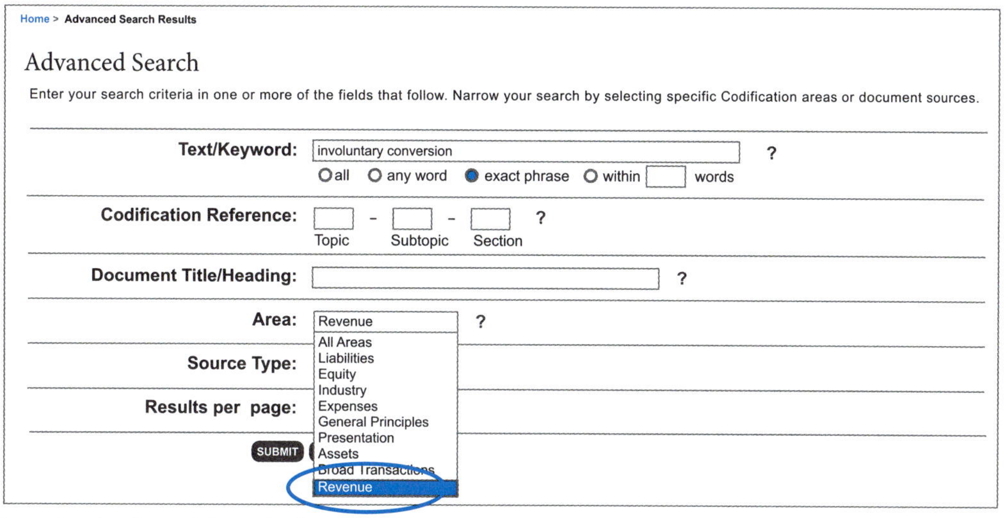

Figure 2-8

Advanced search for an exact phrase, limited by area

Reproduced with permission of the Financial Accounting Foundation.

Identifying Search Terms

Keyword searches are based on specific language. Therefore, you must use proper **search terms** (terms that are actually found in the guidance), or you will not find the appropriate guidance.

Search terms are obviously necessary for performing keyword searches, but they have other uses, as well. For example, search terms can be used to quickly find key guidance on a page during a browse search (using the "find word on page" shortcut, or "ctrl+f"). Search terms also can help a researcher maintain focus during Codification searches, as beginning researchers can occasionally start reading guidance and lose sight of what they were looking for. Keep your search terms at top of mind to maintain efficiency and focus during a search for guidance.

Identifying search terms can be a sort of brainstorming exercise. Write down all possible terms that you think might be useful, including words that may be synonymous with other search terms you have identified. With time, you'll learn the terms used most commonly in the accounting literature.

After entering a search term, a researcher will be directed to a search results page. At this point, a researcher can choose to pursue one or several search results, or the researcher could use the results to generate ideas for other search terms that might be effective.

Following are steps a researcher can take to determine whether a result he or she has pursued is relevant (and if not, what to do):

1. If you see a paragraph in the search results that appears to be directly on point, follow your instinct! Read that paragraph and determine whether it is responsive to your question.

2. If, however, the search results just lead you to a topic but no perfect paragraph, begin by reviewing the Overview and Background section of that topic. See whether the guidance appears to be on the right track for your search.

3. Next, review the scope section for the topic. Is your issue within the scope of this guidance?

4. As you perform the preceding steps, take note of other useful terms, or links to other related guidance. Perhaps these clues will lead to more relevant guidance, if what you're reading is not already on point.

5. Finally, if you have hit a "dead-end" (the guidance doesn't appear to apply, and you have not successfully identified alternate search terms), scroll down to Section **60** of that topic (Relationships). This section includes links to other related standards; reviewing this list might trigger ideas, as well.

Following are two examples illustrating the brainstorming exercise involved in identifying search terms. Note that a "researchable question" has been identified for each situation below. Researchable questions are discussed further in Chapter 3.

EXAMPLE

Situation 1:

Company A (your company) has acquired 51% of the common stock of Company B.

- Researchable question: How should Company A account for its investment in Company B?
- Possible search terms: equity investment, acquisition, investment, equity method, consolidation, consolidate, majority owner

Commentary—Situation 1:

Very little information is given about this situation; additional facts would be needed before an accounting position could be selected. That said, we have sufficient information to brainstorm some possible initial searches.

Unfortunately, beginning researchers often have to learn through trial and error which search paths are most effective for a given situation. For example, guidance on *whether* to consolidate an investee is located under the topic "Consolidation" (under the "Broad Transactions" area). A search for the term "acquisition," on the other hand, will generally land you in business combinations guidance, which describes *how* to consolidate a majority-owned subsidiary. In this case, therefore, a search for "consolidation" would be more effective than guidance on "acquisitions," since you need to decide whether consolidation is required.

A search for the terms "majority" or "majority owner" are likely to lead a researcher to click on the Consolidation topic, so these terms would be effective. However, a search for the term "equity investment" or "equity method" will land researchers in guidance that does not apply, given that this situation involves a purchase of greater than 50% of the outstanding common shares of an entity. Reviewing the Overview or the Scope guidance in these topics will indicate to the researcher that another search term should be tried.

With a little experience, you will learn to browse right to the "Consolidation" topic for this issue. This is appropriate because a purchase of greater than 50% of an entity's common stock generally results in consolidation (assuming the investee's capital structure is fairly simple). The Consolidation topic also addresses the accounting for an investor's involvement in more complex "variable interest entities."[8]

EXAMPLE

Situation 2:

Company A (original debtor) has paid $10 million to Company B to assume its liability to pay off a 10-year loan obligation, payable to Bank. Bank agrees to release Company A from its payment obligation, but only on the condition that Company B assumes the obligation and that Company A will still pay if Company B defaults.

- Researchable question: Can Company A remove the loan obligation to Bank from its financial statements?
- Possible search terms: debt extinguishment, liability extinguishment, liability derecognition, secondary liability, guarantee, primary obligor, secondarily liable

Continued

---

[8] FASB Accounting Standards Codification topic 810-10 (Consolidation).

> **Commentary—Situation 2:**
>
> Ultimately, the most relevant guidance for this research question would be found by keying "secondarily liable" into the search bar. Researchers would be directed to the derecognition section of the Liability Extinguishments topic (**ASC 405-20-40**), which indicates that the original debtor becomes a guarantor and must recognize a guarantee obligation.
>
> Researchers entering "debt extinguishment" into the search bar will be led to guidance that includes links to the liability extinguishments topic; however, researchers unfortunately might overlook those links and get stuck reading a lot of guidance that does not apply.
>
> A search of the term "guarantee" would result in guidance indicating how to value a guarantee, but such guidance doesn't indicate whether this arrangement should be recorded as a guarantee. A link to liability extinguishment guidance is available in the Relationships section of the guarantee topic.

The lesson: Using the wrong search term will often get you close to the right guidance. You just have to keep your eye out for links, and follow one source of guidance to the next. Do not try to fit a round peg in a square hole; if it seems like the guidance page you are reading isn't clear in responding to your question, look for links to related content or try another search term.

Identifying Search Terms

Read the following practice scenarios, then brainstorm search terms you would use to look for relevant guidance. Identify at least two possible search terms.

Now
YOU
Try
2.4

1. A company ships its widgets to a customer on December 31 but has not yet collected payment from the customer. The customer has promised to pay within 30 days but has never purchased goods from the company before.

   Possible search terms to use in researching the company's accounting for the sales?

   a. _____

   b. _____

2. A customer is suing the local grocery store for a slip-and-fall incident. The grocery store believes the lawsuit will likely be considered frivolous and rejected by the court.

   Possible search terms to use in determining whether the grocery store should record or disclose the matter?

   a. _____

   b. _____

3. An investor is suing a corporation that has just absorbed another entity in a merger. The investor is alleging that the corporation overstated the values of certain equity investments on its balance sheet, which were acquired during the merger.

   Possible search terms to use in determining how the corporation should have valued the acquired investments?

   a. _____

   b. _____

Often, even using the wrong search term initially will lead you to the right answer eventually, if you keep following "leads" that appear to be potentially relevant. This is all part of the process; you will become more efficient with time.

TIP from the Trenches

Caution: In some circumstances, keyword searches are inefficient (which is why, when possible, browse searches are preferable). Assume you need guidance on accounts receivable. A simple search for this term returns 47 search results, as shown in Figure 2-9. Notice how these search results would have a researcher running every which way, trying to identify the most relevant guidance. Of course, a researcher could "Narrow" the search by area or related term, but wouldn't a browse search for this topic be much simpler?

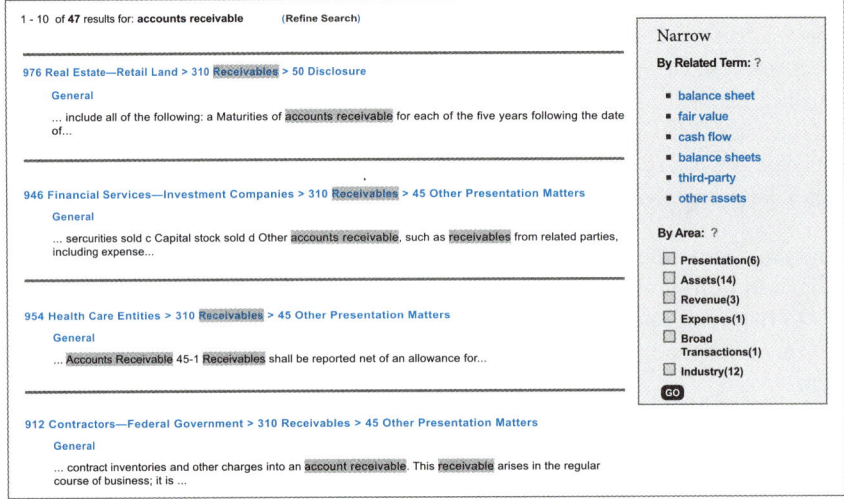

Reproduced with permission of the Financial Accounting Foundation.

Knowledge ✓ Check

13. **When is it most appropriate to use the keyword search feature?**

Search by ASC Reference Number

Researchers can use the "Go To" feature to jump directly to specific content, by typing in the content's ASC reference number. Figure 2-10 illustrates the use of this feature. In this example, entering **605-10-25-1** in the box at top left takes the researcher directly to revenue recognition guidance.

Figure 2-10

Using the Go-To box

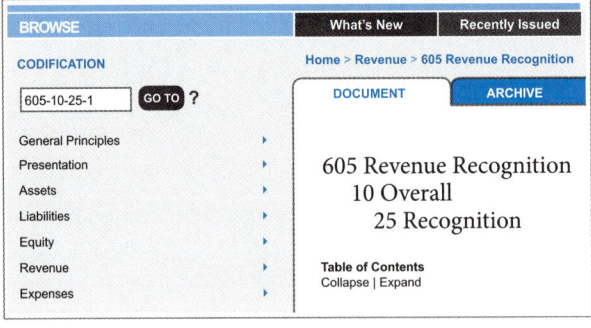

Reproduced with permission of the Financial Accounting Foundation.

Cross Reference Tab

The **Cross Reference** feature allows users to link Codification topics with the original standards that were used to populate the Codification. Users can either key in the number of an original standard and be directed to the corresponding Codification topic, or they can key in the Codification topic number to find the original standard number. For example, entering **FASB Statement No. 157**, *Fair Value Measurements* (**FAS 157**) into a cross-reference search directs users to **ASC Topic No. 820** (Fair Value Measurement), as illustrated in Figure 2-11.

Figure 2-11

Utilizing the Cross Reference feature to find the ASC topic number corresponding to FAS 157

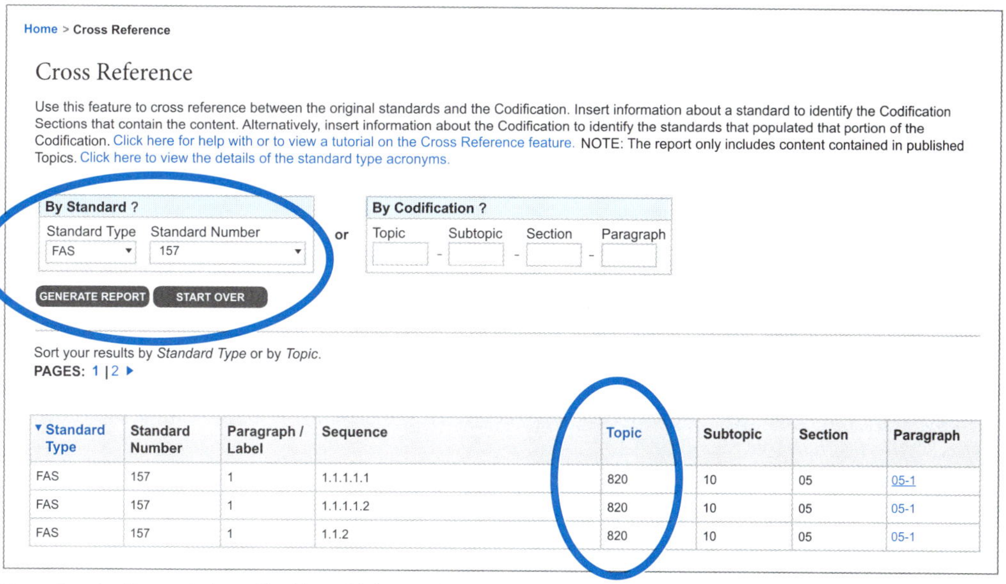

Reproduced with permission of the Financial Accounting Foundation.

The FASB continues to make its original pronouncements available on its website, as well as through a link included in the Codification (to "Pre-Codification Standards"). Chapter 4 discusses circumstances in which it can be valuable to reference pre-Codification standards.

Master Glossary

The **Master Glossary** is another useful starting point for researchers seeking further information about a specific term. Click on any term in the Master Glossary, and you will be directed to where that term is used within the Codification. Beware that some terms listed in the Glossary are listed more than once, and the definitions may differ slightly depending on what topic they are used in. Review all duplicate terms before deciding which context best fits the topic you are searching. Individual topics also include Glossaries (Section 20), which define terms specific to that topic.

CHAPTER SUMMARY

The FASB Codification is the essential source of authoritative accounting guidance for nongovernmental entities. Over the years, the guidance in the Codification has been created by a number of standard setters, but today it is the FASB that carries the torch, continually revising guidance included within the Codification. Content within the Codification is organized by topic, and then further segregated into subtopics and sections. For a research effort to be thorough, certain of these sections must be included in every search. Although several methods are available for searching the Codification, users will likely find that user-directed "Browse" searches are most efficient. With practice, you will become increasingly comfortable searching the Codification.

REVIEW QUESTIONS

1. Explain what it means for the Codification's guidance to be "authoritative."
2. Aside from the FASB, name three other standard-setting bodies whose guidance is included in the Codification.
3. What entities does guidance in the Codification apply to?

4. Is all SEC guidance contained within the Codification, and is SEC guidance considered authoritative for all entities?

5. In which area of the Codification would a researcher begin a Browse search for the Leases topic?

6. Which section, within the Inventory topic, is most relevant if you are interested in understanding the effects of inventory obsolescence?

7. Which section, within the Revenue Recognition topic, tells you whether revenue can be recorded at the time of sale for a product with a right of return attached?

8. Which search method does the FASB suggest that researchers use as a starting point when conducting research? (This is also generally the most efficient search method.)

9. Which additional areas in the guidance are considered "required reading" for a researcher who has found general guidance in the Initial Measurement section, but who needs to be sure his or her search was thorough? (Name three other areas the researcher should consider.)

10. What is the name of the guidance currently issued by the FASB to update the Codification? Is this guidance considered "authoritative" in its own right?

11. When should a researcher rely on guidance shown under "Pending Content" instead of existing content?

EXERCISES

Use the FASB Codification to answer the following questions. There is a specific, correct answer to each of the following questions. Keep looking in the Codification until you find the reference that directly responds to these questions.

1. Suppose you wanted to understand which types of receivables should be classified (presented) on the balance sheet as "current assets."
   a. Show how you would navigate to the appropriate guidance using the "browse topics" feature on the left side of the screen. (example: liabilities-contingencies-loss contingencies-initial measurement)
   b. Now provide the numerical ASC reference for the relevant guidance, *down to the paragraph*.
   c. What search term(s) might I enter, if I wanted to perform a keyword search to locate this guidance?
   d. What is the Codification reference (ASC xxx-xxx) if I were looking specifically for guidance on agriculture receivables? *Hint:* This is an industry-specific topic.

2. Go to the tab entitled "cross reference" on the Codification homepage. What is the ASC overall topic (ASC XXX) that corresponds to FASB Statement No. 154?

3. Use the "advanced search" feature (search by exact phrase) to answer part (a).
   a. Find the ASC reference (ASC xxx-xx-xx-x) for the following guidance excerpt:
      "Rent shall be charged to expense by lessees (reported as income by lessors) over the lease term as it becomes payable (receivable)."
   b. Does this guidance (that is, the ASC topic just identified) apply to mineral exploration (mining) rights? Describe why or why not. Cite your source.

4. What is the ASC reference (ASC XXX)—*down to the paragraph level of detail*—for the following? Please respond using complete sentences.
   a. Criteria for determining whether a lease should be classified as capital versus operating
   b. Criteria for determining whether information about an operating segment should be reported separately (i.e., as a *reportable segment*) in the notes to a company's financial statements
   c. Guidance on whether Treasury share transaction guidance in the Codification applies to nonpublic entities
   d. Guidance indicating which assets are generally classified on the balance sheet as "current assets"

5. Answer the following using the FASB Codification and cite your sources (down to the paragraph[s]). Please respond using complete sentences.
   a. Is SEC guidance considered authoritative GAAP, and is all SEC guidance housed within the Codification?
   b. Provide two examples from the Codification of "nonauthoritative" sources of GAAP.
   c. Name a circumstance in which a company selling a product subject to a customer right to return cannot recognize revenue at the time of sale.
   d. In determining whether the equity method should be applied to an investment in common stock, an investor should consider whether it can exercise significant influence. Significant influence is characterized by certain quantitative factors (20% ownership) and qualitative factors. What are two of the qualitative factors an investor should consider?

CASE STUDY QUESTIONS

For the following case studies, please respond in a brief paragraph (for part 1 of each case study). Start a new paragraph to respond to part 2. In your responses, remember that you are being asked not only to locate the appropriate guidance, but also to *apply* it to the case facts presented.

Sales Incentives Rainbow Printers ("Rainbow") offers its customers payment terms of 2/10, n/30, where purchasers making payment within 10 days of product receipt will receive a discount of 2% off the purchase price, or must pay the full balance due within 30 days. Rainbow has just received payment from a new customer who paid within the 10-day window and is thus entitled to the 2% discount. This discount will not result in a loss to Rainbow on the sale of the product. Rainbow needs your help to determine when the 2% sales incentive should be recognized, and how it should be recorded—as a reduction in revenue, or as a cost of sales?

2.1

Required:
1. Citing guidance from the Codification, explain how Rainbow should account for the sales incentive.
2. Explain to Rainbow's management how you located the relevant guidance, including search method used and which section you searched within the appropriate topic.

Derecognition of a Liability Alliance Corp has a $1 million note payable due to its founder, Tom Baker. Mr. Baker is recently deceased and has no heirs that Alliance Corp's executive team is aware of. Alliance Corp has asked for your help to determine whether it is appropriate to *derecognize the liability* from its financial statements.

2.2

Required:
1. Citing guidance from the Codification, respond to Alliance Corp.
2. Explain to Alliance Corp's management how you located the relevant guidance, including search method used and which section you searched within the appropriate topic.

Asset Classification Jones Brothers purchased U.S. Treasury notes 5 years ago, which are now 2 months away from maturity. Jones Brothers has asked you whether it is appropriate to reclassify these notes into the "current assets" category of its balance sheet.

2.3

Required:
1. Citing guidance from the Codification, respond to Jones Brothers.
2. Explain to Jones Brothers' management how you located the relevant guidance, including search method used, and which section you searched within the appropriate topic.

Chapter 3

The Research Process and Guidelines for Effective Documentation

Linda is an audit senior who has been assigned to the audit of Flyaway.com ("Flyaway" or the "Company"). Flyaway sells airline tickets to customers through an online platform, where customers can select an airline and travel schedule of their choice. Once a customer purchases a ticket, Flyaway remits payment for the travel to the airline and retains a commission (roughly 10% of the ticket's value). The airlines set all ticket prices. If a flight is canceled, the airline must refund the customer. On the other hand, if the customer's payment is invalid, Flyaway assumes credit risk.

Flyaway management is grappling with a fundamental reporting issue: Should the Company report its ticket revenue on a gross basis (as a principal), or net (as an agent)? The Company has expressed a preference for reporting the revenue gross, and is planning to prepare documentation in support of that treatment, but has asked the audit team to weigh in.

Linda finds herself in need of two skills: 1) the ability to apply a step-by-step research process to develop her own conclusion on this critical issue, and 2) the ability to effectively document her research. Given the potential for differences of opinion on this issue, Linda knows that her documentation will need to be airtight.

After reading this chapter and performing the exercises herein, you will be able to

1. **Describe** the objectives of performing accounting research.

2. **Apply** the research process to open-ended accounting issues.

3. **Identify** "researchable questions" and related keywords.

4. **Draw** a picture to illustrate relationships in a transaction.

5. **Examine** alternative viewpoints in an accounting research analysis.

6. **Draft** effective emails and issues memoranda to communicate research results.

Learning Objectives

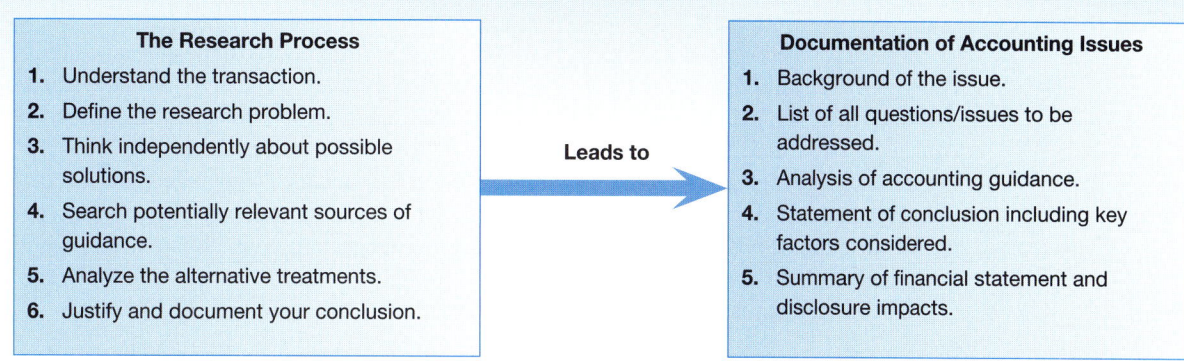

The Research Process	Documentation of Accounting Issues
1. Understand the transaction.	1. Background of the issue.
2. Define the research problem.	2. List of all questions/issues to be addressed.
3. Think independently about possible solutions.	3. Analysis of accounting guidance.
4. Search potentially relevant sources of guidance.	4. Statement of conclusion including key factors considered.
5. Analyze the alternative treatments.	5. Summary of financial statement and disclosure impacts.
6. Justify and document your conclusion.	

Leads to →

Organization of This Chapter

This chapter begins by discussing the objectives of performing accounting research. This discussion is followed by guidance on the accounting research process, followed by discussion of how to communicate results of accounting research. The section on communication encompasses (1) drafting effective emails, (2) preparing accounting research memoranda, and (3) utilizing appropriate guidance references and proper style in these communications.

Two of the major lessons in this chapter—learning the process of performing research and learning to communicate research—may seem iterative. However, it is important to first understand *how to research* an issue before we can discuss *how to communicate* the research, as shown in the illustration.

OBJECTIVES OF PERFORMING ACCOUNTING RESEARCH

It may seem obvious, based on our discussion in prior chapters, that the objective of performing accounting research is to get to the "right" answer when determining how to account for a certain transaction or item. However, the objectives of accounting research are generally twofold:

1. To account for transactions or items in a manner that is appropriate and **supportable** based on authoritative guidance, and
2. To create **documentation** describing the research performed and supporting the conclusion reached.

The first objective echoes the discussion in Chapter 2; that is, a company's accounting must comply with authoritative guidance in order for the company to receive an unqualified audit opinion. However, let's take a moment to discuss the importance of documenting the accounting conclusions reached. When you create accounting research documentation, you are summarizing in one place all relevant background on an issue, the guidance considered, and the basis for your selected accounting position. Documenting the basis for accounting positions is especially critical in circumstances where the accounting for a transaction is judgmental (for example, if two or more alternatives are present).

Documentation is critical to accounting research because

- Creating documentation of the basis for accounting positions creates an audit trail. Not only will the files be useful for historical reference, but current documentation can be shared with the company's auditors, helping the auditors understand and review the company's accounting judgments in real time.

- This transaction sets precedent for future transactions. Without proper documentation, company accountants could risk reaching a different conclusion if this type of transaction is later repeated. This could result in inconsistent accounting or, worse, restatement if company accountants conclude that the prior transaction's accounting is improper and the transaction is material.

- If your company's accounting position on a transaction is ever questioned (for example, through an SEC comment letter, in the event of a lawsuit, or by regulators), ideally, your company's rationale for the accounting would already be neatly summarized into a memo. In theory, such a memo could be forwarded straight over to the SEC in response to their inquiry, for example.

- Auditors must also maintain documentation evidencing their reviews of judgmental client accounting positions. This documentation shows that the auditor was diligent in researching and evaluating whether client positions are appropriate.

The next section of this chapter describes the process involved in performing accounting research. Following this, we will discuss methods for effectively communicating accounting research, including how to prepare an accounting issues memorandum. As you read these sections, you will see that documenting your research is integral to the process of performing the research.

Knowledge✔ Check

1. Why is documentation critical to accounting research?

THE PROCESS OF PERFORMING ACCOUNTING RESEARCH

This section of the chapter aims to introduce beginning researchers to the research process, from understanding the facts of a transaction to reaching a conclusion and documenting your results. Master each step of this process, and you may soon find yourself being asked to participate on higher-level projects—offering you valuable opportunities to grow in knowledge and skills.

Note that multiple variations of the accounting research process exist (for example, in other textbooks, in accounting firm literature, etc.); this book describes just one of many possible approaches. The approach in this book is particularly geared to the beginning researcher, who may require a few extra steps in order to fully analyze an issue. Generally speaking, the similarities among the various research approaches tend to outnumber their differences.

The research process described in this book consists of the following steps:

1. Understand the facts/background of the transaction.

2. Define the problem. That is, identify the "researchable question."

3. Stop and think: What accounting treatment will likely be most appropriate?

4. Search potentially relevant sources of guidance, copying any relevant guidance into a Word document.

5. Analyze alternatives, documenting your consideration of each.

6. Justify and document your conclusion.

Step 1: Understand the Facts/Background of the Transaction

Let's assume that your involvement in this whole transaction review process began when your supervisor dropped a contract on your desk and said: "Read this and tell me what you think the accounting should be." What would you do first?

Your first challenge in any accounting research assignment is to *fully understand* the transaction and *why* it is being entered into. Obtaining this understanding often starts with

- Reading transaction documents, including draft or final contracts, and

- Talking to parties within your organization who have knowledge of the transaction. This can help you understand the purpose of the transaction, plus clarify any unique terms of the transaction.

After considering the two preceding resources, think about whether you understand the big picture for this transaction. Do you have a clear understanding of *who* the parties are to this transaction, and *why* they are entering into it? Do you clearly understand the *economics (financial costs and benefits)* and *cash flows* of the arrangement? Without realizing it, beginning researchers may go through several rounds of research with incomplete information, gathering additional facts each time they stop to ask ("frequent fliers" to the boss's office). Save yourself time and effort by trying to form a complete picture during this first step of the research process. It might help at this point for you to sketch out—for your own benefit—a picture of the transaction. Instructions for doing this are provided later in this chapter.

As discussed in Chapter 1, researching the accounting for a transaction should ideally occur before the transaction takes place (and before contracts are finalized). Be careful, however. An accounting position documented based on *draft* agreements could change as contracts are edited and finalized. Changes to contracts and final drafts should be reviewed to ensure that they do not change the accounting analysis.

Once you have a working understanding of a transaction, consider whether the following resources would shed additional light on the transaction:

- Has my company undertaken any transactions similar to this in the past? If so, try to get your hands on any memos documenting the background and accounting positions taken for those transactions. This will not only save you time and effort in researching the issues, but it may also provide additional context as to the company's business purpose in entering this transaction.

■ Have peers in my industry completed similar transactions? If so, look for discussion of these transactions in

● Peer companies' public filings (Form 10-Ks), press releases, or responses to SEC comment letters (where the company may describe to the SEC its rationale for accounting positions taken).

● Industry-specific publications, such as whitepapers or accounting guides.

Take note of the accounting elections or judgments addressed by your peers that may be relevant to your transaction; be aware, however, that differences in terms may exist between the transactions.

See Chapter 4 for further discussion of SEC comment letters and accounting firm resources.

■ Should specialists be involved? Certain transactions can be highly nuanced and may require the involvement of individuals with specialized knowledge. Examples of such nuanced transactions include business combinations, securitizations, so-called hybrid debt offerings, or transactions related to a company's pension obligations, to name a few. If such specialized knowledge is not available within your own company, your auditors may be a good resource. Types of specialists include

● Technical accounting specialists

● Actuaries

● Valuation specialists, and

● Legal counsel.

Any steps that you are able to take to fully understand the purpose and economics of a transaction should be taken.

In some cases, however, you might be given only limited background on an issue (verbally, or in writing) and told what to research. That is, in some cases, your supervisor may not want to divulge all relevant facts of the transaction to you, and may only be asking for your help with one aspect of the research. This may be especially true early in your career. Even in such cases, it is helpful to go through the preceding list of steps as a sort of checklist; ask yourself: "Can I still perform this step for my limited-scope research question?" Often, even without access to contracts, many of the listed steps will still apply, such as consideration of company past practices and comparison to peer transactions.

 **Knowledge Check**

2. **In addition to reading transaction documents (contracts), what are two other possible methods for obtaining background on a transaction?**

Step 2: Define the Problem. That Is, Identify the "Researchable Question."

The next step of your research process is to define the problem; that is, identify the **researchable question(s)**. Doing so will help to focus your research efforts. Avoid long or complex questions; if your question has multiple parts, break that issue into two or more questions.

Following are examples of researchable questions that might come to mind during your initial review of a contract:

■ *If my company will receive money under the contract*: Will we recognize revenue for this? Will receiving these funds cause us to incur a liability? Have we received any capital contributions? Have we entered into a lease arrangement?

■ *If my company will pay money under the contract*: Have we created or purchased an asset? Have we incurred an expense? Have we entered into a lease arrangement?

■ *If my company purchased an ownership interest in our counterparty to the contract*: Will my company have to consolidate the counterparty? Alternatively, will my company have to record an investment in the counterparty?

Notice that each of these question includes a topic that you could navigate to in the Codification, as a starting point for your research. For example,

- To respond to the question: "Will we recognize revenue for this?", an appropriate starting point for a browse search would be

    Revenue Recognition (**Topic 605**) > Overall (**10**) > Recognition (**25**)

- An appropriate starting point for the question: "Have we entered into a lease arrangement?" would be

    Broad Transactions > Leases (**Topic 840**) > Overall (**10**) > Scope (**15**)

In some cases, it might make sense to focus your researchable questions on the *type of transaction* you are assessing. This is most effective in the case of structured, or complex transactions for which the accounting is unique to that class of transaction (such as topics listed in the Broad Transactions area of the Codification).

For example, assume that you are asked to review a contract related to a securitization of accounts receivable (i.e., the sale of investments in a portfolio of accounts receivable). In this case, knowing that this is a unique type of transaction that may be governed by its own set of rules, you should begin your search by looking for guidance specific to this type of transaction. In this case, your first researchable question might be: "Should this transaction be accounted for as a securitization?"

- An appropriate starting point for this question would be

    Broad Transactions > Transfers and Servicing (**Topic 860**)
    Sales of Financial Assets (**20**) > Scope (**15**)

Alternatively, if you are reviewing a contract involving *commodities* (e.g., gas, oil, gold) or *currency*, consider the question: "Does this contract contain a derivative?"

- An appropriate starting point for this question would be

    Broad Transactions > Derivatives and Hedging (**Topic 815**) > Overall (**10**) > Scope (**15**)

The questions just illustrated are provided with the intent of helping beginning researchers draw connections between contract terms and research questions. As such, these questions have been intentionally kept broad. In practice, however, it is often appropriate for questions to be more specific. For example, the question: "Does this transaction qualify for the milestone method of revenue recognition?" would likely be more effective than: "Will we recognize revenue for this transaction?" As you work through the research process, you will find that you can become more specific with your questions.

Finally, additional researchable questions will often become apparent as you work through the research process. For example, assume that a researcher has determined use of the milestone method is appropriate for a transaction (a scope issue). Next, the researcher must determine *how to apply* this method, and might identify the following additional questions:

- Which milestones in the contract are considered "substantive" and thus eligible for recognition as revenue?
- How much revenue should be recognized for each substantive milestone?
- What disclosures are required for transactions accounted for under the milestone method?

Notice that these questions are worded as specifically as possible, as this provides a good framework for conducting research.

Identifying the Researchable Question

Take a moment to practice identifying a single, researchable question for the following issues.

1. A company ships its widgets to a customer on December 31 but has not yet collected payment from the customer. The customer has promised to pay within 30 days but has never purchased goods from the company before.

    Researchable question? _____

Now
YOU
Try
3.1

2. A customer is suing the local grocery store for a slip-and-fall incident. The grocery store believes the lawsuit will likely be considered frivolous and rejected by the court. The grocery store must decide whether to record or disclose this matter.

    Researchable question? _____

3. An investor is suing a corporation that has just absorbed another entity in a merger. The investor is alleging that the corporation overstated on its balance sheet the values of certain equity investments that were acquired during the merger. The investor's attorney needs to understand how the equity investments should have been valued.

    Researchable question? _____

Step 3: Stop and Think: What Accounting Treatment Will Likely Be Most Appropriate?

The third step of the research process requires researchers to "stop and think." That is, before you turn to the Codification for guidance, stop and think on your own: What accounting treatment do *you* think would be most appropriate for this transaction or event? Coming up with your own, independent idea of how a transaction should be accounted for will help you to stay objective as you look for guidance in the Codification and can help you avoid anchoring to the first possible solution you find.

This is not your first accounting course—you have the knowledge to think through accounting issues independently. Use that knowledge now. Think through one or two accounting alternatives for this transaction that make logical sense to you, and jot these alternatives down.

A final step before you turn to the Codification for guidance is to take a moment to jot down possible **search terms** related to your researchable question and your initial thoughts about the accounting treatment. As noted in the introduction to search terms in Chapter 2, it's not uncommon for beginning researchers to get bogged down in Codification guidance, losing sight of what they were looking for. Keep your research question, and the list of search terms you have identified, at top of mind in order to maintain efficiency and focus as you perform your search.

Step 4: Search Potentially Relevant Sources of Guidance, Copying Any Relevant Guidance into a Word Document

Now that you have identified the researchable question, thought through the issue, and identified possible search terms, you are ready to find relevant guidance. This section provides only a high-level discussion of how to collect relevant guidance; tips for searching the Codification are available in Chapter 2.

If you know which Codification topic applies to your research question, browse to that topic in the FASB Codification. To save yourself time, always start your research by locating the topic that you expect to be most relevant. If you don't know which topic is appropriate for your search, use the Codification's keyword search feature instead. Follow all leads (search results) that appear to be relevant, as the keyword may lead you to several useful sources of guidance.

As a beginning researcher, you may end up exploring a lot of places in the Codification before you find guidance that is directly on point. Keep track of potentially relevant guidance that you find by copying sections of the guidance into a Word document. Finding potentially relevant guidance can still be, essentially, a brainstorming exercise. Look for guidance that is either directly on point or, if not available, guidance that may be relevant by analogy (for example, guidance that is on point, but for a similar transaction that differs from your transaction). Be exhaustive in your search; attempt to find all possible relevant guidance that can be used to answer your research question. In this stage of the research process, you may also choose to consult nonauthoritative sources of guidance, which are discussed further in Chapter 4.

At the end of this step, review the guidance you have collected. Ideally, you will have found some guidance that is on point, and some that upon further review does not appear to be as relevant. At this point, you may weed out (that is, delete from your Word document) sources that are less relevant, focusing instead on the guidance that is most applicable to your research question.

This step 4 is particularly geared toward beginning researchers. As you gain experience with research, you may find it easier to identify—as you go—whether or not a source is relevant, and whether it's worth pursuing. Eventually, you will be able to determine in real time which sources are most responsive to your research question.

3. **Describe the process recommended in this step, for collecting then narrowing down guidance.**

 **Knowledge Check**

Step 5: Analyze Alternatives, Documenting Your Consideration of Each

Now that you have found guidance that appears to be relevant to your issue, the next step is **analyzing** that guidance, or evaluating how that guidance applies to your research question. This process can involve judgment; that is, guidance in the Codification may not offer specific answers to the researcher's precise issue, or the Codification may allow for alternative accounting treatments. In such circumstances, it is essential for a researcher to clearly identify and analyze the relative merits of the alternative treatments available.

Recall our Flyaway.com example from the beginning of this chapter. In that example, an auditor (Linda) must research whether her client, an online ticket broker, should recognize revenue for the full amount of airline tickets sold or for the amount of its commission only. Linda has found guidance relevant to this issue in **ASC 605-45** (Revenue Recognition—Principal Agent Considerations) and has identified two alternative accounting treatments for her client:

1. Recognize revenue for the gross amount billed to the customer (the full ticket price); or

2. Recognize revenue for the net amount retained, as a commission, after paying the airline.

Even if one treatment is obviously preferable to the other based on the facts of these transactions, Linda should still present *both* alternatives when documenting the issue. Given that alternative treatments are available, it would be disingenuous to say: "Revenue must be recognized on a net basis," pointing only to guidance supporting this one alternative. Linda's analysis should clearly show how the guidance for both alternatives applies to the fact pattern, and it should clearly show the factors she considered in deciding that one treatment was preferable to another.

In some cases, two acceptable alternatives may appear to be available. In such cases, you must weigh the relative merits of each alternative, considering the following:

■ If authoritative guidance (i.e., the Codification) does not express a preference as to which alternative should be used, do sources of nonauthoritative guidance (e.g., accounting firm publications) address this issue? See Chapter 4 for further discussion of nonauthoritative sources.

■ Does one alternative appear to better reflect the economics of the transaction (to users of the financial statements)?

■ Which alternative is most consistent with the company's prior practices, if the company has entered into similar transactions in the past?

■ Is this position consistent with the positions elected by peers in my company's industry?

■ Have I vetted this accounting position with the appropriate levels of management?

■ Finally, do our auditors agree with this treatment?

Document all factors considered in your analysis of the alternative treatments. Start with the guidance you collected from your search of the Codification, providing discussion (in your own words) of how you considered that guidance relative to your company's fact pattern. After you have presented the authoritative guidance, next you should document all "other" factors considered in your analysis (including any meaningful consideration you gave to the bulleted items just listed).

Be wary of selecting an alternative that represents a departure from a past practice of your company, or of companies in your peer group. Such a departure should be addressed in your analysis, as well as discussed with management and your auditors. Your company may risk being questioned by investors or by the SEC if you elect a position (on a material transaction) that is inconsistent with past practices or unique among those in your industry.

TIP from the Trenches

> The only way someone reading your documentation will trust your conclusion is if you have clearly identified the available alternatives.
>
> In the past, I have asked students to document the accounting required for a certain transaction, knowing that when they began to explore the guidance, they would be presented with two alternatives.
>
> ■ The "A" papers are the ones where students say: "Two alternatives exist (method A and method B). Method A appears to be more appropriate for this situation because . . ."
>
> ■ The "B" or "C" papers are the ones where students say: "Method A should be followed because . . ." without mentioning that an alternative treatment is available.
>
> As an employer, I would place more trust in the work of the "A" students. Even if I disagree with their choice of accounting method, at least I have been made aware that two choices exist. In contrast, the "B" or "C" papers did not give me the full story. When reviewing future submissions from these "employees," I would likely perform the extra step of rechecking the guidance they cite for completeness.

To illustrate this point, complete the following **Now YOU Try** exercise, considering the facts about Flyaway.com presented in the opening scenario of this chapter.

Now YOU Try 3.2

Comparing Alternative Accounting Treatments

1. **ASC 605-45** (Revenue Recognition—Principal Agent Considerations) provides the following indicators of gross reporting. In the boxes below, indicate how each relates to the Flyaway.com example. In cases where the fact pattern does not provide sufficient information to respond, answer "not applicable."

Indicators of Gross Reporting	Indicator present? Not present? Or, not applicable?
The entity is the primary obligor in the arrangement (i.e.,responsible for providing the product or service desired by the customer).	a. _____
The entity has general inventory risk (or must pay the service provider even if the customer does not accept the service).	Entity does not have this risk. This indicator of gross reporting is not present.
The entity has latitude in setting the transaction price.	b. _____
The entity changes the product or performs part of the service desired by the customer.	c. _____
The entity has discretion to pick the supplier to perform the service.	d. _____
The entity is involved in determining the product or service specifications.	e. _____
The entity has the risk of physical inventory loss.	Not applicable
The entity has credit risk (risk of loss if customer payment is not fully collected).	f. _____

2. Following are indicators of net reporting from **ASC 605-45**. Indicate how each applies to Flyaway.com.

Indicators of Net Reporting	Indicator present? Not present? Or, not applicable?
The entity's supplier is the primary obligor.	a. _____
The amount the entity earns is fixed (a fixed dollar amount, or a stated percentage).	b. _____
The supplier has credit risk.	c. _____

3. Consider your analysis of these indicators (in questions 1 and 2). Now, also consider that two indicators (primary obligor, and having general inventory risk) are considered "strong" indicators. Weighing all of these considerations, which accounting treatment generally appears to be more supportable for this fact pattern and why?

_____

_____

_____

4. Why would it have been inappropriate to document consideration of that alternative only?

_____

So, which of these indicators belong in your memo? Nearly all of them. Any indicator that you weighed (positively or negatively) in evaluating an issue should be documented. It is not necessary, however, to include discussion of those indicators that were "not applicable" to this fact pattern. In practice, the researcher might also look to how other similar companies account for this type of transaction; this analysis should be also documented, immediately following the Codification analysis in a memo.

Step 6: Justify and Document Your Conclusion

The final step of the research process is to reach a conclusion—that is, determine which accounting treatment is most appropriate given the authoritative literature you have analyzed. Document this conclusion, summarizing salient points from your analysis of the guidance and other factors considered.

Once you reach the point of documenting your conclusion, in many cases it may already be fairly obvious from your analysis which treatment is most appropriate. In such cases, your conclusion can be fairly brief. For example:

> **ASC 605-45** indicates that it is a matter of judgment to determine which method of accounting—gross or net—is most appropriate for a transaction but provides indicators that should be considered in selecting an alternative. As described in the analysis above, certain indicators [namely, x and y] were met that would indicate gross reporting is appropriate. However, other indicators [a and b] indicate that net reporting would be appropriate. Given that certain indicators should be weighted more heavily than others [namely, c and d], and given that these conditions were [met/not met], Flyaway.com has concluded that it should report revenues on a [gross/net] basis. This is also consistent with how other ticket resellers account for similar transactions.

Notice that, even in this example of a brief conclusion, the author summarized the most compelling points in the analysis as support for the conclusion. It is not sufficient to say:

In conclusion, these transactions will be accounted for on a net basis.

Rather, the following underlined text should be added to such a conclusion, restating the rationale for the conclusion:

In conclusion, <u>because of factors x, y, and z</u>, these transactions will be accounted for on a net basis.

<table>
<tr><td>[**TIP**] from the Trenches</td><td>Don't "jump to" conclusions. Make sure your conclusion includes your rationale (for example, "because of factors x, y, and z"), rather than simply naming the alternative selected.</td></tr>
</table>

In cases where the choice between two or more alternatives is highly judgmental, the conclusion should be longer and more detailed. The conclusion should clearly explain which requirements from the guidance, along with other factors considered, were compelling in selecting an alternative. The rationale articulated in the conclusion could later become a critical part of the audit trail if the accounting for the transaction is ever called into question.

Knowledge ✔ Check

4. **Why is a Conclusion section necessary, if guidance excerpts have already been provided in the Analysis section of an issues memo?**

COMMUNICATING ACCOUNTING RESEARCH

Now that you have learned about the research process and the role that documentation plays in the process, let's take a closer look at how to communicate the results of your research. We will explore two common methods for communicating accounting research:

- Emails
- Accounting issues memoranda

Emailing the Results of Research Questions

Email is often useful for communicating the results of limited-scope research questions. This is often the case when you are not the "owner" of the issue (i.e., the party responsible for documenting or concluding on the complete issue), but rather are helping provide relevant guidance to some aspect of an issue that a colleague is managing.

Here is an example of a professional email responding to a limited-scope research question. In this example, John, a staff member on the audit of Flyaway.com, has been asked to help Linda research whether ASC 605–45 (Revenue Recognition—Principal Agent Considerations) is the appropriate starting point for Linda's research into the client's accounting. John's response is as follows:

Linda,

You asked me to research whether Flyaway.com's revenue recognition falls within the scope of **ASC 605–45** (Revenue Recognition—Principal Agent Considerations). Given my understanding of Flyaway.com's business model, I am assuming the Company will not be providing any of the flight services itself (rather, the flights will be provided by third-party airlines). However, let me know if that's not the case.

ASC 605-45 lists transactions that are within the scope of this guidance, as follows:

> **15-2**   The guidance in this Subtopic may apply to, but is not limited to, the following transactions and activities:
>
>> a.   Arrangements with third-party suppliers to drop-ship merchandise on behalf of the entity.
>> b.   Services offered by an entity that will be provided by a third-party service provider.
>> c.   . . .

Par. 15-2(b) lists "services offered by an entity that will be provided by a third-party service provider" as an example of a transaction that is within the scope of this guidance. As Flyaway.com sells flights on its website that will be provided by third-party airlines, it appears that these arrangements are within the scope of this guidance.

Furthermore, implementation guidance within ASC 605–45 includes an example, in par. 55-39 through 55-45, illustrating gross versus net reporting considerations for discount airline ticket sellers, which are similar to the role of Flyaway.com. Therefore, ASC 605–45 appears to be the appropriate guidance to consider for this arrangement.

Let me know if you need anything further. Thanks for letting me assist with this question.

John

The sample email above exhibits qualities that you should generally try to include in your professional email communications. Here are some of the lessons learned from this email:

- Keep it brief. The sample email above is concise, yet complete in its response to the question raised.

- Re-state the question: "You asked me to research . . ."

- Include an excerpt from authoritative guidance to support your response.

- Use complete sentences.

- If you made any assumptions in researching the issue, state what you assumed. It's likely that you will have to make assumptions if you have only limited background on an issue.

- Reread, possibly print, the email before you send it. This will help you identify confusing or weak language, as well as grammatical errors.

- Do not say "I think/feel"; this isn't about you. It's about what guidance is on point. If you are unsure about how guidance should be read, you can say: "It appears . . ."

- Avoid exclamation points, in order to keep your tone as professional as possible.

- Include an offer to be of further assistance.

TIP *from the* **Trenches**

One of my former **accounting research** colleagues made it a habit to print and reread *every* substantive email to a client or supervisor before sending it. She wanted to always put her most professional self forward. Her thoughtful approach to research—combined with her attention to detail—has paid dividends for her career; she went on to work in the national office of a major firm, then moved into a position in the SEC's Office of the Chief Accountant.

Now **YOU** **Try** **3.3**

Drafting a Professional Email

You are a staff auditor reviewing the Statement of Cash Flows for Auto Corp (the client). The senior on your audit team (Matt) has asked you to research whether the client has appropriately classified the proceeds from the sale of its manufacturing facility as cash flows from investing activities.

Draft an email response to Matt's question. Use the Codification guidance in Figure 3-1 to support your response.

Figure 3-1

Codification excerpt for email exercise (ASC 230-10, Statement of Cash Flows)

> **Classification**

45-10   A statement of cash flows shall classify cash receipts and cash payments as resulting from investing, financing, or operating activities.

> > **Cash Flows from Investing Activities**

45-11   Cash flows from purchases, sales, and maturities of available-for-sale securities shall be classified as cash flows from **investing activities** and reported gross in the statement of cash flows.

45-12   All of the following are cash inflows from investing activities:

  a. Receipts from collections or sales of loans made by the entity and of other entities' debt instruments (other than cash equivalents and certain debt instruments that are acquired specifically for resale as discussed in paragraph **230-10-45-21**) that were purchased by the entity

  b. Receipts from sales of equity instruments of other entities (other than certain equity instruments carried in a trading account as described in paragraph **230-10-45-19**) and from returns of investment in those instruments

  c. Receipts from sales of property, plant, and equipment and other productive assets . . .

Reproduced with permission of the Financial Accounting Foundation.

Your response here _____

_____

_____

_____

_____

_____

_____

_____

_____

_____

Drafting an Accounting Issues Memorandum

Documentation in the form of an accounting issues memorandum is generally warranted when a transaction is complex, judgmental, or highly material. Each company should have policies in place for when such documentation is required, and at what point in the transaction review process. It is considered a best practice to evaluate and document the accounting for a transaction at or before the time the transaction is executed. In certain cases, such "contemporaneous" documentation is *required*, as discussed further in Chapter 1.

Accounting issues memos are generally organized into the following format (see Figure 3-2), subject to some variation by company. Nevertheless, we'll refer to this as the "standard memo format."

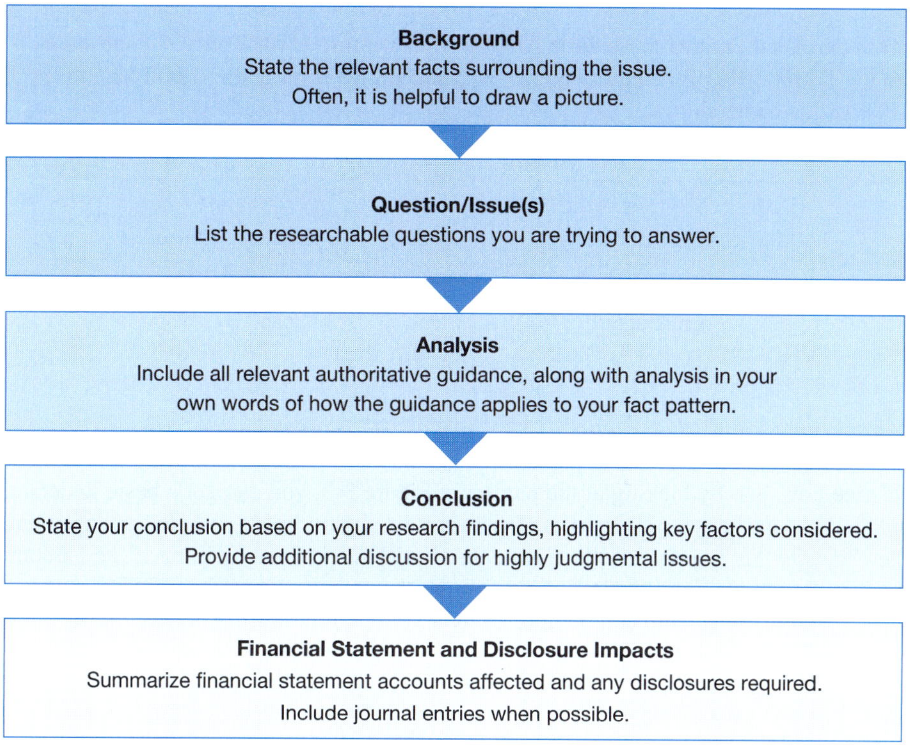

Background
State the relevant facts surrounding the issue.
Often, it is helpful to draw a picture.

Question/Issue(s)
List the researchable questions you are trying to answer.

Analysis
Include all relevant authoritative guidance, along with analysis in your own words of how the guidance applies to your fact pattern.

Conclusion
State your conclusion based on your research findings, highlighting key factors considered.
Provide additional discussion for highly judgmental issues.

Financial Statement and Disclosure Impacts
Summarize financial statement accounts affected and any disclosures required.
Include journal entries when possible.

Figure 3-2

Standard memo format

The issues memorandum should include all of the categories in Figure 3-2. Present these categories in bold to improve the readability of your memo.

> Your ultimate goal with the issues memo is to create a "one-stop shop" for knowledge about this transaction and its accounting. A reader, after picking up your memo, should not have to do additional digging to fully understand the background or the support for the accounting conclusion. After reading your memo, if a reader finds it necessary to get additional key facts from the contract, or to read additional guidance from the Codification, then you have failed to make your memo a one-stop shop.

TIP from the Trenches

Background

The Background section of an issues memo should include all relevant background necessary for understanding the transaction and its accounting. This section should be concise, but not sparse. Aim to provide enough detail about the issue that a party uninvolved with the matter could pick up the memo—even years later—and understand the issue well enough to form an opinion as to whether or not the accounting treatment is appropriate.

Step 1 of the research process, described earlier in this chapter, outlines the process necessary to understand the facts and background of a transaction. Be thoughtful in your fact-gathering; it is not uncommon for beginning researchers to go back two or three times to ask additional questions, based on incomplete initial information.

Transactions are often complex. A *picture of a transaction*, included within the Background section of a memo, can greatly enhance a reader's understanding of the relationships and parties involved in the issue. These can be fairly easy to create using the "shapes" feature in Word. In the picture, try to show as much information about the relationships among the parties as you can (parent/subsidiary relationships, what each party gives or gets from the other, etc.).

For example, here is a simple picture for the following arrangement:

■ Two unrelated entities are entering into a joint venture (JV). Entity A contributes $1,000 to the JV for 50% of the equity ownership, and Entity B makes a $2,000 loan to the JV for 50% of the ownership.

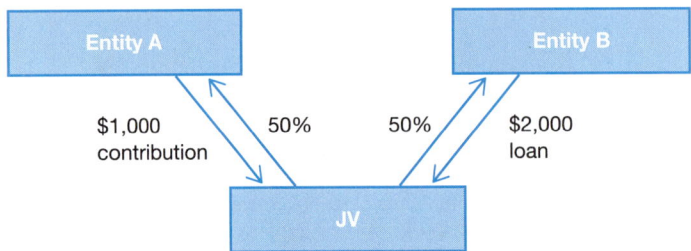

Notice how, just by looking at the picture in Figure 3-3, you can get a basic understanding of the relationships between the parties. To illustrate a slightly more complex arrangement, let's add new facts to this example. Let's assume that Entity A is owned by Entity 1, and assume that Entity B is owned by Entity 2. Let's also assume that a bank loans the JV $500. Often when drawing a picture, ownership can be implied by a vertical relationship between two entities.

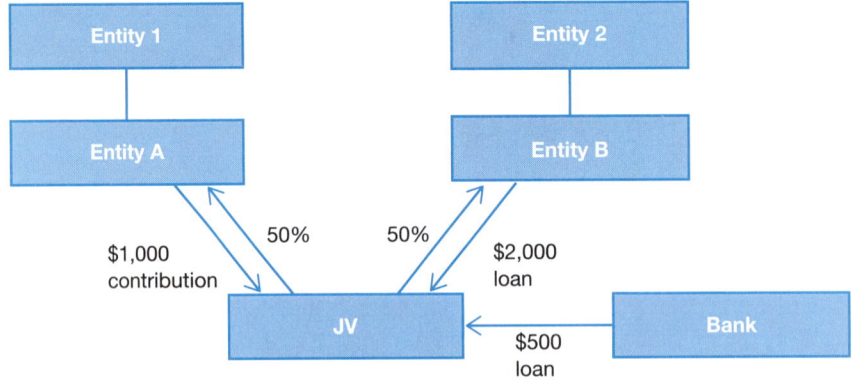

Notice a few things about the picture in Figure 3-4. First, even without "100%" written next to the line connecting Entity 1 and Entity A, the vertical relationship implies full ownership. Second, as the bank is not involved as an owner, it is not drawn in a vertical relationship; it is shown to the side of the JV to indicate that it is an outside, third party.

There is no magic to drawing a picture for inclusion in a memo. The idea is just to portray relationships in a way that readers can easily understand.

Drawing a Picture

Draw a picture for the following arrangement:

- Entity A owns Entity B and Entity C. Entities B and C enter into a joint venture ("the JV"). Entity B contributes $20,000 for 99% of the equity ownership. Entity C contributes $500 for 1% of the equity and will serve as manager of the JV. Bank lends the JV $1 million.

- Hint: Beside the line representing Entity C's contribution of $500, you can also write "manager," as this is a type of service that Entity C is contributing to the JV.

Your picture here

Question/Issue(s)

The Question/Issue(s) section of the memo should follow immediately after the background. Under the header "Issue(s)," list your researchable question(s). Often, there may be multiple questions to address. For example, assume that Entity A is evaluating the accounting for its relationship with the JV in Figure 3-4. In that case, the following research questions would be relevant:

Issues:

1. Does Entity A have a variable interest in the joint venture?

2. Does the joint venture qualify for the business scope exception in par. 15-17(d) of **ASC 810-10** (Consolidations)?

3. If no scope exception is available, does the joint venture meet the definition of a variable interest entity in par. 15-14 of **ASC 810-10**? (and so on)

Each issue should be phrased in the form of a question. Given that this example deals with a rather complex accounting topic, you'll notice that each question builds on the previous one. Had this been a simpler topic, a single issue ("Issue 1") might suffice to determine the accounting, and a second issue ("Issue 2") might address required disclosures.

For a more detailed example of a variable interest entity evaluation, see the Chapter 5 Appendix.

Analysis

The Analysis section of the memo should address each issue listed, one at a time, with the issue name in bold print. Title the first Analysis section, for example, **Analysis of Issue 1: Does Entity A have a variable interest in the joint venture?**

The Analysis section is arguably the most critical component of a well-written issues memo. In this section, you will include excerpts from relevant guidance, along with commentary in your own words about how the guidance applies to your transaction. Include enough guidance to respond completely to each issue. The Analysis section is where you will include discussion of all potential alternative treatments, weighing their relative merits.

Remember the "one-stop shop" concept; you need to include actual quotations from authoritative guidance in your memo to support your analysis. Use enough guidance so that a reader will not also have to reperform a search of the Codification in order to understand your analysis. Nonauthoritative guidance may be used as additional support for your analysis but should not be your primary source of guidance. Remember that if an auditor or the SEC comes knocking, your goal is to be able to hand them a well-reasoned, guidance-supported position paper.

The "Analysis" section of your memo is aptly named, because commentary in your own words is critical to this section. As a general rule of thumb, your own comments should *precede and follow* all guidance excerpts.

Ever heard of the interpersonal communication concept of a "compliment sandwich"? It goes something like this: If you're going to criticize someone, say something nice before and after the criticism. For example, "Joe, I like your tie today. I really wish you would do something about your bad breath. By the way, nice job on that report."

Think of your analysis section as a series of *guidance sandwiches*, with your commentary preceding and following all guidance excerpts.

EXAMPLE

The following sample guidance sandwich was used in John's email to Linda, regarding Flyaway.com. When Linda is ready to document her research on Flyaway.com's revenue recognition, she can include this guidance sandwich in the Analysis section of her issues memo.

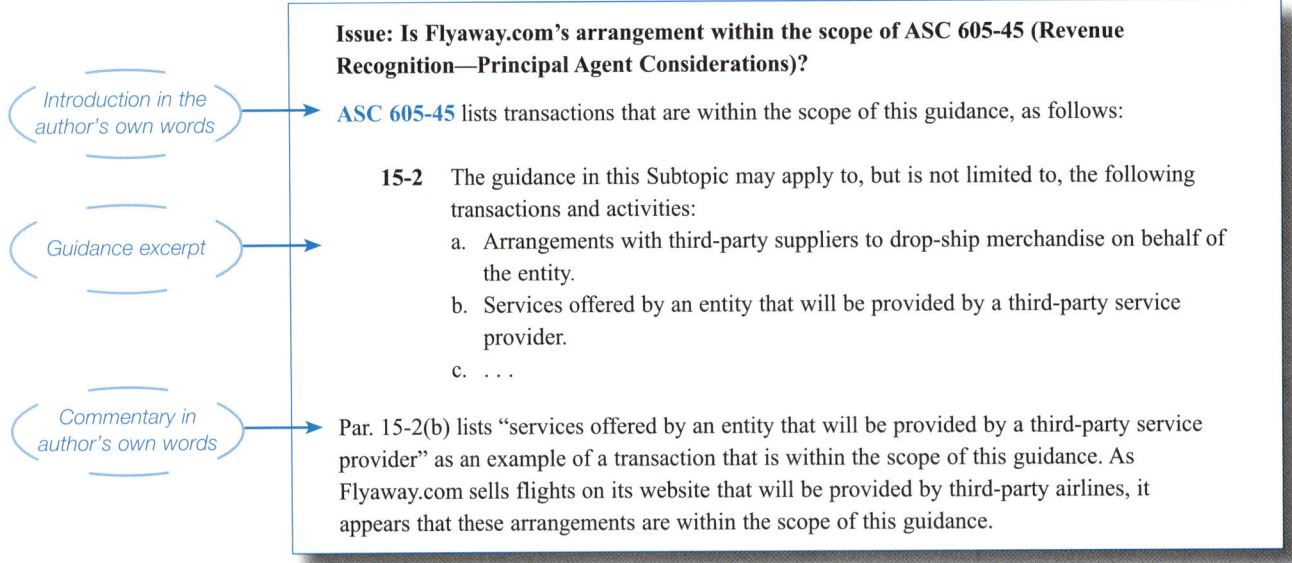

> **Issue: Is Flyaway.com's arrangement within the scope of ASC 605-45 (Revenue Recognition—Principal Agent Considerations)?**
>
> *Introduction in the author's own words*
>
> **ASC 605-45** lists transactions that are within the scope of this guidance, as follows:
>
> *Guidance excerpt*
>
> 15-2   The guidance in this Subtopic may apply to, but is not limited to, the following transactions and activities:
> a. Arrangements with third-party suppliers to drop-ship merchandise on behalf of the entity.
> b. Services offered by an entity that will be provided by a third-party service provider.
> c. . . .
>
> *Commentary in author's own words*
>
> Par. 15-2(b) lists "services offered by an entity that will be provided by a third-party service provider" as an example of a transaction that is within the scope of this guidance. As Flyaway.com sells flights on its website that will be provided by third-party airlines, it appears that these arrangements are within the scope of this guidance.

Notice how the example provides commentary in John's own words before and after the guidance excerpt. The first sentence of the example introduces the guidance and states why it is being considered. The quote from the guidance is inserted next. Finally, the last sentence applies the guidance to the company's own set of facts.

Now YOU Try 3.5

Guidance Sandwiches

Remember the email you drafted to your audit senior (Matt) regarding the Statement of Cash Flows for Auto Corp? Take a moment now to identify the guidance sandwich you used in that email (or, take a moment to create one now). Recall that you are responding to Matt's question about whether the client has appropriately classified the proceeds from the sale of its manufacturing facility as cash flows from investing activities.

Hint: Your guidance sandwich could start with, for example:

■ **ASC xxx** states that cash flows from investing activities include . . . "(x)."

Your response here _____

_____

_____

Now that you understand guidance sandwiches, let's focus on how to perform a thoughtful guidance analysis.

Very commonly, a researcher's analysis of guidance must be more robust than our simple revenue recognition scope example. The researcher must thoughtfully describe how each requirement in the guidance relates to his or her specific transaction. A leading professor in accounting research described the importance of the analysis section as follows:

> *The Analysis section is really the key and what I often find most lacking in students' reports. That's because they don't do a good job of reasoning from the facts of the case, using the literature they found, to reach the appropriate conclusion. Rather, their process is more like: here are the facts, here is research, here is a conclusion.*

A thoughtful Analysis section should include the researcher's reasoning as to why the words in certain literature led the researcher to believe that the described item or transaction should be accounted for in a particular way. You will see that "guidance sandwiches" are critical to an in-depth analysis, as well.

The following example, which evaluates whether an investment should be accounted for under the cost or equity method of accounting, illustrates a robust analysis involving the consideration of two accounting alternatives. Recall from our previous discussion that when multiple acceptable alternatives are present, the researcher should tell the full story and include these alternatives in his or her documentation.

EXAMPLE

Well-Reasoned Analysis

Facts: Investor, Inc. recently purchased 15% of the outstanding common stock of ABC Corp, a nonpublic company. Along with this purchase, Investor, Inc. also was given the ability to appoint five new members (out of ten total members) to ABC Corp's Board of Directors. Additionally, Investor, Inc. will be leading a restructuring (such as a refinance) of ABC Corp's current outstanding debt, as a condition of its equity investment.

Analysis: Should Investor, Inc account for its investment under the cost method, or under the equity method?

Investor, Inc has evaluated the appropriate accounting treatment for its investment in 15% of ABC Corp's stock. Because this is a noncontrolling (less than 50%) ownership interest, two alternatives were considered: 1) Account for the investment under the "cost method", or 2) Account for the investment under the "equity method".

Use of the cost method is addressed in **ASC 325-20** ("Investments - Other, Cost Method Investments"), as follows:

05-2   Investments are sometimes held in stock of entities other than subsidiaries, namely corporate joint ventures and other noncontrolled entities. These investments are accounted for by one of three methods—the cost method (addressed in this Subtopic), the fair value method (addressed in Topic 320), and the equity method (addressed in Topic 323).

05-3   While practice varies to some extent, the cost method is generally followed for most investments in noncontrolled corporations, in some corporate joint ventures, and to a lesser extent in unconsolidated subsidiaries, particularly foreign.

The guidance above indicates that the cost method can be used to account for investments in "noncontrolled corporations." It is true that Investor, Inc does not control ABC Corp. However, this topic (**ASC 325-20**) does not offer additional interpretive guidance for determining which transactions are within the scope of the cost method. (Note that the scope guidance for cost method investments is minimal, and is not on point, and implementation guidance is not available for this topic). Therefore, it is appropriate to consider what guidance is available regarding use of the equity method.

ASC 323-10 (Investments—Equity Method) identifies investments that fall within the scope of this topic, as follows:

15-3   The guidance in the Investments—Equity Method and Joint Ventures Topic applies to investments in common stock or in-substance common stock... that give the investor the ability to exercise significant influence (see paragraph 323-10-15-6) over operating and financial policies of an investee even though the investor holds 50% or less of the common stock or in-substance common stock . . .

Therefore, par. 15-3 states that common stock giving the investor the ability to exercise significant influence should be accounted for under the equity method. Additional scope guidance available in par. 15-6 and 15-8 states the following for determining whether "significant influence" is present:

15-6   Ability to exercise significant influence over operating and financial policies of an investee may be indicated in several ways, including the following:
a. Representation on the board of directors
b. Participation in policy-making processes
c. Material intra-entity transactions
d. Interchange of managerial personnel
e. Technological dependency
f. Extent of ownership by an investor in relation to the concentration of other shareholdings (but substantial or majority ownership of the voting stock of an investee by another investor does not necessarily preclude the ability to exercise significant influence by the investor).

15-8   . . . an investment of less than 20 percent of the voting stock of an investee shall lead to a presumption that an investor does not have the ability to exercise significant influence unless such ability can be demonstrated...

In this case, Investor, Inc purchased 15% of ABC Corp's stock. Therefore, par. 8 indicates that there is a presumption that Investor, Inc does not have significant influence. However, this presumption can be overcome if other indicators of significant influence are present, such as those listed in par. 6. Along with Investor, Inc's purchase of the stock, Investor Inc was given the ability to nominate five of ten total members to ABC Corp's Board. Investor, Inc will also be leading a restructuring of ABC Corp's current debt load. As such, indicators (a) and (b) of par. 6 are present, indicating that Investor, Inc does have the ability to exercise significant influence and should therefore the investment should be accounted for under the equity method.

In this example, notice how the author performed a complete analysis, in his or her own words, of how the guidance relates to Investor, Inc.'s fact pattern. To support this analysis, the author incorporated excerpts from authoritative guidance. Notice too the author's determination that, while this investment is theoretically within the scope of both the cost and equity methods, use of the equity method is more appropriate given the entity's ability to exercise significant influence.

In some cases, you will encounter guidance with multiple conditions, often shown as "and" or "or" conditions. Generally speaking, "and" conditions must all be met in order for a certain accounting treatment to apply. With "or" conditions, only one condition must be met. For example, for a contract to meet the definition of a derivative, it must meet three conditions: has a notional and an underlying (e.g., a quantity and a price), *and* requires no initial net investment, *and* is capable of net settlement.

In such cases where multiple conditions are present, it is a best practice to evaluate each condition provided. To do so, first present the full guidance excerpt. Next, evaluate each of the conditions from the guidance in turn. Figure 3-5 provides a template for analyzing guidance which includes multiple conditions.

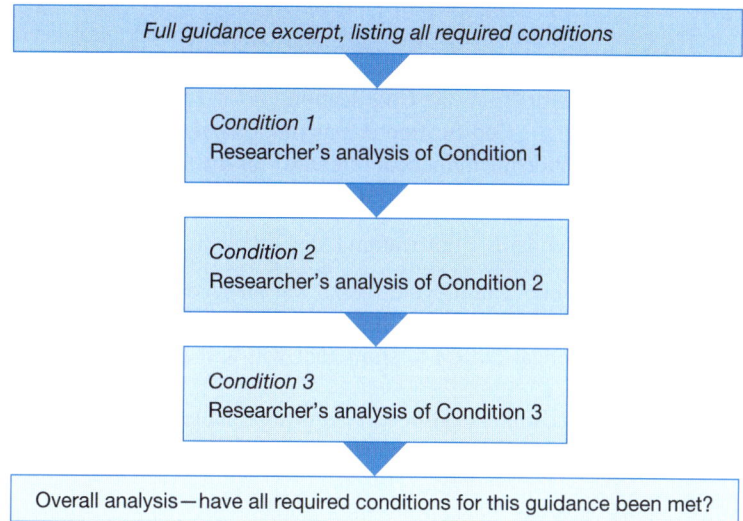

Figure 3-5

Template for completing an analysis of guidance with multiple conditions

Finally, in addition to analyzing the requirements of accounting guidance (both from authoritative and nonauthoritative sources), the Analysis section of an issues memo is also the appropriate place for discussion of other key factors considered in determining an appropriate accounting treatment. Present your consideration of these other factors following your review of the applicable authoritative literature. For example, How are peer companies accounting for this type of transaction? How has our company handled this type of transaction historically?

Conclusion

Conclude your discussion of each separate issue with a clearly written **conclusion**. In our Investor, Inc. example, the company determined through its analysis that use of the equity method is appropriate. In the conclusion section of its memo, Investor, Inc. should summarize key points from this analysis and describe the conclusion reached. See additional discussion of justifying and documenting conclusions earlier in the chapter under "The Process of Performing Accounting Research."

> **TIP** from the Trenches
>
> If your company consulted subject matter experts or other professionals in its evaluation of an accounting issue, this "consultation" should be documented in the issues memo. This consultation could be described just before, or immediately following, the Conclusion section of the issues memo (depending on whether the consultation was considered in reaching, or just to confirm, the company's accounting position).

Financial Statement and Disclosure Impacts

When applicable, conclude your memo with a summary of **financial statement and disclosure impacts**. Journal entries can be useful in describing anticipated financial statement impacts.

PROPERLY REFERENCING ACCOUNTING GUIDANCE

How Do I Reference a Passage from the Codification?

Excerpts from authoritative guidance are critical to effective accounting research communications. Paraphrasing guidance (that is, summarizing it into your own words) is not enough; authoritative guidance is far more impactful in a memo than a summary of guidance in your own words. Additionally, quoting "Codification excerpts" from articles or textbooks is inappropriate; always get authoritative guidance directly from the Codification. This discussion focuses on how to properly cite guidance excerpts from the Codification.

The first time you refer to the Codification in a memo, give its full title ("FASB Accounting Standards Codification"). Include the numerical reference for the topic you are citing, as well as a parenthetical description of the topic name. For example:

- Per FASB Accounting Standards Codification (ASC) topic 840-10-20-1 (Leases), . . .

Remember that not everyone reading your memo was an accounting major and understands the acronym ASC. Therefore, it is important initially to provide the full name of the Codification, then to use the parenthetical (ASC) to show that you will abbreviate this term in future references within the memo.

After your initial reference to the Codification, it is acceptable to refer to the topic using the abbreviation "ASC," and omitting the parenthetical topic name (Leases). For example,

- Per ASC 840-10-20-2: . . .

Note how these sample numerical references go all the way down to the paragraph level. Always provide as much detail as possible. Your reference would be lacking if you sent readers to Topic 840-10, as that leaves them with pages of guidance to sort through to find what you are trying to reference. Do your readers the favor of getting them directly to the appropriate paragraph within the guidance.

In citing guidance, don't get creative with sentence structure. Following are examples of both strong and weak references. Stick to the strong references, and your memos will have a more professional tone.

- Strong references:
  - According to ASC xxx, "Quote"
  - ASC xxx states or ASC xxx requires: "Quote"
  - Per ASC xxx: "Quote"
  - ASC xxx provides the following guidance: "Quote"
  - The rate of return shall be based on: "Quote" (ASC xxx).
  - The rate of return shall be based on: "Quote" [fn 1]
    (at end of page) Footnote 1: ASC xxx

- Weak references:
  - **ASC xxx** asks readers to . . . "Quote"
  - **ASC xxx** believes . . . "Quote"
  - The Codification writes . . . "Quote" (**ASC xxx**)
  - The FASB says . . . "Quote" (**ASC xxx**)
  - I found the following guidance . . . "Quote" (**ASC xxx**)

Take careful note of the language and punctuation used in the preceding examples. "Per **ASC xxx**" is followed by a colon (:). "According to **ASC xxx**" is followed by a comma (,). All of the lead-ins just listed should be followed by excerpts from the guidance. Additionally, each excerpt includes a reference to the source of the guidance (**ASC xxx**). Note that these numerical references should get down to the paragraph-level of detail, since each provides a quotation directly from a paragraph of the guidance.

Referencing the Codification

Fill in the blanks using strong reference words.

1. _____ ASC 840-20-50-1, "For all **operating leases**, the lessee shall disclose . . ."

2. ASC 840-20-50-1 _____: "For all **operating leases**, the lessee shall disclose . . ."

3. _____ ASC 840-20-50-1: "For all **operating leases**, the lessee shall disclose . . ."

Now **YOU** Try **3.6**

Should I Ever Use Footnotes in Professional Memos?

The use of footnotes and endnotes (that is, numerical references leading readers to a "works cited" source at the end of a page or document) should be fairly rare in accounting research memos. That is, you should primarily expect to cite the Codification or other authoritative sources of guidance, and these source references can be included in the body of your memos.

Footnotes or endnotes are appropriate, however, if you are referencing a less-common source of guidance, which requires a lengthier source citation. For example, if you find guidance in an academic paper or in a professional journal, a footnote or endnote citation is appropriate, as the reference must include not only the author's name, but the article name, date published, title of journal, edition number, and page number. Including all of this detail in the body of your research memo would bog down memo readers.

When Should I Use Quotation Marks?

Any guidance copied directly from the Codification must be enclosed in double quotation marks, *and* you must cite the source of the guidance down to the paragraph-level of detail (e.g., Per **ASC xxx-xx-xx-xx . . .**).

> For example, **ASC 715-30-35-47** (Compensation—Pension) states: "The expected long-term rate of return on plan assets shall reflect the average rate of earnings expected on the funds invested or to be invested to provide for the benefits included in the projected benefit obligation."

Notice the use of double quotation marks to enclose the quote, and notice the full reference to the Codification source.

There is one (and only one) instance in which quotation marks are not required: If you are including a long excerpt—roughly three lines or more—from the Codification, and you *indent the guidance*. Indenting long excerpts (as opposed to integrating the quotation within other text) can also improve the readability of your memo.

EXAMPLE

> ASC 715-30 (Compensation—Pension) requires that companies consider future expected returns on investments in selecting an expected return on assets assumption:
>
> > **35-47**   The expected long-term rate of return on plan assets shall reflect the average rate of earnings expected on the funds invested or to be invested to provide for the benefits included in the projected benefit obligation. In estimating that rate, appropriate consideration shall be given to the returns being earned by the plan assets in the fund and the rates of return expected to be available for reinvestment . . .
>
> Therefore, an asset return assumption is appropriate if management believes this rate is achievable in the future.

Notice how this example includes both: (1) a reference (**ASC xxx**) down to the paragraph level of detail and (2) guidance that is indented, indicating that it is a direct quote.

When Is It Appropriate to Alter an Excerpt from the Guidance?

It is only appropriate to alter an excerpt from the guidance if (1) in doing so, you do not change the meaning of the guidance, and (2) you clearly tell the reader what you have altered. Use brackets [ ] to identify any words you have changed, or to acknowledge that you have added emphasis to part of a quote.

For example, note the following altered excerpt from **ASC 840-10** (Leases—Overall):

> **15-6.**   ". . . The right to control the use of the underlying [PP&E] is conveyed if **any** of the following conditions is met . . ." [Emphasis added]

In the preceding example, the author omitted the words "property, plant, or equipment" in favor of using the bracketed term [PP&E]. Additionally, the author added boldface type to the term "any," and acknowledged this change by stating "[Emphasis added]." As neither change alters the meaning of the guidance, and as both changes were identified with brackets, these changes are appropriate.

When Is It Appropriate to Use Ellipses?

Ellipses, or those three dots in a row (. . .) are used when a writer *omits* some text in a quote or *doesn't quote the full sentence or paragraph*. As you begin writing technical emails and memos, you may find that ellipses are useful in trimming fat; that is, eliminating irrelevant sections from a paragraph may improve the readability of your analysis. While guidance is critical to a strong issues memo, too much guidance can be burdensome.

EXAMPLE

> Here is original guidance from **ASC 405-20** (Extinguishments of Liabilities) describing how a debtor's secondary liability should be recorded as a guarantee.
>
> > **40-2**   If a creditor releases a debtor from primary obligation on the condition that a third party assumes the obligation and that the original debtor becomes secondarily liable, that release extinguishes the original debtor's liability. However, in those

> circumstances, whether or not explicit consideration was paid for that guarantee, the original debtor becomes a guarantor. As a guarantor, it shall recognize a guarantee obligation in the same manner as would a guarantor that had never been primarily liable to that creditor, with due regard for the likelihood that the third party will carry out its obligations. The guarantee obligation shall be initially measured at fair value, and that amount reduces the gain or increases the loss recognized on extinguishment. See Topic **460** for accounting guidance related to guarantees.

Here's an example of the proper use of an ellipsis to abbreviate a sentence from the preceding text.

40-2 "However . . . , ~~in those circumstances~~, whether or not explicit consideration was paid for that guarantee, the original debtor becomes a guarantor."

Here's an example illustrating the proper use of an ellipsis when the full paragraph is not being quoted. Here, the ellipsis shows that the paragraph continues on, even beyond this excerpted text.

40-2 "If a creditor releases a debtor from primary obligation on the condition that a third party assumes the obligation and that the original debtor becomes secondarily liable, that release extinguishes the original debtor's liability. However, in those circumstances, whether or not explicit consideration was paid for that guarantee, the original debtor becomes a guarantor . . ."

While ellipses may become a great tool in your toolbox, you must always *check and double check* that the text you are skipping over is not critical to the understanding of a passage, and that using the ellipsis does not change the meaning of the original guidance.

Here's an improper use of an ellipsis. Notice how pertinent guidance has been omitted.

40-2 "If a creditor releases a debtor from primary obligation on the condition that a third party assumes the obligation . . . ~~and that the original debtor becomes secondarily liable~~, that release extinguishes the original debtor's liability."

STYLE TIPS FOR PROFESSIONAL COMMUNICATIONS

We'll conclude our chapter on communication by discussing a few points on style. Attention to style will improve the professionalism of your work products.

Use Proper Voice in Your Memos

Avoid saying "I" or "we" or "you" in accounting research communications. Technical accounting memos are not about you; they should not be written in the first person.

- For example, do not say: "We found the guidance in **ASC 605**."
- Do not say: "I think" or "We have concluded" in a memo.
- Do not say: "You have asked us for the appropriate accounting treatment . . ." in a memo.

When referring to a company, do not say "they." Rather, call the company by its name initially, and identify (in parenthesis) any abbreviations you plan to use for the company name thereafter.

■   For example, Flyaway.com ("Flyaway" or "the Company") shall recognize revenue on a net basis. This is appropriate given the Company's role as agent.

Notice how this example initially introduces Flyaway.com using its full name, and then uses the parenthetical ("Flyaway" or "the Company") to show how the company will be described in future references within the memo.

Keep Your Language Neutral (Avoid Strong Words)

To improve the professionalism of your writing, keep your language neutral. I once asked students to review a company's accounting election and to comment on whether it was supportable based on guidance from the Codification. A few students described the company's position as "wrong," and one may have even called the company's accounting "ridiculous."

The lesson here: Try to leave your emotions out of technical writing. Keep your language neutral. Here are examples of more appropriate ways to comment on an accounting position. The accounting is

■   "Appropriate/not appropriate."

■   "Consistent/not consistent with" the guidance.

■   "Supported/not supported by" the guidance.

Also, try to avoid "absolutes" in your technical writing. It's better to play it safe and use qualifying words.

■   Use the word "generally" rather than "always."
   ●   Analysts "generally" (not "always") listen to companies' earnings calls for the purpose of understanding more of the qualitative factors behind a company's performance.

■   Use the word "could" instead of "will."
   ●   The company "could" (not "will") have to restate later if it chooses an accounting position that is not supported by the guidance.

Get the Grammar Right

Grammatical errors in your writing can undermine the quality of your whole research effort. Before submitting a memo to your supervisor or to a client, carefully reread it for proper grammar, spelling, and clarity. Even an offense as seemingly minor as a misplaced comma can tarnish the polish on an otherwise great paper.

Following is a brief refresher on commas. If this is a trouble area for you, please review this section carefully.

■   Use commas between "independent clauses"—each with a *subject* and a *verb*:
   ●   *I went* to the store, and *you went* home.
   ●   Comparative *income statements must* be presented for three years, but comparative *balance sheets must* be presented for two years.
   ●   Note: Each of these clauses could be a sentence all by itself, so a comma is needed between them.

■   Use commas after an *introductory phrase*:
   ●   *Although the company's earnings were below expectations*, the company's stock price did not change.
   ●   *If two alternatives are available*, both should be analyzed in your memo.
   ●   Note: Note that each phrase has its own subject and verb; the introductory phrase also includes a transition (if, although, after, before, etc.). Separate these two phrases with a comma.

- Use commas when you insert a phrase into a sentence that isn't necessary for understanding the sentence.
  - He said, *with an encouraging nod*, that I should read more.
  - Nonauthoritative guidance, *which is available from a number of different sources*, can often be useful in supporting authoritative references.
  - Note: If the phrases "with an encouraging nod" or "which is available from different sources" were stricken from these sentences, the sentences would still read just as clearly. As these phrases are purely descriptive, and not necessary for understanding the sentence, they are set off in commas.

CHAPTER SUMMARY

The accounting research process is necessary for ensuring that accounting treatments chosen by financial statement preparers are appropriate and supportable by authoritative guidance. The process starts with the accountant obtaining an understanding of the transaction, and concludes with the accountant documenting and justifying the conclusion reached. Key accounting judgments must be documented, not only to support the current accounting judgment and to facilitate the auditors' review, but also to serve as a historical record of the company's rationale in selecting an accounting position. Accountants who are effective at these research and communication processes will see that these skills can pay dividends in their careers.

REVIEW QUESTIONS

1. What are two objectives of performing accounting research?
2. Cite two reasons why documentation of accounting positions is critical to accounting research.
3. Identify three resources a researcher might consult when gathering facts and background necessary to understand a transaction.
4. Why is it important to identify the "researchable question(s)" early in the research process?
5. When alternative accounting methods are available, why is it essential for a researcher to identify these possible alternatives in his or her documentation?
6. Explain why researchers should include actual excerpts from the guidance in accounting memoranda, rather than paraphrases of guidance (in the researcher's own words).
7. Which section of an accounting issues memorandum is often enhanced by a picture (or diagram) of the transaction?
8. What does the term "guidance sandwiches" mean? Where would you find these in an accounting issues memorandum?
9. How should a researcher refer to guidance from the Codification, the first time it is cited in a memo?
10. Which of the following Codification references is stronger? Explain.
    - *Per* ASC xxx: "Quote"
    - ASC xxx *asks readers to* . . . "Quote"
11. Describe what "voice" should be used in accounting research communications. (Feel free to respond by describing what voices "should not" be used.)
12. Explain what it means for the language in an accounting memorandum to be "neutral."

EXERCISES

1. Identify at least one researchable question for each of the following issues.
    - An online travel agency sells a $300 airline ticket to a customer; of this amount, the travel agency must remit $270 to the airline, and the travel agency will retain a $30 commission related to the sale of the ticket.
    - Acknowledging publicly that its Auto division is its most unprofitable business unit, Conglomerate, Inc. has announced the sale of the Auto Division's 8 manufacturing facilities, along with planned layoffs of Auto

Division's manufacturing employees. Conglomerate, Inc. is hoping to segregate the results of the Auto Division's operations in its financial statements.

- ■ Onyx, Inc. (i.e., "the original polluter") has paid $10 million to a waste disposal company to clean a contaminated site, and to assume its environmental liability (currently recorded as a $10 million liability on Onyx's financial statements). State regulators have signed off on the liability transfer and now look to the waste disposal company as the responsible party for the cleanup. What is Onyx's researchable question?

2. Certain businesses may choose to invest in projects that provide them with tax credits (such as a developer who builds low-income housing developments). In some cases, these tax credits can be sold or traded, when these investor businesses have more credits than they can use. Assume that your company has entered into a contract for the purchase of tax credits from a developer and has asked you to evaluate the accounting implications. You are in the first step of the research process (understanding the facts/background of the transaction). Identify three resources you could consult to gather additional background/precedent for this issue.

3. List the two alternative accounting treatments available for recognizing costs incurred for advertising. Cite your source.

4. What are two types of "Accounting Changes" described in the Codification? Identify these "alternative" types of accounting changes, and cite where you found these listed in the Codification.

5. Your audit firm has a new client in the cable television industry. The audit partner, Dan, has asked you to find out whether the client can recognize revenue immediately for hookup services provided to new customers. Assume that the client's hookup revenues generally approximate $75 per customer, and related direct selling costs generally amount to approximately $10 per customer. Draft an email to Dan, responding to this question.

6. Draw a picture illustrating the following fact pattern:

   Company A is exchanging its building in Ohio, plus $500,000 cash, for a patent from Company B. Company A has taken out a loan for $500,000 from Little Bank in anticipation of the exchange. Little Bank is a wholly owned subsidiary of Big Bank.

7. Draw a picture illustrating the following fact pattern:

   Company A has issued bonds with a fixed 5% rate to investors (in exchange for cash), with interest payable semiannually. Company B has issued bonds that pay LIBOR (a floating rate) to investors (in exchange for cash). Company A and Company B enter into an interest rate swap. In this swap, Company A will pay LIBOR to Bank (a financial intermediary); in turn, Bank passes this payment on to Company B. Company B will pay a fixed 5% rate to Bank, which in turn passes this payment on to Company A. (Through this derivative transaction, Company A has essentially converted its payment obligation from a fixed to a floating rate; Company B has converted its obligation from floating to fixed).

   (*Hint:* To begin this picture, draw four boxes in a row horizontally, to depict, respectively, Investors, Company A, Company B, Investors. There should be lines between each company and its investors depicting the consideration they exchange. Above this horizontal row, draw one box for Bank.)

8. Green Products, a producer of natural cleaning products, has purchased a new production plant and has asked you: *Over what period* should our new plant be depreciated? The plant's estimated useful life is 40 years. Using a guidance sandwich, respond to this question. That is, introduce the issue, quote relevant guidance, then summarize how the guidance applies to the issue in your own words.

9. Read the following issue. Next, add an ellipsis to par. 25-10, to reflect the removal of any guidance not considered relevant to this issue.

   Issue: A company is executing a business combination in stages. Assume that the acquirer has not recognized any business combination-related amounts in other comprehensive income in prior reporting periods.

   ASC 805-10-25-10 (Business Combinations, Recognition)

   25-10 In a business combination achieved in stages, the acquirer shall remeasure its previously held equity interest in the acquiree at its acquisition-date **fair value** and recognize the resulting gain or loss, if any, in earnings. In prior reporting periods, the acquirer may have recognized changes in the value of its equity interest in the acquiree in other comprehensive income (for example, because the investment was classified as available for sale). If so, the amount that was recognized in other comprehensive income shall be reclassified and included in the calculation of gain or loss as of the acquisition date.

10. Starting with the *second sentence* of the following, correct any errors in the paragraph, or fix any areas where the professionalism of the writing could be improved. Consider proper voice, language, and punctuation. You do not need to use the Codification to complete this exercise.

   > You indicated that Zeta Corp ("the Company") is planning to close a plant and therefore plans to lay off a number of its employees. They are planning to apply the guidance in 715-30 (Compensation, Defined Benefit Pensions) to this event. You asked me to determine whether the guidance they've chosen is right or wrong. Their conclusion is wrong because I found guidance in Code section 712-10-05 (Compensation—Nonretirement Postemployment Benefits) saying that severance is covered by that guidance so they will need to follow that guidance.

CASE STUDY QUESTIONS

Interim Reporting of Earnings per Share, Writing an Email Your audit senior, Quinn, is reviewing the second-quarter financial statements prepared by Holder, Inc., a publicly traded company, and thinks the client may have omitted an important item. Quinn has asked you to research whether interim financial statements are required to include earnings per share amounts. Prepare an email responding to Quinn's question. Comment on any other potential ramifications of Holder, Inc.'s omission that come to mind, which you can offer to research. Ensure that you use professional grammar and style.   **3.1**

Determining Whether an Instrument Meets the Definition of a Derivative (Writing the Analysis Section of an Issues Memo)   **3.2**

Facts: You are in the controller's group of Alpha Corp. Today's date is 12/31/20x1. You've been asked to review a contract in which Alpha Corp agrees to purchase 100 shares of IBM from Beta Corp (seller) in 1 year (on 12/31/20x2), for $100 per share. Said another way, Alpha Corp has entered into a forward contract for the purchase of stock.

Required: Analyze whether this contract meets the definition of a derivative. This is a question of scope. Assume that no scope exceptions apply to this contract. In your response, include guidance sandwiches, with excerpts from the guidance and discussion (in your own words) of how the guidance applies to Alpha Corp's fact pattern. Consider the template in Figure 3-5, for analyzing guidance with multiple conditions, when preparing your response.

In your research, you need only consider the following paragraphs from the guidance. However, do not include all of these paragraphs as support for your analysis—choose only those paragraphs that are most compelling and relevant to your analysis.

   ASC 815-10-05-4
   ASC 815-10-10-1
   ASC 815-10-15-83, 15-88, 15-92, 15-96
   ASC 815-10-15-119 and 120

Your typed response should be approximately two pages. Act as though you are writing just the Analysis section of an issues memo, and use the header:

   Analysis—*Does Alpha Corp's contract with Beta meet the definition of a derivative?*

Inventory Valuation, Writing an Issues Memo You are in the controller's group of Charlie Corp. You have been asked to draft a (brief, 1 to 1.5 page) issues memorandum (a memo "to the files") documenting the accounting for the following issue.   **3.3**

   > Charlie Corp has leased a mine, from which it recently extracted 100 kilograms of gypsum (a mineral that can be used to produce drywall). Charlie Corp plans to sell the gypsum to building materials manufacturers. Charlie Corp is analyzing whether its gypsum inventory can be carried at its selling price per ASC 330-10-35-16(b). Assume that quoted market prices are generally available for gypsum, and that the market for gypsum is active.

Using the template for analyzing guidance with multiple conditions from Figure 3-5 of this chapter, analyze whether all necessary conditions are met for the accounting treatment proposed. If assumptions are needed to fully evaluate the guidance, identify those assumptions in your analysis. For this particular memo, you are not required to present alternative treatments; assume for this issue that you have solely been asked to document whether the conditions in ASC 330-10-35-16(b) are met. Present your response in the "standard memo format," including all required issues memo headings.

Chapter 4

A Researcher's Essential Skill: Using Nonauthoritative Sources to Supplement Codification Research

Occasionally, guidance in the Codification may require further explanation, even for the most seasoned of researchers. Just ask Lisa, a senior corporate accountant. She has been asked to evaluate her company's recent purchase of a 5% equity ownership stake in EquityElite, a privately held investment company.

Lisa has carefully reviewed the terms of the investment and has spoken to her manager for additional background. While EquityElite's shares will trade among only a handful of investors, the company's only business activity will be to invest in large, publicly traded companies. Lisa wonders whether her company should account for the investment using the cost method (Topic **325-20**) or using the fair value method, as an available for sale security (Topic **320**). She consults the scope section of each topic to understand which is more appropriate.

(continued)

(continued)

Learning Objectives

After reading this chapter and performing the exercises herein, you will be able to

1. **Understand** the value that nonauthoritative sources add to the research process.
2. **Identify** sources of nonauthoritative guidance and understand when it is appropriate to use these sources.
3. **Answer** research questions using the FASB's Concepts Statements.
4. **Locate** the FASB's basis for conclusions in pre-Codification standards and Accounting Standards Updates.
5. **Locate** guidance within accounting firm publications.
6. **Understand** when peer benchmarking is appropriate and how it is performed.
7. **Identify** circumstances in which references to IFRS may be appropriate.

(continued from previous page)

Key to this scope question is establishing whether the investment in EquityElite has a "readily determinable fair value." This is a condition for application of the guidance in Topic 320. Seeing limited interpretive guidance for this definition in the Codification, Lisa sets out to locate additional examples. She finds a copy of Ernst & Young's guide book, *Certain Investments in Debt and Equity Securities*[1] and locates scope guidance using the table of contents. Lisa soon learns that companies should not "look through" an investee to its underlying holdings in determining whether the investee has a readily determinable fair value. Accordingly, the investment is not within the scope of Topic 320; Lisa will now consider whether the cost method applies.

By supplementing Codification research with a nonauthoritative source, Lisa found plain-English guidance that improved her understanding of the Codification's requirements. She can now document both sources considered (the Codification and Ernst & Young's guidance) in her issues memo.

Using Nonauthoritative Sources of Guidance

1. What is nonauthoritative guidance, and *when* should it be considered?

2. What are common sources of nonauthoritative guidance?
   - FASB Concepts Statements
   - Accounting Standards Updates (ASUs), and pre-Codification standards
   - Accounting firm resources
   - AICPA resources
   - Peer benchmarking
   - International Financial Reporting Standards (IFRS)

3. Citing nonauthoritative sources

Organization of This Chapter

This chapter begins by describing when it is appropriate to utilize nonauthoritative sources, citing guidance from the Codification that permits the use of these sources in certain circumstances.

Next, the chapter introduces several important sources of nonauthoritative guidance, indicating when each source may be used and providing examples demonstrating the use of each source. Included in this discussion is an introduction to the AICPA's new *Financial Reporting Framework for Small- and Medium-Sized Entities* (the FRF for SMEs).

The chapter concludes with guidance on citing nonauthoritative sources.

The preceding graphic illustrates the organization of material in this chapter.

---

[1] Ernst & Young, Financial Reporting Developments: *Certain Investments in Debt and Equity Securities.* October 2011. Page i.

INTRODUCTION TO NONAUTHORITATIVE GUIDANCE

What is Nonauthoritative Guidance?

Nonauthoritative guidance is any source of accounting guidance or practice not included within the FASB Codification. Because this guidance is not included within the Codification, it is not considered part of GAAP.[2] Therefore, in the event of inconsistencies between nonauthoritative guidance and Codification guidance, nonauthoritative guidance generally would not support an unqualified audit opinion.

While the guidance included within the Codification is extensive, there are a few reasons that it may not offer guidance on every possible accounting issue:

- First, the body of guidance making up the Codification was developed over time, in a manner that responded to practitioners' needs as they arose—often, for very specific fact sets. The guidance was never methodically created in such a manner that all possible accounting topics or financial statement line items would be addressed.

- Second, transactions are often unique, and it would be impossible for guidance to be on-point for every unique set of facts.

Codification Topic **105** (Generally Accepted Accounting Principles) describes the relationship between authoritative and nonauthoritative accounting guidance. The browse path for accessing Topic 105 is shown in Figure 4-1.

Figure 4-1

Browse path for accessing ASC 105, Generally Accepted Accounting Principles

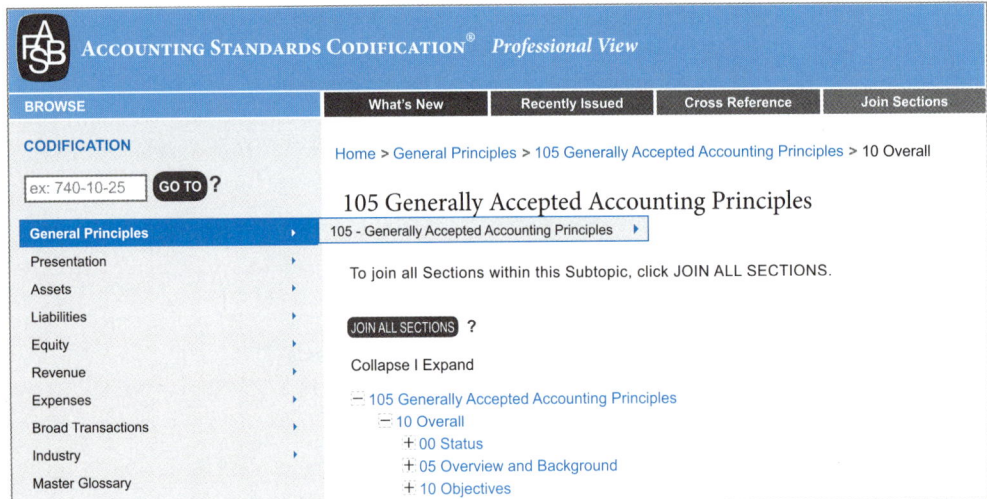

Reproduced with permission of the Financial Accounting Foundation.

In particular, Topic 105

- Establishes the Codification as "the source of authoritative [GAAP] recognized by the FASB to be applied by nongovernmental entities."[3] Guidance from the SEC is also authoritative for public companies.

- Acknowledges that there are circumstances in which authoritative guidance may not be available for a specific transaction. In such circumstances, a practitioner should first consider whether authoritative guidance is available (by analogy) for similar transactions. If not, nonauthoritative sources may be consulted.

---

[2] This statement is consistent with Rule 203, Interpretation 203-1, of the AICPA's Code of Professional Conduct, which states: "Reference to generally accepted accounting principles (GAAP) in Rule 203, Accounting Principles [sec. 203 par. .01], means those accounting principles promulgated by bodies designated by council . . .".

[3] FASB Accounting Standards Codification (ASC) Topic 105-10-05-1 (Generally Accepted Accounting Principles, Overview and Background).

■ States that sources of accounting guidance outside of the Codification are considered nonauthoritative.

Following is an excerpt from **ASC 105-10**, which illustrates this guidance.

05-1   This Topic establishes the *Financial Accounting Standards Board (FASB) Accounting Standards Codification*® (Codification) as the source of authoritative generally accepted accounting principles (GAAP) recognized by the FASB to be applied by nongovernmental entities. Rules and interpretive releases of the Securities and Exchange Commission (SEC) under authority of federal securities laws are also sources of authoritative GAAP for SEC registrants. In addition to the SEC's rules and interpretive releases, the SEC staff issues Staff Accounting Bulletins that represent practices followed by the staff in administering SEC disclosure requirements, and it utilizes SEC Staff Announcements and Observer comments made at Emerging Issues Task Force meetings to publicly announce its views on certain accounting issues for SEC registrants.

05-2   If the guidance for a transaction or event is not specified within a source of authoritative GAAP for that entity, an entity shall first consider accounting principles for similar transactions or events within a source of authoritative GAAP for that entity and then consider nonauthoritative guidance from other sources. An entity shall not follow the accounting treatment specified in accounting guidance for similar transactions or events in cases in which those accounting principles either prohibit the application of the accounting treatment to the particular transaction or event or indicate that the accounting treatment should not be applied by analogy.

05-3   Accounting and financial reporting practices not included in the Codification are non-authoritative. Sources of nonauthoritative accounting guidance and literature include, for example, the following:
  a. Practices that are widely recognized and prevalent either generally or in the industry
  b. FASB Concepts Statements
  c. American Institute of Certified Public Accountants (AICPA) Issues Papers
  d. International Financial Reporting Standards of the International Accounting Standards Board
  e. Pronouncements of professional associations or regulatory agencies
  f. Technical Information Service Inquiries and Replies included in AICPA Technical Practice Aids
  g. Accounting textbooks, handbooks, and articles.

The appropriateness of other sources of accounting guidance depends on its relevance to particular circumstances, the specificity of the guidance, the general recognition of the issuer or author as an authority, and the extent of its use in practice.

As you can see from the list in par. 05-3, there are many possible sources of nonauthoritative guidance. This chapter introduces just a few of the sources that you may find most useful as a practitioner.

Benefits of Nonauthoritative Guidance

You might be wondering whether it's better to just play it safe, and to steer clear of sources that are not authoritative. However, experienced researchers would argue that nonauthoritative sources are often indispensable to their understanding of complex guidance.

Nonauthoritative guidance can be useful for providing

- Guidance for issues not addressed by the Codification.
- Interpretive guidance to help researchers understand and apply Codification requirements.
- Additional context for understanding the intent of Codification guidance.

First, nonauthoritative guidance may address items or transactions (or similar items and transactions) not included in the Codification. For example, there is no definition included in the Codification for the terms "assets" and "liabilities." Researchers seeking guidance on these definitions must consult the FASB's Conceptual Framework (a nonauthoritative source).

Second, nonauthoritative sources can offer **interpretive guidance**, or additional explanations and illustrations, for complex accounting topics. Accounting guidance can be highly nuanced; that is, while the words in authoritative literature may seem straightforward, there are often hidden areas of judgment involved in applying the guidance. Interpretive guidance can help users identify and understand the nuances and areas of complexity within the Codification.

Interpretive guidance is frequently issued by the major accounting firms, in the form of accounting guides and technical accounting whitepapers. Examples of interpretive guidance include

- Questions and answers (Q&As) about the application of a particular standard or requirement within the guidance,
- Illustrative examples of how guidance can be applied to specific situations, and
- Decision trees for applying complex guidance.

Third, nonauthoritative guidance can offer additional context to existing authoritative requirements. In particular, reading a standard setter's **basis for conclusions**, located within the original standard, can occasionally be useful in applying guidance requirements in the manner intended by the standard setter.

Nonauthoritative Sources and the Research Process

Recall the research process introduced in Chapter 3. In the third step, "Search potentially relevant sources of guidance," a researcher gathers all potentially relevant guidance. This step should include a search for both authoritative and nonauthoritative sources of guidance. Relevant guidance gathered in this step of the research process is then included in the Analysis section of an accounting issues memo.

Citing nonauthoritative guidance can be done in one of two ways:

- Ideally, nonauthoritative guidance should be cited *in addition to* Codification references, to support or further clarify Codification guidance.
- Only as necessary, nonauthoritative guidance may be cited as support for accounting positions when Codification guidance is not available.

Ideal–Nonauthoritative Guidance as a Supplement to Codification Guidance

When cited in addition to Codification guidance, nonauthoritative guidance can be included in an accounting issues memo along with Codification excerpts. Codification excerpts should always be quoted first, preceded and followed by commentary in the researcher's own words (recall the "guidance sandwiches" introduced in Chapter 3). Next, nonauthoritative guidance may be cited if it is expected to enhance a reader's understanding of the Codification requirements.

Recall that our opening scenario focused on Lisa's search for guidance on whether her company's investment in EquityElite has a "readily determinable fair value." Recall that EquityElite is a private company whose primary business activity is investing in large, public companies. Here is the Analysis section of Lisa's issues memo, where she evaluates whether this investment is within the scope of ASC 320.

Issue: Is the investment within the scope of ASC 320-10 *(Investments—Debt and Equity Securities)?*

ASC 320-10 lists the instruments within the scope of this guidance: ← *Lisa's words*

15-5. The guidance in the Investments—Debt and Equity Securities Topic establishes standards of financial accounting and reporting for both of the following:
  a. Investments in equity securities that have readily determinable fair values
  b. All investments in debt securities, including debt instruments that have been securitized.

← *Guidance excerpt,* **Authoritative**

The glossary of ASC 320-10 defines "readily determinable fair value," in part, as follows: *Lisa's words*

  a. The fair value of an equity security is readily determinable if sales prices or bid-and-asked quotations are currently available on a securities exchange registered with the U.S. Securities and Exchange Commission (SEC) or in the over-the-counter market . . .
  . . . c.   The fair value of an investment in a mutual fund is readily determinable if the fair value per share (unit) is determined and published and is the basis for current transactions.

← *Guidance excerpt,* **Authoritative**

In this case, the investee (EquityElite) does not have a published per-share value. However, determining the company's per share value could be accomplished by looking at the value of the company's underlying holdings. The Codification does not discuss whether it is appropriate to "look through" an investment. However, Ernst & Young's guide book, *Certain Investments in Debt and Equity Securities*, provides the following guidance on this issue:[4]

← *Lisa's words, analysis*

> When determining whether a security is in the scope of ASC 320, an entity should be careful not to look through the form of its investment to the nature of the securities held by an investee.
>
> **Illustration 1-1: Determining whether a security is in scope**
>
> Company A holds an interest in an unconsolidated entity and the form of the interest meets the definition of an equity security, but does not have a readily determinable fair value. If substantially all of the investee's assets consist of investments in debt securities and/or equity securities that have readily determinable fair values, it would be not be appropriate for Company A to look through the form of the investment to the nature of the securities held by the investee. The investment would be considered an equity security that does not have a readily determinable fair value and ASC 320 would not apply to that type of investment.

← *Excerpt,* **nonauthoritative** *guidance*

As EquityElite does not itself have a readily determinable fair value, and as companies should not "look through" an investment, we have concluded that ASC 320 (Investments—Debt and Equity Securities) does not apply to this investment. Next, we will explore whether application of ASC 325-20 (Cost Method) is more appropriate.

← *Lisa's words, analysis*

In the preceding example, even though guidance from the Codification addressed Lisa's question, Lisa included interpretive, nonauthoritative guidance in her memo as a sort of "value add." Readers of her memo will appreciate that Lisa has included guidance specific to the issue her company is facing.

---

[4] Ernst & Young, Financial Reporting Developments: *Certain Investments in Debt and Equity Securities.* October 2011. Section 1.3.2.1, page 5.

Not Ideal—Nonauthoritative Guidance Used by Itself

On the other hand, using guidance from nonauthoritative sources as your only source of support for an accounting position is not ideal (as it is not GAAP). Nonauthoritative guidance should only be used, by itself, after a researcher has conducted an exhaustive search of the Codification. Even then, nonauthoritative sources can occasionally point you back to the right place within the Codification. Figure 4-2 illustrates steps necessary for determining when you have exhaustively searched the Codification.

Figure 4-2

Was my search effort exhaustive?

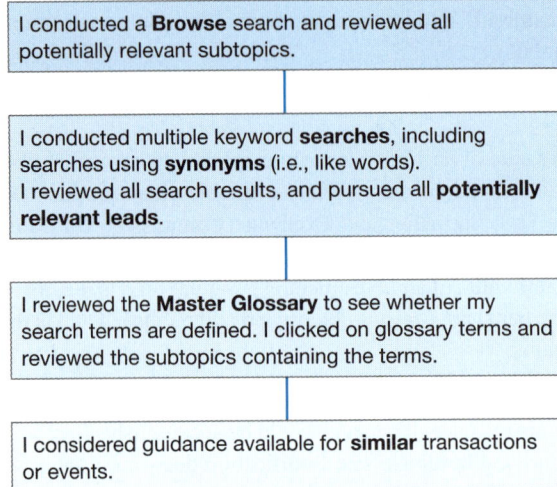

As noted previously, there are instances where the Codification may not contain guidance on a particular topic, such as the definitions of assets and liabilities. However, before concluding that a particular asset or liability is not addressed by the Codification, a researcher should perform the search steps illustrated in Figure 4-2. Many Codification topics define specific assets, such as inventory or receivables. A researcher should only turn to the nonauthoritative, Conceptual Framework definition of assets after concluding that more specific guidance is not available within the Codification.

Searching Nonauthoritative Guidance

Nonauthoritative sources are commonly organized into chapters, and they often begin with a detailed table of contents. To optimize your efficiency in searching these sources, start your search by consulting the table of contents. From there, you can often advance directly to the content that addresses your issue.

For example, assume you have a question about how to account for a trademark acquired in a business combination. Open an accounting firm guide to business combinations, and scan the table of contents for the topic "Recognition of Intangible Assets." You should generally be able to jump right to the guidance you need.

[**TIP**] from the Trenches   Never start a search of nonauthoritative guidance by skimming through the chapters; this search method is inefficient, and you will get lost in detailed guidance!

Now that you understand the role of nonauthoritative guidance, let's explore some common sources that you may encounter in practice.

SOURCES OF NONAUTHORITATIVE GUIDANCE

FASB Concepts Statements

The first nonauthoritative source we will cover is the FASB Concepts Statements (CON), also known as the Statements of Financial Accounting Concepts (SFAC), or the Conceptual Framework. The Conceptual Framework is a set of principles and objectives that are intended to improve the consistency and quality of financial accounting standards. Although issued by the FASB, Concepts Statements are not considered authoritative GAAP and are not included within the Codification. Rather, the Concepts Statements can be accessed on the FASB website (www.fasb.org), under "Standards."

The purpose of the Concepts Statements is generally twofold: first, this guidance gives the FASB a common framework, or language, to guide the development of new standards. Second, the Concepts Statements are intended to provide practitioners with key objectives and principles to consider in the preparation of financial statements.

First and foremost, the Concepts Statements are intended to set forth the fundamental objectives and concepts on which new standards are based. From the brief history provided in Chapter 1, you may recall that the FASB's predecessors (the CAP and APB) were criticized for their failure to develop such a framework. Accordingly, creation of the Conceptual Framework became a key objective of the FASB upon its establishment in 1973. The Board issued Concepts Statements No. 1-6, covering guidance including objectives of financial reporting and guidelines for recognition, between 1978 and 1985; Concepts Statement No. 7, on present value measurement, was issued in 2000.

In recent years, the FASB has made limited progress on a project to replace all of its existing Concepts Statements with a single document, which is expected to read like a chapter book. So far, Chapters 1 and 3 of CON 8 have been issued (as part of a joint project with the IASB), and these chapters focus on the objectives and qualitative characteristics of financial reporting. Today, the IASB has individually resumed its Conceptual Framework project, but the FASB has not yet indicated whether it plans to follow suit. If and when the FASB resumes this project, the Board is expected to reconsider the authoritative status of the Conceptual Framework, and may decide to elevate the Conceptual Framework to authoritative GAAP.[5]

A secondary benefit of the Concepts Statements is that they provide practitioners with objectives to consider in the preparation of financial statements. This function is described in the preamble to CON 8, as follows:

> The objectives and fundamental concepts [of this Concepts Statement] also may provide some guidance in analyzing new or emerging problems of financial accounting and reporting in the absence of applicable authoritative pronouncements.[6] [Explanation added]

That is, CON 8 acknowledges that practitioners may find the broad principles in the Concepts Statements useful when more specific guidance is not available in the Codification.

Test Your Familiarity with the Conceptual Framework

Put a check mark next to the following phrases that sound familiar to you. These phrases reflect key concepts from the Conceptual Framework—you may have learned these in an introductory accounting course. Then count the check marks to see how you scored.

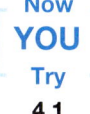

Now
YOU
Try
4.1

_____ The primary objective of general purpose financial reporting is to provide information that is useful to users.
_____ For information to be useful, it must be relevant and a faithful representation.

Source: CON 8, Ch.1 (*The Objective of General Purpose Financial Reporting*), par. OB2, and Ch. 3 (*Qualitative Characteristics of Useful Financial Information*), par. QC4.

Continued

---

[5] FASB Exposure Draft, Proposed Statement of Financial Accounting Concepts: *Conceptual Framework for Financial Reporting: The Reporting Entity.* Issued March 11, 2010. Page vii, paragraph P12.

[6] FASB Statement of Financial Accounting Concepts No. 8, *Conceptual Framework for Financial Reporting,* preamble. September 2010.

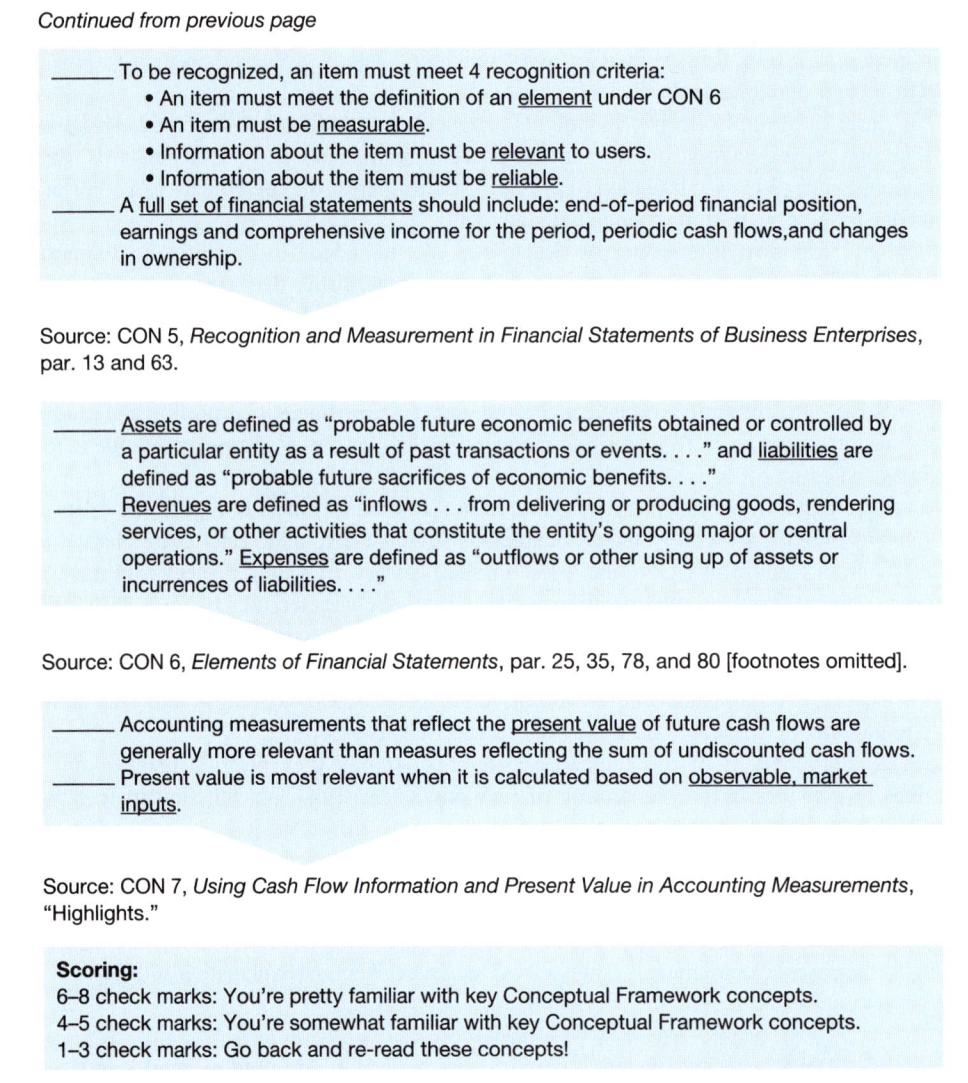

Continued from previous page

_____ To be recognized, an item must meet 4 recognition criteria:
  • An item must meet the definition of an <u>element</u> under CON 6
  • An item must be <u>measurable</u>.
  • Information about the item must be <u>relevant</u> to users.
  • Information about the item must be <u>reliable</u>.
_____ A <u>full set of financial statements</u> should include: end-of-period financial position, earnings and comprehensive income for the period, periodic cash flows,and changes in ownership.

Source: CON 5, *Recognition and Measurement in Financial Statements of Business Enterprises*, par. 13 and 63.

_____ <u>Assets</u> are defined as "probable future economic benefits obtained or controlled by a particular entity as a result of past transactions or events. . . ." and <u>liabilities</u> are defined as "probable future sacrifices of economic benefits. . . ."
_____ <u>Revenues</u> are defined as "inflows . . . from delivering or producing goods, rendering services, or other activities that constitute the entity's ongoing major or central operations." <u>Expenses</u> are defined as "outflows or other using up of assets or incurrences of liabilities. . . ."

Source: CON 6, *Elements of Financial Statements*, par. 25, 35, 78, and 80 [footnotes omitted].

_____ Accounting measurements that reflect the <u>present value</u> of future cash flows are generally more relevant than measures reflecting the sum of undiscounted cash flows.
_____ Present value is most relevant when it is calculated based on <u>observable, market inputs</u>.

Source: CON 7, *Using Cash Flow Information and Present Value in Accounting Measurements*, "Highlights."

Scoring:
6–8 check marks: You're pretty familiar with key Conceptual Framework concepts.
4–5 check marks: You're somewhat familiar with key Conceptual Framework concepts.
1–3 check marks: Go back and re-read these concepts!

When Should You Use Guidance from the Concepts Statements?

Before turning to the Concepts Statements for guidance, always first look to the Codification to see whether transaction, or item-specific guidance is available.

That said, the Concepts Statements are, in some circumstances, the only place to find certain guidance that can be critical to accounting research. Please take a few minutes to understand some common circumstances in which the Concepts Statements may be utilized.

■ To classify elements of financial statements. The broad meanings of the terms "Asset," "Liability," "Equity," "Revenues," and "Expenses" are not defined in the Codification. For definitions of these, you will need to consult CON 6. This guidance contains both brief definitions, as well as a detailed discussion of characteristics that are essential to meeting these definitions.

> CON 6 is commonly used to assist in determining whether a cost should be classified *as an asset or as an expense.*

■ To understand the computation, and objectives, of present value. If accounting literature requires that a certain item be measured at present value, practitioners may choose to consult CON 7. Notably, practitioners are encouraged to consult this guidance only after considering present value guidance within **ASC 820** (Fair Value Measurement), as discussed further in Chapter 8.

> CON 7 may be used to understand how *present value* should be computed.

■ To determine whether an event or item should receive financial statement recognition. In the event that the Codification does not address a particular class of transactions or items, it may be necessary to consult CON 5. CON 5 establishes four recognition criteria, including that an item must meet the definition of a financial statement element, be measurable, and that information related to the item must be relevant and reliable.

> CON 5 establishes *four fundamental recognition criteria*; however, it is not used frequently in practice.

Let's take a moment now to practice performing research using the Concepts Statements. The following questions focus on applying the definitions of financial statement elements.

Researching with the Conceptual Framework

Scenarios 1–2: Asset versus Expense

Use the following excerpts from CON 6 to respond to Scenarios 1 and 2 that follow. Notice that CON 6 presents general principles in the body of the standard (e.g., par. 25–28), while guidance in an appendix to CON 6 (e.g., Appendix B) elaborates on these principles.[7]

Assets

25. Assets are probable future economic benefits obtained or controlled by a particular entity as a result of past transactions or events.

Characteristics of Assets

26. An asset has three essential characteristics: (a) it embodies a probable future benefit that involves a capacity, singly or in combination with other assets, to contribute directly or indirectly to future net cash inflows, (b) a particular entity can obtain the benefit and control others' access to it, and (c) the transaction or other event giving rise to the entity's right to or control of the benefit has already occurred . . .

. . . 28. The common characteristic possessed by all assets (economic resources) is "service potential" or "future economic benefit," the scarce capacity to provide services or benefits to the entities that use them. In a business enterprise, that service potential or future economic benefit eventually results in net cash inflows to the enterprise . . .

Appendix B: CHARACTERISTICS OF ASSETS, LIABILITIES, AND EQUITY OR NET ASSETS AND OF CHANGES IN THEM

Characteristics of Assets

171. Paragraph 25 defines assets as "probable future economic benefits obtained or controlled by a particular entity as a result of past transactions or events." Paragraphs 26–34 amplify that definition. The following discussion further amplifies it and illustrates its meaning under three headings that correspond to the three essential characteristics of assets described in paragraph 26: future economic benefits, control by a particular entity, and occurrence of a past transaction or event.

Future Economic Benefits

172. Future economic benefit is the essence of an asset (paragraphs 27–31). An asset has the capacity to serve the entity by being exchanged for something else of value to the

Continued

---
[7] Footnotes to CON 6 references incorporated in this chapter have been omitted.

Continued from previous page

entity, by being used to produce something of value to the entity, or by being used to settle its liabilities.

173.   The most obvious evidence of future economic benefit is a market price. Anything that is commonly bought and sold has future economic benefit, including the individual items that a buyer obtains and is willing to pay for in a "basket purchase" of several items or in a business combination. Similarly, anything that creditors or others commonly accept in settlement of liabilities has future economic benefit, and anything that is commonly used to produce goods or services, whether tangible or intangible and whether or not it has a market price or is otherwise exchangeable, also has future economic benefit. Incurrence of costs may be significant evidence of acquisition or enhancement of future economic benefits (paragraphs 178–180).

174.   To assess whether a particular item constitutes an asset of a particular entity at a particular time requires at least two considerations in addition to the general kinds of evidence just described: (a) whether the item obtained by the entity embodied future economic benefit in the first place and (b) whether all or any of the future economic benefit to the entity remains at the time of assessment.

175.   Uncertainty about business and economic outcomes often clouds whether or not particular items that might be assets have the capacity to provide future economic benefits to the entity (paragraphs 44–48), sometimes precluding their recognition as assets. The kinds of items that may be recognized as expenses or losses rather than as assets because of uncertainty are some in which management's intent in taking certain steps or initiating certain transactions is clearly to acquire or enhance future economic benefits available to the entity. For example, business enterprises engage in research and development activities, advertise, develop markets, open new branches or divisions, and the like, and spend significant funds to do so. The uncertainty is not about the intent to increase future economic benefits but about whether and, if so, to what extent they succeeded in doing so. Certain expenditures for research and development, advertising, training, start-up and preoperating activities, development stage enterprises, relocation or rearrangement, and goodwill are examples of the kinds of items for which assessments of future economic benefits may be especially uncertain . . .

Control by a Particular Entity

183.   Paragraph 25 defines assets in relation to specific entities. Every asset is an asset of some entity; moreover, no asset can simultaneously be an asset of more than one entity, although a particular physical thing or other agent that provides future economic benefit may provide separate benefits to two or more entities at the same time (paragraph 185). To have an asset, an entity must control future economic benefit to the extent that it can benefit from the asset and generally can deny or regulate access to that benefit by others, for example, by permitting access only at a price.

184.   Thus, an asset of an entity is the future economic benefit that the entity can control and thus can, within limits set by the nature of the benefit or the entity's right to it, use as it pleases. The entity having an asset is the one that can exchange it, use it to produce goods or services, exact a price for others' use of it, use it to settle liabilities, hold it, or perhaps distribute it to owners . . .

Occurrence of a Past Transaction or Event

190.   The definition of assets in paragraph 25 distinguishes between the future economic benefits of present and future assets of an entity. Only present abilities to obtain future economic benefits are assets under the definition, and they become assets of particular entities as a result of transactions or other events or circumstances affecting the entity. For example, the future economic benefits of a particular building can be an asset of a particular entity only after a transaction or other event—such as a purchase or a

Continued

lease agreement—has occurred that gives it access to and control of those benefits. Similarly, although an oil deposit may have existed in a certain place for millions of years, it can be an asset of a particular entity only after the entity either has discovered it in circumstances that permit the entity to exploit it or has acquired the rights to exploit it from whoever had them.

191.   Since the transaction or event giving rise to the entity's right to the future economic benefit must already have occurred, the definition excludes from assets items that may in the future become an entity's assets but have not yet become its assets. An entity has no asset for a particular future economic benefit if the transactions or events that give it access to and control of the benefit are yet in the future. The corollary is that an entity still has an asset if the transactions or events that use up or destroy a particular future economic benefit or remove the entity's access to and control of it are yet in the future. For example, an entity does not acquire an asset merely by budgeting the purchase of a machine and does not lose an asset from fire until a fire destroys or damages some asset.

Scenario 1: A company purchased 50 hole punchers for its office staff. Each hole puncher cost $5 and should be in service for 5 years or more.

Should the cost of these hole punchers be recorded as an asset or as an expense? Support your answer using references to paragraphs from CON 6.

1.   Analysis—Should the hole punchers be recorded as an asset or expense?

_____

_____

_____

_____

_____

In Scenario 1, note that while you could support your position using *only* the definition of an asset (par. 25), your answer is stronger if you support your conclusion with excerpts from detailed Appendix B implementation guidance, as well. For judgmental issues, reference to this detailed interpretive guidance can be essential.

Scenario 2: Using the definition and characteristics of an asset above, explain why advertising costs are generally recorded as expenses, rather than as assets.

2.   Analysis—Why are advertising costs generally recorded as expenses, rather than as assets?

_____

_____

_____

_____

Scenario 3: Revenues and Expenses

CON 6 includes the following guidance defining revenues and expenses.

Revenues

78.   Revenues are inflows or other enhancements of assets of an entity or settlements of its liabilities (or a combination of both) from delivering or producing goods, rendering services, or other activities that constitute the entity's ongoing major or central operations.

Continued

Continued from previous page

Characteristics of Revenues

79.   Revenues represent actual or expected cash inflows (or the equivalent) that have occurred or will eventuate as a result of the entity's ongoing major or central operations. The assets increased by revenues may be of various kinds—for example, cash, claims against customers or clients, other goods or services received, or increased value of a product resulting from production. Similarly, the transactions and events from which revenues arise and the revenues themselves are in many forms and are called by various names—for example, output, deliveries, sales, fees, interest, dividends, royalties, and rent—depending on the kinds of operations involved and the way revenues are recognized.

Expenses

80.   Expenses are outflows or other using up of assets or incurrences of liabilities (or a combination of both) from delivering or producing goods, rendering services, or carrying out other activities that constitute the entity's ongoing major or central operations.

Characteristics of Expenses

81.   Expenses represent actual or expected cash outflows (or the equivalent) that have occurred or will eventuate as a result of the entity's ongoing major or central operations. The assets that flow out or are used or the liabilities that are incurred may be of various kinds—for example, units of product delivered or produced, employees' services used, kilowatt hours of electricity used to light an office building, or taxes on current income. Similarly, the transactions and events from which expenses arise and the expenses themselves are in many forms and are called by various names—for example, cost of goods sold, cost of services provided, depreciation, interest, rent, and salaries and wages—depending on the kinds of operations involved and the way expenses are recognized.

Gains and Losses

82.   Gains are increases in equity (net assets) from peripheral or incidental transactions of an entity and from all other transactions and other events and circumstances affecting the entity except those that result from revenues or investments by owners.

Characteristics of Gains and Losses

84.   Gains and losses result from entities' peripheral or incidental transactions and from other events and circumstances stemming from the environment that may be largely beyond the control of individual entities and their managements. Thus, gains and losses are not all alike. There are several kinds, even in a single entity, and they may be described or classified in a variety of ways that are not necessarily mutually exclusive.

Scenario 3: Assume that a manufacturing company usually pays a waste company (by the pound) to haul away manufacturing waste. Recently, a landfill gas company offered to buy a small portion of the waste for cash, saving the manufacturing facility a portion of its disposal costs and providing it with proceeds from the disposal.

The sale of manufacturing waste is not a primary business activity of the manufacturer; however, it will now result in an inflow of cash.

Which is more appropriate—classifying this transaction as an increase in revenue, a decrease in expense, or as a gain?

3.   Analysis—Record the transaction as increase in revenue or decrease in expense? Alternatively, should the transaction be recorded as a gain?

    _____

    _____

    _____

    _____

    _____

Scenario 4: Definition of a Liability

CON 6 includes the following guidance defining liabilities.

Liabilities

35. Liabilities are probable future sacrifices of economic benefits arising from present obligations of a particular entity to transfer assets or provide services to other entities in the future as a result of past transactions or events.

Characteristics of Liabilities

36. A liability has three essential characteristics: (a) it embodies a present duty or responsibility to one or more other entities that entails settlement by probable future transfer or use of assets at a specified or determinable date, on occurrence of a specified event, or on demand, (b) the duty or responsibility obligates a particular entity, leaving it little or no discretion to avoid the future sacrifice, and (c) the transaction or other event obligating the entity has already happened. Liabilities commonly have other features that help identify them—for example, most liabilities require the obligated entity to pay cash to one or more identified other entities and are legally enforceable. However, those features are not essential characteristics of liabilities. Their absence, by itself, is not sufficient to preclude an item's qualifying as a liability. That is, liabilities may not require an entity to pay cash but to convey other assets, to provide or stand ready to provide services, or to use assets. And the identity of the recipient need not be known to the obligated entity before the time of settlement. Similarly, although most liabilities rest generally on a foundation of legal rights and duties, existence of a legally enforceable claim is not a prerequisite for an obligation to qualify as a liability if for other reasons the entity has the duty or responsibility to pay cash, to transfer other assets, or to provide services to another entity. [Footnotes omitted]

Scenario 4: Assume you are the owner of a building for which you have just entered into a 2-year lease agreement. Due to the short-term nature of the arrangement, the lease will likely be classified as an operating lease.

The FASB is currently proposing fundamental changes to lease accounting, based in part on their view that a lessor's obligation to make an asset available during the lease period meets the definition of a liability. Using language from CON 6, state whether you believe the lessor's obligation meets the definition of a liability.

4. Analysis—Why might a lessor's obligation meet the definition of a liability?

_____

_____

_____

_____

_____

Accounting Standards Updates and Pre-Codification Standards

The second nonauthoritative source we will cover is FASB's Accounting Standards Updates and pre-Codification standards.

■ The term **Accounting Standards Updates** (ASUs) refers to the guidance periodically issued by the FASB for the purpose of making changes to the Codification. ASUs are not considered authoritative in their own right.

■ **Pre-Codification standards** refers to all GAAP that predates the Codification. For example, all then-effective FASB Statements, EITF Abstracts, APB Opinions, and Accounting Research Bulletins were used to populate the Codification in 2009, then were superseded when the Codification became effective.

It's worth taking a moment to understand these resources. In some cases, these standards contain content relevant to a topic, but which was deemed "nonessential" and not carried forward by creators of the Codification. Following are three circumstances in which these resources can be useful:

■ To access **grandfathered content**—This is guidance which is no longer effective for new transactions, but which companies are allowed to continue following if they were already, as of the Codification's effective date in 2009, accounting for a transaction using this guidance.

■ To read a standard setter's **basis for conclusions**—In most cases, the Board's basis for reaching its conclusions on each standard has been omitted from content moved into the Codification. Understanding the rationale for Board decisions can often be useful in applying guidance requirements in the manner intended by the Board.

■ To locate **historical guidance**—This is guidance that applied in the past, but that has since been superseded. Practitioners may need to read historical guidance when dealing with restated (historical) financial statements, or in order to understand prior guidance requirements.

Accounting Standards Updates

Let's take a moment to further discuss ASUs. Each ASU begins with a summary of its key provisions and an explanation of why the Codification is being updated. Next, each ASU details the changes it will make to the Codification, then describes the Board's rationale (its basis for conclusions).

For example, ASU 2012-02, *Testing Indefinite-Lived Intangible Assets for Impairment,* was the second ASU issued in the year 2012. Figure 4-3 depicts the cover (at left) and an excerpted page (at right) of this guidance.

Figure 4-3

Excerpts from ASU 2012-02, *Testing Indefinite-Lived Intangible Assets for Impairment*

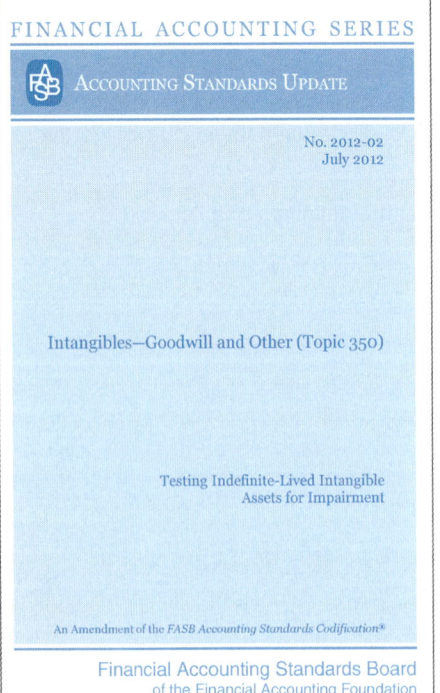

Reproduced with permission of the Financial Accounting Foundation.

- On the cover, notice that this ASU amends the guidance contained in Topic 350 (Intangibles—Goodwill and Other), and notice how the guidance is described as "An Amendment of the FASB Accounting Standards Codification."

- On the excerpted page, notice how changes to existing Codification content are marked. Underlined text reflects new Codification requirements; strike-outs reflect deleted content.

To identify the ASUs that have resulted in changes to a given topic, consult the topic's **Status** section (-**00**).

We will use a **Now YOU Try** to illustrate the use of a pre-Codification standard.

Using Pre-Codification Standards

Now
YOU
Try
4.3

ASC 730-10 (Expenses—Research and Development) requires that certain elements of research and development costs shall be expensed as incurred. One such element is described as follows:

> 25-2(a). ". . . the costs of materials, equipment, or facilities that are acquired or constructed for a particular research and development project and that have no alternative future uses (in other research and development projects or otherwise) and therefore no separate economic values are research and development costs at the time the costs are incurred."

That is, if a physical structure is built as part of a research and development activity, but has no future use, that structure may not be capitalized as an asset.

A researcher wanting more background on this requirement could consult FASB Statement No. 2, *Accounting for Research and Development Costs* (FAS 2). This is the pre-Codification standard that cross references to ASC 730. Appendix B (Basis for Conclusions) of FAS 2, states:

> 33. Consideration was given to the alternative that the costs of materials, equipment, or facilities that are acquired or constructed for a particular research and development project and that have no alternative future uses . . . be apportioned over the life of the project rather than treated as research and development costs when incurred. The Board reasoned, however, that if materials, equipment, or facilities are of such a specialized nature that they have no alternative future uses, even in another research and development project, those materials, equipment, or facilities have no separate economic values to distinguish them from other types of costs such as salaries and wages incurred in a particular project. Accordingly, all costs of those materials, equipment, and facilities should be treated as research and development costs when incurred.

Questions:

1. Explain the Board's rationale for requiring that materials, equipment, and facilities with no alternative future use be expensed as incurred.

_____

_____

2. How would a researcher know that ASC 730 cross references to FAS 2? (*Hint:* This search method was introduced in Chapter 2.)

_____

_____

Accounting Firm Resources

Major public accounting firms often encourage a handful of employees within the firm to become technical accounting specialists, whose role in the firm is to specialize on one or several technical topics and to educate other members of the firm on proper application of the topic. These individuals often work in the firm's national office or may be part of an accounting advisory group. As illustrated in Figure 4-4, specialists might include, for example, a "securitization specialist" or a "derivatives specialist."

In addition to advising peers and clients, technical specialists often write interpretive guidance for their firm and for clients' use in applying complex topics. This guidance frequently offers additional examples to supplement, as well as plain-English discussion and interpretation of, guidance found in the Codification. In certain, limited cases, firm specialists may "clear" any highly judgmental interpretations with the FASB staff before their issuance, to ensure that Codification requirements are correctly interpreted. Although nonauthoritative, imagine how helpful it would be to find a recent firm guide book illustrating a transaction just like one that you are reviewing.

Figure 4-4

Specialists you might find within public accounting firms

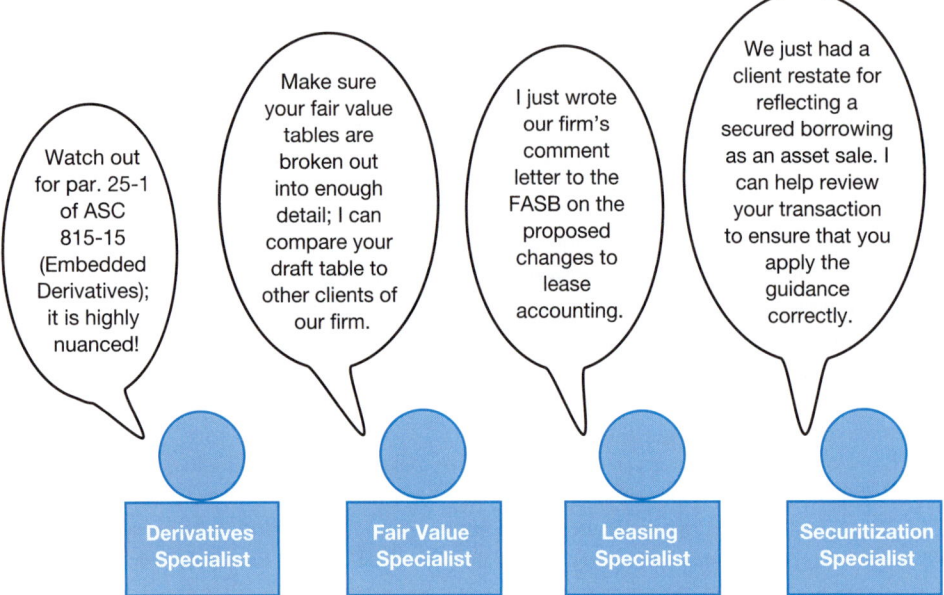

Resources commonly issued by firm technical specialists include:

- Firm research databases (clients of the firm must log in to view content)
- Firm-published guide books by topic
- Technical accounting alerts and "hot topics" whitepapers

Additionally, firm auditors may have access to the following useful resources:

- National office consultation databases (where certain audit firms maintain records of inquiries submitted to their national office)
- Auditor's verbal inquiries of his or her peers (how are other clients in this industry handling this issue, or interpreting this new guidance?)

We will discuss each of these resources in turn.

Research Databases

Several of the large public accounting firms maintain online accounting and auditing research databases for the benefit of their employees, clients, and paid public subscribers. These databases are generally free of charge to firm employees; all other users are generally charged a subscription fee (free 30-day trials are often available, however). Firm databases provide users with access to authoritative guidance including the FASB Codification, along with auditing guidance, SEC guidance, and firm-generated interpretive guidance. These databases include

- Deloitte's *Technical Library* accounting research tool, which includes access to Deloitte's interpretive guidance
- Ernst &Young's *Global Accounting and Auditing Information Tool* (GAAIT), which includes access to the Ernst & Young Accounting Manual
- Grant Thornton's *Client Experience Portal*, which offers clients access to CCH's Accounting Research Manager, along with Grant Thornton–developed content, such as educational webcasts and interpretive whitepapers
- KPMG's *Accounting Research Online* (ARO), which includes access to the KPMG Accounting and Reporting Guide
- PwC's *Comperio* database, which includes access to PwC's Accounting and Reporting Manual (ARM)

In addition to firm research databases, CCH (an independent company) maintains the *Accounting Research Manager* database, which includes authoritative and interpretive guidance, updated daily. Additionally, the AICPA offers subscriptions to its *AICPA Online Professional Library*, which includes access to accounting and auditing literature and interpretive guidance.

As noted in the preceding descriptions, many of the firm research databases contain accounting manuals published by the firm sponsoring the database. These manuals often present requirements directly from the Codification, followed by the firm's own interpretive guidance. Accounting manuals are generally organized into chapters by topic (similar to the Codification's organization) and can be searched like the Codification (i.e., via keyword or browse searches). Users of these research databases often become so comfortable with the plain-English delivery of the content that they often consult firm guidance even before searching the Codification.

Figure 4-5 includes an image from the homepage of PwC *Comperio* and may be helpful in understanding how firm research databases are frequently presented. The layout of this page should remind you of the Codification's layout (browse tree on the left, "quick search" and advanced search features at top right). Notice in the browse tree that a researcher's search options include the FASB Codification, a folder of PwC material, a folder of AICPA auditing guidance, and SEC guidance. The search box located below the Browse tree list allows a researcher to perform a keyword search within a highlighted branch.

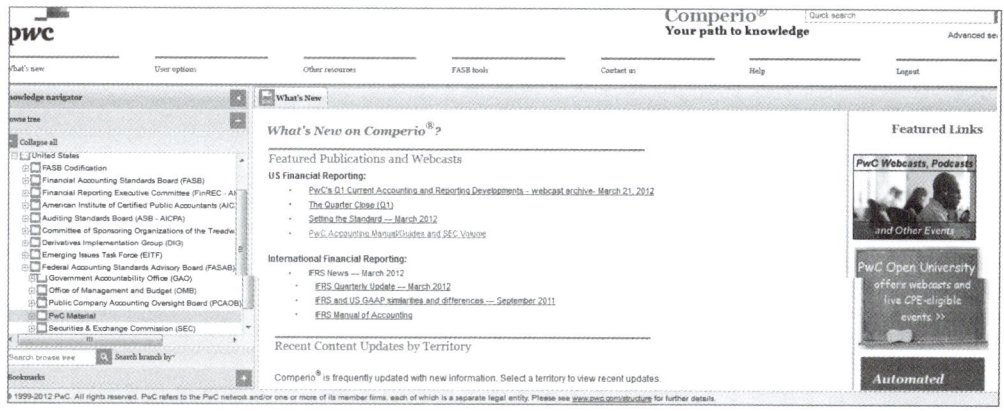

Figure 4-5

Homepage: PwC's *Comperio* database

✓ **Knowledge Check**

1. Using the homepage of PwC *Comperio* (illustrated in Figure 4-5), explain how you would search for the term "debt extinguishment" within the "FASB Codification" branch. Describe what content you would highlight in the browse tree and where you would enter the search term.

2. **Also using Figure 4-5, explain how you would search for PwC interpretive guidance for the keyword "debt extinguishment."**
3. **Where, within the browse tree, would you expect to find the FASB Concepts Statements?**

Guide Books

In addition to maintaining research databases, major public accounting firms also frequently write topic-specific guide books. These guide books are intended to provide interpretive guidance and illustrative examples for complex accounting topics (such as those listed under "Broad Transactions" in the Codification). Examples of guide book topics include

- Fair value measurement
- Consolidation of variable interest entities
- Software revenue recognition
- Derivatives and hedging
- Stock compensation
- IFRS/U.S. GAAP similarities and differences

Some firms even publish guide books summarizing the recent year's SEC comment letters to public companies, as depicted in Figure 4-6.

Figure 4-6

Sample accounting firm guide books.

At left: Ernst & Young's derivatives guide book, at 569 pages plus appendices, offers extensive interpretive guidance. At right: Deloitte's SEC Comment Letters guide book is published annually, to summarize comments and questions sent by the SEC to financial statement preparers.

© Ernst & Young LLP. Used with permission.
Copyright © 2011–2012 Deloitte Development LLC. All rights reserved.[8]

---

[8] This publication contains general information only and Deloitte is not, by means of this publication, rendering accounting, business, financial, investment, legal, tax, or other professional advice or services. This publication is not a substitute for such professional advice or services, nor should it be used as a basis for any decision or action that may affect your business. Before making any decision or taking any action that may affect your business, you should consult a qualified professional advisor.

- Deloitte shall not be responsible for any loss sustained by any person who relies on this publication.

- As used in this document, "Deloitte" means Deloitte & Touche LLP, a subsidiary of Deloitte LLP. Please see www.deloitte.com/us/about for a detailed description of the legal structure of Deloitte LLP and its subsidiaries. Certain services may not be available to attest clients under the rules and regulations of public accounting.

One great thing about accounting firm guide books is that they are frequently available for free on the Internet. Search for them by naming the topic, the word "guide," and the firm name. For example, a Google search for "Accounting for income taxes guide Deloitte," will direct you to Deloitte's 505-page guide on this topic. Firm guide books are also generally available within firm research databases, to database subscribers. In some cases, creating a no-cost login may be required to view these guides (such as for PwC or Ernst & Young materials). Ernst & Young's guides are referred to as "Financial Reporting Developments"—this term can be substituted for the word "guide" below.

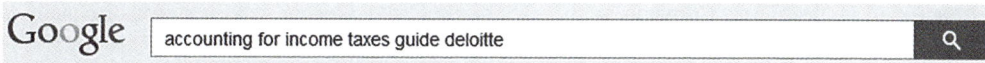

Google and the Google logo are registered trademarks of Google Inc., used with permission.

Firm guide books are often daunting in size. However, they generally include a very detailed table of contents, and are often organized like an accounting standard (e.g., scope issues, followed by recognition, and so on). Start with the table of contents when reviewing a guide book; from there, you can often jump to the exact issue you need to research.

> Firm publications, including guide books, may be nonauthoritative, but they are *incredibly* useful. Top technical accountants both in the Big 4 and in industry frequently refer to guide books published by their own firm, and by other firms, for interpretive guidance on complex issues.

[TIP] from the Trenches

Accounting Firm Technical Updates / Whitepapers

Guide books and accounting manuals take time to develop. For issues that are emerging, or that deal with newly issued guidance, practitioners often turn to firm whitepapers and technical alerts.

KPMG's "Issues In-Depth" series, illustrated in Figure 4-7, addressed time-sensitive implementation issues raised by firm clients in the process of adopting fair value guidance.

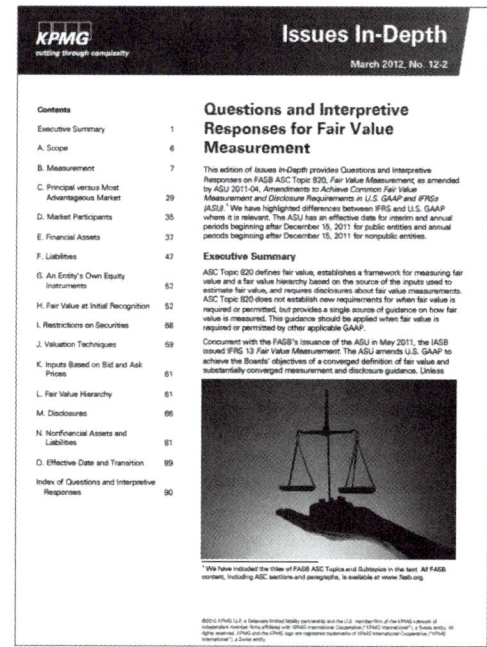

Reprinted with permission of KPMG.

Figure 4-7

Example accounting firm whitepaper—KPMG's "Issues In-Depth" series

Firms frequently distribute these emerging issues whitepapers by email; simply sign up for technical accounting alerts on the accounting firm's website, and you will be alerted as the firm issues new interpretive guidance. Chapter 13 provides additional strategies for selecting email subscriptions.

Auditor Inquiry

Auditors are often able to avail themselves of additional sources of interpretive guidance, described next.

- Some firms maintain a database of inquiries received by their national offices. In some cases, auditors are able to search this database to determine whether a specific client inquiry has been previously addressed by the national office.

- Auditors are frequently able to make verbal inquiries of their peers, to understand how other clients in an industry are handling a specific issue. For example, if an auditor is addressing a question at Healthcare Company A, he may contact his colleague who performs the audit of Healthcare Company B to ask how the client plans to address the same issue. This practice is generally acceptable as long as the auditors are not sharing confidential or nonpublic information.

When (and How) Should You Use Accounting Firm Resources?

Accounting firm guidance can be used either as a starting point for research or as additional support for a researcher's reading of the Codification. As noted previously, some auditors routinely begin their research with firm manuals. Other researchers may turn to firm guidance only as needed to search for examples of application issues or Q&As.

However you use firm guidance, bear in mind these two notes of caution:

1. Your primary support for accounting positions must still always be authoritative guidance. Nonauthoritative sources can play a supporting role, at best, in your accounting issues memos.

2. There's always a chance that the firm guidance you are reading could be outdated. The FASB continually issues new ASUs that change the content in the Codification, and accounting firm publications may have a lag in reflecting these changes. Therefore, once you find relevant firm guidance, establish a practice of always going back to the Codification to confirm that the guidance you are relying on is still current, then quote from the Codification whenever possible.

That is, researchers who start their searches with firm guidance should establish a practice of going back to the Codification to pull authoritative excerpts for their accounting memos. It is *not okay* to cite firm excerpts where Codification excerpts are available.[9]

EXAMPLE

Here are actual student examples of proper and improper use of firm guides:

- **Incorrect**: Ernst & Young defines a bargain purchase option as "(definition)."
- **Correct**: ASC 840-10-20 (Leases) defines a bargain purchase option as: "(definition)." Ernst & Young's guide book, *Lease Accounting* (2011) offers the following additional, interpretive guidance for situations in which a lessee has the option to renew his lease or purchase the leased property:

> In some cases, if the lessee elects to renew the lease, the renewal lease payments are at amounts that exceed estimated fair value. In some cases, the economic disincentive for continuing to lease the property is so significant that it is reasonably assured that the lessee will exercise the purchase option. . . . [This] serves to convert an ordinary purchase option into a bargain . . .[9]

In the latter example, the student appropriately first used available authoritative guidance before supplementing with a nonauthoritative source.

---

[9] Ernst & Young, Financial Reporting Developments: *Lease Accounting*. Revised October 2011. Section 2.4.2 "Economic Penalty Creates a Bargain Purchase Option," page 31.

Caution—As with other sources of nonauthoritative guidance, firm guidance is helpful for *interpreting* the Codification, but it should not *replace* your use of authoritative guidance. Guidance citations in accounting memos should primarily come from authoritative sources.

TIP from the Trenches

EXAMPLE

Using Accounting Firm Resources

Imagine a scenario in which you are evaluating a contract for the purchase of all output from a manufacturing plant to determine whether it is a lease. In the contract, the term "contract price" is defined as the sum of

1. A fee based on the variable operating costs of the plant (such as electricity / water usage of the plant), plus
2. An amount based on the current market price of the output.

In the Codification, one of the conditions necessary for an arrangement to qualify as a lease is, in part[10]

". . . the price that the purchaser (lessee) will pay for the output is . . . [not] equal to the current market price per unit of output as of the time of delivery of the output" (ASC 840-10-15-6c). [Emphasis added]

Assume that you are unsure how the term "market price per unit" is defined, and interpretive guidance for this is not available within the Codification. You turn to Ernst & Young's guide book, *Lease Accounting* (2011) for additional guidance on this issue (see excerpted table of contents in Figure 4-8).

Contents

© Ernst & Young LLP. Used with permission.

Continued

Figure 4-8

Excerpted table of contents from Ernst & Young's guide book, *Lease Accounting* (2011)

---

[10] ASC 840-10-15-6, Leases—Overall—Scope, identifies three conditions, and if any one of these conditions is met, the contract meets the definition of a lease. This example illustrates just part of one of these three conditions. The full condition reads:

   c· Facts and circumstances indicate that it is remote that one or more parties other than the purchaser will take more than a minor amount of the output or other utility that will be produced or generated by the property, plant, or equipment during the term of the arrangement, and the price that the purchaser (lessee) will pay for the output is neither contractually fixed per unit of output nor equal to the current market price per unit of output as of the time of delivery of the output.

Continued from previous page

Ernst & Young's guide book describes market price as follows:

> ". . . market price per unit means the cost is solely a market cost without other pricing factors (e.g., market price per kwh plus percent change in price of natural gas would not be market)."[11] [Emphasis added]

In the contract you are evaluating, the contract price includes variable operating costs, described by Ernst & Young as "other pricing factors." Accordingly, the purchaser in this contract will pay a price that is *not* equal to market, and this condition for lease accounting is met.

In your accounting memo, you could cite both the Codification guidance plus the Ernst & Young guide as support for the conclusion that this condition for lease accounting is met.

Now
[YOU]
Try
4.4

Locating Guidance within Firm Guide Books

As you know by now, searches of nonauthoritative guidance should generally begin with the table of contents. Using the excerpted table of contents of Ernst & Young's guide book in Figure 4-8, where might you start to look for guidance on the issue just described?

AICPA Resources

The AICPA offers a number of nonauthoritative resources which can be useful to practitioners. These include (1) a newly established reporting framework for small and medium-sized nonpublic entities and (2) interpretive guidance to assist practitioners in applying U.S. GAAP. We will discuss each of these in turn.

The FRF for SMEs

Issued in 2013, the AICPA's *Financial Reporting Framework for Small- and Medium-Sized Entities* ("FRF for SMEs" or the "Framework") offers an alternative to the use of U.S. GAAP for small- and medium-sized entities and responds to concerns that U.S. GAAP is currently too complex for certain private companies to apply. In fact, prior to the issuance of this Framework, certain private companies even elected to receive qualified opinions from their auditors, rather than complying in full with current U.S. GAAP. For their part, these companies' lenders and creditors would often accept these qualified opinions, understanding the high costs of full U.S. GAAP compliance.

The FRF for SMEs is expected to benefit certain preparers by providing a more concise, simple reporting framework with fewer required disclosures. The Framework is considered an **other comprehensive basis of accounting** (OCBOA), meaning a reporting framework that is not GAAP; use of this framework is entirely optional for preparers.

Notably, this framework does not replace the work of the FASB's Private Company Council, which is exploring modifications to authoritative GAAP for private companies.

Other AICPA Resources

Other nonauthoritative resources from the AICPA include the following:

■   AICPA Audit and Accounting Guides ("A&A Guides")—These guides summarize Codification and audit standards and provide practical guidance to practitioners. A&A

---

[11] Ernst & Young, Financial Reporting Developments: *Lease Accounting*. Revised October 2011. Section 1.1.3 "Right-to-use property, plant or equipment," page 5.

Guides are often issued for specific industries (e.g., the *Health Care Entities* A&A Guide) as illustrated in Figure 4-9. The AICPA also issues Audit Guides (e.g., *Audit Sampling*).

◼ *Accounting Trends and Techniques* publication (Trends)—This publication compiles examples from the disclosures of hundreds of public companies, as well as statistical data summarizing disclosure trends. The Trends publication is intended to save corporate accountants and auditors the effort of searching, one by one, for examples within company financial statements of how other preparers are complying with accounting and disclosure requirements.

◼ Technical Hotline—The AICPA offers this sort of "advice hotline" on matters including the application of accounting and auditing guidance to complex issues. Practitioners can call or email their questions into the Technical Hotline service, but only after doing their own research and involving the highest levels of their own organizations. The AICPA technical staff will provide its views; these views do not represent official positions of the AICPA.

Small businesses and small or regional CPA firms, which may not have a national office to serve as a resource for such complex questions, may find the AICPA Technical Hotline to be a valuable resource when they have exhausted their internal options.

◼ *Technical Practice Aids* and Q&As—Developed in large part based on inquiries received through its Technical Hotline service, the AICPA often posts Q&As on its website addressing recent questions its technical staff has received. Periodically, these Q&As are compiled and issued in the form of a book—the AICPA's *Technical Practice Aids*. This publication also includes implementation guidance issued by the PCAOB, relating to professional services.

Figure 4-9

AICPA's Audit and Accounting Guide, *Health Care Entities* (2011)

Now
YOU
Try
4.5

Utilizing AICPA Resources

Each AICPA resource described above serves a different function. Identify the AICPA resource that might best fit each scenario described next.

Situation	AICPA Resource to Consult?
Amy is new to the audit team of an airline and is seeking a resource that will assist her in understanding industry-specific accounting and auditing matters.	1. _____
Doug works in the 10-K reporting group at a mid-sized corporation. For years, his team has "rolled forward" the company's pension disclosure, updating numbers but making few changes to content. The company's Controller has asked his team to revisit this disclosure and to see how it can be improved. Doug wants to know how other companies approach this disclosure.	2. _____
After extensive research, the CFO of a small company has hit a dead-end on determining the appropriate accounting treatment for a complex transaction. His accounting firm does not have specialists in this area. He'd like a sounding board for resolving this issue.	3. _____

Peer Benchmarking

Often, it is not enough for companies to simply apply GAAP correctly; companies and their auditors also want to be sure that what they're reporting is consistent with how other companies are addressing the same issues.

Peer benchmarking is a common practice in which companies (and their auditors) review the reporting and disclosures of others within the company's industry. Benchmarking is particularly relevant for companies interested in seeing how their peers have implemented the latest FASB guidance. It is also useful for companies wanting to identify best practices, or to ensure consistency with their peers' methods for disclosing items or transactions.

Companies must occasionally go outside their peer group for benchmarking compliance with just-issued FASB guidance. That is, companies may be limited to reviewing disclosures of early adopters (i.e., companies who choose to apply new guidance prior to its mandatory effective date).

As discussed earlier in this chapter, the AICPA's *Accounting Trends and Techniques* publication summarizes disclosures and trends from hundreds of companies. However, the AICPA's publication is not customized by industry; in some cases, companies themselves want to hand-select the peer group companies that they compare to (e.g., same industry, same size). Additionally, companies may need to access recently issued corporate filings and cannot wait for updates to this publication.

Search for Company Filings

Through its Edgar database, the SEC provides free access to all public filings, including companies' annual (10-K) and quarterly (10-Q) reports. This database is as "real time" as it gets—filings are generally available and searchable to the public immediately upon their receipt by the SEC. Individuals can search for filings by company or by keyword.

Figure 4-10 illustrates two methods for searching the SEC website (www.sec.gov):

- First, a researcher can search for SEC documents using the keyword search box at top right. However, this will not show company filing results. For these, click the "Company Filings" link just below the search box.

- Alternatively, a researcher can navigate to "Filings" then "Search for Company Filings" to view additional search options.

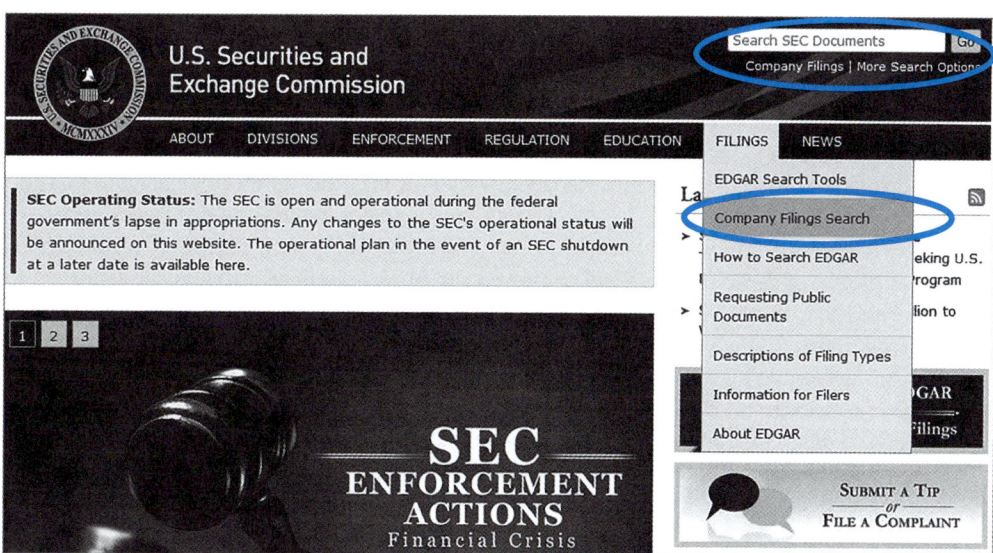

Figure 4-10

Searching company filings on the SEC website

The Edgar database is available free of charge; however it allows for only one search at a time, and only includes public companies. Companies desiring additional functionality can pay a fee to subscribe to professional research databases, such as Morningstar Document Research, SNL Financial, LexisNexis, Mergent Online, or S&P NetAdvantage. These databases offer advanced search options, including searches by industry, within a predefined peer group, and searches of private company financial statements.

Corporate annual and quarterly reports are also generally available on companies' websites, often through the link "Investors" or "Investor Relations." Figure 4-11 shows the link on GE's website to its public filings.

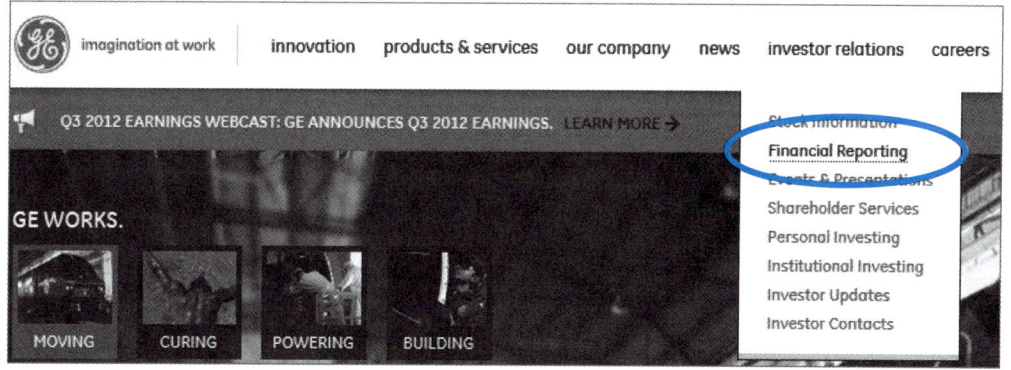

Copyright General Electric. Used with permission.

Figure 4-11

Navigating to GE's public filings, through its "Investor Relations" page

Review of SEC Comment Letters

In addition to searching company filings, a review of **SEC correspondence**, including company responses to SEC comment letters, is another valuable means for understanding peer companies' rationale in selecting or applying accounting policies.

For example, consider the following response from Apple Inc. to an SEC comment letter, regarding Apple's disclosures of the estimated selling price for iPhone upgrades.

> *SEC comment: Please tell us if you considered specifying in your disclosures what products you considered to be "similar offerings" in determining the estimated selling price of unspecified upgrades for the iPhone and Apple TV (e.g., specified software upgrades sold for the iPod Touch and AppleCare).*

Continued

Continued from previous page

Apple response:
As noted in our previous response letter dated March 4, 2010, in determining estimated selling prices (ESPs) for unspecified software upgrade rights for iPhone and Apple TV the Company considered evidence provided by pricing of actual sales of specified upgrades for iPod touch, iPhone AppleCare (APP) contracts, and upgrades to our iLife and iWork application suites. The Company did consider providing additional specific disclosure regarding selling prices of these products and the relevance of these selling prices to the ESPs… However, the Company concluded such additional disclosure would potentially be misleading. This conclusion was based on the fact the actual selling prices of these products were not considered direct proxies for the ESPs determined for iPhone and Apple TV upgrade rights but instead provided evidence to help define a reasonable range of potential ESPs for those rights. The Company concluded the potential to mislead and confuse its financial statement users by providing the complex and extensive additional disclosure needed to describe in detail the use of this evidence outweighed the limited benefit such disclosures would provide. The Company believes the disclosure it has provided fully informs investors as to its use and development of ESPs for iPhone and Apple TV software upgrade rights and fulfills the disclosure requirements of ASC Topic 605-25.[12]

In its response, Apple provides the rationale behind its disclosure of estimated selling price and also offers insight into how it determined estimated selling price for upgrades. This discussion of Apple's measurement methods, and its choice of disclosures, could be quite useful to Apple's peers with similar accounting issues.

To locate public company correspondence with the SEC:

1. Go to Company Filings on www.sec.gov, then search for a company. In the field for Filing Type, type in "corresp."

2. Researchers with access to advanced research databases (subscription required), may have more advanced search options. Audit Analytics intelligence service, for example, allows its subscribers to search for SEC correspondence by Codification citation, company name, topic name, date range, and so on. A researcher could therefore type **ASC 605-25** into the database to be directed to this Apple comment letter (and other comment letters on this subtopic). Westlaw Livedgar also has comment letter search capabilities.

When Should You Perform Peer Benchmarking?

Peer benchmarking can be valuable, for example,

-   When evaluating how other companies have complied with new financial reporting or disclosure requirements.

-   To identify best practices, or opportunities to improve on existing disclosures, by reviewing other companies' filings.

-   To determine whether information presented in existing disclosures is consistent with peers' presentation.

Of course, companies must always consider their own individual circumstances when determining what level of reporting and disclosures are appropriate and meaningful to investors.

Finally, a note of caution: Just because your peers are disclosing an item in a certain way, that doesn't mean that their reporting complies with GAAP. There is always a chance that your peers are misinterpreting GAAP. Keep in mind that your responsibility, first and foremost, is to comply with the authoritative requirements of the Codification. Consistency with your peers should be secondary to that responsibility.

---

[12] Apple Inc. response to SEC comment letter, dated April 1, 2010. Written by Peter Oppenheimer, CFO of Apple Inc.

EXAMPLE

Imagine your client is in the banking industry and is evaluating whether the fair value hierarchy levels (1, 2, or 3) it has disclosed, in accordance with **ASC 820** (Fair Value Measurements), are consistent with others in its peer group. To provide context to your client's decision, you prepare a brief summary of fair value hierarchy disclosures from the peer group's annual reports.[13] An excerpt of your analysis is shown next.

Company	Equity Securities	U.S. Treasury and U.S. Agency Securities	Corporate Bonds	Asset-Backed Securities
Bank A	1	1, 2	2	2, 3
Bank B	1	1, 2	2	2
Bank C	1	1, 2	2	2
...				

Using this summary, your client can more clearly determine whether its disclosures are consistent with its peers.

Form 10-K filings can be lengthy. To skip directly to the financial statements within these filings, (1) look for links within the table of contents (generally located within the first few pages of the filing), or (2) perform a word search (ctrl + f) for "independent registered." These keywords will jump you ahead to the independent auditor's report, which immediately precedes the financial statements.

 TIP from the Trenches

International Financial Reporting Standards (IFRS)

Recall from our earlier discussion of **ASC 105** (Generally Accepted Accounting Principles) that it is acceptable for companies following U.S. GAAP to consult IFRS when authoritative GAAP does not address a particular issue. In such instances, IFRS would be considered a nonauthoritative source of guidance.

When Should You Use IFRS as a Source of Guidance?

References to IFRS should be rare for most U.S. preparers. Given that IFRS guidance strives to be principles-based, it is generally rare for IFRS guidance to offer clarity where U.S. GAAP falls short.

When possible, before turning to IFRS, a researcher should try to resolve his or her issue using US GAAP. For example, if a researcher does not find guidance within the Codification, the researcher might next search for guidance within nonauthoritative U.S. sources, which may offer interpretive guidance on how to analogize other U.S. literature to the issue.

When researchers do utilize IFRS guidance, they should cite it as they would cite other nonauthoritative sources. That is, ideally, the guidance should be used *in addition to* Codification excerpts. This demonstrates to readers of your accounting memo that the IFRS guidance you are relying on is consistent with broad principles presented under U.S. GAAP, when applicable.

---

[13] Sample fair value hierarchy comparison table is based on the following source documents. Note that asset category names may not exactly match the annual reports, as in some cases they differ slightly across companies. They are presented in this book with similar names for comparison purposes. Levels shown in summary table indicate predominant levels reflected for these asset categories but may not exhaustively reflect levels actually disclosed in annual reports. This table is presented for illustration only.

• Wells Fargo's 2011 Form 10-K, Exhibit 13, p. 195.

• Citigroup's 2011 Annual Report, p. 171.

• Bank of America's 2011 Annual Report, p. 241.

Researchers pointing to IFRS requirements, in the absence of directly applicable U.S. GAAP, are often said to be **analogizing to** IFRS guidance. This means that authoritative guidance for the researcher's specific transaction is not available or does not address a particular nuance of the transaction. Therefore, the researcher must rely on specifics within IFRS guidance that is based on similar transactions or principles.

Note that there is some weakness inherent in applying guidance by analogy; essentially, you are applying guidance that was not originally intended to apply to your situation. This strategy should be used sparingly.

EXAMPLE

Referencing IFRS Guidance "By Analogy"

When companies build new manufacturing facilities, they often perform test production runs to test the facility's ability to produce its intended product. You are researching whether the cost of a test production run can be capitalized as part of the property, plant, and equipment (PP&E).

U.S. GAAP's guidance is vague on the issue of which costs may be capitalized as PP&E:

> . . . the historical cost of acquiring an asset includes the costs necessarily incurred to bring it to the condition and location necessary for its intended use.[14]

Further, test production runs are not addressed in the Codification's implementation guidance.

Capitalization of PP&E under IFRS is based on a similar principle:

> The cost of an item of property, plant and equipment comprises . . . (b) any costs directly attributable to bringing the asset to the location and condition necessary for it to be capable of operating in the manner intended by management. . . .[15]

However, IFRS elaborates on this principle, listing "costs of testing whether the asset is functioning properly"[16] as an example of a directly attributable cost that should be capitalized.

In this circumstance, given that IFRS guidance offers more specifics than U.S. GAAP, but is based on the same principle, it may be appropriate to analogize to IFRS guidance, in addition to citing the U.S. GAAP broad principle, as support for the decision to capitalize costs of test production.

IFRS

[Now **YOU** Try **4.6**]

The 2009 economic stimulus bill (American Recovery and Reinvestment Act of 2009) offered federal grant funds to certain qualifying clean energy projects. This left some utility companies engaged in clean energy projects faced with a new accounting issue: How should a for-profit company account for the receipt of federal government funds? U.S. GAAP does not provide guidance directly for this issue, as described in a PwC 2009 whitepaper:

---

[14] ASC 360-10-30-1 (Property, Plant, & Equipment).

[15] International Accounting Standard No. 16, *Property, Plant and Equipment* (IAS 16). Par. 16.

[16] IAS 16, par. 17e.

US generally accepted accounting principles (GAAP) provides limited guidance on the accounting for government grants received by for-profit companies. As such, there may be more than one acceptable alternative for the accounting for government grants. Companies should understand the conditions and restrictions (e.g., repayment conditions) of the government grant and match accounting decisions with the economics and substance of the government grant.

We believe it would be acceptable for companies to apply the guidance in the International Accounting Standard IAS 20, *Accounting for Government Grants and Disclosure of Government Assistance* (IAS 20), by analogy. It should be noted that the AICPA issues paper *Accounting for Grants Received from Governments*, dated October 16, 1979, currently indicates that it has been superseded by IAS 20.[17]

For example, assume that a utility company plans to build a solar power production facility, and was awarded a government grant to proceed with the project. The utility might look to the following guidance in IAS 20, given that U.S. GAAP is not available for this issue.

Presentation of grants related to assets

24.   Government grants related to assets, including non-monetary grants at fair value, shall be presented in the statement of financial position either by setting up the grant as deferred income or by deducting the grant in arriving at the carrying amount of the asset.

Questions:

1.   What are the two alternative treatments presented in IAS 20, for recording the receipt of grant money?

_____

_____

2.   Reread the requirements for citing nonauthoritative sources in **ASC 105-10-05-2** (excerpted earlier in this chapter). State why this analogy to IFRS guidance is permissible.

_____

_____

STYLE CHECK: CITING GUIDANCE FROM NONAUTHORITATIVE SOURCES

Citing Concepts Statements

Following is an example of an appropriate reference to a FASB Concepts Statement. The following format is also acceptable for citing pre-Codification standards (such as FASB Statements).

■   FASB Concepts Statement No. 6, *Elements of Financial Statements* (CON 6), defines assets as:

". . . probable future economic benefits obtained or controlled by a particular entity as a result of past transactions or events" (par. 25).

---

[17] PwC: *In Pursuit of Government Grants*. Page 10. July 2009. Etheridge, Herman, Hanlon. © PricewaterhouseCoopers LLP ("PwC"). Not for further reproduction or use without the prior written consent of PwC.

Note the following required elements included in the preceding citation:

- The type of standard: "FASB Concepts Statement No."
- The title of the standard is fully written out, and italicized
- The paragraph number
- The abbreviation, in parenthesis, that the author intends to use for future references to the standard (i.e., CON 6)

Citing Accounting Firm Guide Books

The objective in citing an accounting firm resource, such as a guide book, is to create a clear trail to exactly where you found the information you're citing. A supervisor or future reader of your memo should have enough information to personally retrace your steps and find the source. For example,

- Deloitte's publication, *A Roadmap to Accounting for Income Taxes* (March 2011), Section 6.02, states: "When disclosing gross DTAs and DTLs, an entity should separately disclose deductible and taxable temporary differences" (page 186).

Notice how this reference includes:

- The title of the guide
- Author or firm publishing the guide (Deloitte)
- Year of publication
- The relevant section and page number

As noted in Chapter 3's style tips for professional communication, sources may be cited in the body of an accounting memo or in a footnote attached to any quotes or guidance used from the source.

CHAPTER SUMMARY

Nonauthoritative sources are often indispensable to the research process, both in circumstances where Codification guidance is available and in cases where it is not. The FASB permits reference to nonauthoritative sources in cases where U.S. GAAP for a particular transaction, or similar transaction, is not available. Sources of this guidance include FASB Concepts Statements, Accounting Standards Updates, accounting firm resources, AICPA literature, and international accounting standards. Researchers should exercise caution when citing nonauthoritative sources, as they alone would not support an unqualified audit opinion. However, when used properly, nonauthoritative sources can add clarity to a researcher's understanding of complex issues and can add value to accounting issues documentation.

REVIEW QUESTIONS

1. Explain what it means for guidance to be "nonauthoritative."
2. Briefly, summarize the key points made in the first sentence of par. 05-1, and in par. 05-2, of ASC 105-10 (Generally Accepted Accounting Principles).
3. Identify two benefits of using nonauthoritative sources.
4. When is it acceptable to quote from only nonauthoritative sources, as support for an accounting position?
5. What is one example of information that a researcher can find in an Accounting Standards Update, but which is not available in the Codification?
6. Describe a circumstance in which reference to a pre-Codification standard may be appropriate.
7. Using the excerpts from the Concepts Statements shown in **Now YOU Try 4.1**, try to identify the objective of each of FASB Concepts Statements No. 6, 7, and 8. For example: "Concepts Statement No. 5 establishes recognition criteria and describes certain required elements of financial statements."

8. Identify three resources available from the AICPA, and state when each might be useful.

9. Name two types of accounting firm publications, and generally describe what each resource offers.

10. What are the required elements for a source citation, assuming the researcher is quoting text from a pre-Codification accounting standard?

EXERCISES

1. Locate FASB Concepts Statement No. 6, *Elements of Financial Statements* (CON 6).
   a. What is the definition of "revenue" in CON 6? Also, cite the paragraph source.
   b. How does revenue differ from "gains"? Cite your paragraph source.

2. Locate CON 5, then summarize the four fundamental recognition criteria identified in CON 5. Cite the paragraph source for this information.

3. Identify the pre-Codification standard that cross-references to ASC 450-20-25-1 (Loss Contingencies). Next, go to par. 59 of that pre-Codification standard. What was the Board intending to prevent by requiring that losses be "reasonably estimable"?

4. Locate ASU 2011-09. What is the title of this standard, and what is a key change effected by this standard? Use the summary at the beginning of this standard to identify a key change.

5. Locate Ernst & Young's guide book (referred to as the "Financial Reporting Developments" series) on share-based payment. Using the table of contents, identify one topic that is addressed (listed) within the Scope section. State the year of publication for the guide you used.

6. Provide the title of two AICPA Audit and Accounting Guides. Please do not use *Health Care Entities*, which was named already in this chapter. Describe how you located these guides.

7. Using the AICPA website, go to "Research" then "Technical Hotline." Locate a recent Technical Q&A on this site and summarize the issue.

8. Using the SEC website, locate General Electric's most recent Form 10-K. When was this form filed? In what footnote can investors read about the company's fair value measurements?

9. Using www.sec.gov, perform a search of Company Filings for Caterpillar Inc. Find Caterpillar's most recent Form 10-K filing (annual report). Within this report, locate the consolidated Caterpillar Inc. income statement and identify the two line items listed under "Sales and Revenues." Also, identify the total "Sales and Revenues" dollar amount for the most recent year.

   (*Hint:* To locate the income statement, open the entire Form 10-K filing then look for "Financial Statements" listed in the table of contents, or use the Interactive Data link next to the Form 10-K filing to link directly to the financial statements.)

10. Using IASB.org (under "IFRS" then "Standards"):
    a. Identify the international accounting standard that corresponds to the FASB's ASC 820, Fair Value Measurement.
    b. Next, compare the definition of fair value, in the technical summary of that IFRS guidance, to the definition of fair value in ASC 820-10-35-2.
    c. Explain, broadly, a circumstance in which a researcher might look to the IASB's fair value guidance.

11. Correct the errors in the following source citation. Assume this is the first time this source is being mentioned in an issues memo.

    Concept 6 defines assets as: *". . . probable future economic benefits obtained or controlled by a particular entity as a result of past transactions or events."*

CASE STUDY QUESTIONS

Asset or Expense (e-mail) You are a corporate accountant for a distribution company that provides distribution services to a large online retailer. Your company extensively uses conveyor belts to move shipping boxes and their contents through its warehouse. The seams in the company's conveyor belts have started to jam periodically, at times bringing the belts to a stop. The company has invested $100,000 to apply a special bonding agent to the belts' seams   4.1

so they won't jam anymore. By applying this bonding agent, the company can avoid replacing the belts to fix this jamming issue. There is a chance that this bonding agent will also result in the belts' useful lives being extended by a few years.

Assume that a plant accountant has contacted you to ask whether the bonding agent should be recorded as an asset or as an expense. Using guidance from the Conceptual Framework, analyze this issue and prepare an email response to the plant accountant.

4.2 **Capital versus Operating Lease Classification, Considering "Big Four" Guidance (issues memo)** You are in the Controller's group of Lessee, Inc. (Lessee) and have been asked to prepare an accounting issues memorandum (using the Standard Memo Format illustrated in the previous chapter) to address the following issue. Support your conclusions with excerpts from the Codification, and remember to include any available, relevant sources from areas of "required reading."

Assume that the lease falls within the scope of lease accounting guidance. Ensure that you use professional grammar and style. For the "Facts" section of the memo, you may copy from the following facts, adjusting as necessary to fit the style of your memo.

> **Facts:** Lessee Inc. (Lessee) is entering into a contract with Landlord Inc. (Landlord) to rent Landlord's newly constructed office building located at 1 Corporate Drive, in Denver, CO. The lease term is 20 years, and the estimated life of the building is 40 years. Lessee will occupy all 10 floors of the building. At the end of the lease term, Lessee agrees to either renew the lease (however, lease payments would be twice the current lease payment price, which is assumed to exceed the fair value of typical lease rental costs), or Lessee agrees to purchase the building at fair value.
>
> Monthly, the Lessee will be required to pay $10,000 to occupy the building, *plus* a monthly supplemental rental cost based on Lessee's sales (1% of sales). From experience, Lessee estimates that 1% of its sales should approximate an additional $15,000 per month. For simplicity, please ignore discounting (use of present value calculations, rates implicit in the lease, etc.) for purposes of this example. The fair value of the leased building is approximately $5 million at lease inception.
>
> There are no residual value guarantees present in this example.

Required: Should the lease arrangement be classified as an operating lease or as a capital lease?

Also, in evaluating whether the lease-end purchase option is a "bargain purchase option," support your response with guidance from *both* the Codification and from Ernst & Young's most recent Lease accounting guide book.

Chapter 5

Using the Codification to Research Issues—Scope

Printout in hand, Julie taps on her boss's door. She is feeling pretty good; she just found a paragraph in the guidance that appears to speak directly to the tax accrual issue her boss asked her to research. As she shows him the guidance, he taps his pen thoughtfully on the desk.

"Are you sure this guidance applies to our type of transaction?" he asks.

He continues, "I think the guidance for franchise taxes (which are based on net worth) differs from guidance for taxes based on income. You've brought me guidance specific to income taxes."

Julie shakes her head; she realizes that she forgot to review the scope section of the guidance that she had printed. "Let me double check the scope section for this guidance," she says. "I'll stop by again later to let you know what I've found."

Confirming that a transaction is within the scope of a Codification topic may seem like an extra step, but much of the guidance within the Codification includes specific instructions for its use. Reviewing the scope section is a critical step to analyzing potentially relevant accounting guidance. Don't get caught like Julie, forgetting to do the appropriate diligence work on guidance that may otherwise appear to be on point.

Learning Objectives

After reading this chapter and performing the exercises herein, you will be able to

1. **Understand** the role that scope guidance plays in professional research.

2. **Review** scope guidance to determine whether a particular transaction is within the scope of a topic.

3. **Identify** certain key judgments involved in applying scope guidance to topics including investments, nonmonetary transactions, stock compensation, income taxes, leases, and derivatives.

> **Understanding and Applying Scope Guidance—**
> **A series of examples**
>
> 1. **Investments**— Determining whether the fair value, cost, or equity method applies
> 2. **Nonmonetary Transactions**—Evaluating the significance of boot, understanding "subsection" scope guidance
> 3. **Stock compensation**—Determining when recipients of stock awards are "employees"
> 4. **Income Taxes**—Evaluating whether a tax is "based on income"
> 5. **Leases**—Determining whether an arrangement contains a lease
> 6. **Derivatives**—Evaluating whether a contract meets the definition of a derivative
> 7. **Industry Guidance**—Evaluating whether an arrangement is subject to specialized industry guidance

Organization of This Chapter

This chapter on "Scope" issues (Section 15 in the Codification) is the first of several chapters focused on accounting issues involving "section" guidance in the Codification. Chapter 6 explores issues of accounting recognition and derecognition (Sections 25 and 40 in the Codification), and Chapters 7 and 8 focus on accounting measurements (Sections 30 and 35 in the Codification), with Chapter 8 focused specifically on fair value.

This chapter begins by discussing broadly the role of scope guidance, including

- When, in the research process, scope guidance should be consulted, and
- What a researcher should look for when reviewing the scope section of a topic.

Next, the chapter illustrates the application of scope guidance to example transactions and provides cases for students to practice their skills applying scope guidance. Actively attempting these examples will not only familiarize students with scope guidance in general, but will improve students' comfort with these technical topics.

This chapter includes the topics depicted in the preceding diagram.

For the practicing accountant, some of the examples that follow may seem overly simplified. However, to the beginning accounting researcher, these examples provide a straightforward introduction to some basics of technical guidance. Armed with these basics, beginning researchers will learn the skills necessary to advance to the more complex issues they will likely face as professionals.

WHAT IS SCOPE GUIDANCE?

Scope guidance indicates which transactions, items, or entities are subject to the guidance within a topic. As discussed in Chapter 2, researchers should view the scope section of each topic as *required reading*. Therefore, before reviewing a topic's recognition or measurement guidance, a researcher should first confirm that the guidance applies to his or her transaction.

The scope guidance for most topics is within Section 15 ("Scope"), usually within Subtopic 10 (the "Overall" subtopic). However, scope guidance may also be found within other individual subtopics and, in some circumstances, might be provided for individual paragraphs within the guidance.

Information within the scope section is commonly presented in one of two ways:

■ The guidance may list transactions that are *not* within the scope.

■ The guidance may contain tests to determine what transactions *should be* included within the scope of the guidance.

When reviewing the Scope section of a topic, a researcher should read any lists of transactions or entities that are excluded from the guidance's scope. If the guidance contains tests, indicating which transactions are within the topic's scope, a researcher should determine whether his or her transaction meets the tests. For example, a scope test may be presented as three conditions, one or all of which must be met for a transaction to be within the scope of a topic.

Often, it is only the most technical and complex of topics that include tests identifying transactions that *should* be within scope (e.g., derivatives, securitizations, variable interest entities, leases). Notice that many of these topics are within the Broad Transactions area, and therefore are subject to specialized accounting. Given the complexity of some of these topics, bear the following in mind if you find yourself faced with one of these tests:

■ Before I perform a detailed scope test, I should read the Overview section of this topic, to make sure that using this topic makes sense.

■ If I have to "test into" this guidance, then this guidance may be highly nuanced. I ought to see whether there is implementation guidance (Section 55) or a nonauthoritative source that can offer additional information on this scope test.

If you find that your transaction is outside the scope of a particular topic, look for references within the Scope section to other topics that might apply. If references are not provided, continue to brainstorm alternative accounting treatments for the transaction you are researching. See Chapter 3 for additional discussion of Codification search methods.

The next section of this chapter illustrates the application of scope guidance for several Codification topics.

APPLYING SCOPE GUIDANCE— INVESTMENTS IN EQUITY SECURITIES

The organization of Investments guidance within the Codification can be a source of confusion to beginning researchers. Following is a brief, simplified summary of how Investments topics apply to different scenarios.

Purchase of a Noncontrolling Interest

The following Codification topics apply to purchases of **noncontrolling interests**. A noncontrolling interest is generally viewed as a purchase of less than 50% of a company's equity securities.[1]

---

[1] ASC 810-10-15-8 (Consolidation): "The usual condition for a controlling financial interest is ownership of a majority voting interest, and, therefore, as a general rule ownership by one reporting entity, directly or indirectly, of more than 50 percent of the outstanding voting shares of another entity is a condition pointing toward consolidation . . . ."

- Investments—Debt and Equity Securities (Topic **320**)—Applies to all investments in debt securities (such as bonds or notes payable), plus investments in equity securities with "readily determinable fair values."[2]

  This topic provides guidance on use of the trading, available-for-sale, or held-to-maturity accounting methods for an investment.

- Investments—Equity Method and Joint Ventures (Topic **323**)—Applies to purchases of equity securities where an investor has **significant influence**. Significant influence is often characterized by a 20% or greater ownership stake in an investee.

- Investments—Other (Topic **325**) —Provides guidance on the cost method of accounting. Generally applies to purchases of equity securities lacking readily determinable fair values, and where an investor lacks significant influence.

Figure 5-1 provides a view from the Codification of topics listed under Investments.

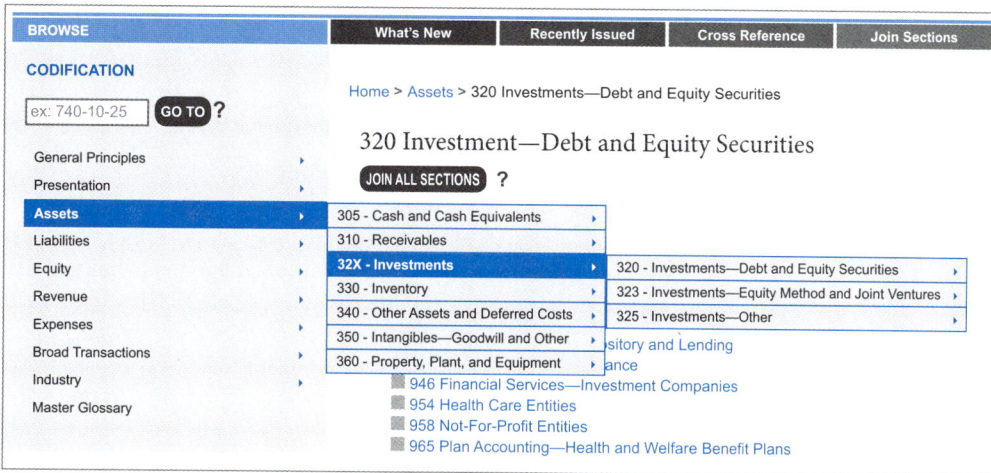

Figure 5-1
Codification topics listed under Investments

Reproduced with permission of the Financial Accounting Foundation.

Determining the appropriate topic to apply to a given investment can involve judgment. In some cases, multiple topics may appear to apply, however, one topic may be more appropriate than another.

Notably, the FASB is currently working on a project that would overhaul financial instrument accounting; this project could significantly change the accounting for the topics described above and could result in a reorganization of Codification guidance related to Investments. Go to www.fasb.org for updates on this project.

Purchase of a Controlling Interest

Investors purchasing a **controlling financial interest** (i.e., a greater than 50% ownership stake) in an investee, or investors who are involved with structured, "variable interest" entities, should consult the Consolidation topic (Topic **810**). The Consolidation topic is located under Broad Transactions within the Codification. The Appendix to this chapter includes a detailed example applying Consolidation scope guidance.

Identify the topic that most likely applies in each of the following scenarios:

1. **ABC Corp purchases 10% of the voting equity shares in a small, private company.**
2. **ABC Corp purchases 30% of the voting equity shares in a small, private company.**
3. **ABC Corp purchases 10% of the voting equity shares in a public company.**
4. **ABC Corp purchases 55% of the voting equity shares in a public company.**
5. **ABC Corp forms a limited-purpose joint venture and lends it $2 million, in exchange for a 50% ownership stake.**

✔ **Knowledge Check**

---

[2] ASC 320-10-15-5 (Investments—Debt and Equity Securities).

APPLYING SCOPE GUIDANCE—
NONMONETARY TRANSACTIONS

Nonmonetary transactions guidance in the Codification (ASC 845) can be somewhat challenging for researchers in that they must consult not only *general* scope guidance for the topic, but must also determine whether a transaction is within the scope of *subsection* guidance (i.e., groups of paragraphs) within this topic. Let's explore this guidance now.

As a researcher, if you ever come across a transaction in which physical assets are being exchanged, consider exploring whether the transaction is **nonmonetary**. According to ASC 845-10:

> **05-2** Most business transactions involve exchanges of cash or other monetary assets or liabilities [for example, cash or accounts receivable] for goods or services. The amount of monetary assets or liabilities exchanged generally provides an objective basis for measuring the cost of nonmonetary assets or services received by an entity as well as for measuring gain or loss on nonmonetary assets transferred from an entity. Some transactions, however, involve either of the following:
>
> a. An exchange with another entity (reciprocal transfer) that involves principally nonmonetary assets or liabilities . . . [Comments added]

That is, in most transactions, goods or services are exchanged for cash or other monetary assets, and the amount of cash generally provides an objective value for the goods being transferred. Nonmonetary transactions therefore present a unique issue, in that they involve assets whose values may not be as objectively determinable. Some monetary consideration (boot) may be involved in a nonmonetary exchange, but this amount cannot be significant (as illustrated in **Now YOU Try 5.1**).

The basic principle in Topic 845 is that nonmonetary exchanges should be recognized at the fair values of the assets exchanged.[3] Often, this fair value measurement can give rise to gain recognition (for example, when the fair value of the exchanged asset exceeds its carrying value). Understandably, the FASB took precautions when developing this guidance to limit this opportunity for gain recognition to circumstances where it was considered most appropriate. Accordingly,

■ Scope guidance within Topic 845 precludes the use of this topic for certain arrangements, such as transactions between entities under common control (e.g., parent-sub, or sub-sub relationships).[4]

■ Measurement guidance within Topic 845 requires that only transactions with commercial substance (e.g., a valid business purpose) may be recognized at fair value.

ASC 845 is organized into the following subsections:

■ General

■ Purchases and sales of inventory with the same counterparty

■ Barter transactions

■ Exchanges involving monetary consideration

■ Exchanges of a nonfinancial asset for a noncontrolling ownership interest

Each of these subsections offers not only unique measurement guidance, but also has unique scope guidance. Therefore, determining whether a transaction is within the scope of ASC 845 is

---

[3] ASC 845-10-30-1 (Nonmonetary Transactions): "In general, the accounting for nonmonetary transactions should be based on the fair values of the assets (or services) involved, which is the same basis as that used in monetary transactions."

[4] ASC 845-10-15-4(b).

a two-step process. Entities must evaluate both (1) "General" Topic 845 scope guidance and (2) subsection scope guidance. Even if a transaction is not precluded from the "general" scope of Topic 845, subsection scope guidance may indicate that the transaction should not be accounted for under Topic 845.

The following examples illustrate application of both the General scope guidance as well as subsection scope guidance.

Exchanges Involving Monetary Consideration

Now
YOU
Try
5.1

Facts: Company A exchanges printing equipment (fair value: $500,000) for a forklift (fair value: $400,000) and $100,000 cash. Company A must determine whether this transaction is within the scope of **ASC 845**.

ASC 845-10 includes the following scope guidance. Par. 15-12 (below) of this topic is somewhat unusual in that it refers readers to the general subsection guidance in order to evaluate what amount of monetary consideration is considered significant. Accordingly, par. 25-6 has been included, to show how "significant" is defined in Topic 845-10.

General

>Entities

15-2 The guidance in the Nonmonetary Transactions Topic applies to all entities.

>Transactions

15-3 The guidance in the Nonmonetary Transactions Topic applies to all types of nonmonetary transactions including:

  a. Nonmonetary exchanges involving boot. Some exchanges of nonmonetary assets involve a small monetary consideration, referred to as boot, even though the exchange is essentially nonmonetary. (See the Exchanges Involving Monetary Consideration Subsection of Section 845–10–15 for situations outside the scope of this Subtopic.)

Exchanges Involving Monetary Consideration

>Overall Guidance

15-12 The Exchanges Involving Monetary Consideration Subsections follow the same Scope and Scope Exceptions as outlined in the General Subsection of this Subtopic, see paragraph 845-10-15-1, and address what level of monetary consideration in a nonmonetary exchange causes the transaction to be considered monetary in its entirety and, therefore, outside the scope of the Exchanges Involving Monetary Consideration Subsections and this Topic.

>Transactions

15-13 The guidance in the Exchanges Involving Monetary Consideration Subsections applies to nonmonetary exchanges involving monetary consideration (boot).

25-6 An exchange of nonmonetary assets that would otherwise be based on recorded amounts but that also involves monetary consideration (boot) shall be considered monetary (rather than nonmonetary) if the boot is significant. Significant shall be defined as at least 25 percent of the fair value of the exchange. . .

As you can see from these excerpts, while the General section scope guidance applies to all entities, the subsection scope guidance sets forth even more specific requirements that can result in transactions being deemed outside the scope of this topic. Considering this guidance and the facts presented, respond to the following.

Questions:

1. Does this transaction meet the General scope guidance within Topic 845?

    _____

    _____

2. Does the transaction meet the scope criteria in the subsection "Exchanges Involving Monetary Consideration"? Explain.

    _____

    _____

    _____

Now

[YOU]

Try

5.2

Exchanges of a Nonfinancial Asset for a Noncontrolling Ownership Interest

Facts: Now assume that Company X exchanges a factory building for a 20% equity ownership interest in Company Y. Recall that ownership of less than 50% of an investee's voting equity is considered a noncontrolling ownership interest. Company X must determine whether this exchange is within the scope of **ASC 845**.

ASC 845-10 includes the following subsection scope guidance:

> **Exchanges of a Nonfinancial Asset for a Noncontrolling Ownership Interest**
>
> **> Overall Guidance**
>
> **15-18** The Exchanges of a Nonfinancial Asset for a Noncontrolling Ownership Interest Subsections follow the same Scope and Scope Exceptions as outlined in the General Subsection of this Subtopic, see paragraph 845-10-15-1, with specific transaction exceptions noted below.
>
> **> Transactions**
>
> **15-19** The guidance in the Exchanges of a Nonfinancial Asset for a Noncontrolling Ownership Interest Subsections applies to nonmonetary transfers of a nonfinancial asset (or assets) for a noncontrolling ownership interest.
>
> **15-20** The guidance in these Subsections does not apply to the following types of transfers:
>
> . . . c. Transfers of real estate in exchange for nonmonetary assets other than real estate (for guidance on the recognition of profit from the exchange, see Subtopic 976-605 [Retail Land - Revenue Recognition] and Section 360-20-40) [Real Estate Sales] [Bracketed text added]

Questions:

1. Are there any scope exceptions within the General scope guidance of Topic 845 that would exclude this transaction from scope? (See guidance in **Now YOU Try 5.1**)

    _____

    _____

2. Does the transaction meet the scope criteria in the subsection "Exchanges of a Nonfinancial Asset for a Noncontrolling Ownership Interest"?

    _____

    _____

    _____

3. Based on your responses to the above questions, does it appear that use of Topic 845 is appropriate to account for this transaction?

_____

_____

_____

In many cases, references to other Codification topics are provided for transactions specifically excluded from the scope of Topic **845**. In this example, the Real Estate Sales topic may be more applicable to this transaction.

APPLYING SCOPE GUIDANCE TO SHARE-BASED COMPENSATION

Companies frequently compensate their employees through a combination of both salary and stock options. The Stock Compensation Topic (Topic **718**), located in the Expenses area of the Codification (under "Compensation"), offers guidance on share-based payments made to employees. Topic 718 requires companies to recognize employee stock awards at their estimated fair value, as determined at the award's grant date. Companies must recognize the award's fair value in compensation expense over the employee's required service period (that is, the period the employee must continue to work before he or she can exercise the option).

The scope of Topic 718 generally extends to all equity awards granted to employees. In some cases, the definition of "employee" comprises certain nonemployee directors of a company. Determining when individuals are subject to this guidance can involve judgment. Following are two examples demonstrating the scope of Topic 718. In certain cases, awards to individuals that are not within the scope of Topic 718 may be subject instead to the guidance in Topic **505** (Equity-Based Payments to Non-Employees).

As you'll see in the following two **Now YOU Try** exercises, glossary terms and implementation or interpretive guidance can assist a researcher in applying scope guidance.

Stock Award to a Board Member for Board Service

Facts: Charles Draper serves on the Board of Directors of Echo Corp and was elected to this position by Echo shareholders. As compensation for his Board service, Echo Corp pays Mr. Draper a fixed salary plus company stock options. Echo is evaluating whether to account for this compensation under **ASC 718**.

Now **YOU** Try

5.3

ASC 718-10 includes the following scope guidance.

> **> Transactions**

15-3 The guidance in the Compensation—Stock Compensation Topic applies to all share-based payment transactions in which an entity acquires employee services by issuing (or offering to issue) its shares, share options, or other equity instruments or by incurring liabilities to an employee that meet either of the following conditions:

  a. The amounts are based, at least in part, on the price of the entity's shares or other equity instruments. (The phrase *at least in part* is used because an award of share-based compensation may be indexed to both the price of an entity's shares and something else that is neither the price of the entity's shares nor a market, performance, or service condition.)

  b. The awards require or may require settlement by issuing the entity's equity shares or other equity instruments.

... **15-5** The guidance in this Topic does not apply to the following payment transactions:

a.   Share-based transactions for other than employee services (see Subtopic 505-50 for guidance on those transactions).

Key to applying this scope guidance is understanding the definition of employee. The glossary of Topic 718-10 defines **employee** as follows:

Employee

An individual over whom the grantor of a share-based compensation award exercises or has the right to exercise sufficient control to establish an employer-employee relationship based on common law as illustrated in case law and currently under U.S. Internal Revenue Service (IRS) Revenue Ruling 87-41...

... A nonemployee director does not satisfy this definition of employee. Nevertheless, nonemployee directors acting in their role as members of a board of directors are treated as employees if those directors were elected by the employer's shareholders or appointed to a board position that will be filled by shareholder election when the existing term expires. However, that requirement applies only to awards granted to nonemployee directors for their services as directors. Awards granted to those individuals for other services shall be accounted for as awards to nonemployees.

Question: Is Echo's award of stock options to Mr. Draper within the scope of Topic 718, Stock Compensation?

_____

_____

_____

_____

[Now **YOU** Try 5.4]

Stock Award to a Board Member, for Professional Services

Facts: Assume the same facts as in the previous example—that is, Charles Draper is an elected Board member of Echo Corp. However, now assume that Mr. Draper also receives stock awards for his work on architectural drawings, which he prepared in order to assist Echo with its plans to build a new facility. Echo is evaluating whether this award is within the scope of **ASC 718**.

Implementation Guidance from Topic 718-10 provides the following example.

Example 2: Definition of Employee

55-91 Nonemployee directors acting in their role as members of an entity's board of directors shall be treated as employees if those directors were elected by the entity's shareholders or appointed to a board position that will be filled by shareholder election when the existing term expires. However, that requirement applies only to awards granted to them for their services as directors. Awards granted to those individuals for other services shall be accounted for as awards to nonemployees in accordance with Section 505-50-25. Additionally, consolidated groups may have multiple boards of directors; this guidance applies only to either of the following:

a.   The nonemployee directors acting in their role as members of a parent entity's board of directors

Continued

b. Nonemployee members of a consolidated subsidiary's board of directors to the extent that those members are elected by shareholders that are not controlled directly or indirectly by the parent or another member of the consolidated group.

In addition, Echo considers the following guidance from Ernst & Young's guide book, *Share-Based Payment* (2011):[5]

2.2.3.2 Example—stock options granted to nonemployee directors

> Illustration 2-1

Company X has four nonemployee members on its board of directors. Members of the board have several years of business experience and possess specific knowledge and expertise within Company X's industry. The nonemployee directors are elected by Company X's shareholders for a three-year term and meet four times a year. Company X grants each non-employee director 500 stock options for each meeting he or she attends. Company X would account for the stock options as employee awards because they were granted to elected nonemployee directors for their services as directors.

In addition, one of the nonemployee directors is also an environmental attorney. During the year, Company X is named as a Potentially Responsible Party (PRP) at a Superfund site. Internal counsel has limited experience with environmental remediation and confers numerous times with the nonemployee director. Prior to presenting the motion to dismiss Company X as a PRP, the nonemployee director spends approximately 100 hours consulting with internal counsel. Ultimately, Company X is successful and is dismissed as a PRP. Company X grants the nonemployee director 7,500 options for his consulting services. Company X would account for the 7,500 stock options under ASC 505-50 because the non-employee director received stock options for services unrelated to his service as a director.

Question: Is the stock award for Mr. Draper's architectural drawings within the scope of Topic 718?

APPLYING SCOPE GUIDANCE FOR INCOME TAXES

Located in the Expenses area of the Codification, the Income Taxes topic (ASC 740) provides guidance on the recognition of taxes based on income. This topic identifies the following primary objectives related to the accounting for income taxes:

a. To recognize the amount of taxes payable or refundable for the current year
b. To recognize deferred tax liabilities and assets for the future tax consequences of events that have been recognized in an entity's financial statements or tax returns. (ASC 740-10-10-1)

The scope of Topic 740 is limited to taxes "based on income."[6] Other GAAP including, for example, Topic 450 (Contingencies) must be applied for taxes not within the scope of Topic 740. Application of other Codification topics to taxes will not result in deferred taxes, as that concept is unique to income tax accounting.

Determining whether a tax is based on income may sound straightforward, but in practice it often requires judgment. Following are two examples illustrating the scope of Topic 740. The

---

[5] Ernst & Young, Financial Reporting Developments: *Share-Based Payment*. Revised October 2011. Page 15.

[6] ASC 740-10-15-3 (Income Taxes, Scope).

first example evaluates whether a "gross receipts tax" (that is, a tax based on revenue) is within the scope of this topic; the second evaluates a so-called "modified gross receipts tax."

Now
YOU
Try
5.5

Determining Whether a "Gross Receipts Tax" Is within the Scope of Income Tax Guidance

Facts: Businesses in New Mexico are subject to a state "gross-receipts tax," ranging in amount from 5.125% to 8.6875%, depending on the business's locale. The tax is imposed on a business's gross receipts, or "the total amount of money or value of other consideration" received from conducting its activities.[7] You must determine whether this gross receipts tax is within the scope of **ASC 740**.

ASC 740-10 includes the following scope guidance:

Transactions

15-3   The guidance in the Income Taxes Topic applies to:
  a.   Domestic federal (national) income taxes (U.S. federal income taxes for U.S. entities) and foreign, state, and local (including franchise) taxes based on income
  b.   An entity's domestic and foreign operations that are consolidated, combined, or accounted for by the equity method. (ASC 740-10-15-3)

The Glossary of Topic 740-10 defines **income taxes** and **taxable income** as follows:

Income Taxes

Domestic and foreign federal (national), state, and local (including franchise) taxes based on income.

Taxable Income

The excess of taxable revenues over tax deductible expenses and exemptions for the year as defined by the governmental taxing authority.

Net income is defined in the Codification's Master Glossary as follows:

Net Income

A measure of financial performance resulting from the aggregation of revenues, expenses, gains, and losses that are not items of other comprehensive income. A variety of other terms such as net earnings or earnings may be used to describe net income.

Finally, PwC's *Guide to Accounting for Income Taxes* states the following with respect to the evaluation of gross receipts taxes under the scope of Topic 740.[8]

A gross-receipts tax is generally based upon a jurisdiction's definition of "taxable gross receipts." In devising this tax, many jurisdictions do not take into consideration any expenses or costs incurred to generate such receipts, except for certain stated cash discounts, bad debts, and returns and allowances. Because the starting point of the computation of a gross-receipts tax is not "net" of expenses, we believe that a gross-receipts tax is not a tax based on income for purposes of determining whether ASC 740 applies.

[7] Source: www.tax.newmexico.gov/All-Taxes/Pages/Gross-Receipts-Tax.aspx.

[8] PwC, *Guide to Accounting for Income Taxes*. 2010 (Revised March 2011). Chapter 1, page 8.
© PricewaterhouseCoopers LLP ("PwC"). Not for further reproduction or use without the prior written consent of PwC.

Question: Is this gross-receipts tax considered a tax based on income, and thus within the scope of Topic 740 (Income Taxes)?

_____

_____

_____

_____

Evaluating Whether a Modified Gross Receipts Tax Is within the Scope of Income Tax Guidance

Now
YOU
Try
5.6

Facts: Michigan's 0.8% "modified gross receipts tax" is based on a company's gross receipts less "purchases from other firms." Purchases from other firms include inventory purchased during the tax year, capital expenditures (depreciable assets acquired), and materials and supplies directly connected to inventory or capital assets.[9] Costs not falling specifically within these categories may not be deducted from gross receipts.

You must evaluate whether Michigan's modified gross receipts tax is a tax based on income and thus within the scope of **ASC 740**.

In addition to the guidance provided for the previous example, consider the following guidance on modified gross receipts taxes from PwC's _Guide to Accounting for Income Taxes_.[10]

> . . . in jurisdictions where the tax is calculated on _modified_ gross receipts, consideration should be given as to whether it is a tax based on income. We believe that a modified gross receipts tax constitutes a tax based on income and should therefore be accounted for in accordance with ASC 740 if it is based on gross receipts that are reduced for certain costs (e.g., inventory, depreciable and amortizable assets, materials and supplies, wages, and/or other expenditures).

Question: Is Michigan's "modified gross receipts tax" within the scope of ASC 740?

_____

_____

APPLYING SCOPE GUIDANCE—LEASES

Located in the Broad Transactions area of the Codification, the Leases topic offers guidance on transactions that require specialized lease accounting. Unlike a typical accrual-accounting contract, application of lease accounting, for a lessee, can result in either:

- In the case of an operating lease, straight-line expense recognition of lease costs.
- In the case of a capital lease, the capitalization of a leased asset and recognition of a related lease payment obligation.

Scope guidance for leases is located in Subtopic 10 (Overall) of Topic **840** (Leases) and applies to all subtopics within Topic 840.[11] This guidance is presented in a few ways: first, the scope guidance includes a test for identifying arrangements that qualify as leases. Second, the

---

[9] http://www.michiganadvantage.org/cm/files/Fact-Sheets/MichiganBusinessTaxreplaceSBT.pdf.

[10] PwC, _Guide to Accounting for Income Taxes_. 2010 (Revised March 2011). Chapter 1, page 8.
© PricewaterhouseCoopers LLP ("PwC"). Not for further reproduction or use without the prior written consent of PwC.

[11] ASC 840-10-15-1 (Leases): "The Scope Section of the Overall Subtopic establishes the pervasive scope for all Subtopics of the Leases Topic. Unless explicitly addressed within specific Subtopics, the following scope guidance applies to all Subtopics of the Leases Topic."

guidance lists specific arrangements that do not qualify for lease accounting. A researcher with a potential lease would have to review the entire scope section before concluding that application of lease guidance is appropriate for his or her transaction.

Transactions that do not qualify for lease accounting should be reviewed for other specialized accounting treatments, including derivative accounting (for example, if the contract involves commodities) or the presence of so-called variable interests (addressed in the Consolidation topic). Contracts that do not require these specialized accounting treatments are frequently accounted for as accrual contracts, with rights and obligations accounted for as they arise.

Following are examples showing both the lease scope test, as well as an example of an arrangement that is excluded from the scope of lease accounting.

The upcoming **Now YOU Try** illustrates how an arrangement conveying the "right to use" property, plant, or equipment can result in lease accounting. Even if a contract is not referred to as a "Lease Agreement," accountants must learn to recognize circumstances in which control over property is being transferred. In the following example, the parties have entered into a contract known as a "power purchase agreement." For accounting purposes, these arrangements can qualify as leases, if certain conditions are met.

In a typical power purchase agreement, a buyer of electricity (often a utility company, which has promised to sell electricity to its own customers) purchases output from a power plant. The buyer could choose to purchase some, or all, of the plant's electricity output. The power plant is typically owned by a third party. Payment for electricity purchased may be fixed per unit of energy purchased (e.g., $0.15 per kilowatt-hour), or in some cases may also include a variable component related to costs of operating the power plant (e.g., plus maintenance costs). See Figure 5-2 for an illustration of this structure.

Figure 5-2	

Example structure for a power purchase agreement

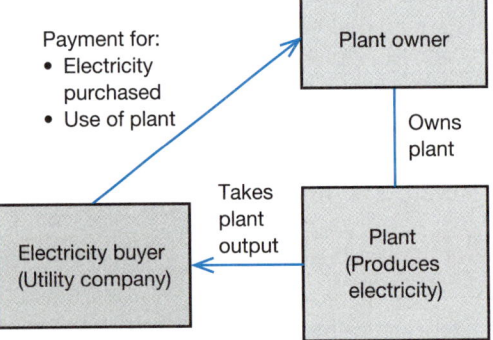

When evaluating a power purchase agreement, the accountant must determine whether the buyer is just purchasing power, or whether the buyer is really getting the right to control the power plant. For example, if the buyer can determine when the plant produces power, and how much, and if the buyer has physical access to the plant, these are indicators that the buyer is leasing the plant. This so-called "power purchase agreement" is not just a simple purchase of power; rather, this activity must be recorded in the financial statements as a lease.

Now
YOU
Try
5.7

Evaluating Whether an Arrangement Contains a Lease—The Lease Scope "Test"

Facts: An electric utility (buyer) has entered into a power purchase agreement (PPA) for the purchase of electricity from a power plant in Summer, Illinois. The PPA states that the buyer will supply all of the fuel (coal) for the plant, will operate the plant, and will take 100% of the output from the plant. The buyer will pay a fee for the electricity based on:

1. the variable operating costs of the plant (such as utility bills, water usage, etc.), **plus**

2. an amount based on the current market price of electricity.

The buyer must now determine whether this arrangement qualifies as a lease.

ASC 840-10 provides the following Lease scope guidance:

Arrangements that Qualify as Leases

15-6   An arrangement conveys the right to use property, plant, or equipment if the arrangement conveys to the purchaser (lessee) the right to control the use of the underlying property, plant, or equipment. The right to control the use of the underlying property, plant, or equipment is conveyed if any of the following conditions is met:

  a.   The purchaser has the ability or right to operate the property, plant, or equipment or direct others to operate the property, plant, or equipment in a manner it determines while obtaining or controlling more than a minor amount of the output or other utility of the property, plant, or equipment. The purchaser's ability to operate the property, plant, or equipment may be evidenced by (but is not limited to) the purchaser's ability to hire, fire, or replace the property's operator or the purchaser's ability to specify significant operating policies and procedures in the arrangement with the owner-seller having no ability to change such policies and procedures....

  b.   The purchaser has the ability or right to control physical access to the underlying property, plant, or equipment <u>while</u> obtaining or controlling more than a minor amount of the output or other utility of the property, plant, or equipment.

  c.   Facts and circumstances indicate that it is remote that one or more parties other than the purchaser will take more than a minor amount of the output or other utility that will be produced or generated by the property, plant, or equipment during the term of the arrangement, <u>and</u> the price that the purchaser (lessee) will pay for the output is neither contractually fixed per unit of output nor equal to the current market price per unit of output as of the time of delivery of the output. [Underlined emphasis added]

The first condition for lease accounting has been evaluated for you, as an example.

Questions:

1.   Is condition (a) for lease accounting met?

  <u>Yes: The buyer has the right to operate the plant. Additionally, given that the buyer will take all output from the plant, it therefore controls more than a minor amount of the output.</u>

Now, evaluate whether condition (b) is met for this arrangement. Be sure to address both parts of condition (b): (1) ability to control physical access and (2) control over output. If you have to make any assumptions in responding to this condition, state what you've assumed.

2.   Is condition (b) for lease accounting met?

  _____

  _____

Next, evaluate whether condition (c) is met for this arrangement. Address both conditions: (1) the likelihood that another party will take more than minor amount of output and (2) whether pricing meets the neither contractually fixed nor equal to market condition.

In your response, consider also the following interpretive guidance from Ernst & Young's *Lease Accounting* guide book (2011):[12]

Market [price] is intended to address those items for which there is a readily available, actively traded market (e.g., electricity). In addition, market price per unit means the cost is solely a market cost without other pricing factors (e.g., market price per kwh plus percent change in price of natural gas would not be market).

---

[12] Ernst & Young, Financial Reporting Developments: *Lease Accounting.* October 2011. Section 1.1.3, Page 5.

3. Is condition (c) for lease accounting met?

_____

_____

Having analyzed each condition in par. 15-6, a researcher should provide an overall conclusion summarizing his or her analysis of the three conditions. Recall from par. 15-6 that an
arrangement meeting *any* of the conditions (a, b, or c) meets the definition of a lease. In the
blanks below, summarize which conditions for lease accounting were met.

4. After evaluating these three conditions from par. 15-6, is this arrangement a lease?

_____

_____

After identifying transactions within the scope of Topic **840** (Leases), the guidance goes on to
list specific arrangements that do not qualify as leases. Arrangements that are not dependent on
specified property, plant, and equipment (PP&E), for example, do not qualify as leases:

> ### ASC 840-10 (Scope)
>
> **>Arrangements that Do Not Qualify as Leases**
>
> **15-10.** . . . although specific property, plant, or equipment may be explicitly identified
> in an arrangement, it is not the subject of a lease if fulfillment of the arrangement is
> not dependent on the use of the specified property, plant, or equipment.

In **Now YOU Try** 5.7, if the utility (buyer) was simply purchasing power from a seller with
access to many power plants, any one of which could be used to produce power for the buyer,
the arrangement would not qualify as a lease. Let's assume the following additional facts about
this example.

Transactions Listed as "Exclusions" from Lease Accounting

Additional Facts: Assume the same facts as in **Now YOU Try** 5.7, but now assume that a power
plant is not named in the agreement documents. However, the plant owner only has one plant
located in Summer, Illinois, and that agreement calls for the utility to purchase power from a coal
plant in Summer, Illinois. Additionally, assume that obtaining power from another source would
not be economically feasible for the seller. The buyer must consider now whether the arrangement is dependent on specific PP&E.

ASC 840 provides the following scope and interpretive guidance regarding the evaluation of
whether an arrangement is dependent on specified PP&E:

> ### ASC 840-10 (Scope)
>
> **15-5.** The identification of property, plant, or equipment in the arrangement need not be
> explicit; it may be implicit. Property, plant, or equipment has been implicitly speci-
> fied if, for example, the owner-seller owns or leases only one asset with which to
> fulfill its obligation to the purchaser and it is not economically feasible or practicable
> for the owner-seller to perform its obligation through the use of alternative property,
> plant, or equipment.
>
> ### ASC 840-10 (Implementation Guidance)
>
> **55-26.** Paragraph 840-10-15-5 states that the identification of the property in the arrange-
> ment need not be explicit; it may be implicit. For example, in the case of a power
> purchase contract, if the seller of the power is a special-purpose entity that owns a

single power plant, that power plant is implicitly specified in the contract because it is unlikely that the special-purpose entity could obtain replacement power to fulfill its obligations under the contract because a special-purpose entity generally has limited capital resources.

Considering the preceding guidance, respond to the following.

Question: Is the arrangement dependent upon specific PP&E?

_____

_____

_____

_____

If you concluded that the arrangement is dependent on specified PP&E, then the arrangement would still be a lease, accounted for under Topic **840** (Leases).

Note that while the guidance from par. 55-26 may not be directly on point (we do not know whether the seller in our example is a special-purpose entity), it helps to further illustrate the guidance in par. 15-5. This example has enough similarities to our power purchase contract that it may be helpful "by analogy" to illustrate when a plant has been implicitly specified in an arrangement.

APPLYING SCOPE GUIDANCE TO DERIVATIVE INSTRUMENTS

Located in the Broad Transactions area of the Codification, Topic **815** (Derivatives) requires that certain instruments must be carried at fair value and marked-to-market (meaning that changes in fair value must be reflected in the asset or liability's recorded value each quarter).

The derivatives topic includes instruments (or contracts) within its scope that "derive" value from changes in some market price or other factor. For example, a contract for the future purchase of oil at a specified price must be carried at fair value. This makes sense because as the value of oil changes, the contract itself will have a positive or negative fair value. The same is true for a contract for the future purchase of a certain stock at a specified price.

In recent years, derivative contracts have evolved into an essential risk-management tool for many companies. Companies frequently turn to derivatives to protect themselves from future commodity price and interest rate changes, in order to improve the predictability of their future cash flows. For example, by early 2012, Southwest Airlines had already entered into contracts locking in prices for 50% of its expected jet fuel purchases for the second half of 2012.[13] Given that these contracts have market-based values that can fluctuate, these contracts must be recorded at their current market value.

Investors like the transparency of derivatives, as they are carried at the contract's current value. Companies, however, may find the frequent effort of re-measuring its derivative contracts burdensome.

Derivatives are defined as instruments with all of the following characteristics:

- It has a stated notional (a quantity) and an underlying (a price).
- It requires little or no initial net investment.
- The contract itself, or the asset sold in the contract, is readily marketable.

Researchers must evaluate whether a contract meets the definition of a derivative, and then must consider whether the contract is eligible for any scope exceptions. Scope exceptions to derivative accounting include, for example, insurance contracts and so-called "normal purchases and normal sales" where an entity can assert that it will use the contracted goods for its own operations.

---

[13] Graham, Rachel. "Jet Fuel Hedging Positions for U.S., Canadian Airlines." Bloomberg online. March 26, 2012.

Following is an example illustrating the use of derivative scope guidance.

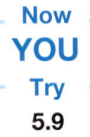

Now
YOU
Try
5.9

Evaluating Whether an Instrument Meets the Definition of a Derivative

Facts: Albert, Inc. sells office supplies. Albert, Inc. is in the process of signing a contract for the purchase of 10,000 staplers in 1 year from its supplier in China. Albert, Inc. will pay $2 per stapler upon delivery. The contract itself does not allow for net settlement between the parties. Albert, Inc. must determine whether the contract meets the definition of a derivative.

ASC 815-10 (Derivatives and Hedging) includes the following scope guidance.

Definition of Derivative Instrument

15-83 A derivative instrument is a financial instrument or other contract with all of the following characteristics:

    a. Underlying, notional amount, payment provision. The contract has both of the following terms, which determine the amount of the settlement or settlements, and, in some cases, whether or not a settlement is required:

        1. One or more underlyings

        2. One or more notional amounts or payment provisions or both.

    b. Initial net investment. The contract requires no initial net investment or an initial net investment that is smaller than would be required for other types of contracts that would be expected to have a similar response to changes in market factors.

    c. Net settlement. The contract can be settled net by any of the following means:

        1. Its terms implicitly or explicitly require or permit net settlement.

        2. It can readily be settled net by a means outside the contract.

        3. It provides for delivery of an asset that puts the recipient in a position not substantially different from net settlement.

ASC 815-10 goes on to provide additional guidance on the terms included in par. 15-83 definition. Excerpts from that additional guidance follow.

Underlying

15-88 An underlying is a variable that, along with either a notional amount or a payment provision, determines the settlement of a derivative instrument. An underlying usually is one or a combination of the following:

    1. A security price or security price index

    2. A commodity price or commodity price index . . .

Notional Amount

15-92 A notional amount is a number of currency units, shares, bushels, pounds, or other units specified in the contract. . . .

Net Settlement Under Contract Terms

15-100 In this form of net settlement, neither party is required to deliver an asset that is associated with the underlying and that has a . . . number of shares, or other denomination that is equal to the notional amount . . .

Primary Characteristics of Market Mechanism

15-110 In this form of net settlement, one of the parties is required to deliver an asset of the type described in paragraph 815-10-15-100, but there is an established market mechanism that facilitates net settlement outside the contract. (For example, an

Continued

exchange that offers a ready opportunity to <u>sell the contract</u> or to enter into an offsetting contract.) . . .

Net Settlement by Delivery of Derivative Instrument or Asset Readily Convertible to Cash

15-119 In this form of net settlement, one of the parties is required to deliver an asset of the type described in paragraph 815-10-15-100, but <u>that asset is readily convertible to cash</u> . . . [Underlined emphasis added]

15-120 An example of a contract with this form of net settlement is a forward contract that requires delivery of an exchange-traded equity security. Even though the number of shares to be delivered is the same as the notional amount of the contract and the price of the shares is the underlying, an exchange-traded security is readily convertible to cash. . . .

15-121 Examples of assets that are readily convertible to cash include a security or commodity traded in an active market and a unit of foreign currency that is readily convertible into the functional currency of the reporting entity.

Questions:

1. Does this contract meet the definition of a derivative?

    a. Does the contract have a notional amount? An underlying?

    _____
    _____

    b. Does the contract require an initial net investment?

    _____

    c. Can the contract be settled net?

    _____
    _____
    _____

    Finally, provide an overall conclusion: Does this contract meet the definition of a derivative? Recall that all three characteristics from par. 15-83 must be met in order for the contract to be a derivative.

2. Overall conclusion: Does this contract meet the definition of a derivative?

    _____
    _____

3. What key factor prevented or caused this contract to be a derivative?

    _____
    _____

APPLYING SCOPE GUIDANCE TO INDUSTRY TOPICS

The Codification includes several industry-specific topics, and guidance in these topics is generally intended to be applied *in addition to* other general Codification requirements. Like other Codification topics, industry topics include scope guidance identifying entities subject to that guidance.

For example, entities in the development stage are subject to special reporting requirements, such as reporting accumulated losses to date and stating on the financial statements that the company is a development-stage entity. In Topic **915** (Development Stage Entities), the Codification limits use of this topic by established extractive industry companies that are engaging in operations with uncertain outcomes (such as oil exploration).[14] In those cases, Topic 915 states that other GAAP should be applied.

The following example illustrates how Topic 915 scope guidance may be applied in addition to other applicable industry guidance.

Now
YOU
Try
5.10

Evaluating the Scope of Industry Guidance

Facts: Big Drills, Inc. is in the extractive industry and is the parent to one successful subsidiary already in operation: Natural Gas, Inc. Big Drills has just announced the creation of a new subsidiary division, Oil, Inc. Big Drills anticipates 5 years of exploration will be necessary before Oil, Inc. will produce revenues. See Figure 5-3 for an illustration of this structure.

Figure 5-3

Big Drills' organizational structure

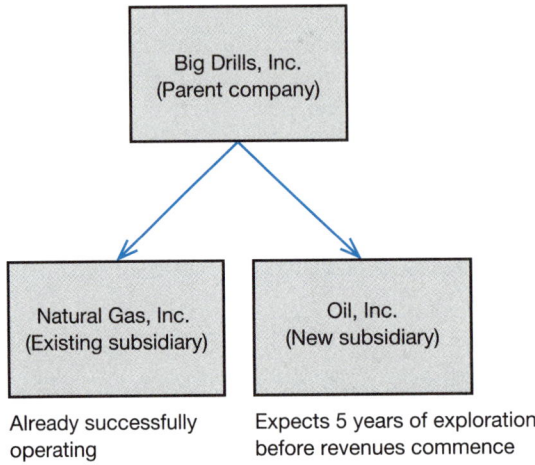

Oil, Inc. is preparing its first-year financial statements and must determine whether to apply the following industry topics: Topic 915, Development-Stage Entities, Topic 932, Extractive Industries—Oil and Gas, or both.

ASC 915-10 (Development Stage Entities) includes the following scope guidance:

> **Overall Guidance**

15-1 The Subtopics within the Development Stage Entities Topic only provide incremental guidance for the entities defined in this Scope Section, or as further defined in the Scope Sections of the individual Subtopics. Entities within the scope of this Topic shall also comply with the applicable guidance not included in this Topic.

> **Entities**

15-2 The guidance in the Development Stage Entities Topic applies to any separate financial statements of:
   a. A development stage subsidiary or other investee of an established operating entity
   b. A separate development stage entity (or of a group of entities that, as a whole, is considered to be in the development stage).

15-3 The term *development stage entity* is used to include a development stage subsidiary or other investee that is issuing separate financial statements.

15-4 The guidance in this Topic applies to development stage entities in all industries.

Continued

---

[14] ASC 915-10-15-5 (Development Stage Entities, Scope).

> **Other Considerations**

15-5 The guidance in the Development Stage Entities Topic does not: ...
    c. Change GAAP currently applicable to established operating entities that are not explicitly addressed in another Topic. For example, this Topic does not change GAAP applicable to the following:
        1. Established operating entities generally in expanding their existing businesses
        2. Established operating entities in the extractive industries in their exploration and development activities . . .

The Glossary of Topic **915-10** defines **development stage entity** as follows:

Development Stage Entity

An entity devoting substantially all of its efforts to establishing a new business and for which either of the following conditions exists:
a. Planned principal operations have not commenced.
b. Planned principal operations have commenced, but there has been no significant revenue therefrom.

Considering the facts and guidance provided, respond to the following.

Questions:

1. Does it appear that ASC 915-10 (Development Stage Entities) applies to the new subsidiary, Oil, Inc.?

_____

_____

2. Does the scope of ASC 915-10 exclude entities in the extractive industry? Explain.

_____

_____

Next, let's consider the scope guidance in **ASC 932-10** (Extractive Industries—Oil and Gas):

15-2   This Topic applies to all entities with oil- and gas-producing activities.
15-2A Oil- and gas-producing activities include the following:
    a. The search for crude oil, including condensate and natural gas liquids, or natural gas in their natural states and original locations
    b. The acquisition of property rights or properties for the purpose of further exploration or for the purpose of removing the oil or gas from such properties
    c. The construction, drilling, and production activities necessary to retrieve oil and gas from their natural reservoirs, including the acquisition, construction, installation, and maintenance of field gathering and storage systems, such as:
        1. Lifting the oil and gas to the surface
        2. Gathering, treating, and field processing (as in the case of processing gas to extract liquid hydrocarbons).
    d. Extraction of saleable hydrocarbons, in the solid, liquid, or gaseous state, from oil sands, shale, coalbeds, or other nonrenewable natural resources that are intended to be upgraded into synthetic oil or gas, and activities undertaken with a view to such extraction.

The Glossary of Topic **932-10** defines **exploration** as follows:

Exploration

Exploration involves both of the following:
a.   Identifying areas that may warrant examination
b.   Examining specific areas that are considered to have prospects of containing oil and gas reserves, including drilling exploratory wells and exploratory-type stratigraphic test wells.

The following questions relate to the application of **ASC 932-10** to Big Drills and its subsidiary, Oil, Inc.

3.   Does the new subsidiary, Oil, Inc. appear to be within the scope of Extractive Industries guidance?

_____

4.   What guidance should Big Drills, Inc. (the parent company) follow when it engages in new exploration projects?

_____

5.   What paragraph from ASC 915-10 above indicated that it is okay to apply Development-Stage Entity guidance in addition to other industry-specific guidance?

_____

APPENDIX 5A: APPLYING SCOPE GUIDANCE TO CONSOLIDATIONS

Consolidation Guidance—Overview

Topic **810** (Consolidation) provides guidance on the two models for determining when consolidation of another entity is required: the voting- and variable-interest models.

- Under the **voting interest model**, entities holding a controlling financial interest in an investee must consolidate the investee.

- Under the **variable interest model**, consolidation is based on which entity has power to direct the activities, and absorb losses or receive returns from a variable interest entity (VIE).

To determine which model applies, Topic 810 requires that entities first evaluate whether an investee is within the scope of variable interest entity guidance (including whether the investee meets the definition of a VIE). If the VIE model does not apply, entities should follow the voting model.[15]

The voting model generally applies to traditional, equity-financed entities, where voting control is held by equity investors. By contrast, VIEs are generally defined as having any one of the following characteristics:

- Insufficiency of equity financing; instead, the entity is primarily financed by debt or other interests (guarantees, derivatives, etc.).

- Power to direct the entity is held by parties other than equity investors.

- Equity investors are not exposed to expected losses of the entity, or do not have the right to expected residual returns of the entity.

Variable interest entities may take the form of an LLC, for example, created by the reporting entity to engage in a specific, limited-scope activity. For example, a reporting entity might create

---

[15] ASC 810-10-15-3 (Consolidation—Overall—Scope).

an LLC for the sole purpose of issuing securities collateralized by a pool of accounts receivable. Alternatively, a VIE could be a research and development joint venture, focused on developing a specific product or technology for one or several sponsoring entities.

Bear in mind that, while only one of the preceding conditions must be present for an entity to be a VIE, it is a best practice to evaluate and document all conditions in the VIE definition.

The following example is intended to familiarize you with the guidance in Topic 810 (Consolidation) defining VIEs.

> Determining whether an entity is a variable interest entity is complex and highly nuanced. Researchers dealing with this topic should take care to read any available interpretive guidance and to consult specialists as needed.

TIP from the Trenches

Evaluating Whether an Entity Is a "Variable Interest Entity"

Facts: Two domestic companies, Manufacturing Company (ManuCo) and Sales Company (SalesCo) are interested in breaking into the Chinese market. They are forming a joint venture LLC ("the JV") to sell ManuCo's products in China. ManuCo will sell its finished goods to the JV at its cost, and the JV will sell the products to Chinese customers at a higher price. To accomplish this, the JV plans to build a distribution center in China.

The JV will be capitalized with an equity contribution of $50,000 from SalesCo (for a 33.3% ownership interest), and the remainder of its capitalization will be a $1 million unsecured loan and a $100,000 equity investment made from ManuCo to the JV (for a 66.6% ownership interest). SalesCo has the right, through a put option, to "put" its equity interest to ManuCo at any time for $50,000. Products sold will be branded with ManuCo's trademark. SalesCo will have sole rights to market ManuCo's products in China. Losses and residual returns of the LLC will be shared in proportion to the entities' equity ownership interests (33%/66%).

ManuCo will appoint a general manager to oversee the day-to-day operations of the JV. The general manager will report to the Board of Directors, which has the ability to hire/fire the general manager. The Board of Directors of the LLC will be comprised of 10 members, 6 nominated by ManuCo, 4 nominated by SalesCo. Figure 5-4 illustrates this transaction.

ManuCo has asked for your help in determining whether the JV is a variable interest entity.

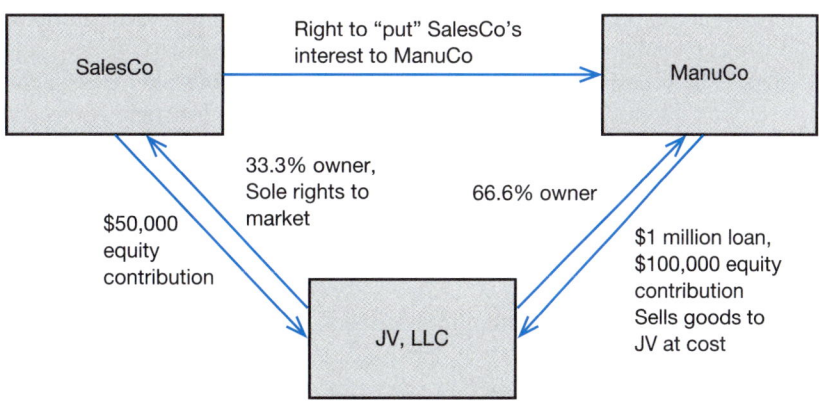

Figure 5-4

Illustration of variable interest entity scenario

ASC 810-10 (Consolidation) includes the following scope guidance:

Entities

15-14 A legal entity shall be subject to consolidation under the guidance in the Variable Interest Entities Subsections if, by design, any of the following conditions exist . . .

Continued

Continued from previous page

    a. The total equity investment (equity investments in a legal entity are interests that are required to be reported as equity in that entity's financial statements) at risk is not sufficient to permit the legal entity to finance its activities without additional <u>subordinated financial support</u> provided by any parties, including equity holders. For this purpose, the total equity investment at risk has all of the following characteristics:

        1. Includes only equity investments in the legal entity that participate significantly in profits and losses . . .

        2. Does not include equity interests that the legal entity issued in exchange for subordinated interests in other VIEs

        3. Does not include amounts provided to the equity investor directly or indirectly by the legal entity or by other parties involved with the legal entity (for example, by fees, charitable contributions, or other payments) . . .

        4. Does not include amounts financed for the equity investor (for example, by loans or guarantees of loans) directly by the legal entity or by other parties involved with the legal entity . . .

    b. As a group the holders of the equity investment at risk lack any one of the following three characteristics:

        1. The power, through voting rights or similar rights, to direct the activities of a legal entity that most significantly impact the entity's economic performance. The investors do not have that power through voting rights or similar rights if no <u>owners</u> hold voting rights or similar rights (such as those of a common shareholder in a corporation or a general partner in a partnership) . . .

        2. The obligation to absorb the <u>expected losses</u> of the legal entity. The investor or investors do not have that obligation if they are directly or indirectly protected from the expected losses or are guaranteed a return by the legal entity itself or by other parties involved with the legal entity . . .

        3. The right to receive the <u>expected residual returns</u> of the legal entity. The investors do not have that right if their return is capped by the legal entity's governing documents or arrangements with other variable interest holders or the legal entity . . .

    c. The equity investors as a group also are considered to lack the characteristic in (b)(1) if both of the following conditions are present:

        1. The voting rights of some investors are not proportional to their obligations to absorb the expected losses of the legal entity, their rights to receive the expected residual returns of the legal entity, or both.

        2. Substantially all of the legal entity's activities (for example, providing financing or buying assets) either involve or are conducted on behalf of an investor that has disproportionately few voting rights . . .

Following is an analysis of each condition from this par. 15-14 guidance.

Is The Joint Venture a Legal Entity?

Notice that the first sentence of par. 15-14 states: "A legal entity shall be subject to consolidation under the guidance in the Variable Interest Entities Subsections if, by design, any of the following conditions exist . . ."

    The glossary of Topic **810-10** defines a **legal entity** as follows:

Legal Entity

Any legal structure used to conduct activities or to hold assets. Some examples of such structures are corporations, partnerships, limited liability companies, grantor trusts, and other trusts.

1. Is the JV a legal entity?

    _____

2. How would your response differ if ManuCo and SalesCo jointly invested in a <u>building</u>, rather than in an LLC?

    _____

Does The JV Have Insufficient Equity At Risk To Finance Its Activities Without Additional Subordinated Financial Support?

The first condition listed in par. 15-14 asks whether the entity has enough equity at risk to finance its activities. If the entity does not have sufficient equity at risk, the entity meets the definition of a VIE. In this case, we must evaluate the $50,000 and $100,000 equity contributions made to the JV.

See par. 15-14a. For equity to be considered at risk, it must meet all four characteristics listed in this paragraph. We'll break this question into two parts: (1) Is the JV's equity at risk? and (2) Is the at-risk equity sufficient to finance the JV's activities?

Is All Of The JV's Equity Considered "At Risk"? That Is, Does It Meet All Of The Conditions In Par. 15-14(a)(1-4) Above?

In your response to part (a)(1), consider potential impacts of SalesCo's put option.

3. Is the JV's equity considered at risk?

    15-14(a)(1): _____

    15-14(a)(2): _____

    15-14(a)(3): _____

    15-14(a)(4): _____

Is The JV's "At Risk Equity" Considered Sufficient For The JV To Finance Its Activities Without Additional-Subordinated Financial Support?

Refer again to condition 15-14(a). The term "subordinated financial support" is defined in **ASC 810-10-20** as

> **Subordinated Financial Support**
>
> Variable interests that will absorb some or all of a variable interest entity's (VIE's) expected losses.

Subordinated financial support refers to investments in the entity that could bear some risk of loss, such as unsecured debt or guarantees. This "insufficiency of equity at risk" characteristic is met if equity investments alone are not sufficient to finance the entity's activities. Sufficiency of equity at risk can generally be evidenced by

■   Demonstration by the entity that its activities can be financed without additional subordinated financial support, or

■   Comparison to the equity capitalization of similar entities.

Think of the activities the JV plans to engage in, then consider the amount of equity deemed "at risk" in part (a). Condition (a) of par. 15-14 requires entities to consider: Is the at-risk equity sufficient to finance the entity's activities?

4. Is equity at risk sufficient to finance the entity's activities?

    15-14(a) _____

Do The JV's At-Risk Equity Investors Lack Power To Direct The Entity? Or, Do The JV's Equity Investors Lack Either The Obligation To Absorb Losses Or The Right To Receive Returns?

Refer again to conditions (b)(1-3) in par. 15-14. These conditions evaluate whether the entity's at-risk equity holders lack (1) power to direct the entity, (2) the obligation to absorb entity losses, or (3) the right to receive entity returns. If the equity holders lack any one of these characteristics, the entity meets the definition of a VIE.

Ernst & Young's guide book on variable interest entities[16] provides the following additional guidance on evaluating the "power to direct" condition:

> Illustration 9-15: Participating rights held by holders of interests that are not equity investments at risk
>
> **Example 1 Facts** Assume that three unrelated enterprises (Enterprises A, B and C) form an LLC. Enterprise A has a 60% equity ownership in the venture, and Enterprises B and C each hold a 20% equity ownership. However, Enterprises B and C can both put their equity interests to Enterprise A at the end of five years for an amount equal to their original equity investment. Enterprise A makes all decisions. However, Enterprise B has the ability to block Enterprise A's decisions.
>
> **Analysis** In this fact pattern, Enterprises B and C are not holders of an equity investment at risk because their ability to put their interests to Enterprise A at the end of five years protects them from having to significantly participate in the losses of the LLC. Enterprise A cannot unilaterally make decisions about the entity's activities because Enterprise B has participating rights. Because Enterprise B (holder of an equity investment that is not at risk) has the unilateral ability to exercise the participating rights, the entity is a VIE.

Additionally, consider the following example from Ernst & Young related to whether sharing returns with a non-equity at risk holder limits the holders of equity at risk from receiving expected residual returns of an entity:

> **Facts** Fortune 500 Company owns and operates ten crude oil refineries in the United States and has been operating in the crude oil refining and marketing business since it first went public in 1956. Fortune 500 Company also has a profit sharing plan that provides its employees with up to 10% of its annual operating profit.
>
> **Analysis** In this example, the provisions of ASC 810-10-15-14(b)(3) are not violated simply because of the existence of the employee profit sharing plan. Sharing of an entity's profits with parties other than holders of the equity investment at risk is permitted as long as that sharing does not cap the at-risk equity holders' returns. Judgment is required to determine whether, by design, the at-risk equity holders' returns are capped.[17]

Consider only the "at risk" equity holders in your response.

5. Do at-risk equity holders lack (1) power to direct, (2) obligation to absorb losses, or (3) right to residual benefits?

    15-14(b)(1): _____

    15-14(b)(2): _____

    15-14(b)(3): _____

---

[16] Ernst & Young, Financial Reporting Developments: *Consolidation of Variable Interest Entities*. Revised June 2011. Page 149.

[17] Ernst & Young, Financial Reporting Developments: *Consolidation of Variable Interest Entities*. Revised June 2011. Example 2, Page 170.

Do The Equity Investors Have Either Of The Following Additional Qualities?

See condition (c) in par. 15-14. This condition says that the "power to direct" condition from par. b(1) is also met if the entity's equity holders (1) have voting rights disproportional to their obligation to absorb losses or their right to receive returns, *and* (2) if substantially all of the entity's activities are conducted on behalf of the investor with disproportionately few voting rights (or, in this case, disproportionately few Board seats).

In this case, the equity investors' voting rights in the JV are essentially "60/40," and their equity ownership percentages are 66.66%/33.33% (ManuCo/SalesCo). However, the put option could result in ManuCo bearing 100% of the JV's expected losses. ManuCo could also bear expected losses of the JV through its $1 million subordinated loan.

6. Are the investors' voting rights proportional to their obligation to absorb expected losses (or their right to receive residual returns) of the JV?

   15-14(c)(1): _____

In evaluating the "substantially all activities" condition in par. (c)(2), Ernst & Young's variable interest entity guide book[18] lists the following considerations. This excerpt does not include all considerations listed by Ernst & Young.

> Factors that should be considered in determining whether the activities involve or are conducted on behalf of with the investor having disproportionately few voting rights include:
>
> ■ Are the entity's operations substantially similar in nature to the activities of the investor with disproportionately few voting rights?
>
> ■ Are the entity's operations more important to the investor with disproportionately few voting rights than the other variable interest holders?
>
> ■ What decisions does the investor with disproportionately few voting rights participate in and to what extent?
>
> ■ Are the majority of the entity's products or services bought from or sold to the investor with disproportionately few voting rights?
>
> ■ . . ." [Footnotes omitted]

7. Are substantially all of the JV's activities conducted on behalf of the investor with disproportionately few voting rights?

   15-14(c)(2): _____

   Overall conclusion on par. 15-14 (c)? Were *both* conditions met? _____

Conclude your analysis with a summary of which conditions, from the definition of a VIE, were met.

8. Paragraph 15-14 states that an entity is considered a VIE if it meets *any* of the conditions in par. 15-14. Based on your analysis, which conditions were met?

   _____
   _____

9. Therefore, is the JV a VIE?

   _____
   _____

[18] Ernst & Young, Financial Reporting Developments: *Consolidation of Variable Interest Entities*. Revised June 2011. Page 176.

CHAPTER SUMMARY

Reviewing scope guidance within the Codification is a critical step in performing accounting research. Scope guidance is presented in various formats; in some cases, only those transactions or entities excluded from the scope of the guidance are listed. In other cases, transactions within the scope of certain guidance may be named, or a scope test may be required. Before performing detailed scope tests for complex guidance, researchers should consult the topic's Overview section to see generally whether the topic is expected to apply. Judgment can be involved in applying scope guidance; in many cases, Codification implementation guidance or accounting firm resources are a useful resource.

REVIEW QUESTIONS

1. What function does scope guidance serve within the Codification?
2. What additional steps should a researcher consider performing, before undertaking a detailed scope test?
3. Name two of the indicators used to determine whether an arrangement contains a lease.
4. Name three Codification topics that could apply to a purchase of equity securities that gives the investor a non-controlling interest.
5. Describe the three characteristics that must be present in order for an instrument to meet the definition of a derivative.
6. Describe what is required for an equity award granted to a nonemployee director to be accounted for under Topic 718, Stock Compensation.
7. Describe why a gross receipts tax is not considered a "tax based on income" and thus included within the scope of Topic 740, Income Taxes.
8. (Refers to material in the Appendix): What process should entities follow when determining whether an investment is subject to the voting- or variable-interest entity model in Topic 810? That is, in what order should a researcher evaluate the two models in Topic 810?
9. (Refers to material in the Appendix): Summarize the three characteristics that could result in variable interest entity classification.

EXERCISES

Respond to the following in complete sentences, and cite your source. If you have to make any assumptions in your response, state what you assumed.

1. Which entities are subject to Earnings Per Share guidance within the Codification?
2. Does the Research and Development topic within the Codification apply to contractual arrangements whereby an entity conducts research and development activities for others?
3. A company has entered into a forward contract for the purchase of gold, in 1 year, for $1500/oz. Does this arrangement meet the definition of a derivative? Analyze all required parts of the definition. (You may simply refer to the guidance excerpts included within this chapter to respond.)
4. Read the guidance in ASC 810-10-15 (Consolidation—Scope), par. 3(a) and 3(b). Based on these paragraphs:
   a. Does it appear that Topic 810 applies to both "variable interest entities" and entities being evaluated for consolidation under the "voting interest" model? What subsections apply to each?
   b. Under the "voting model" described in par. 3(b), what is the usual condition for a controlling financial interest (and therefore, consolidation)?
5. Name two examples of transactions to which the Principal Agent Considerations subtopic (of Revenue Recognition) might apply.
6. What is an example of a transaction excluded from the scope of lease accounting (or which is described as "not qualifying as a lease"? (Do not use the example already included in this chapter).
7. Does the Codification's guidance on Environmental Obligations apply to environmental remediation actions undertaken at the discretion of management?

8. Name three examples of organizations that are within the scope of not-for-profit entities industry guidance.

9. Locate Deloitte's most recent guide to income tax accounting, *A Roadmap to Accounting for Income Taxes*. Does Deloitte believe that not-for-profit foundation excise taxes (e.g., taxes on the sale of goods or production of income) are within the scope of Topic 740 (Income Taxes)? Why or why not?

CASE STUDY QUESTION

Asset Exchange (Drafting an Issues Memo)—Advanced Material   5.1

Facts: Acer Corp transfers factory equipment to Theta Corp in exchange for the receipt of $1 million cash and a 25% equity ownership stake in Theta. Acer's book basis in the transferred equipment was $6 million, and the equipment was recently appraised for $6.5 million. The fair value of the investment in Theta is $5.5 million, and this fair value was reliably determined. The investment gives Acer significant influence over Theta but is not a controlling financial interest in Theta. Theta is in the business of making and selling tissues (such as Kleenex) and will use the building for tissue production.

Prior to transferring the equipment, Acer used the equipment to produce paper plates and napkins. However, significant overseas competition has caused profit margins and demand for the domestic production of paper plates and napkins to fall. Production using the equipment had recently been cut down to only 1 × 8-hr shift per day. Tissues are expected to be a more profitable output, with steady consumer demand. Theta expects to run the equipment for 3 × 8-hr shifts per day. Acer hopes the investment in Theta will revive its slowing growth prospects.

Required: You are in the controller's group of Acer and need to determine the appropriate accounting for this transaction.

First, evaluate whether this transaction is within the scope of the applicable topic. In doing so, please also evaluate whether this transaction is a monetary or nonmonetary exchange, based on the cash exchanged.

Next, determine the appropriate accounting for this transaction. In doing so, please be sure to evaluate whether the transaction has commercial substance (you may evaluate just one of the two conditions for commercial substance, of your choice).

Organize Acer's accounting issues into a memo, including journal entries for this transaction, and explain the authoritative basis for all journal entries recorded. Consider including a picture to enhance the "Background" section of the memo.

Note: Par. 25-6 (of the relevant topic) may be used to consider whether a transaction is "monetary" or "nonmonetary." However, do not look to this paragraph when determining how to account for the value exchanged in this transaction.

Also, assume that Acer will account for the ownership stake in Theta using the equity method.

Chapter 6

Using the Codification to Research Issues— Recognition and Derecognition

It's Sunday morning. Dan, the senior auditor on the Grant Construction Co. engagement, opens the morning newspaper and reads that his client has just announced a commitment to donate $1 million annually, for 5 years, to the town's local Habitat for Humanity chapter. Dan is not sure whether this promise will result in a liability for his client; however, he makes himself a note to research the Codification's requirements on accounting for contributions when he returns to work on Monday. If this commitment requires financial statement recognition, Dan wants to make sure that his client records it.

After reading this chapter and performing the exercises herein, you will be able to

1. **Determine** when an issue involves accounting recognition or derecognition.

2. **Review** recognition guidance to determine when and how a transaction should be recorded in the financial statements.

3. **Identify** certain key judgments involved in applying recognition guidance to revenue, liabilities, leases, income taxes, and subsequent events.

4. **Apply** derecognition guidance to certain liabilities and equity-method investments.

Learning Objectives

Applying Recognition Guidance— A Series of Examples	Applying Derecognition Guidance— A Series of Examples
1. **Revenue Recognition** • Sale of product with right of return • Sale of product with a separately priced warranty • Sales of products on consignment 2. **Liability Recognition** • Loss contingencies • Contributions made 3. **Lease Recognition:** Capital versus operating lease classification 4. **Recognition of Uncertain Tax Positions** • Applying the more-likely-than-not threshold • Evaluating effective settlement 5. **Subsequent Events:** Recognized versus unrecognized	1. **Liability Extinguishment** • Legal and in-substance defeasances • Debt modifications and extinguishments 2. **Equity Method Investments:** Recognition and derecognition

Organization of This Chapter

Recognition guidance (Section 25) is arguably one of the most important sections within the Codification. The objective of this chapter is to familiarize readers with the application of certain recognition guidance, and to help readers develop an understanding of which issues involve accounting recognition. Having exposure to this guidance can improve readers' understanding and efficiency in navigating Codification guidance as professionals, and provides opportunities to practice skills required for the CPA exam, as well.

Nearly every Codification topic includes unique guidance on recognition; clearly, it would be impossible to cover every topic in this chapter. Rather, this chapter includes various issues intended to be representative of questions that researchers might encounter in practice. These include, for example, issues related to revenue recognition, liability recognition, classification of leases, and recognition of uncertain tax positions. A few limited examples are also provided to illustrate the application of Derecognition guidance (Section 40) within the Codification.

This chapter begins with the question: "What is accounting recognition?" To answer this, we will briefly review the objectives and criteria for accounting recognition from the FASB's Conceptual Framework. Next, readers can practice applying recognition guidance to the topics listed in the diagram at the top of this page.

WHAT IS ACCOUNTING RECOGNITION?

Accounting recognition broadly describes the "criteria, timing, and location (within the financial statements)" for recording an item.[1] That is, recognition describes *what* should be recorded (e.g., is an item or event required to be recognized?), *when* it should be recorded (e.g., can revenue be recognized at the time of sale?), and *how* (i.e., where within the financial statements) the item should be recorded.

Although many individual topics within the Codification separately address recognition, it is also useful to consider the overall objectives of recognition set forth in the FASB's Conceptual Framework. Concepts Statement No. 5, *Recognition and Measurement in Financial Statements of Business Enterprises* (CON 5), describes recognition as follows:

> 6.   Recognition is the process of formally recording or incorporating an item into the financial statements of an entity as an asset, liability, revenue, expense, or the like. Recognition includes depiction of an item in both words and numbers, with the amount included in the totals of the financial statements . . .

CON 5 establishes the following four **fundamental recognition criteria**:

> **Fundamental Recognition Criteria**
>
> 63.   An item and information about it should meet four fundamental recognition criteria to be recognized and should be recognized when the criteria are met, subject to a cost-benefit constraint and a materiality threshold. Those criteria are:
>
>> *Definitions*—The item meets the definition of an element of financial statements.
>> *Measurability*—It has a relevant attribute measurable with sufficient reliability.
>> *Relevance*—The information about it is capable of making a difference in user decisions.
>> *Reliability*—The information is representationally faithful, verifiable, and neutral.
>
> All four criteria are subject to a pervasive cost-benefit constraint: the expected benefits from recognizing a particular item should justify perceived costs of providing and using the information. Recognition is also subject to a materiality threshold: an item and information about it need not be recognized in a set of financial statements if the item is not large enough to be material and the aggregate of individually immaterial items is not large enough to be material to those financial statements. [Footnotes omitted]

That is, items meeting these four fundamental criteria should be recorded in the financial statements, subject to two additional tests:

1.   The benefit of recognizing the item must exceed the cost of doing so.
2.   The item should be considered material to financial statement users.

From time to time, practitioners have historically asserted to the FASB that disclosure is a reasonable substitute for financial statement recognition.[2] However, in CON 5, the FASB emphasizes that recognition is the preferred method of conveying information that is material to financial statement users; the FASB does not view disclosure to be an adequate substitute for

---

[1] FASB *Notice to Constituents (v4.6) About the Codification*. January 9, 2012. Page 18.

[2] For example, during the development of FASB Statement No. 123, *Accounting for Stock-Based Compensation* (FAS 123), many constituents urged the Board to require disclosure only, of share-based compensation arrangements, rather than change the accounting recognition of stock awards (see par. 59, FAS 123).

recognition.[3] While it is important to be aware of the recognition principles in CON 5, they are rarely utilized in practice by accounting researchers; rather, their primary role is to serve as a foundation for the FASB's standard-setting process.

In most cases, recognition guidance is available within Section **25** of each topic in the Codification. However, the following additional sources can also provide valuable recognition guidance:

- Other Presentation Matters (Section **45** in the Codification) also frequently describes *how* items should be recorded in the financial statements.

- Implementation Guidance (Section **55**) and SEC content (Sections **S-25** or **S-99**) may offer additional clarification and examples illustrating recognition guidance.

- In limited cases, FASB Concepts Statement No. 6, *Elements of Financial Statements* (CON 6), can be useful in determining how items should be recorded (such as asset versus expense determinations).

Derecognition guidance describes *when* and *how* an asset, liability, or equity item may be removed from the financial statements. The Conceptual Framework does not currently address the issue of derecognition; however, this issue is addressed within individual topics of the Codification, where applicable.

The following section includes examples illustrating recognition guidance for various accounting issues.

1. **What are four sources a researcher might consult for recognition-related guidance?**

Knowledge Check

REVENUE RECOGNITION

Definition and Broad Criteria for Recognition

Our discussion of revenue recognition begins with a refresher on the conceptual definition of revenue and the criteria for its recognition. On the surface, revenue recognition concepts may seem simple (recognize when earned and realized). However, did you know that over 100 individual pieces of revenue recognition guidance were used to populate the Codification? In some cases, this abundance of guidance can lead to different accounting (based on a company's industry) for economically similar transactions. Simplifying the principles for revenue recognition has long been an objective of the FASB, and it is a project that is ongoing today. Currently, the Revenue Recognition topic contains 36 subtopics, with unique guidance offered for many transactions and industries.

Conceptual Definitions of Revenue

CON 6 broadly defines revenues as increases in assets or decreases in liabilities:

> 78. Revenues are inflows or other enhancements of assets of an entity or settlements of its liabilities (or a combination of both) from delivering or producing goods, rendering services, or other activities that constitute the entity's ongoing major or central operations.

By contrast, CON 5 offers a slightly different view, emphasizing that revenue recognition "involves consideration of two factors, (a) being realized or realizable and (b) being earned . . ." (par. 83).

One objective of the FASB's current revenue recognition project is to remove the potential for inconsistencies between these two models for determining when revenue may be recognized. Under the CON 5 approach, revenue recognition focuses on the earnings process, while the CON 6 approach emphasizes that revenue arises from changes in assets and liabilities.

---

[3] FASB Concepts Statement No. 5, *Recognition and Measurement in Financial Statements of Business Enterprises*, par. 9.

The FASB's proposed model would move away from use of the terms "earned and realized" and instead is intended to focus on revenue arising from changes in assets and liabilities; but even under that model, many pages of the proposed standard are devoted to describing when performance has occurred and revenue may be recognized.

General Requirements for Revenue Recognition

Within the Codification, Topic **605-10** (Revenue Recognition, Overall) offers the following criteria for recognizing revenue. Revenue can generally be recognized when

■ It has been realized or is realizable, and

■ It has been earned.[4]

These criteria are shown in full here.

> ### > Revenue and Gains

25-1 The recognition of revenue and gains of an entity during a period involves consideration of the following two factors, with sometimes one and sometimes the other being the more important consideration:

   a. Being realized or realizable. Revenue and gains generally are not recognized until realized or realizable. Paragraph 83(a) of FASB Concepts Statement No. 5, *Recognition and Measurement in Financial Statements of Business Enterprises*, states that revenue and gains are realized when products (goods or services), merchandise, or other assets are exchanged for cash or claims to cash. That paragraph states that revenue and gains are realizable when related assets received or held are <u>readily convertible</u> to known amounts of cash or claims to cash.

   b. Being earned. Paragraph 83(b) of FASB Concepts Statement No. 5, *Recognition and Measurement in Financial Statements of Business Enterprises*, states that revenue is not recognized until earned. That paragraph states that an entity's revenue-earning activities involve delivering or producing goods, rendering services, or other activities that constitute its ongoing major or central operations, and revenues are considered to have been earned when the entity has substantially accomplished what it must do to be entitled to the benefits represented by the revenues. That paragraph states that gains commonly result from transactions and other events that involve no earning process, and for recognizing gains, being earned is generally less significant than being realized or realizable.

In addition to Codification requirements, public companies must also become familiar with the SEC's interpretations of the basic revenue recognition criteria. Located in the "**S99**" section of Topic 605-10, the SEC has developed four additional criteria for interpreting the FASB's concepts of "realized and earned."

The staff believes that revenue generally is realized or realizable and earned when all of the following criteria are met:
• Persuasive evidence of an arrangement exists,
• Delivery has occurred or services have been rendered,
• The seller's price to the buyer is fixed or determinable, and
• Collectibility is reasonably assured.[5] [Footnotes omitted] (par. 1)

---

[4] ASC 605-10-25-1 (Revenue Recognition).

[5] SAB Topic 13.A.1, Revenue Recognition—General, as accessed in ASC 605-10-S99.

Be aware that, within the Codification, these criteria are accompanied by extensive interpretive guidance and examples. The full original text of this SEC guidance is also available on the SEC's website.

Armed with these basic revenue recognition concepts, we will now practice applying revenue recognition guidance to several examples. These examples illustrate revenue recognition guidance for products (**ASC 605-15**), services (**ASC 605-20**), and for consignment sales (using SEC guidance in **ASC 605-10**).

Sale of a Product with a Right of Return

Now
YOU
Try
6.1

Facts: RetailMart just sold a customer a big-screen TV for $1,500, and the customer has the option to return the TV for a full refund within 30 days. The customer paid cash for the product. RetailMart has no further obligations to the customer after the sale, except the requirement to stand ready to accept the customer return within 30 days, if necessary. RetailMart must determine whether it is appropriate to recognize revenue at the time of sale.

In addition to the general principle for revenue recognition in **ASC 605-10** (excerpted in the preceding discussion), subtopic 605-15 (Revenue Recognition—Products) provides guidance for product sales. The following guidance from **ASC 605-15** describes when it is appropriate to recognize revenue for product sales with a right of return.

> ### > Sales of Product when Right of Return Exists

25-1 If an entity sells its product but gives the buyer the right to return the product, revenue from the sales transaction shall be recognized at time of sale only if all of the following conditions are met:

a. The seller's price to the buyer is substantially fixed or determinable at the date of sale.

b. The buyer has paid the seller, or the buyer is obligated to pay the seller and the obligation is not contingent on resale of the product. If the buyer does not pay at time of sale and the buyer's obligation to pay is contractually or implicitly excused until the buyer resells the product, then this condition is not met.

c. The buyer's obligation to the seller would not be changed in the event of theft or physical destruction or damage of the product.

d. The buyer acquiring the product for resale has economic substance apart from that provided by the seller. This condition relates primarily to buyers that exist on paper, that is, buyers that have little or no physical facilities or employees. It prevents entities from recognizing sales revenue on transactions with parties that the sellers have established primarily for the purpose of recognizing such sales revenue.

e. The seller does not have significant obligations for future performance to directly bring about resale of the product by the buyer.

f. The amount of future returns can be reasonably estimated (see paragraphs 605-15-25-3 through 25-4). Because detailed record keeping for returns for each product line might be costly in some cases, this Subtopic permits reasonable aggregations and approximations of product returns. As explained in paragraph 605-15-15-2, exchanges by ultimate customers of one item for another of the same kind, quality, and price (for example, one color or size for another) are not considered returns for purposes of this Subtopic.

Sales revenue and cost of sales that are not recognized at time of sale because the foregoing conditions are not met shall be recognized either when the return privilege has substantially expired or if those conditions subsequently are met, whichever occurs first.

Continued

Continued from previous page

25-2   If sales revenue is recognized because the conditions of the preceding paragraph are met, any costs or losses that may be expected in connection with any returns shall be accrued in accordance with Subtopic <u>450-20</u>.

Questions:

1.   Does RetailMart meet the par. 605-15-25-1 conditions for recognition of revenue at the time of sale?

_____

_____

_____

_____

2.   Which condition may require further review?

_____

_____

Assume that RetailMart sells big-screen TVs frequently, and knows from its historical experience that approximately 2% of its sales usually result in returns. **ASC 605-15** provides the following additional guidance regarding an entity's ability to reasonably estimate future returns.

25-3   The ability to make a reasonable estimate of the amount of future returns depends on many factors and circumstances that will vary from one case to the next. However, any of the following factors may impair the ability to make a reasonable estimate:
  a.   The susceptibility of the product to significant external factors, such as technological obsolescence or changes in demand
  b.   Relatively long periods in which a particular product may be returned
  c.   Absence of historical experience with similar types of sales of similar products, or inability to apply such experience because of changing circumstances, for example, changes in the selling entity's marketing policies or relationships with its customers
  d.   Absence of a large volume of relatively homogeneous transactions.
25-4   The existence of one or more of the factors in the preceding paragraph, in light of the significance of other factors, may not be sufficient to prevent making a reasonable estimate; likewise, other factors may preclude a reasonable estimate.

Additional Questions:

3.   Based on consideration of this additional guidance, is recognition at the time of sale appropriate, and what entry (entries) should be made?

_____

_____

_____

4.   What entry is required by par. 25-2, to account for expected returns? Page [144] of this chapter includes the relevant excerpt from **ASC 450-20**. Assume the accounts involved are "Sales Return Expense" and "Allowance for Sales Returns".

  dr. _____ $_____

        cr. _____ $_____

Sale of a Product with a Separately Priced Extended Warranty

Now
YOU
Try
6.2

Facts: Assume that in addition to selling the customer a TV for $1,500, RetailMart also sold the customer its optional extended warranty coverage for $240 cash. This coverage allows the customer to receive, within 2 years of the date of purchase, a full refund, replacement, or repair service for any product defects. Assume that costs to honor the warranty are equally likely to occur at any time during the contract period. These costs are not expected to exceed the sales price of the warranty contract. RetailMart did not incur any direct costs related to the sale of this warranty. RetailMart must now determine when it should recognize revenue and related costs from the sale of the extended warranty.

Although the product being sold is a television, the extended warranty contract is considered a service. The Revenue Recognition—Overall subtopic (**ASC 605-10**) indicates that guidance for separately priced extended warranty contracts is included in the Services subtopic:

> **05-1** . . .This Topic includes the following Subtopics:
>   a.   Overall. The Overall Subtopic [605-10] provides guidance on the following:
>   1.   Revenue and gains
>   2.   . . .
>   b.   Products. The Products Subtopic [605-15] provides guidance on the following:
>   1.   Sales with a right of return
>   2.   . . .
>   c.   Services. The Services Subtopic [605-20] provides guidance on the following:
>   1.   Separately priced extended warranty and product maintenance contracts . . .
>   [Bracketed numerical references and emphasis added]

Accordingly, we must look to revenue recognition guidance in Topic **605-20** to determine when it is appropriate to recognize the warranty sale.

> > Separately Priced Extended Warranty and Product Maintenance Contracts
> . . . **25-3** Sellers of extended warranty or product maintenance contracts have an obligation to the buyer to perform services throughout the period of the contract and, therefore, revenue shall be recognized in income over the period in which the seller is obligated to perform. That is, revenue from separately priced extended warranty and product maintenance contracts shall be deferred and recognized in income on a straight-line basis over the contract period . . .
> **25-4** Costs that are directly related to the acquisition of a contract and that would have not been incurred but for the acquisition of that contract (incremental direct acquisition costs) shall be deferred and charged to expense in proportion to the revenue recognized. All other costs, such as costs of services performed under the contract, general and administrative expenses, advertising expenses, and costs associated with the negotiation of a contract that is not consummated, shall be charged to expense as incurred.

Questions:

1.   When is it appropriate for RetailMart to recognize revenue from the sale of the extended warranty?

_____

_____

2. When should the costs of performing warranty services be recognized?

    _____

    _____

3. Explain which subtopics the researcher had to consult for guidance on the product sale (with right of return attached), then for guidance on the sale of the extended warranty contract.

    _____

    _____

Now, provide the journal entries required to reflect the warranty revenue and warranty costs for each of the following circumstances.

4. What initial entry is required to record the transaction with the customer at the time of sale?

    dr. _____ $_____

        cr. _____ $_____   (Par. _____)

5. What monthly journal entry is required thereafter?

    dr. _____ $_____

        cr. _____ $_____   (Par. _____)

6. What journal entry would be required at month 6, assuming repair costs of $50 were paid in cash to a third-party repair company?

    dr. _____ $_____

        cr. _____ $_____   (Par. _____)

7. Finally, contrast the accounting for separately priced warranty contracts, versus the accounting for the retailer's liability for potential future product returns.

    _____

    _____

Sales of Products on Consignment

Consignment sales are generally characterized by a manufacturer (the "consignor") sending a quantity of goods to a "consignee," who acts as a selling agent for the consignor. Risk of loss for consigned goods is generally retained by the consignor until goods are sold, and payment for consigned goods is generally remitted to the consignor when the goods are sold. Any unsold goods held by the consignee at the end of a trading period are generally returned to the consignor.

FASB content within the Codification does not specifically address revenue recognition for consignment arrangements. However, the SEC sections within the Codification, applicable to public companies, do provide guidance on consignment sales. Nonpublic companies may find it useful to analogize to this guidance, in addition to applying the general recognition principles in **ASC 605-10** (Overall) and **605-15** (Products). The SEC's guidance for consignment arrangements is highlighted in the following example.

Now
YOU
Try
6.3

Sales of Products on Consignment

Facts: GoodScents (consignor), a perfume manufacturing company, sells fragrances in retail stores on a consignment basis. The retailer (consignee) remits payment to GoodScents only when inventory is sold to the end customer. Title to the inventory, and risk of loss related to the inventory, remains with GoodScents until such time as the inventory is sold. Inventory not sold by the consignee may be returned to GoodScents, and GoodScents pays handling fees for the return of merchandise. In exchange for its selling effort, consignee is entitled to receive a fixed percentage of the sale. GoodScents must determine whether it should recognize revenue at the time perfume is delivered to consignees, or upon sale to the ultimate customer.

The SEC provides guidance on consignment sales in SAB Topic 13.A.2[6] (available in the Codification at **ASC 605-10-S99**). This guidance, presented in question and answer format, interprets the SEC's revenue recognition condition that "persuasive evidence of an arrangement exists."

> Facts: Company Z enters into an arrangement with Customer A to deliver Company Z's products to Customer A on a consignment basis. Pursuant to the terms of the arrangement, Customer A is a consignee, and title to the products does not pass from Company Z to Customer A until Customer A consumes the products in its operations. Company Z delivers product to Customer A under the terms of their arrangement.
>
> Question: May Company Z recognize revenue upon delivery of its product to Customer A?
>
> Interpretive Response: No. Products delivered to a consignee pursuant to a consignment arrangement are not sales and do not qualify for revenue recognition until a sale occurs. The staff believes that revenue recognition is not appropriate because the seller retains the risks and rewards of ownership of the product and title usually does not pass to the consignee.

Questions:

1. Considering the SEC's guidance on consignment arrangements, should GoodScents recognize revenue at the time perfume is delivered to consignees, or upon sale to the ultimate customer?

   _____

   _____

2. Where, within the Codification, would a researcher go to access this SEC guidance?

   _____

   _____

As the preceding examples have illustrated, revenue recognition guidance is varied and extends across a number of unique subtopics within **ASC 605** (Revenue Recognition). Each subtopic describes the appropriate approach to revenue recognition for a given situation or set of circumstances; for this reason, it is critical for a researcher to carefully consider which subtopic is most directly applicable to his or her situation.

In some cases, recognition guidance from the SEC is integral to applying general requirements from the Codification; a researcher should always consider whether SEC guidance is available for a given recognition issue.

TIP from the Trenches

LIABILITY RECOGNITION

Recall that liabilities are defined in CON 6 as "probable future sacrifices of economic benefits arising from present obligations" (par. 35). When an item meets the definition of a liability and meets the other basic recognition criteria, it must be recognized in the financial statements. But what happens when the existence of a liability is uncertain?

Recognizing a Contingent Loss

Topic **450** (Contingencies) addresses circumstances where an uncertain event (gain or loss) requires financial statement recognition. Topic 450-10 acknowledges that estimates are inherent in the preparation of financial statements but contrasts recurring estimates with gain or loss contingencies, where the existence of an asset or liability is uncertain.

---

[6] SAB Topic 13.A.2, Persuasive Evidence of an Arrangement, as accessed in ASC 605-10-S99.

05-6   Not all uncertainties inherent in the accounting process give rise to <u>contingencies</u>. Estimates are required in financial statements for many ongoing and recurring activities of an entity. The mere fact that an estimate is involved does not of itself constitute the type of uncertainty referred to in the definition of a loss contingency or a gain contingency . . .

> > Estimates Used in Accruals

55-3   Amounts owed for services received, such as advertising and utilities, are not contingencies even though the accrued amounts may have been estimated; there is nothing uncertain about the fact that those obligations have been incurred.

Loss contingencies must be recognized in the financial statements if two conditions are met:

■   First, it must be probable that an asset has been impaired or that a liability has been incurred.

■   Second, the amount of loss must be reasonably estimable.

Following is an example illustrating the application of loss contingency guidance.

Now
YOU
Try
6.4

Contingent Losses

Facts: In 2012, two major manufacturers of smart phones were involved in a patent infringement lawsuit, in which the market leader (plaintiff) accused a competitor (defendant) of copying its smart phone design, software features, and hardware design. Recently, a U.S. district court judge found the defendant guilty of patent infringement and awarded the plaintiff $1 billion in damages. No amount has been paid yet, and experts speculate that the defendant could appeal the case all the way to the U.S. Supreme Court. Alternatively, the parties may agree to a settlement out of court. The defendant has not yet determined whether it will appeal the verdict or consider settlement, however, it believes that a loss amounting to between $0.5 and $1.5 billion is likely. The defendant must determine whether this contingent loss must be recognized, in accordance with **ASC 450-20**.

ASC 450-20 (Loss Contingencies) includes the following recognition guidance:

25-2   An estimated loss from a loss contingency shall be accrued by a charge to income if both of the following conditions are met:
a.   Information available before the financial statements are issued or are available to be issued (as discussed in Section <u>855-10-25</u>) indicates that it is probable that an asset had been impaired or a liability had been incurred at the date of the financial statements. . . .
b.   The amount of loss can be reasonably estimated. . . .

The glossary of Topic 450-20 defines **probable** as:

The future event or events are likely to occur.

In assessing whether a loss can be **reasonably estimated**, ASC 450-20 provides the following guidance:

25-4   The condition in paragraph <u>450-20-25-2(b)</u> is intended to prevent accrual in the financial statements of amounts so uncertain as to impair the integrity of those statements.

Continued

25-5 That requirement shall not delay accrual of a loss until only a single amount can be reasonably estimated. To the contrary, when the condition in paragraph <u>450-20-25-2(a)</u> is met and information available indicates that the estimated amount of loss is within a range of amounts, it follows that some amount of loss has occurred and can be reasonably estimated . . .

Questions:

1. Is the loss probable?_____

2. Is the loss reasonably estimable?_____

3. Overall conclusion: Should the defendant recognize a contingent loss?

_____

_____

Notice that the preceding example determines only *whether* a loss must be recorded, but it does not provide guidance on what amount of liability must be recorded. For this information, a researcher would continue on to read the initial measurement section of Topic 450-20.

Recognizing a Liability for Contributions Made

Guidance on "contributions made" is located within the Expenses area of the Codification (see Figure 6-1). Generally speaking, this guidance applies to charitable giving by an entity, and entities are required to record a liability for contributions made (including unconditional promises to give) at fair value.

For reference, entities searching for guidance from the recipient's perspective would look to "contributions received" guidance in the Not-For-Profit industry topic (**ASC 958-605**). While the receipt of contributions is primarily an issue encountered by not-for-profit entities, business entities receiving contributions are also generally permitted to apply contributions received guidance.[7]

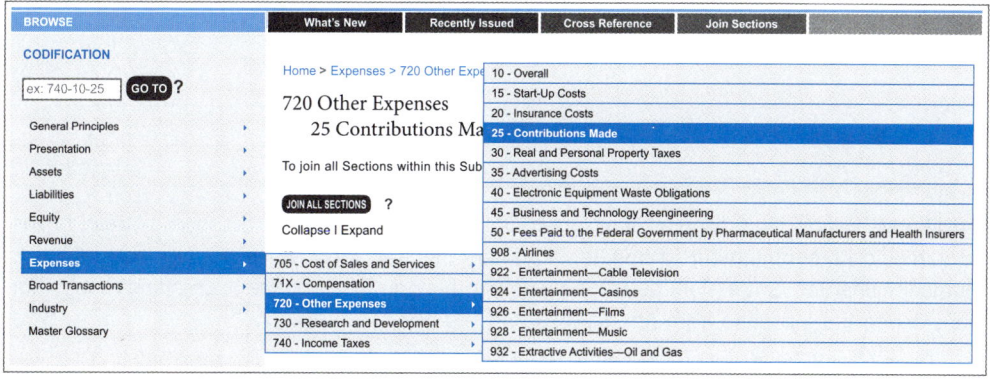

Figure 6-1

Contributions Made guidance is available within Topic 720-25 (Other Expenses— Contributions Made)

Reproduced with permission of the Financial Accounting Foundation.

---

[7] ASC 958-605-15-4 (Not-for-Profit Entities - Revenue Recognition): "Accounting for <u>contributions</u> is an issue primarily for <u>not-for-profit entities</u> (NFPs) because contributions are a significant source of revenues for many of those entities. However, except for Section <u>958-605-45</u>, the guidance in the Contributions Received Subsections applies to all entities (NFPs and business entities) that receive contributions unless otherwise indicated."

Now
YOU
Try
6.5

Contributions Made

Facts: Grant Construction Co., a regional homebuilder, plans to make a series of contributions to its local Habitat for Humanity chapter, of $1 million each year for 5 years. The company has not yet informed the charity of its planned contribution but has included the planned contribution in its internal budgets. Grant is researching whether it must record this planned contribution as a liability.

ASC 720-25 includes the following recognition guidance:

> **25-1** Contributions made shall be recognized as expenses in the period made and as decreases of assets or increases of liabilities depending on the form of the benefits given. For example, gifts of items from inventory held for sale are recognized as decreases of inventory and contribution expenses, and unconditional promises to give cash are recognized as payables and contribution expenses . . . [Emphasis added]

The glossary of Topic 720-25 defines **unconditional promise to give** as

> A promise to give that depends only on passage of time or demand by the promisee for performance.

The glossary of Topic 720-25 defines **promise to give** as

> A written or oral agreement to contribute cash or other assets to another entity. A promise carries rights and obligations—the recipient of a promise to give has a right to expect that the promised assets will be transferred in the future, and the maker has a social and moral obligation, and generally a legal obligation, to make the promised transfer. A promise to give may be either conditional or unconditional.

Questions:

1. Must Grant Construction Co. record this planned contribution?

   _____

   _____

   _____

Additional Facts: Now assume that Grant Construction Co. has just issued a press release announcing its commitment to donate $1 million annually, for 5 years, to its local Habitat for Humanity chapter. Grant must determine whether this promise requires accounting recognition, considering the guidance from ASC 720-25.

2. Does Grant Construction's verbal commitment to donate require recognition?

   _____

   _____

   _____

As you may recall from our discussion in Chapter 4, the term *liability* is not currently defined in the Codification. Rather, a researcher must look to the Conceptual Framework for this definition.

However, notice how the definition of liabilities—"probable future sacrifices of economic benefits arising from present obligations"—is foundational to the guidance provided in both ASC 450-20 (Loss Contingencies) and ASC 720-25 (Contributions Made). Both of these subtopics operationalize the definition of a liability, each for different circumstances.

In both cases, applying the recognition guidance in these subtopics also involves consideration of glossary terms, such as the term *probable* in ASC 450-20 and the term *promise to give* in ASC 720-25.

RECOGNITION OF LEASES

Application of lease accounting guidance, for a lessee, can result in either

- In the case of an **operating lease**, straight-line expense recognition of lease costs.
- In the case of a **capital lease**, the capitalization of a leased asset and recognition of a related lease payment obligation.

That is, in an operating lease, the lessee must only report periodic lease expense. In a capital lease, the lessee must record lease-related assets and liabilities on its balance sheet. Currently, to determine which accounting model is appropriate, lessees and lessors must apply four lease classification criteria, which are provided in the Overall subtopic for leases (ASC 840-10):

- Does the lease agreement transfer ownership to the lessee at the end of the lease term?
- Does the lease include a bargain purchase option?
- Is the lease term equal to 75% or more of the leased asset's economic life?
- Are the lease payments (as defined in the Codification) 90% or more of the leased asset's fair value?[8]

Leases meeting any one of the four above criteria are considered capital leases.

This model has been criticized for its use of so-called "bright lines"; that is, under this model, leases with only slight differences in terms may receive very different accounting treatments. Consequently, the FASB and **International Accounting Standards Board** (IASB) are jointly undertaking a project to dramatically change lease accounting. Go to www.fasb.org for updates on this project. The following example illustrates the very different accounting treatment for capital versus operating leases.

Recognizing Capital and Operating Leases in the Financial Statements

Now
YOU
Try
6.6

Facts: Lessee, Inc. (Lessee) is entering into a contract with Landlord Inc. (Landlord) to rent Landlord's newly constructed office building. The lease term is 30 years, and the estimated economic life of the building is 40 years. Lessee will occupy all 10 floors of the building. Assume that

- Title to the building does not transfer to the Lessee at the end of the lease term,
- There is no bargain purchase option present in the lease, and
- Lease payments do not exceed 90% of the fair value of the leased asset.

Recall that the criteria for classifying leases are provided in the Overall subtopic for leases (ASC 840-10). By contrast, guidance specific to the recognition and measurement of operating and capital leases is available within the Operating Leases and Capital Leases subtopics, respectively (840-20 and 840-30).

Using the preceding introduction to leases and the recognition guidance that follows, respond to the questions that follow.

---

[8] ASC 840-10-25-1 (Leases).

ASC 840-20 (Operating Leases) provides the following broad recognition guidance:

> **25-1**   Rent shall be charged to expense by lessees (reported as income by lessors) over the lease term as it becomes payable (receivable). If rental payments are not made on a straight-line basis, rental expense nevertheless shall be recognized on a straight-line basis unless another systematic and rational basis is more representative of the time pattern in which use benefit is derived from the leased property, in which case that basis shall be used.

ASC 840-30 (Capital Leases) states:

> **25-1**   The lessee shall recognize a capital lease as an asset and an obligation.

Questions:

1. Should this lease be classified as a capital or an operating lease?

    _____
    _____
    _____

2. In what subtopic of ASC 840 would a researcher find this classification guidance?

    _____

3. How would the lease be recorded in Lessee's financial statements?

    _____

4. How would the accounting differ if the lease term was only 29 years?

    _____

Recall that the objective of recognition guidance is to identify what, when, and how an item should be recorded in the financial statements. Researchers must determine how a lease should be classified (based on recognition guidance in the Overall subtopic), then must determine what entries should be recorded based on that classification (based on recognition guidance in the Operating or Capital Lease subtopics).

RECOGNITION OF UNCERTAIN TAX POSITIONS

Differences between an entity's financial reporting amounts and its tax basis in assets and liabilities can give rise to temporary differences. These temporary differences can result in future taxable or deductible amounts and are reflected in the financial statements as deferred tax assets and liabilities.

Reporting deferred tax assets and liabilities in the financial statements can involve judgment. **ASC 740-10** (Income Taxes) establishes a two-step process for the recognition of tax positions.[9] First, entities must determine whether a tax position meets the **more-likely-than-not** threshold for recognition. Next, if this recognition threshold is met, entities must determine the appropriate measurement of the tax position. This chapter discusses only the first step in this process (recognition).

Par. 25-6 and 25-7 introduce the basic recognition principle for income tax accounting:

> **25-6**   An entity shall initially recognize the financial statement effects of a tax position when it is more likely than not, based on the technical merits, that the position will be sustained upon examination. The term *more likely than not* means a likelihood of more than 50 percent; the terms *examined* and *upon examination* also include resolution of the related appeals or litigation processes, if any . . .

Continued

---

[9] ASC 740-10-25-5 (Income Taxes): "This Subtopic requires the application of a more-likely-than-not recognition criterion to a tax position before and separate from the measurement of a tax position . . .".

25-7 In making the required assessment of the more-likely-than-not criterion:

    a. It shall be presumed that the tax position will be examined by the relevant taxing authority that has full knowledge of all relevant information.

    b. Technical merits of a tax position derive from sources of authorities in the tax law (legislation and statutes, legislative intent, regulations, rulings, and case law) and their applicability to the facts and circumstances of the tax position . . .

    c. Each tax position shall be evaluated without consideration of the possibility of offset or aggregation with other positions.

Once it has been established that a tax position meets the "more-likely-than-not" threshold for recognition, a preparer must then evaluate measurement guidance to determine what *amount* of the tax position should be recorded.

Applying the More-Likely-Than-Not Threshold—Uncertain Tax Positions

Now
YOU
Try
6.7

Facts: A newly formed entity has incurred net operating losses for its first 2 years in operation. However, it has seen a consistent increase in customers and improving gross profit margins year-over-year. The company believes it can record a deferred tax asset or liability (that is, the net operating losses reported in its first two tax returns can be used to offset future years' taxable income). However, realizing the benefit of its net operating losses depends on having positive future taxable income. The company believes it is probable (or at least 75% likely) that its third and fourth years of operations will result in positive taxable income. Companies have a 20-year period in which net operating losses may be applied against future taxable income. Historically, the company's owners (in previous endeavors) have not let loss carryforwards expire unused. The company must determine whether this carryforward meets the more-likely-than-not threshold for recognition.

The basic principles regarding this issue are outlined in par. 25-6 and 25-7 above. Additionally, consider the following glossary and implementation guidance from **ASC 740-10**:

Carryforwards (ASC 740-10-20)

Deductions or credits that cannot be utilized on the tax return during a year that may be carried forward to reduce taxable income or taxes payable in a future year. An operating loss carryforward is an excess of tax deductions over gross income in a year; . . .

55-7 Subject to certain specific exceptions . . . a deferred tax liability is recognized for all taxable temporary differences, and a deferred tax asset is recognized for all deductible temporary differences and operating loss and tax credit carryforwards . . .

Questions:

1. Does the company's operating loss carryforward appear to meet the more-likely-than-not threshold for recognition? Explain why this does or doesn't seem appropriate.

    _____

    _____

    _____

2. How shall the loss carryforward be reported (as a deferred tax asset or liability)?

    _____

    _____

    _____

Effective Settlement of a Tax Position

Tax positions that do not initially meet the more-likely-than-not threshold for recognition may be recognized when certain conditions are met. Par. 25-8 of **ASC 740-10** states:

> **25-8** If the more-likely-than-not recognition threshold is not met in the period for which a tax position is taken or expected to be taken, an entity shall recognize the benefit of the tax position in the first interim period that meets any one of the following conditions:
>
>   a. The more-likely-than-not recognition threshold is met by the reporting date.
>   b. The tax position is effectively settled through examination, negotiation or litigation.
>   c. The statute of limitations for the relevant taxing authority to examine and challenge the tax position has expired.

Determining when a tax position has been **effectively settled** (per "b" above) can involve judgment. The following example illustrates guidance on effective settlement.

Now
YOU
Try
6.8

Effective Settlement

Facts: A company claims a research and development (R&D) tax credit on its 2012 tax return. Determining which costs qualified for the R&D credit was judgmental, and the company is concerned that the IRS may question some of the individual costs comprising its amount claimed for the R&D credit. That is, the company is not sure whether, if examined, the IRS would allow the full amount of its R&D credit claimed. Accordingly, the company concluded that only a portion of the credit claimed met the more-likely-than-not threshold for recognition in its 2012 financial statements.

The company filed its 2012 tax return in February 2013, and the return showed a net tax refund due to the company. In April 2013, the company received a tax refund check from the federal government.

See par. 25-8 above. Additionally, **ASC 740-10** offers the following guidance on effective settlement.

> **25-9** A tax position could be effectively settled upon examination by a taxing authority. Assessing whether a tax position is effectively settled is a matter of judgment because examinations occur in a variety of ways . . .
>
> **25-10** As required by paragraph 740-10-25-8(b) an entity shall recognize the benefit of a tax position when it is effectively settled. An entity shall evaluate all of the following conditions when determining effective settlement:
>
>   a. The taxing authority has completed its examination procedures including all appeals and administrative reviews that the taxing authority is required and expected to perform for the tax position.
>   b. The entity does not intend to appeal or litigate any aspect of the tax position included in the completed examination.
>   c. It is remote that the taxing authority would examine or reexamine any aspect of the tax position. In making this assessment management shall consider the taxing authority's policy on reopening closed examinations and the specific facts and circumstances of the tax position. Management shall presume the relevant taxing authority has full knowledge of all relevant information in making the assessment on whether the taxing authority would reopen a previously closed examination.

Questions:

1. What are the three conditions that would allow for recognition of a tax position that was not previously recognized? (See excerpt from par. 25-8 on the previous page.)

_____

_____

2. Given the company's receipt of a refund check, is it appropriate to conclude that the tax position has been effectively settled (and thus, is the full tax credit eligible for financial statement recognition)?

_____

_____

Additional Facts: Assume the same facts as the previous example, but now assume that tax return has been selected for an IRS audit. The IRS staff member conducting the review has called the company to say that the audit is nearly complete, and the IRS does not have any findings. However, before the staff member can send the IRS's final written clearance of the tax year in question, the audit must be reviewed by the staff member's supervisor. The supervisor's review could result in changes to the staff member's preliminary conclusions. Management believes that, once the final audit report is received, the likelihood of the IRS re-opening this tax year for audit is remote.

3. May the company now consider its tax position to be effectively settled, and thus eligible for recognition? If not, what additional factors should be considered?

_____

_____

_____

SUBSEQUENT EVENTS RECOGNITION

A **subsequent event** is an event that takes place after the balance sheet date, but before financial statements are issued. Guidance for subsequent event recognition is available in Topic **855** (Subsequent Events), within the Broad Transactions area of the Codification. For public companies, the period by which financial statements must be filed is stipulated by the SEC; for nonpublic companies, the timing depends on the needs of their specific users. For public companies, for example, the SEC requires that annual financial statements be filed within 60 to 90 days of the company's fiscal year end, with the specific timing depending in part on the company's size.[10]

Companies are required to evaluate subsequent events through the date that financial statements are issued or are available to be issued. For public companies, the issue date generally corresponds with the date financial statements are filed with the SEC. Nonpublic companies should generally evaluate subsequent events through the date financial statements are available to be issued (that is, complete and approved by management).[11]

For example, General Electric Co. (GE) has a calendar year-end and generally files with the SEC in late February. For its 2012 annual financial statements, GE's subsequent events period therefore spanned from January 1 to February 26, 2013. This period is illustrated in Figure 6-2.

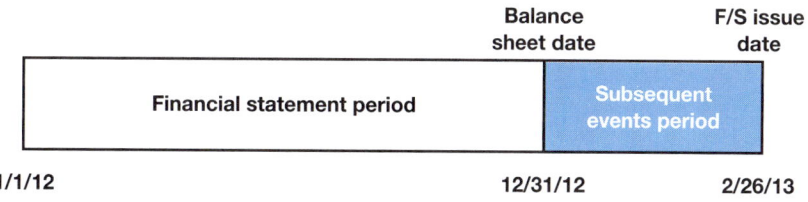

Figure 6-2

GE's year-end 2012 subsequent events period, shaded

_____

[10] Per Section 13(a) of the 1934 Securities Exchange Act. Also as described in Section 1330.1 "Exchange Act Report Dates" of the SEC Division of Corporate Finance *Financial Reporting Manual*. Updated as of June 30, 2012. Page 37.

[11] ASC 855-10-25-1 through 25-3 (Subsequent Events).

The Codification describes two types of subsequent events:[12]

■ **Recognized subsequent events:** Events that provide additional evidence about conditions existing at the balance sheet date, including estimates inherent in preparing the financial statements

■ **Unrecognized subsequent events:** Events that provide evidence about conditions that did not exist at the balance sheet date, but which arose after the balance sheet date

Recognized subsequent events, as the name implies, require adjustment to the financial statements. Unrecognized subsequent events do not require adjustment to the financial statements. However, disclosure of such events may be required to keep the financial statements from being misleading.

Implementation guidance within Topic **855-10** provides examples of events classified as recognized versus unrecognized. The following paragraphs can be used to respond to **Now YOU Try 6.10**.

> > **Recognized Subsequent Events**

55-1 The following are examples of recognized subsequent events addressed in paragraph 855-10-25-1:

  a. If the events that gave rise to litigation had taken place before the balance sheet date and that litigation is settled after the balance sheet date but before the financial statements are issued or are available to be issued, for an amount different from the liability recorded in the accounts, then the settlement amount should be considered in estimating the amount of liability recognized in the financial statements at the balance sheet date.

  b. Subsequent events affecting the realization of assets, such as receivables and inventories or the settlement of estimated liabilities, should be recognized in the financial statements when those events represent the culmination of conditions that existed over a relatively long period of time. For example, a loss on an uncollectible trade account receivable as a result of a customer's deteriorating financial condition leading to bankruptcy after the balance sheet date but before the financial statements are issued or are available to be issued ordinarily will be indicative of conditions existing at the balance sheet date. Thus, the effects of the customer's bankruptcy filing shall be considered in determining the amount of uncollectible trade accounts receivable recognized in the financial statements at balance sheet date.

> > **Nonrecognized Subsequent Events**

55-2 The following are examples of nonrecognized subsequent events addressed in paragraph 855-10-25-3:

  a. Sale of a bond or capital stock issued after the balance sheet date but before financial statements are issued or are available to be issued

  b. A business combination that occurs after the balance sheet date but before financial statements are issued or are available to be issued (Topic 805 requires specific disclosures in such cases.)

  c. Settlement of litigation when the event giving rise to the claim took place after the balance sheet date but before financial statements are issued or are available to be issued

  d. Loss of plant or inventories as a result of fire or natural disaster that occurred after the balance sheet date but before financial statements are issued or are available to be issued

Continued

---

[12] ASC 855-10-25-1 through 25-3.

e. Losses on receivables resulting from conditions (such as a customer's major casualty) arising after the balance sheet date but before financial statements are issued or are available to be issued

f. Changes in the fair value of assets or liabilities (financial or nonfinancial) or foreign exchange rates after the balance sheet date but before financial statements are issued or are available to be issued

g. Entering into significant commitments or contingent liabilities, for example, by issuing significant guarantees after the balance sheet date but before financial statements are issued or are available to be issued.

Subsequent Events

Using the guidance in par. 55-1 and 55-2 above, determine whether the following events, occurring on January 15, 20X2, should be classified as recognized or unrecognized by a company whose fiscal year ended on December 31, 20X1. Include specific guidance references (e.g., 55-1a) to support your responses.

Now **YOU** Try **6.9**

Event	Recognized or Unrecognized	Paragraph supporting your response
A customer files for bankruptcy, resulting in the write-down of the customer account receivable.		
A fire damages corporate headquarters, resulting in an impairment of the asset value.		
The company issues bonds (that is, engages in a borrowing).		
Court delivers a ruling on litigation that commenced prior to the balance sheet date.		
Equity securities in the pension fund suffer a significant decline in value.		

DERECOGNITION ISSUES

Although provided a separate category within the Codification, Derecognition guidance (Section "40") within the Codification is fairly limited. The FASB staff has described this guidance as follows:

> Section 40, Derecognition, addresses the criteria, the method to determine the amount of basis, and the timing to be used when derecognizing a particular asset, liability, or equity item for purposes of determining gain or loss, if any.[13]

That is, derecognition guidance describes the removal of certain items from the balance sheet, along with related gain or loss recognition (when applicable). However, it's worth noting that assets, liabilities, and equity can also be "removed" from the balance sheet through other means, for example, through amortization or impairments. These other means are generally addressed within the Subsequent Measurement section of a topic (Section "35"). Chapters 7 and 8 of this book address measurement issues.

---

[13] Financial Accounting Standards Board: *FASB Learning Guide: For the Codification Research System* (March 1, 2012). Lesson 3, Page 24.

Liability Extinguishment

ASC 405-20 (Extinguishments of Liabilities) provides guidance on when it is appropriate to derecognize a liability (see browse path depicted in Figure 6-3). The guidance acknowledges that entities may choose to settle a liability in a number of ways, including

- By paying a creditor,
- By obtaining a release from the creditor (e.g., due to default or nonpayment), or
- By setting aside assets dedicated to the eventual settlement of a liability.[14]

Given that numerous forms of debt settlement may exist, accounting guidance has established its own criteria for determining when it is appropriate to derecognize a recorded liability. **ASC 405-20** states:

> **40-1** A debtor shall derecognize a liability if and only if it has been **extinguished**. A liability has been extinguished if either of the following conditions is met:
> a. The debtor pays the creditor and is relieved of its obligation for the liability. Paying the creditor includes the following:
>   1. Delivery of cash
>   2. Delivery of other financial assets
>   3. Delivery of goods or services
>   4. Reacquisition by the debtor of its outstanding debt securities whether the securities are cancelled or held as so-called treasury bonds.
> b. The debtor is legally released from being the primary obligor under the liability, either judicially or by the creditor . . . [Emphasis added]

Following are examples demonstrating application of this guidance.

Figure 6-3

Browse path for Liability Extinguishments topic (ASC 405-20)

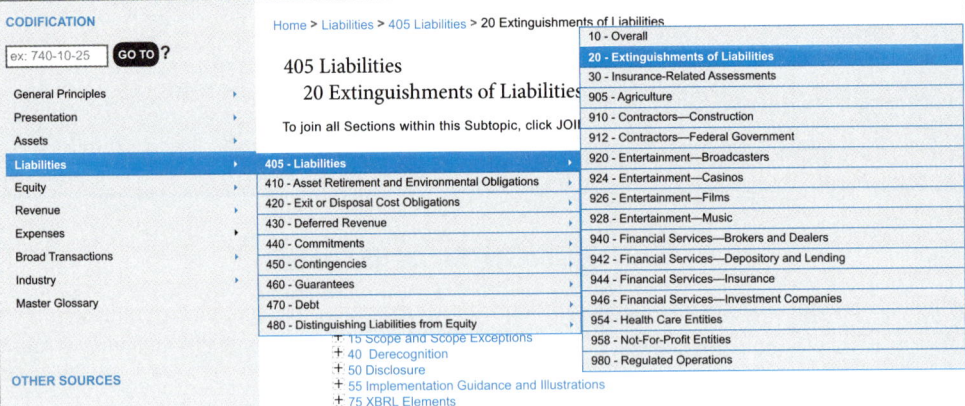

Reproduced with permission of the Financial Accounting Foundation.

In-Substance Defeasance

Now YOU Try

6.10

Facts: A private business owner has taken out a loan from a bank, and he has created a separate trust fund with cash equivalents (short-term U.S. treasury bonds and short-term certificates of deposit) sufficient to pay the debt. The business owner is researching whether he must continue to record the loan payable on his financial statements.

The Codification refers to the setting aside of assets, as planned payment of a debt, as an "in-substance defeasance."

---

[14] ASC 405-20-05-2 (Extinguishments of Liabilities).

The Codification[15] defines **in-substance defeasance** as:

> Placement by the debtor of amounts equal to the principal, interest, and prepayment penalties related to a debt instrument in an irrevocable trust established for the benefit of the creditor.

In addition to applying the general derecognition principle in par. 40-1, researchers should consider the following implementation guidance from **ASC 405-20** specific to in-substance defeasances.

> > > In-Substance Defeasance Transactions

55-3 In an in-substance defeasance transaction, a debtor transfers essentially risk-free assets to an irrevocable defeasance trust and the cash flows from those assets approximate the scheduled interest and principal payments of the debt being extinguished.

55-4 Under the financial-components approach, an in-substance defeasance transaction does not meet the derecognition criteria for either the liability or the asset. The transaction lacks the following critical characteristics:

a. The debtor is not released from the debt by putting assets in the trust; if the assets in the trust prove insufficient, for example, because a default by the debtor accelerates its debt, the debtor must make up the difference.

b. The lender is not limited to the cash flows from the assets in trust.

c. The lender does not have the ability to dispose of the assets at will or to terminate the trust.

d. If the assets in the trust exceed what is necessary to meet scheduled principal and interest payments, the transferor can remove the assets.

e. Subparagraph superseded by Accounting Standards Update No. 2012-04.

f. The debtor does not surrender control of the benefits of the assets because those assets are still being used for the debtor's benefit, to extinguish its debt, and because no asset can be an asset of more than one entity, those benefits must still be the debtor's assets.

Question: Does the business owner's so-called "in-substance defeasance" allow him to derecognize the liability? Explain.

_____

_____

_____

Legal Defeasance

Facts: Now assume that the private business owner has taken out a loan from a bank but is unable to repay the loan. The business owner files for bankruptcy protection; the court with authority over this matter has not yet approved the terms of a bankruptcy settlement. The business owner is researching whether he can now derecognize the liability.

ASC 405-20 offers the following guidance regarding extinguishments via **legal defeasance**:

55-9 In a legal defeasance, generally the creditor legally releases the debtor from being the primary obligor under the liability. Liabilities are extinguished by legal defeasances if the condition in paragraph <u>405-20-40-1(b)</u> is satisfied. Whether the debtor has in fact been released and the condition in that paragraph has been met is a matter of law . . .

Now
YOU
Try
6.11

---

[15] ASC 470-50-20 (Debt—Modifications and Extinguishments).

Recall that the condition from par. 40-1(b) states:

> b.   The debtor is legally released from being the primary obligor under the liability, either judicially or by the creditor . . .

Question: Is it now appropriate for the business owner to derecognize the liability? If not, what additional hurdle must be met for derecognition to occur?

_____

_____

_____

Debt Modifications and Extinguishments

ASC 470-50 (Debt Modifications and Extinguishments) applies the broad liability extinguishment principles in ASC 405 to debt instruments. Figure 6-4 illustrates the browse path for accessing this topic. The instruments addressed in ASC 470 range from traditional loans payable to more complex debt instruments, such as debt that is convertible into equity shares.

ASC 470-50 differentiates between debt modifications and debt extinguishments, with each subject to a different accounting treatment. Generally speaking, a **debt modification** occurs when a debtor exchanges similar debt instruments with the same creditor. A **debt extinguishment** occurs when debt instruments with substantially different terms are exchanged. The accounting for these events is as follows:

- In a debt modification, the debtor determines a new interest rate for the modified instrument, based on the original loan's carrying amount and the revised cash flows, and applies that rate to the instrument prospectively.[16]

- In a debt extinguishment, the debtor recognizes the new instrument at fair value, derecognizes the original debt instrument, and records a gain or loss for any difference.[17]

Derecognition guidance within ASC 470-50, included within the example below, can be used to determine which of these accounting methods should be applied.

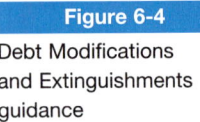

Figure 6-4

Debt Modifications and Extinguishments guidance

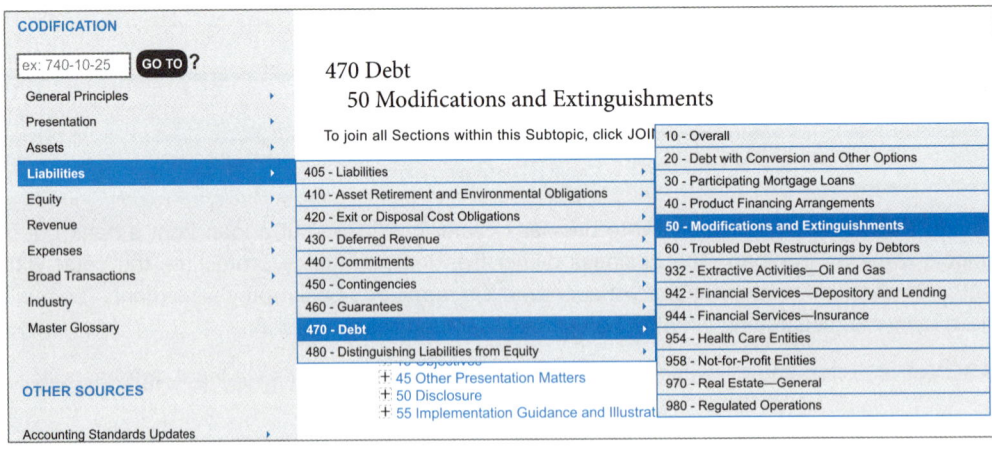

Reproduced with permission of the Financial Accounting Foundation.

---

[16] ASC 470-50-40-14.

[17] ASC 470-50-40-13.

Debt Modifications and Extinguishments

Now
YOU
Try
6.12

Facts: Taking advantage of record-low interest rates, a business refinances its commercial property mortgage but stays with the same lender. The business changed its loan from a 30-year, 5.0% fixed rate mortgage to a 15-year, 3.75% fixed rate mortgage. The business is researching how to account for this refinance transaction.

According to **ASC 470-50**, the exchange of one mortgage loan for another shall be accounted for as a debt extinguishment if the new debt has terms that are substantially different from the original debt, as described below.

> **> Modifications and Exchanges**

40-6 An exchange of debt instruments with substantially different terms is a debt extinguishment and shall be accounted for in accordance with paragraph <u>405-20-40-1</u>. A debtor could achieve the same economic effect as an exchange of a debt instrument by making a substantial modification of terms of an existing debt instrument. Accordingly, a substantial modification of terms shall be accounted for like an extinguishment.

In a refinance transaction, the debtor often pays off his existing mortgage loan with the proceeds from borrowing under the new mortgage loan. This is described in par. 40-9, as follows:

40-9 Transactions involving contemporaneous exchanges of cash between the same debtor and creditor in connection with the issuance of a new debt obligation and satisfaction of an existing debt obligation by the debtor would only be accounted for as debt extinguishments if the debt instruments have substantially different terms, as defined in this Subtopic.

"Substantially different terms" is described in par. 40-10 as a 10% or greater change in cash flows between the existing and new debt instruments.

40-10 From the debtor's perspective, an exchange of debt instruments between or a modification of a debt instrument by a debtor and a creditor . . . is deemed to have been accomplished with debt instruments that are substantially different if the present value of the cash flows under the terms of the new debt instrument is at least 10 percent different from the present value of the remaining cash flows under the terms of the original instrument . . .

Question: What analysis must the business perform, in order to determine whether the refinance transaction shall be accounted for as an extinguishment of its original debt?

_____

_____

_____

Equity Method Investments—Recognition and Derecognition

A purchase of voting stock in another entity is accounted for under the "equity method" when the investor has significant influence over, but a noncontrolling interest in, the investee. A noncontrolling interest is generally characterized by an interest in less than 50% of an investee's stock,[18] and significant influence is generally presumed to exist when an investor owns 20% or more of the investee's stock.[19]

Under the equity method in **ASC 323-10**:

> **25-2** An investor shall recognize an investment in the stock of an investee as an asset.

That is, the purchase of stock gives rise to an Investment asset. Subsequent to initial recognition, the investor records his share of investee net income as an increase in the recorded investment asset and as income. Conversely, an investor shall reduce his recorded Investment asset for his share of investee losses.

> **35-4**   Under the equity method, an investor shall recognize its share of the <u>earnings or losses of an investee</u> in the periods for which they are reported by the investee in its financial statements rather than in the period in which an investee declares a dividend. An investor shall adjust the carrying amount of an investment for its share of the earnings or losses of the investee after the date of investment and shall report the recognized earnings or losses in income.

Notice that, although equity method losses can lead to partial or full asset *derecognition* by an investor, guidance for recording these losses is located within the *subsequent measurement* section of Topic **323** (Equity Method Investments).

By contrast, the Derecognition section in **ASC 323-10** consists of just one paragraph, which addresses an investor's accounting for share issuances by an investee.

> **> Investee Capital Transactions**
>
> **40-1**   An equity method investor shall account for a share issuance by an investee as if the investor had sold a proportionate share of its investment. Any gain or loss to the investor resulting from an investee's share issuance shall be recognized in earnings.

We will now take a moment to apply this simple equity method recognition and derecognition guidance.

Now YOU Try 6.13

Equity Method Investments—Recognition and Derecognition

Facts: Investor purchases 25% of the voting stock of Investee. At the time, Investee has 100 total shares outstanding. Investor pays $25 cash for the shares (which amounts to $1 each × 25 shares).

---

[18] ASC 810-10-15-8 (Consolidation): "The usual condition for a controlling financial interest is ownership of a majority voting interest, and, therefore, as a general rule ownership by one reporting entity, directly or indirectly, of more than 50 percent of the outstanding voting shares of another entity is a condition pointing toward consolidation."

[19] ASC 323-10-15-3 (Equity Method Investments): "Subsequent references in this Subtopic to common stock refer to both common stock and in-substance common stock that give the <u>investor</u> the ability to exercise <u>significant influence</u> (see paragraph <u>323-10-15-6</u>) over operating and financial policies of an <u>investee</u> even though the investor holds 50% or less of the common stock or in-substance common stock (or both common stock and in-substance common stock)."

Questions:

1. What journal entry should Investor record for his investment in Investee? Cite the paragraph from **ASC 323-10** above that provides this recognition guidance.

   dr. _____ $_____

       cr. _____ $_____   (Par. _____)

Additional Facts: The next period, Investee issues 20 additional shares (for a total of 120 shares now outstanding) at a price of $1 per share. Investor does not purchase any of these additional shares, therefore the issuance reduces Investor's ownership in the company to 20.8%. Said another way, the issuance caused Investor to lose value of $4.2 (investment valued at $25 now valued at $20.8) due to the share issuance. Investor does not receive any proceeds from the share issuance.

2. How should Investor report the Investee's issuance of additional shares? Paragraph reference?

   dr. _____ $_____

       cr. _____ $_____   (Par. _____)

Additional Facts: The next period, Investee reports losses of $50. Investor's share of this loss is computed as $50 × 20.8% = $10.4.

3. How should Investor report this loss? Paragraph reference?

   dr. _____ $_____

       cr. _____ $_____   (Par. _____)

4. What observations can you make regarding the **entries** recorded in Questions 2 and 3 above, and regarding the **location of Codification guidance** for the two different events described in questions 2 and 3?

   _____

   _____

In this example, notice how both the investee's share sale, and the investee's loss, result in the reduction of Investor's recorded investment value. However, the guidance for recording these events is provided within different sections of Topic **323-10**.

Two additional points are worth noting related to this example:

■ First, investee capital transactions that have the effect of reducing an investor's percent ownership below the level of significant influence can cause the investee to discontinue use of the equity method.[20]

■ Additionally, if an investor's recognition of investee losses causes the Investment asset to be reduced to zero, the equity method investor shall discontinue use of the equity method.[21]

In this example, neither the share issuance nor recognition of investee losses were significant enough to cause the investor to discontinue use of the equity method.

---

[20] ASC 323-10-35-36: "An investment in voting stock of an investee may fall below the level of ownership described in paragraph 323-10-15-3 from sale of a portion of an investment by the investor, sale of additional stock by an investee, or other transactions and the investor may thereby lose the ability to influence policy, as described in that paragraph. An investor shall discontinue accruing its share of the earnings or losses of the investee for an investment that no longer qualifies for the equity method."

[21] ASC 323-10-35-20: "The investor ordinarily shall discontinue applying the equity method if the investment (and net advances) is reduced to zero . . .".

CHAPTER SUMMARY

Recognition guidance describes what, when, and how items should be recorded in the financial statements. Determining when an item qualifies for financial statement recognition involves consideration of the objectives of recognition (as outlined in the FASB's Conceptual Framework), consideration of cost/benefit constraints, and consideration of topical guidance within the Codification. While the cases in this chapter were fairly straightforward, judgment is often involved in a researcher's application of recognition guidance. In many cases, the Codification's Implementation Guidance section should be consulted in addition to the Recognition section of a topic.

REVIEW QUESTIONS

1. In addition to the four fundamental recognition criteria from CON 5, what two additional factors should a financial statement preparer consider before recording an item?

2. What four additional criteria has the SEC developed for interpreting the FASB's requirement that revenue must be "realized and earned"?

3. What guidance should a retailer, selling products with the right of return, use to account for any costs or losses that are expected in connection with product returns?

4. What are the criteria for recognition of a loss contingency?

5. Are "unconditional promises to give" required to be recognized as liabilities?

6. What is the basic threshold for recognition of an uncertain tax position?

7. How does the recognition of an operating lease differ from the recognition of a capital lease?

8. Explain what it means for a subsequent event to be "unrecognized"? Provide one example.

9. How does an in-substance defeasance differ from a legal defeasance? Can both result in the extinguishment of a liability?

10. Differentiate between a debt modification and a debt extinguishment.

EXERCISES

Respond to the following in complete sentences, and cite your source. *Hint:* Use Recognition guidance (Section 25 of each applicable topic) from the Codification to respond.

1. How is a cost method investment recognized in an investor's financial statements?

2. Vendor distributes $1 off coupons for its retail product in the Sunday paper. The coupon will not result in a loss to vendor on the sale of its product. At what point should Vendor recognize the cost of this sales incentive?

3. Assume that you own a construction company and frequently purchase bathtubs for installation in customer homes. One bathtub manufacturer has offered you $1,000 cash back after your tenth bathtub purchase. So far this year, your company has purchased 9 tubs and expects to place its tenth bathtub order later this month. Should this probable rebate be recognized, and how?

4. ASC 350-40 (Intangibles—Internal Use Software) specifically states that capitalization of costs (in an internal use software project) may begin when two criteria are met. What are these two criteria?

5. At the "inception of a guarantee," what must be recognized in the guarantor's statement of financial position? You can limit your response to the one most relevant "recognition" section paragraph.

6. A customer slipped and fell in ABC Corp's showroom on June 30, 20x1 and initiated a lawsuit. At December 31, 20x1, the company estimated its probable loss to be $150,000. In January, 20x2, before issuance of ABC Corp's financial statements, a judge ruled in favor of the customer and awarded the customer $200,000 in damages. Must the company recognize the effects of this ruling in its 20x1 financial statements?

7. An employer offers each of its 10 employees 15 vacation days per year. As of February, no employees have taken vacation; however, each employee has earned 2 days. Vacation days that are unused at the end of the year may be carried forward to the following year. The employer encourages employees to use their full vacation allotment and thus does not anticipate forfeitures. Must the employer record a liability for the employees' vacation days earned thus far?

8. In a sales arrangement with multiple deliverables (such as the sale of a washing machine with a 1-year mainte-nance contract), what are the criteria for the seller treating a delivered item as a separate unit of accounting?

9. When is it appropriate for a not-for-profit entity to recognize the receipt of an unconditional promise to give (a "contribution receivable") from another entity?

CASE STUDY QUESTIONS

Asset Retirement Obligation, Changes in Estimate versus Errors, Writing an Issues Memo   6.1
Background information (general): By law, entities must handle and dispose of certain types of asbestos in a special manner. Specifically, if a factory containing asbestos undergoes major renovations or is demolished, the asbestos will require remediation. Companies generally record such remediation obligations as "Asset Retirement Obligations."

Asset retirement obligations (AROs) are liabilities that companies must record if they own, acquire, or build assets with legal requirements related to their disposal. For example, telephone poles, treated with chemicals so they will last for many years, have associated AROs due to requirements related to their safe disposal. Nuclear plants, given the radioactive materials they handle, are assigned significant AROs. Asset retirement obligations are generally estimated when an asset is built or purchased and are recorded at the present value of the eventual disposal obligation. AROs are generally recorded with a debit to the asset (increasing the asset value by the present value amount of its retirement cost), and a credit to ARO, for example:

dr. Factory (asset retirement cost) -	$5 million
cr. Asset retirement obligation - Factory	$5 million

Facts: Big Company's corporate headquarters, built in 1970, has asbestos in its insulation. The Company's financial statements reflect a $4 million asset retirement obligation (ARO) for the eventual remediation of the asbestos. This ARO was initially estimated and recorded in 2005 when the company adopted FIN 47, *Accounting for Conditional Asset Retirement Obligations*. (Note: Amounts recorded for AROs are generally estimated, because it is not always possible to know how much remediating asbestos—or other like issues—will ultimately cost.) Big Company is a public company with a calendar year-end.

While performing routine maintenance work on the facility, additional sampling identified the presence of asbestos in more places than the Company had documented during its initial estimate. The Company now believes the total cost to remediate the asbestos will be $8 million. The initial estimate ($4 million) was based on sampling around the plant for areas containing asbestos. The newly-discovered areas with asbestos were in a part of the facility that was not sampled.

Required: Assume that you are in the controller's group of Big Company and have been asked to prepare an account-ing issues memorandum documenting your consideration of the following issues.

1. The Company's controller is questioning whether this liability for asbestos disposal is even necessary at all. He argues that asbestos must only be remediated if it is disturbed (such as through renovations), and points out that the company does not have any immediate plans to renovate the building. Respond to his question using authoritative guidance—is a liability even necessary, if the company's plans for disposal or renovation of this building are uncertain?

2. Determine whether the additional liability for the newly discovered asbestos is considered a change in account-ing estimate or an error. Note that this is *not* a change in accounting principle. Support your answer using authoritative guidance.

3. Describe how the company should record this $4 million change (prospectively, or through a retrospective adjust-ment)? What accounts should be debited/credited? You can disregard use of present value for this example.

Post-Employment Benefits, PP&E Classification, Issues Memo   6.2
Facts: The Johnstown auto assembly plant plans to terminate all operations on December 30, 20X2. That is, the plant will shut down, and employees serving at the plant will be terminated. Cruiser Corp, the owner of the plant, is a public company with a calendar year-end.

The plant currently employs 300 workers, 100 of whom are unionized. Per union contracts, union employees who are terminated are entitled to 25% of the average of their "high 3" years of pay for 3 years, with payments beginning immediately upon termination. Assume the average of these employees' "high 3" years' pay amounts to

$70,000 annually per employee. These termination payments will be separate and apart from any retirement benefits to which union workers are entitled. Union workers are contractually required to continue working until the last day of the plant's operations.

On August 1, 20X2, knowing that a plant closure was likely, Cruiser Corp offered a voluntary severance package to its nonunion employees of $30,000 each, payable ratably over 6 months beginning on 1/1/X3. Employees were required to notify the Company of their intention to accept a voluntary severance package by September 1, 20X2. By September 1, 20X2, 150 employees had accepted the voluntary termination package and terminated their employment. The 50 employees who elected to not take the package will not receive special termination benefits upon their ultimate termination from the company.

Cruiser Corp plans to make payments to severed employees directly out of its corporate assets; a fund for this event was not established in advance. Additionally, all 300 workers have been offered another postemployment benefit: the option to enroll in a job training and counseling program at Cruiser Corp's expense. At 9/30/X2, Cruiser Corp estimates that 25% of the terminated employees are probable of signing up for this training, at a cost of $300 per enrolled individual.

Cruiser Corp publicly announced its plans to close, and to sell, the plant on 9/30/X2, via a press release. The plant currently has a "for sale" sign on its lawn and is being advertised on the multiple-listing service (MLS) as for sale, at a price deemed appropriate for the area by a local realtor. Cruiser Corp estimates that the fair value less costs to sell the plant is $3 million. The plant is currently carried on the financial statements at $3.2 million.

Assume this does not qualify as a discontinued operation, for financial statement reporting purposes.

Required: Assume that you are in the controller's group of Cruiser Corp and have been asked to prepare an accounting issues memorandum documenting the accounting issues related to the Johnstown plant closure. This memo should include consideration of the following issues.

1. Determine the appropriate accounting for the different employee termination benefits (union, nonunion, job training). Identify the journal entries and appropriate dates for recording each promised benefit, documenting your basis for the date selected for each journal entry. You may disregard effects of discounting (present value measures) when computing required journal entries. *Hint:* All three of these benefits are addressed together within 1 topic in the Codification.

2. Determine how the company should record the soon-to-be-closed plant (as PP&E held for sale, or as PP&E to be held and used?), and determine what impact this has on the plant's (1) carrying amount (this is an issue of subsequent measurement) and (2) financial statement presentation.

If you conclude that the asset is "held and used," you are not required (for purposes of this example only) to perform an impairment test while the asset is classified as such, as this test is quite involved. However, you *should* consider the plant's carrying amount for any periods where the plant is considered to be "held for sale."

6.3   *Gross versus Net Revenue Recognition Guidance*

ASC 605-45 (Revenue, Principal-Agent Considerations) provides guidance on revenue recognition for situations where a principal-agent relationship exists. For example, a travel agent might seek out this guidance in order to determine whether to recognize revenue gross (for the full price of an airline ticket sold) or net (for the amount of his or her commission only). Yet, ASC 605-45 does not include a section on "Recognition." Identify where, within this topic, a researcher can find information on gross versus net revenue recognition. Briefly (in one or two sentences), brainstorm why gross versus net guidance is located within this section, rather than being located in the "recognition" section of ASC 605-45.

Chapter 7

Using the Codification to Research Measurement Issues

Ellen is observing an inventory at her client's warehouse and notices several shelves of boxes marked with the date "20X1." She pauses: that date was nearly 5 years ago! Upon further evaluation, Ellen learns that the inventory is still being sold, but infrequently.

Back at her desk, Ellen pulls up **ASC 330** (Inventory) and begins reading about the requirement that inventory should be recorded at the lower of its cost or market value. She wonders: Does this mean that she should also refer to **ASC 820** (Fair Value Measurement)? Is market value the same as fair value?

After some quick research, Ellen understands that inventory is not measured at fair value; rather, the term "market" refers to a measurement defined specifically within **ASC 330**.

As with other key Codification sections, applying measurement guidance can require judgment and experience. In fact, some measurement issues may require years of experience to master. The next two chapters of this book aim to speed up your journey along this learning curve.

After reading this chapter and performing the exercises herein, you will be able to

1. **Identify** key measurement attributes used within the Codification.

2. **Locate** sources of measurement guidance, primarily within the Codification.

3. **Understand** the appropriate timing for accounting measurements, including differences between initial and subsequent measurements.

4. **Apply** measurement principles to sample issues involving initial and subsequent measurements.

Learning Objectives

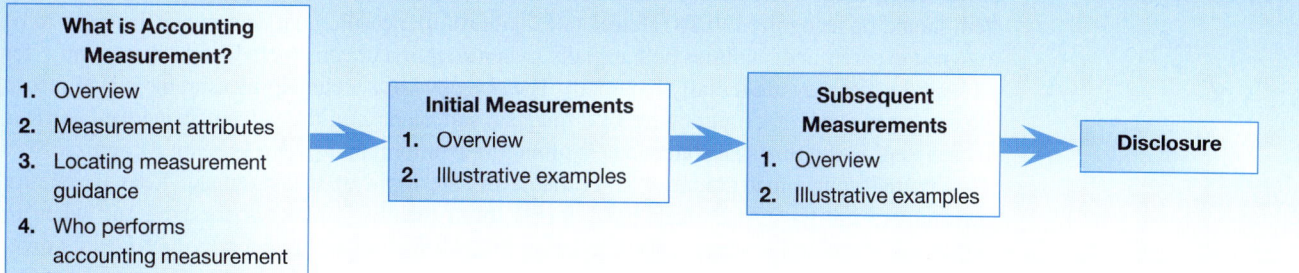

Organization of This Chapter

This chapter is the first of two that focus on accounting measurements. This chapter addresses researching measurement issues in general; Chapter 8 focuses on researching fair value measurements.

This chapter begins with background on accounting measurements, including an overview of key **measurement attributes** (or measurement methods) found in the Codification. Next, this chapter highlights differences between initial and subsequent measurements and explains why measurement may be required at different times for different assets and liabilities. Illustrative examples are provided, giving readers the opportunity to apply guidance to various types of measurements. Finally, this chapter emphasizes the need for transparent disclosure to accompany key financial statement measurements.

The preceding graphic illustrates the organization of content in this chapter.

The examples selected for the two measurement chapters in this book are by no means all-inclusive. Admittedly, these chapters will only scratch the surface of the possible measurement issues you could face as a professional. However, it is a surface worth scratching. Without any overview of measurement, you will be faced with a significant learning curve as you learn this information on the job.

The examples within this chapter have been intentionally kept simple; however, in practice measurement can be highly nuanced and may require the involvement of specialists.

Our discussion of measurement primarily focuses on asset and liability measurements because, as described within the Codification's fair value topic, they are generally considered to be a "primary subject of accounting measurement."[1]

---

[1] ASC 820-10-05-1D (Fair Value Measurement).

WHAT IS ACCOUNTING MEASUREMENT?

Overview and Conceptual Background

Accounting measurement describes at what value (i.e., for how much?) a financial statement item should be recognized. Also referred to as **valuation**, measurement determines the value to be assigned to assets and liabilities both initially (when acquired or constructed) and subsequently (for all periods after they are initially recorded). The objective of accounting measurement is to record the economic value of a transaction. To a financial statement user, the *value* management ascribes to each item in the financial statements is often just as important as *what* is being recognized.

Limited conceptual guidance is available on the topic of measurement. That is, neither practitioners nor the FASB itself have access to an overall framework for how and when to perform accounting measurements. Rather, each Codification topic generally provides its own, independent instructions for measurement, with the notable exceptions of items measured at fair value and present value.

That said, two of the FASB's Concepts Statements (Concepts Statements Nos. 5 and 7) do provide limited measurement guidance, as follows:

- Concepts Statement No. 5 (*Recognition and Measurement*):
  - Lists "measurability" as one of the four key criteria necessary for an item to receive financial statement recognition:

  > *Measurability*—It has a relevant attribute measurable with sufficient reliability.[2]

  - Identifies and defines various measurement attributes, including historical cost, current cost, current market value, net realizable value, and present value. States that the use of each is fact-dependent.
- Concepts Statement No. 7 (*Cash Flow Information and Present Value*):[3]
  - Describes how to measure present value and describes why present value information is relevant in certain cases.

However, these principles are considered to be of limited use in today's environment, in part because they are now somewhat dated. For example, notice how CON 5 (issued in 1984) does not even include fair value in its list of key measurement attributes. Also, present value guidance in CON 7 (issued in 2000) has more or less been replaced by present value guidance in ASC 820 (Fair Value Measurement). And to be clear, the Conceptual Framework is nonauthoritative and therefore should be considered only in limited circumstances, such as when authoritative guidance is not available.

The FASB and IASB recently started then stopped a joint project to create a Conceptual Framework chapter focused on measurement, with the objective of establishing principles to guide future decision making by the boards. During 2013, the IASB (but not the FASB) resumed this project on an individual basis. In the joint model the Boards had been developing, the new measurement chapter was expected to continue to support the notion that the choice of measurement attributes is fact-dependent and would not have been expected to change current practice. The chapter was also expected to emphasize the benefits of fair value, encouraging its use where relevant and cost-beneficial.

Measurement Attributes

As noted, each Codification topic generally sets its own rules for measurement. With the exception of *fair value* and *present value*, which are defined and described in detail in ASC 820, there is no consistent definition, or framework for applying, most measurement attributes.

---

[2] FASB Concepts Statement No. 5, *Recognition and Measurement in Financial Statements of Business Enterprises* (CON 5), par. 63.

[3] Concepts Statement No. 7, *Using Cash Flow Information and Present Value in Accounting Measurements*.

Nevertheless, it is helpful to consider the broad definitions of measurement attributes that are available. Let's begin by considering CON 5's list of measurement attributes and examples of these attributes, depicted in Figure 7-1.

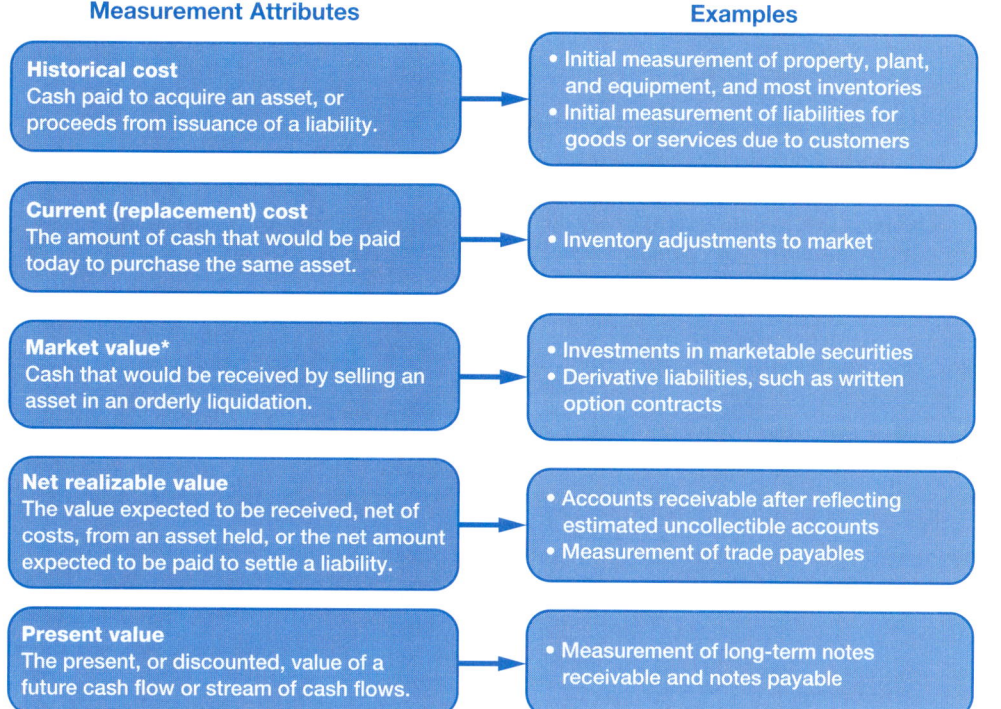

Measurement Attributes

Historical cost
Cash paid to acquire an asset, or proceeds from issuance of a liability.

Current (replacement) cost
The amount of cash that would be paid today to purchase the same asset.

Market value*
Cash that would be received by selling an asset in an orderly liquidation.

Net realizable value
The value expected to be received, net of costs, from an asset held, or the net amount expected to be paid to settle a liability.

Present value
The present, or discounted, value of a future cash flow or stream of cash flows.

Examples

• Initial measurement of property, plant, and equipment, and most inventories
• Initial measurement of liabilities for goods or services due to customers

• Inventory adjustments to market

• Investments in marketable securities
• Derivative liabilities, such as written option contracts

• Accounts receivable after reflecting estimated uncollectible accounts
• Measurement of trade payables

• Measurement of long-term notes receivable and notes payable

Figure 7-1

Measurement attributes and examples from CON 5

*Today, CON 5's description of market value is encompassed within the definition of fair value.

While these measurement attributes from CON 5 may be observed within individual Codification topics, these broad definitions generally do not appear in the Codification.

By contrast, the Codification defines only a handful of measurement attributes; often, these defined attributes only apply to one or two specified topic(s). For example,

■ Two definitions of *net realizable value* are provided, and each definition applies narrowly to a specific topic (Inventory, Agriculture Receivables).

■ *Historical cost* is defined, but the definition only applies narrowly to Topic **255** (Changing Prices).

■ *Amortized cost* is defined, but the definition only applies narrowly to Topic **320** (Investments—Debt and Equity Securities).

Given this lack of broadly defined measurement attributes (fair value and present value excepted), the Codification instead relies on measurement models that are often topic-specific. For example,

■ Loss contingencies are measured at management's *best estimate* of a possible loss or, if no one amount in a range is a better estimate than other amounts, at the minimum amount in the range.

■ Equity method investments are initially measured at cost, then are adjusted each period for the investor's share of investee earnings or losses. This measurement model reflects the investor's *proportionate ownership share* in the investee.

■ Uncertain tax positions that meet the more-likely-than-not threshold for recognition are measured as the *greatest amount of benefit* likely to be realized upon settlement with a taxing authority.

■ In multiple-element arrangements, the total arrangement consideration is allocated to individual deliverables based upon the deliverables' *relative selling prices*, assuming each deliverable qualifies for separate recognition.

Guidance on applying each of these measurement attributes is available within the related Codification topic. Given the uniqueness of each topic's measurement guidance, individual topics are therefore a researcher's best source for measurement guidance.

Now that you have a general understanding of the *variety* of measurement attributes available in the Codification, we will explore how a researcher can *locate* measurement guidance within the Codification.

Where Can I Find Measurement Guidance?

As noted, the first step in locating measurement guidance is to consult individual Codification topics. Specifically, measurement guidance is included within Sections **30** (Initial Measurement) and **35** (Subsequent Measurement) of certain topics. Figure 7-2 illustrates the location of sample topic-specific measurement guidance.

Figure 7-2

Location of topic-specific measurement guidance within the Codification

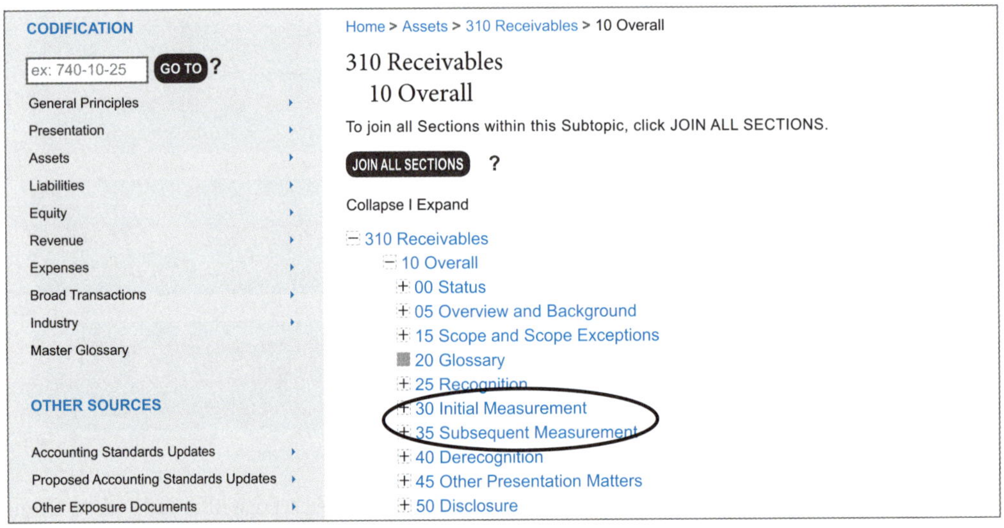

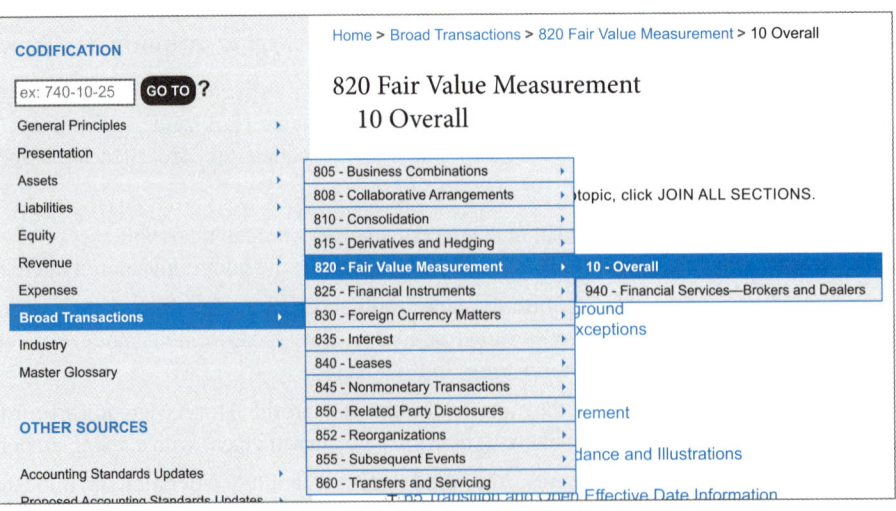

Reproduced with permission of the Financial Accounting Foundation.

For topics requiring *fair value* measurements, researchers should also consult Topic **820** (Fair Value Measurement). Within Topic 820, researchers will find detailed measurement and disclosure requirements for assets and liabilities measured using fair value. This guidance should be used *in addition to* the individual topic requiring the fair value measurement.

Figure 7-3 illustrates the browse path for accessing fair value measurement guidance.

Figure 7-3

Browse path for accessing fair value measurement guidance (ASC 820-10)

Reproduced with permission of the Financial Accounting Foundation.

For topics requiring *present value* measurements, researchers should also consult the "Present Value" section within Topic 820's Implementation Guidance (Section 55). Additionally, CON 7 may be a useful resource for present value guidance, in rare cases where Topic 820 is not fully responsive to an issue. Again, this guidance should be used *in addition to* the individual topic requiring the present value measurement.

Figure 7-4 illustrates two sources of present value guidance (ASC 820 and CON 7).

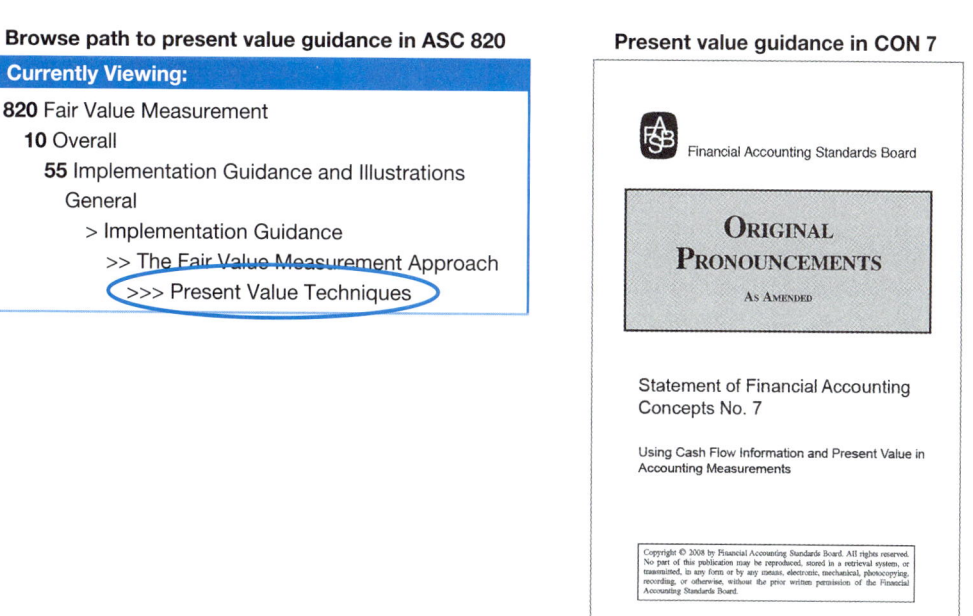

Reproduced with permission of the Financial Accounting Foundation.

Figure 7-4

Two sources of present value guidance: ASC 820 and CON 7

Figure 7-5 illustrates an effective approach to researching measurement guidance.

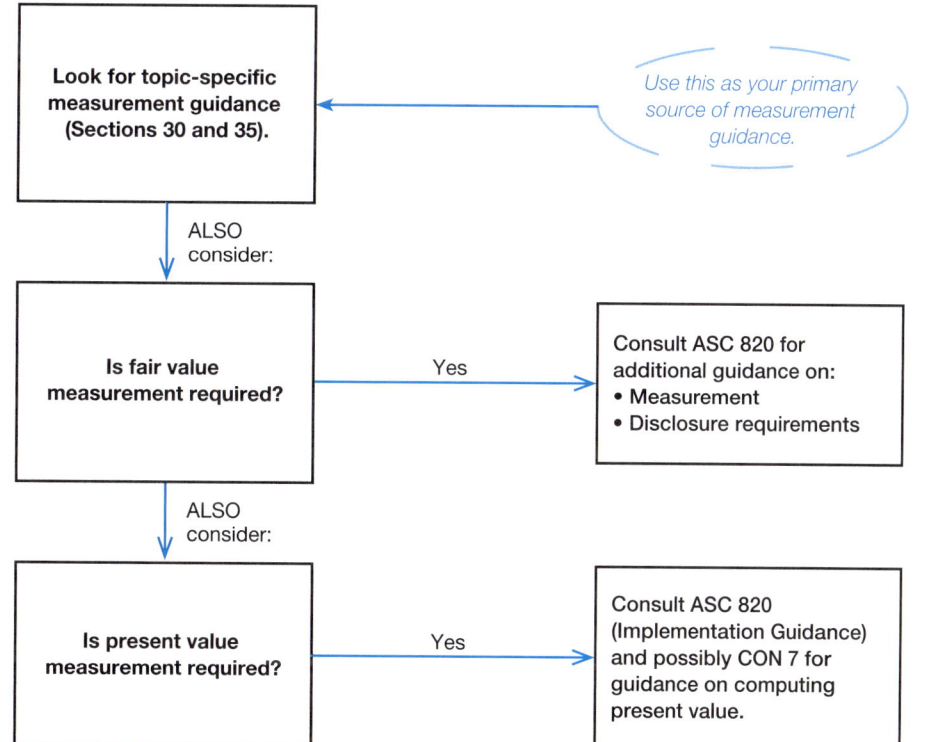

Figure 7-5

Approach to researching measurement guidance

Chapter 8 of this book provides additional discussion of fair value and present value measurements.

[TIP] from the Trenches

> As with all accounting research efforts, your search for measurement guidance may not be limited to a single topic. Consideration of other related Codification topics, or of nonauthoritative resources (such as firm guide books) may be necessary to enhance your understanding of certain material.

Who Performs Accounting Measurement In Practice?

Accounting measurement has become increasingly complex in recent years, as new structured (complex) transactions have emerged, and as standard setters have placed increasing emphasis on the use of fair value measurements. Corporate accountants and auditors alike are expected to have a basic working knowledge of accounting measurement issues, yet they must also understand when an issue warrants the involvement of a specialist.

More and more, management and auditors are engaging **valuation specialists** to assist them with complex measurements. These individuals include, for example,

- Accounting firm valuation specialists, who may be engaged to advise management on methods for measuring complex instruments and transactions such as stock compensation, bond issuances, and acquired businesses

- Actuaries, who often assist management in measuring their pension and retiree healthcare costs and obligations

- Independent valuation providers, whom management can engage on a fee-for-service basis to value complex instruments (such as the fair value of a company's bond issuances, the fair value of portfolios of investment securities, etc.)

Following is a brief **Knowledge Check** that emphasizes key points from this introductory section of the chapter.

Knowledge ✓ Check

1. **What is the first resource researchers should consult when seeking measurement guidance for an issue?**
2. **If fair value is required, should a researcher consult ASC 820 instead of, or in addition to, the original guidance topic?**
3. **What are two sources for guidance on present value measurements?**

INITIAL MEASUREMENTS

Overview

Initial measurement occurs when an item is first recorded in the accounting system. That is, assets are initially measured when they are acquired, and liabilities are initially measured when they are incurred. This is also referred to as a "day 1" measurement. For example, generally speaking,

- Investments in equity securities are initially measured at the transaction date, at an amount equal to their purchase price.

- Notes payable (an incurrence of a liability) are initially measured at the issuance date, at an amount based on their issuance price.

- Many assets and liabilities acquired in business combinations are initially measured at the acquisition date, at their acquisition date fair values (subject to potential adjustments).

- Loss contingencies are initially measured when an entity determines that a loss is probable, and that the amount of loss can be reasonably estimated; loss contingencies are recorded at management's best estimate of the loss amount.

When a single asset is acquired or liability incurred, in an arm's-length transaction, the item received is generally recorded at its transaction price. Transaction price, in arm's-length transactions, is frequently presumed to equal fair value. Assuming cash is exchanged, the asset or liability is recorded for the amount of cash exchanged, and no real "measurement" is required to initially record the item.

Fair value guidance in **ASC 820-10** supports that transaction prices are frequently reflective of fair value:

> **30-3**   In many cases, the transaction price will equal the fair value (for example, that might be the case when on the transaction date the transaction to buy an asset takes place in the market in which the asset would be sold).

For this reason, even different measurement attributes (e.g., historical cost, fair value) are often recorded at the same amount initially.

That said, initial measurement can be complicated for certain transactions, such as (to name a few):

- Capital assets or inventories that are self-constructed (rather than acquired), where the entity must determine which costs should be included in the capitalized value of the asset;

- Exchanges where the transaction price must be allocated among multiple acquired assets;

- Transactions where cash flows are long-term in nature and therefore must be discounted;

- Events with uncertain cash flows, such as contingent events; and

- Nonmonetary exchanges, where cash is not an available measure for determining the value of goods exchanged.

Following are illustrative examples of initial measurements; assume that all examples in this chapter occur at arm's-length.

Applying Initial Measurement Guidance

The following **Now YOU Try** scenarios demonstrate initial measurement guidance using different measurement attributes:

- Acquired versus self-constructed inventory (historical cost)

- Multiple-element arrangements (relative selling price method)

- Notes receivable and accounts receivable (present value)

Initial Measurement of Inventory Assets (Historical Cost)

Here's what we know: Inventory is initially measured at cost, and subsequently measured at the lower of cost or market. Simple, yes?

Maybe, maybe not. Assume that you purchase finished goods for resale to your customers. To determine the cost of the goods, you would look to the transaction price you paid to the manufacturer, plus or minus any applicable freight, discounts, and taxes. However, what if you produce the inventory in-house? In that case, judgment will be required to determine which costs should be included in the inventory's cost basis. For example, should direct labor (employee) costs be included in the inventory's cost basis? Can factory overhead costs be included?

The following **Now YOU Try** illustrates the application of initial measurement guidance for inventory. This example does not cover the determination of which inventory should be charged to expense when sold (e.g., use of the FIFO and LIFO methods); rather, this example focuses solely on the appropriate *cost basis* for capitalized inventory.

Now
YOU
Try
7.1

Initial Measurement of Inventory

Facts: TireMart operates a retail tire sale and repair shop. TireMart purchases tires from its supplier at a cost of $50 per tire, and incurs freight charges of $5 per tire (payable to a third-party delivery company).

In addition, TireMart runs its own production facility, which is dedicated to producing a line of TireMart's own brand of sporty rims. The materials cost per rim is $25. Direct labor costs for the month, a variable production cost based on hours worked, are $3,000, and the cost of utilities (light and heat) in the factory amounted to $1,000 for the month. The cost of sales personnel amounted to $2,000 for the month, and TireMart incurred $100 in direct-mail advertising expenses. TireMart had a normal production run this month, producing 100 rims.

In this example, you will be asked to determine the following:

■ What amount should TireMart include in Inventory related to its tires purchased?

■ Which costs should TireMart include in Inventory related to its production of rims?

■ Which costs must be charged to expense as incurred?

The following excerpt from **ASC 330-10** (Inventory) provides guidance for the initial measurement of inventory.

> ### > Cost Basis

30-1 The primary basis of accounting for inventories is cost, which has been defined generally as the price paid or consideration given to acquire an asset. As applied to inventories, cost means in principle the sum of the applicable expenditures and charges directly or indirectly incurred in bringing an article to its existing condition and location. It is understood to mean acquisition and production cost, and its determination involves many considerations.

30-2 Although principles for the determination of <u>inventory</u> costs may be easily stated, their application, particularly to such inventory items as work in process and finished goods, is difficult because of the variety of considerations in the allocation of costs and charges.

30-3 For example, variable production overheads are allocated to each unit of production on the basis of the actual use of the production facilities. However, the allocation of fixed production overheads to the costs of conversion is based on the normal capacity of the production facilities. Normal capacity refers to a range of production levels. Normal capacity is the production expected to be achieved over a number of periods or seasons under normal circumstances, taking into account the loss of capacity resulting from planned maintenance. . . .

30-7 Unallocated overheads shall be recognized as an expense in the period in which they are incurred. Other items such as abnormal freight, handling costs, and amounts of wasted materials (spoilage) require treatment as current period charges rather than as a portion of the inventory cost.

30-8 Also, under most circumstances, general and administrative expenses shall be included as period charges, except for the portion of such expenses that may be clearly related to production and thus constitute a part of inventory costs (product charges). Selling expenses constitute no part of inventory costs. The exclusion of all overheads from inventory costs does not constitute an accepted accounting procedure . . .

Questions:

1. First, brainstorm the "browse path" you would use, to locate guidance for this issue.

Example: Assets > Receivables (ASC 310) > Overall (-10) > Recognition (-25)

Assets > _____ (ASC _____) > Overall (-10) > _____ (-____)

2. *Purchased tires*

What per-tire amount should TireMart include in Inventory for tires purchased? $ _____

Explain the guidance from par. 30-1 supporting this conclusion: _____

_____

3. *Rims produced by TireMart*

For each cost listed below, indicate whether it should be included in the capitalized "Rim Inventory" asset account, or whether it must be charged to expense as incurred:

Materials cost of $25 per rim (Example)
Per-rim amount to capitalize? $25
Rationale from guidance?
Par. 30-1 requires entities to measure inventory based on the consideration given to acquire an asset. These include amounts paid directly to bring an asset to its existing condition. These direct materials charges were incurred to bring the rims to their desired condition.

Direct labor cost of $3,000 for the month
Per-rim amount to capitalize? $_____
Rationale from guidance? (Hint: Use par. 30-1.)

_____

Cost of utilities (light and heat) for the month ($1,000)
Per-rim amount to capitalize? $_____
Rationale from guidance?

_____

Cost of sales personnel for the month ($2,000)
Per-rim amount to capitalize? $_____
Rationale from guidance?

_____

Cost of direct-mail advertising expenses ($100)
Per-rim amount to capitalize? $_____
Rationale from guidance?

_____

Total per-rim amount capitalized in Inventory: $_____
Total period expenses: $_____

Whether acquired or self-constructed, the initial measurement attribute for inventory is "cost." However, as this example demonstrates, determining the historical cost of acquired assets, where there is a third-party transaction that provides an objective basis for the inventory's value, is often more straightforward than determining which costs should be assigned or allocated to self-constructed assets.

Initial Measurement of Multiple-Element Arrangements (Relative Selling Price)

When multiple goods or services are delivered in an arrangement, entities must determine, first, *whether* revenue can be allocated separately to the deliverables and, second, *how* revenue should be allocated. The second question (*how* to allocate revenue) is an issue of initial measurement; to answer this, the Codification's Revenue Recognition—Multiple Element Arrangements guidance (**ASC 605-25**) introduces a measurement attribute that is unique to multiple-element transactions.

Per **ASC 605-25**, the consideration received by a vendor in a multiple-element arrangement should be allocated based on the deliverables' **relative selling prices**:

> **30-2**   Arrangement consideration shall be allocated at the inception of the arrangement to all deliverables on the basis of their relative selling price (the relative selling price method), except as specified in paragraphs 605-25-30-4 through 30-5. When applying the relative selling price method, the selling price for each deliverable shall be determined using vendor-specific objective evidence of selling price, if it exists; otherwise, third-party evidence of selling price (as discussed in paragraph 605-25-30-6B). If neither vendor-specific objective evidence nor third-party evidence of selling price exists for a deliverable, the vendor shall use its best estimate of the selling price for that deliverable (as discussed in paragraph 605-25-30-6C) when applying the relative selling price method . . .

Knowledge ✓
Check

4. **Par. 30-2 provides a 3-part "hierarchy" for determining the selling price of each deliverable in a multiple-element arrangement. Identify the three measurement options in this hierarchy:**
    i) **Use "vendor-specific objective evidence" of selling price, if it exists; if not,**
    ii) _____
    iii) _____

Following is a **Now YOU Try** exercise which illustrates the **ASC 605-25** guidance for determining the relative selling prices of deliverables.

Multiple-Element Arrangements

Now
YOU
Try
7.2

Facts: Friendly Appliance is an appliance retailer. Assume that Friendly sells a washing machine and installation services together to a customer for $600. As of 12/31/X1, the washing machine has been delivered, but the delivery crew (also trained to perform installations) was missing a part necessary to perform the installation service. The delivery crew has scheduled a return visit to the customer's home for 1/2/X2, to complete the installation.

Friendly has determined that these two "deliverables" meet the **ASC 605-25** criteria for separate recognition, namely,

1. The delivered item (the washing machine) has value to the customer on a stand-alone basis;

2. Although the customer has the right to return the washing machine, Friendly considers its performance of the installation service to be probable and substantially within its control.

Friendly's management must now determine what value to assign to each deliverable.

ASC 605-25 defines each method for determining relative selling price, as follows:

> **30-6A**   Vendor-specific objective evidence of selling price is limited to either of the following:
> a. The price charged for a deliverable when it is sold separately
> b. For a deliverable not yet being sold separately, the price established by management having the relevant authority (it must be probable that the price, once

Continued

established, will not change before the separate introduction of the deliverable into the marketplace).

30-6B Third-party evidence of selling price is the price of the vendor's or any competitor's largely interchangeable products or services in standalone sales to similarly situated customers.

30-6C The vendor's best estimate of selling price shall be consistent with the objective of determining vendor-specific objective evidence of selling price for the deliverable; that is, the price at which the vendor would transact if the deliverable were sold by the vendor regularly on a standalone basis. The vendor shall consider market conditions as well as entity-specific factors when estimating the selling price. [Emphasis added]

Friendly's management has gathered the following information:

i. The price of a washing-machine installation service, when performed by other vendors, is $150.

ii. Friendly Appliance currently offers customers the option to buy (1) just the washing machine, for $500, or (2) the washing machine plus installation service for $600. Friendly Appliance does not sell installation service separately to non-customers.

iii. Friendly Appliance estimates that if it did sell installation services separately, it would likely charge $150 for this service.

a. Vendor-specific objective evidence
b. Third-party evidence
c. Vendor's best estimate of selling price

Questions:

1. Considering the guidance from par. 30-6, what type of evidence (a, b, or c) corresponds to each numbered piece of information from Friendly's management?

   i. _____ ii. _____ iii. _____

2. Considering the graphic above and the hierarchy in ASC 605-25, which *sources of information* provide the best evidence of standalone selling price for:

   ◼ The washing machine? _____

   ◼ The installation service? _____

3. What browse path would you use, to locate this multiple-element transaction measurement guidance in the Codification?

   Revenue Recognition (ASC 605) > _____ (-25) > _____ (-30)

As you read in par. 30-2, the arrangement consideration in multiple-element arrangements should be allocated to deliverables on the basis of their relative selling prices. The formula for determining the relative selling price of each deliverable is:

$$\text{Total arrangement consideration} \times \frac{\text{Estimated selling price of 1 deliverable}}{\text{Total estimated selling prices of both deliverables}}$$

Accordingly, in the preceding example, Friendly would recognize revenue as follows:

- Washer: $600 arrangement consideration × [$500/(500 + 150)] = $462
- Installation: $600 × [$150/(500 + 150)] = $138

Notice that the estimated standalone selling prices for the washing machine and installation were based on two different methods for estimating selling prices, but each was determined to provide the best estimate of that deliverable's standalone value.

This "hierarchy" for determining relative selling price is a measurement attribute unique to multiple-element arrangement guidance. Researchers seeking information on this measurement should consult the individual topic (ASC 605-25) and, as needed, interpretive publications (such as firm accounting manuals).

Initial Measurement of Receivable Assets (Present Value)

ASC 310 (Receivables) provides guidance applicable to a range of receivables, including trade receivables, notes receivable, loan syndications (loans involving a group of lenders), and more. Yet within this topic, differences exist in the accounting prescribed for each type of receivable, just as differences exist in the nature of each receivable. For example, the terms of various receivables may differ (trade receivables generally have a short term, while notes receivable—also known in the Codification as "loans"—tend to have longer terms). Also, trade receivables are often satisfied in a single payment, while notes receivable tend to require multiple payments and often include an interest component.

Following is a simple introduction to the initial measurement guidance provided for notes receivable. Initial measurement guidance is not provided for other types of receivables within the Receivables topic. This **Now YOU Try** is intended to be a simple introduction and does not touch on all potential complexities, such as discounting, or unit of account issues (e.g., measure the receivables individually, or as a group?), and so on. These topics are, however, addressed in Chapter 8 of this book.

Now **YOU** Try

7.3

Measuring Receivable Assets

Facts: Assume that an entity has received a note receivable in exchange for providing significant goods and services to a customer. This transaction gives rise to the question: How should the exchange be measured? Recall that when an exchange involves cash, cash sets the "fair value" of the exchange. When a receivable is received instead of cash, an entity must determine an appropriate value for that receivable.

ASC 310-10 provides the following initial measurement guidance for notes receivable.

> **Notes Exchanged for Cash**

30-2 . . . when a note is received solely for cash and no other right or privilege is exchanged, it is presumed to have a present value at issuance measured by the cash proceeds exchanged . . .

> **Notes Exchanged for Property, Goods, or Services**

30-4 As indicated in paragraph 835-30-25-2, if determinable, the established exchange price (which, presumably, is the same as the price for a cash sale) of property, goods, or services acquired or sold in consideration for a note may be used to establish the present value of the note. That paragraph explains that, when notes are traded in an open market, the market rate of interest and quoted prices of the notes provide the evidence of the present value. That paragraph notes that these methods are preferable means of establishing the present value of the note.

Questions:

1. Brainstorm the "browse path" you would use, to locate guidance on the initial measurement of notes receivable.

    Assets > _____ (ASC ____) > Overall (-10) > _____ (-____)

2. Per ASC 310, at what value should notes receivable initially be recorded: present value, fair value, or cost?

    _____

3. How is the present value of a note exchanged for cash generally determined?

    _____

4. Par. 30-4 describes two ways in which the present value of a note exchanged for property, goods, or services can be determined. Identify these two options for determining a note's present value.

    i) _____

    ii) _____

In this example, if a cash transaction cannot be used to establish the present value of a note receivable, researchers must look to other information. Although present value measurements are defined generally within **ASC 820** (Fair Value Measurements), researchers should also look to specific guidance within the Receivables topic, for determining the present value of notes receivable.

SUBSEQUENT MEASUREMENTS

Overview

Subsequent measurements, or "day 2" measurements, are necessary for reporting changes in recorded assets or liabilities. Subsequent measurement guidance provides both (1) information on *what subsequent value* to report for assets and liabilities and (2) information on *how to report* those changes (in which financial statement line item). Changes in recorded assets and liabilities can arise, for example, due to sales of assets or settlements of liabilities, or due to changes in the condition or market value of assets or liabilities. Examples of subsequent measurements include

- Recording an estimate of uncollectible accounts receivable
- Recording the effects of inventory obsolescence
- Adjusting the recorded value of investment securities held to match market prices
- Testing goodwill for impairment
- Recording depreciation for fixed assets
- Determining whether an item of property, plant, or equipment should be impaired

Each topic within the Codification specifies when subsequent measurements must be performed. In some cases, subsequent measurements may be required every period; in other cases, these measurements are only required when events or changes in circumstances (e.g., "triggering events") indicate that the carrying amount of an asset may not be recoverable. Still other cases may require assessment at different periods (such as quarterly or annually).

Following are examples of the required timing for certain subsequent measurements:

- Investments in equity securities classified as "trading" or "available for sale" must be measured at fair value every period for which financial statements are presented (quarterly or annually).

■ Depreciation of fixed assets must be recorded every period; however, the fixed assets them-selves are not generally remeasured each period.

■ Goodwill must be tested for impairment annually (or between annual tests, depending on the circumstances).[4]

■ Property, plant, and equipment held and used is tested for impairment if a triggering event occurs; property, plant, and equipment held for sale is tested for impairment each period.

Following are examples illustrating the appropriate timing and valuation for sample subse-quent measurements.

Applying Subsequent Measurement Guidance

The following **Now YOU Try** scenarios continue two of our earlier illustrations: inventory and accounts and notes receivable valuations. However, notice how the measurement attributes have changed from those illustrated in our earlier examples, given that the upcoming examples involve subsequent measurements.

■ Inventory (lower of cost or market)

■ Notes receivable, accounts receivable (net realizable value)

Additional scenarios illustrating subsequent measurements are included within the fair value measurement chapter of this book (Chapter 8). Those scenarios involve (1) recording unrealized gains on investment securities classified as trading and available-for-sale and (2) fixed asset impairment testing.

Subsequent Measurement of Inventory Assets (Lower of Cost or Market)

Inventory guidance within the Codification (**ASC 330**) requires that, in periods subsequent to initial measurement, inventory must be recorded at the lower of its cost or market value. In apply-ing this requirement, it is important for researchers to understand that ASC 330's definition of "market" is unique to ASC 330, and it is separate and distinct from the concept of fair value. ASC 330 provides detailed guidance necessary for determining the "market" value of inventory assets.

The fair value topic (**ASC 820-10**) further supports this distinction between "market" and "fair value," indicating that inventory measurements are not within the scope of fair value guidance:

> **15-2(b)(2)** The guidance in the Fair Value Measurements and Disclosures Topic does not apply . . . Under Sections, Subtopics, or Topics that require or permit measurements that are similar to fair value but that are not intended to measure fair value, including . . . **Topic 330**. [Bold and underlined emphasis added]

The glossary of ASC 330-10 defines the term **market** as follows:

> As used in the phrase "lower of cost or market," the term *market* means current replacement cost (by purchase or by reproduction, as the case may be) provided that it meets both of the following conditions:
> a. Market shall not exceed the net realizable value [estimated selling price less reasonably predictable costs of completion and disposal]
> b. Market shall not be less than net realizable value reduced by an allowance for an approximately normal profit margin. [Explanation added]

---

[4] Notably, in 2013, the FASB and its Private Company Council issued a proposal that would give private companies the option to amortize goodwill, rather than perform annual goodwill impairment tests. This proposal would not change the annual impairment test requirement for public companies.

Par. 35-1 through 35-5 of ASC 330, included below, provide guidance on the subsequent measurement of inventory. This guidance essentially requires a two-step evaluation to determine whether an inventory's market value has fallen below its cost:

1. First, compare the recorded inventory cost to its replacement cost (market value as previously defined).

2. If replacement cost is less (in step 1), recognize a loss if the retailer does not expect to earn normal profits upon sale of the inventory.

The following **Now YOU Try** continues our earlier TireMart inventory valuation example and illustrates consideration of this subsequent measurement guidance.

Inventory Subsequent Measurement

Now **YOU** Try

7.4

Facts: Recall our earlier TireMart example. Due to declines in consumer demand, the per-unit replacement cost for rims similar to those sold by TireMart is now $60. Assume TireMart's rims are carried in inventory at a cost of $65 per rim and that the estimated per-unit sales price, less estimated sales commissions, is $58. Assume that 50 rims remain in inventory. TireMart is considering whether the recorded value of its rims requires adjustment. TireMart's historical practice has been to record inventory obsolescence through Cost of Goods Sold.

ASC 330-10 offers the following guidance on subsequent measurements of inventory.

> **> Adjustments to Lower of Cost or Market**
>
> **35-1** A departure from the cost basis of pricing the <u>inventory</u> is required when the utility of the goods is no longer as great as their cost. Where there is evidence that the utility of goods, in their disposal in the ordinary course of business, will be less than cost, whether due to physical deterioration, obsolescence, changes in price levels, or other causes, the difference shall be recognized as a loss of the current period. This is generally accomplished by stating such goods at a lower level commonly designated as <u>market</u>. . . .
>
> **35-4** As a general guide, utility is indicated primarily by the current cost of replacement of the goods as they would be obtained by purchase or reproduction. In applying the rule, however, judgment must always be exercised and no loss shall be recognized unless the evidence indicates clearly that a loss has been sustained. There are therefore exceptions to such a standard. Replacement or reproduction prices would not be appropriate as a measure of utility when the estimated sales value, reduced by the costs of completion and disposal, is lower, in which case the realizable value so determined more appropriately measures utility.
>
> **35-5** Furthermore, when the evidence indicates that cost will be recovered with an approximately normal profit upon sale in the ordinary course of business, no loss shall be recognized even though replacement or reproduction costs are lower.

Questions:

1. Brainstorm the "browse path" you would use, to locate guidance on subsequent measurements of inventory.

   Assets > _____ (ASC _____) > Overall (-10) > _____ (-___)

2. Under what circumstances must companies re-evaluate the recorded cost of their inventory? (See par. 35-1)

3. Considering the guidance above, name three factors that might indicate a decline in the utility of a good.

_____

_____

4. What journal entry should TireMart record, to reflect the decline in its inventory value?

dr. _____ $_____

    cr. _____ $ _____

Citing from the guidance, explain how you arrived at this journal entry.

_____

_____

_____

This example highlighted two measurement attributes—net realizable value and lower of cost or market, both of which were necessary to consider in determining the appropriate subsequent measurement for TireMart's inventory.

Subsequent Measurement of Receivables (Net Realizable Value)

Subsequent to initial measurement, the value of recorded receivables may require adjustment for several reasons, including:

■ To reflect cash collections

■ To reflect interest accruals (for interest to be collected from borrowers) and interest income collected

■ To reflect losses from uncollectible receivables or impaired loans.

Concepts Statement No. 5 states that "net realizable value" is generally the measurement attribute used to measure short-term accounts receivable. CON 5, par. 67(d) describes net realizable value as the undiscounted amount of cash "into which an asset is expected to be converted in due course of business less direct costs. . . ."

Our next **Now YOU Try** focuses on how to measure the net realizable value of receivables; specifically, this example focuses on how to record losses related to estimated uncollectible receivables and impaired loans. Recording such losses is generally a two-step process:

■ First, if an account is expected to be uncollectible (or a loan is believed to be impaired), an allowance account should be established, with a corresponding charge to income.

■ Next, if an actual loss occurs (that is, if a customer defaults or the account is written off), the allowance account should be adjusted to reflect the loss.

Subsequent measurements of both trade receivables and loans can be complex in that measuring customer credit risk (that is, the likelihood of customer nonpayment) can involve significant judgment. Additionally, the measurement of estimated credit losses can be complicated by variables such as the unit of account being measured (e.g., assess impairment for individual receivables or groups of receivables?) and the use of present value to estimate impairment allowances.

Notably, the FASB recently proposed changes to the accounting for receivables (including, for example, loans, debt securities, and trade receivables) that would require companies to recognize their current estimate of expected credit losses at each reporting date through the use of an allowance account, with subsequent changes in expected credit losses (both favorable and unfavorable) recognized in earnings.

The objective of the following example is to illustrate the concept of net realizable value, and to illustrate the process for charging off losses from receivables. For simplicity, unit of account and discounting are not covered in this example; however, these topics are addressed in Chapter 8.

Receivables—Subsequent Measurement

This **Now YOU Try** illustrates the two-step process involved in recording losses related to estimated uncollectible receivables and impaired loans, and the guidance related to this process.

Step 1: Establish an Allowance Account

The process for establishing an allowance account under **ASC 310-10** depends on what type of receivable is being measured. The first guidance we will review applies to *trade receivables* and to *groups of small-balance loans* where individual loans within the group have not been individually evaluated for impairment. Following that, we will consider guidance on evaluating individual loans for impairment. Considering the excerpts provided, respond to the questions that follow.

> > **Losses from Uncollectible Receivables**

35-7 The conditions under which receivables exist usually involve some degree of uncertainty about their collectibility, in which case a contingency exists.

35-8 Subtopic 450-20 [Loss Contingencies] requires recognition of a loss when both of the following conditions are met:

  a. Information available before the financial statements are issued or are available to be issued . . . indicates that it is probable that an asset has been impaired at the date of the financial statements.

  b. The amount of the loss can be reasonably estimated.

35-9 Losses from uncollectible receivables shall be accrued when both of the preceding conditions are met. Those conditions may be considered in relation to individual receivables or in relation to groups of similar types of receivables. If the conditions are met, accrual shall be made even though the particular receivables that are uncollectible may not be identifiable.

Questions:

1. Brainstorm the "browse path" you would use, to locate guidance on subsequent measurements of receivables.

    Assets > _____ (ASC _____) > Overall (-10) > _____(-___)

2. In order to record an allowance for uncollectible receivables, what two conditions must be met?

    _____

    _____

3. What other Codification topic is referenced in the preceding ASC 310 excerpt, and how should it be considered?

    _____

Next, let's review the section from ASC 310-10 relating to *individual loans* that are being individually evaluated for impairment. Various factors may indicate that individual evaluation is necessary. For example, a customer's credit risk could become a concern if the customer becomes seriously delinquent in making payments (as indicated in past due reports); alternatively, knowledge that a particular customer is experiencing business interruptions or operating losses could cause an entity to question whether the customer's account is collectible.

The following guidance should be considered in determining whether individual loans, once identified for evaluation, are considered to be impaired. Guidance from this topic permitting the aggregation of similar loans has been omitted for simplicity.

> > Assessing Whether a Loan Is Impaired

35-16 A loan is impaired when, based on current information and events, it is probable that a creditor will be unable to collect all amounts due according to the contractual terms of the loan agreement. All amounts due according to the contractual terms means that both the contractual interest payments and the contractual principal payments of a loan will be collected as scheduled in the loan agreement . . .

35-18 The term *probable* is used consistent with its use in Subtopic 450-20 [Loss Contingencies] . . .

> > Measurement of Impairment

35-20 Measuring impairment of a loan requires judgment and estimates, and the eventual outcomes may differ from those estimates. Creditors shall have latitude to develop measurement methods that are practical in their circumstances.

35-22 When a loan is impaired (see paragraphs 310-10-35-16 through 35-17), a creditor shall measure impairment based on the present value of expected future cash flows discounted at the loan's effective interest rate, except that as a practical expedient, a creditor may measure impairment based on a loan's observable market price, or the fair value of the collateral if the loan is a collateral-dependent loan. If that practical expedient is used, Topic 820 [Fair Value Measurement] shall apply.

35-24 . . . If the present value of expected future cash flows (or, alternatively, the observable market price of the loan or the fair value of the collateral) is less than the recorded investment in the loan . . . a creditor shall recognize an impairment by creating a valuation allowance with a corresponding charge to bad-debt expense or by adjusting an existing valuation allowance for the impaired loan with a corresponding charge or credit to bad-debt expense . . .

4. What general principle applies, for determining *whether* a loan is impaired?

    _____

5. What three methods are described in par. 35-22 for *measuring* an impairment loss?

    _____

6. Where might a researcher go to find additional guidance on the expected cash flow method of measuring present value? *Hint:* Locating guidance for present value measurements was discussed earlier in this chapter.

    _____

7. If an impairment must be recognized, what two accounts should the creditor adjust?

    _____

Step 2: Charge-offs to reflect actual losses

Recall that the second step in recognizing impairment losses, generally after recording an allowance for estimated losses, is to write off accounts deemed uncollectible. The following guidance from ASC 310-10 provides guidance for this entry.

> Credit Losses for Loans and Trade Receivables

35-41 Credit losses for loans and trade receivables, which may be for all or part of a particular loan or trade receivable, shall be deducted from the allowance. The related loan

Continued

or trade receivable balance shall be charged off in the period in which the loans or trade receivables are deemed uncollectible. Recoveries of loans and trade receivables previously charged off shall be recorded when received.

8. What journal entry is generally required when a credit loss occurs?

dr. _____

cr. _____

This example demonstrated the process for performing "day 2" measurements of certain receivables. It's worth noting, however, that this guidance does not apply equally to all industries. Certain industries have specialized accounting practices for receivables; for example, companies in the financial services—mortgage banking industry are required to report certain loans at the lower of cost or fair value.

Through the preceding examples, you have had the opportunity to think critically about, and to apply, several measurement attributes from the Codification. The next section of this chapter briefly describes the relationship between measurement and disclosure.

DISCLOSURE SHOULD ACCOMPANY KEY MEASUREMENT JUDGMENTS

Transparent disclosure should accompany key financial statement measurements, regardless of the measurement attribute used.

Disclosure provides management with the opportunity to explain its choices of measurement methods and the judgments involved in calculating reported amounts. Additionally, disclosure provides financial statement regulators and users with transparency into these methods and judgments.

The Securities and Exchange Commission (SEC) has historically been a strong proponent of transparent disclosure, emphasizing that companies should clearly explain key financial statement measurements and measurement policies. At times, the SEC has expressed its concerns about disclosure transparency to individual companies (in the form of comment letters), in "Dear CFO" letters issued to public companies in general, and in public speeches. In certain cases, if the SEC determines that corporate disclosures are false or misleading, or otherwise violate securities laws, the agency may bring enforcement actions against individuals or corporations.

Financial statement users also frequently request more transparent disclosures about measurement. During the deliberations of FASB Statement No. 157, *Fair Value Measurements* (later codified as ASC 820), for example, investors encouraged the Board to require expanded disclosures of fair value measurements based on unobservable inputs:

> Those users strongly supported the expanded disclosures. They indicated that the expanded disclosures would allow users of financial statements to make more informed judgments and segregate the effects of fair value measurements that are inherently subjective, enhancing their ability to assess the quality of earnings broadly.[5]

Given the importance of accompanying measurements with clear disclosure, challenge yourself as a researcher to always consult Section 50 ("Disclosures") when performing research related to measurement issues.

---

[5] FASB Statement No. 157, *Fair Value Measurements*, par. C98.

CHAPTER SUMMARY

Given the lack of broad framework for applying most measurement principles, researchers must consult individual Codification topics for measurement guidance specific to each topic. Within each topic, measurement guidance generally describes when measurement is required, how changes in values should be measured, and how these changes should be reported in the financial statements. Fair value and present value measurements are unique in that a consistent definition of these measurement attributes has been established, as we will discuss further in Chapter 8.

This chapter only scratched the surface of the wide range of measurement issues that researchers may encounter in practice; however, it is only with practice that researchers will become familiar with these issues.

Given the judgment and complexity that can be involved in accounting measurement, accountants must take care to provide transparent and thoughtful disclosures about the selection of measurement bases and measurement assumptions. Specialists should be involved, as necessary, in helping to interpret complex measurement guidance.

REVIEW QUESTIONS

1. Inventory costing is a matter of (initial/subsequent?) measurement. Inventory obsolescence is a matter of (initial/subsequent?) measurement.

2. What is a measurement attribute? Are most measurement attributes defined in the Codification?

3. What does it mean, for most of the Codification's measurement guidance to be "topic-specific"? What implications does this have for a researcher, looking for measurement guidance in the Codification?

4. Describe two circumstances in which a valuation specialist might be engaged to assist with an accounting measurement.

5. Complete the following sentence: Transaction price, in an arm's-length transaction, is generally presumed to equal _____.

6. What is the initial measurement attribute for inventory? What are some considerations that could result in complexity in initially measuring inventory?

7. What researchable question did the multiple-element revenue example address?

8. What hierarchy applies for determining the relative selling price of deliverables, in multiple-element revenue arrangements?

9. Name two examples of subsequent measurements.

10. Describe the process for determining whether the value of inventory should be written down, below its cost.

11. Explain why disclosure should accompany key measurement judgments, and provide two examples of parties who lobby for increased transparency in disclosures.

EXERCISES

Respond to the following using guidance in the Codification. Cite your sources for all responses.

1. Perform a keyword search for the term "unit of account" in the Codification. List two of the topics highlighted in your search results, where "unit of account" is a consideration.

2. In periods subsequent to initial measurement, is goodwill amortized? Explain and cite the Codification reference for your response.

3. Generally, how are guarantees initially measured?

4. Several assumptions are involved in an employer's measurement of its liability for defined benefit pension benefits. Name three of these assumptions. *Hint:* This is located under the topic related to an *employer's* accounting for pensions; this differs from a pension *plan's* accounting.

5. Is measurement guidance (in Sections 30 or 35 of the applicable topic) available regarding employer obligations for compensated employee absences (such as vacation accruals)? If not, think: Where else might a researcher look for such measurement guidance within this topic?

6. What basic measurement principle exists for the measurement of nonmonetary transactions? What are two examples in which modifications to the basic principle apply?

7. Once an entity has determined that it is probable of having an environmental remediation liability, what costs must the entity initially include in its estimated environmental remediation liability (an "environmental obligation")?

8. In periods subsequent to the acquisition date in a business combination, what guidance is available regarding the measurement (by an acquirer) of contingent liabilities assumed? Assume the contingencies were recognized as of the acquisition date.

9. Under Topic 835-20 (Capitalization of Interest), what amount of interest may initially be capitalized as part of the initial investment in an asset, for certain qualifying assets? How should a company determine its "capitalization rate" for capitalizing interest?

10. When should an investor, applying the "equity method" of accounting for an investment, recognize equity method income—in the period the investee reports earnings, or in the period the investee declares a dividend?

CASE STUDY QUESTIONS

Accrual for a Lawsuit, Writing an Issues Memo Your company has just been named as defendant in a lawsuit related to a leak of chemicals, from one of your company's plants onto private property. The plaintiff is suing for $5 million in damages; your company's attorneys believe the ultimate amount of loss could range between $1 million and $3 million, with no amount in the range more likely than other amounts in the range. The lawsuit is expected to be resolved in the middle of next year.   **7.1**

Citing from authoritative literature, prepare a brief accounting issues memo to the files addressing (1) whether a loss should be accrued, and for what amount, and (2) what disclosures should be made in the company's financial statements.

Determining Whether an Impairment Is "Other Than Temporary," Writing an Email Assume you are an auditor, and your client is a public company with a large portfolio of available-for-sale equity securities. The client reports these securities at fair value, with unrealized gains and losses recognized in "other comprehensive income," an equity account, each period.   **7.2**

The client is preparing its quarterly financial statements and is again—for the second consecutive quarter—recording a decline in market value for several of the securities. These securities' fair values are now below their cost. From experience, you know that losses on available-for-sale securities must be recognized in *earnings* if (1) the securities are considered *impaired* (i.e., cost basis in excess of fair value) and (2) if the impairment is considered "other than temporary." Your client has asserted that it has the ability and intent to hold the securities, at least until their value recovers, and believes that the losses need only be recognized in OCI.

Locate the relevant accounting guidance, then draft an email to your audit supervisor (Sean) that

- tells him about this issue,
- explains the general requirement regarding impairment of available-for-sale securities, describes your evaluation of whether the change in security values should be considered an other-than-temporary impairment (and therefore recognized in earnings), and
- suggests next steps.

It may be difficult to reach a definitive conclusion regarding whether impairment is required; however, it is important that you make your supervisor aware of this issue and the relevant guidance. Consider all sources of "required reading" in your response. Try to be succinct, while fully addressing the issue (try not to overwhelm your supervisor with an overly lengthy email).

Measurement attributes used in public company balance sheets Working with a group, choose a U.S. public company, and locate its most recent year-end balance sheet in the company's 10-K. Your goal is to understand, and describe, how each balance sheet item is measured, citing guidance from the Codification indicating the requirements for the measurement.   **7.3**

The following table and notes show an example of the deliverable you should provide. Follow this format, listing the balance sheet item, amount, and a brief summary of its measurement basis. Use additional notes to show (concisely) the Codification justification for this measurement, as well as to add any discussion that helps a reader's understanding of the item, or to share any facts you find interesting.

Use your own words in your explanations; do not copy directly from the company's financial statements. If you must use the company's words, provide a reference (cite the financial statements, and specific page number, as a source). In particular, when you come across balance sheet items that are industry- or company-specific, provide additional discussion of the items.

Do not choose a company just because its balance sheet is short. Aim for a minimum of 15 total items on the balance sheet. You may elect to take a "pass" on up to two balance sheet items, for example, if you have difficulty locating, understanding, or explaining the item's measurement basis. However, please explain your rationale for any "passes" you elect to take.

Your group's final deliverable should be no more than 4 to 5 pages (including roughly 1 page for the table). Present a deliverable that is polished. Also, feel free to be creative with your explanations/value add in your notes. For example, you can contrast your company's practices to other companies', point out items unique to your company's industry, highlight any recent changes in measurement method, and so on.

Once your group has selected a company, post your selection on the class discussion board, if available. Once a company is chosen by a group, other groups should not choose this company.

Example:

ABC Company, year-end 20X1 balance sheet

Financial Statement Item	Amount	Basis of measurement	Reference (to notes below)
Inventory	100,000	Lower of cost or market	Note 1
Loans receivable, net	200,000	Cost less uncollectible accounts reserve	Note 2

Note 1:

ABC Company has inventory, primarily in the form of purchased fuel, which it carries at cost. This is appropriate in accordance with ASC XXX-XX, which states: " ". One thing that is unique about ABC Company's inventory is that the Company . . .

Note 2:

ABC Company, through its Finance division, routinely makes loans to customers. These loans are carried at cost less a reserve for uncollectible accounts. ASC XXX-XX permits this practice, stating: " ". In 20X1, the auditors for ABC Company found that the Company's uncollectible accounts reserve policy was insufficient and issued a qualified audit opinion.

. . . and so on.

Chapter 8

Fair Value Measurements in the Codification

Jay is a plant accountant for NewTech Corp, a hardware manufacturing company which produces parts for customers ranging from manufacturers of cell phones, to tablet computers, to smart watches. Jay is reviewing the recorded value of equipment used by NewTech to produce hardware for desktop computers. The equipment, which has a carrying value of $10 million at 12/31/X1, represents NewTech's only major investment in its PC hardware line. Unfortunately, decreased market demand for personal computers has caused NewTech to reassess its expected future cash flows associated with the equipment. As a result, Jay is now researching whether the equipment should be tested for impairment.

But Jay is not sure where to go from here – should he evaluate this issue using fair value measurement guidance, or guidance for property, plant, and equipment? Once he locates this guidance, how should he even begin to perform such an analysis? Read on, as this chapter will introduce the guidance sources, approaches, and inputs used to perform fair value measurements, and will revisit NewTech's impairment question. Understand the basics of fair value measurement guidance in the Codification, and you will be well on your way to having a stronger understanding of an issue that challenges many accountants: valuation.

After reading this chapter and performing the exercises herein, you will be able to

1. **Broadly,** understand the definition of fair value and the approaches for measuring fair value.

2. **Navigate** ASC 820, the Codification topic on fair value measurements.

3. **Apply** measurement principles to sample recurring and nonrecurring fair value measurements.

4. **Review** valuation technique disclosures and identify key information about management's measurement approach.

Learning Objectives

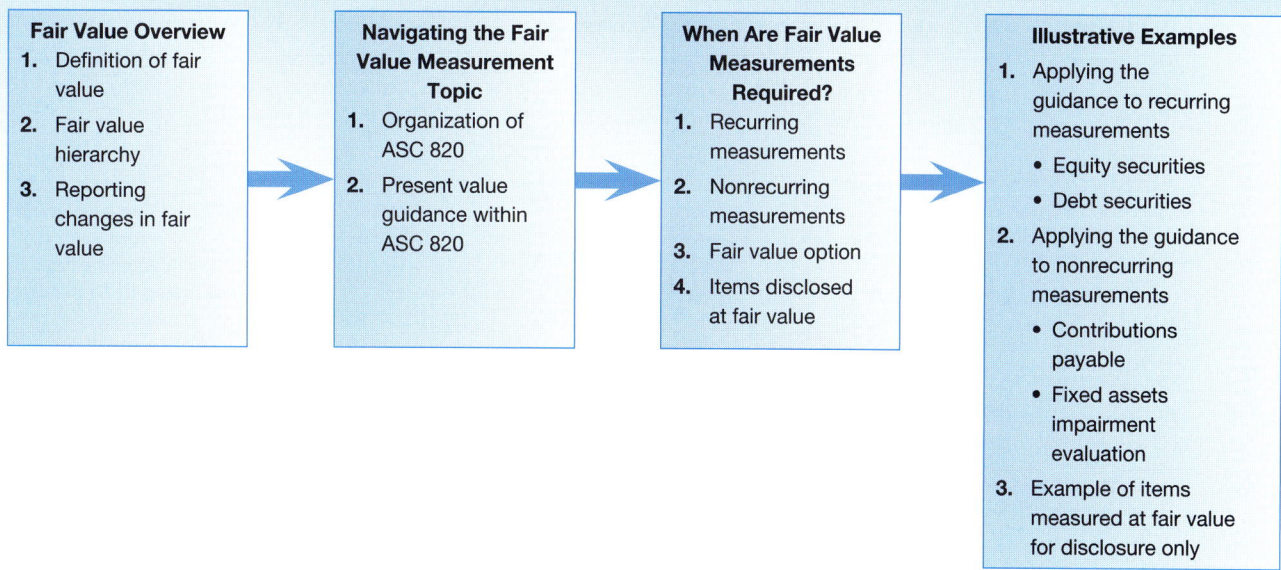

Fair Value Overview	Navigating the Fair Value Measurement Topic	When Are Fair Value Measurements Required?	Illustrative Examples
1. Definition of fair value 2. Fair value hierarchy 3. Reporting changes in fair value	1. Organization of ASC 820 2. Present value guidance within ASC 820	1. Recurring measurements 2. Nonrecurring measurements 3. Fair value option 4. Items disclosed at fair value	1. Applying the guidance to recurring measurements • Equity securities • Debt securities 2. Applying the guidance to nonrecurring measurements • Contributions payable • Fixed assets impairment evaluation 3. Example of items measured at fair value for disclosure only

Organization of This Chapter

A growing attribute for both initial and subsequent measurements is fair value. With this in mind, this chapter has been devoted to fair value measurements, including discussion of the definition of fair value, information for navigating fair value guidance, and examples of recurring and nonrecurring fair value measurements.

Within this chapter, readers will have the opportunity to apply fair value concepts, guidance, and research skills to topics ranging from market-based fair value measurements, to present value techniques based on expected cash flows. In addition, the chapter will highlight the importance of the fair value measurement attribute to the measurements of financial instruments.

The preceding graphic illustrates the organization of concepts in this chapter.

Fair value measurement is a vast and complex topic; this chapter does not claim to be a complete, all-inclusive lesson on fair value accounting. However, this chapter does strive to improve your research skills, understanding of, and ability to apply critical concepts involved in performing fair value measurements.

As with previous chapters, examples within this chapter have been simplified for teaching purposes; in practice, fair value measurements can be highly nuanced and may require the involvement of specialists.

FAIR VALUE OVERVIEW

Unlike other measurement attributes in the Codification (present value excepted), fair value is unique in that its definition, and guidance for computing fair value, is applied consistently across all Codification topics requiring the use of fair value.

Located under Broad Transactions, **ASC 820** (Fair Value Measurement) is the primary source for fair value measurement and disclosure guidance within the Codification. This guidance should be consulted any time a topic requires the use of fair value. Although ASC 820 provides guidance on *how* to measure fair value, it does not require fair value measurements in addition to those already required by other Codification topics.[1] Fair value measurement guidance should always be considered *in addition to* the individual topic requiring the fair value measurement.

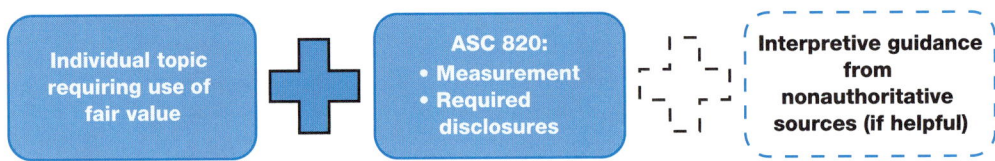

Extensive nonauthoritative resources are also available on the topic of fair value measurement and disclosure. Firm guide books, plus chapters within firm research manuals, for example, exist that are devoted to the topic of fair value measurement. As noted in Chapter 4 (regarding nonauthoritative resources), these sources can be useful in *supplementing* authoritative guidance but should not *replace* use of the Codification.

Definition of Fair Value

The glossary of ASC 820-10 defines **fair value** as:

> The price that would be received to sell an asset or paid to transfer a liability in an orderly transaction between market participants at the measurement date.

This definition reflects the following principles:

- Market participant perspective: Entities should focus on how potential buyers and sellers (market participants) would value their asset or liability.

- Exit price notion: Entities should focus on the value they expect to receive or pay when they rid themselves of (i.e., exit) the asset or liability.

- Orderly transaction: Entities should assume that a hypothetical sale would occur between informed, willing market participants.

Fair value is measured using one or more of the following three approaches:

- A market approach, where the valuation is based on market prices for identical or similar assets or liabilities;

- A cost approach, where the valuation is based on the current replacement cost of an asset, as determined from a hypothetical market participant's perspective; or

- An income approach, which uses valuation techniques (such as present value) that convert future cash flow amounts (or future income and expenses) into a single current amount.

---

[1] ASC 820-10-05-1A (Fair Value Measurement).

These approaches can be used individually or in combination to approximate the fair value of an asset or liability.

Finally, it is important to understand that the **unit of account** being measured can have a significant impact on the value assigned to assets or liabilities. The unit of account determination involves, for example, deciding whether assets should be measured individually or in combination with other assets, as a group. ASC 820 provides only limited guidance for determining the appropriate unit of account for fair value measurements; in most cases, researchers should consult the original Codification topic (that required the use of fair value) for unit of account guidance.

1. Considering the *definition of fair value*, do you think that both of the following measurements are at "fair value"? Explain below.

 **Knowledge Check**

> **i. Investments in trading securities**
> Management values its portfolio of trading securities using quoted stock market prices.

> **ii. Private company investments**
> To value its investment in a nonpublic company, management uses a valuation model that considers:
> • projected future income from the investee, and
> • the trading values of similar publicly-traded companies.

Explain. _____
_____
_____

2. Considering your understanding of the three *valuation approaches*, match the following sample valuations with the valuation approach used.

> i. Management estimates the value of its corporate bonds by determining the present value of the bonds using a market-based interest rate.

a. Market approach
b. Income approach
c. Cost approach

> ii. Management estimates the value of its specialized machinery by determining the current cost of all inputs necessary to rebuild (and replace) the machine, including construction and installation costs.

> iii. Management values its actively traded crude oil futures using quoted prices from the Chicago Mercantile Exchange.

Provide the letter corresponding to each valuation.
i. _____ ii. _____ iii. _____

The Fair Value Hierarchy

In the first **Knowledge Check** question above, you may have concluded that both measurements meet the definition of fair value. If you did, you were correct. Both measurements are intended to reflect an exit value for the investments, using information that market participants would also use to value the items.

That said, the first measurement used a market approach, based on quoted (observable) trade prices of identical securities in the market. The second measurement used a combination of the market approach (considering trading values of similar companies) and income approach (projected future income from the investee).

Clearly, however, the measurement of the trading securities is more **observable** (objective, based on market data from independent sources) than the mixed-model measurement, which relies in part on projected future income (an unobservable input). ASC 820 requires entities to ". . . maximize the use of relevant observable inputs and minimize the use of unobservable inputs to meet the objective of a fair value measurement . . . ."[2]

Given that fair value measurements can vary in their degree of observability, ASC 820 introduced a fair value measurement hierarchy, which prioritizes the use of observable inputs. For each asset or liability measured at fair value, companies must disclose the hierarchy level of the measurement. The fair value hierarchy is as follows:

- Level 1: Measurement is observable, price is quoted by market.

- Level 2: Measurement is mostly observable (e.g., a quoted price is available for similar assets or liabilities).

- Level 3: Measurement relies heavily on unobservable inputs (such as management assumptions).

This hierarchy does not change how items are measured; it merely classifies measurements into a hierarchy of observability, for disclosure purposes.

The Debits and Credits: Reporting Changes in Fair Value

When an item is periodically remeasured at fair value, the asset or liability value is adjusted. But what is the offsetting debit or credit to that adjustment?

Changes in an asset or liability's value may be recorded:

- In the income statement ("fair value through earnings");

- In other comprehensive income ("fair value through OCI"); or

- In the case of certain hedged items, changes in fair value may be reported in earnings but largely offset by changes in the fair value of a related asset or liability.

To be clear, all of these measurements are considered fair value measurements, but even fair value measurements can differ in how they are recorded. Subsequent measurement guidance, available within individual Codification topics, indicates how changes in fair value must be recorded. Later in this chapter, in the section on recurring fair value measurements, we have included an example illustrating how changes in fair value are recorded for a portfolio of equity securities.

TIP	from the Trenches

Leave out the word *market* when you search for guidance on fair value. The term *fair market value* is rarely used in the Codification, and it may make you sound funny in conversation. In research and in your communications, simply refer to this measurement attribute as *fair value*.

NAVIGATING THE FAIR VALUE MEASUREMENT TOPIC

Organization of ASC 820

ASC 820 (Fair Value Measurement) is organized in a manner similar to other Codification topics; that is, ASC 820 is divided into sections, including a section for Scope, Recognition, Initial Measurement, and so on. Figure 8-1 illustrates the sections included within ASC 820.

---

[2] ASC 820-10-35-16AA.

Home > Broad Transactions > 820 Fair Value Measurement > 10 Overall

820 Fair Value Measurement
10 Overall

To join all Sections within this Subtopic, click JOIN ALL SECTIONS.

JOIN ALL SECTIONS ?

Collapse I Expand

− 820 Fair Value Measurement
   − 10 Overall
      + 00 Status
      + 05 Overview and Background
      + 15 Scope and Scope Exceptions
      ▨ 20 Glossary
      + 25 Recognition
      + 30 Initial Measurement
      + 35 Subsequent Measurement
      + 50 Disclosure
      + 55 Implementation Guidance and Illustrations
      + 60 Relationships
      + 65 Transition and Open Effective Date Information
      + 75 XBRL Elements

Figure 8-1

Organization of ASC 820-10, Fair Value Measurement

Yet, the subject matter covered by ASC 820 is clearly different from other Codification topics. That is, the objective of ASC 820 is to define the fair value measurement attribute, and to provide guidance necessary to apply that definition. Because the subject matter of ASC 820 is so unique, we will take a moment now to describe how information is organized within this topic.

Arguably, the most important section of ASC 820 is Section 35 (Subsequent Measurement). Within this section, researchers will find the definition of fair value, as well as extensive guidance on how to apply this definition. For example, Section 35 introduces the three valuation techniques for estimating fair value and discusses the classification of valuation inputs within the fair value hierarchy. Figure 8-2 illustrates the organization of content within Section 35.

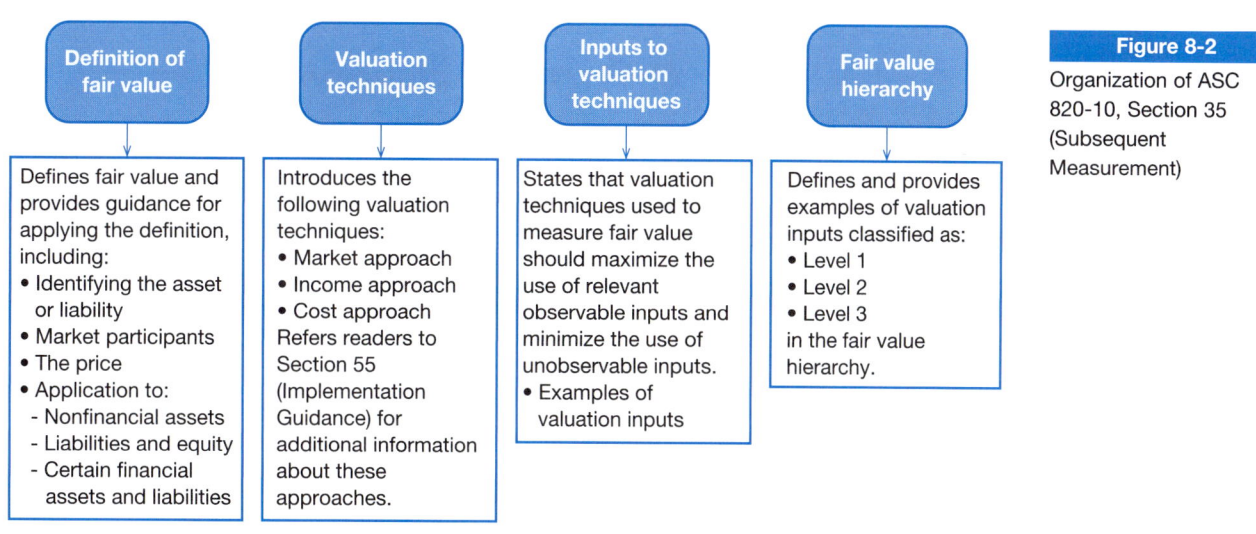

Figure 8-2

Organization of ASC 820-10, Section 35 (Subsequent Measurement)

Other notable sections within ASC 820, along with a brief (not all inclusive) description of their content, are shown in Figure 8-3.

Figure 8-3

Other notable sections from ASC 820, and a brief description of their content

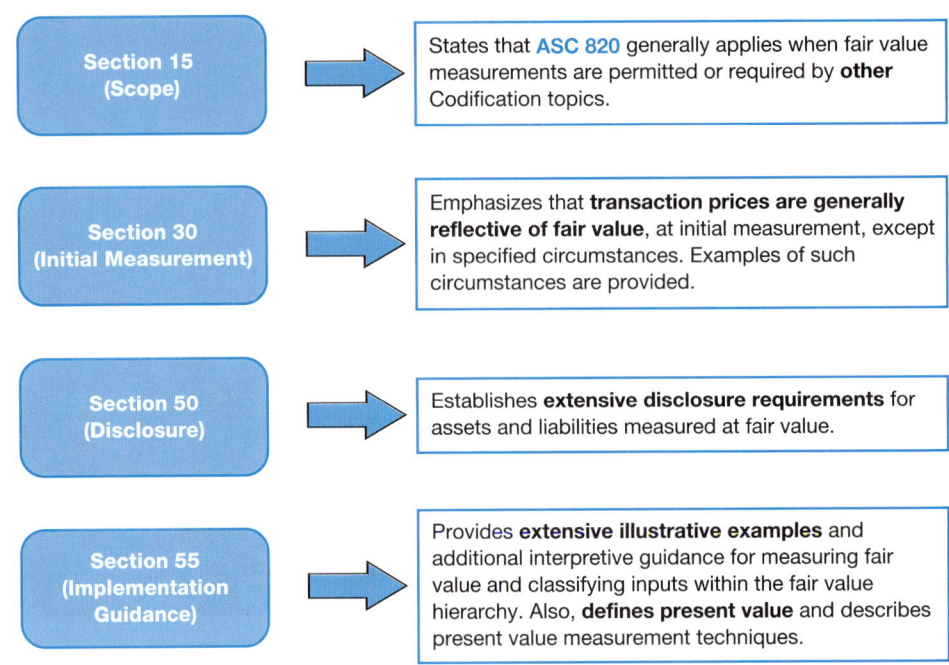

Recall from Chapter 2 of this book that researchers should treat certain content from the Codification as required reading. This rule of thumb also applies to ASC 820; when researching fair value measurement issues, researchers should consider all "required" sections, including for example the scope section, related paragraphs (as indicated by >>), relevant implementation guidance, and relevant SEC guidance (particularly for public companies).

Present Value Guidance within ASC 820

Historically, present value has been thought of as distinct from "market" value, and present value was even at one point made the focus of an entire FASB Concepts Statement (CON 7—Present Value Measurements). Today, however, our view of the relationship between these measurement attributes has shifted to the following:

Present value is a method for measuring fair value.

There are two reasons for which a researcher might use a present value measurement:

- First, a Codification topic may require the use of present value.

- Or second, a Codification topic may require the use of fair value, and a researcher may determine that the income approach, using present value, is an appropriate method for measuring fair value.

In either case, researchers looking for present value measurement guidance should consult ASC 820-10, Section 55 (Implementation Guidance), in addition to considering guidance from the individual topic requiring the use of present value. Within Section 55, alternative methods for measuring present value are described: the discount rate adjustment technique, and the expected present value technique.

That said, in the unlikely event that present value guidance within ASC 820, Section 55, is not fully responsive to a researcher's questions, CON 7 (Present Value Measurements)—a nonauthoritative source of guidance—may also be consulted.

Knowledge
Check

3. Refer to Figure 8-2. What are four major topical areas covered in Section 35 of the Fair Value Measurement topic (ASC 820-10)?

4. Where, within the Fair Value Measurement topic, would a researcher find present value guidance?

WHEN ARE FAIR VALUE MEASUREMENTS REQUIRED?

Depending on the circumstances, and on the asset or liability being measured, fair value measurements may be required or permitted at different times. Generally, assets and liabilities may be measured at fair value (1) on a recurring basis, (2) on a nonrecurring basis, (3) if the fair value option has been elected, or (4) for disclosure purposes only.

Recurring Fair Value Measurements

Certain financial assets and liabilities are required to be measured and reported at fair value each quarterly and annual period (and are therefore referred to as **recurring** fair value measurements). Recurring fair value measurements include, for example,

- Derivative assets and liabilities,
- Marketable debt and equity securities classified as trading or available-for-sale, and
- Financial assets and liabilities for which the fair value option has been elected (as discussed further below).

The value of each of these assets and liabilities is adjusted to fair value each period, with changes generally reported in earnings, other comprehensive income, or primarily as an offset to a related asset or liability (e.g., in a hedged transaction).

Nonrecurring Fair Value Measurements

Some items are only measured at fair value in certain circumstances. These fair value measurements are described as **nonrecurring**.

Items measured at fair value on a nonrecurring basis might otherwise be measured, initially and subsequently, using some other measurement attribute or attributes (such as amortized cost, net realizable value, etc.). Measurement at fair value may only be required, for example, upon the occurrence of a triggering event indicating that the item's fair value may have fallen below its recorded amount, or due to some other nonrecurring event (such as a business closure or business combination).

Nonrecurring fair value measurements include, for example,

- Impairments of fixed assets, such as property, plant, or equipment (PP&E),
- Impairments of goodwill or other intangible assets,
- Measurement of assets and liabilities acquired in a business combination, and
- Measurement of exit or disposal activity costs.

As an example, let's discuss why goodwill—tested annually—is considered a nonrecurring fair value measurement.

Although goodwill is *tested for impairment* annually, it is only *reported* at fair value and disclosed as a fair value measurement if an impairment occurs (that is, if the carrying value of goodwill exceeds its fair value). If no impairment occurs, goodwill shall continue to be reported on the balance sheet at its carrying value. Accordingly, goodwill is only measured and disclosed at fair value on a *nonrecurring* basis, when an impairment occurs.[3]

> Recurring and nonrecurring fair value measurements require extensive disclosure, including (but not limited to) information about **valuation techniques** (a required fair value disclosure) and the fair value hierarchy level for each class of assets and liabilities measured at fair value.
>
> Notably, items measured at fair value on a nonrecurring basis are only subject to these disclosure requirements for fair value measurements that occur subsequent to an item's initial measurement.

---

[3] As noted in the previous chapter, in 2013, the FASB and its Private Company Council issued a proposal that would give private companies the option to amortize goodwill, rather than perform annual goodwill impairment tests. This proposal would not change the annual impairment test requirement for public companies.

Option to Measure at Fair Value

The **fair value option** may also be elected for certain financial instruments not required to be measured at fair value. This option allows entities to measure certain financial assets and liabilities at fair value on a recurring basis.

Although initially issued as a sort of sister standard to FAS 157 (*Fair Value Measurements*), FAS 159 (*The Fair Value Option for Financial Assets and Financial Liabilities*) guidance is included within a separate Codification topic: **ASC 825** (Financial Instruments). See Figure 8-4 for the browse path to this topic.

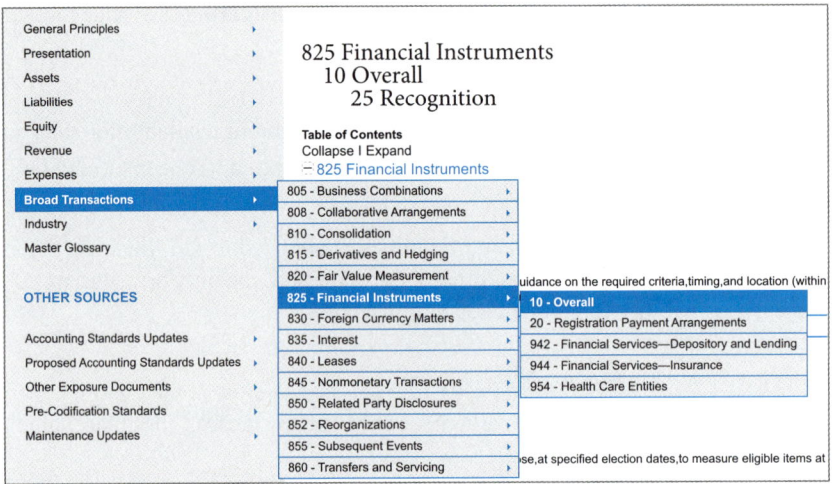

Reproduced with permission of the Financial Accounting Foundation.

But how would a researcher know to look for "Fair Value Option" guidance within ASC 825? Although the placement of this guidance may seem counter-intuitive, consider this:

The fair value option primarily permits the use of fair value for measuring financial assets and financial liabilities.

For example, scope guidance from ASC 825-10 indicates that entities may elect the fair value option for most financial assets and liabilities, as well as for certain other instruments (such as loan commitments and warranty rights and obligations):

> **15-4** All entities may elect the <u>fair value</u> option for any of the following eligible items:
> a.   A recognized <u>financial asset</u> and <u>financial liability</u>, except any listed in the following paragraph
> b.   A <u>firm commitment</u> that would otherwise not be recognized at inception and that involves only financial instruments . . .
> c.   A written loan commitment
> d.   The rights and obligations under [certain] insurance contracts . . .
> e.   The rights and obligations under [certain] warrant[ies] . . .
> f.   A host financial instrument resulting from the separation of an embedded nonfinancial derivative from a nonfinancial hybrid instrument . . .

That said, certain financial assets and liabilities are not eligible for the fair value option. For example, the fair value option cannot be elected for employers' pension obligations and for capital lease payment obligations (both financial liabilities). Researchers should carefully consult scope guidance in ASC 825-10 when determining whether the fair value option may be elected.

The existence of fair value option guidance reflects the FASB and IASB's interest in increasing the prevalence of fair value measurements, particularly for financial assets and liabilities. Currently, many financial assets and liabilities continue to be measured using other measurement attributes (for example, cost- and equity-method investments, held-to-maturity securities, etc.). In addition to offering this fair value option in ASC 825, the FASB and IASB are also working on a priority joint Financial Instruments project that they hope will expand the use of fair value in measuring financial instruments.

Understanding the Meaning of "Financial Assets" and "Financial Liabilities"

As discussed above, the FASB and IASB have emphasized that fair value is a desirable measurement attribute for many financial assets and liabilities and, accordingly, require fair value measurements and/or disclosures for many financial assets and liabilities.

It is therefore important to understand what is meant by the terms "financial asset" or "financial liability" when discussing the topic of fair value. Following are excerpts from the Codification describing these instruments.

Financial assets are defined as

Cash, evidence of an ownership interest in an entity, or a contract that conveys to one entity a right to do either of the following:

- Receive cash or another financial instrument from a second entity, or
- Exchange other financial instruments on potentially favorable terms with the second entity.*

Financial liabilities are defined as

A contract that imposes on one entity an obligation to do either of the following:

- Deliver cash or another financial instrument to a second entity, or
- Exchange other financial instruments on potentially unfavorable terms with the second entity.*

Together, financial assets and liabilities are referred to as **financial instruments.**

Nonfinancial assets are defined as

An asset that is not a <u>financial asset</u>. Nonfinancial assets include land, buildings, use of facilities or utilities, materials and supplies, intangible assets, or services.*

Nonfinancial liabilities are not defined in the Codification but can generally be viewed as liabilities that are not financial liabilities. Examples include obligations to deliver goods or services.**

*Source: FASB Codification Master Glossary.   **Source: ASC 820-10-35-18.

Financial Assets and Liabilities

1. Using the preceding definitions, complete the following table, indicating what part of the definition of "financial asset" or "financial liability" is met for each item.

Financial Assets/Liabilities	Part of definition met?
Cash	
Accounts receivable	Example: A contract that conveys "the right to receive cash"
Investments in equity securities (shares of stock)	
Stock purchase warrant (a right to buy stock at specified price)	
An in-the-money forward contract to buy shares of IBM (a derivative asset)	A contract that conveys the right to exchange financial instruments (cash for shares) on potentially favorable terms.
Accounts or notes payable	
Derivative liabilities, such as an out-of-the-money forward contract to buy shares of IBM	

2.   What term is used to collectively refer to "financial assets" and "financial liabilities"?

Items Disclosed at Fair Value

Also included in **ASC 825** (Financial Instruments) is a requirement that public (and large non-public) companies must disclose most financial instruments at fair value, regardless of whether they are measured at fair value within the financial statements. For example, many financial liabilities (like notes payable) are measured at cost (assuming the fair value option has not been elected), but must still be disclosed at fair value.

Within this disclosure, companies must reflect the instrument's carrying amount, fair value, and the fair value hierarchy level of the measurement. Companies must also describe their valuation techniques for measuring the instruments' fair values.

It's worth noting that certain financial assets and liabilities are exempted from these disclosure requirements, including for example capital lease payment obligations and employer pension liabilities.

As previously mentioned, while not all financial instruments are measured or disclosed at fair value, the FASB and IASB have expressed an objective of increasing the use of this measurement attribute for financial instruments. Therefore, even if a financial asset or liability is not reported at fair value, a researcher's antenna should go up when dealing with such assets or liabilities, as they may be subject to fair value disclosure requirements.

The next section of this chapter takes readers through illustrative examples of fair value measurements, including recurring, nonrecurring, and disclosure-only measurements at fair value.

APPLYING THE GUIDANCE: RECURRING FAIR VALUE MEASUREMENTS

The following examples illustrate the application of fair value measurement and disclosure guidance to recurring fair value measurements. The first example, focused on investments in equity securities, illustrates how changes in fair values of equity securities may be recorded on the income statement, or through other comprehensive income (OCI).

The second example describes valuation techniques for determining the fair values of investments in debt securities.

Equity Securities: Reporting Changes in Fair Value

ASC 320 (Investments—Debt and Equity Securities) applies to debt securities and to equity security investments that have "readily determinable" fair values. Subsequent measurement guidance within **ASC 320** requires that

- Securities classified as "trading" must be recorded at fair value with changes reported in current income.
- Securities classified as "available for sale" must be recorded at fair value with unrealized gains and losses reported in other comprehensive income (OCI, an equity account).

Although the securities in both cases are measured at fair value, the change in value is reported differently, as illustrated in the following example.

Fair Value of Equity Securities

Facts: An entity has the following two investments in marketable securities, whose fair values have changed this period:

1. An equity security, classified as "trading," whose quoted market price has increased by $10 this period.

2. An equity security, classified as "available for sale," whose quoted market price has increased by $10 this period.

The entity is researching what journal entries are required to report the changes in these securities' values.

The following excerpt from **ASC 320-10** (Investments—Debt and Equity Securities) provides guidance for the subsequent measurement of investments in marketable equity securities.

> **35-1** Investments in debt securities and equity securities shall be measured subsequently as follows:
>
> a. <u>Trading securities</u>. Investments in debt securities that are classified as <u>trading</u> and equity securities that have <u>readily determinable fair values</u> that are classified as trading shall be measured subsequently at <u>fair value</u> in the statement of financial position. Unrealized <u>holding gains and losses</u> for trading securities shall be included in earnings.
>
> b. <u>Available-for-sale securities</u>. Investments in debt securities that are classified as available for sale and equity securities that have readily determinable fair values that are classified as available for sale shall be measured subsequently at fair value in the statement of financial position. Unrealized holding gains and losses for available-for-sale securities (including those classified as current assets) shall be excluded from earnings and reported in other comprehensive income until realized...
>
> c. <u>Held-to-maturity securities</u>. Investments in debt securities classified as held to maturity shall be measured subsequently at amortized cost in the statement of financial position . . .

Questions:

1. Brainstorm the "browse path" you would use, to locate guidance for subsequent measurements of investments with readily determinable fair values.

    Assets > _____ (ASC _____) > Overall (-10) > _____ (-_____)

2. What journal entry is required for the "trading" security? Provide the paragraph reference from the guidance that supports this journal entry.

    dr. _____ $_____

        cr. _____ $_____   (Par. _____)

3. What journal entry is required for the "available-for-sale" security? Provide the paragraph reference from the guidance that supports this journal entry.

    dr. _____ $_____

        cr. _____ $_____   (Par. _____)

4. Are both securities required to be measured at fair value? Explain.

    _____

5. What approach (market, income, or cost) appears to have been used to determine the securities' fair values? Explain.

    _____

As a reminder, because **ASC 320** requires a fair value measurement, entities applying this guidance should also look to **ASC 820** (Fair Value Measurement) for fair value measurement and disclosure guidance. For example, the following guidance from **ASC 820-10** is relevant to the measurement of these investments:

> **35-36B** In all cases, if there is a quoted price in an active market (that is, a Level 1 input) for an asset or a liability, a reporting entity shall use that quoted price without adjustment when measuring fair value . . .

In this example, while Topic **320** *required the use of* fair value and identified *how an entity should report changes* in fair value, Topic **820** provided guidance on *how to measure* fair value.

Notably, the FASB is currently in the process of proposing fundamental changes to its current model for financial instrument accounting. These changes could do away with the concepts of "trading" and "available-for-sale" securities, instead requiring all equity investments not subject to the equity method of accounting to be measured at fair value through net income. However, the proposed changes would allow companies to apply a practicability exception for equity investments without a readily determinable fair value, which may be measured at cost (as adjusted for impairment or observable price changes). Visit the FASB website for updates on this project.

Debt Securities: Measuring and Disclosing Fair Value

Companies' investment portfolios often include a mix of debt and equity securities. The previous example illustrated the accounting for certain equity securities; this example provides insight on valuation techniques used to measure certain debt securities. In particular, this example features two corporate disclosures, describing methods used by each company to value and categorize debt securities in the fair value hierarchy.

Like investments in certain equity securities, debt securities classified as "trading" or "available-for-sale" are required by **ASC 320** (Investments—Debt and Equity Securities) to be measured at fair value, with changes recorded through income or through OCI. (Notably, this accounting could change as part of the FASB's current project on financial instrument accounting; the proposed model would require companies to classify debt securities based on the securities' cash flow characteristics, and based on the company's business model related to those securities.)

Back to our current example, companies with investments in debt securities often hold the following two security types within their investment portfolios:

- Investments in "risk-free" U.S. Treasury Notes (i.e., government bonds)
- Investments in corporate bonds (such as IBM bonds, GE bonds, etc.)

Imagine that you have been asked to assign a value to these two types of debt securities (government bonds and corporate bonds). Given that most debt securities' trade prices are not quoted on public exchanges, where would you even begin?

Debt securities are frequently traded through brokers, and recent pricing data for these trades can be used as an observable input to determine the price of the same, or similar, debt securities. If recent trade data for a similar debt security is available, adjustments may be required to reflect differences in the specific securities (e.g., adjustments for differences between the issuers' credit standing, or adjustments for the trading volume of different securities). Therefore, valuing debt often involves consideration of multiple inputs, given that quoted prices may not be readily available.

Often, companies rely on market pricing services in order to value large portfolios of debt and equity securities. For example, some companies engage "pricing vendors" to determine the value of each security within their portfolio as of the balance sheet date. In addition, companies with significant investment portfolios may subscribe to services that allow them to perform their own market research. For example, companies that lease Bloomberg terminals can use the terminals to query the real-time values of debt securities, which are based on recent trade data.

Techniques for Determining the Fair Value of Debt Securities

Now YOU Try 8.3

Facts: Following are excerpts from the annual reports of General Electric Company (GE) and Morgan Stanley, which describe each company's valuation techniques related to investments in certain government and corporate debt securities. Using these excerpts, you will be asked to respond to the questions that follow.

GE's 2011 Annual Report describes GE's valuation technique for estimating the fair value of government and corporate debt securities, as follows:

> Since many fixed income securities do not trade on a daily basis, the methodology of [our] pricing vendor[s] uses available information as applicable such as benchmark curves, benchmarking of like securities, sector groupings, and matrix pricing . . . Thus, certain securities may not be priced using quoted prices, but rather determined from market observable information. These investments are included in Level 2 and primarily comprise our portfolio of corporate fixed income, and government, mortgage and asset-backed securities.[4]

Next, the following excerpt from Morgan Stanley's 2011 Annual Report discusses Morgan Stanley's valuation techniques related to Treasury and corporate debt securities:[5]

> **U.S. Treasury Securities**
>
> U.S. Treasury securities are valued using quoted market prices. Valuation adjustments are not applied. Accordingly, U.S. Treasury securities are generally categorized in Level 1 of the fair value hierarchy.
>
> **Corporate Bonds**
>
> The fair value of corporate bonds is determined using recently executed transactions, market price quotations (where observable), bond spreads or credit default swap spreads [an indicator of credit risk] obtained from independent external parties such as vendors and brokers. . . . When position-specific external price data are not observable, fair value is determined based on either benchmarking to similar instruments or cash flow models with yield curves, bond or single name credit default swap spreads and recovery rates as significant inputs. Corporate bonds are generally categorized in Level 2 of the fair value hierarchy; in instances where prices, spreads or any of the other aforementioned key inputs are unobservable, they are categorized in Level 3 of the fair value hierarchy. [Comments added]

Questions:

1. What information does GE's pricing vendor use to measure its debt securities' fair values?

2. What inputs does Morgan Stanley use in valuing corporate debt securities?

---

[4] GE 2011 Annual Report, p. 82.

[5] Morgan Stanley 2011 Annual Report. PP. 150–151.

3. Contrast GE's fair value hierarchy level assigned to government (Treasury) securities to the level assigned by Morgan Stanley. Explain your understanding of why these differ.

As you have likely noticed, the valuation of debt securities can be complex and involves consideration of many variables. Additionally, assigning the appropriate fair value hierarchy level to investments can involve judgment; for example in this case, the two companies chose a different fair value hierarchy level for similar instruments (Treasury securities).

APPLYING THE GUIDANCE: NONRECURRING FAIR VALUE MEASUREMENTS

Following are two examples illustrating nonrecurring fair value measurements. The first example illustrates the fair value measurement of a contribution payable using an income approach. The second example illustrates the evaluation of PP&E for impairment, using a combination of the market and income approaches to determining fair value.

Contributions Payable: Measuring Fair Value Using an Income Approach

Per ASC 720-25 (Contributions Made), contributions payable are initially recorded at fair value.

> **30-1** Contributions made shall be measured at the fair values of the assets given or, if made in the form of a settlement or cancellation of a donee's liabilities, at the fair value of the liabilities cancelled.

Contributions payable are considered nonrecurring fair value measurements because they are not required to be remeasured at fair value in periods subsequent to initial measurement.

Section 35 (Subsequent Measurement) of Topic 820 provides certain guidance specific to the fair value measurement of liabilities. In particular, Topic 820-10 provides a hierarchy for measuring the fair value of liabilities, prioritizing methods that result in the most observable valuations.

> **35-16BB** . . . a reporting entity shall measure the fair value of the liability or equity instrument as follows:
> a. Using the quoted price in an active market for the identical item held by another party as an asset, if that price is available
> b. If that price is not available, using other observable inputs, such as the quoted price in a market that is not active for the identical item held by another party as an asset
> c. If the observable prices in (a) and (b) are not available, using another valuation technique, such as:
>   1. An income approach (for example, a present value technique that takes into account the future cash flows that a market participant would expect to receive from holding the liability or equity instrument as an asset; see paragraph 820-10-55-3F)
>   2. A market approach (for example, using quoted prices for similar liabilities or instruments classified in shareholders' equity held by other parties as assets; see paragraph 820-10-55-3A). [Emphasis added]

In other words, the use of present value techniques to determine the fair value of a liability is generally acceptable when quoted market prices for the same, or similar, liabilities are not available.

ASC 820-10 describes different techniques for measuring present value under the income approach:

- The **discount rate adjustment technique**, which measures the present value of future cash flows using an estimated market discount rate.

- An **expected present value technique**, using a combination of expected cash flows (which may/may not be adjusted for risk) and discount rates (which may or may not be adjusted for risk). Two variations of this technique are available.

The first technique is considered to be most appropriate when future cash flows are fixed or contractual in amount, per ASC 820-10:

> **55-10** The **discount rate adjustment technique** uses a single set of cash flows from the range of possible estimated amounts, whether contractual or promised (as is the case for a bond) or most likely cash flows . . . The discount rate used in the discount rate adjustment technique is derived from observed rates of return for comparable assets or liabilities that are traded in the market . . . [Emphasis added]

The following example illustrates use of an income approach and, specifically, use of the discount rate adjustment technique, for measuring fair value.

Measuring Fair Value Using an Income Approach

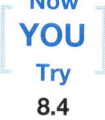

Facts: Assume that Herbert Financial, LLC has just announced its commitment to donate $1 million to its local Chamber of Commerce, in 2 years.

Herbert has concluded that:

- This promise to give is not an actively-traded contract. Rather, it is a unique contract between two parties (donor and recipient). Therefore, no quoted price is available in an active (or inactive) market for identical or similar contracts.

- Therefore, use of an income approach (such as a present value technique) is appropriate.

Given that Herbert's future cash flows are fixed in amount, Herbert has determined that use of the discount rate adjustment technique is appropriate for measuring present value. Under this technique, Herbert will use its contractual cash flows, and will discount these cash flows using an observable, market rate for comparable company liabilities.

Herbert observes the interest rates offered on 2-year corporate bonds, of companies with a credit rating similar to its own (assume a BB rating), and notes that these rates approximate 10%. Accordingly, Herbert concludes that a 10% discount rate is appropriate for the measurement of its contribution liability.

Herbert computes the present value of its liability as follows:

Year	Contractual Cash Flow	Risk-Adjusted Discount Rate	Present Value
2	$1 million	10%	$826,446*

*Present value = Future value / $(1 + \text{interest})^{\text{time}}$. That is, PV= $1M / (1.1^2)

Questions:

1. What browse path did Herbert follow to identify the measurement requirements for contribution liabilities?

   Expenses > Other Expenses (720) > _____ (-25) > _____ (-30)

2. What *measurement attribute* must Herbert use to measure its contribution liability? Cite the guidance supporting your response.

    _____

3. What fair value measurement approach (market or income) did Herbert select, and how (based on ASC 820-10-35-16BB, did Herbert conclude that this was appropriate?

    _____

    _____

    _____

4. Which present value measurement approach (discount rate adjustment, or expected cash flows) did Herbert select, and why?

    _____

    _____

5. Explain what it means for a discount rate to be based on "observed" rates of return.

    _____

    As noted earlier in this chapter, fair value measurements performed on a nonrecurring basis are only subject to fair value disclosure requirements in periods subsequent to initial measurement. So in Herbert's case, this initial measurement at fair value is not required to be included in Herbert's fair value measurement disclosures.

Fixed Assets: Testing for Impairment Using Fair Value

Long-lived assets (excluding those acquired in a business combination) are initially measured at historical cost and are subsequently measured at amortized cost (i.e., cost net of depreciation).

However, in certain circumstances, entities must test the cost basis of long-lived assets (or asset groups) for impairment. The timing of this testing depends upon how the PP&E is classified under **ASC 360** (Property, Plant, & Equipment):

- If PP&E is classified as *held and used*: The cost basis shall be tested for recovery when events or changes in circumstances (i.e., "triggering events") indicate that the carrying amount of the asset or asset group may not be recoverable. Triggering events might include, for example, a significant decrease in the market price for an asset or asset group, or current period operating losses related to operation of an asset or asset group.

- If PP&E is classified as *held for sale*: For every period that an asset is considered "held for sale," entities must compare the asset (or asset group)'s current carrying value to its fair value less costs to sell.

Classification as "held and used" versus "held for sale" depends upon an entity's plans for the asset (e.g., whether the asset is being used in operations, or whether it is available for immediate sale). The model for measuring impairments differs between these two classifications; this discussion will focus only on assets classified as "held and used."

The following two-step test shall be used to determine whether an impairment loss must be recognized for an asset classified as "held and used."[6]

---

[6] ASC 360-10-35-17 (Property, Plant, and Equipment): "An impairment loss shall be recognized only if the carrying amount of a long-lived asset (asset group) is not recoverable and exceeds its fair value. The carrying amount of a long-lived asset (asset group) is not recoverable if it exceeds the sum of the undiscounted cash flows expected to result from the use and eventual disposition of the asset . . . An impairment loss shall be measured as the amount by which the carrying amount of a long-lived asset (asset group) exceeds its fair value."

> **Step 1.** Determine whether the asset's carrying value exceeds the sum of the undiscounted cash flows expected to result from the entity's own use and eventual disposal of the asset.

If carrying value exceeds entity's internal cash flow projections, go to Step 2.

> **Step 2.** Measure an impairment loss for the amount by which the asset's carrying amount exceeds its fair value.

That is, if during an impairment evaluation, an entity concludes that the cost basis of an asset held and used is not recoverable, the asset's carrying value shall be adjusted to fair value. Future depreciation shall be recorded based on this new cost basis.

The following example illustrates an impairment test for PP&E to be held and used.

Testing Property, Plant, and Equipment for Impairment: Step 1

Now
YOU
Try
8.5

Facts: Recall NewTech Corp, the hardware manufacturing company introduced in our opening scenario to this chapter. Let's revisit the valuation of NewTech's equipment, considering the following facts.

Recall that NewTech owns specialized equipment used to produce a hardware component for desktop computers. This equipment, having a carrying value of $10 million at 12/31/20X1, represents NewTech's only major investment in its PC hardware line, and cash flows from the equipment are largely independent of cash flows from NewTech's other assets. Therefore, NewTech has concluded that the equipment, by itself, is the appropriate unit of accounting for this asset. The equipment's estimated useful life is 3 years, and the equipment is expected to have a residual value of $0.5 million at that time.

As noted previously, changes in the business climate for personal computers have caused NewTech to reassess its future cash flow projections associated with the equipment. Specifically, the increasing market share occupied by the tablet computer market has decreased the demand for NewTech's hardware, and has caused NewTech to lower its earnings projections related to sales of its hardware. Given this change in business climate and projected earnings, plant accountants believe it is necessary to test the equipment for impairment.

Questions:

1. Before we continue further into this example, take a moment to brainstorm the browse path you would use, to locate guidance on impairments of PP&E.
    Assets > _____ (ASC _____) > Overall (-10) > _____ (-_____)

2. Also, identify the "triggering event" that caused NewTech to perform this impairment test.

    _____

To perform step 1 of the impairment test, NewTech accountants considered the following guidance from **ASC 360-10**:

> **35-29** Estimates of future cash flows used to test the recoverability of a long-lived asset (asset group) shall include only the future cash flows (cash inflows less associated cash outflows) that are directly associated with and that are expected to arise as a direct result of the use and eventual disposition of the asset . . .
>
> **35-30** Estimates of future cash flows used to test the recoverability of a long-lived asset (asset group) shall incorporate the entity's own assumptions about its use of the asset (asset group) . . .

Notice that the step 1 test does not involve a "fair value" measurement, which would focus on market participant assumptions. Instead, the step 1 test indicates that an entity should use its own, undiscounted assumptions about use of the asset. In this case, NewTech has taken into consideration two alternatives for the asset's use and disposal, and the possible cash flows generated under each alternative.

The following box illustrates "step 1" of NewTech's impairment test.

Step 1 test: Determine whether the asset's carrying value exceeds the undiscounted cash flows expected to arise from use and disposal of the asset.

Carrying value: Expected cash flows (in millions):

$10 million vs.	Scenarios for use/disposal of equipment	Cash flows from use of assets	Cash flows from disposition	Likelihood of realizing these cash flows	Probability-weighted cash flows	Likelihood of selling in 1 year, vs 3 years	Total
	Sell in 1 year . . .	3	6	50% × (3 + 6)	4.5		
		4	6	50%	5.0		
	Total for scenario				9.5	60%	5.7
	Sell in 3 years . .	7.5	0.5	50%	4.0		
		9.5	0.5	50%	5.0		
	Total for scenario				9	40%	3.6
	Expected cash flows (undiscounted)						9.3

---

3. Does carrying value exceed the entity's own total expected cash flow projections? _____

   Therefore, should NewTech go on to step 2 of the impairment test? _____

4. If NewTech sells the equipment in 1 year, what two possible cash flow amounts might it expect to generate from *use* of the asset? _____ or _____.

5. Which scenario (sell in 1 year versus sell in 3 years) results in higher probability-weighted cash flows? Explain.

   _____

6. Does NewTech believe that it is more likely it will sell the equipment in 1 year, or that it will sell the equipment in 3 years? Explain.

   _____

7. Was this "step 1" test intended to determine the fair value of the equipment? Explain.

   _____

Step 2 of the impairment test requires entities to measure an impairment loss for the amount by which the asset's carrying value exceeds its fair value. The following guidance from **ASC 360-10** applies to this test.

Measurement of an Impairment Loss

35-17 . . . An impairment loss shall be measured as the amount by which the carrying amount of a long-lived asset (asset group) exceeds its fair value.

Continued

Fair Value

35-36 For long-lived assets (asset groups) that have uncertainties both in timing and amount, an expected present value technique will often be the appropriate technique with which to estimate fair value.

That is, entities must record an impairment loss for the amount by which an asset's carrying amount exceeds its fair value. The fair value of long-lived assets is frequently measured using an expected present value technique.

ASC 820-10 (Fair Value Measurements) provides the following additional guidance on measuring fair value for nonfinancial assets, which involves consideration of the asset's *highest and best use*.

35-10A "A fair value measurement of a nonfinancial asset takes into account a market participant's ability to generate economic benefits by using the asset in its highest and best use or by selling it to another market participant that would use the asset in its highest and best use." **Highest and best use** is defined as: . . . "the use of an asset by market participants that would maximize the value of the asset . . ."[7]

Finally, ASC 820-10 provides the following present value measurement guidance which can assist in determining the fair value of long-lived assets.

55-5 Present value (that is, an application of the income approach) is a tool used to link future amounts (for example, cash flows or values) to a present amount using a discount rate. A fair value measurement of an asset or a liability using a present value technique captures all of the following elements from the perspective of market participants at the measurement date:
a. An estimate of future cash flows for the asset or liability being measured.
b. Expectations about possible variations in the amount and timing of the cash flows representing the uncertainty inherent in the cash flows.
c. The time value of money, represented by . . . a risk-free interest rate . . .
d. The price for bearing the uncertainty inherent in the cash flows (that is, a risk premium).
e. Other factors that market participants would take into account in the circumstances. . . .[Emphasis added]
55-13 The expected present value technique uses as a starting point a set of cash flows that represents the probability-weighted average of all possible future cash flows (that is, the expected cash flows) . . .
55-15 Method 1 of the expected present value technique adjusts the expected cash flows of an asset for systematic (that is, market) risk . . .
55-16 In contrast, Method 2 of the expected present value technique adjusts for systematic (that is, market) risk by applying a risk premium to the risk-free interest rate . . .

Recall that expected present value is one possible technique for measuring present value (with another possible approach being the "discount rate adjustment technique"). Under an expected present value technique, cash flow scenarios are assigned probabilities, and then discounted.

Companies using an expected present-value technique can choose to "risk-adjust" their cash flow scenarios (Method 1), or can choose to "risk-adjust" the discount rates used to determine the expected present value (Method 2), as described in the preceding guidance excerpt.

Using this information, let's now perform step 2 of NewTech's impairment test.

---

[7] ASC 820-10-20 (Fair Value Measurement, Glossary).

Testing Property, Plant, and Equipment for Impairment: Step 2

Facts: NewTech has reviewed the preceding guidance from **ASC 360-10** and **ASC 820-10** regarding approaches to determining fair value, highest and best use of nonfinancial assets, and present value estimation techniques.

Based on consideration of par. 35-36 of **ASC 360-10**, NewTech believes an *expected present value technique* (an income approach) is appropriate for estimating the fair value of its equipment, given that the timing and amount of future cash flows that will be generated by the equipment is uncertain. NewTech believes an income approach is most appropriate given that it does not have reliable inputs available for estimating fair value under the market or cost approaches.

Additionally, NewTech reviewed the par. 35-10 guidance in **ASC 820-10**, regarding highest and best use of nonfinancial assets, and believes the highest and best use of its equipment would be achieved if a market participant uses the equipment to support an existing line of desktop computers. This could increase the possible applications for the equipment and could increase the potential future cash flows from the equipment. Like NewTech, a market participant would likely realize a residual value of $0.5 million upon disposal of the equipment in 3 years.

Finally, in considering how to apply the expected cash flow approach to estimating present value, NewTech has elected to use Method 2, adjusting its assumed discount rates to reflect market risks. NewTech will estimate these discount rates using the assumed rates that a *market participant* would expect to pay to borrow money.

NewTech has performed step 2 of its impairment test, as follows.

Step 2 test: Measure impairment loss as the amount by which carrying value exceeds fair value.

Carrying value: Expected present value technique (in millions):

$10 million vs.

Year of equipment's life	Possible cash flows from use of equipment	Probability of realizing	Expected cash flows (undiscounted)	Discount rate	Expected present value
Year 1.........	4.0	50%	2.00		
	5.0	50%	2.50		
Total year 1			**4.50**	**10%**	**4.09**
Year 2.........	3.5	50%	1.75		
	4.0	50%	2.00		
Total year 2			**3.75**	**10%**	**3.10**
Year 3.........	3.0*	50%	1.50		
	3.5*	50%	1.75		
Total year 3			**3.25**	**10%**	**2.44**
Total expected present value........					**9.63**

* Includes esimated residual value of $0.5

Questions:

1. An impairment loss _____ (should/ should not) be recognized. The amount of the loss is $_____, which represents the amount by which carrying value exceeds the asset's _____.

2. Explain the significance of the second column in the "expected present value" table (possible cash flows from use of equipment). What does this mean?

_____

3. Why are the cash flows in the step 1 test not discounted, but the cash flows in the step 2 test are? As necessary, look back at guidance on both steps of the test to respond.

_____

4. What is the new carrying value for the equipment, on which depreciation will be calculated?

_____

Debrief—PP&E Impairment Example

In summary, step 1 focused on NewTech's own, undiscounted cash flow projections; the measurement called for in this step is not "fair value," but rather a topic-specific measurement attribute defined in ASC 360, applicable to PP&E impairment tests. Step 2 compared the expected cash flows, discounted, that a market participant would expect to generate from use of the asset, to the asset's carrying value. Step 2 involved a fair value measure, and thus NewTech was required to carefully consider fair value principles in developing this estimate.

Now that you have performed this simplified PP&E impairment test, you should have a general understanding for the process involved. In practice, performing impairment tests can be very complex and can require the involvement of specialists. Companies must take great care to select appropriate assumptions, such as appropriately estimating future cash flows, evaluating the likelihood of various scenarios and vetting those with management, and identifying market-appropriate discount rates, for example.

One assumption that was kept simple in this example was the "unit of account" determination. Determining whether an individual asset, versus an asset group, should be evaluated for impairment can have significant bearing on the results of the impairment test. In this example, the unit of accounting was determined to be a single asset (the specialized equipment). However, if the cash flows of this asset had been viewed as inseparable from the cash flows of other assets, increases in the fair value of other assets could have offset decreases in the fair value of this asset, avoiding the need for an impairment charge.

NewTech should be aware that this impairment will give rise to certain disclosure requirements, including disclosure as a "nonrecurring" fair value measurement in NewTech's current period financial statements. Additional disclosures are also required under ASC 360, including discussion of the facts and circumstances giving rise to the impairment, the amount of loss recorded, and methods for determining fair value.

EXAMPLE OF ITEMS MEASURED AT FAIR VALUE FOR DISCLOSURE ONLY

Recall that ASC 825 (Financial Instruments) requires public and large nonpublic companies to disclose their financial instruments at fair value, whether measured at fair value on the balance sheet or not. Therefore, even an entity's own debt, such as bond issuances recorded at amortized cost, must be disclosed at fair value given that an entity's own debt is a financial liability.

For example, Figure 8-5 illustrates a disclosure from Wells Fargo's third quarter 2012 10-Q filing. Wells Fargo's disclosures state that the table presents the fair value of financial instruments not measured at fair value on a recurring basis, and for which the term is greater than 1 year.

Figure 8-5

Wells Fargo disclosure, "Disclosures about Fair Value of Financial Instruments"

| (in millions) | September 30, 2012 | | | | | December 31, 2011 | |
| | Carrying Amount | Estimated Fair Value | | | | Carrying Amount | Estimated Fair Value |
		Level 1	Level 2	Level 3	Total		
Financial assets							
Cash and due from banks (1)	$ 16,986	16,986	—	—	16,986	19,440	19,440
Federal funds sold, securities purchased under resale agreements and other short-term investments (1)	100,442	3,887	96,555	—	100,442	44,367	44,367
Mortgages held for sale (2).......	3,762	—	2,751	1,075	3,826	3,566	3,566
Loans held for sale (2)..........	126	—	103	29	132	162	176
Loans, net (3)	746,868	—	56,334	698,830	755,164	731,308	723,867
Nonmarketable equity investments (cost method)	8,061	—	4	9,395	9,399	8,061	8,490
Financial liabilities							
Deposits	952,239	—	889,179	64,367	953,546	920,070	921,803
Short-term borrowings (1).......	51,957	—	51,957	—	51,957	49,091	49,091
Long-term debt (4)	130,506	—	122,085	11,461	133,546	125,238	126,484

(1) Amounts consist of financial instruments in which carrying value approximates fair value.

(2) Balance reflects MHFS and LHFS, as applicable, other than those MHFS and LHFS for which election of the fair value option was made.

(3) Loans exclude balances for which the fair value option was elected. Loans exclude lease financing with a carrying amount of $12.3 billion and $13.1 billion at September 30, 2012 and December 31, 2011, respectively.

(4) The carrying amount and fair value exclude balances for which the fair value option was elected and obligations under capital leases of $77 million and $116 million at September 30, 2012 and December 31, 2011, respectively.

Wells Fargo & Company's Report on Form 10-Q for the Quarter Ended September 30, 2012, p.144. © 2012 Wells Fargo & Company. All rights reserved. Used with permission.

This table is accompanied by discussion of the valuation techniques used to measure fair value. For example, Wells Fargo states the following regarding the fair value measurement of its own debt:

LONG-TERM DEBT

Long-term debt is generally carried at amortized cost. For disclosure, we are required to estimate the fair value of long-term debt. Generally, the discounted cash flow method is used to estimate the fair value of our long-term debt. Contractual cash flows are discounted using rates currently offered for new notes with similar remaining maturities and, as such, these discount rates include our current spread levels.

Wells Fargo & Company's Report on Form 10-Q for the Quarter Ended September 30, 2012, p.123. © 2012 Wells Fargo & Company. All rights reserved. Used with permission.

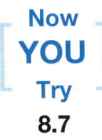

Now **YOU** Try **8.7**

Items Measured at Fair Value for Disclosure Only

Considering the excerpts from Wells Fargo's quarterly report, respond to the following questions.

1. In its valuation technique disclosure, why does Wells Fargo state that it is required to estimate the fair value of its debt?

2. Describe the valuation method used by Wells Fargo to estimate the fair value of its own long-term debt.

_____

3. What level in the fair value hierarchy is predominantly assigned to Wells Fargo's long term debt? Explain, in light of the valuation technique, why this level is appropriate.

_____

CHAPTER SUMMARY

Fair value measurements are unique in that a consistent definition of this measurement attribute is available and must be applied consistently across all topics requiring its use. Not only is fair value clearly defined in the Codification, but **ASC 820** (Fair Value Measurement) provides extensive guidance for applying this definition to different assets and liabilities.

Accordingly, when a topic requires use of a fair value or present value measurement, researchers must consult not only the original topic, but also ASC 820 for key measurement and disclosure guidance.

Fair value measurements may be required on a recurring basis (e.g., quarterly or annually) or on a nonrecurring basis. Entities may also elect the fair value option for certain financial instruments, essentially choosing to report and disclose items at fair value on a recurring basis. Finally, certain financial assets and liabilities are required to be disclosed at fair value, despite the fact that they are recorded in the financial statements using other measurement attributes. Because of the complexity and potential for judgment involved in fair value measurements, extensive disclosure requirements apply to all assets and liabilities measured at fair value.

Applying fair value measurement guidance can be complex and can involve a specialized skill set; while this chapter attempted to introduce certain fair value principles, this is no substitute for actual experience. Consultation with valuation specialists may be necessary, in practice, to ensure that fair value measurements are performed in accordance with the guidance and with industry standards.

REVIEW QUESTIONS

1. Describe three _sources of guidance_ a researcher might consult, when he or she comes across an individual topic requiring the use of fair value.

2. Identify the three approaches available for measuring fair value, and briefly describe each.

3. What is the fair value hierarchy used for? What information (or, specifically, what characteristic) about a measurement does the hierarchy attempt to convey to financial statement users?

4. Identify three ways that changes in fair value might be recorded. For example, if an asset is debited to reflect an increase in its fair value, what are three possible ways the credit might be recorded?

5. Where can researchers find information on present value measurements? Specifically, identify the authoritative and nonauthoritative sources of guidance available.

6. Name two alternative techniques for measuring present value. Which technique generally applies when cash flows are fixed or contractual in amount?

7. Identify three assets or liabilities for which the fair value option may be elected.

8. Where would a researcher find guidance regarding the fair value option?

9. Name one example of a financial asset and one example of a financial liability, and describe how these items meet the definition of financial asset or financial liability.

10. Most debt securities are not quoted on public exchanges. So, how might a financial statement preparer go about valuing a debt security?

11. Explain the difference between step 1 and step 2 of the PP&E impairment test, for assets held and used.

EXERCISES

Identifying Measurement Attributes for Various Assets and Liabilities

1. Using content from this chapter and the previous chapter (on measurement), indicate whether you would expect the following accounts (list loosely based on a prior GE balance sheet) to be (1) measured at fair value, (2) tested for impairment at fair value, or (3) measured on some other basis. Explain.

Assets (selected)	Measurement
Cash and equivalents	
Investment securities	
Current receivables	
Inventories	
Property, plant and equipment	
Investment in GECS (assume is an equity-method investee)	
Goodwill	
Other intangible assets	
Assets of businesses held for sale	

Exercises to Improve Your Familiarity with Guidance in ASC 820   Respond to the following, citing your sources for all responses.

2. Briefly summarize, then explain the significance of, par. 15-1 (scope) of ASC 820-10 (Fair Value Measurement).

3. Briefly summarize par. 30-3 (initial measurement) of ASC 820-10 and provide one example listed in par. 30-3A of an instance when transaction price may not be reflective of fair value.

4. Briefly summarize par. 35-3 (subsequent measurement) of ASC 820-10. Next, look for guidance describing circumstances that might indicate that a transaction is not orderly.

5. Assume that a wealthy investor owns 20% of a single, publicly traded company. In what level of the fair value hierarchy should this measurement be classified, and should the investor adjust the fair value to reflect the fact that its position would be too large to sell in a single day (without negatively impacting the share price)? Such adjustments may be described as "blockage" factors.

6. Locate the present value guidance within Topic 820. What two methods are available for performing the expected cash flow technique, and how do they differ?

7. Identify one disclosure requirement that is unique to level 3 fair value measurements.

Other Fair Value Measurement Research Questions

8. How are trading securities measured, in periods subsequent to initial measurement? How does this differ from how available-for-sale securities are subsequently measured?

9. Refer back to the list of "required reading" areas identified in Chapter 2 of this book. Applying this list to ASC 820, list all areas of "required reading" a researcher should consider when researching fair value measurement questions.

10. Explain when the condition of impairment is considered to exist for goodwill.

11. Can the carrying value of PP&E held for sale ever be "written up" (increased)?

CASE STUDY QUESTIONS

8.1   **Corporate Fair Value Disclosures**   Locate the most recent 10-K filing for a company of your choice. Using this filing, respond to the following, explaining each response:

1. What are some of the company's most significant assets and liabilities that are measured at fair value on a recurring basis?

2. For the #1 most significant (by dollar amount) asset or liability, locate the company's "valuation technique" disclosure. Briefly summarize the company's approach to measuring this item.

3. Next, locate the Codification guidance requiring this (most significant) asset or liability to be measured at fair value. Specifically, please include an excerpt from the exact paragraph requiring the asset or liability to be measured at fair value.

4. What, if any, nonrecurring fair value disclosures did the company disclose? Explain.

5. Locate the company's disclosure of financial assets and liabilities disclosed at fair value, but which are not reported at fair value in the financial statements. Describe the most significant of these assets and liabilities; was the difference between carrying value and fair value significant?

Changes to Financial Instrument Accounting Research the current status of the FASB and IASB's "Financial Instruments" project. Assume you are writing an email to your supervisor, briefing her on this project. What measurement attribute(s) does the project propose (or require) companies to use for financial assets and liabilities, both at initial and subsequent measurement? What is the current status of this project, and when is guidance expected to become effective? How will this project change the current accounting for financial instruments? What might be the reasons for this difference?   **8.2**

Comparing Corporate Fair Value Disclosures Locate the most recent 10-K filings for two companies of your choice, but which are in the same industry. Compare their fair value disclosures. What are some differences between the categories of assets and liabilities the companies measure at fair value on a recurring basis? What are some differences in the hierarchy levels used by these companies? Explain these differences, using a tabular format with footnotes as necessary to summarize and explain differences noted.   **8.3**

For example,

Assets and liabilities included by Company 1 only	Assets and liabilities included by Company 2 only	Assets and liabilities for which different hierarchy levels were used
-List and describe- . . . and so on	-List and describe-	-List and describe-

Chapter 9

Audit and Professional Services Research

You are a new staff member on the audit of Big Box Entertainment, Inc. (Big Box). You have recently befriended a first-year analyst in the controller's group at Big Box, and that individual has invited you to see a movie this weekend. The analyst receives free tickets to Big Box–affiliated theaters and has offered you one of his free tickets. It seems like a silly question, but you start to wonder whether this simple movie invitation could put your professional independence at risk. Erring on the side of caution, you research the audit professional standards and discuss the issue with your supervisor on the engagement.

As a professional, it is important to understand not only *when* audit or ethics research is required, but also to understand *where to find* relevant research. This chapter explores types of research and sources of professional standards for circumstances where an auditor needs guidance regarding his or her own professional conduct.

Learning Objectives

After reading this chapter and performing the exercises herein, you will be able to

1. **Perform** the four steps of the audit research process.

2. **Differentiate** between types of professional services, understanding which services require independence.

3. **Identify** key sources of, and standard setters for, audit and professional services research guidance.

4. **Apply** audit research guidance to sample ethics and independence issues.

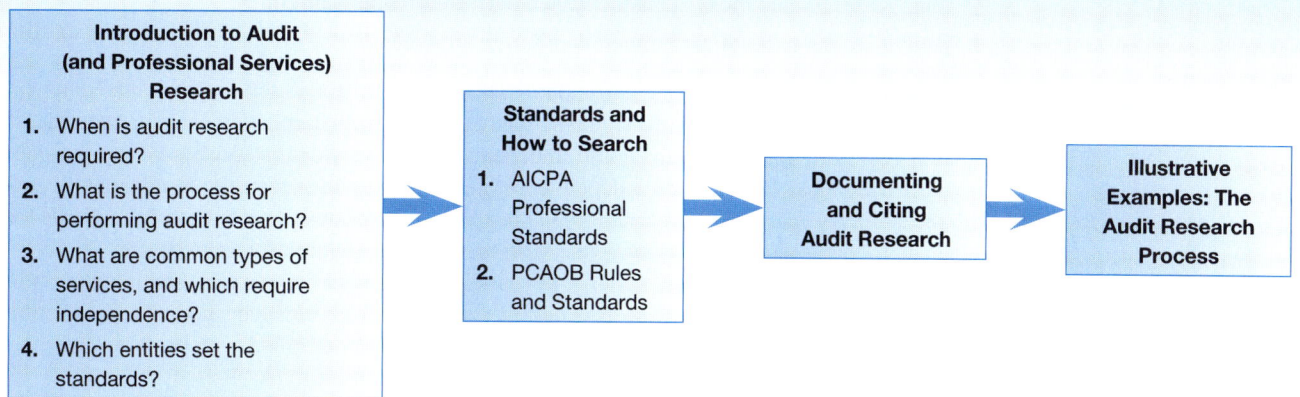

Introduction to Audit (and Professional Services) Research

1. When is audit research required?
2. What is the process for performing audit research?
3. What are common types of services, and which require independence?
4. Which entities set the standards?

Standards and How to Search

1. AICPA Professional Standards
2. PCAOB Rules and Standards

Documenting and Citing Audit Research

Illustrative Examples: The Audit Research Process

Organization of This Chapter

Previous chapters in this book have focused on accounting research; that is, research supporting an entity's financial reporting. By contrast, this chapter provides guidance on **audit and professional services research**, or research related to an accountant's own professional responsibilities and conduct. At times, this chapter collectively refers to professional services research as "audit research."

This chapter begins with an introduction to audit and professional services research, including the research process, differences between types of professional services, and the standard setters with authority for these services (namely, the AICPA and PCAOB).

Following this introduction, the chapter discusses key rules and standards forming the body of professional services guidance. These include the professional services and ethics standards of the AICPA as well as the rules and standards of the PCAOB. We will discuss these sources of guidance in turn, describing how to search these standards and the differing degrees of authority carried by various AICPA and PCAOB standards and publications.

Finally, this chapter concludes by discussing the importance of proper documentation in audit research and by providing examples that apply the research process to sample ethics and independence issues.

The preceding graphic illustrates the organization of content within this chapter.

This chapter focuses on services provided to U.S. public and nonpublic companies. Guidance for services provided to governmental entities is presented in Chapter 10 of this book. Guidance on international auditing standards is provided in the appendix to Chapter 12.

INTRODUCTION TO AUDIT RESEARCH

When Is Audit Research Required?

Both as a CPA exam candidate and as a professional, you will undoubtedly encounter circumstances in which you need guidance regarding your own professional conduct. For example, you could encounter the following issues:

- If I accept gifts from my client, will my independence be impaired?
- If I disagree with my audit supervisor but don't speak up, could I be held accountable?
- What requirements must I consider when performing audit sampling?
- What documentation must be included in my audit files?

Both before and during your participation in any professional services engagement, you should become familiar with professional standards related to that engagement. For example, if you are performing an audit, you should understand the professional standards governing both (1) your own ethical conduct and independence and (2) procedures required to adequately perform the audit. As you perform the audit, you may periodically consult professional standards for guidance on how to comply with evidence, testing, and documentation requirements.

As with accounting research, areas of key risk and judgment may require documentation in the form of a research memo. In professional services research, however, your documentation might focus on whether your audit methodology and approach complied with professional standards for auditors, rather than focusing solely on the application of GAAP.

As a practicing accountant, compliance with professional standards is essential. Consequences for noncompliance can range from PCAOB inspection findings to possible license suspension and/or criminal charges. Take the time now to become familiar with key sources of professional guidance so that you can quickly reference this information when you need it.

The Audit Research Process

The audit, or professional services, research process differs from the accounting research process in that, rather than researching transactions, accountants are researching standards for their own conduct. Accordingly, the audit research process is unique in that accountants must first identify the type of client service being provided and the applicable standard setter, before they are able to identify sources of professional guidance. Figure 9-1 depicts the audit research process.

Figure 9-1

The audit research process

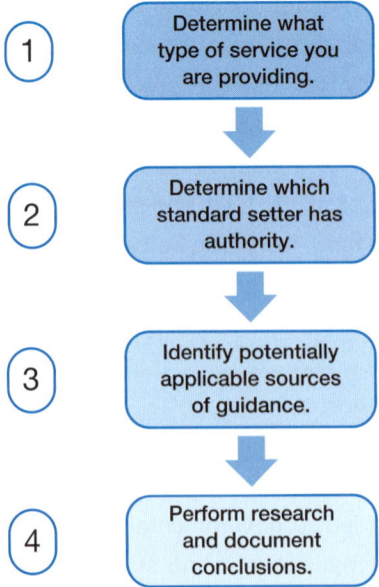

1. Determine what type of service you are providing.

2. Determine which standard setter has authority.

3. Identify potentially applicable sources of guidance.

4. Perform research and document conclusions.

The steps in this process are as follows:

1. Determine the type of service you are providing. For example, does the engagement involve providing a consulting service or an assurance service?
2. Determine which standard setter has authority. This determination depends on the type of service being provided (e.g., consulting or assurance) as well as the type of client being served (public or nonpublic).
3. Identify potentially applicable sources of guidance. In this step, researchers should brainstorm and list out potentially relevant sources of professional services guidance.
4. Perform research and document conclusions. Generally, conclusions are documented within engagement workpapers.

The fourth step of the audit research process involves an effort similar to the process for performing accounting research. That is, researchers must gather relevant facts about the issue, identify a researchable question and keywords, and then—using the list of potentially relevant sources identified in step 3—perform browse and keyword searches of the guidance to find information that is on point. Like the accounting research process, researchers should conclude this process by documenting their analysis of the guidance and describing the basis for conclusions reached.

The next section of this chapter introduces the various types of professional services. Understanding differences between these services will enable researchers to perform the first step of the audit research process.

Types of Services—Assurance versus Consulting

As a professional, you will likely have the opportunity to choose from among a diverse range of client service offerings. Given the extensive education requirements, training, and ethical standards set for CPAs, individuals with this designation are frequently entrusted to independently report on both financial and nonfinancial information.

Understanding the type of client service you are providing is the first step in determining what professional guidance applies. Therefore, let us briefly review several types of professional services generally performed by accountants. We will divide these services into two broad categories: services for which independence is required and services for which independence is not required. These two broad categories are illustrated in Figure 9-2.

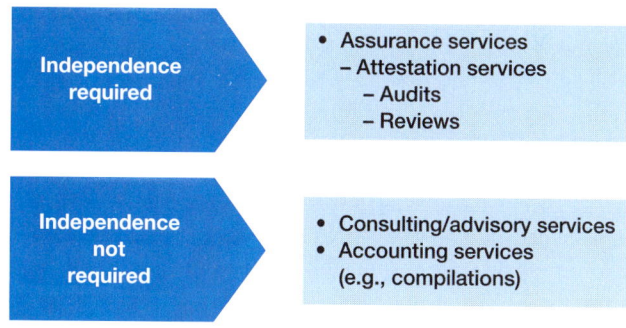

Figure 9-2

Professional services for which independence is/is not required

Independence Required (Assurance, Attestation, and Audit Services)

Let's begin with the broadest category of services for which independence is required: assurance. The AICPA defines **assurance services** as

> independent professional services that improve the quality or context of information for decision makers.[1]

---

[1] "Welcome to Assurance Services." American Institute of Certified Public Accountants, April 6, 2005. Archived copy, retrieved December 27, 2012.

Assurance services generally involve three components:

■ Information or a process that is being evaluated

■ An independent accountant, who evaluates the information or process

■ An information user, who is interested in the accountant's independent evaluation

We introduce the term "assurance service" first, as it is a broad term that encompasses attestation and audit services. The objective of an assurance service is to report on whether information (financial or nonfinancial) is reliable, or whether a process is working effectively. Assurance engagements can be tailored to the needs of the business or information user.

Key to the definition and objectives of an assurance engagement is that the accountant be *independent*, and therefore able to objectively perform the service.

Examples of assurance services include:

■ Performing a financial statement audit

■ Evaluating and reporting on a company's compliance with industry-specific regulations

■ Reviewing and reporting on the security of a company's information systems

■ Reviewing and reporting on the accuracy of management's internal reporting and forecasting

Assurance services can be performed for the benefit of an organization internally (for example, when management wishes to have an independent review of its processes) or externally (for example, for the benefit of regulators, financial statement users, etc.).

Increasingly, accountants are leveraging their role as independent, trusted business advisors to sell additional value-added assurance services. For example, notice how KPMG-UK markets its assurance services to potential clients:

> The financial statement audit can provide invaluable business insight of course. But increasingly, business leaders need and can benefit from assurance that goes beyond the traditional external audit. . . .
>
> As auditors we can apply the same skills, rigour and robust challenge to <u>many areas of your business that can be quantified and measured</u>. We thrive on complexity and seek to give greater peace of mind <u>wherever there are high levels of uncertainty and concern</u>. Importantly, without the right level of assurance, it's difficult to know if your governance and risk management is right. This is as much about helping you to capitalise on new business opportunities, as it is about mitigating risk.[2] [Emphasis added]

The underlined text in the previous quote is indicative of how broadly assurance services may be defined; in this case, KPMG indicates that it may be able to add value to a range of business areas.

An **attestation service** is a type of assurance service in which an accountant reports on the reliability of an *assertion* that is the responsibility of a third party. Often, the accountant will issue a report naming the assertion reviewed and the accountant's conclusions on that assertion. Attestation engagements include, for example, financial statement reviews, agreed-upon

---

[2] "Article reprinted from (Assurance Services www.kpmg.com/uk/en/services/audit/assuranceservices/pages/default.aspx), Copyright: © 2013 KPMG LLP, a UK limited liability partnership, is a subsidiary of KPMG Europe LLP and a member firm of the KPMG network of independent member firms affiliated with KPMG International Cooperative, a Swiss entity. All rights reserved."

"All information provided is of a general nature and is not intended to address the circumstances of any particular individual or entity. Although we endeavor to provide accurate and timely information, there can be no guarantee that such information is accurate as of the date it is received or that it will continue to be accurate in the future. No one should act upon such information without appropriate professional advice after a thorough examination of the facts of a particular situation."

"For additional news and information, please access KPMG's global website on the Internet at http://www.kpmg.com."

procedures (i.e., limited-scope procedures as requested by a client), and reporting on prospective financial information prepared by a client.

Finally, an **audit** is a specific type of attestation service in which an independent accountant provides an *opinion* on management's assertions, issued in the form of a report. Two of the most common audit services performed today are

- ■ Financial statement audits
- ■ Audits of internal controls over financial reporting

The Sarbanes-Oxley Act of 2002 ("the Sarbanes-Oxley Act") requires public company auditors to express an opinion both on the fairness of management's financial statements and on the effectiveness of a company's internal controls over financial reporting (together referred to as an **integrated audit***).*

In summary, assurance services, including attestation and audit engagements, improve the quality of information used in making decisions, both internally (by management) and externally. Maintaining independence is key to an accountant's ability to objectively provide these services.

Independence Not Required (Consulting/Advisory Services, Compilations)

In **consulting** (or "**advisory**") **services**, an accountant or other service provider performs a value-added service for the benefit of management. In contrast to assurance services, where historical information is reviewed, consulting services are often focused on establishing recommendations for future events or processes.

Two parties are generally involved in consulting engagements: the service provider (accountant) and management. Independence is not required for consulting engagements; rather, the accountant acts as a partner to management, identifying possible strategic improvements and best practices for the client.

CPA firms market their consulting services as opportunities for clients to strategically grow their businesses. Figure 9-3 illustrates content adapted from Big Four websites, where each firm emphasizes its ability to add value to its clients.[3]

> ### *"Transform your business"*
> #### *"Grow and innovate"*
> ## *"Uncover insights that create new futures"*
> #### *"Turn strategy into reality"*

Figure 9-3

Big Four firms market their consulting services (adapted website content)

Consulting engagements include, for example,

- ■ Designing a new information system for a client
- ■ Analysis of a potential merger or acquisition
- ■ Litigation support services
- ■ Loaned staff services, for example, where a CPA firm loans one or more members of its staff to a client to perform routine controllership functions

---

[3] (1) "Management Consulting", KPMG. http://www.kpmg.com/Global/en/services/Advisory/management-consulting/Pages/default.aspx: "Successful organizations are using this time to transform their business . . .".
(2) "Consulting", PwC. http://www.pwc.com/us/consulting: "Grow and innovate".
(3) "Consulting", Deloitte. http://www.deloitte.com/view/en_US/us/Services/consulting/index.htm: ". . . we help organizations build value by uncovering insights that create new futures . . ."
(4) "Advisory Services: How we work", Ernst & Young. http://www.ey.com/GL/en/Services/Advisory/About-Advisory-Services: " We help turn strategy into reality."
All accessed on December 27, 2012.

Accountants may also provide other accounting services, such as **compilations**, to non-public clients. In a compilation, an accountant prepares financial statements using information obtained from management, but does not provide any assurance over the information compiled. Additionally, the accountant must generally prepare a compilation report, describing the accountant's role in preparing the financial statements. Independence is not required for compilation engagements; however, a lack of independence must be disclosed in the compilation report.

The Sarbanes-Oxley Act prohibits auditors of public companies from providing specified services to audit clients (such as, for example, certain tax consulting services).[4] By contrast, accountants may provide consulting services to nonpublic audit clients in certain circumstances. However, the AICPA (as the applicable rulemaking body) cautions that CPAs must maintain their objectivity and independence for all matters related to the attestation engagement. Before accepting consulting engagements, CPAs should consider whether providing these services would create a conflict of interest, impairing the CPA's objectivity.[5]

Knowledge Check

1. Name three examples of engagements for which independence is required.
2. Which type of service involves only two parties—the CPA and management?
3. Can firms provide consulting services to their audit clients?

The Standard Setters: The AICPA and the PCAOB

The AICPA and PCAOB are responsible for setting audit and other professional standards for accountants. Figure 9-4 illustrates their authority.

Figure 9-4

Areas of PCAOB versus AICPA authority

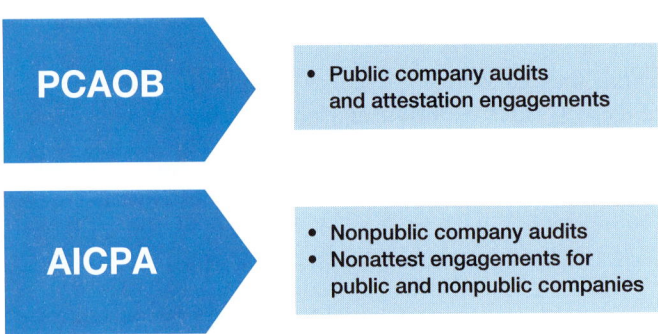

PCAOB
- Public company audits and attestation engagements

AICPA
- Nonpublic company audits
- Nonattest engagements for public and nonpublic companies

The PCAOB is a private entity established under the Sarbanes-Oxley Act, following large-scale public company audit failures. As its name implies, the "Public Company Accounting Oversight Board" (PCAOB's) objective is to oversee accountants providing audit or attest services to public companies, or **issuers**.[6] Prior to creation of the PCAOB, the accounting profession had been largely "self-regulated" (that is, there was no external organization designated to oversee the profession).

Today, accounting firms providing auditing services to issuers must register with the PCAOB, and the PCAOB monitors these **registered public accounting firms**' compliance with PCAOB rules and standards and with applicable securities laws. To that end, the PCAOB is required to perform annual inspections of certain large public accounting firms. The PCAOB has the authority to investigate and impose sanctions on accounting firms and auditors who are suspected of violating professional standards or securities laws.

---

[4] The Sarbanes-Oxley Act of 2002, Title II (Auditor Independence), Sec. 201(g), "Prohibited Activities."

[5] AICPA, Statement on Standards for Consulting Services No. 1, par. 9 and footnote 3.

[6] For simplicity, this book uses the terms public company and issuer interchangeably, and it uses the terms nonpublic company, private company, and nonissuer interchangeably. In practice, slight differences may exist between these definitions.

Like the FASB, the PCAOB is funded through accounting support fees assessed to public companies. The SEC has oversight authority over the PCAOB, including authority to approve the PCAOB's proposed rules, standards, and budget.

> The PCAOB's guidance applies to *accountants providing services* to public companies. However, the PCAOB does not actually regulate *public companies*. Please take note of this difference.

Audits of **nonissuers**, or nonpublic companies, are subject to AICPA guidance. Additionally, AICPA standards apply to nonattestation services provided to both public and nonpublic companies.

Regardless of whether they are subject to AICPA or PCAOB audit standards, all CPAs must comply with the AICPA's Code of Professional Conduct. In addition to complying with PCAOB ethics and independence rules, public company auditors must also comply with certain professional conduct standards issued by the SEC.

Which Standard Setter Has Authority?

If I am auditing a public company (i.e., an "_____"), then I must follow:

- The _____'s audit standards.

- The _____'s Code of Conduct.

- And the _____ and _____'s professional conduct and ethics standards.

> **Now YOU Try 9.1**

Standards Overlap

As our discussion of AICPA and PCAOB standards will further describe, there is significant duplication between the standards available for public company and nonpublic company auditors.

When the PCAOB began operations in 2002, it did not start with a clean slate. Rather, it started by borrowing heavily from the professional standards already in place, most of which were issued by the AICPA.

In the years since its formation, the PCAOB has replaced its "interim" use of certain AICPA standards with its own original PCAOB standards, but continues to use many AICPA standards as interim. At the same time, the AICPA has continued to revise its own standards, in many cases without the PCAOB acknowledging or reflecting these updates on its own website. The bottom line? Our profession must now carefully adhere to these two similar, but increasingly divergent, sets of standards. The overlap between our current professional standards can be confusing for even experienced researchers.

> To ensure that you are using an appropriate source of guidance, always start your research by clearly determining which standard setter has authority: the PCAOB or the AICPA. Then conduct your research by focusing primarily on that standard setter's materials. Do not assume that an auditing standard (i.e., "AU-C") you find on the AICPA's website is the same as the corresponding AU you find on the PCAOB's website.

> **TIP** from the Trenches

The decision tree in Figure 9-5 illustrates the process for identifying the applicable standard setter for an engagement.

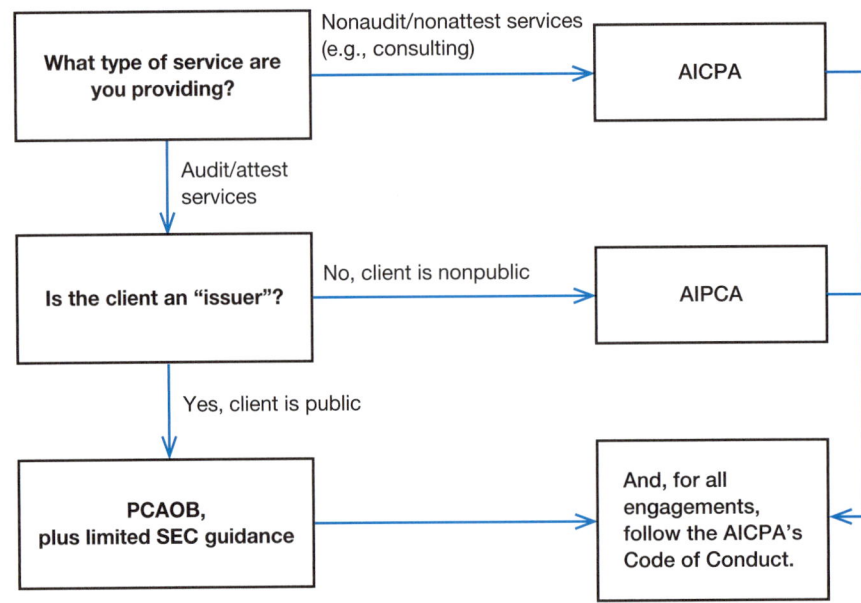

Understanding relevant sources of professional standards will improve both (1) your ability to comply with these professional standards and (2) your efficiency in researching issues as a professional. The next section of this chapter introduces professional standards and other interpretive publications issued by the AICPA.

AICPA PROFESSIONAL STANDARDS

The AICPA refers to its body of professional services guidance as **professional standards.** These include, for example, standards for client service engagements (such as audit and consulting standards) and independence and ethics standards.

We will begin our discussion of the AICPA's professional standards with the Code of Conduct.

Code of Professional Conduct (ET)

The AICPA's **Code of Professional Conduct** (the "Code of Conduct" or the "Code") establishes mandatory ethics requirements applicable to all CPAs, regardless of the type of service being performed or the type of client being served. Individuals who violate provisions of the Code can be sanctioned by the AICPA.

Maintained by the Professional Ethics Executive Committee (PEEC) of the AICPA, the Code is divided into multiple sections, abbreviated "ET" for ethics. Periodically, the PEEC updates the Code as necessary to clarify its provisions or to reflect new ethics interpretations and rulings. For example, in 2013, the Committee revised Ethics Interpretation No. 102-4, *Subordination of Judgment*, to clarify how AICPA members should respond to potential compliance threats. An example illustrating this revised interpretation is provided at the end of this chapter. As changes to the Code are approved and implemented, AICPA members are notified through updates in the AICPA's *Journal of Accountancy*.

Guidance in the Code of Conduct is organized as follows:

- Introduction
- Section 50—Principles of Professional Conduct
- Section 90—Rules: Applicability and Definitions
- Section 100—Independence, Integrity and Objectivity

- Section 200—General Standards Accounting Principles
- Section 300—Responsibilities to Clients
- Section 400—Responsibilities to Colleagues
- Section 500—Other Responsibilities and Practices

The Code's **Principles of Professional Conduct** (ET Section 50) set forth broad expectations regarding a CPA's commitment to ethical behavior. These principles establish a framework for applying the Code's rules. Take a moment to familiarize yourself with these principles, excerpted in Figure 9-6.

Section	Principle
ET Section 52—Article I—Responsibilities	In carrying out their responsibilities as professionals, members should exercise sensitive professional and moral judgments in all their activities.
ET Section 53—Article II—The Public Interest	Members should accept the obligation to act in a way that will serve the public interest, honor the public trust, and demonstrate commitment to professionalism.
ET Section 54—Article III—Integrity	To maintain and broaden public confidence, members should perform all professional responsibilities with the highest sense of integrity.
ET Section 55—Article IV—Objectivity and Independence	A member should maintain objectivity and be free of conflicts of interest in discharging professional responsibilities. A member in public practice should be independent in fact and appearance when providing auditing and other attestation services.
ET Section 56—Article V—Due Care	A member should observe the profession's technical and ethical standards, strive continually to improve competence and the quality of services, and discharge professional responsibility to the best of the member's ability.
ET Section 57—Article VI—Scope and Nature of Services	A member in public practice should observe the Principles of the Code of Professional Conduct in determining the scope and nature of services to be provided.

Figure 9-6

Principles of Professional Conduct, excerpted

Sections 100–500 of the Code of Conduct establish ethics rules, referred to as the **Rules of Conduct**. ET Section 91 requires CPAs to adhere to these rules, as follows:

.01 The bylaws of the AICPA require that members adhere to the rules of the Code of Professional Conduct. Members must be prepared to justify departures from these rules.[7]

Content within Sections 100–500 of the Code is generally organized as shown in Figure 9-7.

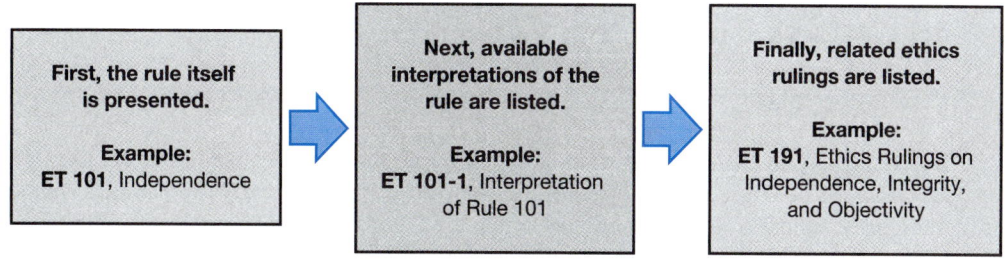

First, the rule itself is presented.

Example:
ET 101, Independence

Next, available interpretations of the rule are listed.

Example:
ET 101-1, Interpretation of Rule 101

Finally, related ethics rulings are listed.

Example:
ET 191, Ethics Rulings on Independence, Integrity, and Objectivity

Figure 9-7

Organization of content within the Code of Conduct

---

[7] AICPA, Code of Professional Conduct (ET) Section 91 (Applicability), par. 1.

Interpretations of the rules (such as ET 101-1) provide detailed guidance for applying specific rules. **Ethics rulings** (such as ET 191) summarize formal ethics cases involving CPA violations of the rules. CPAs should treat interpretations and ethics rulings as integral to fully understanding each rule.

Knowledge ✓ Check

4.   **What source of guidance applies to all CPAs, regardless of client served, and relates to a CPA's own ethical conduct?**
5.   **Describe the role of interpretive guidance and ethics rulings within the AICPA's Code of Conduct.**

EXAMPLE:

Code of Conduct Rules, Interpretations, and Ethics Rulings

The following guidance is excerpted from the Code of Conduct, Section 300, Responsibilities to Clients. Specifically, this example illustrates Rule 301, Confidential Client Information.

■   The *Rule* briefly states the ethics requirement. Per Rule 301, par. 1:

> A member in public practice shall not disclose any confidential client information without the specific consent of the client. (ET 301.01)

■   *Interpretations* illustrate the application of the rule to a specific scenario. In this case, assume that you are researching how to handle client information in the event your CPA firm is being sold to another firm. Per ET 301-3, par. 4 (an interpretation of Rule 301), Confidential information and the purchase, sale, or merger of a practice:

> . . . The member must take appropriate precautions (for example, through a written confidentiality agreement) so that the prospective purchaser does not disclose any information obtained in the course of the review, since such information is deemed to be confidential client information.

■   *Ethics Rulings* provide further interpretive guidance, in the form of Q&As, illustrating application of the rule to a specific scenario. Per Ethics Ruling ET 391.7 (Revealing Names of Clients):

> .013   *Question*—May a member in public practice disclose the name of a client for whom the member or the member's firm performed professional services?

> .014   *Answer*—It is permissible under rule 301 [ET section 301.01] for a member to disclose the name of a client, whether publicly or privately owned, without the client's specific consent unless the disclosure of the client's name constitutes the release of confidential information. For example, if a member's practice is limited to bankruptcy matters, the disclosure of a client's name would suggest that the client may be experiencing financial difficulties, which could be confidential client information.

Take a moment to read Rule 301. Did you notice that the rule does not define *confidential client information*? Rules generally provide very little detail; for this reason, researchers should treat interpretive guidance and ethics rulings within the Code as required reading. The additional information provided by these sources is necessary to appropriately apply each Rule of Conduct.

Understanding and Citing from the Code of Conduct

Now **YOU** Try **9.2**

Answer the following, using the guidance from ET 301, ET 301-3, and ET 391 as applicable.

1. What is one precaution a member might take to protect confidential client information in the event the member's firm is being evaluated by a potential purchaser?

    Per _____, one precaution a member might take is _____

    _____ .

2. Could a researcher have answered question 1 using only the guidance in Rule 301? Or, was interpretive guidance necessary to answer this question? _____

    _____ .

3. Using *Rule 301* from the preceding Code of Conduct illustration, identify two acceptable ways of referencing rules from the Code of Conduct.

    _____ 301, par. 01   _____ 301.___

Note that either of the above citations may be used to reference rules from the Code of Conduct.

Notably, during 2013 the AICPA released a proposal to revise its Code of Conduct, based on a *threats and safeguards* approach. The AICPA anticipates that its proposed changes would facilitate research for its members. Visit www.aicpa.org to learn more about the status of this project.

AICPA Auditing Standards (AU-C)

The AICPA's **auditing standards** provide auditors with guidance on the proper conduct of an audit, from acceptance, to planning, to fieldwork, to preparing documentation and issuing an audit report. The Auditing Standards Board of the AICPA issues **Statements on Auditing Standards** (or "SAS"), which are then organized into sections of the professional standards, referred to as "AU-Cs". Auditing standards issued by the AICPA comprise the body of guidance referred to as **generally accepted auditing standards** (GAAS).

During 2012, the Auditing Standards Board completed a project (the "Clarity Project") to improve existing auditing standards and to converge U.S. auditing standards with International Standards on Auditing (ISAs), issued by the International Auditing and Assurance Standards Board (IAASB). As a result of this project, AU-C numbers now generally correspond to ISAs, wherever a comparable ISA is available. This project replaced all pre-Clarity auditing standards, referred to as AUs.

The AICPA's clarified auditing standards have been codified into sections, as follows:

- AU-C 200—299: General Principles and Responsibilities
- AU-C 300—499: Risk Assessment and Response to Assessed Risks
- AU-C 500—599: Audit Evidence
- AU-C 600—699: Using the Work of Others
- AU-C 700—799: Audit Conclusions and Reporting
- AU-C 800—899: Special Considerations
- AU-C 900—999: Special Considerations in the United States

Each section of the auditing standards (i.e., each "AU-C") is further organized as follows:

- Introduction: Describes the purpose, scope, and effective date of the section.

- Objective: Provides context for the requirements, establishes a framework for auditor judgment.
- Definitions: Defines key terms used within the section.
- Requirements: Sets forth the requirements of the standard and expectations for auditors.
- Application and Explanatory Material: Provides examples and other explanatory information necessary for applying guidance requirements. Also includes special considerations, such as applying the guidance to small company audits and government audits.

Let's discuss a few of these areas in more detail: objectives, requirements, and application material.

Having *objectives* in audit standards provides auditors with an overall context for the requirements of the standard. Knowing what's trying to be achieved by the rules can help auditors exercise judgment, as necessary, in applying the requirements of a standard. In some cases, an auditor may conclude that procedures *beyond* those required by a standard are necessary to achieve the standard's objectives.[8]

[TIP] from the Trenches

As a CPA, you are expected to rely frequently on your own professional judgment. Each auditing standard now includes a section for Objectives; this section is intended to provide auditors with a framework for exercising good professional judgment.

Within the *requirements* of audit standards, auditors should understand the meaning of two terms, in particular:

- **Must**: The auditor must follow the guidance without departure.
- **Should**: Auditor must comply or, in rare circumstances, may depart from the requirement by performing alternate procedures that achieve the intent of the requirement, provided the auditor documents the justification for departure.

These terms are also described within audit standards as "unconditional" and "presumptively mandatory" requirements, respectively.

Finally, remember how we referred to Implementation Guidance (Section **55** in the FASB Codification) as "required reading"? A similar rule holds true for the *application and explanatory material* within auditing standards: auditors should view these sections as required reading. According to AU-C 200 (Overall Objectives of the Independent Auditor):

> .21 The auditor should have an understanding of the entire text of an AU-C section, including its application and other explanatory material, to understand its objectives and to apply its requirements properly.
>
> .22 The auditor should not represent compliance with GAAS in the auditor's report unless the auditor has complied with the requirements of this section and all other AU-C sections relevant to the audit.

That is, AU-C 200 (par. .21–.22) states that the application and explanatory sections of AU guidance are considered integral to understanding a standard. Furthermore, only auditors who comply fully with AU-C guidance, including application guidance, may state in the audit report, "We conducted our audit in accordance with auditing standards generally accepted in the United States of America."

---

[8] AICPA, AU-C Section 200, *Overall Objectives of the Independent Auditor and the Conduct of an Audit in Accordance With Generally Accepted Auditing Standards.* Par. .23(a).

AICPA Attestation Standards (AT)

Next, let's briefly introduce another source of client service guidance issued by the AICPA: attestation standards. The AICPA's **Statements on Standards for Attestation Engagements** (SSAEs), organized into sections referred to as "ATs," provide guidance on attestation services provided to nonpublic companies. Attestation standards, notably, do not apply to certain attest engagements that are covered by other guidance, such as financial statement audits and reviews.

CPAs performing attest engagements are expected to conduct their engagements in accordance with these standards. Attestation standards include, for example,

- Guidance for performing agreed-upon procedures engagements (AT 201)
- Guidance for performing reviews of pro-forma financial information (AT 401)
- Guidance for performing examinations of internal controls that are integrated with an audit of the financial statements (AT 501)

Interpretive guidance is available for certain of the attestation standards; this interpretive guidance often applies only narrowly, to specified industries or circumstances. For example, AT 501 (Examinations of Internal Controls) is interpreted by AT 9501, which addresses the application of AT 501 to insured depository institutions (e.g., banks). Accountants providing attestation services should always check interpretive guidance, when available, to determine whether it applies to their engagement.

During 2013, the Auditing Standards Board of the AICPA proposed changes to its attestation standards as part of its Clarity project. Among the proposed changes, current attestation standards would be reorganized (in a manner similar to the organization of AU-Cs) and renumbered. Visit www.aicpa.org to learn more about the status of this project.

Compilation and Review Standards (SSARS)

Issued by the AICPA's Accounting and Review Services Committee, **Statements on Standards for Accounting and Review Services (SSARSs)** cover compilation and review services provided to nonissuers. These standards are codified in the professional standards as "AR" sections.

Accountants providing compilation and review services should become familiar with the requirements in AR Section 60, *Framework for Performing and Reporting on Compilation and Review Engagements*. As its name implies, this standard provides a framework (that is, overall instructions) for accountants performing compilation or review services. For example, AR 60 describes differences between compilation and review services and sets forth reporting requirements for accountants performing these engagements.

Other Sources of AICPA Guidance

Other Professional Standards

In addition to the standards described above, the AICPA's professional standards also include:

- Consulting services standards—Statement on Standards for Consulting Services (SSCS)
- Quality control standards—Statements on Quality Control Standards (SQCSs)
- Peer review standards—Standards for Performing & Reporting on Peer Reviews (PRP)
- Tax standards—Statements on Standards for Tax Services (SSTSs)
- Valuation services standards—Statements on Standards for Valuation Services (SSVS)

As you can see from the above list, these standards cover client services (such as consulting and tax services) as well as guidance on firms' internal quality control procedures. Tax standards (SSTSs) are described in Chapter 11 of this book.

Interpretive Publications

The AICPA issues a number of **interpretive publications**, which accountants are expected to consider in addition to professional standards. Following are the AICPA's four interpretive publications for audits:

- Auditing interpretations of GAAS

- Exhibits to GAAS

- Auditing guidance included in AICPA Audit and Accounting Guides

- AICPA Auditing Statements of Position (SOP)[9]

The term "interpretive publications" carries a certain level of authority, as explained by AU-C Section 200:

> Interpretive publications are recommendations on the application of GAAS in specific circumstances, including engagements for entities in specialized industries. An interpretive publication is issued under the authority of the ASB after all ASB members have been provided an opportunity to consider and comment on whether the proposed interpretive publication is consistent with GAAS. (par. .A81)

As noted in this excerpt, interpretive publications are reviewed by the Auditing Standards Board; this is the same body that creates the AICPA's auditing standards. Accordingly, interpretive publications are not as authoritative as the actual audit standards issued by that body, but they are more authoritative than other publications (such as journal articles).

AU-C Section 200 (Overall Objectives of the Independent Auditor) states that an auditor "should consider applicable interpretive publications in planning and performing the audit" (par. 27).

Notice the use of the term *should*, which indicates a presumptively mandatory requirement. Auditors should consider interpretive publications in addition to complying with audit standards.

Following is additional guidance on each of the audit interpretive publications.

1. Auditing Interpretations of GAAS

Interpretations are available for certain audit standards and often apply only narrowly, to specified industries or circumstances. When researching an audit standard, the auditor should take a moment to consider whether an interpretation is available for that standard and, if so, whether the interpretation is relevant to the engagement.

For example, AU-C 500 (Audit Evidence) is interpreted by AU-C 9500, which addresses "The Effect of an Inability to Obtain Audit Evidence Relating to Income Tax Accruals."

2. Exhibits to GAAS

Certain AU-C guidance contains exhibits, which are intended to illustrate or emphasize key points from the guidance. For example, AU-C Section 580 (Written Representations) is accompanied by several exhibits illustrating sample management representation letters and schedules.

Exhibits to GAAS are easily located, generally at the end of the related audit standard.

3. AICPA Audit and Accounting Guides

The AICPA's Audit and Accounting Guides (A&A Guides) provide detailed, practical guidance on a range of topics. These topics include, for example, how to perform certain audit procedures, and how to audit certain industries. Following are examples of A&A Guides:

- Audit & Accounting Guide, *Health Care Entities*

- Audit & Accounting Guide, *Airlines*

- Audit Guide, *Analytical Procedures*

- Audit Guide, *Audit Sampling*

---

[9] AU-C 200, par. 14 (Definitions). Definition of "interpretive publications."

4. Auditing Statements of Position

The AICPA's Auditing Statements of Position (SOPs) are also intended to provide additional guidance on certain areas related to audit procedures and industries. Auditing SOPs can be found within the AICPA's *Technical Practice Aids* publication. This publication also includes extensive Q&As regarding audit and attestation services, as well as select PCAOB staff Q&As.

Note that the AICPA's use of the term *interpretive publications* is not limited to audit guidance. For example, AR Section 60 (Framework for Compilations and Reviews) requires accountants providing compilation and review services to consider interpretive publications for these services. Interpretive publications for compilations and reviews are defined as (1) compilation and review interpretations of SSARSs; (2) appendixes to SSARSs; (3) compilation and review guidance included in A&A Guides; and (4) AICPA Statements of Position, where applicable to compilation and review engagements.[10] Again, only these four resources carry the authority of "interpretive" publications.

Other Publications

The AICPA issues publications for a wide range of service offerings and industries. Described within the professional standards as "other resources," these publications do not have the same authority as professional standards or interpretive publications, but can be helpful to an accountant's understanding of professional standards.

AICPA publications include, for example,[11]

- The *Journal of Accountancy*, which includes articles on a range of services;
- The AICPA's The *CPA Letter* publication;
- The AICPA's annual *Compilation and Review Alert*; and
- The AICPA Guide, *Compilation and Review Engagements*.

These, along with resources issued by groups outside of the AICPA (such as firm auditing guides, audit programs, or checklists) may be helpful to professionals, but compliance with these publications is not required by the AICPA.

Summary

Accountants should generally prioritize the AICPA's sources of professional guidance as depicted in Figure 9-8:

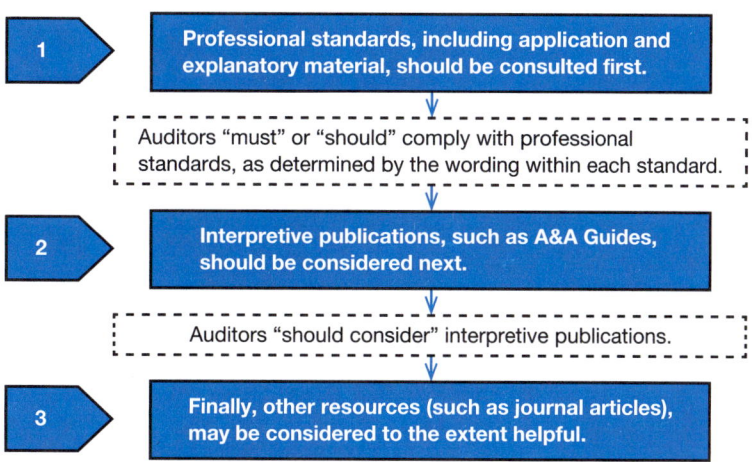

Figure 9-8
Priority of AICPA guidance sources

---

[10] AICPA, AR Section 60, *Framework for Performing and Reporting on Compilation and Review Engagements.* Par. .18, "Interpretive Publications."

[11] AICPA, AR Section 60, par. 20, "Other Compilation and Review Publications."

Clearly, accountants should carefully comply with the hierarchy of professional services guidance above. But accountants should also know that their best safeguard against the risk of professional errors is to arm themselves with knowledge. Read the *Journal of Accountancy* regularly, as well as firm publications describing issues relevant to the profession. Awareness of current, or high-risk issues will make you better prepared to identify and manage areas of risk.

Knowledge ✓
Check

6. **Describe the "hierarchy" of professional guidance sources issued by the AICPA. Which are mandatory, and which are simply considered "helpful"?**

7. **Which type of standard should an accountant apply, if he or she is performing a financial statement review for a client? Also, what specific standard number provides a framework for performing review engagements?**

How Do I Search AICPA Guidance?

Using Research Databases

Individuals with access to subscription research databases (for example, Deloitte's *Technical Library*, or KPMG's *Accounting Research Online*) can perform keyword searches of, or can browse directly to, AICPA guidance within these tools. Trial subscriptions are frequently available to researchers interested in trying out these databases. These search options are similar to how a researcher would find Codification or firm guidance within these research tools.

Figure 9-9 illustrates a search, using Deloitte's *Technical Library*, for the keyword "documentation." Notice how the researcher has specified the AICPA guidance fields in which to search for the term.

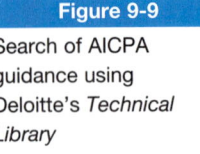

Figure 9-9

Search of AICPA guidance using Deloitte's *Technical Library*

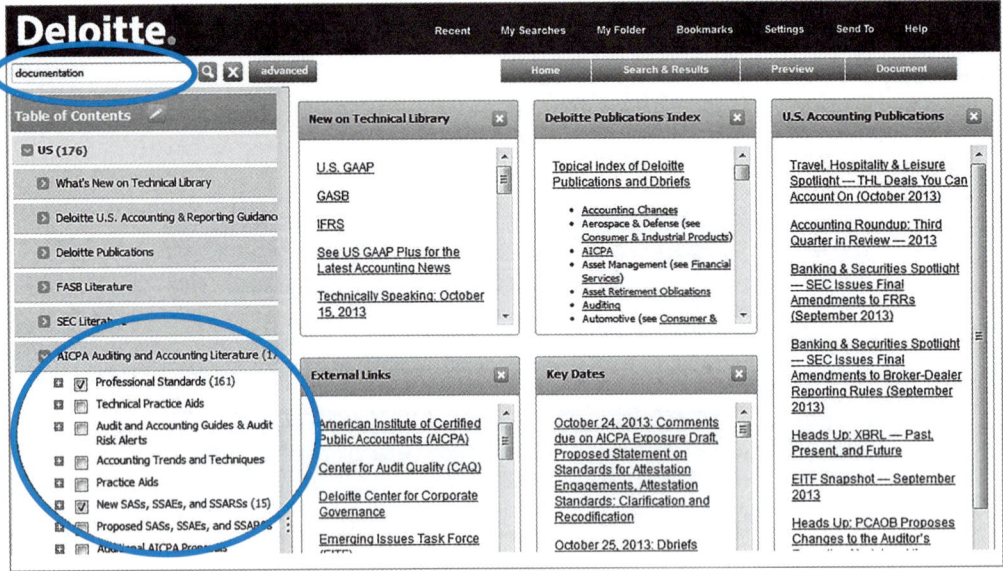

---

[12] See Ch. 4, fn [10].

Using the AICPA Website

Researchers without access to firm research databases can search for literature using the AICPA's website: www.aicpa.org. Searches can generally be performed in one of two ways:

- By searching for a term from the homepage. Figure 9-10 illustrates a search for the term "independence" within the "Research" area of the AICPA's website.

- Or, by browsing to the AICPA's standards and performing a keyword search on the standards page. Notice in Figure 9-10 that researchers can access the "Standards" page under the tab "Research."

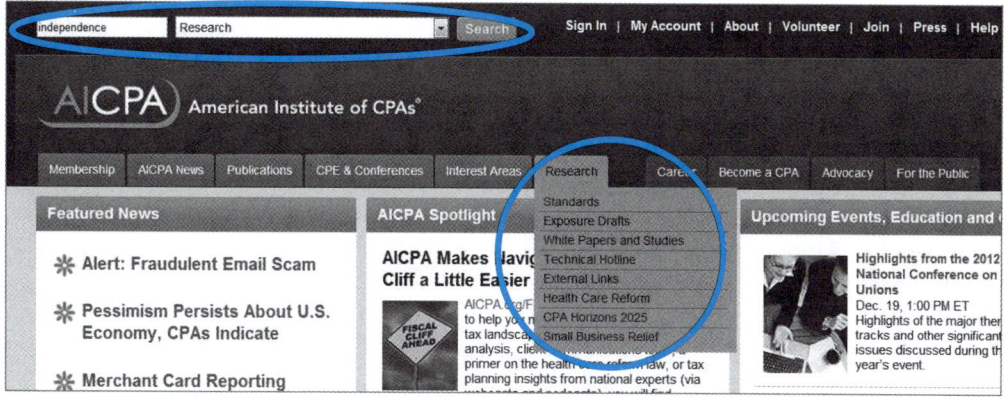

Figure 9-10

Performing searches using the AICPA's website

Copyright AICPA; Used with permission.

Once on the Standards page, researchers can browse to the appropriate type of standard (e.g., audit standards, peer review standards). The Standards page is illustrated in Figure 9-11.

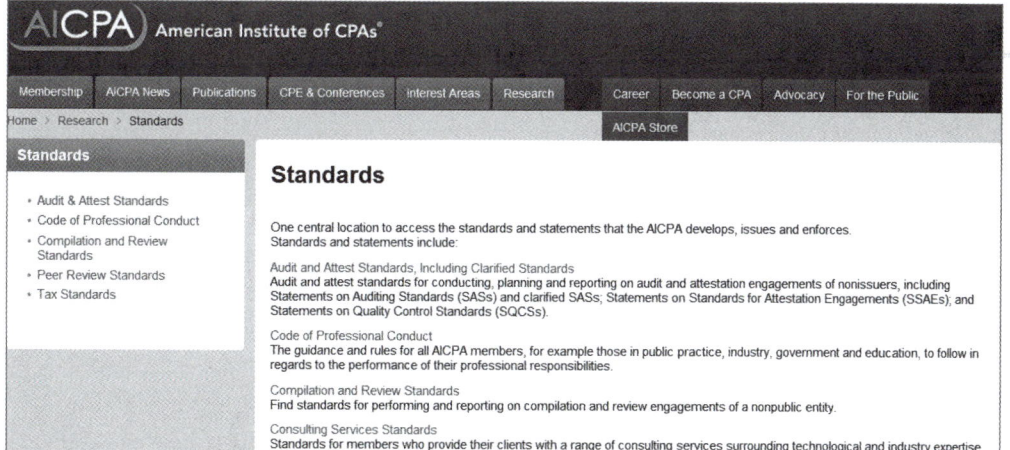

Figure 9-11

The AICPA's "Standards" page, where researchers can browse to various AICPA standards

Copyright AICPA; Used with permission.

Next, researchers can search for the appropriate standard by searching the page by keyword. For example, a "ctrl + f" (i.e., "find") search on the page for relevant keywords allows researchers to jump to relevant standards. Figure 9-12 illustrates a keyword search, within audit standards, for the term "documentation." The first search result is SAS No. 122, or AU-C Section 230, *Audit Documentation*.

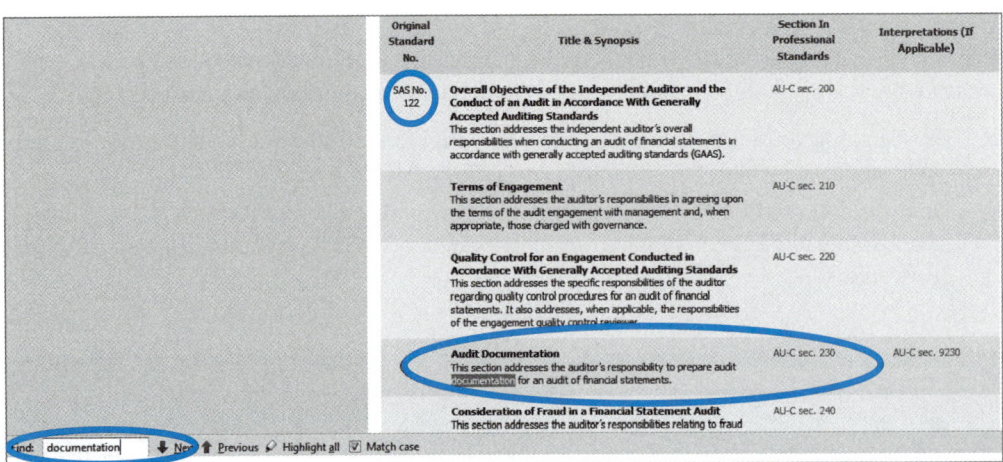

Copyright AICPA; Used with permission.

Now that you have a general understanding of AICPA guidance sources and search methods, let us turn to the rules and standards of the PCAOB.

PCAOB RULES AND STANDARDS

Why Does the PCAOB Issue Auditing Standards?

Before we discuss specifics about the PCAOB's rules and standards, it is helpful first to understand the context in which these standards are, and have been, issued. First, the PCAOB was mandated by the Sarbanes-Oxley Act to issue auditing, quality control, and ethics and independence rules and standards,[13] because the public generally believed that our profession had failed at regulating itself. Within these standards, the PCAOB was instructed to provide guidance on certain specific matters, as discussed further below. Second, one of the PCAOB's objectives in issuing standards is to facilitate their own inspections and enforcement activities. Unlike accounting standards, where the standard setter (the FASB) differs from the enforcer/regulator (the SEC), the PCAOB has authority to issue the standards that it also enforces.

Let us discuss each of these points in a little more detail.

First, the PCAOB issues auditing standards for registered public accounting firms, because the Sarbanes-Oxley Act directed it to do so. Under Sarbanes-Oxley, the PCAOB was given the option to, at its discretion (1) issue its own original rules and standards or (2) to the extent deemed satisfactory by the PCAOB, adopt for its own use standards issued by other organizations. In all cases, standards issued by the PCAOB are subject first to SEC approval.

Sarbanes-Oxley required the PCAOB's standards to include certain new requirements for public company auditors. These requirements include:

- Auditors must describe their testing of internal controls, within the financial statement audit report.

- Firms must subject all audit reports to a concurring or second partner review and approval.

- Auditors must maintain workpapers for a period of at least 7 years following an audit.[14]

In 2003, less than a year after the PCAOB was established, the Board voted to adopt certain AICPA audit standards for use as its own interim guidance. Since that time, the PCAOB has replaced certain of these standards with its own guidance, including standards that address the requirements outlined above.

---

[13] Sarbanes-Oxley Act, Sec. 103. "Auditing, Quality Control, and Independence Standards and Rules." Par. (a)(1), and par. (b)(1).

[14] Sarbanes-Oxley Act, SEC. 103. Par. (a)(2)(A)(i–iii).

Second, issuing audit standards and rules facilitates the PCAOB's inspections and enforcement activities. The PCAOB views its standard-setting activities as essential to establishing clear expectations for its annual inspections of registered accounting firms and, when necessary, enforcement actions.

The PCAOB refers to its body of rules and standards (including its interim use of AICPA guidance) collectively as **the standards of the Public Company Accounting Oversight Board (United States)**. In preparing audit reports of issuers, auditors may not refer to PCAOB guidance as "generally accepted auditing standards." Instead, audit reports of issuers must now state:

> We conducted our audits in accordance with the standards of the Public Company Accounting Oversight Board (United States).[15]

The PCAOB anticipates that its standards will continue to evolve as necessary to meet the needs of our changing profession. James R. Doty, appointed to the PCAOB as chairman in 2011, stated the following in a conference before members of the accounting profession:

> We don't rewrite standards just for the sake of change. Since its earliest days, the PCAOB has endeavored to develop instructive standards that comprise the real intellectual content of what auditors do. The standards ought to be a living set of principles that a learned profession can believe in and resort to for support.[16]

Chapter 13 of this book describes steps that accountants can take in order to stay current with the changing body of accounting and auditing standards.

The following sections of this chapter introduce the rules and standards of the PCAOB, including the PCAOB's interim use of AICPA guidance.

PCAOB Rules of the Board

The PCAOB's **Rules of the Board** serve a somewhat hybrid purpose; they both (1) govern the PCAOB's conduct as an organization and (2) establish certain standards for auditor conduct. For example, the rules establish the frequency of the Board's required inspections of registered accounting firms, while also requiring members of registered firms to maintain independence from audit clients.

The Rules of the Board are organized as follows:

- Section 1: General Provisions (including definitions, such as "issuer")
- Section 2: Registration and Reporting
- Section 3: Professional Standards
- Section 4: Inspections (conducted by the PCAOB, of registered public accounting firms)
- Section 5: Investigations and Adjudications
- Section 6: International
- Section 7: Funding (of the PCAOB)

Using the titles of Sections 1–7, take a moment to complete the **Now YOU Try** exercise below, intended to familiarize you with content from the PCAOB rules. These section titles should be sufficiently descriptive to allow you to complete this exercise.

[15] PCAOB Auditing Standard No. 1, *References in Auditors' Reports to the Standards of the Public Company Accounting Oversight Board*. Appendix: Illustrative Reports.

[16] James R. Doty, PCAOB Chairman. AICPA National Conference on Current SEC and PCAOB Developments. Keynote address. December 3, 2012.

Locating Information within the PCAOB's Rules

Provide the section number and title (from the PCAOB's Rules of the Board) that you would consult for guidance on the following issues.

1. Does the receipt of "contingent fees" impair an auditor's independence?

    Section No. _____: _____ (title of section)

2. Would providing tax advice to an audit client impair an auditor's independence?

    Section No. _____: _____

3. Under what circumstances is a public accounting firm required to register with the PCAOB?

    Section No. _____: _____

4. How are accounting support fees (the PCAOB's funding mechanism) allocated among public companies?

    Section No. _____: _____

5. What disciplinary sanctions might a registered firm face, if it is found to be in violation of PCAOB rules?

    Section No. _____: _____

6. How frequently does the PCAOB conduct inspections of registered public accounting firms?

    Section No. _____: _____

As an auditor, you may find yourself referring most often to Section 3 (Professional Standards) of the PCAOB's rules. Certain content from this section (specifically, rules numbered 35xx) forms the body of the PCAOB's **ethics and independence standards**. Section 3 includes, for example, Rule 3520, "Auditor Independence":

> A registered public accounting firm and its associated persons must be independent of the firm's audit client throughout the audit and professional engagement period.

In addition, Section 3's professional standards include Rule 3101, "Certain Terms Used in Auditing and Related Professional Practice Standards." This rule defines the following terms used within PCAOB standards:

(1) **Unconditional Responsibility**: The words "must," "shall," and "is required" indicate unconditional responsibilities. The auditor must fulfill responsibilities of this type in all cases in which the circumstances exist to which the requirement applies. Failure to discharge an unconditional responsibility is a violation of the relevant standard and Rule 3100.

(2) **Presumptively Mandatory Responsibility**: The word "should" indicates responsibilities that are presumptively mandatory. The auditor must comply with requirements of this type specified in the Board's standards unless the auditor demonstrates that alternative actions he or she followed in the circumstances were sufficient to achieve the objectives of the standard. Failure to discharge a presumptively mandatory responsibility is a violation of the relevant standard and Rule 3100 unless the auditor

Continued

demonstrates that, in the circumstances, compliance with the specified responsibility was not necessary to achieve the objectives of the standard.

Note: In the rare circumstances in which the auditor believes the objectives of the standard can be met by alternative means, the auditor, as part of documenting the planning and performance of the work, must document the information that demonstrates that the objectives were achieved.

(3) **Responsibility To Consider**: The words "may," "might," "could," and other terms and phrases describe actions and procedures that auditors have a responsibility to consider. Matters described in this fashion require the auditor's attention and understanding. How and whether the auditor implements these matters in the audit will depend on the exercise of professional judgment in the circumstances consistent with the objectives of the standard. [Bold emphasis added]

These terms from Rule 3101 might call to mind the "must" and "should" requirements introduced in AICPA standard AU-C 200. Take a moment now to flip back to those AICPA definitions, then complete the following exercise.

Must and Should Requirements

Now
YOU
Try
9.4

1. Both the PCAOB and AICPA state that *unconditional* responsibilities can be indicated by the word: _____.

   The PCAOB's definition states that unconditional responsibilities can *also* be indicated by the terms: _____ and _____.

2. Both the PCAOB and AICPA state that *presumptively mandatory* responsibilities can be indicated by the word: _____.

3. Unlike the AICPA definition, the PCAOB definition includes *consequences* for auditors of noncompliance with unconditional and presumptively mandatory responsibilities. Complete the following statement using the definition of "unconditional responsibility":

   Failure to discharge an unconditional responsibility _____

   _____ .

4. Which of the three types of responsibility is unique to the PCAOB? What words indicate this type of responsibility?

   Responsibility unique to PCAOB: _____

   Words that indicate this responsibility: _____

Recall that these terms from Rule 3101 describe an auditor's responsibility to comply with PCAOB audit standards. Let's discuss these audit standards next.

PCAOB Auditing Standards, and Interim Use of AICPA Auditing Standards

Auditors subject to the PCAOB's authority must use a combination of both

- The PCAOB's own **auditing standards** (abbreviated "AS") and
- Certain AICPA guidance (AU) adopted as interim by the PCAOB.

As the PCAOB issues its own standards, it generally discontinues its interim use of related AICPA guidance. For example, upon issuing AS 3, *Audit Documentation*, the PCAOB discontinued its interim use of SAS 96, the AICPA's original audit documentation standard. (The AICPA has also since replaced its own use of this guidance). With the issuance of AS 3, the PCAOB met one of Sarbanes-Oxley's directives—to issue requirements for audit workpaper retention.[17]

The PCAOB lists its own audit standards, as well as interim AICPA guidance, together on its website (see Figure 9-13).

The PCAOB has not adopted the changes effected by the AICPA's Clarity Project and, therefore, does not use the AU-C standards currently in use by the AICPA. Rather, in 2013 the PCAOB began a project intended to reorganize its existing interim and PCAOB-issued standards into the following categories:

- General auditing standards
- Audit procedures
- Auditor reporting
- Matters related to filings under federal securities laws
- Other matters associated with audits

This reorganization, once complete, would not be expected to result in changes to the content of existing standards.

Figure 9-13

PCAOB standards and interim standards are listed together on the PCAOB's website

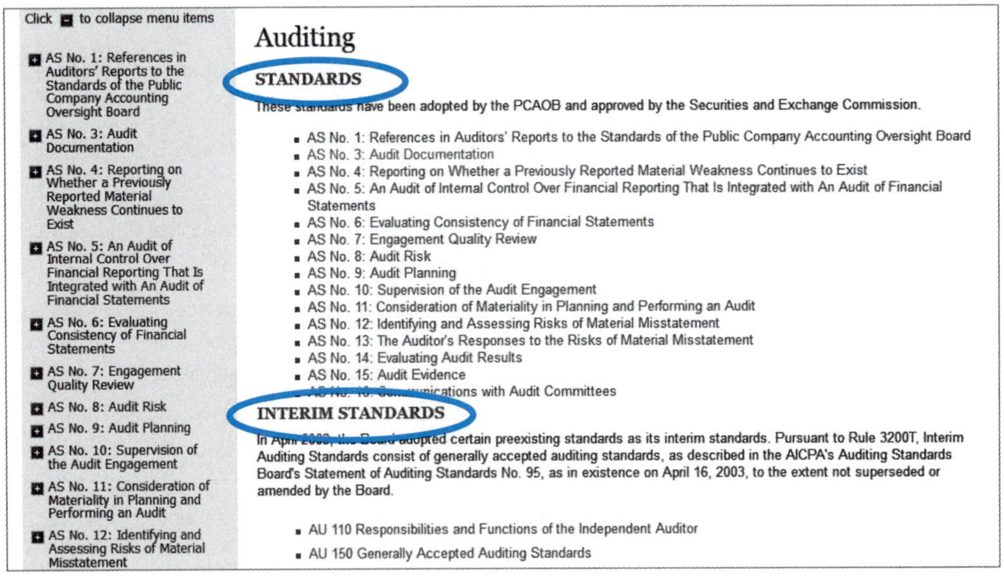

© PCAOB. Used with permission.

Researchers navigating to individual PCAOB standards will see that a summary table of contents is provided at the beginning of each standard. Figure 9-14 illustrates the summary table of contents for AS 5 (Integrated Audits[18]). Using links within the table of contents, researchers can quickly navigate to the content most relevant to their research. Or, when reviewing a standard for the first time, researchers may find it most valuable to first read the standard's Introduction.

---

[17] PCAOB Auditing Standard No. 3, *Audit Documentation* (AS 3). Par. 14.

[18] PCAOB Auditing Standard No. 5, *An Audit of Internal Control Over Financial Reporting That Is Integrated with an Audit of Financial Statements.*

<table>
<tr><td>

Auditing Standard No. 5

An Audit of Internal Control Over Financial Reporting That Is Integrated with An Audit of Financial Statements

Supersedes Auditing Standard No. 2

Effective Date: Fiscal years ending on or after November 15, 2007

Final Rule: PCAOB Release No. 2007-005A

SUMMARY TABLE OF CONTENTS
(1 - 8) Introduction
(9 - 20) Planning the Audit
(21 - 41) Using a Top-Down Approach
(42 - 61) Testing Controls
(62 - 70) Evaluating Identified Deficiencies
(71 - 84) Wrapping-Up
(85 - 98) Reporting on Internal Control
Appendix A Definitions
Appendix B Special Topics
Appendix C Special Reporting Situations

</td><td>

Figure 9-14

Summary table of contents for PCAOB's AS 5 (Integrated Audits)

</td></tr>
</table>

© PCAOB. Used with permission.

Also as shown in Figure 9-14, certain PCAOB standards are accompanied by appendices, which often contain illustrative examples and the standard setter's basis for conclusions. Appendices can provide researchers with valuable context for understanding the guidance.

Other PCAOB & SEC Guidance

Following are other sources of guidance issued by the PCAOB and its staff, as well as a brief introduction to certain SEC rules for public company auditors.

Other PCAOB Standards

The PCAOB has the authority to develop standards for the following additional areas. To date, however, the PCAOB has primarily relied upon the use of interim AICPA guidance in these areas.

- Attestation standards: The PCAOB has adopted, as interim guidance, the AICPA's attestation standards ("AT").

- Ethics and Independence standards: In addition to its own Rules of the Board, the PCAOB has adopted (as interim) certain ethics and independence guidance from the AICPA Code of Conduct ("ET") and from the Independence Standards Board.

- Quality Control standards: The PCAOB has adopted, as interim guidance, the AICPA's quality control standards ("QC"), as well as certain additional requirements published by the SEC.

PCAOB Staff Releases

The PCAOB's staff issues the following guidance intended to highlight emerging or noteworthy audit practice issues, and to interpret rules and standards of the Board:

- Staff Audit Practice Alerts

- Staff Q&As

These resources are located under "Standards," and then "Guidance" on the PCAOB's website. Figures 9-15 illustrates the page containing these sources of staff guidance. Auditors can stay alert to changes in this list of staff guidance through subscriptions to firm email alerts, discussed further in Chapter 13.

Guidance

STAFF AUDIT PRACTICE ALERTS

Staff Audit Practice Alerts highlight new, emerging, or otherwise noteworthy circumstances that may affect how auditors conduct audits under the existing requirements of PCAOB standards and relevant laws. The statements contained in Staff Audit Practice Alerts are not rules of the Board and do not reflect any Board determination or judgment about the conduct of any particular firm, auditor, or any other person.

- Alert No. 10: Maintaining and Applying Professional Skepticism in Audits (Dec. 4, 2012) 🗎
- Alert No. 9: Assessing and Responding to Risk in the Current Economic Environment (Dec. 6, 2011) 🗎
- Alert No. 8: Audit Risks in Certain Emerging Markets (Oct. 3, 2011) 🗎
- Alert No. 7: Auditor Considerations of Litigation and Other Contingencies Arising from Mortgage and Other Loan Activities (Dec. 20, 2010) 🗎
- Alert No. 6: Auditor Considerations Regarding Using the Work of Other Auditors and Engaging Assistants from Outside the Firm (July 12, 2010) 🗎
- Alert No. 5: Auditor Considerations Regarding Significant Unusual Transactions (April 7, 2010) 🗎
- Alert No. 4: Auditor Considerations Regarding Fair Value Measurements, Disclosures, and Other-Than-Temporary Impairments (April 21, 2009) 🗎
- Alert No. 3: Audit Considerations in the Current Economic Environment (Dec. 5, 2008) 🗎
- Alert No. 2: Matters Related to Auditing Fair Value Measurements of Financial Instruments and the Use of Specialists (Dec. 10, 2007) 🗎
- Alert No. 1: Matters Related to Timing and Accounting for Option Grants (July 28, 2006) 🗎

STAFF QUESTIONS AND ANSWERS

Staff questions and answers set forth the staff's opinions on issues related to the implementation of the standards of the PCAOB. The PCAOB publishes questions and answers to help auditors implement, and the Board's staff administer, the Board's standards. The statements contained in the staff questions and answers are not rules of the Board, nor have they been approved by the Board.

- Auditing Standard No. 7, Engagement Quality Review (Feb. 19, 2010) 🗎

RELATED INFORMATION
- Current Activities

RULES
- Standard-Setting Rules

© PCAOB. Used with permission.

SEC Ethics Requirements

In addition to complying with PCAOB rules and standards, auditors of public companies must comply with certain professional standards of the SEC. Among these, the SEC's Regulation S-X sets forth certain requirements for auditors, including the following:

- Auditor qualifications requirements
- Requirements related to auditor independence
- Required elements of the audit report
- Requirements for audits performed by multiple firms[19]

Regulation S-X is available on the SEC's website, www.sec.gov.

How Do I Search PCAOB Guidance?

Similar to performing searches of AICPA guidance, researchers will likely find that the most efficient way to search PCAOB guidance is through a research database, such as Deloitte's *Technical Library*.

Figure 9-16 illustrates a search for the keyword "documentation" using Deloitte's *Technical Library*. Notice how the researcher has specified the PCAOB literature sources in which to search for this term.

---

[19] SEC, Regulation S-X, Reg. § 210.2-01 (parts a and b): "Qualifications of Accountants"; Reg. § 210.2-02: "Accountants' Reports"; Reg. § 210.2-05 "Examination of Financial Statements by More than One Accountant."

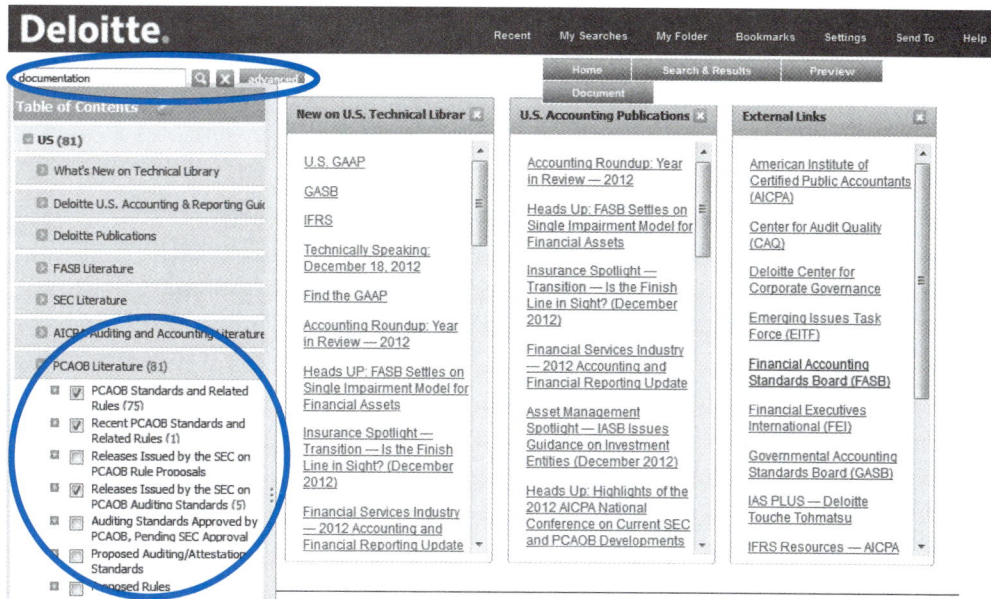

Figure 9-16

Search of PCAOB guidance using Deloitte's *Technical Library*

Researchers without access to firm research databases can search for literature using the PCAOB's website: www.pcaobus.org. These searches can begin

- By searching for a term from the homepage. Notice in Figure 9-17 the search for the term "independence" within the "Auditing and Professional Standards" section of the PCAOB's website.

- Or, by browsing to the PCAOB's standards and rules from the homepage. Notice in Figure 9-17 that researchers can browse to PCAOB standards and rules from a few locations on the homepage.

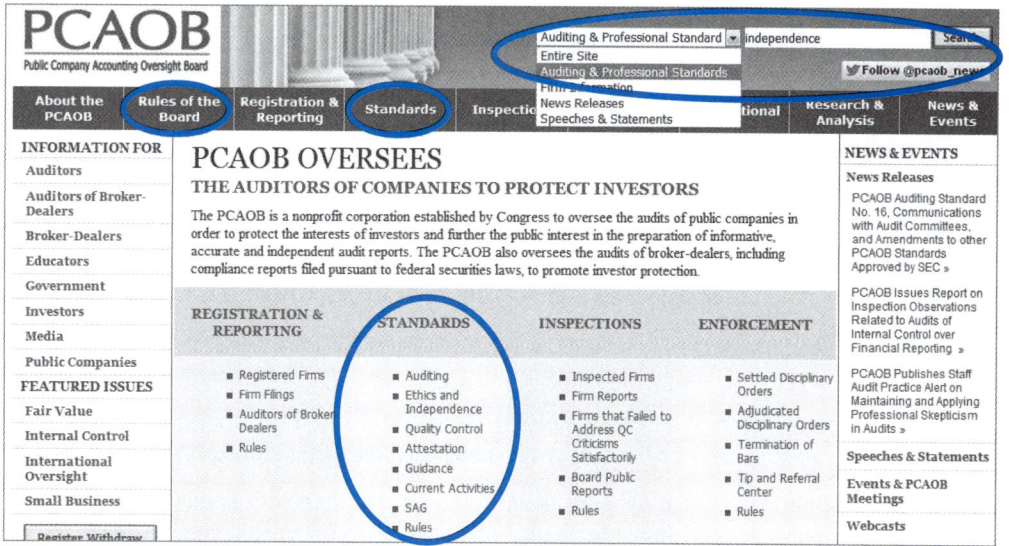

Figure 9-17

Performing searches using the PCAOB's website

---

[20] See Ch. 4, fn [10].

Once a researcher has browsed to the appropriate type of standard (e.g., auditing standards, ethics standards), researchers can then search on the page by keyword.

For example, Figure 9-18 illustrates a keyword search (using "ctrl + f") for the term "documentation" on the audit standards page. Note the highlighted search result: AS 3, *Audit Documentation*.

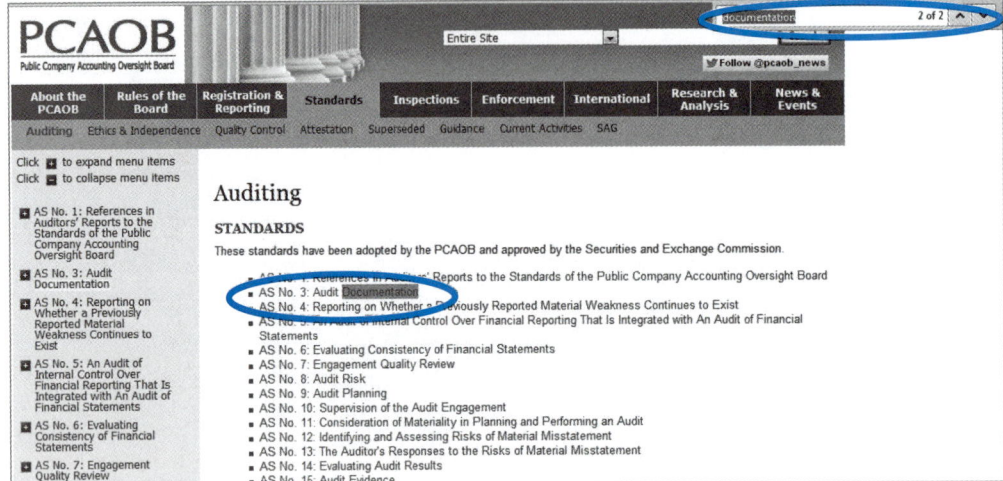

© PCAOB. Used with permission.

DOCUMENTATION OF PROFESSIONAL SERVICES RESEARCH

You know from previous chapters that *accounting* positions must be supported with documentation. Now let's take a moment to discuss why documentation is also important from the *service professional's* perspective.

Creating and maintaining sufficient **documentation**, or working papers, is critical to professional service engagements. Particularly for attestation engagements (such as audits), where the accountant must attest to the validity of an assertion, documentation is necessary to demonstrate the basis for the accountant's conclusions, and to demonstrate that the engagement complied with relevant professional standards. Audit documentation includes, for example, memoranda, confirmations, correspondence, schedules, audit programs, and letters of representation.

As noted previously, one of the first audit standards issued by the PCAOB was AS 3, *Audit Documentation*. The PCAOB prioritized the issuance of this standard, because it viewed audit documentation as one of the "fundamental building blocks" of the Board's oversight function.[21] Shortly thereafter, the AICPA also updated its own guidance on audit documentation.

Within their audit documentation standards, the PCAOB and AICPA sets forth requirements for the

■ Required elements of audit documentation.

■ Retention period for audit documentation.

■ Process for making changes to audit documentation after the audit report is issued.

To comply with AICPA and PCAOB documentation requirements, auditors are required to document the procedures performed, evidence obtained, and conclusions reached with respect to financial statement assertions. Additionally, auditors must document any significant audit findings or issues and how these matters were resolved. Both the PCAOB and AICPA require

---

[21] AS 3, Appendix A: Background and Basis for Conclusions. Par. A4.

auditors to place particular emphasis, within their documentation, on areas with the greatest risk of material misstatement.

Recall from our discussion of accounting research that research memoranda should include quotations from authoritative literature as support for conclusions reached. Similarly, auditors should support their choice of audit procedures and conclusions with citations from both professional standards and accounting standards. References to audit research may be included within audit schedules, or within memoranda documenting significant audit issues, depending on the complexity of the issue. Guidance for citing from audit standards is provided within the next section of this chapter.

Whether you are performing services for issuers or for nonissuers, *prepare documentation with the expectation that it will be reviewed by an external party*. Documentation may be reviewed, for example, in the event of

- Quality control reviews (from other partners in the CPA firm),
- Peer reviews (performed by other CPA firms),
- PCAOB inspections,
- SEC inquiries, or
- Litigation involving the audit client or audit firm.

The threat of a review can be disconcerting to some auditors; in recent years, the SEC and PCAOB have sanctioned numerous accountants who have gone back into their workpapers, just before an inspection was to begin, to add key documents or schedules that supported the audit opinion. Such was the case for the auditors described in Case Study 9-2, located at the end of this chapter. Don't jeopardize your career; before the workpapers for an engagement are finalized, think again about whether your documentation is sufficient to support a review.

An auditor's best defense for supporting his or her professional judgments is sufficient, contemporaneous, and complete documentation. In fact, the process alone of documenting an issue can often shed light upon whether the position is supportable. Identify the areas of greatest risk in the audit, then consider whether your documentation of these issues is sufficient to withstand review.

 **TIP** from the Trenches

Citing Professional Standards

Following are examples of appropriate initial and subsequent references to professional standards. After each citation, notice the list of "required elements" included in the citation.

Initial Reference:

AU-C section 700, *Forming an Opinion and Reporting on Financial Statements* (par. 27), states that audit reports "should describe management's responsibility for the preparation and fair presentation of the financial statements."

This initial reference includes the following required elements:

- The type of standard is named: "AU-C section XXX."
- The title of the standard is fully written out, and italicized.
- The paragraph number is provided.
- Excerpts from the guidance are enclosed in quotes.

Subsequent References (once the standard has already been named in your documentation):

Audit reports should be in writing (AU-C 700.22).

This second citation includes the following required elements:

- The type of standard (AU-C) is named.
- The standard number and paragraph are provided (700.22).

When in doubt, err on the side of providing *too much* detail about the source of guidance you are citing. Your objective in clearly citing professional standards is to allow readers to retrace your steps and locate the guidance that you are relying on. Remember that a "reader" of your documentation could be anyone ranging from an audit supervisor to a PCAOB inspector.

APPLYING THE AUDIT RESEARCH PROCESS

The following example illustrates the audit research process using various sections of the AICPA Code of Conduct.

Now YOU Try 9.5

Independence (Using the Code of Conduct)

Facts: Assume that your recently-deceased grandfather left you an inheritance, which includes a direct investment in shares of WellCorp, your audit client. You are the partner on the WellCorp engagement; WellCorp is a privately held company.

Required: Determine whether it is appropriate to keep the inherited shares of WellCorp stock. To answer this question, complete the following steps in the audit research process.

1. Step 1: What type of service are you providing? _____

2. Step 2: Which standard setter has authority? _____

3. Step 3: Which sources of guidance might apply to this service?

   Brainstorm: _____

Step 4: Perform research and document conclusions. See discussion below.

We know from the facts that you have received an investment in an audit client. Next, we will research the following three questions:

- Are you required to be independent of WellCorp? That is, are you a "covered member" with respect to this client?
- If so, does receipt of this inheritance impair your independence?
- Finally, what steps must you take to dispose of the inheritance?

Are you a covered member with respect to this client, and thus required to be independent?

The AICPA's Code of Conduct, ET Section 92 (Definitions) defines a **covered member** as follows:

.07   **Covered member.** A covered member is—
    a.   An individual on the attest engagement team;
    b.   An individual in a position to influence the attest engagement;

Continued

    c.   A partner or manager who provides nonattest services to the attest client . . .;

    d.   A partner in the office in which the lead attest engagement partner primarily practices . . .;

    e.   The firm, including the firm's employee benefit plans; or

    f.   An entity whose operating, financial, or accounting policies can be controlled . . . by any of the individuals or entities described in (a) through (e) or by two or more such individuals or entities if they act together.

5.   In this case, you are a covered member because: _____

   _____ .

6.   Assume that you are writing a research memo and including this source. How would you reference this source, the first time it appears in your memo?

   _____

Does receipt of this inheritance impair your independence?

Consider the following guidance from ET 101 (also known as "Rule 101" in the Code of Conduct) and its interpretations.

   .01   Rule 101 - Independence

   A member in public practice shall be independent in the performance of professional services as required by standards* promulgated by bodies designated by Council. [Asterisk added]

*AU-C 200, par. 15 states: "The auditor must be independent of the entity when performing an engagement in accordance with GAAS . . ."

   .02   101-1—Interpretation of Rule 101.

   Independence shall be considered to be impaired if:

     A.   During the **period of the professional engagement** a **covered member**

       1.   Had or was committed to acquire any direct or material indirect financial interest in the **client**. [Footnotes omitted.]

7.   According to ET _____, par. _____, independence is impaired if you have either a _____ or a material _____ interest in the client.

Notice that the term "material" precedes only indirect interests, indicating that *all* direct interests are a concern, but only *material* indirect interests are a concern.

Is this interest a direct or indirect financial interest?

ET 101-15 defines direct and indirect financial interests as follows:

A **financial interest** is an ownership interest in an equity or a debt security issued by an entity, including rights and obligations to acquire such an interest and derivatives directly related to such interest.

A **direct financial interest** is a financial interest:
1. Owned directly by an individual or entity . . . ; or
2. Under the control of an individual or entity . . . ; or
3. Beneficially owned through an investment vehicle, estate, trust, or other intermediary . . .

Continued

Continued from previous page

> An **indirect financial interest** is a financial interest beneficially owned through an invest-
> ment vehicle [such as a mutual fund], estate, trust, or other intermediary . . . when the ben-
> eficiary neither controls the intermediary nor has the authority to supervise or participate in
> the intermediary's investment decisions. [Comments added, footnotes omitted]

8.   Which type of interest did you inherit—direct or indirect? _____

9.   Could this interest cause your independence to be impaired, and why? _____

What steps must you take to dispose of the inheritance?

ET 101-15 provides the following guidance regarding "unsolicited" financial interests.

> **.17 101-15—Financial Relationships**
>
> **Unsolicited Financial Interests**
>
> Independence would not be considered to be impaired if an unsolicited financial interest in
> a client is received, such as through gift or inheritance, and the financial interest is disposed
> of as soon as practicable, but no later than 30 days after the covered member has knowledge
> of and the right to dispose of the financial interest . . .

10.   According to ET _____, par. _____, this inheritance is referred to as an
      _____ financial interest. To maintain independence from WellCorp,
      you must _____ .

11.   ET 101-15 is an _____ of Rule 101 (Independence).

Debrief—Independence Example

The first three steps of the audit research process should have led you to conclude that you were
performing an audit, of a nonissuer, and thus that AICPA guidance is applicable to this service.
In the brainstorming exercise, you likely identified the Code of Conduct as a possible source of
guidance for this service.

   In responding to the research questions regarding independence, you may have noticed that
very little detail was provided in Rule 101. As this chapter has discussed, a thorough search
requires consideration of interpretive and explanatory material; remember that these are considered an integral part of any professional standard. In this case, ET 101-1 and ET 101-15 provided
interpretive guidance that was responsive to this specific independence issue.

Subordination of Judgment (Using Audit Standards and Ethics Guidance)

According to the AICPA, historically one of the most common areas of ethics violations for
CPAs relates to the **subordination of judgment**.[22] That is, CPAs should never subordinate their
professional judgment, or keep quiet about important concerns, just because they are a junior
member of the engagement team or corporate group.

   The following example illustrates the audit research process, for the audit of an issuer,
involving the subordination of judgment.

---

[22] AICPA, *Ethics Decision Tree: For CPAs in Business and Industry*. "One of the most common ethics violations by
CPAs in business & industry relates to Ethics Interpretation 102-4 on Subordination of Judgment." Copyright AICPA,
2002. Page 1.

Facts: You are a new staff member on the audit of Public Company, Inc. Following instructions from your audit supervisor, last week you sent out confirmation requests related to certain of Public Company's accounts receivable. Those "positive" confirmation requests asked respondents whether they agreed with the receivable balance shown on the request.

This week, you have received responses from two of the respondents, indicating that they do not owe your client any money. You are concerned that the accounts receivable balances are not accurate or, worse, have been falsified. Your supervisor does not appear to share your concern and has indicated that the account balances are not material enough to include in the list of audit findings. Your supervisor asks that you move on to another area of the audit due to time and budget constraints.

Required: Determine what action should be taken to resolve the two non-conforming responses to the accounts receivable confirmation request. To answer this question, complete the following steps in the audit research process.

1. Step 1: What type of service are you providing? _____

2. Step 2: Which standard setter has authority? _____

3. Step 3: Which sources of guidance might apply to this service?

    Brainstorm: _____, _____

Step 4: Perform research and document conclusions. See discussion below.

You must research the following issues, in order to appropriately address this matter.

- First, you need to review what is required of an auditor, when confirming accounts receivable balances and when considering exceptions identified.

- Next, you need to determine what steps should be taken, in order to avoid subordinating your judgment to another individual.

What are the requirements for confirming accounts receivable?

To locate audit guidance applicable to confirmations, we must begin our search on the PCAOB website. There, under Audit Standards, we can search for the keyword "confirmations." The relevant guidance is AU 330, *The Confirmation Process*. This is AICPA guidance adopted as interim by the PCAOB.

AU 330 includes the following guidance regarding evaluating the results of confirmation procedures:

> .33   After performing any alternative procedures [applied to nonresponses, if applicable], the auditor should evaluate the combined evidence provided by the confirmations and the alternative procedures to determine whether sufficient evidence has been obtained about all the applicable financial statement assertions. In performing that evaluation, the auditor should consider (*a*) the reliability of the confirmations and alternative procedures; (*b*) the nature of any exceptions, including the implications, both quantitative and qualitative, of those exceptions; (*c*) the evidence provided by other procedures; and (*d*) whether additional evidence is needed. If the combined evidence provided by the confirmations, alternative procedures, and other procedures is not sufficient, the auditor should request additional confirmations or extend other tests, such as tests of details or analytical procedures. [Comments added, underlined emphasis added]

4. According to AU 330, par. 33, what additional steps should be taken related to the two questionable accounts?

    _____

    _____

    _____

5. Based on this research, do you agree with your supervisor's conclusion that you should not investigate these two accounts further? _____

_____

What steps should an auditor take, to avoid subordinating his or her judgment to another individual?

The PCAOB has adopted ET Section 102, *Integrity and Objectivity* (from the AICPA Code of Conduct) as interim ethics guidance. Rule 102 states:

01. In the performance of any professional service, a member shall maintain objectivity and integrity, shall be free of conflicts of interest, and shall not knowingly misrepresent facts or subordinate his or her judgment to others.

Interpretation 102-4, *Subordination of judgment by a member*, states, in part:

.05 ...If a member and his or her supervisor...have a difference of opinion relating to the application of accounting principles; auditing standards; or other relevant professional standards... then self-interest, familiarity, and undue influence threats to the member's compliance with Rule 102 may exist. Accordingly, the member should apply appropriate safeguards so that the member does not subordinate his or her judgment when the member concludes the difference of opinion creates significant threats to the member's integrity and objectivity.

In assessing the significance of any identified threats, the member should form a conclusion, after appropriate research or consultation, about whether the result of the position taken by the supervisor or other person

a. fails to comply with professional standards, when applicable;
b. creates a material misrepresentation of fact; or
c. may violate applicable laws or regulations.

If the member concludes that the position taken is not in compliance with professional standards but does not result in a material misrepresentation of fact or a violation of applicable laws or regulations, then threats would not be considered significant. However, the member should discuss his or her conclusions with the person taking the position.

If the member concludes that the position results in a material misrepresentation of fact or a violation of applicable laws or regulations, then threats would be considered significant. In such circumstances, the member should discuss his or her concerns with the supervisor. If the difference of opinion is still not resolved, then the member should discuss his or her concerns with the appropriate higher level(s) of management within the member's organization. . .

If after discussing such concerns with the supervisor and appropriate higher level(s) of management within the member's organization, the member concludes that appropriate action was not taken, then the member should consider [additional safeguards, see ET 102-4]. . . .

If the member concludes that no safeguards can eliminate or reduce the threats to an acceptable level or if the member concludes that appropriate action was not taken, then he or she should consider his or her continuing relationship with the member's organization and take appropriate steps to eliminate his or her exposure to subordination of judgment. . . .

6. Was Rule 102, by itself, responsive to this question? Explain. _____

_____

7. Considering the excerpt from ET 102-4, describe the steps an auditor should take to avoid a subordination of judgment.

   i) ET 102-4 states that if a position taken is not in compliance with professional standards but does not result in a material misrepresentation of fact or a violation of applicable laws, the member should

   _____

   _____

   ii) However, if the position results in a material misrepresentation of fact or a violation of applicable laws or regulations, then threats are considered _____

   The member should

   - First, _____

   - Next, if the matter is still not resolved,

   _____

   _____

8. In this case, your supervisor has instructed you to *move on*, and to not follow up on exceptions related to confirmation requests. Considering the guidance in ET 102-4, what is the first step you might take in order to avoid subordinating your judgment?

   _____

   _____

Debrief—Subordination of Judgment Example

ET 102-4 emphasizes that CPAs are responsible to act ethically, regardless of their level in an organization. As noted toward the end of the ET 102-4 excerpt, a member may need to go so far as to terminate his or her employment with an organization if he or she is not satisfied that threats have been reduced to an acceptable level. ET 102-4 goes on to caution members that "resignation may not relieve the member of his or her responsibilities in the situation, including any responsibility to disclose to third parties, such as regulatory authorities or the employer's (former employer's) external accountant." That is, in some cases even terminating your employment may not relieve you of the obligation to voice your concerns to outside parties.

Becoming familiar with professional standards, and knowing how to efficiently research these standards, can serve as your own *safeguard*, of sorts, against the risk of acting unethically or without complete information.

A CPA in the preceding example should carefully document all audit procedures performed and the authoritative support for these procedures, as well as all conversations and actions taken to ensure compliance from an ethics perspective.

CHAPTER SUMMARY

Compliance with professional standards is more than a "nice to know." As a professional, your career depends on it. Accounting professionals are held accountable for compliance with numerous professional services standards and ethics rules. Determining which standards to follow often depends on the type of engagement being performed, and on the type of client being served. The two primary standard setters for professional guidance are the AICPA and the PCAOB.

The two sets of guidance available from the PCAOB and AICPA currently have significant overlap. Accountants should strive to only search for guidance on the website (or related firm research database content) of the rulemaker with authority for each engagement.

Finally, paying careful attention to documentation requirements may be an accountant's best defense against professional risk. Documentation should focus in particular on key risk areas, and should adequately support the accountant's opinions, as well as the sufficiency of procedures performed.

REVIEW QUESTIONS

1. Name the four steps of the audit research process.

2. What are some of the differences between assurance and consulting services?

3. In what circumstances is an accountant subject to the rules and standards of the PCAOB?

4. Does the AICPA's Code of Conduct apply to a CPA who is performing an audit of an issuer? Explain.

5. Explain the AICPA's definitions of "must" and "should." In what section of an audit standard would you expect to find these terms?

6. Identify the sources of AICPA audit guidance that are considered "interpretive publications." Are auditors required to comply with these sources?

7. Aside from issuing audit and ethics standards, what are some of the PCAOB's other responsibilities?

8. Are PCAOB standards referred to as "generally accepted auditing standards"?

9. What are the three levels of responsibility defined in PCAOB Rule 3101? What are the words that may be used (such as "must" and "should") within the guidance to indicate these types of responsibility?

10. Explain why documentation is critical to audit research.

EXERCISES

Answer the following using www.aicpa.org or www.pcaobus.org, as appropriate. If the question involves audit standards, use "Clarified" standards. Also: Cite the source for each response (include paragraph numbers, where applicable).

1. List three examples of individuals who are considered "covered members," using the AICPA's Code of Conduct.

2. Using the AICPA's Code of Conduct, identify an issue summarized under the Ethics Rulings on "independence."

3. Using the AICPA website, locate AR Section 60, *Framework for Performing and Reporting on Compilation and Review Engagements.*
   a. What is the corresponding Statements on Standards for Accounting and Review Services (SSARSs) number for this guidance? SSARS No. _____
   b. Using guidance from AR 60, briefly summarize how a compilation service differs from a review or an audit of financial statements.
   c. Using guidance from AR 60, briefly summarize how a review differs from an audit of financial statements.

4. What are some examples of alternative procedures that an auditor (subject to AICPA standards) might apply, if he or she has not received responses to external confirmation requests?

5. Does accepting contingent fees impair an auditor's independence? Use the PCAOB website to respond.

6. Go to the PCAOB's website and list one proposed audit standard named on the site. Where did you navigate within the site to find this?

7. Locate the PCAOB standard (AS) on supervision of an audit engagement.
   a. Who does the guidance say is responsible for the engagement and its performance?
   b. Who else is required to comply with the requirements of this AS?

8. Locate the PCAOB's audit standard on performing integrated audits. When an auditor is reporting on the results of an audit, must the auditor issue separate or combined reports on the company's financial statements and internal controls?

9. Under "Inspections" on the PCAOB's website, locate the link to Firm Inspection Reports. Review a firm inspection report and describe some of the findings cited by the PCAOB. In particular, look for firm inspection reports that say: "QC criticisms are now public."

CASE STUDY QUESTIONS

Auditor Independence Utilize the AICPA website to respond.

Facts: Jake Jones is an audit partner in a CPA firm, and Jake recently invested in a diversified mutual fund managed by Fidelity Investments. He owns less than 1% of the total shares outstanding of the mutual fund itself. One of the mutual fund's holdings is shares of ABC Corp. ABC Corp is one of Jake's clients and is a nonpublic company.

Required: What guidance tells Jake that he must be independent of ABC Corp, *and* does his investment impair his firm's independence on this audit?

Respond to these questions in the form of an issues memo. Explain your analysis, citing from the guidance to support your response. If the guidance states that a "covered member" must be independent, you will need to define covered member to fully explain your analysis. Make a clear, reasoned argument, using a logical discussion of relevant guidance. You can use the following headers to begin your response.

> *Issue 1: What guidance requires Jake to be independent of ABC Corp?*

> *Issue 2: Does this investment impair Jake's firm's independence on this audit?*

PCAOB Disciplinary Orders Utilize the PCAOB website to respond.

9.1

9.2

Facts: On August 1, 2011, the PCAOB issued Orders formally barring two former Ernst & Young auditors from future audits of public companies.[23] Peter C. O'Toole and Darrin G. Estella, as partner and senior manager for a public company audit, respectively, were charged with violating PCAOB rules and auditing standards with the improper creation, addition, and backdating of audit documentation prior to a PCAOB inspection.

Following is part of the PCAOB's summary findings related to this matter. This is from the PCAOB's Order related to Mr. O'Toole.

> Respondent improperly created, added, and backdated a working paper in advance of the Board's inspection of the Audit. Others under his supervision and authorization improperly created, added, and backdated other working papers in advance of the Board's inspection. Respondent, and others supervised and authorized by him, provided misleading documents and information to the Board, in violation of Rule 4006. This conduct also violated AS3 because the documents added to the working papers did not indicate the dates that documents were added to the working papers, the names of the persons preparing the additional documentation, and the reason for adding the documentation months after the documentation completion date.[24]

The PCAOB's Order goes on to describe the workpaper that was added to the audit files (postaudit, but in advance of the PCAOB inspection), as one that supported audit work related to the client's valuation of a key investment. According to the PCAOB's report, Mr. O'Toole anticipated that the valuation of that investment would be a key focus of the PCAOB inspection.[25]

Required: Evaluate this case in the form of an accounting issues memorandum. In the Facts section of your memo, use the facts presented above, along with any salient points from the PCAOB Order, to describe the issues at hand.

Next, list then analyze the following two issues:

1. How were the auditors' actions in violation of PCAOB Rule 4006? What should the auditors have done differently?
2. How were the auditors' actions in violation of AS 3? What should the auditors have done differently?

In your analysis, present relevant excerpts from the applicable auditing rules and standards alongside your consideration of the case facts and details from the PCAOB Order. Finally, present a brief conclusion which summarizes your analysis.

---

[23] PCAOB Release No. 105-2011-004, August 1, 2011, and Release No. 105-2011-005, August 1, 2011.

[24] PCAOB Release No. 105-2011-005, August 1, 2011. Page 3, par. 3.

[25] PCAOB Release No. 105-2011-005, August 1, 2011. Pages 5–6, par. 13.

Chapter 10

Governmental and Industry Accounting Research

Jon has just been scheduled to work on the audit of a school district, starting on Monday. He is a staff auditor at a regional public accounting firm, and this is his first governmental audit client. He wonders how this engagement will differ from his private-sector experiences. Jon knows that state and local governments must follow GASB accounting standards but has otherwise forgotten much of what he learned about governmental accounting (let alone governmental audits). Now, Jon is unsure of how to prepare for work on Monday and feels uncomfortable holding himself out as a "government auditor."

As Jon likely knows by now, much of the training that auditors receive takes place on the job. That is, much of his initial audit work will involve reviewing prior year workpapers, then performing specific steps required by the current year audit program.

But Jon also wants to be able to understand the broader context for the audit steps he will perform. That's why he decides to take a few simple steps, this weekend, to educate himself for the week ahead. First, he dusts off his old governmental accounting textbook. Flipping through the table of contents provides him with a much-needed refresher on issues that are unique to governmental accounting. Second, Jon looks up the client's comprehensive annual financial report (CAFR) from last year, to get a feel for the final product

Continued

Learning Objectives

After reading this chapter and performing the exercises herein, you will be able to

1. **Identify** the standards and standard setters involved in governmental accounting and auditing.

2. **Perform** research using sources of governmental accounting and auditing literature.

3. **Become** familiar with industry accounting resources, including professional organizations and standards.

(continued from previous page)

his audit team will be working toward. Finally, Jon scans the GASB's website to see what's new in the world of state and local government accounting. There, he reads the headlines then accesses a few short video clips on GASB activities, which he enjoys from the comfort of his couch.

A little bit of preparation will go a long way in making Jon feel confident when he reports to the client's site on Monday. This preparation will also allow Jon to better understand each step he performs in the audit program, allowing him to exercise professional care as an auditor.

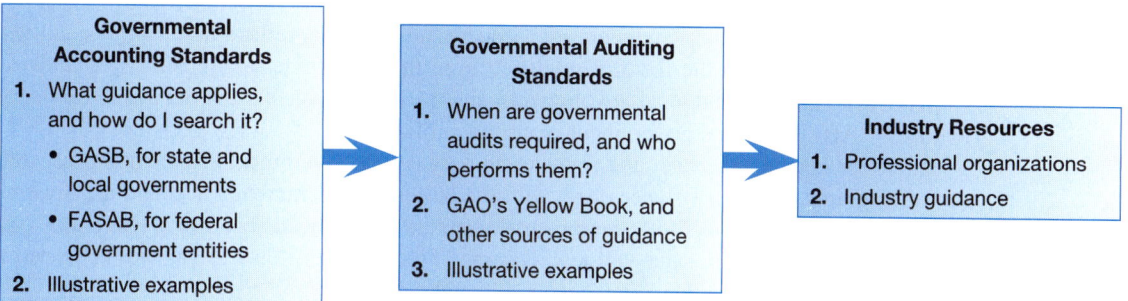

Organization of This Chapter

As you now know, guidance in the FASB Codification only applies to *nongovernmental* entities. So where should preparers of government financial statements go for guidance? And what professional standards apply to governmental auditors?

This chapter introduces sources of governmental accounting and auditing guidance, as well as several resources for industry (i.e., "management") accounting guidance. Readers will have the opportunity to apply guidance from each of these sources to sample research questions. However, consistent with the lesson from our opening scenario, this chapter emphasizes that understanding the basic principles of governmental accounting is the first, most critical step necessary for success in performing governmental research.

In addition to describing key authoritative sources of guidance, this chapter describes select nonauthoritative resources used in practice by government accountants and auditors, and by accounting professionals in industry.

The preceding graphic illustrates the organization of topics within this chapter.

Let's begin now with the guidance applicable to governmental accounting.

GOVERNMENTAL ACCOUNTING RESEARCH

The first thing to understand about governmental accounting research is that the *research process* itself is no different from the process performed for nongovernmental entities. Like the accounting research process described in Chapter 3, governmental research starts with obtaining an understanding of the transaction, identifying the researchable question, then searching the literature and documenting conclusions.

What is unique about governmental accounting research, however, is the *body of knowledge* required to perform it. Governmental accounting differs fundamentally from private-sector accounting for a number of reasons. These include:

■ The purposes of these entities differ. Governments exist for the public good, while private-sector companies exist for the benefit of their owners (shareholders).

■ Governments generate revenues through taxation; private-sector companies generate revenues through sales of goods or services.

■ Governments offer services for which they do not receive reciprocal value, such as social services; private-sector companies sell their goods and services in arm's-length exchanges to obtain profit.

■ The community of government financial statement users, and their motivations, differ from those interested in private-sector financial statements.

Governmental financial statements are based on standards that reflect these unique qualities. These standards come in the form of guidance from the Governmental Accounting Standards Board (GASB) for state and local governments, and the Federal Accounting Standards Advisory Board (FASAB) for federal government reporting entities.

As in our opening scenario, the first step in performing governmental accounting research is to refamiliarize yourself (if necessary) with the basics of governmental accounting. Governmental accounting textbooks (or governmental chapters in advanced accounting textbooks) can be a good resource for this. Once you review some of these basics, you will be ready to research more specific issues in governmental accounting and auditing.

The next sections of this chapter introduce, first, the standards for state and local government financial statements and, next, standards for federal government financial statements.

State and Local Accounting Standards

Financial statements are an important means by which state and local governments and agencies can demonstrate their accountability to the public. The laws of many individual states, in fact, require that audited financial statements be prepared at the state and local government levels. Users of these financial statements range from parties interested in understanding the government's priorities (such as citizens and taxpayer groups) to lawmakers interested in setting future agendas and to parties interested in government bond issuances (such as investors, analysts, rating agencies, and municipal bond insurers).

The **Governmental Accounting Standards Board** (GASB) establishes accounting standards for state and local government entities. The AICPA Audit and Accounting Guide, *State and Local Governments*, par. 1.01, defines **governmental entities** as follows:

Public corporations and bodies corporate and politic are governmental entities. Other entities are governmental entities if they have one or more of the following characteristics:
- Popular election of officers or appointment (or approval) of a controlling majority of the members of the organization's governing body by officials of one or more state or local governments;
- The potential for unilateral dissolution by a government with the net assets reverting to a government; or
- The power to enact and enforce a tax levy.

Continued

Furthermore, entities are presumed to be governmental if they have the ability to issue directly (rather than through a state or municipal authority) debt that pays interest exempt from federal taxation. However, entities possessing only that ability (to issue tax-exempt debt) and none of the other governmental characteristics may rebut the presumption that they are governmental . . . [Footnotes omitted]

Figure 10-1 provides examples of state and local government entities subject to the GASB's guidance.

Figure 10-1

Examples of state and local government entities subject to GASB guidance

GASB guidance is considered *authoritative* for state and local government entities. In other words, these entities must apply GASB guidance in order for their financial statements to be "in conformity with generally accepted accounting principles," which is necessary for a government to receive an unqualified audit opinion. Although the GASB cannot force compliance with the standards it sets, the audit process and state laws requiring GAAP financial statements compel certain governments to comply.[1] In addition, many state and local governments are required, under borrowing agreements, to provide lenders with audited financial information.

Located just downstairs from the FASB in Norwalk, Connecticut, the GASB is an independent organization focused on creating and improving standards for state and local governments. The objective of these standards is to facilitate governments' public accountability, and to provide information that is useful to financial statement users. Like the FASB, the funding and administration of the GASB are overseen by the Financial Accounting Foundation (FAF). The GASB is funded primarily through an accounting support fee assessed to broker-dealers and investors in the municipal bond trading market.[2] Additionally, a portion of the GASB's funding comes from sales of its publications.

Guidance Issued by the GASB

The GASB issues the following guidance:

■ Standards (Statements of Governmental Accounting Standards, or GASB Statements)

■ Interpretations

■ Technical Bulletins

■ Implementation Guides (Q&As), issued by GASB staff

■ Concepts Statements (Statements of Governmental Accounting Concepts)

---

[1] GASB, *GASB At A Glance*. July, 2012. Page 2.

[2] This fee was established in 2012 through the Dodd-Frank Wall Street Reform and Consumer Protection Act.

The GASB uses the hierarchy depicted in Figure 10-2 to prioritize authoritative sources of state and local government accounting guidance:[3]

Figure 10-2

Hierarchy of generally accepted accounting principles for state and local entities

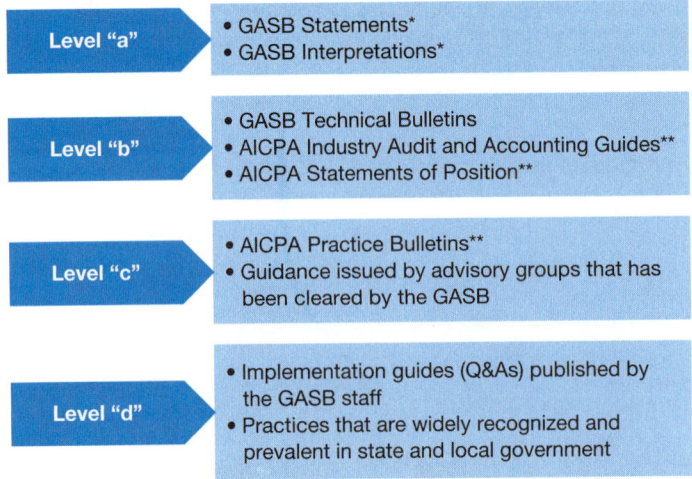

Level "a"
- GASB Statements*
- GASB Interpretations*

Level "b"
- GASB Technical Bulletins
- AICPA Industry Audit and Accounting Guides**
- AICPA Statements of Position**

Level "c"
- AICPA Practice Bulletins**
- Guidance issued by advisory groups that has been cleared by the GASB

Level "d"
- Implementation guides (Q&As) published by the GASB staff
- Practices that are widely recognized and prevalent in state and local government

*Includes standards and interpretations of the National Council on Governmental Accounting (NCGA), the GASB's predecessor. Note that the terms "Statements" and "Standards" are used interchangeably.
**Authoritative only if specifically made applicable to state and local governmental entities and cleared by the GASB.

All sources in Figure 10-2 hierarchy are considered "authoritative"; however, the degree of their authority varies. Preparers of government financial statements should prioritize the use of level "a" sources; when such guidance is not available, the other levels may be used in declining order. Notice that level "b" includes certain AICPA guides; these include, for example, the AICPA Audit Guide, *State & Local Governments*.

If none of the categories (a–d) provide relevant guidance for a transaction, nonauthoritative sources may be considered. These include guidance for similar transactions, or other accounting literature including, first and foremost, GASB Concepts Statements, then other resources such as FASB guidance, international standards, textbooks, and so on.

It's worth noting that the GASB currently has a project underway to reevaluate this hierarchy; one possible outcome may be a model where only two levels of authority exist: authoritative or nonauthoritative, like the model used by the FASB.

Researching GASB Guidance

GASB guidance can generally be accessed (1) using the GASB's *Governmental Accounting Research System* (**GARS Online**) database or (2) using original standards on the GASB website.

GARS Online

The GARS Online database, depicted in Figure 10-3, includes access to the **GASB Codification** plus other related resources.

Much like the FASB Codification, the GASB Codification organizes authoritative guidance by topic and is the preferred method for accessing state and local government accounting guidance. Researchers can generally access the full GARS Online database in one of two ways: (1) through a paid subscription to GARS Online purchased from the GASB or (2) through low-cost academic access from the American Accounting Association ($250 per school, per year). The GASB Codification portion of this database can also be accessed within certain—but not all—accounting research databases (such as CCH's *Accounting Research Manager* and PwC's *Comperio* database).

---

[3] GASB Statement No. 55, *The Hierarchy of Generally Accepted Accounting Principles for State and Local Governments,* par. 3 (codified in GASB Cod. Sec. 1000.101).

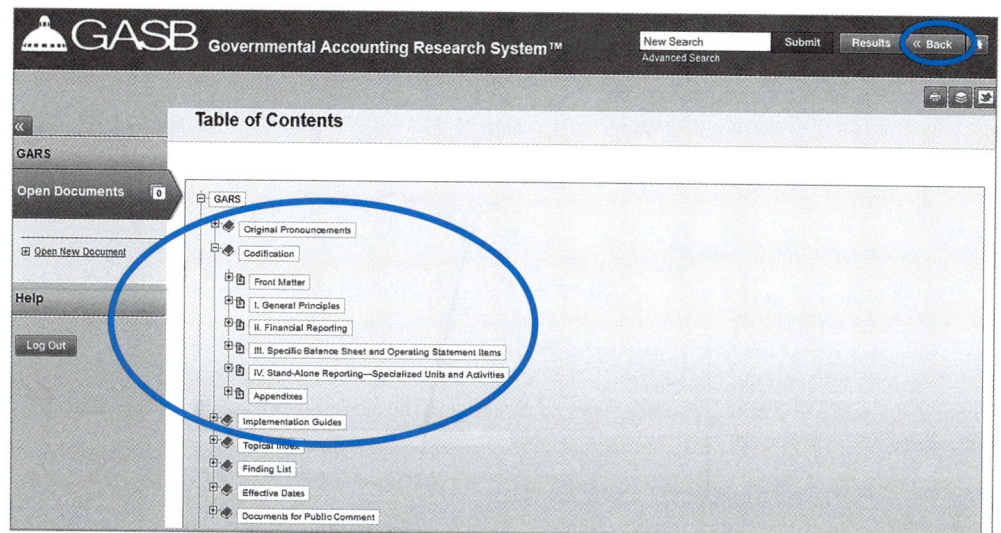

Figure 10-3

Homepage of GARS
Online (blue circles
added)

Reproduced with permission of the Financial Accounting Foundation.

Notice in Figure 10-3 that authoritative content (namely, the Original Pronouncements, the Codification, and Implementation Guides) has been circled for emphasis. Unlike the situation for FASB guidance, GASB original pronouncements (to the extent not superseded) remain an authoritative source of guidance, despite the existence of the Codification.

To access guidance in the Codification, click the + signs next to each heading (or else you'll just be directed to the preface of each section, if you click the heading itself). Also circled is the GARS Online "Back" button (use this, rather than your browser's "back" button, which may cause you to be logged off of GARS Online). Figure 10-4 further describes the content included within GARS Online.

GARS Link	Content
Original Pronouncements	Includes all original sources of governmental accounting guidance, such as: GASB Standards and Interpretations, Technical Bulletins, Concepts Statements, certain AICPA guidance, and Standards and Interpretations of the GASB's predecessor (the NCGA).
Codification	Includes the following currently-effective content, organized by topic: • GASB (and NCGA) Standards, Interpretations, and Technical Bulletins • References to relevant AICPA Audit & Accounting Guides and Statements of Position • Links to related Implementation Guides
Implementation Guides	Includes: • The current-year "Comprehensive Implementation Guide" (Q&As), which includes all currently-effective implementation guidance organized by topic • Original Implementation Guides by standard, as issued
Finding List	Cross references each original pronouncement, by paragraph, to its location in the GASB Codification. Also identifies those paragraphs considered "background information" and thus not incorporated into the Codification.
Effective Dates	Lists the effective dates for each original pronouncement.
Documents for Public Comment	Links to guidance currently being proposed by the GASB.

Figure 10-4

Content included within
GARS Online

Knowledge ✔ Check

Using the GARS Online screenshot from Figure 10-3 and the content descriptions in Figure 10-4, identify which resource a researcher would use:

1.   For Q&A's on a particular topic?
2.   To find background information or the basis for conclusions in an original GASB standard?
3.   If a researcher wants to locate the Codification reference for GASB Statement No. 34, par. 2?

Also, respond to the following:

4.   What two sources of "level a" GAAP make up the *main body* of content included in the GASB Codification?

You may have noticed in Figure 10-3 that the GASB Codification includes four parts (I–IV) plus appendices; let's take a moment now to understand how guidance is organized within these four parts.

The Four Parts of the GASB Codification

Figure 10-5 illustrates the four parts of the GASB Codification, describes how guidance from each part should be referenced, and summarizes types of content located within each part. Take a moment to review Figure 10-5, then respond to the questions that follow.

Figure 10-5

The four parts of the GASB Codification, plus appendices

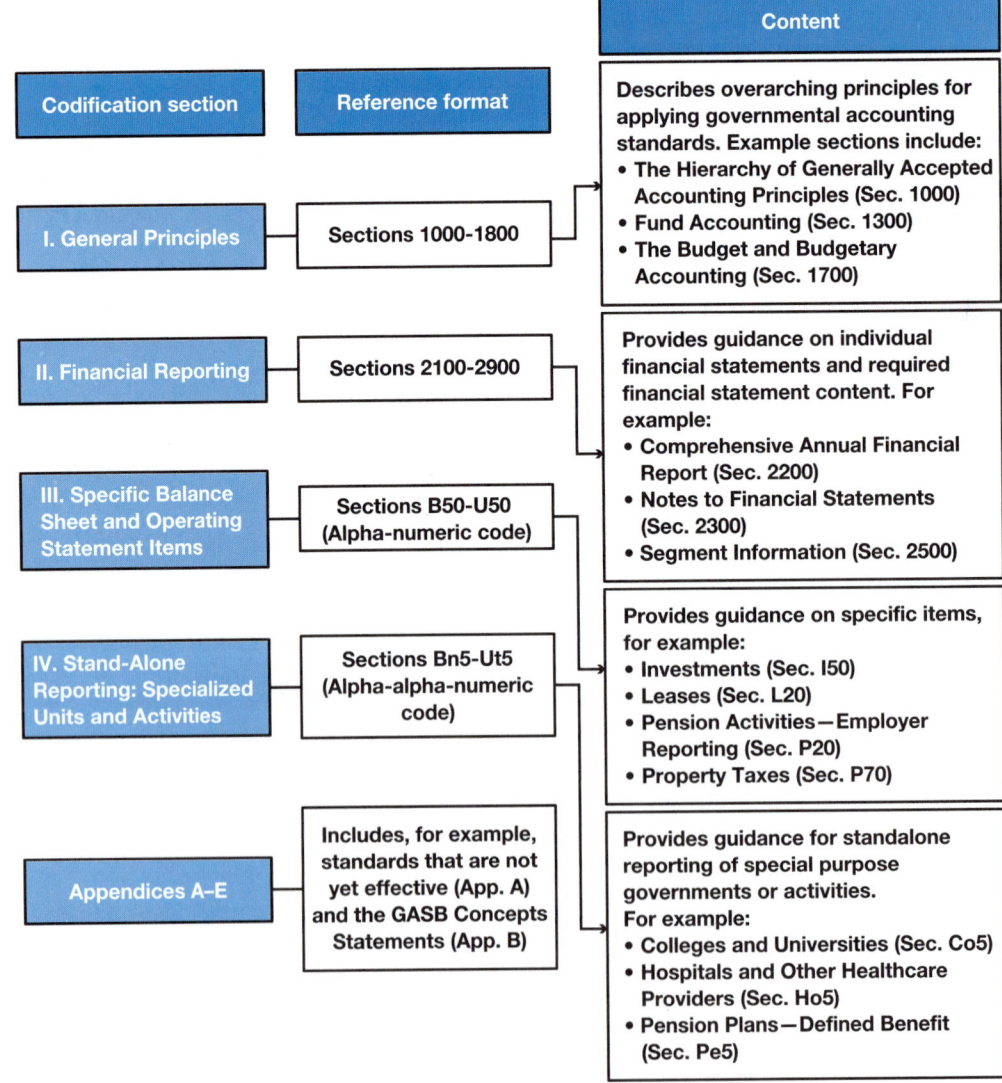

Using Figure 10-5, respond to the following.
In what part (I, II, III, or IV) of the Codification might a researcher find:

Knowledge Check

5. **Sections entitled "Defining the Financial Reporting Entity" and "Cash Flow Statements"?**
6. **Guidance on differences between the cash and accrual bases of accounting?**
7. **Sections entitled "Bankruptcies," "Pension Plans," and "Regulated Operations"?**
8. **Sections entitled "Inventory" and "Nonmonetary Transactions"?**

Browse Searches within GARS Online As you know from prior chapters, a "browse search" means little more than attempting to navigate directly to appropriate guidance within a research database. In this case, researchers must first determine which "part" of the GASB Codification to search, then should look for relevant topics within that part. Browse searches are generally preferable to keyword searches in that they allow a researcher to understand how an issue fits into the broader context of the Codification.

Because the GASB Codification contains guidance with varying degrees of authority (recall the hierarchy of authoritative guidance), each paragraph within the Codification indicates its source material. This is also helpful to researchers looking for background information that is included within original standards, but which has not been included within the Codification. Also, where relevant, topics link to separately located content such as Implementation Guides (level d) and certain AICPA content (levels b and c). Certain topics also include paragraphs .901–.999, which indicate Nonauthoritative Discussion—supplemental guidance and illustrations.

To illustrate the format of an individual topic, Figure 10-6 depicts the top-of-page matter for Topic Po50 (Postemployment Benefit Plans Other Than Pension Plans). Notice that the page lists the topic's source material ("Sources") and provides links to related topics (under "See Also"). Also circled in Figure 10-6 is the link to *Implementation Guidance* related to this topic.

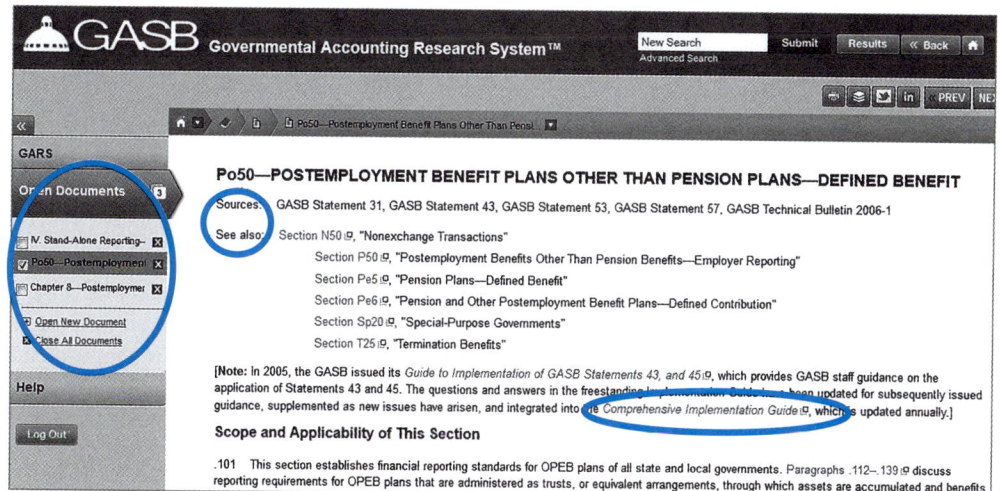

Figure 10-6

Sample GASB Codification section, Po50 (Postemployment Benefit Plans Other Than Pension Plans), blue circles added

Reproduced with permission of the Financial Accounting Foundation.

Researchers should treat any available Implementation Guidance as required reading, as it may influence how a standard is applied. Additionally, researchers can use the "See Also" links for additional direction if an initial search proves fruitless.

The list of "Open Documents" on the left side of Figure 10-6 keeps a running list of any documents a researcher views. Click two of the checkboxes, and you'll have the option to view two documents concurrently.

> **TIP** from the Trenches
>
> When researching an issue that is new to you, chances are pretty good that you won't always end up in the right place the first time. Take advantage of the "See Also" links within each standard to generate ideas about possible other, or related, areas to search for relevant guidance.

Keyword Searches within GARS Online Keyword searches within GARS Online are generally most appropriate when a researcher has a search term in mind but is not familiar with how that term fits into the literature.

The keyword search function within GARS Online is fairly straightforward, particularly for researchers familiar with FASB Codification searches. This function is depicted in Figure 10-7.

Figure 10-7

Advanced keyword search of GARS Online, circle added

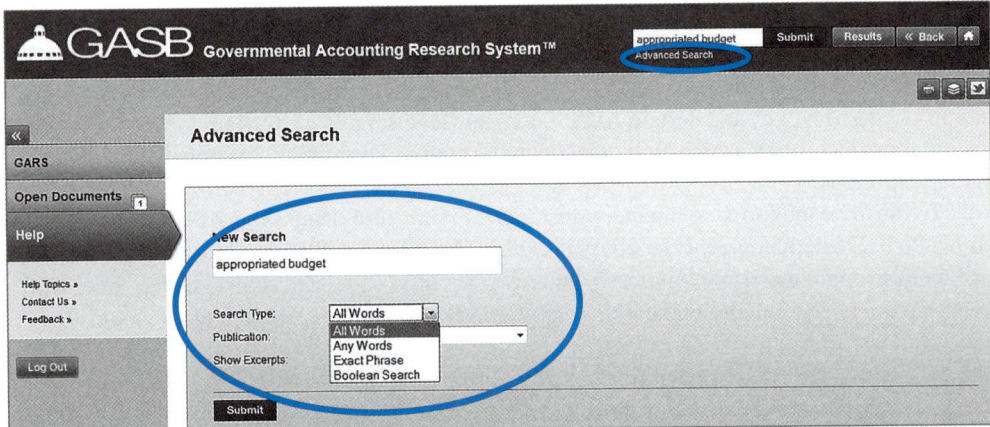

Reproduced with permission of the Financial Accounting Foundation.

As illustrated in Figure 10-7, a researcher can choose to search for all words, any words, an exact phrase, or using a "Boolean operator" search (where the terms "and," "or," or "not" are inserted between two search terms). Additional guidance on conducting Boolean searches is available under the GARS Online help menu (see left-hand link in Figure 10-7). Also in Figure 10-7, the search field "Publication" allows researchers to specify whether to search just within the Codification or within another area of GARS Online (such as Original Pronouncements only). Your best bet? Stick with the default option, to search the full GARS Online database, and your results will be organized by part anyway (e.g., "2 results in Original Pronouncements," "2 results in GASB Codification").

For researchers using other databases to access the GASB Codification, the mechanics of performing a keyword search will differ slightly. For example, Figure 10-8 illustrates a sample keyword search of the GASB Codification for the term "infrastructure" using CCH's *Accounting Research Manager* database.

Notice in Figure 10-8 that {Government, GASB, and GASB Codification} have been selected in the fields for {Subject, Author, and Book}, respectively. If, for example, a researcher is interested in interpretive governmental content authored by CCH, he or she could select "Government" as the subject, then "CCH" as the author. Alternatively, suppose a researcher is searching for a keyword within the GASB's original pronouncements; in this case, the researcher could select "GASB" as the author, then "GASB Statements" as the book.

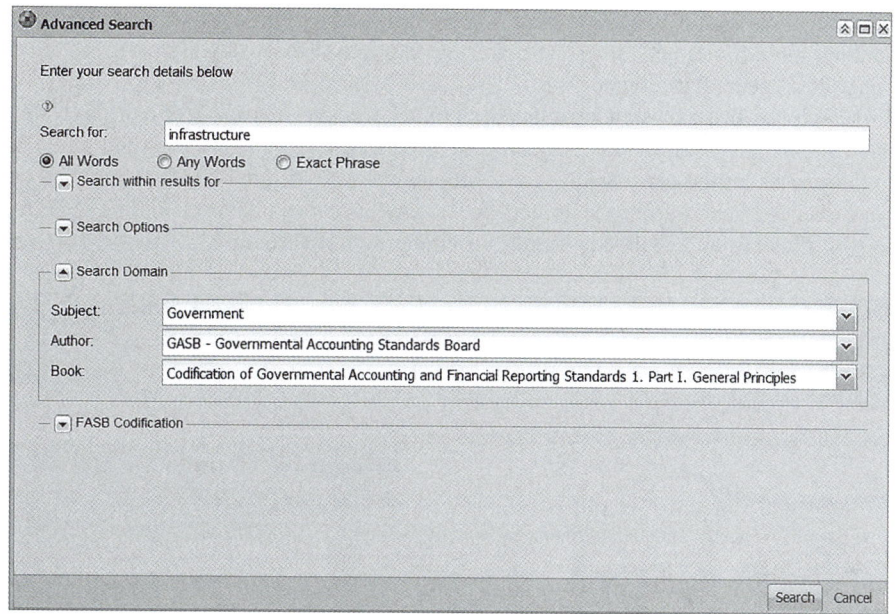

Figure 10-8

Keyword search of the GASB Codification using CCH's *Accounting Research Manager*

✓ **Knowledge Check**

9. Using Figure 10-6, name one of the original standards that serves as the *source* material for Section Po50 (Postemployment Benefit Plans).
10. Using Figure 10-6, name one related topic that links to Section Po50.
11. Notice in Figure 10-8 the fields for Subject and Author in CCH's advanced search feature. If the Subject were changed to "Accounting" (i.e., nongovernmental content), what is one "Author" search option that you might expect to see?

> An extended example applying guidance from the GASB Codification to a local government's sales and property tax revenues is provided in the **Appendix** to this chapter. Intended to expose beginning researchers to a range of issues, the example touches upon revenue recognition, application of the accrual/modified accrual bases of accounting, and fund accounting.

Now that you have a basic understanding of GARS Online and the GASB Codification, let's discuss another (albeit less desirable) option for accessing GASB guidance.

Accessing Standards on the GASB Website

A less ideal way to research GASB literature is by accessing full texts of the GASB's original standards free of charge on its website, www.gasb.org, under "Pronouncements." This manner of searching is less than ideal because

■ These standards are only available in their original, *as issued* form on the GASB website and do not reflect revisions that may have occurred since their issuance.

■ Guidance is not organized by topic. Therefore, in some cases, researchers must navigate through multiple standards and interpretations in order to understand the guidance applicable to a single topic.

■ Finally, the GASB website does not include the full population of guidance applicable to government financial statements. For example, certain AICPA literature is considered authoritative for government financial statements but is neither accessible nor clearly referenced on the GASB's website.[4]

---

[4] For example, the 2013 AICPA Audit & Accounting Guide, *State and Local Governments*, is included within the GASB Codification and is available for purchase from the AICPA, but is not listed on the GASB's website.

Researchers using the GASB website therefore risk using outdated, or incomplete, sources. Recognizing these limitations, the GASB website cautions that its standards page is intended to serve only as a "general reference."[5]

To search for original standards on the GASB website, researchers can navigate to the Pronouncements page (under the Standards & Guidance tab). There, researchers can perform keyword searches on the page (using, for example, ctrl + f). Alternatively, researchers can perform an Advanced Search from the homepage, for any instances of a term on the GASB website. Figure 10-9 illustrates an advanced search for the term "infrastructure."

Reproduced with permission of the Financial Accounting Foundation.

The current **status** of standards listed on the GASB website varies; certain standards are still fully applicable, while others may be fully or partially superseded. Figure 10-10 illustrates the standards list from the GASB website, including links to status information. Notice, for example, that Statement No. 22 has been fully superseded. Notice also the link to the Status page for each standard (such as under Statement No. 24).

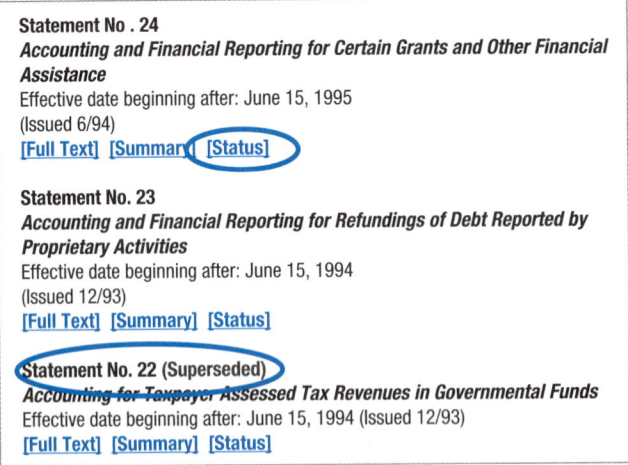

Reproduced with permission of the Financial Accounting Foundation.

When accessing standards on the GASB website, it is essential to review a standard's Status page. On this page, a researcher can determine how a given standard has been *affected by* subsequent guidance issuances, can identify ways this standard *affects* (or has changed) other

---

[5] www.GASB.org, Pronouncements. Accessed on 10/19/2013.

standards, and can find references to *Other Interpretive Literature* related to the standard. It is critical to understand how current a standard is before relying upon it.

> The GASB's website can be a useful reference but should not be relied on as a source of authoritative guidance if you are performing governmental accounting in practice. There is just too much risk involved—you could inadvertently apply outdated guidance or miss an important interpretive source.

[TIP] from the Trenches

Additional Sources for State and Local Guidance

Numerous nonauthoritative resources are available to assist government accountants in the preparation of financial statements. These resources may offer, for example, practical explanations of authoritative requirements, illustrations, and checklists. For example,

1. GFOA's "Blue Book," *Governmental Accounting, Auditing, and Financial Reporting (GAAFR)*

First published in 1934, the "Blue Book" of the Government Finance Officers Association (GFOA) provides practical guidance for state and local governments' accounting, auditing, and financial reporting. The Blue Book also includes reference materials, such as a model comprehensive annual financial report (CAFR), and chapters devoted to specialized topics (such as capital assets and derivatives). In addition to the Blue Book, the GFOA also offers training programs and program checklists designed to assist government financial statement preparers.

Notably, the GFOA is also responsible for the Certificate of Achievement for Excellence in Financial Reporting Program, which is awarded to state and local governments for high quality financial reporting. Figure 10-11 illustrates the seal awarded to recipients of this distinction.

Used with permission from GFOA.

Figure 10-11

The GFOA's "Certificate of Achievement" seal for excellence in government reporting

2. PPC's *Guide to Preparing Governmental Financial Statements*

Practitioners Publishing Company, (PPC), offers several practical guides for government accountants, including PPC's *Guide to Preparing Government Financial Statements*. Pulling together requirements from GASB standards, interpretations, technical bulletins, and AICPA material, the guide walks users step-by-step through issues involved with preparing financial statements, from recognition of assets, to fund accounting, to disclosures.

3. Resources from the Association of Government Accountants (AGA)

The AGA, a professional organization for government accountants, offers online toolkits, guides, and training materials intended to improve the quality of government financial reporting. Its research publications, including its quarterly magazine, the *Journal of Government Financial Management,* assist government accountants in staying current with important industry news.

4. Interpretive Guidance within Firm Research Databases

Certain research databases offer subscribers access to interpretive guidance and tools for government accounting. CCH's *Accounting Research Manager*, for example, gives subscribers access to CCH's governmental GAAP practice manual, a governmental GAAP guide, audit tools, and checklists.

Next, we will discuss the accounting standards applicable to federal government financial statements.

Federal Accounting Standards

The **Federal Accounting Standards Advisory Board** (FASAB) establishes accounting standards applicable to U.S. government financial statements. Under the CFO Act of 1990, the U.S. government and its "component entities," or federal reporting entities, are required to prepare annual, audited financial statements.

Specifically, the CFO Act required executive branch entities of the U.S. government to prepare audited financial statements; legislative and judicial branch entities are generally not subject to this requirement and instead report limited cash-basis financial information.[6] Annually, the financial statements of entities from each branch of the U.S. government are aggregated to create the government-wide **consolidated financial report** (CFR). This report is audited by the Government Accountability Office (GAO).

Figure 10-12 illustrates several of the executive branch entities (depicted as *significant reporting entities*) that are required to prepare audited financial statements.[7] Note, however, that not all entities required to comply with the CFO Act are shown in this graphic.

Figure 10-12

Organization of the U.S. government, including "significant" executive branch reporting entities required to prepare audited financial statements

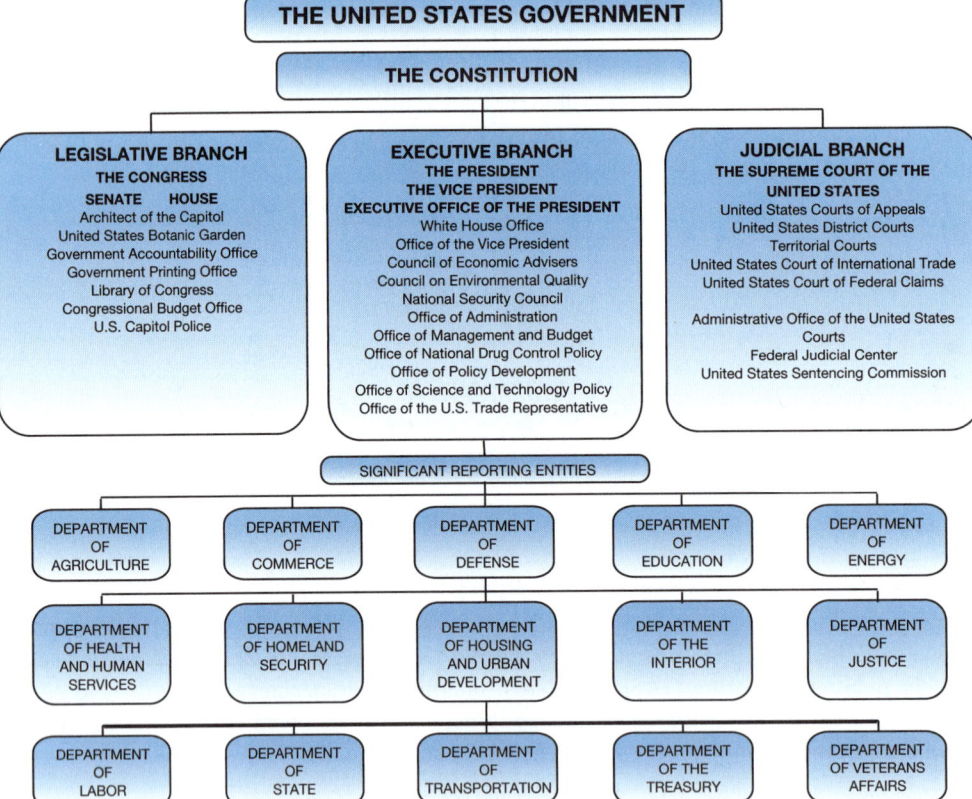

Image excerpted from 2011 Financial Report of the U.S. Government, issued by the U.S. Department of Treasury.[8]

---

[6] 2011 *Financial Report of the U.S. Government*, Note 1A: Reporting Entity. Page 51.

[7] This illustration was excerpted from the 2011 Financial Report of the U.S. Government, Management's Discussion and Analysis, Exhibit 1, page 2. The original illustration (not reproduced in full in this chapter) also lists several of the "other significant reporting entities" (such as the Securities and Exchange Commission) required to prepare audited financial statements.

[8] id.

The FASAB was established in 1990 in order to create accounting standards for the financial reports required under the CFO Act. Federal officials representing the Department of the Treasury and the Office of Management and Budget (OMB), both Executive Branch entities, and the Government Accountability Office (GAO), a legislative branch agency—having the authority to set these standards—created the FASAB and delegated to it their standard setting responsibilities.

Collectively, the Department of Treasury, the OMB, and the GAO (i.e., the "sponsor agencies") fund the FASAB. Of the FASAB's nine-member board, three members are appointed by the sponsor agencies, and six members are selected from the public. Two of the FASAB's sponsor agencies, the GAO and OMB, have the right to review and, at their discretion, object to, FASAB standards before they are issued as final.

Guidance Issued by the FASAB

Guidance issued by the FASAB is referred to as **GAAP for federal entities**. The FASAB's authoritative sources of guidance are compiled and codified together in the *FASAB Handbook of Federal Accounting Standards and Other Pronouncements* (the "**FASAB Handbook**"), available free of charge at www.fasab.gov, under "Standards." The FASAB Handbook, depicted in Figure 10-13, reflects the current population of FASAB guidance and is generally updated annually. Individual standards issued between updates are also available on the FASAB's website.

FASAB guidance can also be accessed in certain, but not all, firm research databases. PwC's *Comperio* database, for example, provides its subscribers access to FASAB's final and proposed guidance.

Figure 10-13

The FASAB Handbook (cover image), as of June 30, 2012

The FASAB Handbook includes the following guidance:

- FASAB Standards, also referred to as Statements of Federal Financial Accounting Standards (SFFAS)
- Concepts Statements, also referred to as Statements of Federal Financial Accounting Concepts (SFFAC)
- Interpretations, also referred to as Interpretations of Federal Financial Accounting Standards
- Technical Bulletins (TB)

■ Technical Releases (TR), also referred to as Federal Financial Accounting and Auditing Technical Releases

■ Staff Implementation Guidance

The hierarchy depicted in Figure 10-14 applies to the use of FASAB guidance.

Figure 10-14

Hierarchy for the use of FASAB guidance[9]

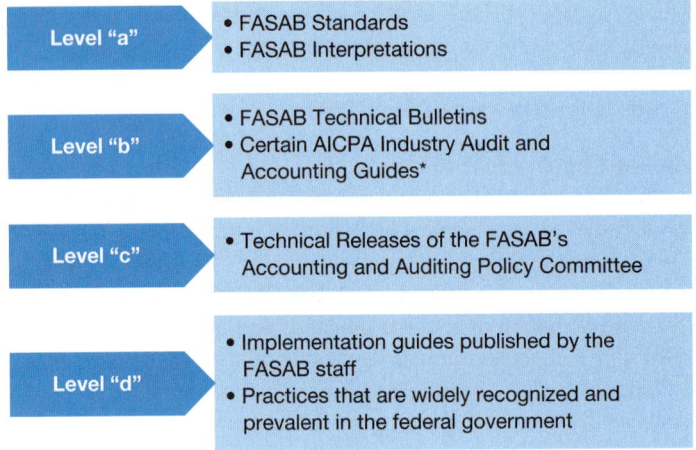

Level "a"
- FASAB Standards
- FASAB Interpretations

Level "b"
- FASAB Technical Bulletins
- Certain AICPA Industry Audit and Accounting Guides*

Level "c"
- Technical Releases of the FASAB's Accounting and Auditing Policy Committee

Level "d"
- Implementation guides published by the FASAB staff
- Practices that are widely recognized and prevalent in the federal government

*If specifically made applicable to federal reporting entities by the AICPA and cleared by the FASAB

Preparers of federal government financial statements should utilize accounting guidance in the order of priority listed. That is, if guidance in level a is unavailable for a transaction, guidance in levels b–d may be applied in descending order. If none of these sources (a–d) offer relevant guidance, entities should consider guidance for similar transactions, then they may consider other sources of guidance such as the FASAB Concepts Statements or FASB, AICPA, GASB, or IASB guidance, articles, or textbooks.

Guidance within the FASAB handbook is organized by standard, and each standard is presented as a separate chapter. The Status page of each standard lists other standards and interpretive guidance that affect, or are affected by, the standard. For example, Figure 10-15 illustrates the Status page of SFFAS 33 (Pensions, Other Retirement Benefits, and Other Postemployment Benefits).

Figure 10-15

Sample "Status" page, showing guidance that affects (or is affected by) SFFAS 33

> ### Statement of Federal Financial Accounting Standards 33: Pensions, Other Retirement Benefits, and Other Postemployment Benefits: Reporting the Gains and Losses from Changes in Assumptions and Selecting Discount Rates and Valuation Dates
>
> ## Status
>
> | | |
> |---|---|
> | **Issued** | October 14, 2008 |
> | **Effective Date** | For fiscal years beginning after September 30, 2009 |
> | **Interpretations and Technical Releases** | None. |
> | **Affects** | • SFFAS 5. pars. 65, 66, 83, 95, and 157, by changing the standard for selecting discount rates.
• SFFAS 7, par. 67.1, by replacing the phrase "best estimate" with "reasonable estimate" and "likely" with "reasonably expected"; par. 67.2 by replacing "best" with "reasonable."
• SFFAS 17, pars. 25, 27(2), and 27(4), by replacing the phrase "best" with "reasonable" and deleted "best," respectively. |
> | **Affected by** | None. |

Source: FASAB Handbook, as of June 30, 2012

---

[9] SFFAS 34, *The Hierarchy of Generally Accepted Accounting Principles, Including the Application of Standards Issued by the Financial Accounting Standards Board*, FASAB Handbook 2012 revision, par. 5.

To search for guidance within the FASAB Handbook, researchers can (1) perform "ctrl+f" (find) keyword searches within the Handbook or (2) scan the Handbook's table of contents to locate standards relevant to their searches. Within each individual standard is a table of contents, which can help researchers efficiently navigate to relevant guidance.

Applying FASAB Guidance

The following example illustrates the accounting for government Medicare obligations (a type of "social insurance"). Readers will have the opportunity to review and apply FASAB guidance applicable to this issue.

Accounting for Medicare

Facts about Medicare: Medicare is a national health insurance program for people ages 65 and older, as well as for certain individuals with disabilities. Generally, U.S. citizens and permanent residents meeting the age requirement are eligible for Medicare if they or their spouse worked for at least 10 years in Medicare-covered employment. Medicare is funded, in part, through a payroll tax levied on employees and employers.

Required: Read the following excerpts from SFFAS 17, *Accounting for Social Insurance*, then respond to the questions that follow.

> 14. The following programs are designated as social insurance and subject to these standards:
>   • Old-Age, Survivors, and Disability Insurance (OASDI or "Social Security");
>   • Hospital Insurance (HI) and Supplementary Medical Insurance (SMI), known collectively as "Medicare";
>   • Railroad Retirement benefits;
>   • Black Lung benefits; and
>   • Unemployment Insurance (UI). . . .
>
> **Characteristics of Social Insurance Programs**
>
> 15. These programs were developed to carry out the responsibilities of the government and generally have characteristics that make them unique. . . . This statement identifies the following five characteristics common among social insurance programs:
>   (1) Financing from participants or their employers,
>   (2) Eligibility from taxes/fees paid and time worked in **covered employment**,
>   (3) Benefits not directly related to taxes/fees paid,
>   (4) Benefits prescribed in law, and
>   (5) Programs intended for the general public.

Now YOU Try 10.1

Questions:

1. First, recall from the reading: Is SFFAS 17 applicable to state and local governments, or to federal government entities? Explain.

_____

2. Read the "Facts about Medicare" above, then explain how you determined (under both par. 14 and 15) that Medicare is within the scope of this guidance:

Par. 14: _____

Par. 15: _____

SFFAS 17 states the following regarding the recognition and measurement of social insurance benefits:

> 22. The expense recognized for the reporting period should be the benefits paid during the reporting period plus any increase (or less any decrease) in the liability from the end

Continued

Continued from previous page

> of the prior period to the end of the current period. The liability should be social insurance benefits due and payable to or on behalf of beneficiaries at the end of the reporting period, including claims incurred but not reported (IBNR).

3. How does SFFAS 17 require governments to measure the liability for social insurance benefits?

_____

_____

4. Brainstorm, recalling from previous financial accounting courses: Is this recognition model consistent with how nongovernmental entities record employee retirement health care obligations?

_____

_____

Referencing Governmental Accounting Guidance

Citing Standards

References to governmental accounting standards follow a similar format as references to other, nongovernmental sources. For example, following are sample references to GASB and FASAB standards:

■ Per GASB Statement No. 1, *Accounting and Financial Reporting for Derivative Instruments* (Statement 1 or GASBS 1) par. 2, Statements of the NCGA (the GASB's predecessor) are recognized by the GASB as being in force until modified by the GASB.

■ Per Statement of Federal Financial Accounting Standards No. 1 (SFFAS 1), *Accounting for Selected Assets and Liabilities*, par. 18, "***intragovernmental assets and liabilities*** arise from transactions among federal entities."

Both citations include the following required elements:

■ The full name of the standard type (e.g., GASB Statement No., or Statement of Federal Financial Accounting Standards No.). This full introduction is necessary whenever guidance is first cited in a memo. Without this, a reader might have difficulty understanding how to locate this guidance.

■ Full name of standard is included, in italics.

■ Paragraph number is included.

■ An indication (in parenthesis) that future references to this source will be abbreviated as "GASBS 1" or "SFFAS 1."

Future references to these standards may simply state: "Per GASBS 1, par. 2" or "Per SFFAS 1, par. 19," for example.

Citing the GASB Codification

References to the GASB Codification can be cited as follows:

> GASB Cod. Sec. 2300.102 states: "The notes to the financial statements should communicate information essential for fair presentation of the basic financial statements that is not displayed on the face of the financial statements."

In this example, identification of the "GASB Cod" is provided initially; future references to the Codification within the same memo can be abbreviated as "Sec. 2300, par. 102."

GOVERNMENTAL AUDITING STANDARDS

In What Circumstances Are Government Audits Required?

Recall from our discussion of governmental accounting standards that many state, local, and federal government entities are required to prepare audited financial statements. These audits may be required by, for example,

- The CFO Act, which requires certain federal entities to prepare annual, audited financial statements;

- The laws of individual states, which may require annual audited state and local government financial statements; or

- Compliance with debt or other covenants, requiring governments (borrowers) to provide audited financial statements.

In addition to financial statement audits, entities may be required to undergo **performance audits** in certain circumstances. The objectives of individual performance audits can vary but might focus on, for example,

- The efficiency and effectiveness of a government program (e.g., Are government resources being expended in the manner intended?);

- An entity's internal controls and governance structure;

- An entity's information security; or

- An entity's compliance with laws and regulations.

Following are two circumstances in which performance audits are currently required.

"Single Audit" Requirement for Recipients of Federal Funding

Entities receiving federal funding in excess of $500,000 are required by the U.S. government's Office of Management and Budget (**OMB**) **Circular A-133** to undergo a **single audit**.[10] Illustrated in Figure 10-16, a single audit is defined as a financial statement audit plus a *program* (aka, performance) audit of programs for which federal funds have been received. Single audits must be conducted in accordance with both Circular A-133 and governmental auditing standards, and these audit requirements apply to both governmental and nongovernmental entities receiving federal funding.

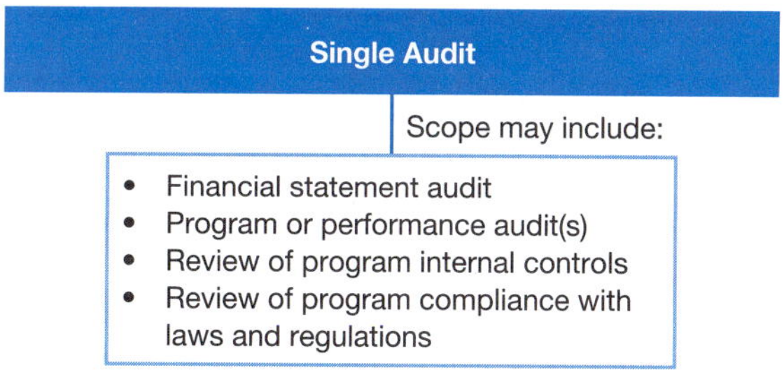

Single Audit

Scope may include:
- Financial statement audit
- Program or performance audit(s)
- Review of program internal controls
- Review of program compliance with laws and regulations

Figure 10-16

A "single audit" combines required financial statement and performance audits, for recipients of federal funds

Annually, the OMB prepares department-specific Supplements to Circular A-133, which provide auditors with guidance for auditing specific federal award programs.

- For example, auditors reviewing the effectiveness of the Department of Justice "JOBS" grants—awarded to local governments for the purpose of hiring additional police officers— must consult the Circular A-133 "Department of Justice Supplement." That supplement

---

[10] OMB Circular No. A-133, "Audits of States, Local Governments, and Non-Profit Organizations". Revised to show changes published in the Federal Register June 27, 2003 and June 26, 2007. Subpart B (Audits), Section .200 (Audit Requirements), par. (a).

instructs local government auditors, when conducting performance audits, to ask: "How many new officers were hired this year?"[11]

Notably, the OMB is currently reviewing potential changes to Circular A-133, including possibly raising the threshold for audit from $500,000 to $750,000 in federal funds received.

State-Required Performance Audits

Certain states require their municipal governments and agencies to submit to periodic performance audits, which can range in their objectives and scope. For example,

- In New York, the Office of the State Comptroller (OSC) conducts performance audits of state agencies, public authorities, and local governments (including towns, villages, school districts, and fire districts). The focus of these audits can vary, from a review of internal controls, to a review of the entity's governance structure, to reviews of specific programs' efficiency and effectiveness. The type of audit required is determined based on a risk assessment by the OSC.

- The need for regular oversight over school district governance and controls, in particular, was underscored by the $11 million, Roslyn, New York, School District fraud, uncovered in a 2005 audit.[12] Perpetrated primarily by the district's Superintendent and the Assistant Superintendent for Business (i.e., school district chief financial officer), this fraud might have been prevented had effective governance and internal controls been in place. In response to this fraud, the New York OSC initiated a 5-year effort to review the internal controls of all New York school districts, in addition to continuing to require annual, independent financial audits of all school districts in the state.[13]

Clearly, government audits can range widely in their objectives and complexity; these examples illustrate just a few of the circumstances in which government audits are required. Next, let's discuss the parties who perform government audits.

Who Performs Government Audits?

You may be wondering: do all "government auditors" work for the government? No; while it's true that internal and external auditors of government financial statements may work for the federal, or for state or local governments, many "government auditors" work in public accounting firms (ranging from local firms to national firms). In many cases, the governmental entity under audit has the opportunity to engage an audit firm of its choice; in other cases, the federal government may conduct (or assign responsibility to another agency for conducting) an audit of a state or local government that receives federal government funds, or state auditors (or another audit agency appointed by the state) may audit municipalities. Many federal agencies have an **Office of the Inspector General** whose mission is, in part, to audit the programs and operations of the agency.[14]

Therefore, even if your future involves working for a public accounting firm, it is possible that *you* will be assigned to a governmental client. Unfortunately, as a profession, our ability to perform quality governmental audits has historically been underwhelming.

EXAMPLE

In a June 2007 project, several federal agencies worked together to test (based on statistical sampling) the audit quality of federal award ("funds") recipients. Of the 208 audits sampled,[15]

Continued

---

[11] OMB Circular No. A-133, Compliance Supplement 2012. Department of Justice supplement: "Public Safety Partnership and Community Policing Grants." Section L(2), Performance Reporting.

[12] Huefner, Ronald J. "Local government fraud: the Roslyn School District case." *Management Research Review,* copyright Emerald Group Publishing Limited. Vol. 33, No. 3, 2010. Page 199.

[13] Division of Local Government and School Accountability, of the Office of the New York State Comptroller. "Making the Grade: Five Years of School District Accountability." 2009 Annual Report. February 2010. Page 2.

[14] Inspector General's Act of 1978, as amended.

[15] President's Council on Integrity and Efficiency, "Report on National Single Audit Sampling Project." June 2007. Page 2.

- 63 audits were found to be "unacceptable" and could not be relied on.
- 30 audits had significant deficiencies and were considered to be of "limited reliability."
- 115 were considered "acceptable" and thus could be relied on.

It's worth noting that the acceptable audits represented an overwhelming majority (92.9%) of the federal awards (in dollars) reviewed. However, based on *numbers of audits*, the results showed significant percentages of unacceptable audits and audits of limited reliability. Per the government report:

> . . . For those audits not in the acceptable group, in our opinion, lack of due professional care was a factor for most deficiencies to some degree. [16]

The report offered the following recommendations to the government and the accounting profession: (1) improve audit standards and guidance, particularly related to documentation and audit sampling; (2) require minimum levels of training for government auditors; and (3) establish clear consequences for unacceptable audits.

Consistent with these recommendations, the next section of this chapter introduces readers to the authoritative guidance applicable to government audits, and describes the "minimum training" requirements applicable to government auditors.

Standards for Government Audits

The U.S. Government Accountability Office—Standard Setter
The U.S. **Government Accountability Office** (GAO) serves as the primary standard setter for government audits, establishing professional standards for audits of financial statements, attestation engagements, and performance audits (including, for example, compliance audits). The GAO's standards, codified in the **Yellow Book** of government auditing standards, are collectively referred to as **generally accepted government auditing standards**, or **GAGAS**.

Despite its important role in setting government auditing standards, to call the GAO simply a standard setter would be an understatement. A legislative-branch, nonpartisan agency, the GAO describes its mission as twofold: (1) to support Congress by providing objective, fact-based information and (2) to help improve the performance and ensure the accountability of the federal government. Also referred to as the "congressional watchdog," the GAO is the audit and investigative arm of Congress, frequently studying the ways taxpayer dollars are spent.[17]

The GAO is headed by the Comptroller General of the United States, who is appointed by the U.S. president to serve a 15-year term. Having long-term requirements supports the agency's independence and the ability of its leaders to develop institutional knowledge.

In addition to issuing auditing standards, the GAO performs certain audits. Notably, the GAO is responsible for auditing the annual federal government-wide financial statements. Audits of individual departments, such as the Department of Energy and the Department of Homeland Security are generally conducted by other federal departments or by public accounting firms. See Figure 10-17 for a sample of CFO Act agencies, auditors, and their fiscal year 2011 audit opinion.

---

[16] President's Council on Integrity and Efficiency, "Report on National Single Audit Sampling Project." June 2007. Page 3.

[17] GAO, *Performance and Accountability Report Fiscal Year 2012*, Page 6. November 15, 2012.

[18] Information excerpted from Statement of Gene L. Dodaro, Comptroller General of the United States. Testimony Before the Subcommittee on Government Organization, Efficiency and Financial Management, Committee on Oversight and Government Reform, House of Representatives." The Federal Government Faces Continuing Financial Management and Long Term Fiscal Challenges." GAO-12-444T, page 20.

Figure 10-17

Sample of fiscal year 2011 CFO Act agencies audited, opinions received, and auditors, from the 2011 *Financial Report of the U.S. Government*[18]

CFO Act Agency	Opinion	Auditor
Department of Agriculture	Unqualified	Office of Inspector General (OIG) of the Agriculture Dept.
Department of Commerce	Unqualified	KPMG LLP
Department of Defense	Disclaimer	OIG of the Defense Dept.
Department of Education	Unqualified	Ernst & Young LLP
Department of Energy	Unqualified	KPMG LLP
Department of Health and Human Services	Unqualified	Ernst & Young LLP
Department of Homeland Security	Qualified	KPMG LLP

Content and Organization of GAO Guidance

The GAO's *Yellow Book* is the authoritative source for government audit requirements, covering a range of topics including auditor ethics, and engagement planning, performance, and reporting requirements.[19] Using AICPA standards as a base, GAGAS adds to and/or modifies these requirements in order to address government-specific audit issues.

It is important to understand that auditors adhering to the Yellow Book *must also comply, in full, with the audit and attestation standards of the AICPA*. The AICPA's audit and attestation standards are **incorporated by reference** into GAGAS, meaning that although AICPA standards have not been copied into the Yellow Book, the Yellow Book requires auditors to fully comply with these standards in addition to government-specific Yellow Book standards. Notably, certain of the AICPA's clarified standards include "governmental consideration" paragraphs specific to governmental audits. PCAOB standards are not incorporated into GAGAS.

Per Chapter 4 (Standards for Financial Audits) of the Yellow Book:

> 4.01 . . . GAGAS incorporates by reference the American Institute of Certified Public Accountants (AICPA) Statements on Auditing Standards (SAS) . . . All sections of the SASs are incorporated, including the introduction, objectives, definitions, requirements, and application and other explanatory material. Auditors performing financial audits in accordance with GAGAS should comply with the incorporated SASs and the additional requirements in this chapter. The requirements and guidance contained in Chapters 1 through 3 also apply to financial audits performed in accordance with GAGAS.
>
> 4.02 GAGAS establishes requirements for performing financial audits in addition to the requirements contained in the AICPA standards. Auditors should comply with these additional requirements, along with the incorporated SASs, when citing GAGAS in their reports.

In the auditor's (or attestation provider's) report, when stating that an engagement was performed in accordance with GAGAS, it is not necessary to state that the engagement also complied with AICPA standards. Because GAGAS incorporates AICPA standards by reference, it is understood that an engagement performed in accordance with GAGAS also complies with AICPA standards.[20]

Following is a brief **Now YOU Try** exercise intended to reinforce the sources of guidance that must be followed under GAGAS.

---

[19] GAO, *Government Auditing Standards* (i.e., the "Yellow Book"). 2011 Revision. Chapter 1, par. 1.04.

[20] GAO, *Government Auditing Standards* (i.e., the "Yellow Book"). 2011 Revision. Chapter 4, par. 4.18; Chapter 5, par. 5.19, 5.51, and 5.61.

Understanding Compliance with GAGAS

Review the excerpt from **par. 4.01** and the preceding discussion, and respond to the following.

1. For an auditor to comply with GAGAS, he or she must also comply with the AICPA's
_____ .

2. Specifically, an auditor must comply with all sections of the AICPA's SAS, including the introduction, objectives, _____ .

3. Financial statement auditors must also comply with Ch. _____ through _____ of the Yellow Book, which establish general standards for auditor conduct.

4. When citing compliance with GAGAS in the auditor's report, it is not necessary to also state that the audit complied with AICPA standards because: _____
_____

Now YOU Try **10.2**

The Yellow Book is accessible on the GAO's website, as follows:

- www.gao.gov/yellowbook; or

- www.gao.gov, then "Resources For" then "Auditing and Accountability" then "Government Auditing Standards."

Figure 10-18 illustrates the cover page and the first table of contents page from the Yellow Book.

Within the Yellow Book, guidance is organized by topic. Therefore, when searching for guidance, researchers may find it most efficient to scan the Yellow Book's table of contents. This offers researchers the benefit of getting a feel for available guidance and seeing how it is organized. Alternatively, researchers can perform keyword searches of the entire document, using ctrl + f.

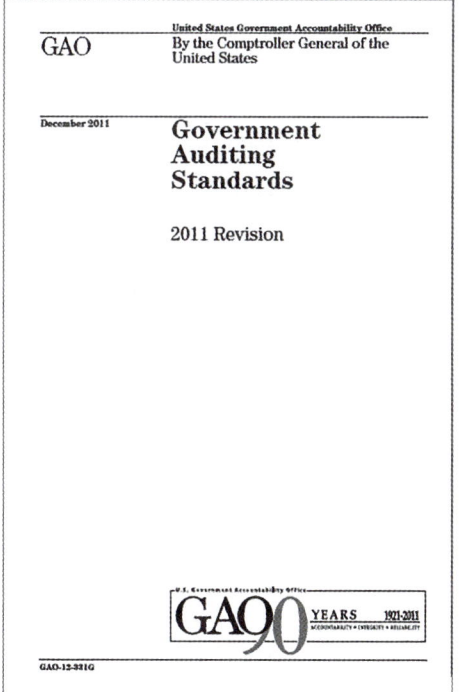
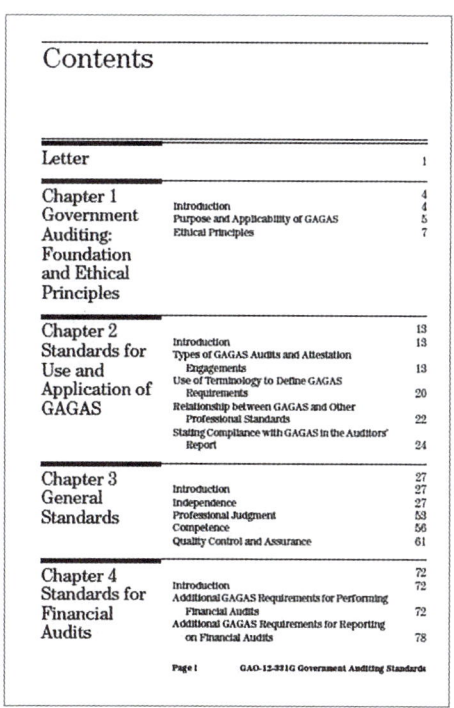

Figure 10-18

GAO's *Government Auditing Standards* (Yellow Book) cover page and excerpt from table of contents

Figure 10-20 lists the chapters and summarizes some of the key content included in the Yellow Book.

Figure 10-19

Yellow Book chapters and content summary

Chapter	Examples of chapter content
Chapter 1, Government Auditing: Foundation and Ethical Principles	• Describes the purpose and applicability of GAGAS (identifies entities subject to) • Role of government auditors • Role of ethics in audits
Chapter 2, Standards for Use and Application of GAGAS	• Defines types of GAGAS engagements (financial/performance audits, attestation engagements) • Defines "unconditional" and "presumptively mandatory" requirements • Describes the relationship between GAGAS and other professional standards (such as AICPA guidance)
Chapter 3, General Standards	• Requires auditors to be independent, to use professional judgment, to possess technical competence • Audit firms must maintain a system of quality control
Chapter 4, Standards for Financial Audits	• Requires auditors to comply with AICPA audit standards in addition to specific GAGAS field work and reporting standards
Chapter 5, Standards for Attestation Engagements	• Requires auditors to comply with AICPA attestation standards in addition to specific GAGAS standards
Chapter 6, Field Work Standards for Performance Audits	• Provides guidance for performance audits, including audit planning, evidence, and documentation
Chapter 7, Reporting Standards for Performance Audits	• Provides guidance on communicating the results of performance audits
Appendixes	• Supplemental guidance • Conceptual Framework for independence

Notably, within Yellow Book Chapter 3 (General Standards), the section on auditor competency includes certain training requirements for government auditors. Specifically, government auditors must earn at least 80 hours of continuing education credits in the fields of audit and attestation every 2 years, and 24 hours of this must pertain specifically to the government environment and government auditing.[21]

Take a moment now to practice your Yellow Book research skills with the following **Now YOU Try** exercise.

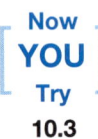

Now **YOU** Try 10.3

Locating Information within the Yellow Book

Provide the chapter number that you would consult for guidance on the following questions.

1. Are GAGAS applicable to nonprofit entities?

   Chapter No. _____

2. What audit evidence is required for auditors engaged to perform "performance" audits?

   Chapter No. _____

3. What are the minimum training requirements necessary for a government auditor to demonstrate "competence"?

   Chapter No. _____

4. Like the AICPA, does GAGAS use the word "must" to indicate an unconditional requirement?

   Chapter No. _____

5. What additional documentation (beyond AICPA requirements) is required for financial statement audits performed under GAGAS?

   Chapter No. _____

---

[21] GAO, *Government Auditing Standards* (i.e., the "Yellow Book"). 2011 Revision. Chapter 3, par. 3.76. Also: GAO, *Guidance on GAGAS Requirements for Continuing Professional Education*, April 2005. Par. 18–19.

Citing GAO Guidance

The following example illustrates an appropriate reference to guidance from the Yellow Book.

■ Per *Government Auditing Standards, December 2011 Revision,* Section 3.02 (Independence):

3.02 In all matters relating to the audit work, the audit organization and the individual auditor, whether government or public, must be independent.

Note that the preceding reference contains the title of the source (*Government Auditing Standards*) as well as the date of revision. As a researcher, err on the side of caution and assume your reader does not know what a "yellow book" is—only use this term after introducing the full title of the source.

Because the Yellow Book is revised periodically, it is necessary to include the date of the revision you have consulted. Without this complete information, future readers of your memo may have difficulty locating your original source.

Note also that section and paragraph numbers (e.g., 3.02) should be included any time specific guidance is cited.

Other Governmental Audit Resources

In addition to the GAO's Yellow Book and the OMB's Circular A-133 and supplements, several other sources of authoritative guidance exist for government audits. These include (but are not limited to):

■ OMB Bulletin No. 07-04, *Audit Requirements for Federal Financial Statements* (as amended), which establishes additional audit requirements for federal government financial statements.

■ FASAB Technical Releases, located within the *FASAB Handbook*, which set forth certain requirements for audits of federal government entities.

■ State-specific audit requirements, often included within individual states' "audit manuals." States may require governmental auditors to comply with these requirements in addition to complying with GAGAS.

Nonauthoritative Resources

A number of practical, nonauthoritative resources are also available to aid government auditors. These include (but are not limited to) the following.

1. GAO/PCIE Financial Audit Manual (FAM)

The GAO, together with the President's Council on Integrity and Efficiency (PCIE), produces an audit manual (the FAM) intended to improve the consistency, efficiency, and effectiveness of government audits. The FAM includes, for example, practical guidance to auditors for identifying and addressing areas of key risk.[22]

2. AICPA Governmental Audit Quality Center

The AICPA's Governmental Audit Quality Center (GAQC) strives to improve on the quality of governmental audits, by providing educational resources, community forums, and practice aids (including audit checklists) to its members.

3. PPC Guides

Publishing company "PPC" publishes practical guides for government audits including, for example, PPC's *Guide to Single Audits* and PPC's *Guide to Audits of Local Governments*. These publications are intended to be a practitioner's "one stop shop" for understanding and performing government audits and include audit programs, checklists, confirmations, auditor's reports, and the like.

---

[22] GAO/PCIE *Financial Audit Manual*, Volume 1. July 2008. Section 110 (Overview), par. 14–15.

Applying Governmental Auditing Standards

Following are two examples illustrating the application of governmental audit guidance. The first example illustrates an audit report for a local government performance audit. The second example illustrates the GAO's audit findings related to its audit of the U.S. federal government.

Now
YOU
Try
10.4

Audit of Local Government's Receipt of Grant Funds

Facts: In 2012, the U.S. Department of Justice's Office of the Inspector General (OIG) conducted a program audit of "COPS" grant money received by the City of Newark, New Jersey. The COPS program offers grant money to local governments in order to enhance their local policing efforts and to upgrade existing police communication systems.

Following is an excerpt from the Yellow Book describing the reporting requirements for performance (including program) audits:

> **7.08** Auditors should prepare audit reports that contain (1) the objectives, scope, and methodology of the audit; (2) the audit results, including findings, conclusions, and recommendations, as appropriate; (3) a statement about the auditors' compliance with GAGAS; (4) a summary of the views of responsible officials; and (5) if applicable, the nature of any confidential or sensitive information omitted.

Following are excerpts from the OIG's audit report on Newark's use of COPS funds.[23]

> The purpose of this audit was to determine whether reimbursements claimed for costs under the grant were allowable, supported, and in accordance with applicable laws, regulations, guidelines, and terms and conditions of the grant, and to determine program performance and accomplishments. COPS awarded Newark $2,787,001 to implement the grant program and required Newark to provide $929,000 in local funds for a total project cost of $3,716,001.
>
> We examined Newark's accounting records, financial and progress reports, and operating policies and procedures and found the deficiencies below resulting in net questioned costs totaling $3,539,432.
>
> - Newark significantly changed the scope of the grant project without prior written approval from COPS.
> - Newark did not achieve the performance objectives related to voice communications funded by the grant.
> - Newark purchased wireless network equipment and services totaling $2,777,569 that were not procured using a competitive process or approved for purchase under the New Jersey State Cooperative Purchasing program, which is in violation of grant regulations requiring competition. . . .
>
> We conducted this performance audit in accordance with generally accepted government auditing standards. Those standards require that we plan and perform the audit to obtain sufficient, appropriate evidence to provide a reasonable basis for our findings and conclusions based on our audit objectives.

Using the excerpted GAGAS requirements and the OIG audit report, respond to the questions that follow.

---

[23] U.S. Department of Justice Office of the Inspector General Audit Division, Audit Report GR-70-12-007. July 2012. Pages i–ii, 17.

Questions:

1. What law or standard, discussed within the chapter, requires certain recipients of federal grant funds to be audited?

_____

2. Describe how the OIG's audit report satisfies the GAGAS requirements excerpted in par. 7.08. (Or note any areas not covered in this excerpt).

   i) _____

   ii) _____

   iii) _____

   iv) _____

   v) _____

Audit Report—Federal Government-Wide Financial Statements

Now
YOU
Try
10.5

Facts: One of the GAO's responsibilities is to audit the consolidated government-wide financial report on an annual basis. However, fiscal year 2011 marked the fifteenth consecutive year that the GAO expressed a disclaimer of opinion on this report.[24] The following example focuses on the GAO's reported internal control findings which were, in part, responsible for this disclaimer of opinion.

Following are excerpts from the Yellow Book describing auditor reporting requirements related to internal controls, followed by excerpts from the GAO audit report describing internal control findings.

> **Reporting on Internal Control and Compliance with Provisions of Laws, Regulations, Contracts, and Grant Agreements**
>
> **4.19**   When providing an opinion or a disclaimer on financial statements, auditors should also report on internal control over financial reporting . . .
>
> **Presenting Findings in the Auditors' Report**
>
> **4.28**   When performing a GAGAS financial audit and presenting findings such as deficiencies in internal control . . . auditors should develop the elements of the findings to the extent necessary . . . If auditors sufficiently develop the elements of a finding, they may provide recommendations for corrective action. [Footnotes omitted]

Following is an excerpt from the GAO's audit report describing reasons for its disclaimer of opinion:

> **Disclaimers of Opinion on the Accrual-Based Consolidated Financial Statements**
>
> Because of the federal government's inability to demonstrate the reliability of significant portions of [its] financial statements . . . principally resulting from limitations related to certain material weaknesses in internal control over financial reporting and other limitations on the scope of our work, we are unable to, and we do not, express an opinion on such accrual-based consolidated financial statements . . .
>
> . . . The underlying material weaknesses in internal control, which generally have existed for years, contributed to our disclaimer of opinion on the accrual-based consolidated financial statements. [These include] the federal government's inability to

Continued

---

[24] 2011 *Financial Report of the U.S. Government*. Management's Discussion & Analysis, page 5.

Continued from previous page

- satisfactorily determine that property, plant, and equipment and inventories and related property, primarily held by DOD, were properly reported in the accrual-based consolidated financial statements;
- reasonably estimate or adequately support amounts reported for certain liabilities, such as environmental and disposal liabilities, or determine whether commitments and contingencies were complete and properly reported;
- support significant portions of the reported total net cost of operations, most notably related to DOD, and adequately reconcile disbursement activity at certain federal entities;
- adequately account for and reconcile intragovernmental activity and balances between federal entities;
- ensure that the federal government's accrual-based consolidated financial statements were (1) consistent with the underlying audited entities' financial statements, (2) properly balanced, and (3) in conformity with GAAP; . . .

Questions:

1. According to par. 4.19 of the *Yellow Book*, when must auditors report on internal controls over financial reporting?

2. What reasons does the GAO give for its disclaimer of opinion?

3. Describe how the GAO's audit report excerpt satisfies the requirements in par. 4.28 of the Yellow Book—and identify any areas not shown in this particular excerpt that are also required by par. 4.28.

Finally, let us turn our attention to several resources available to management accountants.

INDUSTRY RESOURCES

The last section of this chapter introduces additional professional resources available to management accountants (also known as "industry" accountants). Namely, we will discuss professional organizations, as well as standards available to management accountants, internal auditors, and government contractors. The population of standards and professional resources described below is not all-inclusive; rather, this discussion is intended to introduce just a few of the many resources available to practicing accountants.

Professional Organizations

Numerous professional groups, or trade organizations, are available for accountants in industry. These organizations offer members the opportunity to network, attend industry-specific training courses, and to exchange best practices. Also, in some cases, these organizations issue standards applicable to professionals in a particular industry. Professional organizations of accountants include, just to name a few:

- The Institute of Management Accountants (IMA)
- Institute of Internal Auditors (IIA)

- The International Federation of Accountants (IFAC)

- Financial Executives International (FEI)

- The Association of Certified Fraud Examiners (ACFE)

As a practitioner, it may be both helpful (or often, necessary) to become familiar with the professional groups applicable to your industry, and the resources they offer.

Next, let's discuss a few sources of industry guidance available to management accountants.

Management Accounting Standards

The Institute of Management Accountants (IMA) is a professional organization focused on the development and advancement of management accountants and finance professionals working inside organizations. Its members include, for example, individuals ranging from CFOs, to treasurers, to staff accountants.

As part of its mission to support management accountants, the IMA issues Statements on Management Accounting (SMAs). These standards are intended to provide valuable, in-depth information, best practices, and implementation guidance on a range of management accounting subjects. SMAs cover topics ranging from leadership and ethics, to cost management, to corporate governance. Application of SMAs is not required; rather, these standards are intended to be useful to individuals and corporations.

Internal Audit Resources

The Institute of Internal Auditors (IIA) is a professional association dedicated to supporting and advancing the internal audit profession. The IIA issues guidance, which is primarily divided into two types: (1) mandatory and (2) strongly recommended. Following are the IIA's "mandatory" sources of guidance:

- Definition of Internal Auditing

- IIA's Code of Ethics

- *International Standards for the Professional Practice of Internal Auditing* (Standards)

These sources receive their authority as "mandatory" through internal audit charters maintained within business organizations. Internal audit charters give the internal audit department access to business unit information and records, while simultaneously establishing expectations for the work and conduct of the internal audit department. For reference, the IIA makes a Model Internal Audit Activity Charter available at its website, www.theiia.org.

The IIA's sources of "strongly recommended" guidance consist of: Position Papers, Practice Advisories, and Practice Guides. Internal auditors are encouraged to comply with these sources of interpretive guidance, as applicable.

The IIA's mandatory standards consist of requirements and interpretive guidance governing the planning, performance, and reporting of internal audit engagements. These standards are contained within a single booklet, accessible on the IIA's website.

Cost Accounting Standards (for Government Contractors and Certain Universities)

The **Cost Accounting Standards Board**, created by the Office of Federal Procurement Policy (an executive branch entity), establishes cost accounting standards (CAS) for government contractors and universities receiving government grants. For contractors, these standards apply in full to entities awarded projects in excess of $50 million (individually, or in the aggregate), and in part to certain contracts of lesser amounts. Government contractors (excluding small businesses) must comply with these standards in the measurement, assignment, and allocation of costs to negotiated contracts with the U.S. government. Among these requirements, contractors must disclose their cost accounting practices in writing to the government (the "CAS Disclosure Statement").

Contracts with the U.S. Department of Defense make up the majority of procurement contracts subject to CAS. As defense contractors submit cost-based contract proposals to the Department of Defense, these costs must be determined in accordance with CAS.

Guidance issued by this board includes CAS, as well as rules and regulations. Collectively, these sources of guidance are codified within the "Code of Federal Regulations" (CFR), at Title 48, Chapter 99. Proposed and final rules are published in the *Federal Register*, a daily news publication of the federal government.

In addition to government contractors, colleges and universities receiving government grants in excess of $25 million are also subject to certain CAS requirements. For example, these entities must disclose their cost accounting policies to the federal government and follow certain project costing guidelines.

[**TIP**] **from the Trenches**   As you begin to specialize as a professional, take the time to become familiar with the organizations and standards available for your industry.

APPENDIX 10A: APPLYING THE GASB CODIFICATION, AN EXTENDED EXAMPLE

Recognition of Tax Revenues, Using Fund Accounting

The following example illustrates the recognition of sales and property tax revenues by a local government. In doing so, the example touches on the different bases of accounting applicable to governments (accrual and modified accrual), as well as the use of fund accounting. For teaching purposes, this example has been kept very simple; however, in practice, these issues can be much more nuanced and can require professional judgment and as necessary, additional research.

Facts: Assume that the Town of Hampton imposes two taxes on its residents:

1. A 10 cents per-gallon fuel tax, charged on purchases of gasoline from gas stations located in the town.

2. A 2% property tax, charged annually on the assessed value of residential properties. This tax is billed in January of each year; collections generally occur within 15 to 30 days.

Respond to the questions that follow using the guidance provided.

Are the Town of Hampton's two taxes considered "nonexchange transactions"?
GASB Cod. Sec. N50.104 (Nonexchange Transactions) defines a "nonexchange transaction" as one where a government "*either* gives value (benefit) to another party without directly receiving equal value in exchange *or* receives value (benefit) from another party without directly giving equal value in exchange."

Per Section N50, par. 104, nonexchange transactions are divided into *four classes*:

■ **Derived tax revenues**, imposed by governments on exchange transactions; examples include taxes on sales of goods or services, and corporate or personal income taxes.

■ **Imposed nonexchange revenues**, based on assessments imposed by a government entity on a nongovernmental entity (excluding assessments on exchange transactions); examples include commercial and residential property taxes, and fines and penalties.

■ **Government-mandated nonexchange transactions**, when a governmental entity provides resources to a lower-level governmental entity and requires the recipient to use the funds for a specific purpose; examples include federal programs that state/local governments must perform (using federal funding), or state programs performed by local governments (using state funding).

■ **Voluntary nonexchange transactions**, resulting from agreements entered into by willing parties; examples include grants and donations.

Questions:

1. First, do the two taxes appear to meet the definition of a "nonexchange transaction"?

   _____

   _____

2. Next, identify which class of nonexchange transaction each Town of Hampton tax falls under. Explain.

   Fuel tax: _____

   Property tax: _____

In What Circumstances Are the Accrual and the Modified Accrual Bases of Accounting Used?

In governmental accounting, revenues may be recognized on an *accrual* basis, or using a *modified accrual* basis. Understanding what basis of accounting applies is an important step in determining how the Town of Hampton should recognize its tax revenues.

Section 1600 (Basis of Accounting) of the GASB Codification describes circumstances in which each basis is most appropriate:

Government-wide Financial Statements (Statement of Principle)

The government-wide statement of net assets and the statement of activities should be prepared using the economic resources measurement focus and the accrual basis of accounting.

Fund Financial Statements (Statement of Principle)

In fund financial statements, the modified accrual or accrual basis of accounting, as appropriate, should be used in measuring financial position and operating results.

a. Financial statements for governmental funds should be presented using the current financial resources measurement focus and the <u>modified accrual</u> basis of accounting. Revenues should be recognized in the accounting period in which they become available and measurable . . .

b. Proprietary fund statements of net position and revenues, expenses, and changes in fund net position should be presented using the economic resources measurement focus and the <u>accrual</u> basis of accounting.

c. Financial statements of fiduciary funds should be reported using the economic resources measurement focus and the <u>accrual</u> basis of accounting. [Underlined emphasis added]

3. Based on the guidance above, explain when each basis of accounting (accrual vs. modified accrual) applies.

   Accrual: _____

   _____

   Modified Accrual: _____

   _____

What Are Some Common Funds Used in Governmental Accounting, and Should the Property and Sales Tax Revenues be Recorded in a Fund?

Next, in order to determine which basis of accounting is most appropriate for its sales and property tax revenues, the Town of Hampton must determine whether the revenues will be recorded within a fund.

Per Section 1300 (Fund Accounting) of the GASB Codification:

Fund Accounting Systems (Statement of Principle)

Governmental accounting systems should be organized and operated on a fund basis. A fund is defined as a fiscal and accounting entity with a self-balancing set of accounts recording cash and other financial resources, together with all related liabilities and residual equities or balances, and changes therein, which are segregated for the purpose of carrying on specific activities or attaining certain objectives in accordance with special regulations, restrictions, or limitations.

Section 1300 requires governments to report governmental, proprietary, and fiduciary funds to the extent that they have activities meeting the criteria for these funds. Following is a list of the three **fund categories** (shown in bold) from Section 1300, each followed by a description of certain funds that are included within that category.

Governmental Funds

.104 The *general fund* should be used to account for and report all financial resources not accounted for and reported in another fund.

.105 *Special revenue funds* are used to account for and report the proceeds of specific revenue sources that are restricted or committed to expenditure for specified purposes other than debt service or capital projects . . .

.106 *Capital projects funds* are used to account for and report financial resources that are restricted, committed, or assigned to expenditure for capital outlays . . .

.107 *Debt service funds* are used to account for and report financial resources that are restricted, committed, or assigned to expenditure for principal and interest . . .

Proprietary Funds

.109 *Enterprise funds* may be used to report any activity for which a fee is charged to external users for goods or services . . . [Such as where a government utility passes its operating costs on to its customers]

.110 *Internal service funds* may be used to report any activity that provides goods or services to other funds, departments, or agencies of the primary government and its component units, or to other governments, on a cost-reimbursement basis . . .

. . . **Fiduciary Funds** should be used to report assets held in a trustee or agency capacity for others and therefore cannot be used to support the government's own programs. . . . [I]ncludes pension (and other employee benefit) trust funds, investment trust funds, private-purpose trust funds, and agency funds. (Par .102(c)). [Emphasis and comments added]

4. What are the three fund categories used to organize governmental accounting systems?

   _____

5. Assume that the Town of Hampton plans to use these tax revenues to fund its general government operations. In this case, which *fund* appears to be appropriate? How did you ascertain this?

   _____

   _____

6. Considering your response to the previous question and the guidance provided above from Section 1600 of the GASB Codification, what basis of accounting applies to that fund?

   _____

Based on This Fund Type and Basis of Accounting, When Can Hampton Recognize Its Sales and Property Tax Revenues?

Broad revenue recognition guidance for non-exchange transactions is provided in GASB Cod. Sec. N50 (Nonexchange Transactions). Additional guidance on the recognition of property tax revenue is also provided in Section P70 (Property Taxes).

Per Section N50:

Revenue Recognition in Governmental Fund Statements

.127 When the modified accrual basis of accounting is used, revenues resulting from non-exchange transactions should be recognized as follows:

a. *Derived tax revenues.* Recipients should recognize revenues in the period when the underlying exchange transaction has occurred and the resources are available.

b. *Imposed nonexchange revenues — property taxes.* Recipients should recognize revenues in accordance with Section P70. [Footnotes omitted]

Per Section P70:

Application of the Modified Accrual Basis to Property Tax Revenues

.104 When a property tax assessment is made, it is to finance the budget of a particular period, and the revenue produced from any property tax assessment should be recognized in the fiscal period for which it was levied, provided the "available" criteria are met. *Available* means collected within the current period or expected to be collected soon enough thereafter to be used to pay liabilities of the current period. Such time thereafter shall not exceed 60 days. Governments should disclose in their summary of significant accounting policies the length of time used to define *available* for purposes of revenue recognition in the governmental fund financial statements.

7. What is the principle applicable to each tax, for determining when the town of Hampton can recognize revenues? Cite your source for each response.

Fuel tax: _____

_____

Property tax: _____

_____

CHAPTER SUMMARY

Audited financial statements are often required for governmental entities ranging from local governments to state governments to individual and consolidated federal agencies. Additionally, certain states require their municipal governments and agencies to undergo periodic compliance audits. While the process for performing governmental accounting and auditing research is no different from the process for performing FASB research, the body of knowledge required to perform governmental engagements is fundamentally different. It is therefore imperative for accountants performing such engagements to educate themselves about how governmental accounting and auditing requirements are unique.

The authoritative sources for governmental accounting standards are the GASB (for state and local governments) and the FASAB (for federal government entities); governmental auditing standards are established by the GAO. In addition to these authoritative sources, practitioners may find value in certain nonauthoritative resources, such as practical guides including interpretive discussion, model financial statements, and checklists, for example.

Finally, several resources are available to management accountants; this chapter named just a few: standards for internal auditors, cost accounting standards, and management accounting standards. Professional trade associations also offer important resources to practitioners, such as industry-specific accounting guides, articles, and networking opportunities. Practicing accountants may find significant value in becoming familiar with the professional organizations and resources available for their specific industry or practice area.

REVIEW QUESTIONS

1. Complete the following chart, identifying the relevant standard setter and type of standards applicable to each preparer or auditor.

Preparer/Auditor	Standard setter	Name of applicable standards
NJ Water Authority's financial statements		
U.S. federal government-wide financial statements		
Department of Energy's financial statements		
PwC auditor, auditing the state of NY		
Government auditor, auditing the U.S. Department of Defense		

2. Does the FASB Codification apply to governmental entities? Explain.

3. Describe two circumstances in which state and local governments might be required to issue audited financial statements.

4. What are some steps a beginning accountant might take, when first assigned to a governmental accounting or audit engagement, in order to become more familiar with fundamentals of governmental accounting and auditing?

5. Aside from general purpose state and local governments, list three other types of entities that may be subject to GASB's accounting standards.

6. What is meant by the term the GASB "hierarchy"? How does the hierarchy work?

7. When searching for GASB guidance, why is it preferable to use the GASB Codification, as opposed to searching for individual standards on the GASB's website?

8. Describe the information available on a standard's "Status" page, on the GASB website.

9. Is guidance issued by the FASAB referred to as "GAAP"? Explain.

10. Which entities are required to comply with FASAB guidance? Explain, and name three examples of specific entities that comply with FASAB guidance.

11. Who audits government financial statements?

12. Are auditors subject to the GAO's Yellow Book also required to comply with AICPA audit standards? Explain the relationship between the Yellow Book and AICPA guidance.

13. Describe whether (or in what circumstances) use of the following sources of industry guidance is considered "mandatory":
   ■ Management accounting standards
   ■ Internal audit standards
   ■ Cost accounting standards

14. Assume you have written a memo and included the following citation. How might you abbreviate future references to guidance from this standard, within the same memo?

   Per Statement of Federal Financial Accounting Standards No. 1, *Accounting for Selected Assets and Liabilities*, par. 18, "***intragovernmental assets and liabilities*** arise from transactions among federal entities."

15. Do the GAO's auditing standards apply solely to audits of financial statements?

EXERCISES

The following exercises require students to access information and guidance using the following websites, as appropriate: GASB standards and GASB Codification (www.gasb.org or www.aaahq.org), FASAB (www.fasab.gov), GAO (www.gao.gov/yellowbook).

1. Assume that the Jones County Water Authority (JCWA), New York, a public utility, has undergone budget cuts and must lay off a number of employees.
   a. Which standard setter has authority to set accounting principles for the JCWA? Explain.
   b. Search for guidance issued by this standard setter, then describe when the JCWA should record a liability and expense for estimated termination benefits (such as severance benefits) payable to its terminated employees.

2. Locate the Status page for GASB Statement No. 26, *Financial Reporting for Postemployment Healthcare Plans Administered by Defined Benefit Pension Plans.* When did this standard initially become effective? What GASB Statement superseded this standard?

3. Assume the Town of Hampton is undergoing a bankruptcy, and a bankruptcy "plan of adjustment," restructuring the town's debt, has been confirmed by a court. Locate the appropriate accounting guidance, then respond to the following questions.
   a. *When* (i.e., at what date) is it appropriate for the town to recognize gains from adjustments to its prebankruptcy debt? Cite your source.
   b. Locate the summary of the original standard for this issue, and describe the objective of this standard.

4. Locate the preamble to FASAB's Statements of Federal Financial Accounting Concepts. Are Statements of Federal Financial Accounting Concepts considered "GAAP"? If they are not considered GAAP, then how should the Concepts Statements be used? Explain.

5. Locate the FASAB's accounting standard on "fiduciary" activities.
   a. What are fiduciary activities, and what are examples of these? Cite your sources for these responses.
   b. According to the Introduction of this standard, should fiduciary assets be recorded on government entities' balance sheets? If not, how should they be addressed in the financial statements?
   c. Using the standard's table of contents, determine whether (and if applicable, identify) any Interpretations or Technical Releases relate to this standard.

6. Locate SFASS 24, *Selected Standards for the Consolidated Financial Report of the United States Government.* Read, then summarize the discussion in par. 1–3; should researchers assume that new FASAB guidance applies just to federal "component entities" or also to the consolidated federal financial report?

7. Locate SFFAS 5, *Accounting for Liabilities of the Federal Government*, then respond to the following:
   a. How does the FASAB define a "nonexchange transaction"? Provide an example of a nonexchange transaction. Cite your sources for these responses.
   b. Should a liability be recognized for federal nonexchange transactions? Cite your source.

8. Imagine you are writing a memo and including the following quote from FASAB guidance:
   > "MD&A should discuss important problems that need to be addressed, and actions that have been taken or planned."

   Locate this quote in the FASAB Handbook and write out the full source citation for this quote. Assume this is the first reference to FASAB guidance that you have included in your memo.

9. Locate the "Yellow Book", *Government Auditing Standards*, 2011 Revision (or more recent if available). What *types of audits* does the Yellow Book say the requirements and guidance in GAGAS apply to?

10. What are the five categories of GAGAS requirements for performing government financial audits, which should be applied in addition to AICPA standards?

11. Locate the 80-hour and 24-hour training requirement (within the Yellow Book) for government auditors. Explain this requirement, citing your source.

12. Locate the auditor's report included within the 2011 federal government-wide financial statements.
    a. On the first page of the auditor's report, what three management responsibilities are described?
    b. Identify one of the auditor's summary findings, on the second page of the audit report.

13. Using FASAB guidance, respond to the following:
   a. What is "general" PP&E? In your response, cite from the actual requirement and not just the summary guidance that describes general PP&E.
   b. How should the cost of general PP&E be initially recorded?
   c. How is depreciation expense calculated for general PP&E?

CASE STUDY QUESTIONS

10.1   **Recent Pension Reporting Requirements**
       Facts: Issued in June 2012, GASB Statement No. 68, *Accounting and Financial Reporting for Pensions*, requires government entities to record their net pension liability (that is, the difference between pension assets and liabilities) in the financial statements for the first time, in a manner similar to the calculation required for nongovernmental pensions. This new requirement is expected to dramatically increase the liabilities reported by state and local governments.

       Required: Locate a recent news article describing the issuance of GASBS 68, then prepare a few paragraphs in response to the following questions.
       1. What are some of the different reactions this guidance has received from the public?
       2. For defined benefit pension plans, how do pre-GASBS 68 pension reporting requirements differ from the GASBS 68 requirements? Focus in particular on how the new guidance affects liability and expense recognition and measurement.

10.2   **Role of Your State Comptroller's Office** Perform a Web search for your state's Comptroller's office (or Treasurer, or other agency responsible for overseeing local government finances within the state). Identify the agency, then describe one oversight function performed by the agency related to state or local government finances. For example, describe any financial audits, compliance audits, or other reporting requirements performed or required by the agency or Comptroller's office. Describe how this oversight function contributes to the state or local government's accountability to the public. Your response should require approximately 1–2 paragraphs.

10.3   **Federal Financial Statements** Locate the most recent audited financial statements of a CFO Act agency (that is, an individual federal reporting entity). Determine who audited the agency. What, if any, audit findings were named? What internal control findings, if any, were described? What other commentary did you identify, in the auditor's report, which was notable to you? Your response should require approximately 1–2 paragraphs.

10.4   **Dissolution of a Village Government (Writing an Issues Memo)**
       Facts: Citing discontent with their increasing property tax rates, residents in the Village of East Glen voted to dissolve their village government, instead agreeing to receive similar services (formerly provided by the Village government) from their county government, Eden County. No consideration must be paid by (or to) the county to effect this transfer. The effects of this transfer/dissolution will be that all village assets and liabilities (cash balances, buildings, infrastructure, and accounts payable) will become property and responsibility of the county, five employees will transfer to the Eden County district offices, and two employees will be involuntarily terminated and given 3 months of severance pay. The two terminated employees were responsible for East Glen's street maintenance division, which will be discontinued.

       Required: You have been asked to write a brief accounting issues memo to the Eden County government files describing the accounting implications of the East Glen dissolution. In your memo, address the appropriate accounting for the transaction: Merger, Acquisition, or Transfer of Operations? Also, address how Eden County should recognize and measure the additional assets and liabilities, and describe—broadly—the accounting implications of the discontinuation of the street maintenance operations and the principle for *recognition* of the related employee terminations. In doing so, assume that the Village of East Glen has prepared financial statements as of the merger date. Feel free to identify other issues that should be considered, as well. In your memo, be sure to appropriately cite the authoritative guidance relevant to this issue and include excerpts from the guidance to support your analysis.

10.5   **Federal Government Accounting: Contingent Liabilities (Writing an Email)**
       Facts: Litigation is pending against a federal government agency for an alleged violation of privacy rights. The plaintiff in the case has requested damages of $5 million, although the federal government agency's lawyers estimate that the plaintiff may be willing to settle for as little as $1 million; at this point, it is not clear what amount within the range will be paid. The government's lawyer believes the plaintiff will "likely" prevail in the lawsuit.

       Required: Act as though you are an accountant for the federal government, and your accounting supervisor (Dan) has asked you to evaluate this issue. Determine whether the federal government should record a liability on its financial statements related to this contingency and, if so, for what amount. Write your response in the form of an email to your supervisor.

Chapter 11

Fundamentals of Tax Research

It is income tax preparation season, and newly minted CPA Nora Smith is preparing her federal income tax return. Ever since her mother lost her job a year ago, Nora has been paying the real property taxes and mortgage on her mother's house in order to help her avoid foreclosure. Now, Nora wants to know whether she can deduct any part of the payments on her personal federal income tax return. Recalling what she learned in her accounting and tax research classes, Nora starts her search for the applicable federal tax law by looking at the most fundamental primary source, the Internal Revenue Code. She then turns to other primary sources of tax law, such as regulations, rulings, and cases, as well as explanations in secondary sources, to reach a conclusion.

As a professional performing tax services—for yourself or for others—it is important to be familiar with the many different sources of tax law and to know how to locate guidance within these sources. This chapter will teach you the fundamentals of tax research and the professional standards applicable to tax services.

After reading this chapter and performing the exercises herein, you will be able to

1. **Understand** the tax research process.
2. **Differentiate** between primary and secondary sources of tax law.
3. **Contrast** and understand the relative precedential values of the different primary sources of tax law.
4. **Gain** familiarity with the use of an online tax research service (RIA Checkpoint).
5. **Identify** the key sources of professional standards for tax services.
6. **Apply** tax research skills to sample tax issues.

Learning Objectives

Organization of This Chapter

Previous chapters in this text have focused on accounting and auditing research related to both governmental and nongovernmental entities. By contrast, this chapter focuses on **tax research**, a type of accounting research specifically focused on determining the proper tax treatment of transactions and events.

Fair warning—learning about federal tax law may make you feel like you're back in a high-school U.S. government class. This chapter will take you through statutory tax law in the form of the Internal Revenue Code, as well as guidance issued by the IRS, and the role of the courts in establishing tax law.

After first identifying *who* generally performs tax research, and *when*, this chapter describes the tax research *process*.

The chapter then describes key sources of federal tax law and their relative importance as precedent. The sources of federal tax law include primary sources, such as the Internal Revenue Code, Treasury Regulations, Internal Revenue Service rulings, and court decisions; and secondary sources, such as treatises and periodicals.

Next, the chapter demonstrates the use of an online tax research service, followed by a discussion of how and when to update tax research, focusing on the use of a citator.

Finally, this chapter concludes by discussing the professional standards that govern a CPA's own conduct for providing tax services.

The preceding graphic illustrates the organization of content within this chapter.

This chapter focuses solely on research related to U.S. federal tax issues and does not address state tax research. The *process* for researching state tax issues is very similar, but the *sources* involved (e.g., individual state tax statutes, state tax agencies' regulations and rulings, and state court decisions) can be quite different.

WHO PERFORMS TAX RESEARCH, AND WHEN?

Tax research is generally performed by in-house corporate accountants and by public accountants for their clients. In addition, because tax research is essentially a type of legal research focused on tax, it is also common for tax research to be performed by tax lawyers on behalf of their clients. For example, a tax lawyer may advise a client on how to structure a transaction or may represent a client in a litigated tax dispute. Finally, individuals working for government tax agencies may also perform tax research, such as in the course of auditing tax returns. This chapter primarily refers to the taxpayer as a "client," but the lessons in the chapter are intended to apply equally to both in-house accountants and public accountants performing tax research.

Tax research is unique in that it focuses on compliance with tax laws. Accordingly, this research may be performed

- For tax and transactional *planning* purposes,
- For purposes of tax *compliance*, and
- During and after tax *audits*.

Tax professionals are often asked to determine the tax treatment of a proposed transaction or event before it occurs. This is called **tax planning**. Accountants who are consulted before a transaction or event occurs may be in a position to not only advise the client as to the tax results of the proposal, but may also be able to suggest other alternative structures that may lower or defer tax.

For example, suppose that a business client has contacted you for advice regarding its plan to sell a warehouse and use the proceeds to purchase a larger warehouse. The client's initial questions might focus on the tax treatment of the sale, such as whether or not the client will have a taxable gain, whether the gain will be ordinary or capital, and ultimately how much tax will be due. Being consulted in advance, however, puts the tax professional in a position of being able to research and suggest an alternative, such as structuring the transaction as a like-kind exchange pursuant to Section 1031 of the Internal Revenue Code, which can produce a better tax result for the client.

Tax research is also performed for **tax compliance** purposes; that is, the preparation and timely filing of accurate tax returns. Sometimes, a tax professional may not learn about a transaction or other event that affects the client's tax return until the return is being prepared. In this context, the primary questions for the tax professional (and which may require research) may be "How is the completed transaction treated for tax purposes?" and "How and where should the transaction be reported on the client's tax return?" Additionally at this time, any prior research performed for proposed transactions (or based on draft contracts) should be reviewed, before filing the tax return on which the transaction is reported.

Finally, tax research may be necessary even after tax returns have been filed, such as when a client is being audited by a governmental tax agency. During an audit, the government tax auditor may review whether transactions or other events were properly reported and, ultimately, whether the correct amount of tax was paid. The tax professional may be asked to research these issues in anticipation of, or in response to, a position taken by the government auditor. Tax research may also be used to support a dispute of the results of a tax audit (e.g., through the administrative process or litigation).

Knowledge Check

1. **Who performs tax research?**
2. **At what points in the life of a transaction might it be necessary to perform tax research?**

THE TAX RESEARCH PROCESS

You will find that the tax research process bears some similarity to the accounting research process introduced in Chapter 3. The major difference is just how unique the subject matter is; this affects how a researcher will perform every step of the process. The following discussion is designed to put you in the mind of a tax researcher. Figure 11-1 depicts the tax research process.

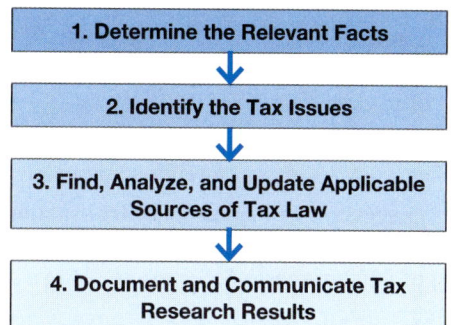

Figure 11-1

The tax research process

To some extent, these four steps are intertwined and often cannot be performed in a straight 1-2-3-4 order. For example, a **tax authority** (i.e., a source of tax law that provides guidance) found in step 3 of the research process may require the researcher to go back to step 1 and ask more questions, which may lead to the identification of additional tax issues (step 2). As a result, tax researchers have to be flexible and open to following where their research takes them.

Let's now discuss each step of the research process in more detail.

Step 1: Determine the Relevant Facts

First, you must gather both the relevant tax and nontax facts related to the issue. Facts may be obtained either directly from the client and/or indirectly from others at the researcher's firm who have directly communicated with the client. Where applicable, facts may also be obtained from, and/or confirmed with, reliable outside sources.

- For example, if the client's records do not indicate how much the client paid for an asset, it may be necessary to request this information from the seller of the asset or from other records (such as county real estate transfer records).

- Similarly, it may be necessary or advisable to obtain an appraisal (prepared by a third-party qualified appraiser) of an asset, such as in the case of a donation to a charity.

  Consider the following questions when gathering **tax facts** relevant to an issue:

- **How is the client generally treated for tax purposes?**
  - Is the client an individual, a business entity, or another type of taxpayer (such as a trust or estate)?
  - Is the client a U.S. domestic taxpayer or a foreign person or entity?
  - If the client is a corporation, is it a C corporation, or has it elected to be treated as an S corporation?
  - If the client is a limited liability company (LLC), is it treated as a disregarded entity, as a partnership, or as a corporation for tax purposes?
  - Is the client subject to special income tax rules, such as those applicable to charitable organizations, real estate investment trusts (REITs), banks or insurance companies?

- **What type of tax is involved?** Does the issue involve income tax, estate tax, excise tax, or another type of tax?

- **What are the client's relevant tax attributes?** The client's tax year; the amounts, if any, of the client's taxable income, net operating loss (NOL) and tax credit carryovers; and the adjusted tax bases of the client's relevant assets are examples of **tax attributes**.

- ■ **When will the transaction take place?** Is this research being performed for a proposed transaction, a completed transaction, or for a tax position that is under audit?

- ■ **Are other parties involved?** If so, are any other parties considered "related parties" for which loss recognition may be limited under the Internal Revenue Code?

- ■ **What tax years are involved?** Does the current year, or another year's, tax law apply to this transaction?

- ■ **What are the dollar amounts involved in the transaction?** Dollar amounts may include, for example, the tax basis of an asset sold, the amount of depreciation or other expense claimed, or the amount of payments received.

- ■ **What is the location of the client and/or the transaction?** This question is particularly relevant when researching state, local, and foreign tax issues.

- ■ **What documentation is necessary to evidence the transaction for tax purposes?** Is contemporaneous documentation (such as in the form of a store receipt or an acknowledgment from a charity for a gift of $250 or more) necessary to claim a deductible expense or credit on a tax return?

A researcher should also consider the **nontax facts** related to a transaction; that is, the client's business purpose or other motivations for undertaking the transaction. Such facts are particularly relevant when determining how best to structure a proposed transaction. Researchers should consider, for example,

- ■ **Why is the client undertaking this transaction?** This may explain why the transaction is being structured in a particular way.
  - ● For example, while it may be desirable for tax purposes for a seller to structure the sale of a corporate business as a stock sale, nontax facts such as environmental liabilities, or a buyer's unwillingness to purchase the corporation's stock, may rule out this option. The tax researcher needs to know these nontax facts to efficiently perform research that is useful to the client.

- ■ **What documentation exists that evidences the transaction?** The tax researcher should review all documentation related to the transaction, including contracts, written correspondence, appraisals, and receipts, to properly research the tax issues and accurately report the transaction on a tax return.

While the list of questions may initially seem overwhelming, with experience, your ability to identify and ask relevant questions will improve. Figure 11-2 lists just a few of the factual questions a researcher might ask in determining the proper income tax treatment of a client's sale of a building.

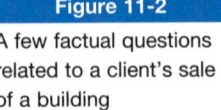

Figure 11-2

A few factual questions related to a client's sale of a building

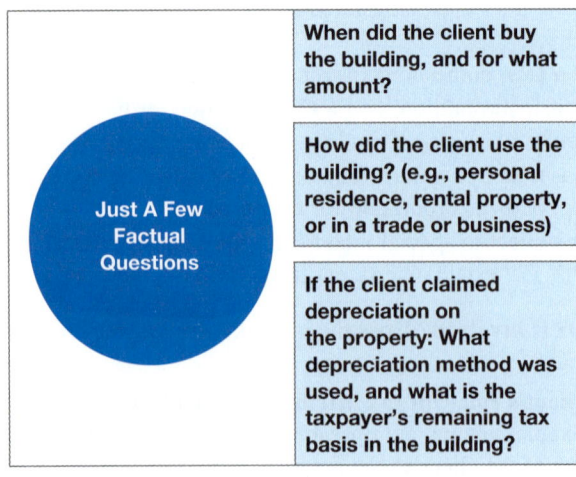

Just A Few Factual Questions

When did the client buy the building, and for what amount?

How did the client use the building? (e.g., personal residence, rental property, or in a trade or business)

If the client claimed depreciation on the property: What depreciation method was used, and what is the taxpayer's remaining tax basis in the building?

3. **What are four "tax facts" questions a researcher might ask during the first step of the tax research process?**
4. **What are two "nontax facts" questions a researcher might ask during the first step of the tax research process?**

✔ **Knowledge Check**

Step 2: Identify the Tax Issues Involved

Armed with the facts of your client's transaction, your next step is to identify the tax issues related to the transaction. For beginning researchers, identifying the tax issues applicable to a given fact pattern may require some trial and error, and may even require some preliminary research. To assist with this learning curve, the following are a number of common income tax issues to consider as a starting point.

First, ask yourself what *type of tax* is involved: Is it an income tax issue? An estate or gift tax issue? An excise tax issue? A sales or use tax (or other state tax) issue? An employment (e.g., FICA/Social Security tax) and withholding tax issue?

Once you determine the type of tax involved, more specific tax issues can be identified. For example, assume you are researching issues related to a client's income tax return. Specific tax issues related to the client's cash receipts might involve, for example,

- Is the item included in gross income for tax purposes?
- Is the item considered ordinary income or capital gain income?
- If the item is capital gain income, is it short term or long term?
- Is the item considered active or passive income?

On the other hand, tax issues related to cash payments might include, for example,

- Is the item deductible as an expense?
- Do any limitations (such as the at-risk and passive activity loss limitations) apply?
- What documentation is required to claim the payment as an expense for tax purposes?
- What year (or years) is the item deductible?
- Is a purchased asset depreciable or amortizable for tax purposes?

The tax issues involved can vary considerably depending upon the facts. Figure 11-3 illustrates just a few of the tax issues involved when evaluating a client's sale of a building, assuming that the building was being rented to an unrelated tenant.

Figure 11-3

A few tax issues involved in a client's sale of a building

Next, list the tax issues that you have identified. Decide which issues require more research and which you are comfortable answering with only minimal, confirming research. With experience, you will become better able to organize and prioritize the tax issues involved.

Take a moment to complete the following **Now YOU Try** exercise, intended to get you thinking about steps 1 and 2 of the research process.

Now
YOU
Try
11.1

Determining Facts and Identifying Tax Issues

Your client, Heather Stark, loves dogs and volunteers for an organization called People for Dogs Inc. ("PFD"). PFD's mission is to temporarily provide foster homes and, ultimately, to find permanent homes for stray dogs. Heather volunteers for PFD, by temporarily fostering several dogs each year. During 2012, Heather spent a considerable amount of time and money on the dogs that she fostered, including paying for dog food, veterinary services, dog toys, feeding dishes, and other supplies. You have been asked to prepare Heather's 2012 federal income tax return.

1. Referring back to the lists of sample questions for determining the facts relevant to an issue, list two tax or nontax facts questions you might ask Heather:

    _____

    _____

2. Identify a relevant "tax facts" question that you might ask the PFD organization:

    _____

3. List two tax issues that you would need to research in order to prepare Heather's 2012 federal income tax return:

    _____

    _____

Step 3: Analyze Tax Research Findings

The third step in the tax research process involves finding, analyzing, and updating tax law that is relevant to the client's issue. Later in this chapter, we will describe the sources of tax law and how to update research results. For now, we will focus on the *process* of identifying and analyzing how tax law applies to a research issue.

Assume that a researcher has located sources of tax law and now must analyze whether each tax authority found is relevant to the client's issue. In analyzing each tax authority, a researcher should consider the following:

- Does the Internal Revenue Code section or regulation being considered apply to the client's situation?
- Are the facts of the case or ruling analogous to the client's situation?
- What are the key differences between the facts of the case or ruling and the client's situation? Does the Code, a regulation, or another case or ruling indicate that these factual differences should lead to a different result?
- What is the reasoning or rationale for the conclusions reached in the case or ruling? Does that reasoning or rationale apply to the client's situation?

Part of analyzing each tax authority found includes considering its relative weight as precedent. You will find, as considered later in the discussion of sources of federal tax law, that not all sources of tax law are equal. At times, the conclusions reached by different sources of tax law may be inconsistent; in these cases, the researcher must take into account the relative **precedential values** of the sources found. The precedential value of a tax authority refers to how strong an authority it is for the client's situation. This takes into account both the relative weights of different sources of tax law and the relevance of each authority to the client's situation.

- For example, as discussed below with respect to court decisions, appellate court decisions (particularly decisions of the U.S. Supreme Court and of the client's applicable Circuit of the U.S. Court of Appeals) have a greater precedential value than trial court decisions.

- Therefore, if a trial court and an appellate court reach different conclusions on a tax issue in cases involving similar facts, the tax researcher would generally give greater weight to the appellate court's decision in his or her analysis.

- However, if one authority ruled on a fact pattern that was more closely aligned with the client's situation than another, greater weight might be given to that (closely aligned) authority.

At times, a tax researcher may only be able to find sources of tax law that are of relatively low precedential value. For example, if a tax issue has not been litigated in court, the only authority that may exist is an IRS ruling interpreting an Internal Revenue Code provision. The ruling is of lower precedential value than some other sources of tax law (such as a Code provision or regulation). In some circumstances, the client may wish to pursue a tax treatment that conflicts with a lower precedent source, as described in the following **TIP from the Trenches**.

> Not all sources of tax law are irrefutable. If the only relevant tax authority is of limited precedential value, the tax researcher may consider recommending taking a contrary position on a tax return. The recommendation should only be made after careful consideration, disclosing the risks (including that it may be necessary to litigate the issue) to the client, and properly disclosing the position taken on the client's tax return to minimize penalties.

[TIP] from the Trenches

It is only through a thorough analysis of the sources of tax law found that the tax professional may arrive at a reasoned conclusion for the issue being researched. As with identifying tax issues, a researcher's ability to analyze tax research findings should improve as the researcher gains experience.

Step 4: Document and Communicate Tax Research Results

As a general rule of thumb, if you find the need to research a tax issue, you should take the time to document the issue.

In documenting research findings, a tax researcher often prepares

- A memorandum to the client's file; and
- A written communication of tax advice to the client.

Part of documenting one's research findings is writing a **memorandum to the client's file**. A file memorandum should be dated and would usually include a statement of the relevant facts (including from whom the facts were obtained), an identification of the tax issue or issues involved, the researcher's conclusion on each identified issue, a discussion of the authority supporting the conclusion(s), and an indication of the next steps to be taken (such as contacting the client or verifying a fact relied on). The discussion of supporting authority should describe and cite the sources of tax law relied on in reaching the conclusion(s), and describe and cite any significant and relevant contrary authority that the researcher ruled out in reaching the conclusion(s).

Documenting tax research results would also usually include printing (or saving digital) copies of relevant sources of tax law relied on, and of any **significant contrary authority** that the researcher has ruled out (such as a source with significantly different facts or of lesser precedential value). The memorandum and related documentation become part of the client file and should be organized so that the original researcher, or another tax professional, can be quickly reacquainted (or acquainted) with the relevant authority at a later date (such as when it's time to prepare the related tax return or defend the conclusion reached during a tax audit).

Communicating tax research results involves providing the client with tax advice that is based on the conclusions reached through research. Tax advice may be provided orally, such as in person or over the telephone. However, it is always suggested (and sometimes required by professional standards) that the tax advisor follow up the oral advice with a written communication to the client. Alternatively, the tax advice may initially be provided in written form.

Tax advice (whether oral or written) should be provided in a way that the client can understand. In communicating tax advice to a client with little or no tax knowledge, for example, the tax professional should usually explain things as simply as possible and should not rely on technical terms that only someone with a sophisticated level of tax knowledge would be expected to understand without explanation. By contrast, when communicating tax advice to a more tax-sophisticated client, the adviser may use technical terms and, depending on the client, may assume a fairly high level of tax knowledge.

Written communication of tax advice to a client may be in the form of a letter or memorandum to the client. In either case, the substance of the communication should include the key elements noted in Figure 11-4.

Figure 11-4

Key elements included in written communication of tax advice to a client

Statement of what the writer was asked to determine

- Identifies the question(s) asked by the client

Summary of the conclusion(s) reached

- This should also include any recommendations made

Statement of the relevant facts

- Indicate any research done to determine the facts
- For client-provided facts: "It is my understanding from you that . . ."
- Indicate sources of facts obtained other than from the client
- Where appropriate, may include statement: "I have relied on the facts as provided by you and have not done any independent investigation regarding them."

Summary of controlling tax law

- Analysis of tax law supporting conclusion(s) reached
- Discussion of alternatives considered and why rejected

Statement of limitations on advice provided

- Indicate assumptions made, including no change in tax law after written advice provided to client

The applicable standards of professional tax practice, briefly described at the end of this chapter, must also be considered in communicating tax advice to the client.

The next section of this chapter introduces the sources of U.S. federal tax law, including primary and secondary sources. Being familiar with these sources, and understanding their relative weights and importance, will help enable researchers to perform the third and fourth steps in the tax research process.

SOURCES OF FEDERAL TAX LAW

Primary Sources of U.S. Federal Tax Law

The **primary sources** of U.S. federal tax law are issued by the U.S. federal government and generally have precedential value, the level of which varies among the primary sources. By contrast, **secondary sources** of tax law (discussed later in this chapter) are not precedential. In addition, taxpayers may incur a substantial understatement penalty under Section 6662 of the Internal Revenue Code for taking a position on a tax return for which there is neither **substantial authority** nor adequate disclosure. Only some of the primary sources of tax law constitute substantial authority. These are listed in Treasury Regulation Section 1.6662-4(d)(3)(iii).

The primary sources of U.S. federal tax law are depicted in Figure 11-5. The sources discussed in this chapter, and that a beginning researcher is most likely to encounter, are noted with an asterisk.

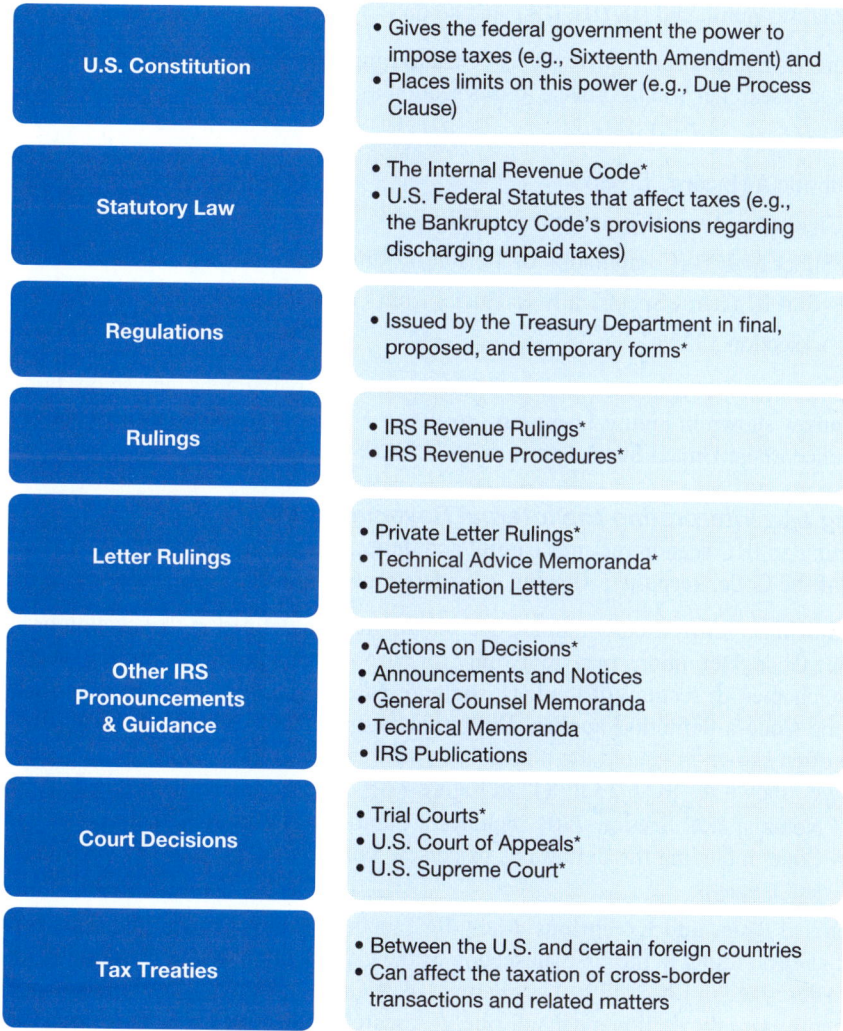

Figure 11-5

Primary sources of U.S. tax law

The Internal Revenue Code

The **Internal Revenue Code** (the "**IRC**" or the "**Code**") is a federal statute and an important primary source of federal tax law and a substantial authority. The IRC is codified at Title 26 of the United States Code ("U.S.C."). The IRC is often amended, and the current version of the

Code is the "Internal Revenue Code of 1986, as amended." The Code is accessible within online tax research services such as RIA Checkpoint (discussed later in this chapter), or for free through the IRS's Web site (www.irs.gov).

Organization of the Internal Revenue Code

The Code is organized in the following order: First into subtitles (lettered A through I), followed by chapters (organized by chapter number), then subchapters (lettered A, B, C, etc.), parts (numbered I, II, III, etc.), and sections (organized by section number).

Each Code section (or §) may be further organized in the following order:

- Subsections lettered (a), (b), (c), and so on;
- Paragraphs numbered (1), (2), (3), and so on;
- Subparagraphs lettered (A), (B), (C), and so on;
- Clauses numbered (i), (ii), (iii), and so on; and
- Subclauses numbered (I), (II), (III), and so on.

Figure 11-6 shows part of IRC § 132, "Certain fringe benefits." To locate Section 132 within the Code, a researcher would browse to this section as follows:

IRC (Title 26 of the U.S. Code)

> Subtitle A (Income Taxes)

>> Chapter 1 (Normal Taxes and Surcharges)

>>>Subchapter B (Computation of Taxable Income)

>>>>Part III (Items Specifically Excluded from Gross Income)

>>>>>Section 132

Within Section 132, a researcher will find subsections, paragraphs, and so on. For example, the last arrow shown in Figure 11-6 points to IRC § 132(e)(2)(B). Alternatively, it can be cited, by reference to the United States Code, as 26 U.S.C. § 132(e)(2)(B).

Reading and Interpreting the Internal Revenue Code

Interpreting an IRC section requires careful and thorough reading and analysis. When reading a section of the Code, keep the following considerations in mind:

- **Definitions.** Terms used within a Code section may be defined in that section or elsewhere in the Code. Definitions may apply only for purposes of a particular portion (such as a subtitle, chapter, or section) of the IRC, so the researcher must always consider to which parts of the Code a definition applies. Definitions are not bold or highlighted in the Code but are often shown in "quotation marks," as you'll notice in the case of the term "de minimis fringe" shown in IRC § 132(e)(1) in Figure 11-6.
  - Notably, IRC Section 7701 includes a number of definitions that apply to the entire Code, including the definitions of person, corporation, partnership, foreign, domestic, and taxpayer.
- **General Rules and Exceptions.** Many IRC sections state a general rule. This is often, but not always, found in the first subsection of the Code section. See, for example, the general rule described in IRC § 132(a) in Figure 11-6. A Code section may also include one or more exceptions to the section's general rule. A researcher must read the entire code section that appears to apply, to be certain a situation is covered by that Code section and to determine its applicable tax treatment. Reading only part of a Code section can result in missing important (and relevant) information, and can lead to providing erroneous tax advice.
- **Effective Dates.** The IRC is frequently amended, so some provisions of the Code only apply to certain tax periods. The applicable period may be very clearly stated in the Code section. If the Code section does not state an effective date (as is the case in Figure 11-6), the researcher may need to refer to amendments to the Code section to determine the effective

Figure 11-6

Internal Revenue Code
Section 132

Internal Revenue Code Section 132 – Certain fringe benefits

Subsection ➤ **(a) Exclusion from gross income**

Gross income shall not include any fringe benefit which qualifies as a—

 (1) no-additional-cost service,

 (2) qualified employee discount,

 (3) working condition fringe,

 (4) de minimis fringe,

 (5) qualified transportation fringe,

 (6) qualified moving expense reimbursement,

 (7) qualified retirement planning services, or

 (8) qualified military base realignment and closure fringe.

(b) No-additional-cost service defined

For purposes of this section, the term "no-additional-cost service" means any service provided by an employer to an employee for use by such employee if—

 (1) such service is offered for sale to customers in the ordinary course of the line of business of the employer in which the employee is performing services, and

 (2) the employer incurs no substantial additional cost (including forgone revenue) in providing such service to the employee (determined without regard to any amount paid by the employee for such service).

(c) [omitted].

(d) Working condition fringe defined

For purposes of this section, the term "working condition fringe" means any property or services provided to an employee of the employer to the extent that, if the employee paid for such property or services, such payment would be allowable as a deduction under section 162 or 167.

Subsection ➤ **(e) De minimis fringe defined**

For purposes of this section—

 (1) In general

 The term "de minimis fringe" means any property or service the value of which is (after taking into account the frequency with which similar fringes are provided by the employer to the employer's employees) so small as to make accounting for it unreasonable or administratively impracticable.

Paragraph ➤ **(2) Treatment of certain eating facilities**

 The operation by an employer of any eating facility for employees shall be treated as a de minimis fringe if—

  (A) such facility is located on or near the business premises of the employer, and

Subparagraph ➤   **(B)** revenue derived from such facility normally equals or exceeds the direct operating costs of such facility.

 The preceding sentence shall apply with respect to any highly compensated employee only if access to the facility is available on substantially the same terms to each member of a group of employees which is defined under a reasonable classification set up by the employer which does not discriminate in favor of highly compensated employees. For purposes of subparagraph (B), an employee entitled under section 119 to exclude the value of a meal provided at such facility shall be treated as having paid an amount for such meal equal to the direct operating costs of the facility attributable to such meal.

(f) – (l) [omitted].

date of any changes made by the amendment. In this case, a researcher might search for amendments to Section 132 to identify the effective date of applicable amendments.

- **Cross References.** A Code section often refers to one or more other sections of the IRC. It is necessary for the tax researcher to actually look at the provisions of the cross-referenced Code sections to conclusively determine the proper tax treatment.

Take a moment to complete the following **Now YOU Try** exercise, intended to improve your familiarity with the guidance included within Code sections.

Now YOU Try 11.2

Code Section 132

Refer to Figure 11-6 to answer the following questions:

1. What three terms are defined in Section 132?

   _____

   _____

   _____

2. To what part of the Code do these definitions apply?

   _____

3. What other Code sections are referred to in IRC § 132?

   _____

4. Assume that your client is an employer who operates a snow-plowing service. The client would like to provide its employees with the benefit of snow-plowing their home driveways for free during the winter. What is the result or tax consequence if it can be established that the snow-plowing benefit provided to the client's employees is a "no-additional-cost service"?

   _____

   _____

- **Common Terms.** Some words used in the Code should be interpreted in accordance with their everyday meanings. Such **common terms** include, for example, references to dollar amounts or time periods and words such as "and" and "or."
  - For example, the phrase "less than $100" includes amounts of $99.99 or less, but not $100. By contrast, "$100 or less" and "not more than $100" do include $100, as well as lesser amounts.
  - If an IRC section provides that a form must be filed "within 30 days" after an event occurs, the tax researcher should know that 30 days is not necessarily the equivalent of one month. The 30-day period would start on the day after the event occurs and would end on the 30th day thereafter.
  - When a list of terms is joined by "and," all items in the list are required to be true or correct. When a list of terms is joined by "or," only one of the items in the list is required to be true or correct.

Take a moment to complete the following **Now YOU Try** exercise, which focuses on the everyday meanings of a few common terms used in the Code.

Now YOU Try 11.3

Common Terms

Answer the first two questions. The common term is highlighted in each question.

1. The phrase "**before** August 1, 2013" refers to the period that ends on what date?

   _____

2. The phrase "**after** August 1, 2013" refers to the period that begins on what date?

Refer again to Figure 11-6 to answer the next two questions.

3. Choose the correct answer (a, b, or c):

    For an employer-provided benefit to be considered a "no-additional-cost service," which of the following is required?

    (a) The service must be offered for sale to customers in the ordinary course of the line of business of the employer in which the employee is performing services.

    (b) The employer cannot incur a substantial additional cost (including forgone revenue) in providing the service to the employee (determined without regard to any amount paid by the employee for the service).

    (c) Both (a) and (b) are required.

---

4. To be excluded from gross income, an employer-provided fringe benefit must be both a working condition fringe and a de minimis fringe. Is the previous sentence true or false? Why?

Understanding Legislative History

Understanding the **legislative history** of tax laws can provide researchers with additional background on, including the intent behind, enacted laws. For federal tax legislation, legislative history comprises

- Reports of the House Ways and Means Committee, and reports of the Senate Finance Committee;

- Reports of the Joint Conference Committee; and

- General Explanations of the Joint Committee on Taxation.

As noted, the IRC is frequently amended by **federal statute**. A legislative bill becomes a federal statute only after it is passed by a majority vote of each house of the U.S. Congress (i.e., the House of Representatives and the Senate) and then signed into law by the President. If the President vetoes a bill, Congress can override the veto by a two-thirds vote of both houses of Congress.

Before being considered by the full House of Representatives or the Senate, proposed tax legislation is generally first considered by committees, who issue reports on their findings:

- The **House Ways and Means Committee** writes and reviews draft tax legislation for the House.

- The **Senate Finance Committee** writes and reviews draft tax legislation for the Senate.

If a tax bill that is passed by the House of Representatives differs from a tax bill passed by the Senate, it is referred to the **Joint Conference Committee** (composed of members of the House Ways and Means and the Senate Finance Committees), which must prepare a compromise version of the proposed legislation for vote by both the House and Senate. The Joint Conference Committee may also issue a committee report that becomes part of the legislative history of the ultimately enacted tax legislation.

In addition, the **Joint Committee on Taxation**, a nonpartisan committee with members from the House Ways and Means and Senate Finance Committees and with a professional staff of economists, attorneys, and accountants,[1] prepares a report that is a general explanation of newly enacted tax legislation.

---

[1] See IRC §8002 and *https://www.jct.gov/about-us/overview.html* for additional information regarding The Joint Committee on Taxation.

Collectively, these reports of the House Ways and Means Committee, the Senate Finance Committee, and the Joint Conference Committee become part of the legislative history of a tax law. The legislative history of a statutory change and the Joint Committee on Taxation's general explanation are considered substantial authority, and reviewing them can aid a tax researcher in understanding the reasons for the legislation (i.e., the "legislative intent") as well as the meaning of the statutory changes. This can be particularly helpful to a tax researcher when reviewing new tax legislation for which there are no regulations or other guidance. Figure 11-7 reviews the process by which tax legislation is adopted.

Figure 11-7

The process of adopting tax legislation

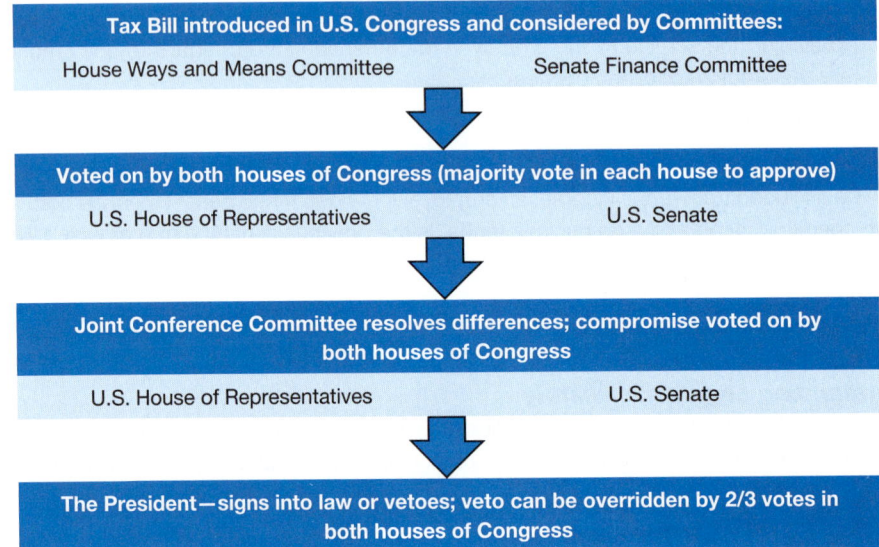

Federal statutes are referred to by **Public Law** (or "**P.L.**") number. A Public Law number includes two numbers with a hyphen in the middle (e.g., P.L. 111-92). The first number indicates the 2-year Congressional Session in which it was enacted, and the second number indicates the number of the bill (in sequential order) enacted by that session of Congress. For example, P.L. 111-92 (the "American Recovery and Reinvestment Tax Act of 2009"), was the ninety-second bill enacted into law by the 111th Session of Congress (2009–2011). Committee Reports reference the related tax legislation by Public Law number.

Federal Tax Regulations

The **Internal Revenue Service (IRS)** is the largest of the U.S. Treasury Department's bureaus and "is responsible for determining, assessing, and collecting internal revenue in the United States."[2] As an administrative agency of the U.S. federal government, the IRS issues many different administrative sources of federal tax law. Figure 11-8 lists the sources of federal tax law issued by the IRS that are discussed in this chapter.

Federal tax **regulations** are the Treasury Department's official interpretation of the IRC, are considered substantial authority, and have the greatest precedential value of any of the sources of federal tax law listed in Figure 11-8. While the Treasury Department is the official issuer of tax regulations, it does so with much IRS involvement; accordingly, Figure 11-8 shows lines from both Treasury and the IRS for regulations.

Authority to issue tax regulations is found in the IRC § 7805, which provides that the Secretary of the Treasury "shall prescribe all needful rules and regulations for the enforcement of this title, including all rules and regulations as may be necessary by reason of any alteration of law in relation to internal revenue." Tax regulations that are issued to interpret a section of the Code

---

[2] _http://www.treasury.gov/about/organizational-structure/bureaus/Pages/default.aspx_.

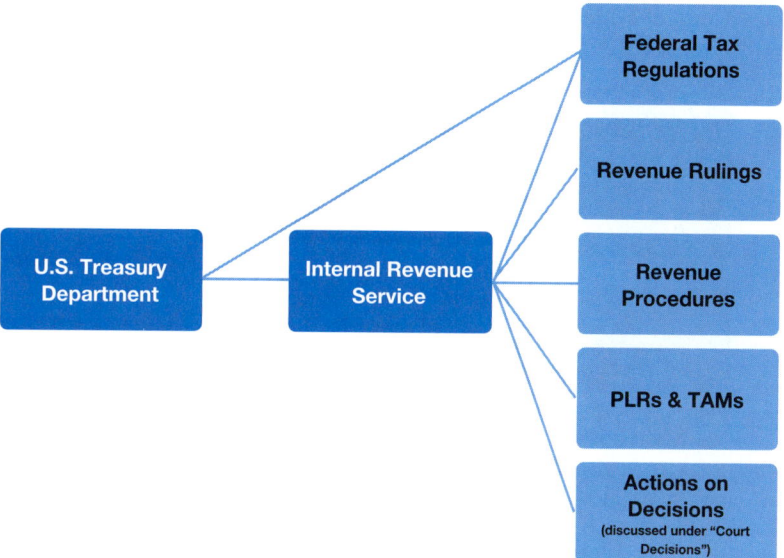

Figure 11-8

Sources of U.S. federal tax law issued by the IRS

under this general grant of authority to issue regulations are sometimes referred to as "**general regulations**" or "**interpretive regulations.**"

Other Code sections give the Secretary authority to set (rather than merely interpret) the requirements for a specific area of tax law. For example, IRC Section 385(a) authorizes the Secretary "to prescribe such regulations as may be necessary or appropriate to determine whether an interest in a corporation is to be treated for purposes of this title as stock or indebtedness (or as in part stock and in part indebtedness)." Regulations issued under such a special grant of authority are sometimes referred to as **legislative regulations**.

Courts use a deferential standard when reviewing regulations (meaning, they often "defer" to the Treasury Department) and will generally uphold a regulation provided that it is based on a permissible construction (interpretation) of the statute.[3] If there is clearly a conflict between a Code provision and a regulation, however, the Code provision controls, as its authority as a statute is of greater precedential value than a regulation.

Federal tax regulations are issued in final, proposed, and temporary formats.

- **Final regulations** are the Treasury Department's final, official interpretations of the tax law and are issued by a **Treasury Decision (T.D.)**.

- **Proposed regulations** are not considered official interpretations of the tax law until they have been through a finalization process. When issuing a proposed regulation, the IRS will generally provide a public comment period (of at least 30 days) and may schedule a public hearing to discuss a proposed regulation. Following this public outreach, the Treasury Department may finalize the proposed regulation, revise and repropose it, or withdraw it for further study.

- **Temporary regulations** are official interpretations of the IRC, but are effective for only a temporary period, usually 3 years. A temporary regulation is usually issued with a proposed regulation to provide some immediate, reliable guidance for a temporary period while the IRS requests and receives comments on the proposed regulation and works towards issuing a final regulation.

Final, proposed, and temporary federal tax regulations are published in three places: the **Federal Register,** the **Internal Revenue Bulletin (I.R.B.),** and the **Cumulative Bulletin (C.B.)**. Final and temporary federal tax regulations are also compiled and published in

---

[3] *Mayo Foundation for Medical Ed. & Research v. U.S.,* 107 AFTR 2d 2011-341, 131 S.Ct. 704 (2011).

Title 26 of the **Code of Federal Regulations (C.F.R.)**. Figure 11-9 compares the Federal Register, I.R.B., C.B., and C.F.R.

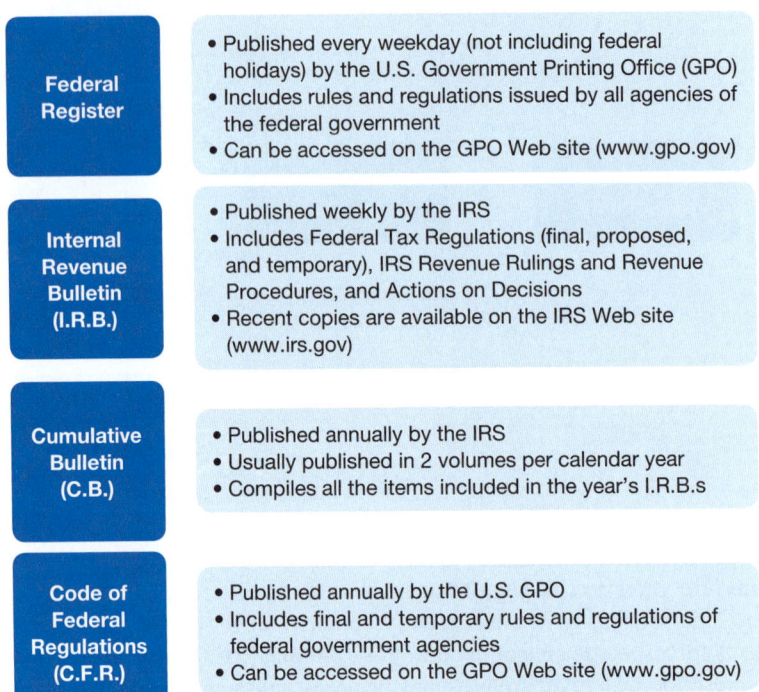

Figure 11-9

Comparison of the Federal Register, I.R.B., C.B., and C.F.R.

Federal tax regulations are organized first by a number that designates the type of tax or regulation involved (followed by a period), and then by IRC section number. The numbering system is as follows:

Number	Type of Tax or Regulation
1	Income tax
20	Estate tax
25	Gift tax
31	Employment tax
301	Procedural regulation

For example, the citation to Regulation § 1.132-3 indicates that it

■ Is an income tax regulation (1),

■ Was issued with respect to IRC § 132 (132), and

■ Is the 3rd final regulation that was issued related to IRC Section 132 (-3).

Similar to Code sections, regulations are broken down by paragraphs, subparagraphs, and clauses. For example, "Regulation § 1.132-3(a)(2)" refers to subparagraph (2) of paragraph (a) of Regulation § 1.132-3. Treasury regulations are often cited using the abbreviation "Treas. Reg." or just "Reg." before the section number. A final regulation can also be cited by reference to the Code of Federal Regulations as "26 C.F.R. § 1.132-3". Again, the "26" in this citation refers to Title 26 of the C.F.R., the title within the C.F.R. where federal tax regulations are codified.

Proposed regulations should be cited with either the word "Proposed" or the abbreviation "Prop." at the beginning of the citation. For example, "Prop. Reg. § 1.351-2" informs the reader that the regulation cited has not been finalized. Temporary regulations include a "T" in the citation to clearly indicate that the regulation cited is only temporary. For example, in "Treas. Reg. § 1.162-4T," the "T" indicates that it is a temporary regulation.

Final, proposed, and temporary regulations may be accessed using an online tax research service such as RIA Checkpoint (introduced below), or for free through the IRS Web site (www.irs.gov). Final and temporary regulations are also available on the U.S. Government Printing Office (GPO) Web site (www.gpo.gov).

Consider the following **TIP from the Trenches** related to finding tax regulations.

Despite that tax regulations can be accessed for free through the GPO and IRS Web sites, the search engines on these sites are limited and best used when the researcher already knows the citation for the regulation and just needs to retrieve it. When searching for regulations without a citation, such as by keyword search or by reference only to the related IRC section, it is generally more efficient to use an online tax research service.

TIP from the Trenches

Revenue Rulings

While the Treasury Department is primarily responsible for issuing federal tax regulations, the IRS issues several of its own sources of federal tax guidance. One such source is an IRS **Revenue Ruling**. Revenue Rulings are issued by the IRS National Office and are published in the I.R.B. A Revenue Ruling is "an official interpretation by the IRS of the internal revenue laws and related statutes, treaties, and regulations"[4] and is considered a substantial authority. Revenue Rulings may

- Involve the application of the Code and regulations to a particular factual situation.
  - As a result, a Revenue Ruling can be an important source of guidance for taxpayers in the same or a similar situation, because it can be relied on in determining the tax treatment of a transaction.
  - However, the IRS cautions against reaching the same conclusion reached in a Revenue Ruling in another case unless the facts and circumstances are essentially the same as those described in the Revenue Ruling.
- Contain informational updates, such as inflation-related adjustments to certain provisions of the Code and changes in the applicable federal rates of interest applicable to certain tax calculations.

The IRS sometimes modifies, revokes, or issues guidance that supersedes a Revenue Ruling. Therefore, the researcher must be certain that any Revenue Ruling relied on is still "good law." Revenue Rulings are cited by number and by reference to where they appear in the I.R.B. or the C.B. Figure 11-10 illustrates sample Revenue Ruling citations.

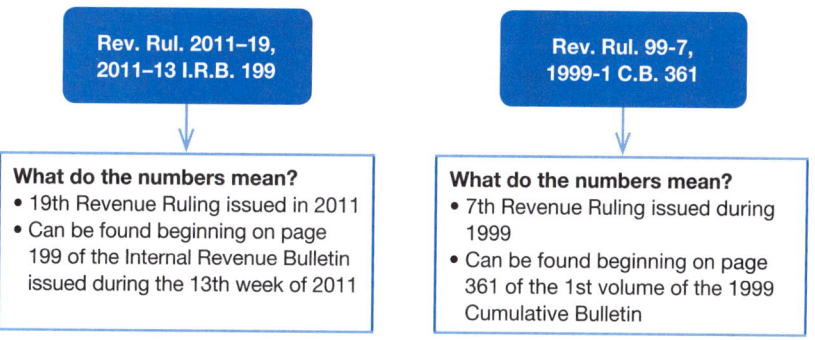

Figure 11-10

Revenue Ruling citations

Rev. Rul. 2011–19, 2011–13 I.R.B. 199

What do the numbers mean?
- 19th Revenue Ruling issued in 2011
- Can be found beginning on page 199 of the Internal Revenue Bulletin issued during the 13th week of 2011

Rev. Rul. 99-7, 1999-1 C.B. 361

What do the numbers mean?
- 7th Revenue Ruling issued during 1999
- Can be found beginning on page 361 of the 1st volume of the 1999 Cumulative Bulletin

Take a moment to complete the following **Now YOU Try** exercise, intended to help you practice properly citing Revenue Rulings.

---

[4] Rev. Proc. 89-14, 1989-1 C.B. 814.

Citing Revenue Rulings

Provide the citation to the following Revenue Rulings:

1. The 52nd Revenue Ruling issued during 2005 and that can be found beginning on page 423 of the 2nd volume of that year's Cumulative Bulletin:

_____

2. The 5th Revenue Ruling issued during 2013 and that can be found beginning on page 525 of the Internal Revenue Bulletin issued during the 9th week of 2013:

_____

Revenue Procedures

A **Revenue Procedure** is an official statement published in the I.R.B. that affects the rights or duties of taxpayers or others under federal tax law.[5] The topics of Revenue Procedures are varied, but generally they involve guidance in the nature of "how to" do something, such as how to request a private letter ruling (discussed below) from the IRS or how to make certain elections under the Code. Revenue Procedures are also considered substantial authority.

Like Revenue Rulings, Revenue Procedures are cited by number and by reference to where they appear in the I.R.B. or the C.B. For example, Revenue Procedure number 2013-4 would be cited as "Rev. Proc. 2013-4, 2013-1 I.R.B. 126," which indicates that

- It is the 4th Revenue Procedure issued in 2013 (2013-4), and
- It can be found beginning at page 126 of the Internal Revenue Bulletin issued during the 1st week of 2013 (126 and 2013-1).

Private Letter Rulings and Technical Advice Memoranda

The IRS National Office issues **Private Letter Rulings** or **PLRs** to taxpayers seeking guidance regarding, or to confirm the tax consequences of, proposed or not-yet-reported transactions. In some cases, the IRS may refuse to issue a requested PLR; this refusal may lead the taxpayer to reconsider and/or restructure a proposed transaction.

The IRS National Office also issues **Technical Advice Memoranda** or **TAMs**. A TAM may be requested by an IRS agent during a federal tax audit, for which the agent seeks National Office input. The TAM describes the IRS's tax analysis and conclusion regarding the audit issue. In some cases, a taxpayer may choose to litigate this decision in court. Figure 11-11 contrasts a Private Letter Ruling and a Technical Advice Memorandum.

Figure 11-11

Comparison of a PLR and a TAM

Private Letter Ruling (PLR)

- Requested by a taxpayer
- Issued by IRS National Office
- Generally regarding a proposed or not-yet-reported transaction
- Purpose:
  - Guidance
  - Assurance

Technical Advice Memorandum (TAM)

- Requested by IRS auditor (sometimes at a taxpayer's request)
- Issued by IRS National Office
- Completed transaction
- Regarding issue(s) raised on IRS audit of a taxpayer's return
- Purpose: IRS analysis & conclusion(s)

Both PLRs and TAMs provide that they "may not be used or cited as precedent." This means that PLRs and TAMs are not precedent that the IRS is required to follow in other cases. However, a

_____

[5] Id.

tax adviser should review relevant PLRs and TAMs (involving facts that are similar to the client's) when researching a tax issue, because they provide guidance as to how the IRS has treated the issue under similar circumstances. PLRs and TAMs are frequently cited when documenting tax research, but with the understanding that they are not binding on the IRS as precedent.

PLRs and TAMs do, however, constitute substantial authority. Therefore, a taxpayer can rely on a PLR or TAM to avoid certain statutory tax penalties (but not the underlying tax) if the IRS takes a different position in a taxpayer's case than it did in the relevant PLR or TAM.

PLRs and TAMs are cited in a similar format, by number. For example, let's "decode" PLR 200601002:

- The first four digits[6] of the PLR refer to the year it was released to the public (2006);

- The next two digits indicate the week it was released ("01" means the PLR was released during the first week of 2006); and

- The final three digits indicate the order in which the ruling was released during the week ("002" means the PLR was the second one released during the week).

Take a moment to complete the following **Now YOU Try** exercise regarding PLRs and TAMs.

PLRs and TAMs

Answer the following questions based on the information just provided.

1. List two ways in which PLRs and TAMs differ.

    _____

    _____

2. What does the citation "PLR 201310022" tell you about this ruling?

    _____

PLRs and TAMs are not published in the I.R.B. or the C.B. However, they are made available for public inspection by the IRS and, more practically, can be accessed using an online tax research service (discussed later in the chapter).

Court Decisions

When the IRS and a taxpayer disagree about the proper tax treatment of a transaction, their dispute may end up being litigated in court. This litigation may result in the court issuing a written decision interpreting other sources of tax law, including the Code and regulations. Court decisions are another primary source of tax law and can provide important guidance for the tax researcher. A relevant court decision is considered substantial authority provided that it has not been overruled or reversed on appeal.

There are a number of different federal courts that hear and decide federal tax cases, including trial courts (where the case is initiated and tried) and appellate courts (which decide appeals of trial or lower appellate court decisions). Understanding each court's **jurisdiction** (i.e., the types of cases the court has authority to hear and decide) helps the researcher to determine whether a decision is precedent for the client's situation being researched. Court decisions appear in **reporters** (volumes in which a number of court decisions are published) and are also accessible using online tax research services.

Trial Courts

The **trial courts** that can hear and decide federal tax cases are the U.S. Tax Court, the U.S. District Court, and the U.S. Court of Federal Claims. Figure 11-12 contrasts these three federal trial courts.

---

[6] For pre-2000 PLRs and TAMs, only the first two digits refer to the year issued. For example, TAM 9715002 (April 11, 1997) was the second ruling issued during the fifteenth week of 1997.

Figure 11-12

Trial courts that decide federal tax cases

U.S. Tax Court	U.S. District Court	U.S. Court of Federal Claims
• Decides only federal tax cases • Based in Washington, D.C.; trials in many U.S. cities • Litigate case before paying tax alleged to be due • No jury	• Decides different types of federal cases • 94 Districts located throughout the U.S. • Refund claims only • May be a jury trial if a question of fact	• Decides only cases involving monetary claims against the U.S. Federal Government • Based in Washington, D.C.; trials in many U.S. cities • Refund claims only • No jury

A taxpayer initiates a case in **U.S. Tax Court** ("Tax Court") by filing a petition, which is generally required to be filed within 90 days of receiving a notice of deficiency from the IRS following a tax audit. The Tax Court is unique in that it is the only court at which the taxpayer may litigate a federal tax deficiency without first paying the tax. The U.S. Tax Court issues three types of decisions: regular decisions, memorandum decisions, and summary decisions. Figure 11-13 briefly summarizes the differences between these three types of Tax Court decisions and their relative precedential values.

Figure 11-13

Types of U.S. Tax Court decisions

Tax Court Regular Decisions

• Often involve issues being decided for the first time by the Tax Court
• Highest precedential value of all Tax Court decisions
• Decisions reported in the Tax Court of the United States Reports (abbreviated "T.C.")
• Can be appealed to an appellate court

Tax Court Memorandum Decisions

• Historically, have involved previously-decided and factual (as opposed to legal) issues
• Have precedential value, but less than Tax Court regular decisions
• Decisions reported in RIA's Tax Court Memorandum Decisions ("RIA T.C. Memo") & CCH's Tax Court Memorandum Decisions ("TCM")
• Can be appealed to an appellate court

Tax Court Summary Decisions

• Applies to small cases; tax and penalties at issue cannot exceed $50,000
• Cannot be used or cited as precedent per IRC §7463(b)
• Decisions not officially published, but available through online tax research services (e.g., RIA's "TC Summary Opinions")
• Cannot be appealed to an appellate court

As shown in Figure 11-13, regular and memorandum Tax Court decisions may be used as precedent, and therefore should be considered when they involve an issue of law relevant to a client's situation. Additionally, despite the prohibition against citing and using summary decisions as precedent for other cases, a researcher should review them to see how the Tax Court has decided cases that are similar to the client's.

As an alternative to filing a petition with the U.S. Tax Court, a taxpayer may choose to pay the tax, penalty, and interest alleged to be due and file a lawsuit seeking a refund of the amount paid either in a **U.S. District Court** or in the **U.S. Court of Federal Claims**.

■ The U.S. District Court with jurisdiction over a taxpayer's refund claim is generally the district in which the taxpayer resides. The U.S. District Court has jurisdiction over federal tax cases—like the Tax Court—as well as cases involving any federal statute or the U.S. Constitution, cases in which the U.S. government is a party, and cases in which the parties are of diverse citizenship (e.g., citizens of different states) and more than $75,000 is at issue.

■ The jurisdiction of the U.S. Court of Federal Claims is limited to cases involving monetary claims against the U.S. federal government (including claims for tax refunds).

Decisions of the U.S. District Courts are reported in the **Federal Supplement** ("**F. Supp.**") or "F. Supp. 2d" (the second series of the Federal Supplement). Decisions of the U.S. Court of Federal Claims are reported in the **Federal Claims Reporter** ("**Fed. Cl.**").

To locate tax decisions within online tax research services, see RIA's American Federal Tax Reports ("A.F.T.R." or "A.F.T.R.2d") or CCH's U.S. Tax Cases ("U.S.T.C."), for example.

5. **What are the three different types of trial courts that hear and decide federal tax cases?**
6. **What types of cases does each of these courts have the jurisdiction to hear and decide?**
7. **Which type of U.S. Tax Court decision has the greatest precedential value?**

✓ **Knowledge Check**

Appellate Courts

The appellate courts that decide appeals of federal tax cases are the U.S. Court of Appeals and the U.S. Supreme Court. Appellate courts do not hold trials of cases. Instead, an appellate court has to decide whether any errors of law (which can include an error in interpreting tax law) were made at the trial court or a lower appellate court. An appellate court is sometimes referred to as a **higher court**, because appellate court decisions are of greater precedential value than trial court decisions, with the U.S. Supreme Court's decisions being of the highest precedential value. Decisions of an appellate court must be followed by trial courts in cases that can be appealed to that appellate court.

A researcher may find court decisions that reach different conclusions on the same issue of tax law. This can be particularly confusing for the novice researcher. Assuming the facts are similar to the client's situation, the researcher should give more weight or importance to the decision of the court with greater precedential value, and less or no weight to the decision of the court with less precedential value. Figure 11-14 illustrates the hierarchy of the different courts that decide federal tax cases (and the hierarchy of regular and memorandum U.S. Tax Court decisions). The higher the court is on this hierarchy, the greater the precedential value of the court's decisions.

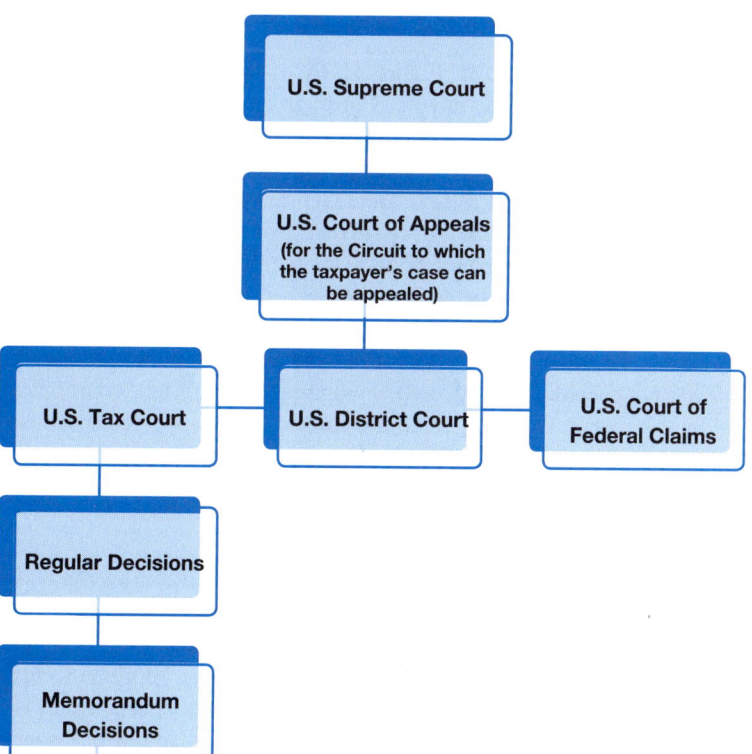

Figure 11-14

Hierarchy of federal courts

U.S. Court of Appeals

The **U.S. Court of Appeals** hears appeals of decisions of the three federal trial courts described previously. There are 13 Circuit Courts of the U.S. Court of Appeals (11 of the Circuits are referred to by number and there are also a D.C. Circuit and a Federal Circuit). An appeal of a Tax Court decision would be to the Circuit that has jurisdiction over the geographic area within which the taxpayer resided when the Tax Court petition was filed. An appeal of a U.S. District Court decision would be to the Circuit that has jurisdiction over the geographic area where the District Court is located. An appeal of a decision of the U.S. Court of Federal Claims is made to the U.S. Court of Appeals for the Federal Circuit. Figure 11-15 depicts the geographic boundaries of the U.S. Court of Appeals.[7]

Figure 11-15

Geographic boundaries of the U.S. Court of Appeals[7]

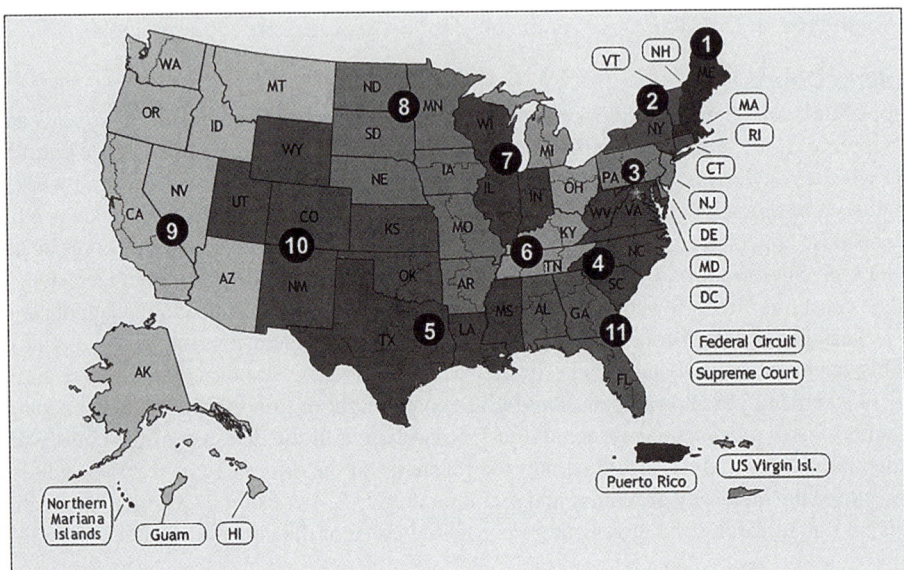

For example, considering the map in Figure 11-15, if a taxpayer lived in Jacksonville, Florida, when she filed her petition with the Tax Court, an appeal of the Tax Court's decision would be filed with the U.S. Court of Appeals for the Eleventh Circuit (which includes Alabama, Florida, and Georgia). The Eleventh Circuit also has jurisdiction over appeals of decisions of the U.S. District Courts located in Alabama, Florida, and Georgia.

Decisions of the U.S. Court of Appeals are reported in the **Federal Reporter**, which is abbreviated "**F.**," "F.2d" (for the second series), or "F.3d" (for the third series). Decisions of the U.S. Court of Appeals in tax cases are also available in online tax research services such as RIA's American Federal Tax Reports ("A.F.T.R." or "A.F.T.R.2d") and CCH's U.S. Tax Cases ("U.S.T.C.").

The different Circuit Courts of the U.S. Court of Appeals may interpret tax law differently, as long as the issue has not been decided by the U.S. Supreme Court. A trial court must follow the law as interpreted by the Circuit Court to which the case could be appealed. Because decisions of the Tax Court are appealed to different Circuit Courts, the Tax Court may interpret the law differently in different cases based on the taxpayer's residence, creating conflicting precedents.

U.S. Supreme Court

The highest appellate court in the U.S. federal court system is the **U.S. Supreme Court**. A decision of the U.S. Supreme Court in a federal tax case must be followed by all trial and appellate courts in federal tax cases involving the same issue. The only exception to this is if the Code (or, in some cases, a regulation) is changed in a way that makes the Supreme Court's decision no longer applicable. There are nine justices on the U.S. Supreme Court, which is located in Washington, D.C. The Supreme Court is primarily an appellate court and, with respect to federal tax cases, may decide a case after an appellate decision is issued by the U.S. Court of Appeals.

---

[7] Source of map: *http://www.uscourts.gov/Court_Locator.aspx*.

The U.S. Supreme Court has discretion over which cases it will decide and issues a **writ of certiorari** if it agrees to hear and decide an appeal. More often, however, the Supreme Court decides not to grant certiorari. When the Supreme Court has granted certiorari, but has not yet decided the case, the citation to the case includes "**cert. granted.**" Finding that certiorari has been granted in a relevant case should put the researcher on alert that the U.S. Supreme Court will be deciding the issue. If the Supreme Court has refused to grant certiorari in a case, the citation to the case includes "**cert. denied.**" The Supreme Court's denial of certiorari is not an indication that the Court agrees with the Court of Appeals' decision in the case. Instead, it is just an indication that the Supreme Court chose not to decide the case.

U.S. Supreme Court decisions are reported in United States Reports ("U.S.") (its official reporter), as well as in the Supreme Court Reporter ("S.Ct.") and the United States Supreme Court Reports, Lawyers' Edition ("L.Ed."). Tax decisions of the U.S. Supreme Court are also published in, and may be cited by reference to, online tax research services such as RIA's American Federal Tax Reports ("A.F.T.R." or "A.F.T.R.2d") and CCH's U.S. Tax Cases ("U.S.T.C.").

Citing Court Decisions

The citation to a court decision generally includes the following information:

■ The names of the parties with a "v." (for versus) in between. Citations of Tax Court decisions generally include only the taxpayer's name and omit "v. Commissioner."

■ The volume number of the reporter in which the decision appears, the abbreviation for the reporter, and the first page number on which the decision appears. Alternatively, the paragraph number for the case may be included in lieu of a page number and/or volume number.

■ An abbreviation indicating the court that decided the case (if not obvious elsewhere in the citation).

■ The year in which the case was decided (if not obvious elsewhere in the citation).

Although citations to court decisions generally refer to volume and page numbers of paper reporters, and some court decisions may also be available on the Web site of the court that issued the decision, it is generally more efficient and thorough to research court decisions using an online tax research service (discussed later in this chapter).

Take a moment to complete the following **Now YOU Try** exercise, intended to acquaint you with case citation format and determining from the citation which court decided the case.

Case Citations

For each of the cases cited below, indicate whether it is a U.S. Tax Court Regular Decision, U.S. Tax Court Memorandum Decision, U.S. District Court Decision, U.S. Court of Federal Claims Decision, U.S. Court of Appeals Decision, or a U.S. Supreme Court Decision.

Now
YOU
Try
11.6

1. *U.S. v. Collins*, 685 F.3d 651 (7th Cir. 2012) **or** 110 A.F.T.R.2d 2012-5128 (CA-7)

_____

2. *Barkley*, TC Memo 2004-287

_____

3. *U.S. v. Home Concrete & Supply, LLC,* 132 S.Ct. 1836 (2012) **or** 109 A.F.T.R.2d 2012-1692 (USSC)

_____

4. *Swallows Holding, Ltd.*, 126 T.C. 96 (2006)

_____

5. *U.S. v. Rigler*, 885 F.Supp. 2d 923 (D.C. Ia. 2012) **or** 110 A.F.T.R.2d 2012-5654 (DCt. I.A.)

_____

6. *Stine v. U.S.*, 106 Fed. Cl. 586 (2012) **or** 110 A.F.T.R.2d 2012-6407 (Ct. Fed. Cl.) **or** 2012-2 USTC ¶50,641 (Ct. Fed. Cl.)

Actions on Decisions

A federal tax case is generally initiated by a taxpayer who disagrees with an IRS decision regarding the taxpayer's tax liability. If the IRS disagrees with the court's decision in a federal tax case involving a significant issue decided in the taxpayer's favor, the IRS may indicate whether or not it will continue to litigate the tax issue decided in the case. The IRS does this by means of an **Action on Decision** (AOD). An IRS **acquiescence** to a case means that the IRS will no longer litigate the issue decided in the case. An IRS **nonacquiescence** to a case means that the IRS does not agree with the court's interpretation of the tax law in a case and will continue to litigate the issue in other cases. The IRS publishes AODs in the I.R.B. AODs are included in the list of substantial authority that can be relied upon to avoid tax penalties. A full citation to a case in which the IRS has acquiesced includes "Acq.," and the full citation to a case in which the IRS has issued a nonacquiescence includes "Nonacq.," followed by the I.R.B. citation where it appears, for example, *Norris,* TC Memo 2011-161, Nonacq. AOD 2011-005, 2011-52 I.R.B.

Secondary Sources of U.S. Federal Tax Law

Secondary sources of U.S. federal tax law include editorial content provided by tax services, tax treatises, and tax periodicals. Although secondary sources are not binding on the IRS or the courts, and are not substantial authority for purposes of avoiding tax penalties, they can be very helpful to a tax researcher, particularly a novice tax researcher, for a number of reasons.

First, consulting a secondary source may be a good first step in your research process. When confronting an issue with which you have little or no experience, you may use a secondary source as background reading to identify and get acquainted with the issue.

Second, a secondary source may help you identify the primary sources of law related to the issue. You can then review the identified primary sources and determine whether they resolve the issue or whether you need to do further research. In either event, you should not rely on the secondary source's discussion of a primary source. It is always necessary to look at the primary source yourself, because the discussion in a secondary source summarizes the primary source. What is left out of the summary may make a difference in the client's case.

Third, you may not be certain of your interpretation of a primary source of tax law. Consulting a secondary source can reinforce your interpretation or may lead you to focus on a different interpretation worth considering.

Tax Services

Tax services generally include a publisher's annotations to and explanations of primary sources of tax law and are periodically updated for new developments. Although these services originated in paper form, they are now generally accessed via an online tax research service that is available by subscription. The primary online services are RIA's Checkpoint and CCH's IntelliConnect. In addition, online legal research services, such as LexisNexis and Westlaw, include access to primary sources of tax law and may also include some secondary sources.

Tax Treatises

Tax **treatises** are published in book form (although some are also accessible via an online tax research service) and provide an in-depth discussion of tax issues. A few examples of tax treatises include:

- Bittker, *Federal Income Taxation of Individuals*
- Bittker & Eustice, *Federal Income Taxation of Corporations & Shareholders*

- Mertens, *Law of Federal Income Taxation*
- Saltzman, *IRS Practice and Procedure*

See the following **TIP from the Trenches** regarding when to consult a treatise.

When the researcher has little or no background knowledge related to the tax issue being researched, a treatise may be the best first place for the researcher to start. Treatises can be used for in-depth background reading to get acquainted with the tax topic involved. Reading the relevant part of a treatise may also help the researcher to better define the issues to be further researched. The treatise will point the researcher to many primary sources of tax law cited within the treatise.

Tax Periodicals

Tax **periodicals** include scholarly and practitioner journals dealing with tax matters. Examples of tax periodicals include the following:

- *The Tax Adviser* (AICPA)
- *TAXES—The Tax Magazine* (CCH)
- *Journal of Taxation* (WG&L)
- *Tax Notes* (Tax Analysts)
- *Daily Tax Report* (BNA)

Tax periodicals include articles that highlight new developments in tax law. Reading tax periodicals on a timely basis helps the tax professional to stay current. Articles in tax periodicals may also be consulted during the research process and provide the researcher with insight in the form of an author's interpretation of tax law.

Consider the following **TIP from the Trenches** regarding using secondary sources for research.

As a beginning researcher, you may find it useful to *start* your research using a secondary source. When using a secondary source, remember that it is not precedent, but can point you in the right direction (towards primary sources) and is often quite user-friendly. For example, beginning tax researchers using RIA Checkpoint (discussed later in the chapter) often find that using the Federal Tax Coordinator is a good starting point, and topics can be searched by table of contents, index, or keyword(s).

Take a moment to complete the following **Now YOU Try** exercise designed to test your knowledge of primary versus secondary sources of tax law.

Primary versus Secondary Sources

For each listed item, indicate what it is a citation for and whether it is a primary source or secondary source of tax law.

1. Reg. §1.351-2(d) _____

2. Bittker & Eustice, *Federal Income Taxation of Corporations & Shareholders*

   _____

3. IRC §1031(a)(2)(A) _____

4. *Tillman*, TC Memo 1996-8 _____

5. *Journal of Taxation* _____

USING AN ONLINE TAX RESEARCH SERVICE TO FIND TAX LAW

With so many sources of tax law, subscribing to and using an online tax research service is a necessity for the professional tax researcher. These services include RIA Checkpoint and CCH IntelliConnect. LexisNexis and Westlaw—two legal research services—also include access to tax law sources. These services are available by paid subscription, and often make arrangements with colleges and universities so that access may be provided free-of-charge to students.

While it may require time and effort to become comfortable using these services, the benefits of doing so are numerous. Researchers can experience efficiency, mobility, and the confidence of knowing you are using a dedicated, professional tax research service designed to help you find accurate and relevant results. The following **TIP from the Trenches** highlights the importance of consulting professional resources in performing tax research.

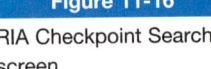

TIP from the Trenches

Researchers should not perform tax research using a general Internet search engine, such as Google or Bing. While some of what the researcher may find will be accurate and authoritative (such as some of the information on the IRS Web site [www.irs.gov]), other results of the search will be secondary authorities (at best) and incorrect information (at worst). Relying on those results in taking a position on a tax return can lead to the imposition of tax, penalties, and interest.

The remainder of this discussion of online tax research services focuses on RIA Checkpoint, which includes access to primary sources of tax law, as well as secondary source material which it classifies as "Editorial Materials" and "News/Current Awareness." Figure 11-16 shows the Search screen (with the Search button circled) for RIA Checkpoint. The Search screen lists the different sources within which the researcher can search on Checkpoint.

Figure 11-16

RIA Checkpoint Search screen

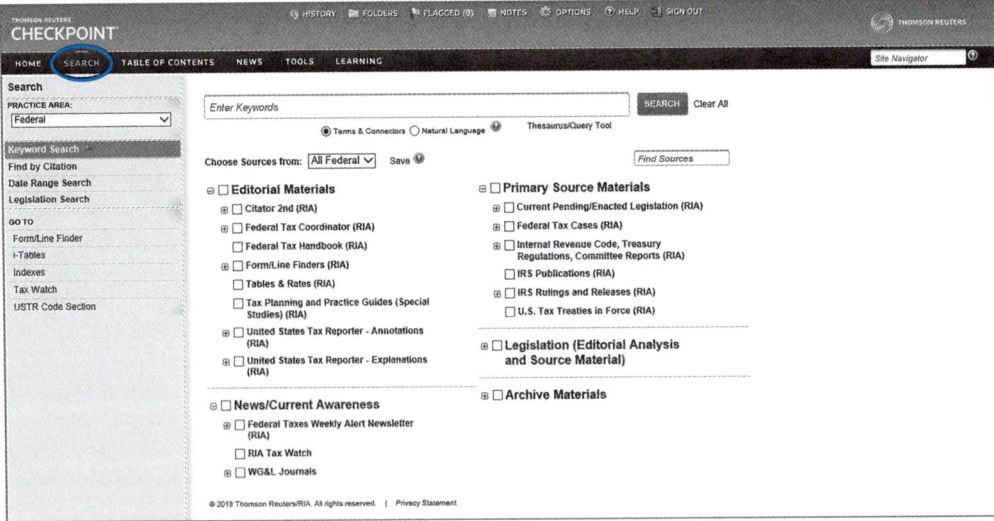

©2013 by Thomson Reuters/RIA. Reprinted with permission. All rights reserved. This information or any portion thereof may not be copied or disseminated in any form or by any means or stored in an electronic database or retrieval system without the express written consent of Thomson Reuters/RIA.

Sources of tax law can be searched in a variety of ways on RIA Checkpoint, as well as on most of the other online tax research services.

Table of Contents and Index Searches on RIA Checkpoint

One way to search on Checkpoint is to think of each database in RIA's Editorial Materials as a large book (or multivolume set). Books have tables of contents and indices and so do these databases. The table of contents of each database may be viewed by clicking on the "Table of Contents" tab followed by clicking on "Federal Library" and then "Federal Editorial Materials." From there, the researcher can click on a database, such as the "United States Tax Reporter" and see its table of contents by groups of Code sections. The researcher can go further, and ultimately access the material in the United States Tax Reporter, by continuing to click onto more and more specific content headings such as one for a particular Code section or its related annotations and explanations. Figure 11-17 illustrates how a table of contents search through the United States Tax Reporter can ultimately lead to accessing its listings for Code Section 61, including the Code section itself, regulations, explanations and annotations.

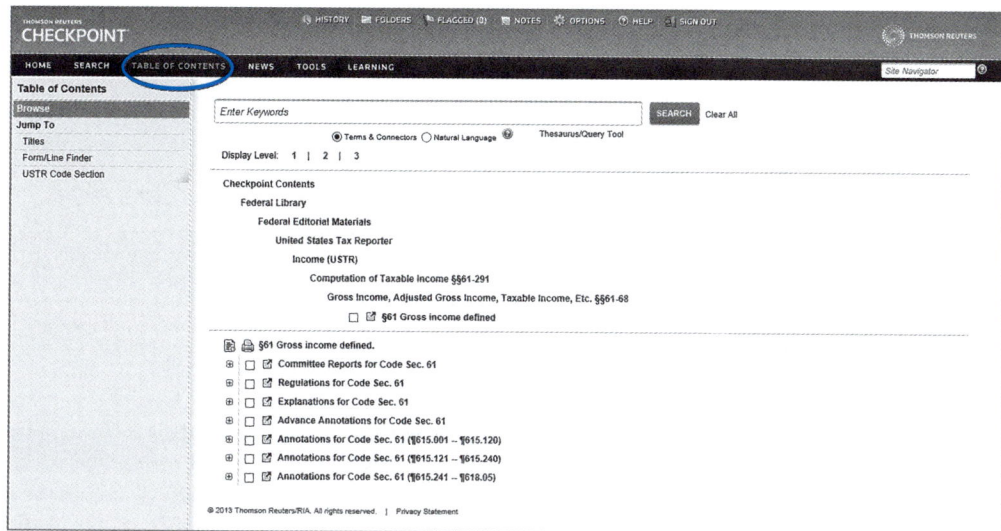

Figure 11-17

Sample table of contents search on RIA Checkpoint

Editorial materials may also be accessed by an index search. This is akin to performing a Master Glossary search within the FASB Codification. To begin an index search on RIA Checkpoint, a tax researcher would again click on the "Table of Contents" tab, followed by "Federal Library," then "Federal Editorial Materials," and then "Federal Indices." From there the researcher can click on a database, such as the "Code Arranged Annotations & Explanations" or the "Federal Tax Coordinator 2d Topical Index," to see the alphabetical index for that database.

When searching in RIA Checkpoint's Editorial Materials, it is important to remember that the results of the search (such as in the form of annotations or explanations) are secondary sources. However, they generally provide links to connect to the primary sources that are annotated or explained in the Editorial Material.

Keyword Searching

An important method for accessing the information on an online tax research service is by searching for keywords in one or more selected databases. This can include primary source material databases, such as "Federal Tax Cases," "Internal Revenue Code, Treasury Regulations, Committee Reports," or "IRS Rulings & Releases," or the databases in RIA's Editorial Materials, or a combination of both. On RIA Checkpoint, a **keyword search** involves using its Search screen (see Figure 11-16), selecting the databases to be searched and entering words (which can be entered using either natural language or Boolean terms and connectors) that one would expect to find in the expected search result documents. The search results will include all documents within the selected database(s) in which the searched words appear and should then be reviewed for relevance and analyzed.

Keyword search results can be limited by making use of the available connectors or expanded by using the Thesaurus/Query Tool, which can be accessed from the Search screen on RIA Checkpoint. RIA's Search Connectors are listed in Figure 11-18.

Figure 11-18

RIA Checkpoint search connectors[8]

Search Connectors

To locate documents:	Use:	Example:
containing any of my keywords	OR, I	funding OR deficiency
containing at least one instance of each of my keywords	space, &, AND	funding deficiency
that contain one keyword but exclude another	^, NOT	funding NOT deficiency
containing my exact phrase	" "	"funding deficiency"
containing variations of my keywords	* (asterisk)	deprecia*
disabling automatic retrieval of plurals and equivalencies	# (pound sign)	#damage (retrieves only damage, not damages)
containing single-character variations	? (question mark)	s????holder (retrieves stockholder, shareholder)
containing compound words	- (hyphen)	e-mail (retrieves e-mail, e mail, email)
containing terms that occur at least # times	atleast#()	atleast5(funding)

To search for a word or phrase:	Use:	Example:
within n words of another (in any order)	/# (where # equals number)	"disclosure exception" /7 negligence
within n words of another (in exact order)	pre/# (where # equals number)	"disclosure exception" pre/7 negligence
within the same sentence (20 words) as another (in any order)	/s	"disclosure exception" /s negligence
within the same sentence (20 words) as another (in exact order)	pre/s	"disclosure exception" pre/s negligence
within one paragraph (50 words) as another (in any order)	/p	"disclosure exception" /p negligence
within one paragraph (50 words) as another (in exact order)	pre/p	"disclosure exception" pre/p negligence

©2013 by Thomson Reuters/RIA. Reprinted with permission. All rights reserved. This information or any portion thereof may not be copied or disseminated in any form or by any means or stored in an electronic database or retrieval system without the express written consent of Thomson Reuters/RIA.

Consider the following **TIP from the Trenches** with respect to index/table of contents searches versus keyword searches.

TIP from the Trenches

Researchers with limited tax knowledge should start their use of an online tax research service by index or table of contents searching. Keyword searching is an "art" that improves as one's knowledge of tax law and its key terms increases. Without sufficient tax knowledge, keyword searches can yield far too many or far too few search results.

---

[8] Checkpoint User Guide at p. 116 (Thomson Reuters 2013).

Citation Searches

Sometimes the tax researcher has the citation for a specific source of tax law, and just needs to retrieve it. The tax researcher can look up the source by using the "Find by Citation" link under the Search tab. For example, if you want to retrieve Revenue Procedure 89-14 by a citation search, click on "Rulings/IRB" under "Find by Citation". This will bring up a "Find a Ruling by Citation" screen on which the researcher can type in "89-14" in the box under "Revenue Procedures," click the "Search" button and immediately start reading Revenue Procedure 89-14. This search is illustrated in Figure 11-19. Similar **citation searches** can be used to find court decisions ("Find Federal Tax Cases") and sections of the Code and regulations ("Find Federal Code & Regs").

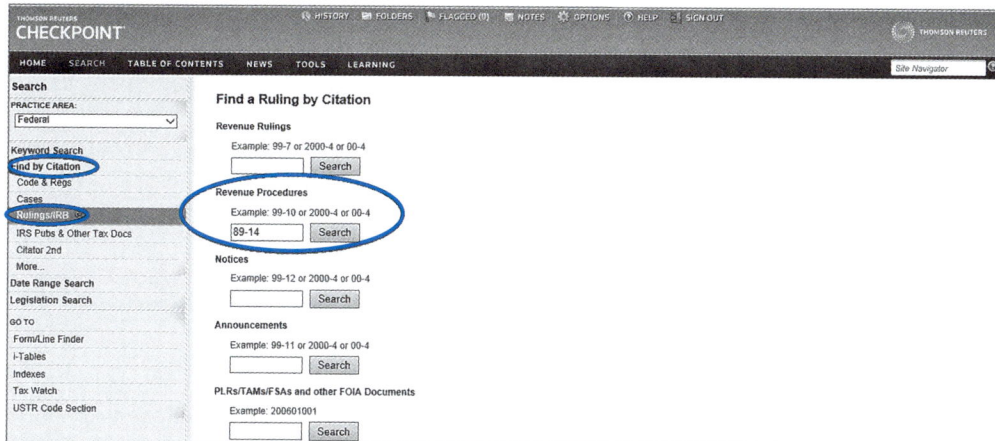

Figure 11-19

Find a Ruling by Citation screen on RIA Checkpoint

Additional Guidance for Using RIA Checkpoint

In addition to the search options described above, online tax research services offer useful links between related sources of tax law. For example, when viewing a Code section on RIA Checkpoint, a number of buttons that link to related material appear above or within the text of the Code section. These buttons link to the following:

- The regulations ("Regs" button) issued with respect to that Code section,
- Legislative history material ("Com Rpts" and "Hist" buttons),
- RIA explanations and annotations ("Expl", "Annot", and "Adv/Annot" buttons),
- Related material in RIA's Federal Tax Coordinator ("FTC" button), and
- For recently amended Code sections, the "New Law Analysis" button.

The "Adv/Annot" button refers to the most recently issued annotations that have not yet been added to the more permanent annotations ("Annot") database. To be current when researching annotations, both "Annot" and "AdvAnnot" should be reviewed. There may also be a "New Law Analysis" button if the Code section has been recently amended.

Figure 11-20 highlights the buttons that appear on RIA Checkpoint above and within Code Section 104.

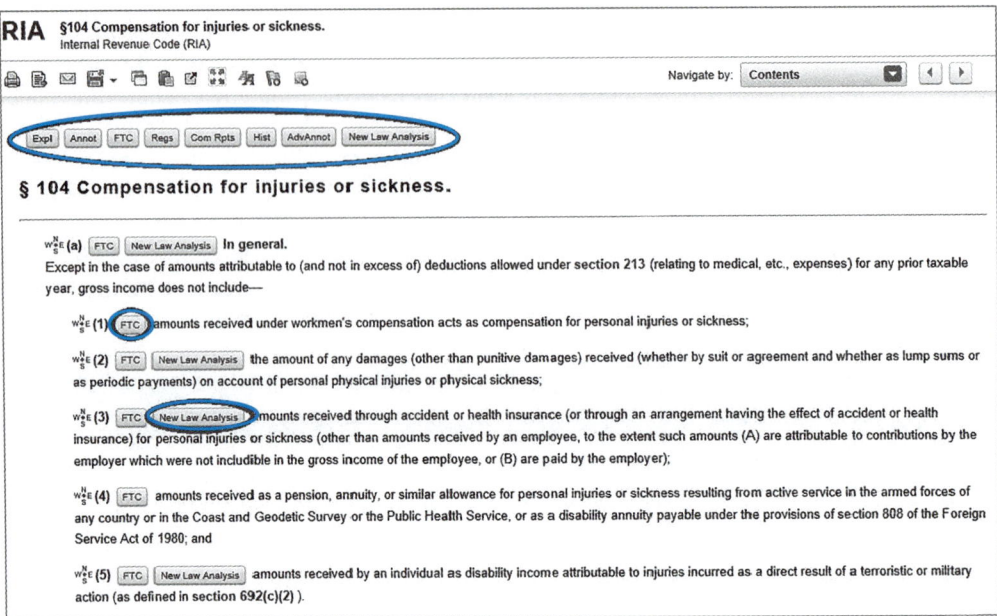

©2013 by Thomson Reuters/RIA. Reprinted with permission. All rights reserved. This information or any portion thereof may not be copied or disseminated in any form or by any means or stored in an electronic database or retrieval system without the express written consent of Thomson Reuters/RIA.

When viewing a regulation, the researcher will see many of the same buttons that appear when viewing the related Code section. In addition, an "IRC" button gives the researcher quick access to the related Code section.

When viewing a case or ruling, the researcher may see buttons linking to where the case or ruling appears in an annotation ("Annot" button) or in the Federal Tax Coordinator ("FTC"). Cases and rulings also include a "Track It" button, where the researcher can choose to be notified by email when the case or ruling being tracked is cited in subsequent sources of tax law, and a "Citator" button (discussed later under Citators).

UPDATING TAX RESEARCH RESULTS

Tax law changes frequently. The Code can be amended by legislation, the Treasury Department can replace a regulation, a court decision may overrule the decision in a different, prior case or may reverse a lower court's decision in the same case, and the IRS may modify or declare obsolete a Revenue Ruling or Revenue Procedure. For these reasons, it is necessary for you to know that you are relying on sources of tax law that are current and still good law.

For amendments to the Code and new or amended regulations, it is generally necessary to look at the Code or regulations themselves. For amendments to the Code, RIA Checkpoint helpfully includes aids such as the "New Law Analysis" button within Code sections that have been recently amended for easy access to information regarding those amendments. The buttons for access to the related Congressional Committee Reports ("Com Rpts") and legislative history ("Hist") are also very helpful.

RIA Checkpoint also provides helpful information when viewing a regulation that has not been amended to reflect relevant amendments to the Code. For example, just above the text of Reg. § 1.162-2 on RIA Checkpoint cautionary information indicates that the regulation has not been amended to reflect changes made by several amendments to Code Section 162. The tax researcher would then look to those Code amendments to determine whether or not IRC § 162 was changed in a way that would make the regulation unreliable in the client's situation.

Updating research findings is part of the third step in the research process (finding, analyzing, and updating applicable sources of tax law). Each time the researcher finds a relevant tax authority, it is necessary to update it to make sure that it is still reliable and authoritative. Tax advice must be current as of the date it is provided to the client. Consider the following **TIP from the Trenches** regarding updating the client on subsequent tax law developments.

Absent an agreement to provide updates to a client, once tax advice has been provided to the client, a CPA is generally not required to provide the client with updates for subsequent tax law developments affecting that advice. From a client relations standpoint, however, it may be advisable to at least alert the client if it appears that a new development could put the client in a worse tax position (or could give the client a more positive tax result) than indicated in the predevelopment advice. It is then the client's decision whether to engage the CPA's services for a more thorough analysis of the affects of the new development on the client's situation. By contrast, in-house corporate tax accountants are generally expected to update the tax advice provided to their employers for relevant tax law developments.

[TIP] from the Trenches

Citators

It is not enough to just locate a case or ruling that is on point. Researchers must also understand whether the case or ruling is still "good law" and whether and how it has been discussed in subsequent cases and rulings. **Citators** are used to update court decisions and IRS Revenue Rulings and Revenue Procedures. For court decisions, a tax researcher can use a citator to learn whether the decision has been affirmed, reversed, modified, or remanded (sent back to the trial court or a lower appellate court) by an appellate court, whether the U.S. Supreme Court has granted or denied certiorari in the case, and whether the IRS has issued an AOD acquiescing or nonacquiescing in the court's decision. Relying on a case that has already been reversed is relying on a discredited authority and can amount to malpractice. Therefore, the tax researcher must check a citator for the subsequent history of the case. The citator will also indicate the other subsequent cases in which the case being checked has been cited and, if so, whether a subsequent case approved, criticized, or otherwise commented on the decision. This information may indicate how reliable the case is. For example, it may not be advisable to rely too strongly on a case that has been criticized in several subsequent court decisions. Citators can also be used to learn the prior history of the case checked on and to access the lower court's decision in the same case.

Similarly, IRS Revenue Rulings and Revenue Procedures can be updated using a citator. In this case, the citator will indicate whether the ruling or procedure has been cited in a court decision, and whether the IRS has clarified, modified, superseded, revoked, or declared the ruling or procedure obsolete. Again, the tax researcher should use this information to determine whether he or she is relying on current, good law or whether it is necessary to look further, such as at a more recent ruling that may have superseded the prior one found by the researcher.

Online tax research services have citators that make updating the law relatively easy. On RIA Checkpoint, the citator is known as "RIA Citator 2nd" and can be accessed in two ways. One way to use RIA's citator is by pushing the "Citator" button when viewing a court decision or ruling. This gives the researcher access to the citator information related to that case or ruling. For example, you might try finding Revenue Procedure 99-14 (hint—the quickest way to do this would be through a Citation Search described above) on RIA Checkpoint and clicking on the "Citator" button. Figure 11-21 shows part of Revenue Procedure 99-14 with the Citator button circled.

Clicking on the Citator button will bring up a reference to the procedure on the left-hand side of the screen. If you click on this reference, you will see the citator results listed for Rev. Proc. 99-14, which are shown in Figure 11-22.

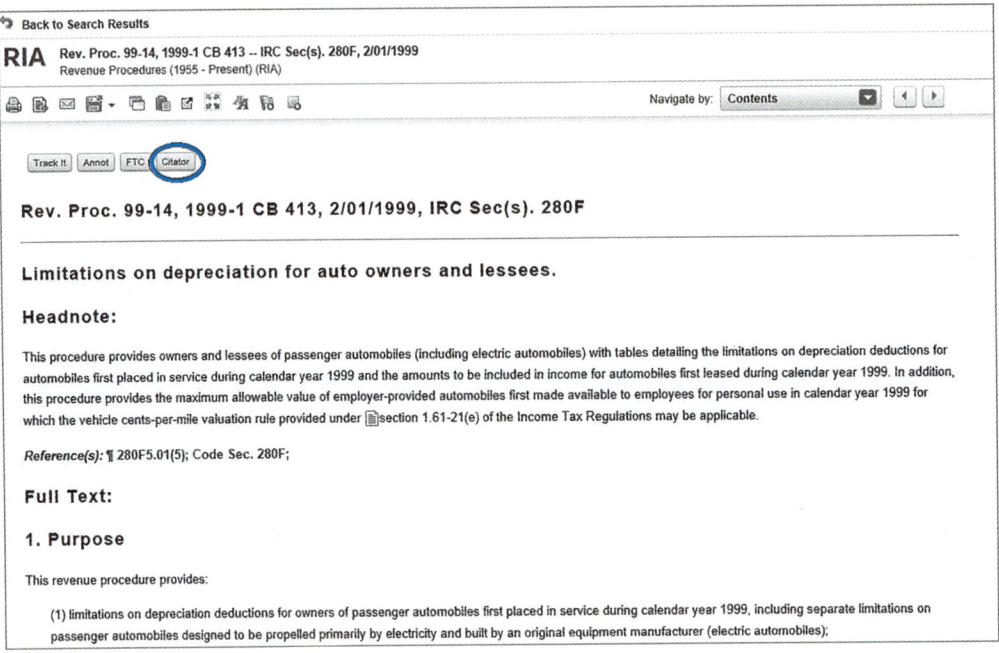

©2013 by Thomson Reuters/RIA. Reprinted with permission. All rights reserved. This information or any portion thereof may not be copied or disseminated in any form or by any means or stored in an electronic database or retrieval system without the express written consent of Thomson Reuters/RIA.

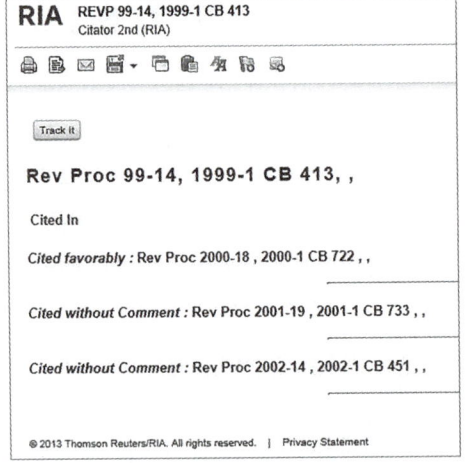

©2013 by Thomson Reuters/RIA. Reprinted with permission. All rights reserved. This information or any portion thereof may not be copied or disseminated in any form or by any means or stored in an electronic database or retrieval system without the express written consent of Thomson Reuters/RIA.

Using the Citator 2nd results, the tax researcher would click on the subsequent procedures listed to review where and how they reference Rev. Proc. 99-14.

The other way to access the RIA Citator 2nd is by clicking on the "Search" tab on Checkpoint. This will bring up the option "Find by Citation" on the left side of the screen. Clicking on "Find by Citation" will bring up the option of finding citations by searching the Citator 2nd by a "Case Name," "Case Citation," or "Ruling Citation." Each of these options has a box where the researcher can type in either a case name or the citation to a court decision or IRS ruling and access the cases and rulings that cite the case or ruling entered, or a list of the cases and rulings cited within the case or ruling entered. At this screen the researcher will also need to indicate whether he or she wants to check the Citator or Advanced Citator. The Advanced Citator would include only the most recent rulings and cases in which the item searched for is cited. In addition, the researcher can check the "Cited" box to search for only the cases and rulings in which the searched for item is cited or can check the "Citing" box to also retrieve the cases and rulings cited within the item searched.

Figure 11-23 illustrates a Citator 2nd search for Ruling Number 99-14. The results of this search will include Revenue Rulings, Revenue Procedures, and other IRS documents numbered 99-14. This is less efficient than finding the ruling and clicking on the Citator button, but may be helpful for finding a document by number when uncertain of its type.

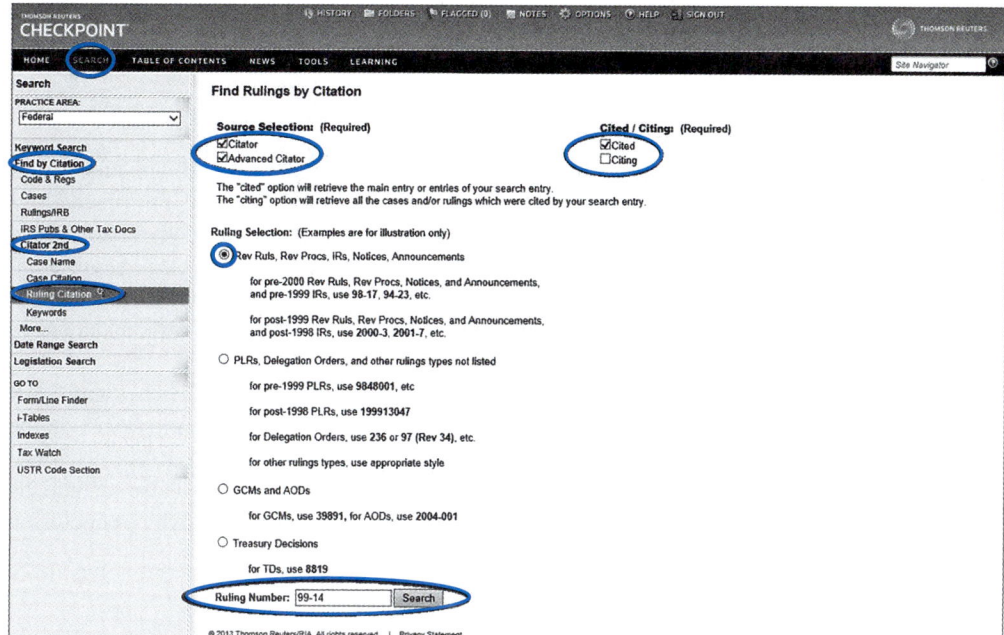

Figure 11-23

RIA Citator 2nd search

STANDARDS OF PROFESSIONAL TAX PRACTICE

Accountants who practice before the IRS, including preparing tax returns and representing clients during tax audits, are subject to rules of practice designed to help maintain the integrity of the federal tax system. The standards for professionals who practice before the IRS are set forth in Circular 230. CPAs are also subject to the American Institute of Certified Public Accountants (the AICPA) Statement on Standards for Tax Services (SSTS).[9] These standards reinforce the need for a tax professional to competently follow the steps of the tax research process to arrive at reasonable and supportable conclusions. These standards are briefly discussed below. A tax professional should be fully familiar with their requirements.

Circular 230

Circular 230[10] is a set of regulations issued by the U.S. Treasury Department that provides the rules of conduct for practicing before the IRS, including who may practice before the IRS and the standards for providing tax advice and issuing tax opinions. Circular 230 provides aspiration-

---

[9] Attorneys practicing before the IRS are also subject to the rules of professional conduct in effect in the jurisdictions within which they practice.

[10] Circular 230 is part of Title 31 of the Code of Federal Regulations. It may be accessed online at *http://www.irs.gov/pub/irs-utl/pcir230.pdf*.

al standards and requirements that should be followed by all professional tax advisers and that are consistent with the tax research process as described in this chapter. As set forth in Section 10.33(a) of Circular 230, the aspirational or "best practices" standards include

- "Communicating clearly with the client regarding the terms of the engagement."
- "Establishing the facts, determining which facts are relevant, evaluating the reasonableness of any assumptions or representations, relating the applicable law (including potentially applicable judicial doctrines) to the relevant facts, and arriving at a conclusion supported by the law and the facts."
- "Advising the client regarding the import of the conclusions reached, including, for example, whether a taxpayer may avoid accuracy-related penalties under the Internal Revenue Code if a taxpayer acts in reliance on the advice."
- "Acting fairly and with integrity in practice before the Internal Revenue Service."

With respect to a "covered opinion" (defined to include, among other things, an opinion in a tax avoidance transaction), Circular 230 sets forth requirements that the tax practitioner must follow, including a prohibition against giving written advice that is based on unreasonable factual or legal assumptions; unreasonably relies on the taxpayer's or anyone else's representations, statements, findings or agreements; does not consider all relevant facts that the practitioner knows or should know; or takes into account the possibility that a return will not be audited or that an issue will not be raised on audit.

Covered opinions must also take into account all significant federal tax issues and must "provide the practitioner's conclusion as to the likelihood that the taxpayer will prevail on the merits with respect to each significant Federal tax issue considered in the opinion" or else must state that the practitioner is unable to reach a conclusion. Covered opinions must also include the reasons for the conclusions reached, including facts and analysis or the reasons why a conclusion could not be reached.[11]

AICPA Statements on Standards for Tax Services

The cover of the AICPA's Statements on Standards for Tax Services is shown in Figure 11-24.[12]

The AICPA's **Statements on Standards for Tax Services** (SSTS) supplement the AICPA's Code of Professional Conduct and Circular 230 and apply to CPAs providing tax services. The SSTS consist of seven Statements, each of which includes an introduction, statement(s), and explanation(s). Many of the statements and explanations are relevant to the tax researcher. For example, paragraph number 4 of SSTS No. 1, regarding taking positions on tax returns, includes the following statement: "A member should determine and comply with the standards, if any, that are imposed by the applicable taxing authority with respect to recommending a tax return position, or preparing or signing a tax return." Determining the applicable standard with which to comply necessarily involves researching the applicable tax law.

SSTS Nos. 2 and 3 primarily relate to obtaining information from the client (the factual investigation portion of tax research). Paragraphs 2 and 3 of SSTS No. 7, regarding the form and content of advice to taxpayers, stresses the need to provide competent tax advice that "compl[ies] with relevant taxing authorities' standards," including "return reporting and disclosure standards" and "the potential penalty consequences of the return position." Explanation paragraph 7 of SSTS No. 7 states that the member should consider a number of factors in deciding the form of advice provided to a taxpayer. The decision as to form includes whether the advice should be provided in writing and, if so, the form and level of detail. These factors include the importance of the transaction, the amount involved, the existence of authority and precedent, the tax sophistication of the taxpayer, and the potential penalty consequences.

---

[11] Circular 230, Section 10.35.

[12] The AICPA's Statements on Standards for Tax Services apply to members of the AICPA and may be accessed online at http://www.aicpa.org/InterestAreas/Tax/Resources/StandardsEthics/StatementsonStandardsforTaxServices/DownloadableDocuments/SSTS,%20Effective%20January%201,%202010.pdf.

Providing competent tax advice to a client involves researching the law and the facts and reaching supportable conclusions that are appropriately communicated to the client. This is necessary both to provide a professional service to the client as well as to comply with the applicable standards imposed on practitioners by the IRS and on its CPA members by the AICPA.

CHAPTER SUMMARY

As a tax professional, you will be expected to provide sound and accurate tax advice to your clients or employer. You will need to ask questions in order to learn the relevant facts, and will need to know how to find and analyze the many sources of tax law to enable you to reach reasoned, supportable conclusions. You will also have to communicate the advice to your client or employer in a way that can be understood. While doing each of these things, you must always remember to comply with the professional standards applicable to providing tax advice as prescribed by the IRS and the applicable professional organization, such as the AICPA.

By following a professional and systematic approach to tax research, exercising good judgment, and following the applicable professional standards, a tax professional can enjoy a successful and rewarding career while establishing and maintaining an ethical reputation.

REVIEW QUESTIONS

1. Identify the four steps in the tax research process.
2. List at least five primary sources of tax law and two secondary sources of tax law. How do primary sources and secondary sources differ?
3. Compare and contrast the Internal Revenue Code and Treasury Regulations with respect to the following questions:
   a. How and by whom are amendments to the Internal Revenue Code adopted? How and by whom are Treasury Regulations promulgated?
   b. Which of these two sources of tax law has greater precedential value?

4. Compare and contrast Revenue Rulings and Revenue Procedures. Where are they published? How do they differ?

5. Compare and contrast Private Letter Rulings and Technical Advice Memoranda. How do they differ?

6. List the trial courts that can hear and decide federal tax cases. For each of these courts, indicate the following:
   a. Is the court's jurisdiction limited to federal tax cases, or can it hear and decide other types of cases? If so, what other types of cases?
   b. Does the taxpayer have to pay the tax alleged to be due before initiating litigation in the court?

7. What is an appellate court? List the appellate courts that may issue decisions in federal tax cases. Which of these courts is the highest judicial authority on issues of U.S. federal tax law?

8. List and briefly describe the three methods of searching using an online tax research service.

9. What is a citator? Why is it important to use a citator when conducting tax research?

10. What professional standards apply to CPAs who represent taxpayers in preparing federal tax returns and providing tax advice to clients? Who sets these standards?

EXERCISES

Except as otherwise noted, answer the following using an online tax research service, such as RIA Checkpoint.

1. Find IRC Section 162. How many subsections does it have? What are they?

2. Find the regulations issued pursuant to IRC Section 132. How many regulations are there? How many are (a) final regulations? (b) proposed regulations? (c) temporary regulations? Properly cite one of each of these types of regulations.

3. Use the Federal Tax Coordinator 2d Topic Index to find all the items in the Federal Tax Coordinator 2d that mention the term "citrus groves."
   a. How many items are listed?
   b. Click on the link to ¶M-1828. What is the title of this paragraph?
   c. Which Internal Revenue Code sections are discussed in ¶M-1828?
   d. List the four other primary sources of tax law discussed in ¶M-1828 and that can be accessed from it (by clicking on the links to those sources).

4. Keyword Searches
   a. Using a Keyword Search in the Federal Tax Cases database search for cases using a "Natural Language" search with the phrase "can an employee deduct the cost of work clothes." How many cases did this search find?
   b. Now change your keyword search to a "Terms & Connectors" search and search for the following set of terms "work clothes employee deduction" (not in quotes and not separated by commas). How many cases did this search find?
   c. Now change your "Terms & Connectors" keyword search to the following set of terms "work /3 clothes employee deduction" (again not in quotes and with no other connectors or commas). How many cases did this search find?

5. Using a Citation Search or a Keyword Search in the IRS Rulings & Releases database, find Revenue Ruling 72-606.
   a. Provide the citation to this ruling.
   b. What Code sections are discussed in the ruling?
   c. What are the facts of the ruling?
   d. What issue is decided in the ruling?
   e. What did the IRS conclude with respect to this issue?
   f. When viewing the ruling, click on the "FTC" button at the top. What is the paragraph number and heading or title under which this ruling is cited in the Federal Tax Coordinator 2d?
   g. When viewing the ruling check the citator to see in what cases and rulings Revenue Ruling 72-606 was cited. What did you find?

6. Using a Citation Search or a Keyword Search in the Federal Tax Cases database, find the 1983 Tax Court Memorandum decision in the *Tuer* case.
   a. Provide a proper citation to the case.
   b. What Code Sections are discussed in the case?

c. What are the facts of the case?

d. What issues were decided in the case?

e. What did the court conclude with respect to these issues?

f. Relying solely on this decision, what position should Nora Smith take on her federal income tax return with respect to the situation described at the very beginning of this chapter?

7. Now check the citator for the 1983 Tax Court Memorandum decision in the *Tuer* case from Exercise No. 6. (*Hint:* Click on the "Citator" button when viewing the *Tuer* decision and then click on the link to the Citator results on the left side of the screen to see the Citator results.)

a. In how many other cases has the Tax Court's decision in *Tuer* been cited?

b. In which of those other cases was the *Tuer* case distinguished?

c. Review the court's decision in that case and briefly summarize how the facts of that case differ from the facts of the *Tuer* case.

8. Using a Citator Search or a Keyword Search in the Federal Tax Cases database, find the *McLeod* case that was decided by a U.S. District Court in Alabama in 1967.

a. Provide the citation to the case.

b. What did the IRS decide after the court decided this case?

c. Indicate how you found this IRS decision and cite it.

9. Using a Citator Search, find IRC Section 351. Using the legislative history material available by clicking on the "Hist," "Com Rpts," and "New Law Analysis" buttons answer the following questions:

a. What is the name and Public Law number of the statute that most recently amended Section 351?

b. How did that statute amend Section 351? In other words, what changes were made to Section 351 by the statute referred to in answer to 9.a?

c. What Committee's report is available with respect to the statute identified in your answer to 9.a? What does that Committee report say about this amendment?

10. Using the AICPA's Statements on Standards for Tax Services (SSTS) (available online at http://www. aicpa.org/InterestAreas/Tax/Resources/StandardsEthics/StatementsonStandardsforTaxServices/Downloadable Documents/SSTS,%20Effective%20January%201,%202010.pdf), answer the following questions and indicate the Statement number and paragraph number of the SSTS where you found each answer:

a. May a CPA rely on information provided by third parties in preparing a client's tax return? When should a CPA not rely on information provided by the client or a third party in preparing the client's tax return?

b. What should a CPA do if he or she discovers an error on a client's previously filed tax return?

c. What should a CPA do if he or she discovers an error on a client's previously filed tax return during the course of representing the client in an administrative proceeding before the IRS regarding that return?

CASE STUDY QUESTIONS

Charitable Contributions of Used Vehicles, Writing a Client Letter

Facts: You have been asked to provide tax advice to a new start up, for-profit corporation named Donate Your Jalopy, Inc. (DYJ). DYJ's business plan is to provide services to its clients, which will be various 501(c)(3) charitable organizations. DYJ's services will primarily consist of accepting used cars that are donated to charities, selling the used cars, and remitting the proceeds of each used car sale (net of a fee payable to DYJ for its services) to the applicable charity. Doug Clunker is DYJ's founder and president. He thinks that this type of business could be quite lucrative, and he wants to make sure that it is successful. Doug realizes that part of that success will be correctly structuring how DYJ provides its services to charities and making sure that DYJ correctly documents the donations for the donors. Doug has asked for your advice on how to structure DYJ's arrangements with its charity clients and what documentation DYJ should provide to the used car donors.

11.1

Required:

First Step: Identify the relevant Code section and regulations and find an IRS Revenue Ruling that addresses DYJ's proposed situation. Be sure to check the citator to make sure that the ruling is current and that subsequent authority has not affected the tax treatment of this situation.

Second Step: Based on your findings in the first step, write a brief letter to Doug at DYJ advising him as to how DYJ should structure its arrangements with its charity clients and what documentation DYJ should provide to the used car donors.

11.2   **Business-Related Education Expense, Writing a Client Letter**

Facts: Your client, Duane, is employed as an Assistant Public Defender by the City of New York. In his position, he represents persons accused of crimes who cannot afford to pay an attorney to represent them. Duane frequently represents persons who speak Spanish. Duane knows a little Spanish, but is considering taking a conversational Spanish course at a local language school to improve his ability to speak with his Spanish-speaking clients. Duane has asked his boss whether there is any money in the Office of the Public Defender's budget to pay for him to take the course, but he was told that there is not. Duane has asked you whether the cost of the course is deductible for federal income tax purposes if he pays for it himself.

Required:

First Step: Identify the relevant Code section and regulations and find a court decision that is relevant to Duane's situation. Be sure to check the citator to make sure that the case is current and that subsequent authority has not affected the precedential value of the decision.

Second Step: Based on your findings in the first step, write a brief letter to Duane telling him whether or not he can deduct the cost of the conversational Spanish course on his federal income tax return.

11.3   **Charitable Gift of Property Subject to a Condition, Writing a Memorandum to the Client's File**

Facts: Your clients, Steve and Linda Grady, recently purchased oceanfront property in Avalon, New Jersey. The Gradys paid $3 million dollars for the property. There is an existing, modest house on the property that was built in 1950. The Gradys purchased the property for the land (and oceanfront location) as opposed to the existing house. The Gradys would like to demolish the house and build a large, multi-million-dollar house on the property. Rather than paying a contractor $30,000 to demolish the existing house, the Gradys are considering donating the house (but not the land) to the Avalon Volunteer Fire Department ("AVFD") with the stipulation that the AVFD will quickly burn it down as part of its firefighter training program.

Required: Is there any authority indicating that Steve and Linda cannot claim a deduction for this donation? Research this question considering the relevant Code Section(s), regulation(s), cases and/or rulings and write a brief memorandum to the client's file that addresses this question.

Chapter 12

The International Research Environment

Let's face it—you're skeptical of whether this chapter will be of much relevance to you. You know that U.S. GAAP is still the predominant reporting framework in the United States, and it is hard to imagine when, or if, that will change.

But the facts are that international accounting and auditing standards are already impacting U.S. accountants. Our economy is becoming increasingly global, and the expectations for professionals and CPA exam candidates have followed suit. For example, as a professional you may be asked to monitor convergence efforts between U.S. and international accounting standard setters for your client; or you may be tasked with preparing financial statements for a company whose parent is incorporated overseas; or perhaps you will participate in implementing changes to your firm's ethics code, resulting from U.S. convergence with international ethics standards.

This chapter aims to provide you with an understanding of the global standard-setting environment, international accounting and auditing standards, and the relevance of these standards to U.S. accounting practitioners. Understanding these concepts will enhance your professional toolkit and will prepare you for the projects you'll encounter as a professional. So read on—and rest assured that your efforts will pay off.

After reading this chapter and its appendix, and performing the exercises herein, you will be able to

Learning Objectives

1. **Understand** the context in which accounting research is performed internationally.

2. **Identify** the organizations with authority to establish international accounting and auditing standards.

3. **Identify** circumstances in which international standards apply to U.S. practitioners.

4. **Navigate** and apply the two prevailing sets of international accounting guidance: full IFRS, and IFRS for small and medium-sized entities (SMEs).

International Accounting Standards	Appendix: International Auditing Standards
1. Introduction—the move toward global standards 2. The IFRS Foundation and its standard setters 3. The relevance of international standards in the United States 4. IFRS, and *IFRS for SMEs*: Sources, content, application 5. Researching international accounting standards 6. Nonauthoritative resources	1. When do international auditing standards apply? 2. The IFAC and its standard setting boards 3. Researching international auditing standards 4. Example: Comparing international and U.S. audit reports

Organization of This Chapter

The first several sections of this chapter focus on international accounting standards. First, we will look at circumstances in which companies prepare financial statements internationally, then will introduce the predominant international standard setter (the IASB), including discussion of its operations, structure, and standards. Next, the chapter describes circumstances in which international accounting standards are relevant to U.S. accountants.

Building on this base knowledge, the chapter will cover skills for navigating international accounting standards and research tools, then will introduce certain nonauthoritative resources that can support a thoughtful research effort.

International auditing and ethics standards are introduced in the appendix to this chapter. This appendix describes the organizations responsible for establishing these standards and describes the relevance of these standards in the United States. The appendix concludes with an example illustrating certain differences between U.S. and international audit reports.

The preceding graphic illustrates the organization of content within this chapter and its appendix.

This chapter and its appendix focuses primarily on IFRS accounting guidance and IAASB auditing standards, both of which are widely used internationally. It's worth noting that other country- or region-specific sources of international accounting and auditing guidance exist, but are not a primary focus of this chapter.

Acknowledging the duplication inherent in this phrasing, for purposes of easy readability, this chapter occasionally refers to International Financial Reporting Standards (IFRS) as: "IFRS standards" or "IFRS guidance." Also, the terms country, jurisdiction, and region are at times referred to collectively as "country" or "jurisdiction."

INTRODUCTION

The Move toward Global Standards

Internationally, as in the United States, financial statements are an important means by which companies report their results of operations to current and prospective investors and lenders, government authorities, and company management and employees. For many "listed" (or public) companies around the world, the issuance of audited financial statements is required by securities regulators. For "nonlisted" (or nonpublic) companies, financial statements are often required by the laws and regulations of individual countries (or "jurisdictions"). Each jurisdiction sets its own criteria for determining which companies must issue such **statutory** (or government-required) financial statements, and determines the applicable financial reporting framework. In some cases, these statutory financial statements are also designed to fulfill tax reporting requirements.

In the past, the applicable financial reporting framework for each country generally was established by its **national standard setter**, each issuing unique accounting standards. For example, Japanese companies relied primarily on standards of the Accounting Standards Board of Japan, and Canadian companies relied primarily on the Canadian Accounting Standards Board.

Today, international regulators and governments are increasingly turning to the standards set by the **International Accounting Standards Board** (**IASB**), often with the continued collaboration of (or required endorsement by) national standard setters. Now required or permitted for use in nearly 120 countries (including two-thirds of the countries in the G20), and available in 46 languages, **International Financial Reporting Standards** (**IFRS**) have become the predominant global accounting standards.[1] Of the countries that have not adopted IFRS, several major economies have plans to adopt in the future or, like China and India, are working to converge key aspects of their standards with IFRS.

While no formal plan has yet been announced to adopt IFRS for U.S. companies, the FASB and IASB are working on several major projects that they hope will result in converged standards.

Begun in 1973 with a goal of harmonizing global accounting standards, the **International Accounting Standards Committee** (**IASC**)—predecessor to the IASB—issued standards that were largely viewed as "voluntary adjuncts" to the use of national standards.[2] The IASC's standards took on a new momentum in June 2000 (shortly before the IASC was replaced in 2001 by the IASB), when the European Commission announced its plans to require listed companies in the EU to adopt international accounting standards by 2005. At that time, "no other country or countries in the developed world had yet announced a commitment to the IASC's standards."[3] In other words, these standards have gone from "0 to 120," nearly, in just over a decade, and the key catalyst for this change was the EU's commitment to adopting these standards.

Supporting this move toward a single set of high-quality global accounting standards are many investors and multinational corporations, many of whom believe that use of a single reporting language reduces the costs of capital. Let's look at one example of a corporate beneficiary of the move toward global accounting standards.

EXAMPLE

HSBC—A Beneficiary of Global Standards

As one of the world's largest banks, HSBC Holdings plc ("HSBC") has been a vocal supporter of the global move toward IFRS. Based in London, and with subsidiaries located around the

continued

---

[1] Source for "46 translations" statistic: 2011 Annual Report of the IFRS Foundation. Page 1. Source for "nearly 120 countries" statistic: IFRS Foundation report, "Who we are and what we do." Revised Jan. 2013. Page 6.

[2] Zeff, Stephen A. "The Evolution of the IASC into the IASB, and the Challenges it Faces." Published in *The Accounting Review* of the American Accounting Association. Vol. 87, No. 3, 2012. Page 834.

[3] Zeff, Page 824.

globe, HSBC's support not only reflects its responsibility to *prepare* consolidated, global financial statements, but also its role as a major institutional investor (i.e., a *user* of global financial statements). Figure 12-1 illustrates the global nature of HSBC's organization, with subsidiaries in 81 countries across Latin America, North America, Europe, the Middle East, and the Asia-Pacific region.[4]

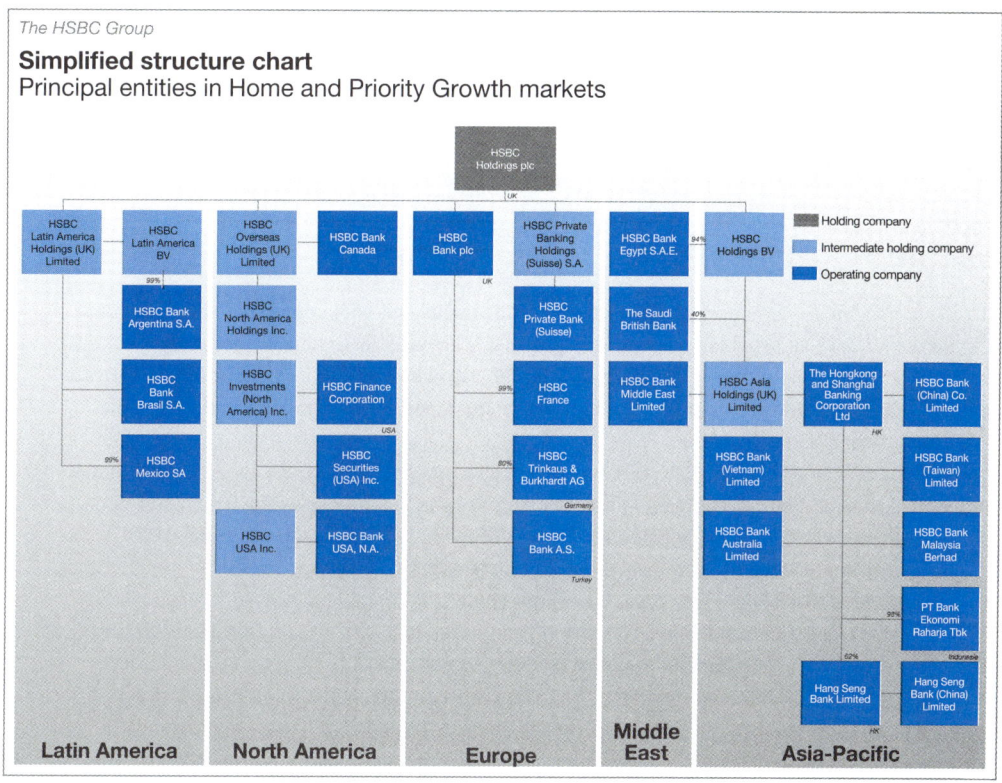

The HSBC Group

Simplified structure chart
Principal entities in Home and Priority Growth markets

1 All entitles wholly owned unless shown otherwise (part ownership rounded down to nearest percent)
2 At 31 December 2012
Image used with permission from HSBC Holdings Plc.

Figure 12-1

HSBC's simplified organizational chart[5]

The following figure, Figure 12-2, illustrates several of the international stock exchanges on which shares of the parent company, HSBC Holdings plc are listed. HSBC's shares are held by approximately 220,000 shareholders in 129 countries and territories around the world.[4]

---

[4] HSBC Holdings plc, Annual Review 2012: *Connecting customers to opportunities*. Page b: "Our network covers 81 countries and territories in Europe, the Asia-Pacific region, the Middle East, Africa, North America and Latin America. Our aim is to be acknowledged as the world's leading international bank." Also: "Listed on the London, Hong Kong, New York, Paris and Bermuda stock exchanges, shares in HSBC Holdings plc are held by about 220,000 shareholders in 129 countries and territories."

[5] The HSBC Group, *Simplified Structure Chart: Principal entities in Home and Priority Growth markets*. As of December 31, 2012. Accessed March 12, 2013 from website, http://www.hsbc.com/about-hsbc/structure-and-network

Figure 12-2

Select markets in which
HSBC Holdings plc
shares are listed

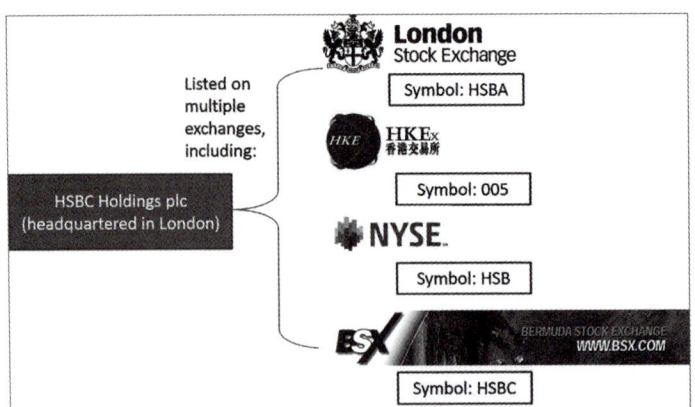

Exchange logos used with permission.
"London Stock Exchange" and the Coat of Arms device are registered trade marks
of London Stock Exchange plc in the UK and other countries and are used under
licence.

Now imagine for a moment the costs that must be associated with complying with individual securities laws and statutory reporting requirements across HSBC's many subsidiary locations! It may come as no surprise, therefore, that HSBC has been vocal in its support for a single set of global accounting standards, arguing that a single reporting framework can decrease the costs of compliance globally.

In a 2009 letter to the U.S. SEC voicing support for the use of IFRS in the United States, HSBC stated: "The costs of maintaining separate ledgers and processes for IFRS and US GAAP are very significant in North America." Allowing U.S. issuers to use IFRS, HSBC wrote, would "eventually eliminate the need to maintain two complete sets of financial records and the need to analyze every transaction under both IFRSs and U.S. GAAP."[6]

This example illustrates the clear benefits afforded to HSBC of the global shift toward IFRS. However, it is important to understand this example in context. As a London-based corporation, HSBC already reports under IFRS in certain jurisdictions and expects to see additional benefits from the continued expansion of IFRS globally. Not all multinational corporations share this view. For example, U.S.-based multinationals Citigroup and Wal-Mart have expressed concern to the SEC that the benefits of an outright adoption of IFRS would not exceed its costs, instead expressing a preference for continued convergence between U.S. GAAP and international standards.[7]

Later in this chapter, we will discuss the status of the U.S.'s consideration of IFRS. But first, let's take a closer look at the organizations responsible for establishing international accounting standards.

---

[6] Iain Mackay, Senior Executive VP and CFO, HSBC North America Holdings Inc. "Comment letter to the SEC." In reference to SEC File Number: S7-27-08. April 20, 2009. Page 2.

[7] Per comment letters in response to SEC File Reference No. S7-27-08, authored by: Robert Traficanti, Citigroup Vice President and Deputy Controller, April 20, 2009. Page 2. Steven P. Whaley, Senior Vice President & Controller, Wal-Mart Stores, Inc., April 20, 2009. Page 2.

The IFRS Foundation and Its Standard-Setting Bodies

Headquartered in London, England, and with a regional office in Tokyo, Japan, the **IFRS Foundation** oversees two independent standard-setting bodies, the IASB and the **IFRS Interpretations Committee (IFRIC)**.

The IFRS Foundation has a challenging mission, as illustrated in Figure 12-3. Its responsibilities, directly and through its standard-setting bodies, include, for example,

- Establishing accounting standards suitable to a wide range of users and responsive to their evolving financial reporting needs;

- Considering input from a broad range of stakeholders, including national and regional standard setters, securities regulators, corporations, accounting firms, and the investor community;

- Continuing convergence efforts with national standard setters, to minimize certain differences in accounting methods;

- Educating preparers and users in an effort to achieve consistent global application of its standards; and

- Encouraging additional jurisdictions, not currently applying IFRS, to adopt.

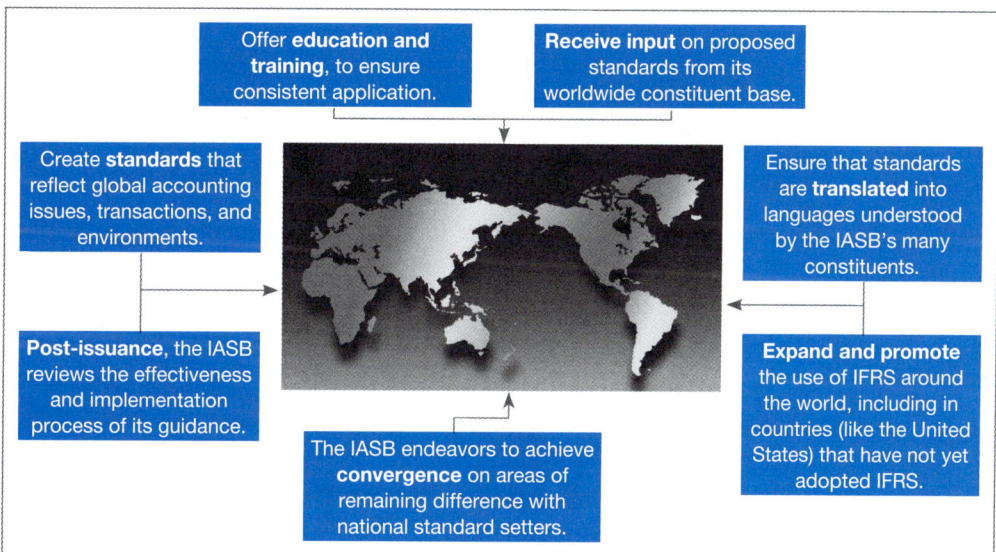

Figure 12-3

The challenging mission of the IFRS Foundation and its standard-setting bodies

Image of world used with permission from Microsoft.

Let's briefly look at how the IFRS Foundation is organized and funded.

Organization and Funding of the IFRS Foundation

The IFRS Foundation and its standard-setting bodies are overseen by the **IFRS Foundation Trustees**, and the Trustees are overseen by the **IFRS Foundation Monitoring Board**. The Foundation's standard-setting bodies are advised by the **IFRS Advisory Council** and the **Accounting Standards Advisory Forum** (ASAF). These relationships are illustrated in Figure 12-4. We will discuss each of these bodies in turn.

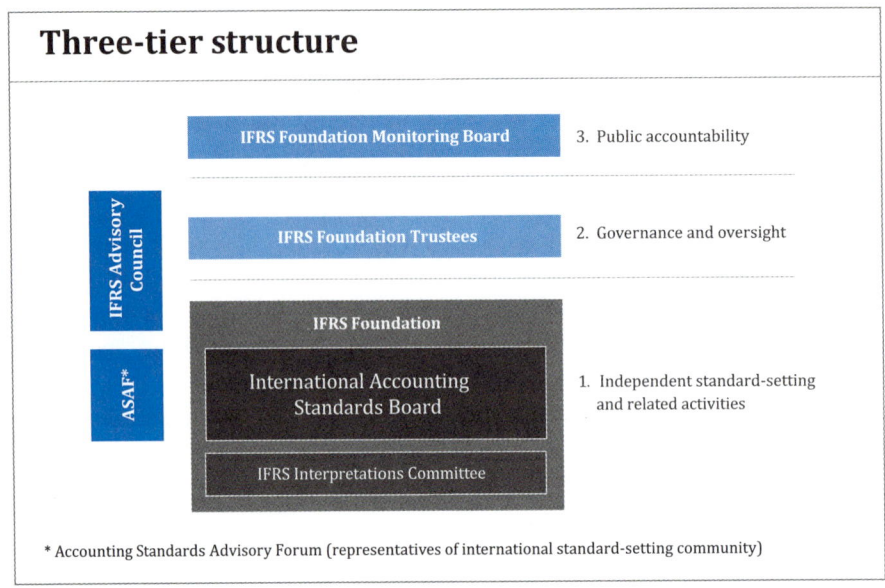

Copyright © IFRS Foundation. All rights reserved.[8]

Source: IFRS Foundation, "Who We Are and What We Do." Revised Sept. 2013. Page 3.

The IFRS Foundation Trustees

Governance of the IFRS Foundation primarily rests with its Trustees, comprised of 22 individuals representing a diversity of geographic regions and professional backgrounds. Responsibilities of the IFRS Foundation Trustees include

- Appointing members to the IASB, the IFRS Interpretations Committee, and the IFRS Advisory Council;

- Providing governance over the independence, funding, and processes of the IASB; and

- Promoting and supporting the use of IFRS globally.

In fulfilling these duties, the Trustees are held publicly accountable to the Monitoring Board (discussed next), to whom the trustees must report at least annually.[9]

The IFRS Foundation Monitoring Board (the "Monitoring Board")

The IFRS Foundation Monitoring Board provides for the formal interaction between the IFRS Foundation and individuals representing the **capital markets authorities** (i.e., securities regulators) it serves. These include

- The U.S. SEC

- The European Commission

- The Financial Services Agency of Japan (JFSA)

- The Emerging Markets and Technical Committees of the International Organization of Securities Commissions (IOSCO)

Recall that under the Securities Exchange Act of 1934, the U.S. SEC was given authority to set U.S. accounting standards, but it chose to delegate this authority to the FASB. In a similar fashion, many international capital markets authorities have chosen to entrust standard setting for listed (e.g., public) companies to the IASB, but still desire oversight over the process in

---

[8] Reproduced by Cambridge Business Publishers Limited with the permission of the IFRS Foundation®. No permission granted to third parties to reproduce or distribute.

[9] IFRS Foundation Constitution, updated January 2013. Par. 13, 15, 19b, 24.

which standards are set. Accordingly, members of this board participate in the appointment of IFRS Foundation Trustees, provide input into the IASB's processes, and—as its name implies—generally "monitor" the activities of the IFRS Foundation.[10]

Members of this board represent capital markets authorities responsible for setting the form and content of financial reporting in their respective jurisdictions. The Monitoring Board is currently seeking to expand its membership to include representatives from major emerging markets. Membership requirements established in 2013 require that members must demonstrate a commitment to the use of IFRS in their jurisdictions, and the jurisdiction must contribute to the IFRS Foundation's funding. Existing members will be evaluated against these criteria beginning in 2016.[11] Given that it has not expressed a commitment to requiring the use of IFRS for U.S. companies, it is unclear whether the SEC will meet the requirements for continued membership at that time.

Advisory Bodies

The IASB regularly receives input from various advisory groups, including the IFRS Advisory Council and the ASAF. Comprised of individuals representing a diversity of geographic and professional backgrounds, the Advisory Council provides a forum for individuals and organizations to provide input into the IASB's standard setting. For example, the Council

■ Advises the IASB on its agenda decisions and priority of projects, and

■ Provides views on existing standard-setting projects.

Members of the IFRS Advisory Council are appointed by the Trustees and meet with members of the IASB at least three times per year.[12]

Established in 2013, the ASAF is intended to formalize the process through which the IASB receives input from regional and national standard setters. This advisory forum, comprising representatives from member standard setters, advises the IASB on its technical projects and will—the IASB hopes—reduce the risk of nonendorsement by various jurisdictions once a standard has been issued.

Other formal advisory bodies to the IASB include, for example, the Emerging Economies Group and the Capital Markets Advisory Group.

Funding for the IFRS Foundation

The IFRS Foundation is funded through a combination of

■ Mandatory levies, imposed by certain countries' governments and regulatory bodies on listed and/or nonlisted companies, similar to (but not as pervasive as) the accounting support fee, which funds the FASB;

■ Contributions from national standard setters and/or governments;

■ Voluntary contributions from public accounting firms and certain U.S. companies (such as Bank of America and Citigroup);[13] and

■ Sales of IASB publications and educational activities.

While the IFRS Foundation has established "target contributions" from its member countries (based in part on each country's GDP), it lacks the authority to impose funding requirements and thus must rely on this mixed-attribute funding system. As of October 2012, approximately 69 of the IFRS Foundation's nearly 120 member countries contributed, directly or indirectly, to

---

[10] Memorandum of Understanding Between the Monitoring Board and the IFRS Foundation Trustees: "Memorandum of Understanding to Strengthen the Institutional Framework of the International Accounting Standards Committee Foundation," April 1, 2009.

[11] IFRS Foundation Monitoring Board, "Monitoring Board Finalizes Assessment Approach for Membership Criteria and Announces Chair Selection," March 1, 2013, available at www.iosco.org.

[12] IFRS Advisory Council, "Terms of Reference and Operating Procedures." February 2012. Par. 1, 3, 7, 11.

[13] 2012 Annual Report of the IFRS Foundation. Page 41.

the operations of the Foundation, a number the IFRS Foundation is working to expand upon.[14] Concern about the Foundation's ability to secure independent funding is a key issue cited by the SEC in its consideration of whether to adopt IFRS.

Now that we have introduced the IFRS Foundation's structure and funding, let us now briefly introduce its two standard-setting bodies—the IASB and the IFRIC. Later in this chapter, we will introduce the guidance promulgated by these bodies.

Standard-Setting Bodies of the IFRS Foundation

The International Accounting Standards Board (IASB)

The IASB is an independent standard-setting organization whose 16 full-time board members represent a diversity of countries and constituencies (including, for example, financial statement users, preparers, auditors, and academics).

The IASB's responsibilities include

- Developing "full" IFRS,
- Issuing guidance for "small-and medium-sized" entities (IFRS for SMEs), and
- Approving the issuance of IFRS interpretive guidance.

The IASB cannot perform these responsibilities in isolation, however, as noted during our discussion of the IFRS Foundation. For the IASB to maintain its authority as global standard setter, it must collaborate extensively with the national and regional standard-setting bodies representing its constituents. The stakes are high. As noted previously, some countries or regions—such as the EU—require their national or regional standard setter or regulators to **endorse** each new IFRS before it is accepted for use in the country. This endorsement process can, at times, result in country-specific variations of IFRS—referred to as **jurisdictional IFRS** (such as "IFRS as adopted by the EU") or in **carve outs** of guidance that a country chooses not to adopt. Such variations can be minor or can result in significant differences across standards. The endorsement process also can result in delays in a country's implementation of newly issued IFRS guidance. Jurisdictional variations of IFRS run counter to the IASB's objective of creating a *single set* of high-quality global accounting standards.

The IASB is hopeful that cooperation with representatives of regional and national standard setting bodies, through its recently established ASAF, will help reduce the risk of nonendorsement of its final standards.

The IFRS Interpretations Committee (IFRIC)

The IFRS Interpretations Committee (IFRIC) issues authoritative guidance on emergent issues that are "likely to receive divergent or unacceptable treatment, in the absence of such guidance."[15] That is, this committee is intended to respond, in a timely manner, to issues that arise regarding the clarity or application of IFRS guidance. The IASB must approve all interpretive guidance before it is issued as final.

In recent years, the IFRIC has been criticized for failing to respond in a timely manner to emergent issues, and for issuing too little interpretive and application guidance. Insufficient (or not timely) interpretive guidance can give rise to diversity in practice, as individual jurisdictions are left to interpret IFRS guidance for themselves. In response to these concerns, the IFRIC recently implemented recommendations (of the Foundation's Trustees) to consider a wider range of issues, and to propose that issues beyond its scope be considered by the IASB.

Before we move on to our discussion of international *standards*, let's first look at how the United States fits into this picture.

---

[14] Report to the Trustees of the IFRS Foundation: *IFRS Foundation staff analysis of the SEC Final Staff Report — Work Plan for the consideration of incorporating IFRS into the financial reporting system for US issuers*, October 22, 2012. Page 7.

[15] IFRS Foundation, *2013 Blue Book*. Preface to International Financial Reporting Standards, par. 14.

When Are International Standards Relevant to U.S. Accountants?

U.S. GAAP and IFRS are generally more alike than they are different, sharing similar conceptual foundations and a similar objective: providing financial information that is useful to investors.

That said, critical differences exist between the two reporting frameworks, which can result in different systems requirements and the need for reconciliations, when comparing results prepared under each framework. While convergence efforts are ongoing between the FASB and IASB in key areas including leases and financial instruments, these "joint projects" do not always result in *converged standards*.

Currently, the SEC requires *U.S. public companies* to prepare their financial statements in accordance with U.S. GAAP. It remains unclear whether and, if so, when the SEC will require or permit these companies to prepare financial statements in accordance with IFRS. In 2008, the SEC issued a roadmap detailing milestones that—if achieved—could lead to the required use of IFRS in the United States.[16] At the time, some U.S. accounting firms believed the move to IFRS was inevitable. Since then, however, the SEC has expressed some concerns about IFRS, including

- Is the IASB's funding mechanism sufficiently developed? Or does the IASB's funding expose it to potential independence concerns?

- Are IFRS being applied consistently globally?

- Is the IASB sufficiently involving (and relying on) regional and national standard-setting bodies in the development of new standards?

- How much cost and effort would be required (by U.S. companies) to adopt IFRS?

- Is the interpretive and industry-specific guidance in IFRS sufficiently developed?[17]

Some speculate that the SEC's (and the U.S. Congress's) greatest concern is the fear of ceding standard-setting authority to an organization outside of the United States.[18] One possible solution to that concern, raised by the SEC, would be the required endorsement by the FASB of IFRS guidance prior to its adoption in the United States.[19] Others speculate that the move to IFRS could ultimately be like the U.S.'s consideration of the "metric system" (a lot of talk about adopting, but ultimately no decision to change). For now, the SEC has left open the possibility that it will reach a decision on this matter; however, the timing of this decision is not clear.

That said, international standards are already relevant in the United States, in certain circumstances. These include

- For U.S. nonpublic companies, who now have the option to apply IFRS;

- Foreign private issuers' filings in the United States; and

- Other areas relevant to U.S. entry-level accountants.

U.S. Nonpublic Companies

While generally not required by the SEC to prepare audited financial statements, recall from earlier chapters that U.S. nonpublic companies may do so to satisfy the needs of their investors and lenders. In order for these financial statements to receive an unqualified audit opinion, they must

---

[16] U.S. Securities and Exchange Commission, Release No. 33-8982: "Roadmap for the Potential Use of Financial Statements Prepared in Accordance with International Financial Reporting Standards by U.S. Issuers." November 14, 2008.

[17] U.S. Securities and Exchange Commission, Final Staff Report: *Work Plan for the Consideration of Incorporating International Financial Reporting Standards into the Financial Reporting System for U.S. Issuers.* July 13, 2012. ("SEC Staff Report, July 2012"). Pages 4–6.

[18] PwC video perspective, *The Quarter Close, Third quarter 2012.* Posted on 9/17/2012 by PwC Assurance Services. From 3:46 to 4:30 (minutes: seconds).

[19] SEC Staff Report, July 2012, page 35. "As it relates to considering the needs of U.S. investors and the U.S. capital markets, the Staff believes that it may be necessary to put in place mechanisms specifically to consider and to protect the U.S. capital markets—for example, maintaining an active FASB to endorse IFRSs."

be prepared in accordance with generally accepted accounting principles. In 2008, the AICPA amended its Rule 203 to recognize the IASB as a designated standard setter, with the authority to establish international accounting principles.[20] This amendment effectively "gives AICPA members the option to use [IFRS] as an alternative to U.S. [GAAP]."[21] The AICPA believes the adoption of IFRS by private companies and not-for-profit organizations will likely be market-driven.[22] While no public information is available on this matter, it is believed that very few, if any, entities actually choose to exercise this option. Notably, recent efforts by the FASB and the Private Company Council to simplify U.S. GAAP for private companies could reduce these companies' interest in using IFRS.

Foreign Private Issuers

Foreign private issuers, listed in the United States, have the option to present financial statements in accordance with U.S. GAAP, IFRS, or their home-country accounting standards (with a reconciliation to U.S GAAP). In 2007, the SEC eliminated the requirement that foreign private issuers must reconcile their IFRS financial statements to U.S. GAAP. The U.S. Exchange Act Rule 3b–4(c) defines "foreign private issuer" as follows:

Any foreign issuer other than a foreign government <u>except</u> an issuer that meets the following conditions:

(1) More than 50 percent of the issuer's outstanding voting securities are directly or indirectly held of record by residents of the United States; <u>and</u>

(2) any of the following:

   (i) The majority of the executive officers or directors are United States citizens or residents;

   (ii) more than 50 percent of the assets of the issuer are located in the United States; or

   (iii) the business of the issuer is administered principally in the United States."[23] [Emphasis added]

While U.S. public companies are required to file a Form 10-K annual report with the SEC, foreign private issuers generally file their annual reports in the United States using Form 20-F.

Considering this definition of foreign private issuer, take a moment to complete the following **Now YOU Try** exercise.

Now YOU Try 12.1

Foreign Private Issuers

Based on our earlier discussion of HSBC Holdings plc (the HSBC parent company), would you generally expect this company to meet the definition of a "foreign private issuer" in the United States? Explain, identifying any assumptions you made in reaching this conclusion.

_____

_____

_____

[20] AICPA Code of Professional Conduct, ET Sections 203, Appendix A: "RESOLVED: That the International Accounting Standards Board (IASB) is hereby designated as the body to establish professional standards with respect to international financial accounting and reporting principles pursuant to Rule 202 [ET section 202.01] and Rule 203 [ET section 203.01]." Since May 18, 2008.

[21] AICPA News Release, "AICPA Council Votes to Recognize the International Accounting Standards Board As a Designated Standard Setter." May 18, 2008.

[22] AICPA website: www.ifrs.com, "IFRS FAQs", developed by the American Institute of Certified Public Accountants. Questions No. 14 and 15. Accessed on March 12, 2013.

[23] U.S. Code of Federal Regulations, definition of "foreign private issuer." 17 CFR 240.3b–4(c). Last updated October 6, 2008.

Other Areas Relevant to U.S. Entry-Level Accountants

U.S. entry-level accountants may face a variety of situations involving the use of IFRS, as illustrated in Figure 12-5.

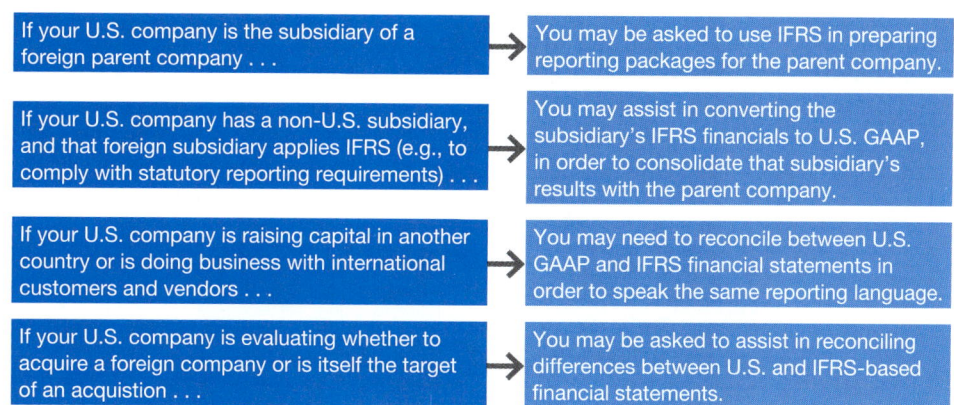

Figure 12-5

Example circumstances in which entry-level U.S. accountants would use IFRS skills

In addition, IFRS skills are relevant to U.S. accountants:

- *On the CPA exam.* For the "foreseeable future," both IFRS and U.S. GAAP will be tested on the CPA exam.[24] Candidates are expected to demonstrate knowledge of international accounting and auditing requirements, as well as familiarity with the international standard-setting environment.[25]

- *As a nonauthoritative source of guidance.* Recall that U.S. accountants may look to IFRS by analogy as a nonauthoritative source of guidance if GAAP is not responsive to a specific issue.

- *To monitor emerging accounting guidance.* Entry-level accountants may be asked to monitor emerging changes in U.S. accounting standards. Decisions reached by the IASB could eventually become mandatory in the United States, or could at least influence future U.S. GAAP requirements.

Finally, consider another benefit of IFRS experience, described in this **TIP from the Trenches**.

Another key benefit of having IFRS experience? It enhances your marketability as a professional. While a U.S. adoption of IFRS remains uncertain, employers (ranging from accounting firms to corporations with international business to institutional investors) seek out individuals with IFRS experience in order to be prepared for evolving accounting requirements impacting their business or their clients' businesses.

The moral of this story? International standards are already relevant, *today*, to U.S. accountants.

✓ **Knowledge Check**

1. Which U.S. entity has authority to decide whether the United States will adopt IFRS for U.S. public companies?
2. Can U.S. nonpublic companies prepare financial statements in accordance with IFRS? Explain.
3. Name four circumstances in which U.S. accountants may be required to apply IFRS.

[24] AICPA.org, Uniform CPA Examination FAQs—International Financial Reporting Standards (IFRS). Accessed October 20, 2013.

[25] AICPA, *Content and Skill Specifications for the Uniform CPA Examination.* Approved May 15, 2009; update approved October 1, 2012. Effective date: January 1, 2014.

INTERNATIONAL FINANCIAL REPORTING STANDARDS (IFRS)

Applicability of IFRS

The IASB issues two types of international financial reporting standards: "full IFRS" and *IFRS for SMEs*, a simplified version of full IFRS. Both sets of guidance are designed to apply to the **general-purpose financial reporting** of profit-oriented entities;[26] full IFRS applies to entities with **public accountability**, and *IFRS for SMEs* applies to entities that do not have public accountability, as illustrated in Figure 12-6.

Notably, in 2013, the IASB created a subset of the *IFRS for SMEs* publication that applies specifically to "micro"-sized entities, such as those with just a few employees.

Figure 12-6

Applicability of full IFRS, versus *IFRS for SMEs*

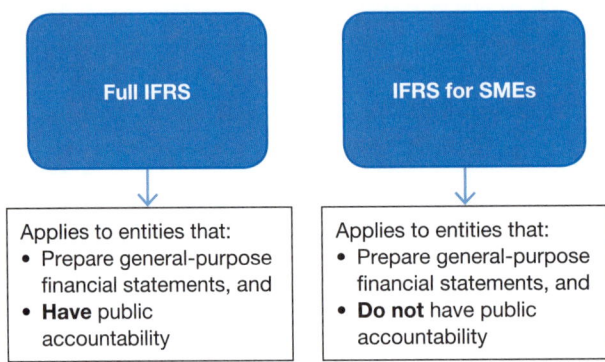

Not-for-profit entities, while not the intended users of IFRS and *IFRS for SMEs*, are permitted to apply this guidance to the extent they believe application is appropriate.[27]

General-Purpose Financial Reporting

The term "general-purpose financial reporting" encompasses (1) **general-purpose financial statements** plus (2) other financial reporting (i.e., information that assists in the interpretation of the financial statements, such as footnote disclosures).[28] The *IFRS for SMEs* glossary defines "general-purpose financial statements" as

> Financial statements directed to the general financial information needs of a wide range of users who are not in a position to demand reports tailored to meet their particular information needs.[29]

That is, many financial statement users (e.g., shareholders, creditors, and employees) cannot individually request financial information from a reporting entity; rather, they must rely on general-purpose financial statements—either presented separately or within an annual report. Such financial statements differ, for example, from financial statements prepared for a specific purpose, such as for tax reporting.

Take a moment to apply your understanding of the term "general-purpose financial statements" in the following **Now YOU Try** exercise.

---

[26] IFRS Foundation, *2013 Blue Book*. Preface to International Financial Reporting Standards, par. 9.

[27] Id. as footnote 26, plus *IFRS for SMEs* Exposure Draft dated Oct. 2013, Basis for Conclusions par. BC23-BC26.

[28] *IFRS for SMEs* (2009), par. P5.

[29] *IFRS for SMEs* (2009), Glossary.

General-Purpose Financial Statements

Assume that a company uses *IFRS for SMEs* as the starting point for its financial statements, then adjusts these statements to comply with requirements specific to its national taxing authority. The entity sends the financial statements to the taxing authority only.

Using the definition of "general-purpose financial statements," consider whether these financial statements would be considered general-purpose or special-purpose financial statements. Explain.

_____

_____

_____

Example based on IFRS Foundation's "Training Material for the *IFRS® for SMEs* (version 2013-1)," Module 1, Page 8, Ex4.

Public Accountability

The *IFRS for SMEs* publication defines *public accountability* as follows:

> 1.3 An entity has public accountability if:
>
> (a) <u>its debt or equity instruments are traded in a public market</u> or it is in the process of issuing such instruments for trading in a public market (a domestic or foreign stock exchange or an over-the-counter market, including local and regional markets), or
>
> (b) <u>it holds assets in a fiduciary capacity for a broad group of outsiders</u> as one of its primary businesses. This is typically the case for banks, credit unions, insurance companies, securities brokers/dealers, mutual funds and investment banks.[30] [Emphasis added]

In other words, entities that *have* public accountability are generally those whose shares or debt securities are traded in a public market, plus banks, credit unions, and other companies that hold assets in a fiduciary capacity for others. The IASB has concluded that any entity with public accountability, *regardless of its size*, should follow full IFRSs.[31]

Scope guidance from the *IFRS for SMEs* publication emphasizes this point:

> If a publicly accountable entity uses this IFRS, its financial statements shall not be described as conforming to the *IFRS for SMEs*—even if law or regulation in its jurisdiction permits or requires this IFRS to be used by publicly accountable entities.[32]

That is, even if directed by a government authority to issue financial statements using *IFRS for SMEs*, entities with public accountability cannot assert that their financial statements comply with *IFRS for SMEs*. Rather, these entities should apply full IFRS or other acceptable standards.

---

[30] *IFRS for SMEs* (2009). Par. 1.3.

[31] *IFRS for SMEs* (2009), Basis for Conclusions. Par. BC76.

[32] *IFRS for SMEs* (2009), Basis for Conclusions. Par. 1.5.

Individual Jurisdiction Considerations

So this is all pretty simple, right?

- Not publicly accountable?—Check.
- Issues general-purpose financial statements?—Check.
- Apply *IFRS for SMEs*.

But wait . . . there's just one more consideration. See, this is just the "intended scope" of the *IFRS for SMEs* publication. Ultimately, the determination of which entities may utilize this guidance rests with authorities in individual countries. To that end, many individual jurisdictions have established additional criteria for determining which entities may report using *IFRS for SMEs* including, for example, criteria based on revenue, assets, employees, or other factors. Certain countries may decide, for example, that entities that are economically significant in that country should be required to use full IFRSs rather than the *IFRS for SMEs*.

Take a moment to apply your understanding of SMEs in the following **Now YOU Try** exercise.

Now
YOU
Try

12.3

Understanding the Scope of *IFRS for SMEs*

Respond to the following, referring back to the preceding discussion as necessary.

Questions:

1. A publicly accountable entity has been required by its national taxing authority to issue financial statements following the guidance in *IFRS for SMEs*.

    Can the entity describe its financial statements as prepared in conformity with *IFRS for SMEs*? Explain.

    _____

    _____

2. An entity meets the IASB's "intended scope" of entities that should apply *IFRS for SMEs*. What other consideration should enter into the entity's decision about whether use of *IFRS for SMEs* is appropriate for its statutorily required financial statements?

    _____

    _____

TIP from the Trenches

> The IASB's issuance of different guidance for entities with and without public accountability differs from U.S. GAAP, where the Codification applies to *all nongovernmental entities*. That said, the number of exceptions available to nonpublic entities in the Codification is expected to grow as a result of the work of the Private Company Council.

The next section of this chapter offers a closer look at "full IFRS."

Understanding "Full" IFRS

Our discussion of full IFRS will begin with a look at sources of IFRS guidance, followed by discussion of the priority in which researchers should consider these sources (the "IAS 8 hierarchy"). Following this introduction, we will discuss methods for researching IFRS guidance.

Sources of IFRS Guidance

To comply with full IFRS, entities must comply with standards of the IASB and its predecessor, the IASC, as well as interpretations of the IFRIC and its predecessor, the SIC. To a lesser extent, entities may also look to the Conceptual Framework for guidance. Figure 12-7 illustrates the guidance comprising full IFRS.

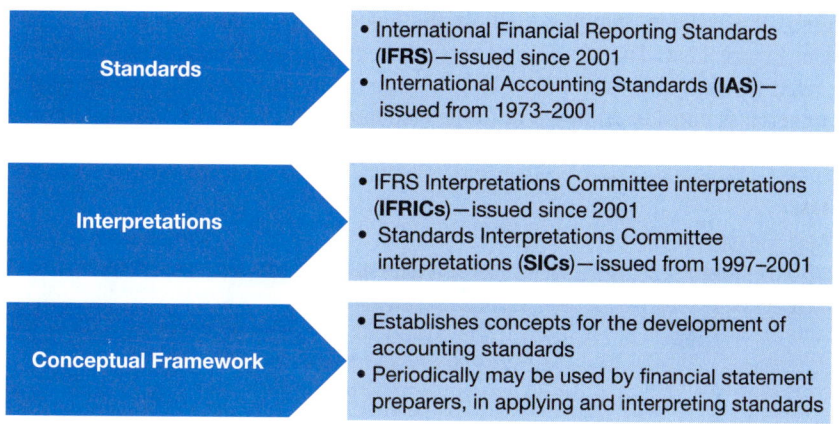

Figure 12-7

Sources of guidance comprising full IFRS

The following sections discuss the nature and content of these sources in further detail.

Standards

Each standard of the IASB and IASC is intended to address a specific accounting topic. For example, observe the individual standard titles listed in Figure 12-8, and notice that each standard's title is indicative of the accounting issue it addresses. This list is an excerpt only and does not show all standards.

2013 Red Book

Document
Preface to IFRS
The Conceptual Framework for Financial Reporting
Changes in this Edition
Introduction to this edition
List of Standards
IFRS 1 First-time Adoption of International Financial Reporting Standards
IFRS 2 Share-based Payment
IFRS 3 Business Combinations
IFRS 4 Insurance Contracts
IFRS 5 Non-current Assets Held for Sale and Discontinued Operations
IFRS 6 Exploration for and Evaluation of Mineral Resources
IFRS 7 Financial Instruments: Disclosures
IFRS 8 Operating Segments
IFRS 9 Financial Instruments
IFRS 10 Consolidated Financial Statements
IFRS 11 Joint Arrangements
IFRS 12 Disclosure of Interests in Other Entities
IFRS 13 Fair Value Measurement
IAS 1 Presentation of Financial Statements
IAS 2 Inventories
IAS 7 Statement of Cash Flows
IAS 8 Accounting Policies, Changes in Accounting Estimates and Errors
IAS 10 Events after the Reporting Period
IAS 11 Construction Contracts

Figure 12-8

Excerpted list of IFRS standards

In effecting changes to this existing set of standards, the IASB's policy has been to amend or replace existing IFRS when appropriate, or to create a new standard if necessary to address comprehensive new issues. Chapter 13 of this book provides further discussion of the IASB's standard-setting process.

Assume for a moment that you click on the link to the standard—IFRS 2—from the standards list in Figure 12-8. The screen that appears next (Figure 12-9) shows a list including the standard itself (always shown in bold), and its accompanying material. Certain of this accompanying material is considered **integral** to the standard (i.e., mandatory guidance), and some is considered **not integral** to the standard (i.e., nonmandatory)**.**

Figure 12-9

IFRS 2 and its accompanying material

Search Results

2013 Red Book

Document	Date of Issue
IFRS 2 Contents	
IFRS 2 Introduction	
IFRS 2 Share-based Payment	2004-02-19
IFRS 2 Appendix A Defined terms	
IFRS 2 Appendix B Application guidance	
IFRS 2 Appendix C Amendments to other IFRSs	
IFRS 2 Approval by the Board of IFRS 2 issued in February 2004	
IFRS 2 Approval by the Board of Vesting Conditions and Cancellations (Amendments to IFRS 2) issued in January 2008	
IFRS 2 Approval by the Board of Group Cash–settled Share–based Payment Transactions (Amendments to IFRS 2) issued in June 2009	
IFRS 2 Basis for Conclusions	
IFRS 2 Implementation Guidance	

IAS 8 (Accounting Policies, Changes in Accounting Estimates and Errors) describes the distinction between integral and not integral guidance as follows:

> IFRSs are accompanied by guidance to assist entities in applying their requirements. All such guidance states whether it is an integral part of IFRSs. Guidance that is an integral part of the IFRSs is mandatory. Guidance that is not an integral part of the IFRSs does not contain requirements for financial statements.[33] [Emphasis added]

That is, researchers are required to apply all guidance that is considered "integral" to a standard. The application of non-mandatory guidance is not *required* per se; however, consideration of this guidance may be useful in helping researchers apply the guidance in the manner intended by the Board.

To identify the content that is integral to each standard, researchers can look to (1) the **authority box** available within the standard's "Contents" page (see Figure 12-10) and (2) information in the header of each appendix, indicating its authority (see Figure 12-11).

Figure 12-10

Authority box for IFRS 2, located within the standard's "Contents" link

International Financial Reporting Standard 2 *Share-based Payment* (IFRS 2) is set out in paragraphs 1–64 and Appendices A–C. All the paragraphs have equal authority. Paragraphs in **bold type** state the main principles. Terms defined in Appendix A are in *italics* the first time they appear in the Standard. Definitions of other terms are given in the Glossary for International Financial Reporting Standards. IFRS 2 should be read in the context of its objective and the Basis for Conclusions, the *Preface to International Financial Reporting Standards* and the *Conceptual Framework for Financial Reporting*. IAS 8 *Accounting Policies, Changes in Accounting Estimates and Errors* provides a basis for selecting and applying accounting policies in the absence of explicit guidance. (Source: 2013 Red Book, IFRS 2 Contents)

---

[33] IFRS Foundation, *2013 Blue Book*. IAS 8, *Accounting Policies, Changes in Accounting Estimates and Errors*. Par. 9.

> **Guidance on implementing**
>
> **IFRS 2 *Share-based Payment***
>
> *This guidance accompanies, but is not part of, IFRS 2.*
>
> **Definition of grant date**
>
> ---
>
> IG1   IFRS 2 defines grant date as the date at which the entity

Copyright © IFRS Foundation. All rights reserved.

Figure 12-11

Header indicating authority of IFRS 2's Implementation Guidance (circle added for emphasis)

In the authority box for IFRS 2 (Figure 12-10), *integral* content is described as follows: "[IFRS 2] is set out in paragraphs 1–64 and Appendices A–C. All the paragraphs have equal authority." By contrast, Figure 12-10 states that "IFRS 2 should be read in the context of" other sources—these sources are *not integral* to the standard.

Within individual standards, all paragraphs have equal authority. Certain paragraphs may be presented in bold type, indicating the standard's main principles. Content within each standard is generally organized into sections similar to those used in the Codification (e.g., Objective, Scope, Recognition, and so on). That said, section headers are not as standardized as the Codification and may be unique to a given topic.

[**TIP**] from the Trenches

> Notice in the authority box to IFRS 2 that the standard's Introduction is not identified as an integral part of the standard. Paragraphs within a standard's Introduction (numbered IN1, IN2, etc.) often *summarize* or *highlight* requirements from the standard but are not themselves considered integral.
>
> Don't make the mistake that some of my students have, of quoting "requirements" from the Introduction, rather than quoting from the standard itself.

4. **Which appendices in IFRS 2 are considered mandatory?**
5. **Name three examples of content—mentioned in the authority box of IFRS 2 or shown above—that is considered nonmandatory in applying this standard.**
6. **What do you think it means for a standard to be read "in the context" of other guidance?**

✓ **Knowledge Check**

Interpretations

Guidance issued by the IFRS Interpretations Committee (IFRIC) is intended to assist researchers in understanding and applying standards. When researching an issue, always scan the list of available interpretations (numbering 24 at press time) to identify any guidance relevant to the research topic.

The following **Now YOU Try** exercise is intended to give readers a feel for the general scope of an IFRIC.

Reading and Understanding an IFRIC

IFRIC 10, *Interim Financial Reporting and Impairment*, resolves a conflict between the requirements of IAS 34 (Interim Financial Reporting) and IAS 36 (Impairment of Assets). Specifically, this IFRIC answers the question: Should an entity reverse an impairment charge recorded for goodwill, if the value of the entity's goodwill recovers in a subsequent interim period?

 Per IAS 36, par. 124, "An impairment loss recognised for goodwill shall not be reversed in a subsequent period." However, "IAS 34 requires year-to-date measures in interim financial state-

Now [**YOU**] Try

12.4

ments. This requirement might suggest that an entity should reverse in a subsequent interim period an impairment loss it recognised in a prior interim period" (IFRIC 10, BC3).

Here's what the IFRIC decided: "An entity shall not reverse an impairment loss recognised in a previous interim period in respect of goodwill." (IFRIC 10, par. 8).

The rationale for this decision is described in IFRIC 10's Basis for Conclusions:

"The IFRIC concluded that the prohibitions on reversals of recognised impairment losses on goodwill in <u>IAS 36</u> . . . should take precedence over the more general statement in <u>IAS 34</u> regarding the frequency of an entity's reporting not affecting the measurement of its annual results." (BC9). [Footnotes omitted]

Questions:

1. Explain the conflicting requirements in IAS 36 and IAS 34 that this Interpretation sets out to clarify.

_____

_____

2. Explain the conclusion reached in IFRIC 10 and the rationale for this conclusion.

_____

_____

3. Why do you suppose the IFRIC addressed this issue, as opposed to the IASB? Explain.

_____

_____

_____

Conceptual Framework

The IASB's *Conceptual Framework for Financial Reporting* (the "Framework") sets forth the conceptual underpinnings for the more specific requirements of IASB Standards and Interpretations. The purpose of the Framework is generally twofold: first, to assist the IASB in the development of new standards, and second, to assist practitioners in applying judgment in the preparation of financial statements, in the absence of more specific guidance.

As illustrated in Figure 12-12 on the next page, the Framework in IFRS *is* considered authoritative, but it has less authority than standards and interpretations of the IASB. Contrast this with U.S. GAAP, where the Conceptual Framework is nonauthoritative. The IASB is currently working on a project focused on improving its Framework, which is expected to result in updates to the following areas: elements of financial statements, measurement, presentation and disclosure, and the reporting entity. Years ago, this project was begun jointly with the FASB, but is now continuing as an individual project.

The IAS 8 Hierarchy

Illustrated in Figure 12-12, the **IAS 8 hierarchy** prioritizes the sources of guidance that entities should consider, in descending order, when developing accounting policies for items or transactions.

That is, if authoritative IFRS guidance is "on point," or directly relevant to a transaction, management should apply that IFRS (source 1 in Figure 12-12). If such guidance is not available, management will have to use its judgment in selecting an appropriate policy; the guidance listed in sources 2–4 should be considered in descending order.

---

[34] IAS 8, par. 7–12.

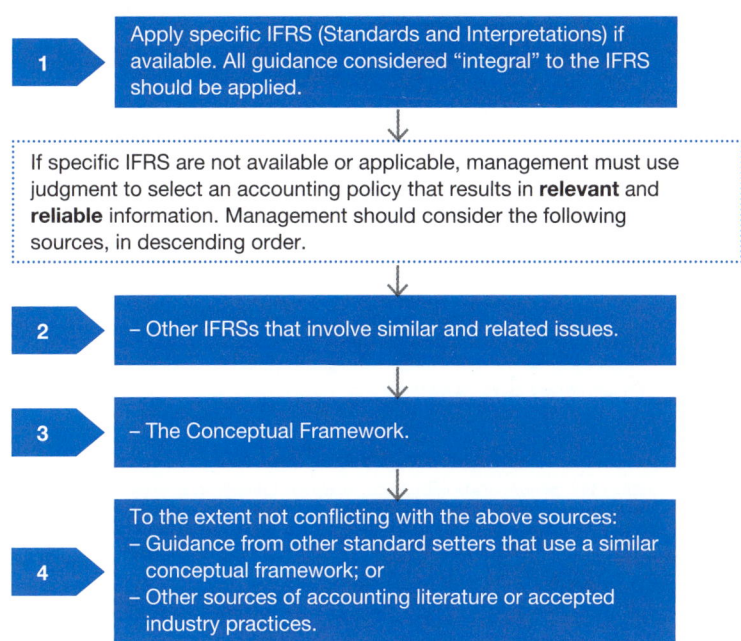

Figure 12-12
The IAS 8 Hierarchy[36]

Researching IFRS

The Research Process

The same research process that applies to U.S. GAAP (see Chapter 3) also applies to international accounting research, subject to a few minor additions.

Recall steps 1 and 2 of the research process: Obtain an understanding of the transaction, and Identify the researchable question. These steps are unchanged in performing international research. However, in the third step: *Explore potentially relevant sources of guidance*, researchers should

- First, determine whether IFRS applies to the particular country and, if so, whether any country-specific variations apply.
- Next, identify the appropriate bound volume of IFRS to consult.

The remainder of the research process, from analyzing results to documenting conclusions, is unchanged in the international research environment. Therefore, let's now discuss these two considerations that are unique to international research.

1. First, Determine Whether IFRS Applies to the Country

As a researcher, how do you know whether IFRS applies to a country, and which entities within that country must comply fully with IFRS as issued by the IASB?

Deloitte's IAS Plus website (www.iasplus.com) is a useful starting point for researchers faced with this question. Under the "Jurisdictions" tab, researchers can select a country, then read about that country's unique financial reporting requirements and access links to more information. For example, Figure 12-13 illustrates a search for the reporting requirements in Nigeria.

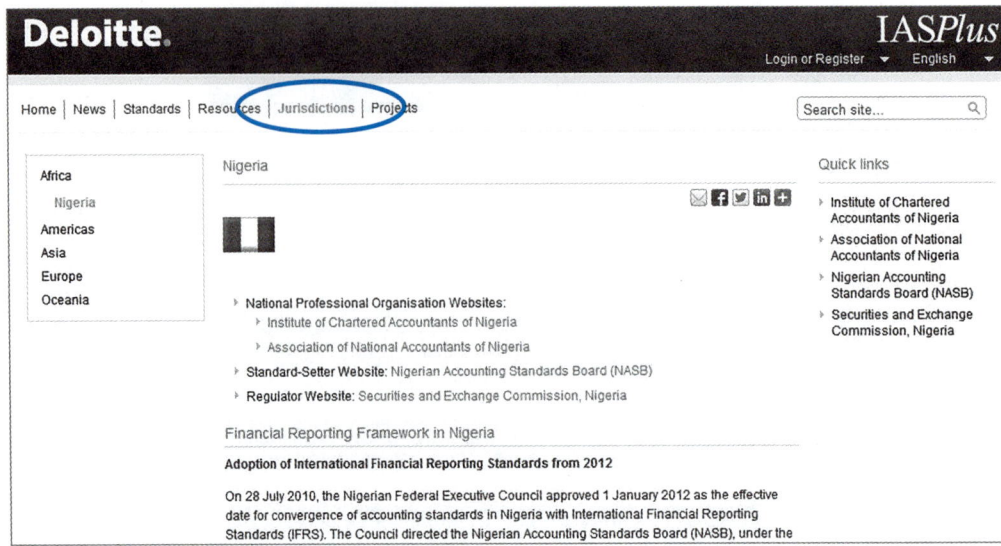

Material on IAS Plus website is © 2012 Deloitte Global Services Limited, or a member firm of Deloitte Touche Tohmatsu Limited, or one of their related entities.[35]

Also helpful is PwC's publication "IFRS Adoption by Country," a 280-page document that lists, by country, the applicable financial reporting requirements and useful references (such as the national standard setter's website). This document is accessible via Web search and can be downloaded free of charge.

Using these resources as a starting point, researchers should take care to understand whether IFRS applies as issued by the IASB, and/or whether other jurisdiction-specific requirements apply. Armed with this understanding, the researcher is ready to begin his or her search of IFRS guidance.

2. Next, Identify the Appropriate Bound Edition of IFRS to Consult

IFRS guidance is organized into three *bound editions*, each available for purchase in printed form or accessible to e-IFRS subscribers online. Before beginning a search of IFRS guidance, researchers are often prompted to select from among these bound editions.

The IFRS **Red Book** includes all IFRS standards and interpretations, including those not yet effective, and related appendices (such as the standard setter's basis for conclusions).

The IFRS **Blue Book** includes *only* the standards, interpretations, and related appendices *that are mandatory for the current financial reporting year*. For example, introductory material within the 2013 Blue Book states:

> This volume <u>does not contain those Standards or changes to Standards with an effective date after 1 January 2013.</u> Readers seeking the consolidated text of IFRS issued at 1 January 2013 (including Standards with an effective date after 1 January 2013) should refer to the two-part 2013 IFRS (Red Book), which is being published in the first quarter of 2013.[36] [Underlined emphasis added]

The IFRS **Green Book**, *A Guide through IFRSs*, presents IFRS guidance as well as extensive cross-references and other annotations intended to serve as *educational material* to

---

[35] Deloitte refers to one or more of Deloitte Touche Tohmatsu Limited, a UK private company limited by guarantee, and its network of member firms, each of which is a legally separate and independent entity. Please see www.deloitte.com/about for a detailed description of the legal structure of Deloitte Touche Tohmatsu Limited and its member firms.

[36] IFRS Foundation, *2013 Blue Book*. "Changes in this Edition, Introduction" sections.

individuals applying IFRS. For example, notice how the following paragraph from IFRS 3 (Business Combinations) in the Green Book includes extensive cross-referencing to explanatory material, such as links to the glossary [G], appendices, and the IASB's basis for conclusions in establishing these requirements:

> 3. An entity shall determine whether a transaction or other event is a <u>business combination</u> by applying the definition in this IFRS, which requires that the assets[G] acquired and liabilities[G] assumed constitute a <u>business</u>. [Refer: <u>Appendix A</u>] If the assets acquired are not a business, the reporting entity shall account for the transaction or other event as an asset acquisition. <u>Paragraphs B5–B12</u> provide guidance on identifying a business combination and the definition of a business.
>
> [Refer: <u>Basis for Conclusions paragraphs BC5–BC21</u>]

Note that the IASB's Conceptual Framework is also included within each of the bound editions.

Think of the Red Book as the book that will help you be **prepaRED** for future transactions. Think of the Green Book like a **green chalkboard**, ready to teach and provide additional explanations.

TIP from the Trenches

When selecting a bound edition to search, researchers are also prompted to select between accessing standards in HTML format or pdf format. Researchers using *pdf format* will notice that the Red, Blue, and Green Books are divided into two parts:

- Part A (the requirements), which contains the Standards, Interpretations, and "integral" appendices
- Part B (accompanying documents), which contains nonmandatory appendices, such as illustrative examples, implementation guidance, bases for conclusions, and dissenting opinions

Generally speaking, researchers may find the HTML format to be more user-friendly than the pdf option, because the HTML format does not divide the guidance into Part A/Part B; rather, all guidance relevant to each standard is listed together, on one screen, and can be easily navigated. For example, Figure 12-9 (shown previously) illustrates the HTML version of IFRS 2.

✔ **Knowledge Check**

7. Which bound edition would be most helpful to a researcher whose company is reviewing the accounting for a proposed transaction, which will likely be executed in 1 year's time?
8. Which bound edition might a researcher consult if he or she is interested in further explanations or context for interpreting the guidance?

Even if you are just preparing current-year financial statements and are most interested in standards with current applicability (such as the standards included in the current-year Blue Book), do not overlook standards with future applicability. Per IAS 8 (par. 30), entities must *disclose* any possible impacts that newly issued IFRS guidance will have, when adopted. Additionally, standards with future applicability could impact management's earnings forecasts.

TIP from the Trenches

Now that you have identified the appropriate source of IFRS to use in performing your research, you are ready to begin searching the guidance.

Searching for IFRS Guidance

To access IFRS guidance online, researchers can (1) subscribe to eIFRS, which gives researchers online access to the bound editions and IFRS search tools, or (2) register at www.ifrs.org for free online access to individual standards.

Subscriptions to eIFRS can be purchased

- Directly from the IFRS Foundation, or

- For students and academics, through a discounted (approximately $20–25) annual subscription from IAAER, the International Association for Accounting Education & Research.

Certain researchers may also have searchable access to IFRS guidance through firm research databases (such as Deloitte's *Technical Library*).

Accessing Guidance Through eIFRS ("Subscribers Only")

The eIFRS homepage is shown in Figure 12-14. From this screen, researchers can browse directly to specific guidance (by clicking on a bound edition), can access the *IFRS for SMEs* publication, or can perform keyword searches within the bound editions (via the Search link at left). A terminology lookup feature is also available in eIFRS, as we will discuss further below.

<table>
<tr><td>

Figure 12-14

Homepage of eIFRS, where researchers can browse to a bound edition or initiate a keyword search

</td><td>

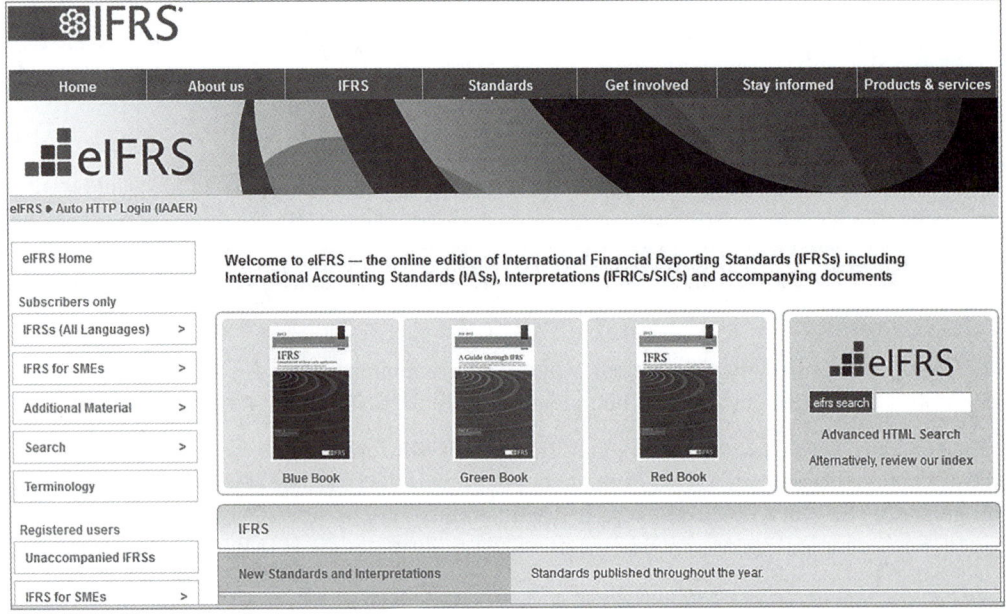

</td></tr>
</table>

Notice that the the left-hand links depicted in Figure 12-14 are divided into "Subscribers Only" (paid content) and "Registered Users" (free) content.

1. Browsing Directly to Standards in eIFRS

Once a researcher has selected, for example, the Red Book in HTML format, the researcher will be directed to a list of standards, like the list shown earlier in Figure 12-8. On this page, researchers can scan the list for relevant standards or can search on the page (for example, using ctrl + f) for keywords in the title of standards.

Assume for a moment that you have selected a potentially relevant standard to search, but have little knowledge of this topic. Where would you begin to determine whether this guidance is relevant to your issue?

While not considered "integral" to the standard, each standard's Introduction section (paragraphs IN1, IN2, and so on) provides a useful, high-level summary of the standard. This section can be a perfect starting point for a researcher who is reading a standard for the first time. Once you determine that the standard is relevant, be sure to consider all guidance considered "integral" to the standard, and look for any relevant interpretations of the standard.

In the wrong place? Look for references to other related standards (sometimes, such references are listed at the top of a standard's Contents page). Or, use keywords and context clues to pursue another browse search option; if this effort is unsuccessful, try a keyword search.

2. Performing a Keyword Search

To perform a keyword search, begin on the eIFRS homepage and click "Search" then "Advanced HTML search." Let's assume that you are searching for the term "self-constructed" within the Blue Book. This search is illustrated in Figure 12-15.

On the Advanced HTML search page, select "Blue Book" in the menu for "Collection," then enter your search term: "self-constructed." Notice the list of search tips shown under the search box in Figure 12-15.

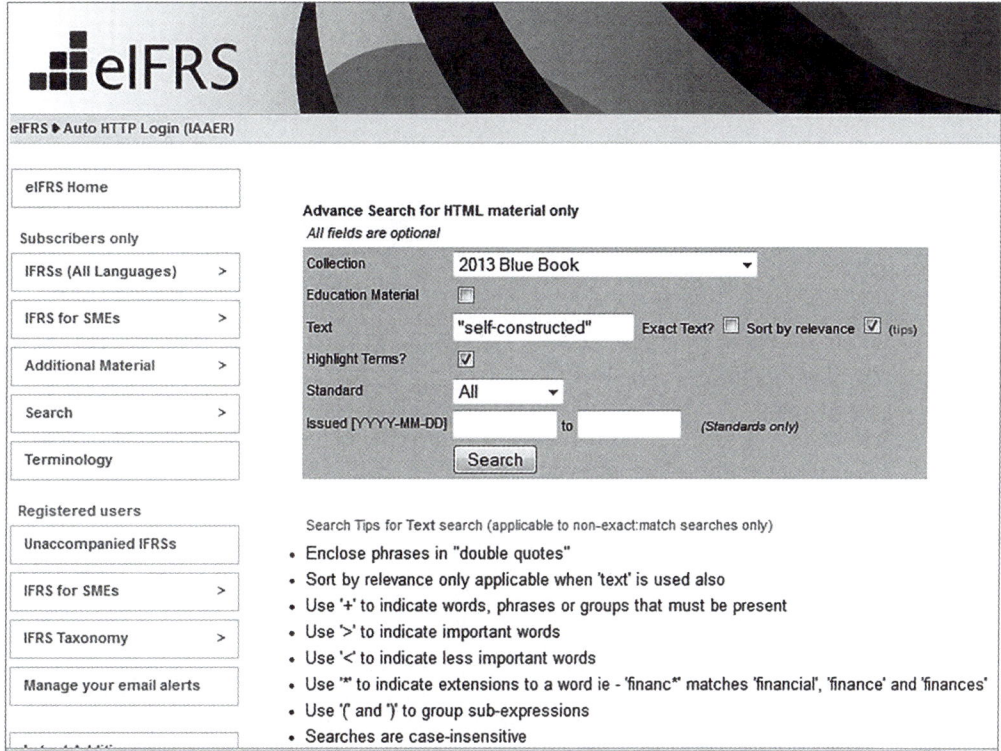

Figure 12-15

Search for the term "self-constructed" within the Blue Book

Before we look at the results of this search, let's first cover a few observations about eIFRS searches:

- Generally, *do not* check the box for **"educational material"**—this appears to search for educational material *instead of* standards. Checking this may result in "No Results Found."

- *Do* check "Highlight Terms" as this will make it easier for you to see where search results appear within a document, and check "Sort by relevance," which ranks search results by relevance.

- Checking "Exact Text" is unnecessary if you use quotes around "exact phrases."

- Interestingly, using the asterisk* after the term "self-construct*" caused the search to return with no results. If this happens to you, try performing the search without use of the asterisk; instead, just try searching the full words: self-constructed, self-construction, for example.

- In your list of search results, *standards* will appear in bold. Other documents (such as appendices) will appear in plain text.

> The eIFRS search system is somewhat quirky. If your search yields few (or no) results, try different variations of your search (with and without check boxes, quotes, hyphens, etc.). Do not immediately assume that the word does not appear in IFRS literature, just because your first search attempt yielded no results.

Figure 12-16 illustrates the results for our search of the term "self-constructed." Notice also that all four search results listed have a score of 100% (their "relevance" score), generally meaning that a researcher can expect to find the search term highlighted within each of these results.

Figure 12-16

Results for search of the term "self-constructed" in the Blue Book

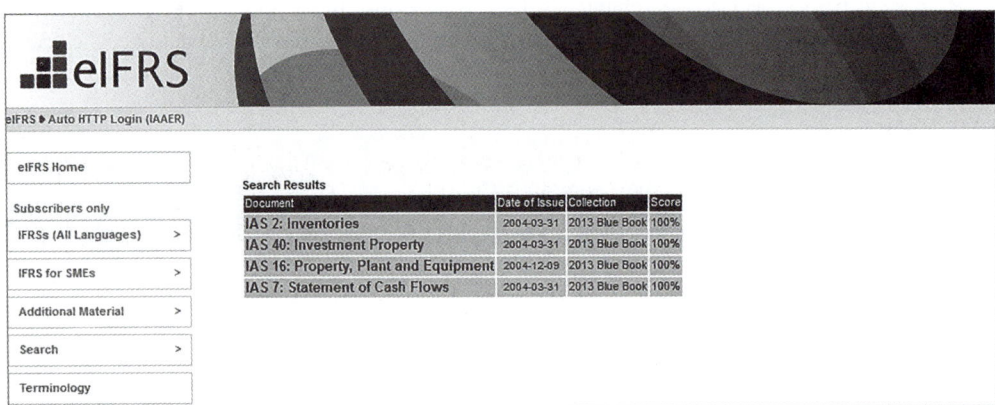

Copyright © IFRS Foundation. All rights reserved.

3. Using the Terminology Lookup Function

The eIFRS system has a Terminology Lookup function that allows researchers to search from among approximately 1,500 key terms used in the official translations of IFRS. This feature and its search results are illustrated, respectively, in Figures 12-17 and 12-18. The Terminology Lookup function is accessible using the left-hand link to "Terminology" on the eIFRS homepage.

Figure 12-17

Terminology Lookup for the term "self-constructed" (circles added for emphasis)

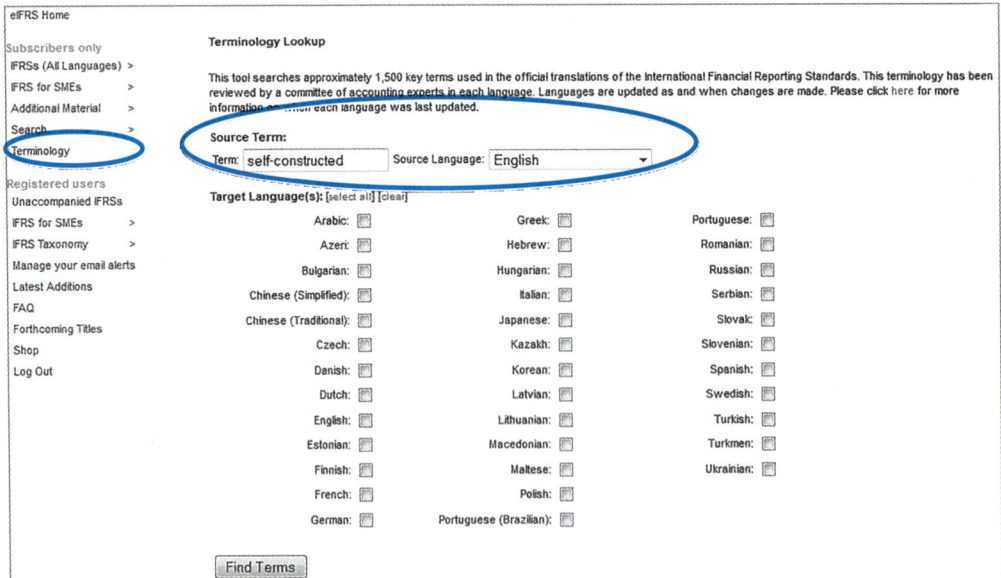

Copyright © IFRS Foundation. All rights reserved.

Terminology Lookup	
1: **self-constructed asset**	
The cost of a self-constructed asset is determined using the same principles as for an acquired asset.	

It is important to understand that this feature only searches within a set population of key terms. That is, other terms may appear within individual standards that are not included within the Terminology Lookup feature. Furthermore, search results are not linked to their source document; so while researchers can find definitions of key terms, they will not be able to link to standards to understand how these terms are used in context.

Researchers may find it more useful to search for terms within the **Master Glossary**, included at the end of each Red Book, Blue Book, and Green Book, which defines terms and links to the standards in which the terms are used.

Accessing Individual Standards on the IFRS Website ("Registered Users Only")

By completing a brief, free online registration, "registered users" of the IFRS website can access current-year "unaccompanied" individual IFRS standards and technical summaries of standards. This access is the equivalent of "part A" of the Red Book, but without the ability to perform searches of the bound editions.

Access to unaccompanied guidance means that the standards are not accompanied by implementation guidance or the IASB's basis for conclusions, and prior year (superseded) guidance is not included.

Statement of Compliance with IFRS

Now that you understand what it takes to research and apply IFRS, let's discuss the requirements for representing compliance with IFRS.

Per IAS 1 (Presentation of Financial Statements), entities whose financial statements comply fully with IFRS must make an explicit and unreserved **statement of compliance** in the financial statement footnotes.[37] As a researcher, you might find it useful to look for this compliance statement (generally located in note 1 or 2 of companies' financial statement footnotes) when determining whether an entity has prepared its financial statements in accordance with IFRS.

Figure 12-19 illustrates the statement of compliance footnote from an annual report of Anheuser-Busch InBev ("AB InBev"), which is based in Belgium.

2. STATEMENT OF COMPLIANCE

The consolidated financial statements are prepared in accordance with International Financial Reporting Standards as issued by the International Accounting Standards Board ("IASB") and in conformity with IFRS as adopted by the European Union up to 31 December 2012 (collectively "IFRS"). AB InBev did not apply any European carve-outs from IFRS. AB InBev has not applied early any new IFRS requirements that are not yet effective in 2012.

In Figure 12-19, notice not only the "unreserved" statement of compliance with IFRS, but also a statement that the financial statements are in conformity with "IFRS as adopted by the European Union." AB InBev also makes a point of stating that it did not apply any EU-specific exceptions to IFRS. But, why all of this explanation?

As noted previously, certain countries (or regions) require their local authorities to "endorse" IFRS before they are adopted for use in the country. In the EU, the Accounting Regulatory Committee (i.e., representatives from member state governments), as advised by the European Financial Reporting Advisory Group (EFRAG), must endorse new IFRSs before they are approved for use in the EU. In the past, this review process resulted in a temporary carve out of key financial

---

[37] IFRS Foundation, *2013 Blue Book*. IAS 1, *Presentation of Financial Statements*. Par. 16.

instruments guidance (the "IAS 39 carve out"); since then, this exception has been resolved. However, *at any given time*, if differences exist between IFRS and "EU IFRS," and these differences are relevant to an entity's financial statements, the entity cannot represent compliance with IFRS.

The following **Now YOU Try** looks at HSBC's IFRS compliance footnote.

Now YOU Try 12.5

The IFRS Compliance Footnote

Read the following excerpt from HSBC Holdings plc's IFRS compliance footnote, then respond to the questions that follow.

> **1 Basis of preparation**
>
> (a) Compliance with International Financial Reporting Standards
>   The consolidated financial statements of HSBC and the separate financial statements of HSBC Holdings have been prepared in accordance with International Financial Reporting Standards ('IFRSs') as issued by the International Accounting Standards Board ('IASB') and as endorsed by the EU. EU-endorsed IFRSs may differ from IFRSs as issued by the IASB if, at any point in time, new or amended IFRSs have not been endorsed by the EU.
>
>   At 31 December 2012, there were no unendorsed standards effective for the year ended 31 December 2012 affecting these consolidated and separate financial statements, and there was no difference between IFRSs endorsed by the EU and IFRSs issued by the IASB in terms of their application to HSBC. Accordingly, HSBC's financial statements for the year ended 31 December 2012 are prepared in accordance with IFRSs as issued by the IASB. (Source: HSBC Holdings Plc, Annual Report and Accounts 2012, Note 1a, page 383.)

Questions:

1. Does HSBC comply in full with IFRS, and does it also comply with "IFRS as endorsed by the EU"?

    _____

2. What is one potential difference, cited by HSBC, that can arise between the EU-IFRS and IFRS as issued by the IASB?

    _____

Let's now turn our attention to the *IFRS for SMEs* publication.

IFRS for Small and Medium-Sized Entities

Overview of *IFRS for SMEs*

Recognizing the complexity of applying full IFRS, the IASB created the 230-page *IFRS for SMEs* publication as a simplified set of guidance for entities without public accountability. In doing so, the IASB acknowledged differences (versus listed companies) in the users and uses of SME financial statements, and the more limited resources generally available to SMEs in preparing financial statements. According to the IASB, such entities are estimated to account for over 95% of all companies around the world.[38]

The *IFRS for SMEs* publication is illustrated in Figure 12-20. Increasingly, individual jurisdictions (and particularly taxing authorities) are turning to this guidance in establishing their statutory reporting requirements.

---

[38] Per ifrs.org website, "About the IFRS for SMEs." Accessed February 7, 2013.

Figure 12-20

The *IFRS for SMEs* publication

To create the *IFRS for SMEs* publication, the IASB started with full IFRS then made certain modifications, as follows:

- Where accounting policy choices exist in full IFRS, the *IFRS for SMEs* allows only the easier option. For example, entities do not have the option to revalue property, equipment, or intangibles.

- Certain principles for recognizing and measuring assets, liabilities, income, and expenses have been simplified. For example, goodwill is amortized, rather than tested for impairment; also, all borrowing and research and development costs are expensed, rather than capitalized in certain circumstances.

- Topics not relevant to SMEs were omitted, such as earnings per share, interim financial reporting, and segment reporting.

- Significantly fewer disclosures are required (roughly a 90% reduction versus full IFRS).[39]

Furthermore, revisions to the *IFRS for SMEs* publication will be limited to once every three years.

Remember this box?

> The *International Financial Reporting Standard for Small and Medium-sized Entities (IFRS for SMEs)* is set out in Sections 1–35 and the Glossary. Terms defined in the Glossary are in **bold type** the first time they appear in each section. The *IFRS for SMEs* is accompanied by a preface, implementation guidance, a derivation table, illustrative financial statements and a presentation and disclosure checklist, and a basis for conclusions. (Source: *IFRS for SMEs* 2009, Contents page)

As shown in the "authority box" from the *IFRS for SMEs* Contents page, the standard itself and the glossary are considered "integral." Other guidance, such as appendices, illustrative

---

[39] Id.

financial statements, a disclosure checklist, and the basis for conclusions, are not integral to the standard.

To assist in application issues related to the *IFRS for SMEs* publication, the IASB established the SME Implementation Group (SMEIG) in 2009. The SMEIG publishes nonmandatory Q&As (to the extent approved for issuance by the IASB), designed to assist practitioners in applying the *IFRS for SMEs*. These Q&A's are accessible on www.ifrs.org, under "IFRS for SMEs."

Judgment Hierarchy and Statement of Compliance

The judgment hierarchy shown in Figure 12-21 applies to an entity's selection of accounting policies under *IFRS for SMEs*.

Figure 12-21

Judgment hierarchy for selecting accounting policies under *IFRS for SMEs*[42]

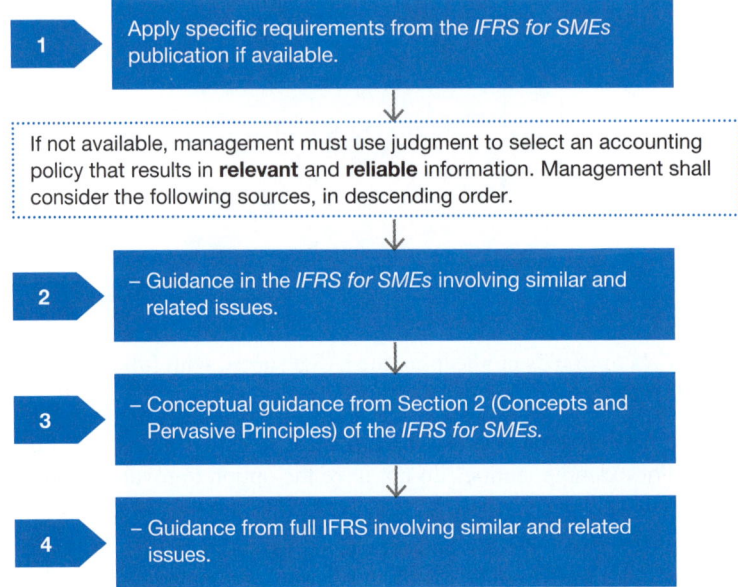

1. Apply specific requirements from the *IFRS for SMEs* publication if available.

If not available, management must use judgment to select an accounting policy that results in **relevant** and **reliable** information. Management shall consider the following sources, in descending order.

2. – Guidance in the *IFRS for SMEs* involving similar and related issues.

3. – Conceptual guidance from Section 2 (Concepts and Pervasive Principles) of the *IFRS for SMEs*.

4. – Guidance from full IFRS involving similar and related issues.

Similar to full IFRS, entities whose financial statements comply with all requirements of the *IFRS for SMEs* must "make an explicit and unreserved statement of such compliance" in their financial statement footnotes,[41] like this illustrative example from the *IFRS for SMEs* publication:

> *Note 2 Basis of preparation and accounting policies*
>
> These consolidated financial statements have been prepared in accordance with the *International Financial Reporting Standard for Small and Medium-sized Entities* issued by the International Accounting Standards Board . . .[42]

Knowledge Check ✔

9. **Why did the IASB create the *IFRS for SMEs* guidance?**
10. **What are two differences between *IFRS for SMEs* and "full" IFRS?**
11. **Which sections of the *IFRS for SMEs* are considered "mandatory"?**

---

[40] *IFRS for SMEs* (2009). Par. 10.3–10.6.

[41] *IFRS for SMEs* (2009). Par. 3.3.

[42] *IFRS for SMEs* (2009). Illustrative Financial Statements, illustrative note 2, "Basis of Preparation and Accounting Policies."

Citing International Accounting Standards

Following are examples of acceptable references to IFRS guidance.

■ Per International Accounting Standard No. 16, *Property Plant and Equipment* (IAS 16), par. 29:

> An entity shall choose either the cost model in paragraph 30 or the revaluation model in paragraph 31 as its accounting policy and shall apply that policy to an entire class of property, plant and equipment.

■ Later references might describe this source as follows: Per IAS 16, par. 29 . . .

Also, following is an acceptable method for citing guidance from the *IFRS for SMEs* publication:

■ Per *IFRS for SMEs* (July 2009 revision), Section 1.1 (Scope): "The *IFRS for SMEs* is intended for use by **small and medium-sized entities** (SMEs)."

It is necessary to include the revision date when citing from the *IFRS for SMEs* publication. It is also helpful to show (in parenthesis) a description of the section from which guidance is being cited. For example, saying "Section 1.1" by itself is not descriptive, so it is helpful (but not necessary) to also describe this section as relating to scope.

NONAUTHORITATIVE RESOURCES

Extensive nonauthoritative resources are available to assist practitioners in understanding and applying international accounting standards. Remember—nonauthoritative guidance can *supplement*, but should not *replace*, the use of authoritative guidance (see Chapter 4 for additional discussion of this point). Also, when it comes to documenting accounting conclusions, researchers should primarily cite authoritative sources.

The following discussion highlights a small sample of available nonauthoritative resources. But first, let's start with a quick **TIP from the Trenches**.

> Asked what nonauthoritative resources she would recommend to beginning researchers, a former IASB project manager was quick to name the following, which she herself frequently consults: (1) Deloitte's "IAS Plus" website; (2) accounting firm IFRS vs. U.S. GAAP comparison guides; and (3) the IASB's own educational resources.

We'll discuss these recommended resources and more in the following section.

Deloitte's IAS Plus Website

A great starting point for researchers applying, or looking for additional information on, IFRS, Deloitte's IAS Plus website (www.iasplus.com) includes news, detailed histories and summaries for each IFRS standard, information about each jurisdiction where IFRS is used, and extensive interpretive guidance (such as guide books for individual IFRS standards) and training resources (such as e-learning modules available for each standard).

Comparison Guides

Comparison guides, generally available free of charge from major accounting firms, summarize key provisions of U.S. GAAP and IFRS and highlight areas of difference. As a beginning researcher, if you were to look at two standards (a U.S. GAAP standard and an IFRS standard) side by side, you may not pick up on nuances implied by different choices of words. Or you may struggle to *efficiently* identify differences in requirements. These guides can efficiently point out such differences.

Before you even log on to eIFRS, consider consulting a comparison guide. Used as a starting point, the guide will (1) identify the names of applicable IFRS (standards and interpretations) that are relevant to a topic and (2) highlight key areas of difference in IFRS versus U.S. GAAP requirements. Both sets of standards frequently change, so be sure that you are using the most current available guide, and always use these guides *in addition to* authoritative sources.

To locate comparison guides, try a Web search for "IFRS vs GAAP," or some variation of this (such as adding the word "comparison" or "guide," for example).

Other Resources

Researchers can also avail themselves of resources ranging from interpretive guidance, to model financial statements, to training modules. The following discussion lists just a sample of the many resources available to practitioners. Caution: When using nonauthoritative guidance, be thoughtful about consulting reputable sources. Avoid unknown websites, and avoid textbooks which could be outdated.

For plain-English *summaries* of IFRS guidance, researchers can consult

- Technical Summaries published by the IASB, available for each standard.
- The IASB's briefing document, *A Briefing for Chief Executives, Audit Committees & Boards of Directors*, which summarizes key principles from each standard of the full IFRS. Updated annually, this document is available under "Educational Materials" in eIFRS.
- Pocket Guides to IFRS, published by the major accounting firms, which summarize IFRS requirements by standard (e.g., Deloitte's *IFRSs in your pocket*, 2013).

For *in-depth analysis* of IFRS requirements, researchers can consult

- IFRS accounting manuals, available for purchase from major accounting firms or available through subscriptions to firm research databases. For example, PwC's *Manual of accounting—IFRS 2013* offers in-depth guidance on the preparation of IFRS financial statements, including examples from company reports and model IFRS financial statements.
- IFRS guide books by topic, such as Deloitte's "iGAAP 2013" series, which includes titles such as *Deloitte iGAAP 2013: Financial Instruments—IFRS 9 and Related Standards*.

For *"model" IFRS financial statements*, researchers can consult, for example,

- Firm websites, such as BDO International and Grant Thornton, which annually publish illustrative financial statements and notes as a technical reference for accountants.
- The Ernst & Young "Core Tools Library," accessible online, which offers industry-specific illustrative IFRS financial statements (e.g., Oil & Gas, Real Estate).

Several firms offer IFRS *training modules* by topic, including

- The IFRS Foundation's training modules explaining and illustrating the application of *IFRS for SMEs*.
- The AICPA's IFRS certification course consisting of multiple online, self-study training courses, covering the basics of IFRS standards plus the opportunity to apply standards to sample scenarios. Enrollment fees apply.
- Firm-produced IFRS learning modules by topic (Web search: "IFRS e-learning" or "learning modules").

The above-named resources are generally accessible via Web search, and most are free of charge.

APPENDIX 12A: INTERNATIONAL AUDITING STANDARDS

When Do International Auditing Standards Apply?

As a private standard-setting organization, the IASB lacks the authority to enforce (i.e., ensure that entities are properly applying) its accounting standards. Rather, enforcement is generally left up to national laws, securities regulators, and the audit process. This section of the text focuses on international auditing standards, focusing in particular on their relevance to U.S. accounting professionals.

Globally, external audits are frequently required for entities with public accountability, as well as for certain statutory financial statements. Governments and securities regulators in individual countries or regions determine the applicable auditing standards for their jurisdictions. Often, these auditing standards are based on the **International Standards on Auditing (ISAs)** issued by the International Auditing and Assurance Standards Board.

In the United States, recall that two organizations are primarily responsible for establishing auditing standards: the PCAOB for public company audits, and the AICPA for nonpublic company audits. Notably, the PCAOB's auditing standards also apply to *foreign private issuers*, as these entities are still considered issuers of securities in the United States—no exception was made under Sarbanes-Oxley for "foreign" issuers.[43] Also notable, the AICPA's auditing standards apply to U.S. nonpublic companies that choose to prepare financial statements in accordance with IFRS (under Code of Conduct Rule 203).

As U.S. accounting firms increasingly perform multinational audits, U.S. auditors are expected to become familiar with international auditing and ethics standards. For example,

- When auditing a U.S. subsidiary of a foreign parent, a U.S. auditor may be expected by the parent company to perform the audit in accordance with international standards.

- The "reverse" is also true—when auditing a U.S. parent with a foreign subsidiary, the audit of the foreign subsidiary may be required by statutory laws to comply with international auditing standards.

The graphic in Figure 12-22 summarizes several scenarios for U.S. auditors, and the applicable auditing standards.

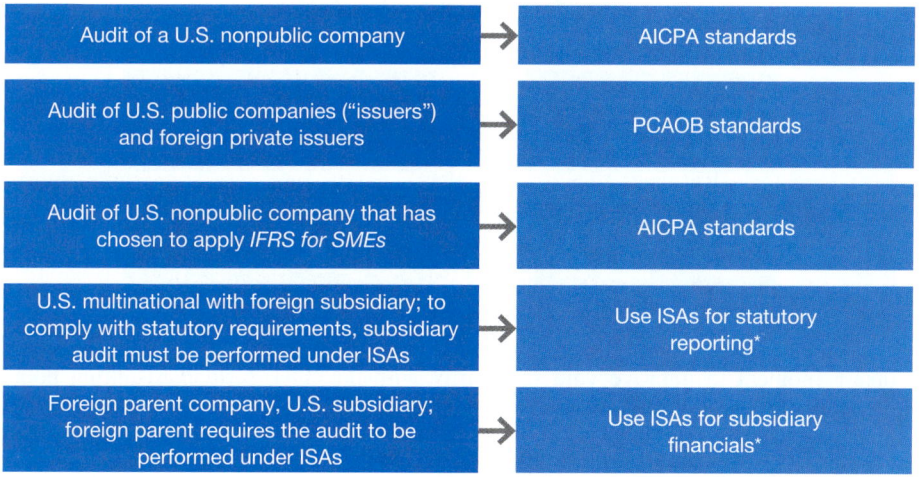

Audit of a U.S. nonpublic company	AICPA standards
Audit of U.S. public companies ("issuers") and foreign private issuers	PCAOB standards
Audit of U.S. nonpublic company that has chosen to apply *IFRS for SMEs*	AICPA standards
U.S. multinational with foreign subsidiary; to comply with statutory requirements, subsidiary audit must be performed under ISAs	Use ISAs for statutory reporting*
Foreign parent company, U.S. subsidiary; foreign parent requires the audit to be performed under ISAs	Use ISAs for subsidiary financials*

Figure 12-22

Sample audit scenarios and applicable source of standards

*To the extent the audit is performed by U.S. auditors, the auditors must also adhere to U.S. auditing and ethical standards.

---

[43] Sarbanes-Oxley Act of 2002, Sections 101(c)(2) and 103(a)(1).

In circumstances where U.S. auditors must comply with international auditing standards, the U.S. auditor is expected to *also* comply with U.S. auditing and ethical standards. Two U.S. auditing standards shed light on the interaction between U.S. auditors and international reporting:

■ AU-C 700, *Forming an Opinion and Reporting on Financial Statements*, permits U.S. auditors to express an opinion on financial statements prepared in accordance with U.S. GAAP, IFRS, or *IFRS for SMEs*.

■ AU-C 910, *Financial Statements Prepared in Accordance with a Financial Reporting Framework Generally Accepted in Another Country*, applies to U.S. auditors engaged to report on financial statements prepared in accordance with *financial reporting frameworks other than U.S. GAAP or IFRS (as issued by the IASB)*, such as audits of financial statements prepared using other national GAAP or jurisdictional variations of IFRS.

   ● This standard describes how auditors should consider both international and U.S. auditing standards in their performance of the audit, and provides guidance for selecting the appropriate form for the auditor's report.

Next, let's look at the organizations responsible for establishing global auditing and ethics standards.

The International Federation of Accountants (IFAC) and Its Standards Boards

Through its four independent standard-setting boards, the **International Federation of Accountants** (IFAC) establishes international standards on ethics, auditing and assurance, accounting education, and governmental (public sector) accounting. The IFAC's mission is, in part, to serve the public interest by "contributing to the development, adoption, and implementation of high-quality international standards and guidance."[44]

The IFAC and its standard-setting boards are illustrated in Figure 12-23. Like the use of IFRS, standards of the IFAC's various boards are progressively gaining worldwide acceptance; as of 2012, IFAC members represented 129 countries and jurisdictions globally.[45]

Figure 12-23

The IFAC and its standard-setting boards

Take a moment to improve your familiarity with the IFAC's standard-setting bodies by completing the following simple **Now YOU Try** exercise.

---

[44] International Auditing and Assurance Standards Board (IAASB), *Handbook of International Quality Control, Auditing Review, Other Assurance, and Related Services Pronouncements,* 2012 Edition, Volume 1. Page 4.

[45] IFAC.org, "Membership". "IFAC is comprised of 173 members and associates in 129 countries and jurisdictions*, representing approximately 2.5 million accountants in public practice, education, government service, industry, and commerce." *As of November 15, 2012. Accessed October 20, 2013.

Now
YOU
Try
12.6

Matching Guidance to Standard Setters

The standard setters illustrated in Figure 12-23 issue guidance that is organized into the following handbooks. Match each handbook to the standard setter that issues it.

Handbook of International Quality Control, Auditing, Review, Other Assurance, and Related Services Pronouncements: _____

Handbook of International Education Pronouncements: _____

Handbook of the Code of Ethics for Professional Accountants: _____

Handbook of International Public Sector Accounting Pronouncements: _____

The IFAC's "member bodies," comprised of global professional accountancy organizations, agree as a condition of membership to adopt or substantially converge with certain of the IFAC's standards, including International Standards on Auditing (ISAs) and the international **Code of Ethics**. To the extent differences exist between these and national standards, member bodies agree to promote standards that are not less stringent than those of IFAC. The AICPA is a member body of the IFAC and thus has agreed to these requirements. As another example, the Financial Reporting Council (of the U.K. and Ireland) uses ISAs as the basis for its own auditing standards.

Following is further discussion regarding each of these standards boards.

International Auditing and Assurance Standards Board (IAASB)

The **International Auditing and Assurance Standards Board** (IAASB) establishes standards for a range of services, applicable to entities of all sizes, including small and medium-sized entities. The IAASB's "Handbook" includes the following standards:

■ International Standards on Auditing (ISAs) for audits

■ ISREs for review engagements

■ ISAEs for assurance engagements

■ ISQCs for quality control

■ ISRS for "related services" (e.g., agreed-upon procedures, compilations)

The IAASB Handbook can be downloaded from www.ifac.org. Researchers can search for guidance within the handbook by perusing the table of contents or by performing keyword searches (using ctrl + f).

While not included within the IAASB Handbook, accountants should also consider the "IESBA Code of Ethics," which applies broadly to all professional accountants, regardless of the service being provided. For audit and assurance engagements, accountants should also consider the IAASB's "International Framework for Assurance Engagements" (the "Framework"), which describes the objectives of assurance engagements and identifies engagements to which the IAASB's auditing and assurance standards apply. While the Framework by itself is not authoritative, accountants are expected to read standards-level guidance for audit and assurance engagements in the context of the Framework. The Framework is not included within the IAASB's Handbook, but is accessible at www.ifac.org.

International Standards on Auditing (ISAs)

For auditors just starting out with international auditing standards, a good starting point is ISA 200 (Objectives of the Independent Auditor, Conduct of an Audit in Accordance with ISAs). ISA 200 sets forth guidance on the proper use and application of ISAs in an audit, for example:

■ An auditor should consider all parts of an ISA in order to properly apply it. This includes consideration of the standard's Objectives section, as well as the Requirements and Application and Explanatory Material sections. If necessary to achieve a standard's Objectives, auditors may need to perform procedures beyond those required within a given standard.

- Requirements within ISAs are described using the word *shall*.

- Similar to the notion of the IFRS "compliance statement," accountants cannot represent compliance with ISAs in their audit reports unless they comply fully with all ISA requirements. Therefore, to the extent jurisdictional variations exist of ISAs, entities may not be able to represent compliance with ISAs unless they still comply fully with ISA standards.[46]

The AICPA's recent Clarity initiative has resulted in substantial convergence between U.S. nonpublic company auditing standards and ISAs. Certain differences remain, where deemed necessary by the AICPA, but in all cases the AICPA's requirements meet or exceed ISA requirements. The PCAOB did not participate in this convergence project.

One notable difference between U.S. and international auditing standards is that ISA standards do not require auditors to report on the effectiveness of internal controls. However, this requirement may be imposed on a jurisdiction-specific basis (e.g., individual countries may require such reporting).[47]

Interpretive Guidance from the IAASB

The IAASB and its staff have issued several sources of nonauthoritative, interpretive guidance related to certain standards included in the Handbook. These include

- IAASB-published "practice notes," designed to provide practical assistance and application guidance for the IAASB's various standards. Practice notes include, for example, the International Auditing Practice Notes (IAPNs).

- The basis for conclusions to each ISA.

- Staff Q&As on the application of standards.

- Training modules for certain standards, including videos and informational slides.

These resources are generally accessible on the "Publications & Resources" page of www.ifac.org.

International Ethics Standards Board for Accountants

The **International Ethics Standards Board for Accountants** (IESBA) issues and maintains a model Code of Ethics for Professional Accountants to be followed by—or to serve as a minimum standard for jurisdiction-specific ethics codes for—professional accountants throughout the world. As noted previously, this Code of Ethics applies broadly: professional accountants must comply with the Code of Ethics in all circumstances, regardless of the functional role, or type of engagement, being performed by the accountant.

Like international auditing standards, individual jurisdictions (to the extent they are members of IFAC) can require compliance with this Code of Ethics, or must establish their own Code of Ethics that is at least as stringent as the IESBA's Code. U.S. accountants are generally expected to abide by the IESBA's Code of Ethics when performing an audit in accordance with ISA auditing standards; otherwise, the AICPA Code of Conduct applies to U.S. accountants.

The Code of Ethics has three parts with differing applicability: [48]

- Part A establishes fundamental principles of professional ethics, including the "conceptual framework" for maintaining compliance with these fundamental principles.

---

[46] ISA 200, *Overall Objectives of the Independent Auditor and the Conduct of an Audit in Accordance with International Standards on Auditing.* Par. 18-20, A55, A58, A70.

[47] ISA 200, Par. A1 (Scope of the Audit): ". . . In some jurisdictions, however, applicable law or regulation may require auditors to provide opinions on other specific matters, such as the effectiveness of internal control, or the consistency of a separate management report with the financial statements. While the ISAs include requirements and guidance in relation to such matters to the extent that they are relevant to forming an opinion on the financial statements, the auditor would be required to undertake further work if the auditor had additional responsibilities to provide such opinions."

[48] International Ethics Standards Board for Accountants, *Handbook of the Code of Ethics for Professional Accountants.* 2013 edition. Par. 100.2 and 100.3.

- Part B applies the framework to public accountants.
- Part C applies the framework to accountants in business.

The Code of Ethics is comprised of standards and interpretations, both of which are authoritative sources, and both of which are issued by the IESBA.

Other IFAC Standards Boards

The IFAC's International Public Sector Accounting Standards Board (IPSASB) establishes minimum standards (**International Public Sector Accounting Standards**, or **IPSAS**) for governments and other public sector entities and strives to promote the use, globally, of an accrual-based approach for the preparation of government financial statements. IPSAS are formulated using IFRS as a starting point, then are revised as necessary to address issues unique to public sector accounting.[49]

The IFAC's **International Accounting Education Standards Board** (IAESB) develops educational standards applicable to member bodies' accountants. For example, the IAESB has established a guideline educational syllabus, outlining educational standards to be achieved by its members. IFAC "member bodies" are required to consider these educational standards while formulating their own educational programs for accountants.

Comparing International Audit Reports

Let's take a moment to review excerpts from audit reports illustrating the use of different accounting and auditing frameworks. For this, we'll return to our example of HSBC.

Figure 12-24 depicts the relationship among the London-based holding company HSBC Holdings plc and a few of its subsidiaries. The North American holding company (HSBC North America) does not issue public securities and generally does not issue financial statements (except for form FR Y-9C, a required filing with the Federal Reserve for bank holding companies). However, the other entities depicted in Figure 12-24 do issue securities, as noted in the illustration.

Figure 12-24

Partial depiction of HSBC Holdings Plc's organizational structure. This illustration is for teaching purposes only and is not a complete depiction of HSBC's subsidiary relationships; not all intermediate subsidiaries and holding companies have been reflected in this illustration.

Comparing International Audit Reports

Using the information in Figure 12-24 and the following audit report excerpts, respond to the questions that follow. The excerpts below are taken from filings with the U.S. SEC and filings in the U.K.

Now
YOU
Try
12.7

---

[49] International Public Sector Accounting Standards Board, *Process for Reviewing and Modifying IASB Documents* (October 2008). Page 1.

I. Report of Independent Registered Public Accounting Firm

. . . We conducted our audits in accordance with the standards of the Public Company Accounting Oversight Board (United States) . . .

In our opinion, the consolidated financial statements referred to above present fairly, in all material respects, the financial position of the Company as of December 31, 2012 and 2011, and the results of its operations and its cash flows for each of the years in the three-year period ended December 31, 2012, and the financial position of the Bank as of December 31, 2012 and 2011, in conformity with U.S. generally accepted accounting principles. [From annual report Form 10-K filed with U.S. SEC]

Questions:

1. In excerpt I, which financial reporting (accounting) framework are the auditors opining on?
   _____

2. What audit standards did the auditors follow, in conducting the audit?   _____

3. Which entity (or possible entities) do you think this opinion relates to?   _____

II. Independent Auditor's Report to the Members of [Company]

. . . Our responsibility is to audit, and express an opinion on, the financial statements in accordance with applicable law and International Standards on Auditing (UK and Ireland). Those standards require us to comply with the Auditing Practices Board's Ethical Standards for Auditors. . . .

In our opinion: . . . the Group financial statements have been properly prepared in accordance with IFRSs as adopted by the EU; the parent company financial statements have been properly prepared in accordance with IFRSs as adopted by the EU and as applied in accordance with the provisions of the Companies Act 2006; . . .

. . . As explained in Note l(a) to the Group financial statements, in addition to complying with its legal obligation to apply IFRSs as adopted by the EU, the Group has also applied IFRSs as issued by the IASB. . . .

[From annual report filed in UK]

4. In excerpt II, which <u>two</u> financial reporting (accounting) frameworks are the auditors opining on?   _____ and _____

5. What audit standards did the auditors follow, in conducting the audit?   _____

6. What ethical standards did the auditors follow?   _____

7. Which entity do you think this opinion relates to?   _____

III. Report of Independent Registered Public Accounting Firm to the Board of Directors and Shareholders of [Company]

. . . We conducted our audits in accordance with the standards of the Public Company Accounting Oversight Board (United States). . . .

In our opinion, the consolidated financial statements referred to above present fairly, in all material respects, the financial position of [Company] . . . and the results of its operations and its cash flows ... in conformity with International Financial Reporting Standards (IFRSs) as adopted by the European Union (EU) and IFRSs as issued by the International Accounting Standards Board (IASB).

[Form 20-F Annual Report, filed with the U.S. SEC]

8. Recall from earlier in the chapter—when does report Form 20-F apply? _____

9. In excerpt III, what <u>two</u> financial reporting (accounting) frameworks are the auditors opining on? _____ and _____

10. What audit standards did the auditors follow, in conducting the audit? _____

11. Which entity do you think this opinion relates to? _____

*Company names have been replaced by bracketed text ("[Company]") for purposes of this exercise.
**References for these excerpts are located immediately following the case studies at the end of this chapter.

CHAPTER SUMMARY

Accounting research skills can serve researchers in a variety of contexts, including both domestic and global. For years, international accounting and auditing standards were established by individual jurisdictions. Today, the international standard-setting environment is becoming streamlined, as the IFRS Foundation and its standard-setting bodies have become established as the predominant global accounting standard setter, and as the IFAC and its standard-setting bodies increasingly lead the way in establishing assurance, ethics, and other standards.

As we've discussed in this chapter, these international standards will likely be impactful to the careers of today's U.S. entry-level accountants. The global context, as well as the research skills, you've acquired from this chapter strive to prepare you for the challenges ahead.

REVIEW QUESTIONS

1. Describe the relationship between the IFRS Foundation and the IASB.

2. Briefly explain why a large multinational corporation, such as HSBC, might be supportive of increasing the global use of IFRS.

3. Does the IASB have the authority to impose funding requirements on its member countries? Contrast the IASB's funding regime with the FASB's funding mechanism.

4. In what circumstances does the IFRS Interpretations Committee handle an issue, and what is the name of the guidance they issue?

5. Are U.S. public companies allowed to issue financial statements in accordance with IFRS? What about U.S. nonpublic companies? Explain.

6. In your own words, how is a "foreign private issuer" defined? What is the significance of this designation?

7. Explain the difference between integral and not integral guidance.

8. Identify the sources of guidance comprising full IFRS.

9. Name two differences between full IFRS and the guidance in *IFRS for SMEs*.

10. When should a researcher turn to the IAS 8 hierarchy? In other words, what is a situation in which that hierarchy might be relevant?

11. Once you have located relevant IFRS or IAS guidance, what interpretive guidance should you also look for?

12. (From Appendix) What is one implication of the U.S. AICPA being a member body of the IFAC?

EXERCISES

To complete these exercises, you will need to become a "registered user" of www.ifrs.org. You will also need to access other resources (such as firm publications, available for free on the Web), where applicable, to respond to the following questions. In all cases, cite the source for your responses.

1. Has South Africa adopted IFRS?

2. Locate an IFRS/US GAAP comparison guide. Name one difference between the U.S. GAAP and IFRS requirements related to *lease classification*.

3. Locate IAS 2, and identify the guidance considered integral to this standard. Explain how you located this information.

4. Locate the most recent annual report of Canada-based Bombardier Inc., a corporation that manufactures planes and trains. Determine whether the financial statements were prepared in accordance with IFRS, and describe the audit standards applied by the auditors. To do this, look for both the auditor's report, and the IFRS compliance statement.

5. Assume that an entity complied with IFRS guidance in all respects, except that the entity has never included an IFRS compliance statement in its financial statement footnote disclosures. Is the entity subject to the guidance for first-time adopters of IFRS? Use authoritative guidance to respond.

6. Locate the IFRIC related to customer loyalty payments. What two options were considered by the IFRIC in determining how a company's obligation for customer loyalty payments (such as discounted goods) should be recognized and measured? What standard numbers are described as being related to this Interpretation (under "References")?

7. Can a subsidiary—whose parent uses full IFRS—use *IFRS for SMEs* if the subsidiary itself is not publicly accountable?

8. (Relates to Appendix topics) Jones & Jones, LLC is in the planning phase for its initial audit of New Client, Inc. It will perform this audit under ISAs. Is Jones & Jones, LLC required to contact New Client's predecessor auditor as part of its engagement planning?

9. (Relates to Appendix topics) Within the handbook of international ethics standards, what are two examples of safeguards (against threats such as client involvement in illegal activities) that an auditor should consider applying during its client acceptance (or "professional appointment") procedures?

10. Correct the following source citation, improving it in any way appropriate.

> IASB standard 5 tells us that "An entity shall classify a non-current asset (or disposal group) as held for sale if its carrying amount will be recovered principally through a sale transaction rather than through continuing use."

CASE STUDY QUESTIONS

12.1   **Property, Plant, & Equipment**

Facts: A Ukranian public company recently built a new manufacturing plant (during fiscal 201X). A few of the costs related to building the plant (or as applicable, incurred after building the plant) were

- Payment of wages and benefits to construction workers, who were already employed by the company. Cost of these wages: $2 million.
- Exterior paint for the building ($50,000).
- A test production run, in which the plant tested its ability to produce its products.
- Payment of wages to construction workers asked to help with additional service issues after the plant was placed in service.

In 201Y, an appraisal by the company's local tax assessor indicated that the building's value had increased by $10 million.

Required:

1. Determine whether the company is subject to the requirements of IFRS (based on the home country). Cite your source for this determination.

2. Locate the relevant guidance, then determine which of the above-listed costs may be included in the initial measurement (i.e., capitalized value) of the plant when the plant is first recognized in 201X. Should any of the costs be expensed, rather than included in the building's cost? Cite your source for each cost. Certain costs may be addressed directly by the guidance; others may require judgment in applying principles from the guidance.

3. Determine whether the property's value should be adjusted in year 2 (201Y).

4. Using an IFRS/U.S. GAAP comparison guide, state how your response to question 3 would differ if this company had been subject to U.S. GAAP. Cite the source for your response.

IFRS for SMEs Now, assume that the Ukranian company's Controller (from Case Study 12.1) has asked whether your response to item 3 (regarding the year 2 value of the plant) would change if the company applied *IFRS for SMEs* (assuming the company was permitted to apply this guidance). Draft a brief email to the company's Controller explaining the different accounting, and cite your source.

12.2

***IFRS for SMEs* Dissenting Opinion** Within the Basis for Conclusions to the *IFRS for SMEs* (2009 revision) a Board member challenged the choice of steps in the *IFRS for SMEs* judgment hierarchy. Recall that this judgment hierarchy is illustrated in Figure 12-21 of this chapter. Locate this Board member's dissenting opinion, and describe the concerns he raised regarding the judgment hierarchy. Additionally, describe one other concern he raised with respect to issuance of the *IFRS for SMEs* publication.

12.3

Your response should require approximately two paragraphs and should clearly reference the source of your research.

Note: Students should be able to access this guidance (the Basis for Conclusions to the *IFRS for SMEs* publication) using Registered User (free) access to www.ifrs.org.

(Relates to Appendix) Smith & Dunn, LLC received a telephone call from a potential client, requesting their assistance in evaluating the accounting treatment for a proposed transaction. The client has laid out a set of hypothetical facts and has asked for Smith & Dunn's general views on the proposed transaction, indicating that its own auditor had a different view than the client's.

12.4

What ethical considerations (from the IESBA Handbook) should Smith & Dunn apply in providing this second opinion to a potential client? Imagine that you are a staff member of the firm and have been asked to email the partners (John & Diana) with your findings.

ADDITIONAL REFERENCES

Now YOU Try 12.7   ** Excerpt No. 1: HSBC USA Inc, 2012 Form 10-K. Page 127; Excerpt No. 2: HSBC Holdings Plc, 2012 Annual Report. Page 369. Excerpt No. 3: HSBC Holdings Plc, 2011 Form 20-F with SE, Page 276.

Chapter 13

Staying Current with Emerging Accounting Guidance

Good news: An effort as simple as "staying current" can help to fast-track your career.

Imagine for a moment Jen, a staff auditor, who is sitting at a picnic table in a cramped room at her client's site. Today, for the first time, Jen will meet the engagement partner, who is dropping in to meet with the client. He will only be in town for a few hours, then he's off to meet with another client.

While the partner is there, Jen receives an email alert: "FASB issues long-awaited Revenue Recognition standard."

Jen turns to the partner and says: "Oh, did you see? The FASB's new revenue recognition standard was just issued. This will affect our client's accounting for software contracts. Maybe you can mention this during your meeting today."

Suddenly, the partner notices a few things about Jen:

First: Jen is not just any staff auditor. She is a staff auditor who *takes the initiative to stay current*.

Second: Jen has the client's interests in mind, and she is thoughtful in considering how emerging guidance will affect *this* client specifically.

Continued

Learning Objectives

After reading this chapter and performing the exercises herein, you will be able to

1. **Understand** the professional advantages of staying current.

2. **Describe,** generally, the standard setters' "due process" for issuing new guidance.

3. **Identify**—and subscribe to—useful resources for staying current.

(continued from previous page)

Third: Jen has effective *communication skills*. Rather than spending the partner's time on small talk, she provided him with information that was clear, succinct, and useful to his meeting with the client.

Jen may not realize it yet, but this simple action will have a lasting impact on the partner's impression of her. Before long, he will begin to request her services on other engagements and will trust her with increasing amounts of responsibility. *This* is how successful careers begin.

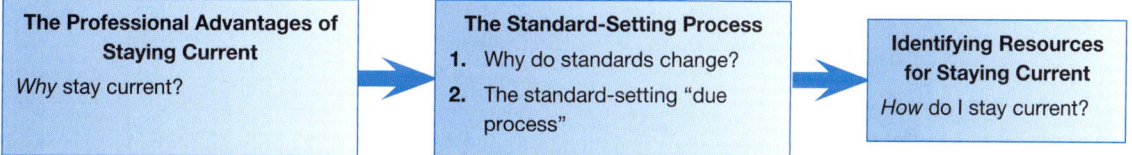

Organization of This Chapter

Accounting research is dynamic. This chapter is designed to teach you the importance of staying informed as the rules for our profession continually change. This chapter will also explain why standards change, standard setters' processes for revising standards, and what you can do to stay current.

The chapter does not provide an exhaustive explanation of standard setting; rather, it is intended to introduce the process and provide you with a general feel for how new guidance is established.

Additionally, this chapter does not present "current events" in standard setting; it would be impossible for this book to keep pace with our rapidly changing profession. However, it will provide you with the tools necessary to take on this challenge yourself.

THE PROFESSIONAL ADVANTAGES OF STAYING CURRENT

What does it mean to "stay current"? It means recognizing that accounting standards are continually changing and making a conscious effort to keep up. This phenomenon of changing standards is not limited to just accounting, however; auditing and ethical standards, regulatory requirements, and international requirements are equally dynamic. By the time you enter the workforce, many of the textbooks that you learned from in school will already be outdated. Staying current involves monitoring not only "final" changes to existing rules, but also being aware of "emerging" guidance that is under development.

Professionals in a variety of roles have the responsibility to stay current, as illustrated in Figure 13-1.

Figure 13-1 Examples of professionals who monitor emerging guidance	

Why I Monitor Emerging Guidance

Auditor:
- I need to ensure that my clients **comply** with all newly effective guidance.
- It's also important to inform my clients about **emerging** changes in standards.
- Finally, my firm may choose to **comment** on standards being developed.

Corporate Accountant:
- **I am expected** to inform management about possible effects of emerging guidance, including changes to:
  - **Budgets** and forecasts,
  - **Systems** requirements,
  - Current **transaction accounting**.
- Periodically, my company submits **comment letters** to the FASB.
- We must **disclose impacts** of issued, but not yet effective, guidance.

Analyst/Investor:
- I actively **communicate to the FASB** information that is most useful to my analysis of financial statements.
- As new requirements become effective, I may need to **adjust my model** for analyzing financial statements.

Of course, the professionals depicted in Figure 13-1 are not the only individuals who monitor emerging guidance. Parties ranging from regulators to attorneys to academics—to the extent they are involved in applying or interpreting accounting standards—have an interest in staying current.

At what level of your career should you be expected to monitor emerging guidance? The opening scenario of this chapter says it all. While some view "emerging accounting" as a partner- or director-level matter, the truth is that professionals at all levels will see significant advantages in their careers from staying current.

The flip side is also true: Imagine the loss of trust that could occur if you, an auditor onsite daily with a client, let an important emerging guidance topic (with relevance to that client) slip by without informing your client that it is out there. *As an auditor, there is a professional expectation that you will help the client stay informed about changes in accounting requirements.* Having conversations with your client, early on, about the impacts of emerging guidance can also minimize differences of opinion later regarding the need to apply, or method of applying, new standards.

Of course, financial statement preparers understand that complying with guidance requirements and monitoring changes is *their own responsibility*; however, preparers appreciate when their auditors can leverage firm resources to share news and insights on emerging issues.

During my career, I was given the advice: "Act like the level you want to be." If a staff accountant starts to perform at a senior level, pretty soon supervisors will notice this, and the individual will be promoted.

Your engagement manager, senior manager, and partner stay informed about emerging issues in the profession; there's no reason you as a first-year associate cannot also be informed. Doing so will actually lighten their load, as they will be able to request your help in monitoring changes to standards and summarizing possible impacts to your clients. Soon, you'll be invited to meetings where these topics are discussed with the client. See? Act like the level you want to be.

TIP from the Trenches

You'll have to weigh the advantages of staying current "on work time" versus the advantages of printing articles to read on your train ride home, or while waiting at the dentist's office. Judge this based on your firm's culture; if reading on the clock is acceptable and expected, go for it. If not, invest in this professional development time after hours.

THE STANDARD-SETTING PROCESS

Why Do Accounting Standards Change?

An accounting standard setter's decision to revise existing guidance, or to issue new guidance, may be driven by a number of considerations. These include, for example,

- *Practitioners, such as preparers or auditors*, may express concern that existing requirements are unclear, and may request clarification from the standard setter. This can result in changes to, or interpretations of, existing guidance.

- *Investors and analysts* might drive the request for changes, concerned that existing reporting or disclosure requirements do not provide sufficient, useful information for decision making.

- As *new types of transactions* emerge, standard setters must keep pace, issuing guidance that appropriately reflects the economics of these activities. For example, mortgage securitizations, repurchase financing transactions, and hedge transactions were all—at one point—viewed as "new" transactions that required standard setters' consideration.

- *Standard setters* are also trying to move away from so-called "bright lines" and toward "objectives-based" guidance that places increased emphasis on professional judgment. Certain standards have become infamous for their use of bright lines, such as the "75% and 90%" tests for lease classification, and the now-superseded rules for Qualifying Special Purpose Entity (QSPE) accounting. In both cases, companies have been known to structure transactions around these rules to achieve a desired accounting result.

- *Convergence with international standard setters* is often another objective of standard-setting projects. Several of the FASB's projects, for example, have been undertaken with the primary objective of eliminating differences between U.S. GAAP and international standards.

Often, standard-setting projects are intended to achieve several of these objectives at the same time, such as issuing objectives-based guidance that is converged with international standards.

As global businesses continually evolve, and as the needs of financial statement users follow suit, expect changing standards to be a constant.

The Standard-Setting "Due Process"

Within this book, we have discussed an alphabet soup of standard setters, including the FASB, GASB, IASB, PCAOB, SEC, and so on. Each of these organizations follows an established process when seeking to make changes to its standards. This process is often referred to as the standard setter's **due process**.

While each standard setter's due process may differ slightly, these processes tend to share some common themes, as illustrated in Figure 13-2.

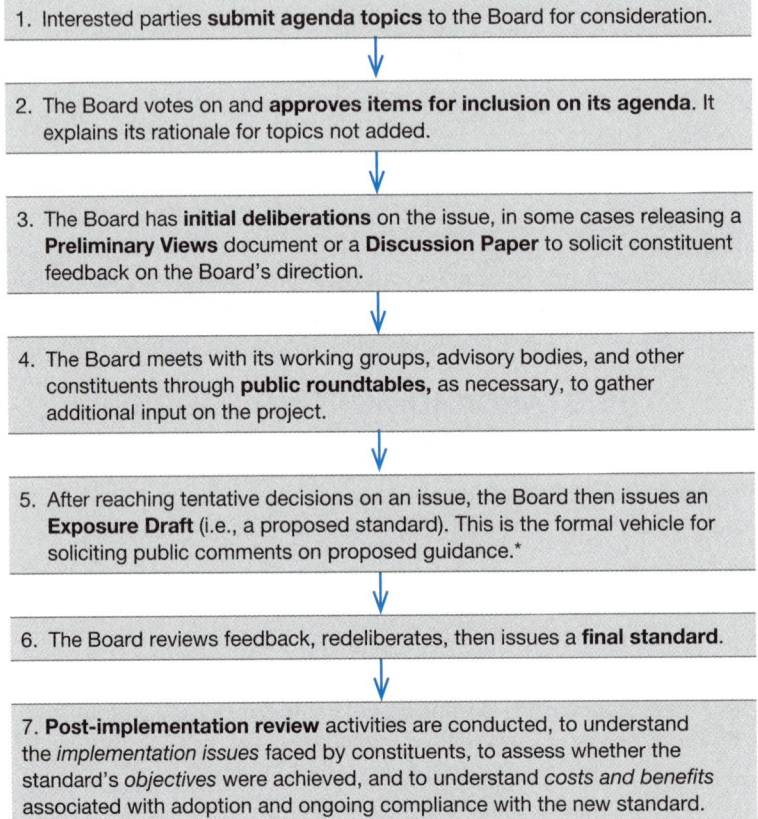

Figure 13-2

Typical standard-setting due process

1. Interested parties **submit agenda topics** to the Board for consideration.

2. The Board votes on and **approves items for inclusion on its agenda**. It explains its rationale for topics not added.

3. The Board has **initial deliberations** on the issue, in some cases releasing a **Preliminary Views** document or a **Discussion Paper** to solicit constituent feedback on the Board's direction.

4. The Board meets with its working groups, advisory bodies, and other constituents through **public roundtables,** as necessary, to gather additional input on the project.

5. After reaching tentative decisions on an issue, the Board then issues an **Exposure Draft** (i.e., a proposed standard). This is the formal vehicle for soliciting public comments on proposed guidance.*

6. The Board reviews feedback, redeliberates, then issues a **final standard**.

7. **Post-implementation review** activities are conducted, to understand the *implementation issues* faced by constituents, to assess whether the standard's *objectives* were achieved, and to understand *costs and benefits* associated with adoption and ongoing compliance with the new standard.

* A second, and sometimes even a third, exposure draft may be necessary if significant changes are proposed following the first exposure draft.

As noted, variations of this process exist for individual standard setters. For example, in the IASB's case, after adding an item to its agenda, it must consider whether to conduct the project alone, or jointly with another standard setter.

In contrast to its "standards level" projects, the IASB also has an **annual improvements process** for making narrow-scope amendments to existing standards. Such amendments may include, for example, minor wording changes, clarifications, or the resolution of minor conflicts between standards, which do not introduce new principles or change existing principles. Annually, these collective improvements are exposed for public comment in a single exposure draft, and become effective in the following year.

Now let's consider for a moment the "form" that final guidance takes at the IASB and FASB. IASB projects generally result in the direct amendment or replacement of existing standards or, as necessary to address new topics, the issuance of a new standard. In contrast, FASB projects culminate in the issuance of a *nonauthoritative* Accounting Standards Update (ASU), a document that explains the reason for the project, the decisions reached, the Board's rationale, and that marks the changes—resulting from this guidance—to be made within the *authoritative* Codification.

For additional discussion of individual standard setters' processes, visit their websites and look for the "standard setting process" page, or a variation of this. This page is located, for example, on www.fasb.org under "About Us," on www.ifrs.org under "Standards Development," or on www.pcaobus.org, under "Standards."

1. **Why do you suppose that accounting standard setters refer to their process as "due process"?**
2. **Which step happens first—exposure draft (proposed standard) or final standard? How do these differ?**

 ✓ **Knowledge Check**

IDENTIFYING RESOURCES FOR STAYING CURRENT

Now that you understand why and how standards change, let's discuss the steps you can take to stay current.

First, Identify the Standard Setters You Want to Monitor

Take a moment to consider which standard setters you will likely need to monitor as a professional. This will greatly depend upon what accounting environment you are working in and what your functional role is, as illustrated in Figure 13-3. The examples in Figure 13-3 are not all-inclusive.

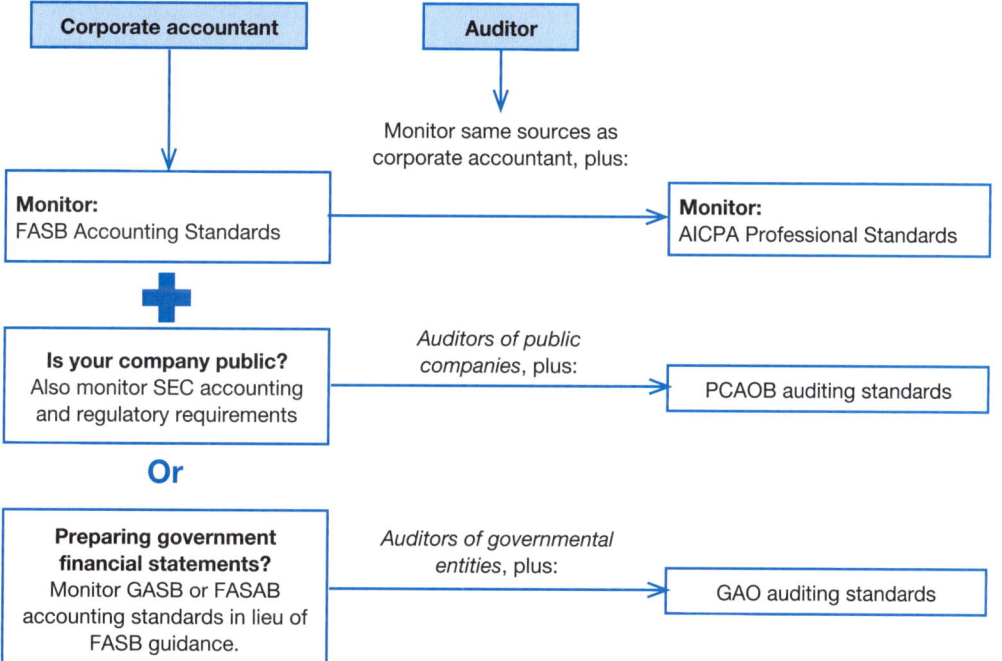

Figure 13-3

Identifying standard setters to monitor

The illustration in Figure 13-3 is meant to serve as a brainstorming tool; in reality, there is no "one size fits all" solution to the set of guidance that each professional should monitor.

Also noteworthy:

■ All professionals can benefit from monitoring broad business news. Newspapers such as the *Wall Street Journal* can be a useful resource for this.

■ *Industry-specific publications* or trade journals are another important reference for both auditors and preparers working in a specific industry.

■ Professionals applying *IFRS or international auditing standards (ISAs)* should monitor changes to those standards.

■ *Tax professionals* should monitor tax law changes and developments. One way to do this is to sign up for periodic update emails through tax research services, such as RIA Checkpoint or CCH IntelliConnect. Tax professionals can also subscribe to paper or online versions of tax periodicals, such as the AICPA's *The Tax Adviser* or Tax Analysts' *Tax Notes*.

Now that you have an idea of which standards to monitor, let's look at some resources that can assist with this effort.

Next, Identify Resources for Monitoring These Standard Setters

The following discussion introduces just a few of the many resources available for monitoring changes in accounting standards. The key is to find the sources of information that are most interesting, and useful, to your needs as a professional.

Subscribe to Weekly Email Updates

If you're looking for a "one-stop shop" for standard setter updates, consider subscribing to weekly emails from a "big 4" or other accounting firm, or from a research provider (like CCH). Subscribers can generally choose from a menu of email options (e.g., Interested in international standards? Governmental? Webcast updates?), then will generally receive a once-per-week email summarizing key standard-setting developments. Notably, the AICPA also offers a free, daily email service (CPA Letter Daily), which summarizes key business and professional news with relevance to accounting professionals.

Often, these email subscriptions offer updates on a broad range of standard setters, including the FASB, PCAOB, SEC, GAO, IASB, and so on. These emails also generally include links to related publications and invitations to educational webcasts. The PwC and Ernst & Young email subscriptions illustrated in the following figures, for example, generally include this content.

First, PwC's CFO Direct website offers updates and insights on standard-setting activities. The link to subscribe to its newsletter service is circled in within Figure 13-4. To locate this page, perform a Web search for "PwC CFO Direct."

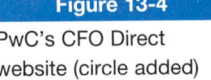

Figure 13-4

PwC's CFO Direct website (circle added)

© PricewaterhouseCoopers LLP ("PwC"). Not for further reproduction or use without the prior written consent of PwC.

Similarly, Ernst & Young's "AccountingLink" website, shown in Figure 13-5, offers standard-setter updates and other educational resources. Subscribers to this website's email alerts (see link circled) can receive Ernst & Young's weekly "US Week in Review" emails. Locate this page by performing a Web search for "Ernst & Young Accounting Link."

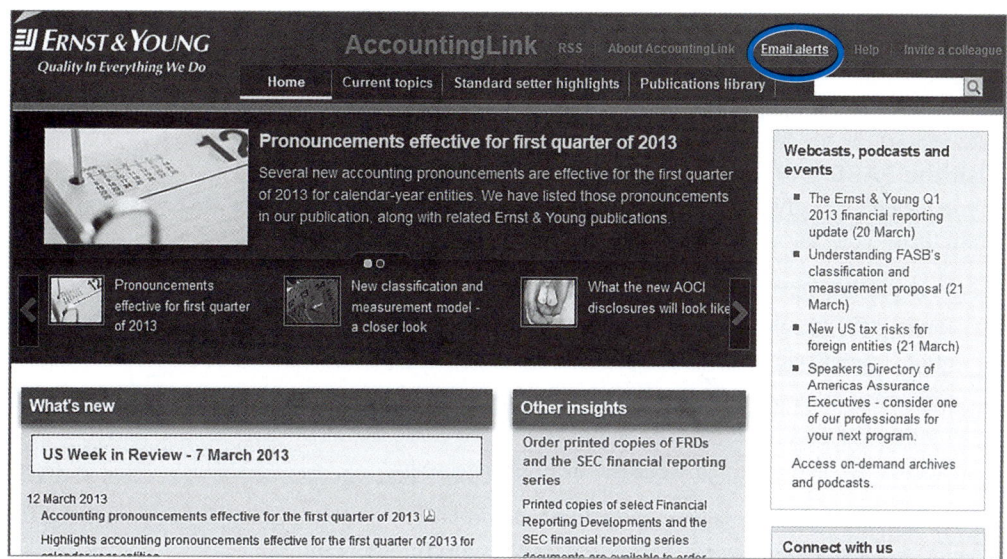

Figure 13-5

Ernst & Young's AccountingLink website (circle added)

Ernst & Young's AccountingLink Website

Identify two resources from Ernst & Young's website (Figure 13-5) that might be of interest to an auditor whose client is preparing their Q1 2013 financial statements.

[Now **YOU** Try **13.1**]

Register for Free Firm Webcasts

Quarterly, the big 4 accounting firms also offer free webcasts on current accounting developments. Locate upcoming webcasts by performing a Web search for: "Deloitte Q4 webcast," for example. These webcasts are often CPE-eligible, meaning that attendees can receive educational credits (necessary to maintain CPA licensure) for participating. Figure 13-6 depicts Deloitte's Quarterly Accounting Roundup webcast.

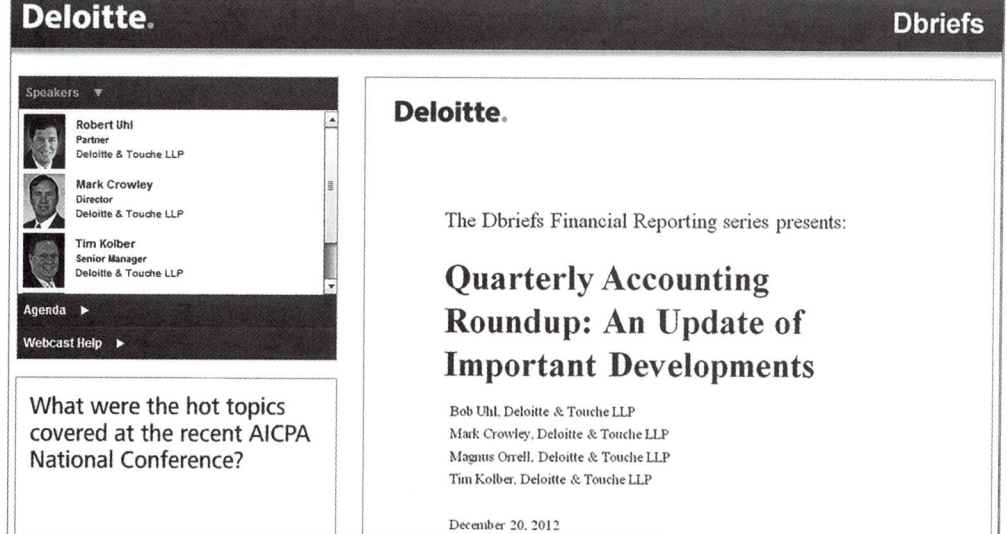

Figure 13-6

Deloitte's Quarterly Accounting Roundup webcast

---

[1] See Ch. 4, fn 8.

In addition to quarterly updates, the big 4 also offer webcasts as new standards are issued. These webcasts generally provide in-depth discussion of the standard's requirements, as well as implications and implementation issues associated with the new standard.

Visit the FASB's Website, Subscribe to "Action Alerts"

If you haven't already done so, take a moment to visit the FASB's website now (www.fasb.org). From there, you can

- View current news and activities of the Board.

- Review the "Project Roster & Status" page, where the FASB lists its current projects and project milestones.

- Sign up to receive **FASB Action Alert** emails, which summarize decisions reached at FASB Board meetings.

- Access live and archived webcasts of FASB meetings.

In addition, researchers can access final and proposed Accounting Standards Updates on the FASB's website, or can access the Codification (subscription required).

Visit the IFRS Website, Subscribe to Email Alerts

Like the FASB website, the IFRS website offers extensive news and updates on its standard-setting activities, plus extensive educational resources.

Under the tab "Stay Informed" on www.ifrs.org, researchers can select from a menu of email alert options, choosing, for example, to be notified whenever new standards are issued, or choosing, for example, to be notified of changes to specific IASB agenda projects. Figure 13-7 illustrates the process for subscribing to IASB email alerts.

Figure 13-7

Subscribing to IFRS email alerts

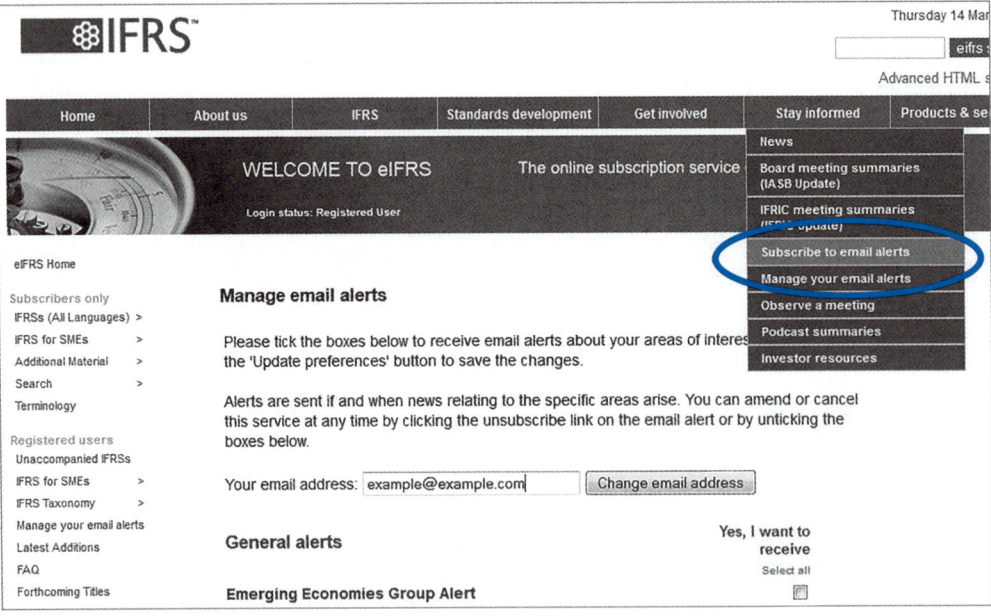

Read the *Journal of Accountancy*

The AICPA's *Journal of Accountancy*, sent monthly to the homes of AICPA members, or available online at www.journalofaccountancy.com, provides updates and practical guidance on a

---

wide range of services including accounting, auditing, taxation, ethics, valuations, and more. Figure 13-8 depicts a *Journal of Accountancy* magazine. If this arrives in your mailbox, take the time to browse it!

Figure 13-8

AICPA *Journal of Accountancy*

Copyright AICPA; Used with permission.

Finally, consider the following **TIP from the Trenches** regarding next steps in your effort to stay current.

Hopefully, this chapter has inspired you to stay informed about changes in our profession. But don't count on always having the enthusiasm to *actively* look up information on your own. Sign up today for **one or two** weekly email updates—these provide a more *passive* way to stay informed on an ongoing basis (the updates will come to you)! Challenge yourself to read *at least one* of these update emails every week.

[**TIP**] from the Trenches

CHAPTER SUMMARY

Many of the accounting principles that you know today will, over time, evolve and change in favor of new requirements. Expect this change, and resolve to keep pace with it.

This chapter reviewed the reasons for, and the process for, effecting changes to existing standards. Now that you generally understand this process, it's time to focus on the real takeaway of this chapter—*Even if it is not expected of you early in your career, stay current.*

Taking the initiative to monitor emerging guidance—and especially being thoughtful about how proposed changes will affect your company or your client's business—will put you at a tremendous professional advantage versus peers who do not make this effort.

Take a few minutes today to sign up for one or two email subscriptions, or subscribe to a professional journal, or resolve to use other resources—regularly—to stay abreast of changes in our profession.

REVIEW QUESTIONS

1. What are some of the reasons that a financial statement preparer would need to stay current with emerging and recently-issued guidance? What are some reasons that an auditor might need to stay current?

2. List three reasons why accounting standards might require change over time.

3. At what level should you, as a professional, begin to monitor emerging guidance? Why?

4. Briefly, describe a typical standard-setting "due process."

5. As a public company auditor, describe some of the resources you might monitor to stay current.

6. Contrast the U.S. FASB's process of issuing new guidance (i.e., involving "ASUs" to update the Codification) to the IASB's process for updating its guidance.

7. Describe what steps you currently take to stay current. Include, for example, newspapers you regularly consult, as well as accounting resources.

EXERCISES

1. Look at the FASB's current technical plan. Are any final standards set to be issued this quarter? Are any exposure drafts ("proposed ASUs") currently out for comment, or expected this quarter?

2. Select one of the FASB's current projects, and describe some of the considerations that led the Board to address this issue.

3. What is one of the topics currently being addressed by the EITF? Why do you suppose that the EITF, and not the FASB, is addressing this issue?

4. Locate the most recently issued Accounting Standards Update, and respond to the following:
   • What was the Board's reason for addressing this issue?
   • What are some of the key changes this standard will make?
   • What Codification topics will this "ASU" amend?
   • Locate the section of the ASU where it shows changes to the Codification. Does this ASU add to, or replace, existing Codification content? Explain.

5. Select one of the IASB's current projects, and describe some of the considerations which led the Board to address this issue.

6. Locate an agenda from an upcoming IASB meeting and list three or four of the topics they plan to cover. Which of these topics do you think may be the most closely watched by the IASB's constituents? Explain.

7. Navigate to the PCAOB's website. Under "Current Activities," describe a project underway at the PCAOB.

8. Navigate to the AICPA website. Locate information regarding activities of the Auditing Standards Board (under Standards, Auditing). What is one issue that this Board is currently addressing?

9. Using the AICPA website, locate a recent edition of the AICPA's *Journal of Accountancy*, and provide the title and date of a recent article. Summarize (in about 1 sentence) what the article is about.

10. Using the FASB website, locate guidance on the FASB's standard setting process (under the About Us tab).
    a. First, briefly describe the significance of due process in standard setting.
    b. Next, identify two ways in which the FASB's standards setting process differs slightly from the general process description in Figure 13-2 of this chapter.

CASE STUDY QUESTIONS

13.1 **Emerging Guidance** Select one current (major) project from the current FASB agenda. In approximately one page, describe the project, including the issue it is addressing (or the practical concern), the proposed changes that could result from the project, key project dates (such as expected timing of exposure drafts, final standards, and so on). If the project is very involved, you may focus on just a few of the project's key issues. Be prepared to discuss this project in your next class meeting.

Use the following format for your response.

Project:

Issue it is addressing:

Possible changes that could result:

Key project dates / next steps:

Selecting and Subscribing to a Resource This chapter covered numerous resources which offer email subscriptions. Research a few options, then select one subscription for yourself. Actually subscribe to it. In an email to your professor, approximately two paragraphs, explain the resources you considered and why you selected this particular subscription.   13.2

Quarterly Financial Reporting Update Webcasts Register to view a "big 4" quarterly financial reporting update webcast. These webcasts generally run approximately 1.5 hours. (Alternatively, at your instructor's direction, read Ernst & Young's most recent quarterly *Financial Reporting Briefs* publication.) While watching, assume that you are a corporate accountant for a publicly traded passenger airline that operates in the United States. Assume that your supervisor asked you to view this webcast and to report back on any issues of relevance to your company. Identify two or three issues with potential applicability to your company.   13.3

Next, draft an email to your supervisor reiterating his or her request, then summarizing the issues you identified and their potential relevance to your company. Also, be prepared to discuss your findings with the class.

Current Events (Newspaper) Locate a newspaper article describing a current event in the accounting or auditing profession. Topics might include, for example, articles describing recent SEC enforcement actions, articles about new accounting or regulatory rules, state or local government accounting issues, and the like. In one page, summarize the issue addressed, and identify the search term you used to locate this article. As always, clearly cite the source of this article (author, journal, etc.). Be prepared to discuss the article with your peers.   13.4

Alternate: After selecting a newspaper article about a current event in the profession, select a publicly-traded company that might be affected by the current event. In 2-3 paragraphs, discuss why you selected this company and the potential impact of this news on the company.   (13.4)

Revenue Recognition—Emerging Guidance Refer back to the Flyaway.com scenario presented at the beginning of Chapter 3. Recall that Linda, an external auditor for Flyaway.com, was researching whether the company should recognize ticket sales revenue gross (as a principal) or net (as an agent).   13.5

Linda has asked for your help—she understands that the FASB is issuing new revenue recognition guidance (expected in late 2013). Linda has asked you to research how the new revenue recognition guidance will affect Flyaway.com's accounting for ticket sales revenues. Respond to Linda in the form of an issues memo. Use the FASB's final standard, if available. If not, use the FASB's January 2012 exposure draft (aka, "Proposed Accounting Standards Update").

Index

Note: The letter "f" refers to the figure on the stated page. For example, 95f is referring to the figure on page 95.

Note: The letter "f" refers to the figure on the stated page. For example, 95f is referring to the figure on page 95.

Note: The letter "f" refers to the figure on the stated page. For example, 95f is referring to the figure on page 95.

Note: The letter "f" refers to the figure on the stated page. For example, 95f is referring to the figure on page 95.

Note: The letter "f" refers to the figure on the stated page. For example, 95f is referring to the figure on page 95.